EARLY TENNESSEE TAX LISTS

Compiled by
BYRON SISTLER *and* **BARBARA SISTLER**

Early Tennessee Tax Lists

© Copyright 1977 by
Byron Sistler and Associates, Inc.
All rights reserved.

Originally published by
Byron Sistler & Associates, Inc.
Evanston, Illinois
1977

Reprinted by
Janaway Publishing, Inc.
2006, 2010

Janaway Publishing, Inc.
732 Kelsey Ct.
Santa Maria, California 93454
(805) 925-1038
www.JanawayPublishing.com

ISBN: 978-1-59641-028-2

Made in the United States of America

INTRODUCTION

Research in Tennessee for the period prior to 1830 poses some difficult problems because no complete census schedules for the state exist before that date. The 1800 census schedules were entirely lost or destroyed, and for 1810 only Rutherford Co. has been saved. The 1820 lists for almost all the eastern counties are missing.

For genealogists seeking county of origin of early settlers the only feasible approach is through the county tax lists, petitions and newspaper accounts. To facilitate this search and simplify the pin-pointing of county of residence we have prepared this index to those early lists. With this "bare bones" information we hope we can send many frustrated ancestor hunters winging on their ways toward the flesh and blood material of which good family histories are made.

This is a single index to 68 county tax lists, petitions, voter lists, and newspaper lists of inhabitants in 34 Tennessee counties. There are about 46,000 entries in all. We believe we have taken all known tax lists into consideration (though not all have been included in the index, since those for years after census schedules are available were not deemed useful and in most cases the transcribing of lists less than 5 years apart would not add significant value to the work).

The earliest list included is from 1787 and the latest 1827. About 2/3 of the state's counties in existence by 1820 are included in one or more lists.

While some tax lists included additional information, such as acreage, number of "polls" etc., there is no data of genealogical value in them other than the name of household head and the county. Since the primary purpose of this book is a directional aid we have omitted this extraneous information.

The index itself is simple enough to follow. You will find the name of the subject followed by a county symbol (see inside front cover) and a date, which represents the year of that particular list.

All of the tax lists are on file at the Tennessee State Library and Archives in Nashville, TN.

Lists represented by this index are as follows:

County	Years	County	Years
Anderson Co.	1805	Lincoln Co.	1812 (newspaper, Fayetteville only)
Bedford	1812		
Bledsoe	1815	Maury	1811, 1816
Blount	1800, 1801, 1805	McMinn	1825
Campbell	1818, 1823	Monroe	1825
Carter	1796, 1798	Montgomery	1798
Claiborne	1803	Rhea	1808, 1819
Cocke	1821, 1827	Roane	1805
Davidson	1788, 1805, 1811	Robertson	1812
Franklin	1812	Sevier	1799
Giles	1812, 1819	Sullivan	1796, 1797, 1812
Grainger	1799, 1803, 1804, 1805, 1810, 1821	Sumner	1787, 1792, 1811, 1816, 1823
Greene	1783, 1805, 1812	Warren	1805, 1812, 1817
Hawkins	1799, 1801	Washington	1814, 1819
Humphreys	1812	White	1811, 1825
Jackson	1802	Williamson	1801, 1806, 1810, 1815
Jefferson	1800, 1822		
Knox	1796, 1799, 1815 (Knoxville only)	Wilson	1804

Byron Sistler
Barbara Sistler

Evanston, IL
August, 1977

KEY TO COUNTY SYMBOLS

A	Anderson	H	Hamilton	Mt	Montgomery
B	Bedford	Ha	Hancock	Mg	Morgan
Be	Benton	Hr	Hardeman	O	Obion
Bl	Bledsoe	Hd	Hardin	Ov	Overton
Bo	Blount	Hw	Hawkins	P	Perry
Br	Bradley	Hy	Haywood	Po	Polk
C	Campbell	He	Henderson	R	Rhea
Ca	Cannon	Hn	Henry	Ro	Roane
Cr	Carroll	Hi	Hickman	Rb	Robertson
Ct	Carter	Hu	Humphreys	Ru	Rutherford
Cl	Claiborne	J	Jackson	S	Scott
Co	Cocke	Je	Jefferson	Se	Sevier
Cf	Coffee	Jo	Johnson	Sh	Shelby
D	Davidson	K	Knox	Sm	Smith
De	Decatur	L	Lauderdale	St	Stewart
Dk	DeKalb	La	Lawrence	Su	Sullivan
Di	Dickson	Le	Lewis	Sn	Sumner
Dy	Dyer	Li	Lincoln	T	Tipton
F	Fayette	M	Macon	V	VanBuren
Fe	Fentress	Ma	Madison	W	Warren
Fr	Franklin	Mr	Marion	Wa	Washington
G	Gibson	Ms	Marshall	Wy	Wayne
Gi	Giles	Mu	Maury	We	Weakley
Gr	Grainger	Mc	McMinn	Wh	White
Ge	Greene	Mn	McNairy	Wi	Williamson
Gu	Grundy	Me	Meigs	Wl	Wilson
		Mo	Monroe		

AAKINSON, William, Wa-1819
AARON, Moses, B-1812
ABBERSON?, Yarby, W-1812
ABBET, Lewis, Fr-1812
ABBOT, Benjamin, Co-1827
    James, Su-1796, Sn-1811
    John, Sn-1811
ABBOTT, James, Su-1797
    William, B-1812
ABBUT, George, Sn-1816
    John, Sn-1816
ABBUTT, James, Sn-1816
ABEL, Cain, R-1819
    James, D-1811
    John, R-1819
ABERNATH, Joseph, Gi-1819
ABERNATHA, David, Mu-1811, D-1811
    Joseph, Mu-1811
    Laban, D-1811
    Laban Jr., D-1811
    Laban Sr., D-1811
    Milly, Mu-1811
ABERNATHY, Allen, Gi-1812
    Charles, Gi-1819
    David, Gr-1805, Gr-1804, Mu-1816
    David Jr., Mu-1816
    John, Gi-1812
    Milton, Mu-1816
    Wm., Gi-1812
ABLE, Cain, Bo-1800, Bo-1801, R-1808
    John, R-1808
    John A., D-1811
ABLES, William, B-1812
ABNER, Elisha, Ct-1796
    Paul, B-1812
ABNEY, George, W-1805, W-1812
    Joshua, W-1805
ABSHER, Isaac, Wh-1825
ACHESON, Robert, Bo-1800
ACHYERD, Frederick, Su-1797
ACKARD, Jacob, Su-1812
    Jacob Jr., Su-1812
ACKART, Adam, Su-1812
ACKERMAN, Jacob, Sn-1811
ACKLEN, Wm., Cl-1803
ACKLIN, Samuel, Cl-1803, Gr-1799
ACKYARD, Jacob, Su-1795, Su-1797
ACOFF, Isaac, Mu-1816
    John, Su-1797(2)
    Timothy, Su-1812, Su-1797
ACOUGH, John, Wh-1825
ACREE, John, Su-1812
ACRES, Daniel, C-1823, C-1818
    John, C-1823, C-1818
    Stephen, Wl-1804
    Uriah, Ge-1783
ACRIDGE, George, Gr-1821
ACRU, John, Su-1812
ACTON, James, Wa-1819
ACUFF, Benjamin, Gr-1804, Gr-1805
    Cain, Gr-1799, Gr-1804, Gr-1805
    Christian, Gr-1804
    Christopher, Gr-1799, Gr-1805
    David, Gr-1821
    Isaac, Mu-1811
    John, Gr-1799, Gr-1804(2), Gr-1805(2)
    John Jr., Gr-1821
    John Sr., Gr-1821
    Richard, Gr-1804, Gr-1805, Gr-1821
    Thomas, Gr-1821
    William, Gr-1804, Gr-1805
ADAIR, Isaac, Mu-1816

ADAIR, James Jr., Wa-1814
    James Sr., Wa-1814
    Joseph, D-1811
    Thomas, A-1805, D-1811
ADAM, Isaac, Mu-1811
    James Sr., Wa-1819
    John, Mu-1811
    Martha E., Sn-1816
    Moses, Wl-1804
    Thomas, Bo-1800
ADAMS, Archabald, B-1812
    Benjamin, D-1805
    Britain, Wi-1815
    Brittean, Wi-1810
    Colin, heirs, Sn-1823
    Collin, Sn-1811
    Collin, Esq., Sn-1816
    Daniel, Wi-1815
    David, B-1812, Ge-1805, Ge-1812
    Edwin, B-1812
    Elisha, Su-1796, Su-1797
    George, Gr-1799(2), B-1812
    Hugh, Gi-1819, Gi-1812
    Isaac, Gi-1812
    Jacob, Wi-1815, Se-1799
    James, Sn-1816, Mt-1798, Je-1800,
        Je-1822, Rb-1812, Gi-1819,
        B-1812
    Jesse, Ct-1796
    John, Wl-1804, Mu-1811, Mu-1816,
        Gr-1799(2), Ge-1812, Wa-1814,
        Mo-1825, Fr-1812, Gi-1819
    John W., Mo-1825
    Jonathan, Gi-1812
    Macajah, Su-1796, Su-1797, Su-1812
    Martin, Wi-1815, D-1811, Mu-1811
    Nathan, Wi-1815
    Peter, W-1812
    Robert, B-1812, K*-1815, Je-1822,
        D-1811(2)
    Romerts Jr., Gr-1799
    Samuel, Dec., Wa-1819
    Sylvester, Hu-1812
    Thomas, Wi-1805, Mu-1811, Mu-1816,
        W-1812, Ge-1812, Bo-1801,
        Fr-1812(2), Wl-1804
    Thos. Jr., Mu-1816
    William, Bo-1800, Bo-1801, B-1812,
        Fr-1812, Gi-1812, Rb-1812(2),
        Sn-1811, Sn-1816, Wl-1804,
        Mu-1811(3), Mu-1816(2), Rb-1812
    Willie, Wi-1810
ADAMSON, Aron, W-1812
    Elenor, Je-1822
    Jesse, Je-1822
    John, Je-1800, Gr-1804
    Jonathan, Je-1800
    Simon, Je-1800, Je-1822
ADAY, Loyd, Gr-1805
    Walter, Gr-1805
ADCOCK, Henry, D-1811
    Joshua, Su-1812
    Lott, Je-1822
    Stinson, Fr-1812
ADDAMS, Willie, Wi-1815
ADEAR, Benjamin, Mu-1811
ADGAR, Andrew, Je-1800
ADGEE, William, Su-1797
ADGES, Benjamin, Su-1797
ADIR, James, Wh-1825
    William, Wh-1825
ADKERSON, John, Wh-1811

ADKIN, Thomas, Gr-1799
ADKINS, Amos, Wi-1810
    Aron, R-1819
    Benjamin, Fr-1812
    Elisha, C-1823
    George, C-1823
    Henry, C-1823
    Isum, Gr-1799
    James, A-1805(2), Gr-1810, Mt-1798
    Jarvis, C-1823
    Jessee, Wh-1825
    John, Wi-1815, C-1823, Gr-1805
    Joshua, A-1805
    Lewis, Gr-1805, Gr-1804, Gr-1821
    Rachel, C-1823
    Richard, Gr-1805, C-1823
    Samuel, R-1819, A-1805
    Sherwood, C-1818
    Thomas, Gr-1799
    Thomas S., Wi-1815
ADKINSON, Charles, Ge-1782
    James, Gi-1819
    Jessee, Wi-1815
    John, Wi-1815
    Samuel, Mu-1811
    William, W-1805, W-1812
ADKISON, Amos, Wi-1801
ADKISSON, John, Fr-1812
ADLEY, Alexander, Mu-1811
ADWELL, John, Su-1796, Su-1797
ADWINS, Sherwood, C-1823
ADY, Levi, Gr-1805
    Loyd, Gr-1805, Gr-1799
    Walter, Gr-1805
AGEE, Isaac, C-1818, C-1823
    James, C-1823, C-1818
    Jesse, C-1823
    William, Su-1796
AGENT, John, Fr-1812
AGILL, William, Fr-1812
AGIOR, John, Wi-1815
AGNEW, James, Gi-1812
AHEAD, Jonas, D-1811
AHSER, Robertson, Gr-1799
AIKEN, John A., Wa-1814, Wa-1819
    Mathew, Wa-1819, Wa-1814
AIKIN, Ezekiel, Mu-1816
    John Sr., Mu-1816
    John Jr., Mu-1816
    Robert, Mu-1816
    Samuel, Mu-1816
    William, Mu-1816
AIKINS, John H., Fr-1812
AILISWORTH, George, Wh-1825
AILSY, Robert, A-1805
AIRCOK, Michael, Ro-1805
AIRES, Contry, Gr 1799
AIRHART, David, D-1805
    Henry, R-1819, R-1808, Bo-1801
    Nicolus, Bo-1801
    Philip & Moses, D-1805
AIRS, Samuel, Wh-1825
AISLEY, John, Sn-1816
AITS, Benjamin, Gr-1805
AJEY, James, A-1805
AKE, Joseph, B-1812
AKIN, Burrell, Mu-1811
    Michael, Gr-1821
    Samuel, Wi-1810, Bo-1801, Wi-1815
AKINS, Ezekiel, Mu-1811
    James, Mu-1811
    John, Mu-1811

AKINS, Robert, Mu-1811
    Samuel, Mu-1811
AKINSON, John, B-1812
AKLES, Moses, B-1812
ALAS, John, Su-1812
ALBART, William, Sn-1811
ALBERT, Elizabeth, Gr-1821
    Martin, Gr-1805
ALBERTS, Henry, Su-1812
ALBRIGHT, Philip, A-1805
ALDER, Barnabas, C-1818
    Barney, C-1823
    John, Gr-1805, C-1818, Gr-1804
ALDERSON, Armstead, Mu-1816, Mu-1811
    James, Sn-1816, Sn-1811
    Jane, Mu-1816
    John, Mu-1816
    S. John, Mu-1816
    William, SN-1811, Mu-1816
    William Sr., Sn-1816
ALDREDG, Nath'l. Jr., K-1799
ALDRIDG, Nath., Wi-1801
ALDRIDGE, Henry, A-1805
    John, B-1812
    Jonathan, Gr-1821
    Nathanl., B-1812
    William, A-1805
ALDRIN?, Job, W-1812
ALENN, Wiley, Sn-1816
ALENSON, John, Bo-1801
    Robert, Bo-1801
ALEORS, John, Wl-1804
ALESAN, David, Wl-1804
ALESON, John, Bo-1800
ALEXANDER, Abner, Bo-1800, Wl-1804
    Adam B., Mu-1816
    Adley, Mu-1816
    Archibald, B-1812(2)
    Arthur, Mu-1811
    B. Alexander, Mu-1811, Mu-1816
    B. John, Wl-1804
    Benjamin, Bo-1801
    Dan, Mu-1816
    Daniel, Sn-1816, Sn-1811, Wh-1811
    David, Mu-1811
    Ebenezar, Bo-1801, Ge-1782, Bo-1800
    Ebinezer, Wi-1810
    Ebenezor, Wi-1815
    Edley, Wl-1804, Wi-1801
    Edwin, Sn-1816, Sh-1811
    Eleazer, Mu-1811
    Eliezer, Wi-1810
    Ezekiel, Mu-1811, Wl-1804
    Ezekius, Wl-1804
    Francis, Wa-1814
    George, Gt 1706, Co 1805(2),
        Ge-1812
    George Sr., Wl-1804
    George Jr., Wl-1804
    Gevins, Bl-1815
    Green, Mu-1816
    Henry, D-1805
    Hiram, Gi-1812
    Hugh, A-1805
    James, Wi-1810(2), Sn-1811,
        Sn-1816, Mu-1811, Mu-1816(2),
        Ge-1783, Gi-1812
    Jeremiah, Bo-1800, Bo-1801
    John, Bo-1800(2), Bo-1801(2),
        Ge-1805, Gi-1819, Mu-1811,
        Su-1797, Wa-1819, Wl-1804

ALEXANDER, John B., Wi-1810
    Joseph, Wi-1815, Wi-1810, Ge-1783,
        Wl-1804, B-1812, Bo-1801,
        Bo-1800, R-1808, Ge-1812,
        R-1819
    Josiah, Mu-1816
    Margaret, Mu-1816
    Matthew, Sn-1811, Sn-1816
    Milton, Mu-1816
    Moses, Fr-1812
    Nathaniel, Wl-1804, Wi-1815,
        Wi-1810, Mu-1816
    Oliver, Bo-1801
    R. Adam, Mu-1811
    Richard, Sn-1816, Sn-1811(2)
    Robert, Wl-1804, Sn-1811
    Silas, Mu-1811, Mu-1816
    Stephen, Ge-1805(2), Ge-1812(2)
    Stephen Sr., Ge-1805
    T. David, Mu-1816
    Thomas, Wi-1815, Wi-1810
    Ge-1805(2), Bo-1800, Bo-1801,
        Fr-1812, Ge-1812(2)
    Will, W-1812
    Will L., Sn-1811
    William, Wl-1804, Mu-1811(2),
        Sn-1816, Mu-1816(2), Wi-1810,
        Bo-1801, Fr-1812, B-1812,
        Gi-1812, Rb-1812, Ge-1812(2),
        Ge-1805(4), R-1819
    Zenis, Mu-1811
ALFORD, Boldy, Wi-1815
    Burtis, Wi-1815
    John, Wi-1815, D-1811
    Nelson, D-1811
ALFRED, JOnathan, Wh-1825
ALINGER, Daniel, Ge-1805
ALISON, Charles, Wa-1814
    David, Ge-1782
    Finley, Su-1812
    John, Su-1812
    Robert, Su-1812, Ge-1783
ALKINSON, William, Gr-1805
ALLAN, John, Sn-1816
ALLARD, M-----, D-1788
ALLAXANDER, William, Wi-1815
ALLBRIGHT, Lewis, Sn-1811, Sn-1816
ALLDREDGE, Nathan, K-1799
    Wm., K-1799
ALLEN, Abraham, Mt-1798, Co-1821
    Alexander, W-1812
    Alexander J., Fr-1812
    Andrew, C-1823
    Archibald, Mt-1798
    Armon, heirs, Wi-1815
    Banjm., W-1812
    Barnet, Gr-1799
    Benjamin, Mc-1825, D-1811, Je-1800
    Carter, D-1811
    Charles, Mu-1816, Mu-1811, Su-1796,
        Su-1797, Su-1812
    Chesly, W-1812
    Christian, Gr-1805
    Clifton, Sn-1811
    D. Henry, Mu-1811
    Daniel, Sn-1811, Su-1797, Su-1796
    David, Sn-1816, Fr-1812
    Drury M., D-1811
    George, Wi-1815, Co-1821, D-1805,
        Mt-1798, Wh-1825, Wi-1810
    George Sr., Gi-1819
    George H., Wi-1810, Wi-1815

ALLEN, George S., D-1811
    Henry, Wi-1815
    Henry S., D-1811
    Isaac, Co-1827
    Jacob, Hu-1812(2)
    James, B-1801, C-1823, Ge-1805,
        Mu-1811, Ro-1805, Su-1796
    James Jr., Mu-1816
    James Sr., Mu-1816
    Jesse, Jr., Wh-1825
    John, B-1812, Bl-1815, Co-1821,
        Co-1827, D-1811(4), Ge-1805,
        Gi-1812, Ro-1805, Sn-1811,
        Sn-1816(2), Sn-1817(2),
        Su-1797, Wh-1811
    John Jr., D-1811, Co-1821
    John W., Wh-1825
    Joseph, Ge-1805, C-1823
    Joss, Wi-1810
    Mas., Sn-1816
    Mathew, D-1811
    Moses, Gi-1812
    Orman, Wi-1801
    Polly H., Wi-1801
    Rachel, Sn-1816
    Reuben, Ge-1805
    Reuben Jr., Co-1821
    Reuben B., Co-1821
    Reuber, Co-1821
    Rhodam, Sn-1811
    Rhody, Sn-1816, Sn-1811
    Richard, Sn-1811, Sn-1816, Hu-1812,
        Ro-1805
    Robert, D-1811, Ge-1805
    Samuel, C-1818, C-1823, D-1811,
        Mt-1798, Wi-1810, Wl-1804
    Samuel H., Wh-1825
    Sarah, Mt-1798
    Thomas, Co-1821, D-1811(2), D-1805,
        Mu-1811(2)
    Valentine, B-1812
    Vallentine, Wi-1810
    William, B-1812, Co-1821, D-1811(2),
        Gr-1799, Hu-1812(2), J-1802,
        Mt-1798, Mu-1811(2),
        Sn-1811(4), Sn-1816, Su-1812,
        Wi-1801, Wi-1815, Wl-1804
    Zachariah, D-1805, D-1811
ALLENTON, Stephen, Sn-1811
ALLEXANDER, Daniel, Sn-1816
ALLEY, Edward, Je-1800
    James, Gr-1799
    John, Gr-1799
    Peter, Sn-1816
    Samuel, Sn-1816
    Willis, Sn-1816
ALLGOOD, John, Su-1812
ALLIN, Andrews, Mt-1798
    Daniel, Sn-1816
    Hilsman, Wl-1804
    James, Ge-1812
    Joseph, Ge-1812
    Porter, Sn-1811
    Robert, Dec., Ge-1812
ALLION, Buddy, Sn-1792
    Ossy, Sn-1792
ALLISON, Andrew, Sn-1811
    David, Ge-1812(2), Ge-1805(2),
        J-1802
    Emin, Ge-1812
    Ewen, Ge-1805
    Francis, Su-1796

ALLISON, Halbert, Gi-1812
    Henry, Su-1812
    Hugh, D-1805, D-1811, C-1818
    James, D-1811, Sn-1816, D-1805(2),
        Wh-1825
    James, Esq., Wi-1810
    Jane, widow of Robert, Wa-1819
    John, Gr-1805, Mu-1816, B-1812(2),
        Wi-1815, Su-1797, Ge-1805,
        Ge-1812
    John, Su-1796 (in Washington)
    John Sr., Wh-1825, Su-1797
    John Sr., Dec., Su-1796
    John Jr., Wh-1825
    Jona, Rb-1812
    Joseph, Wh-1825
    Martha, Wi-1810
    Robert, Su-1797(2), Wa-1814
    Robert, Esq., Su-1796
    Robert, Dec., Wa-1819
    Thomas, Wi-1810, B-1812, Mu-1816
    Thophilus, Mu-1816
    Wm., Rb-1812
ALLON, Joseph, Wi-1810
ALLRED, Isaac, B-1812
    James, B-1812
    Solomon, K-1799
    Thos., K-1799 (Allner?)
    William, B-1812
    William Jr., B-1812
ALLSTODT, Jno. N., Wh-1825
ALLSUP, David, Sn-1816
ALLY, Benjamin, Sn-1811
    Herbert, Rb-1812
    Joseph, Sn-1811
    Samuel, Sn-1811
    Samul, Sn-1816
ALMAN, James, Mt-1798
ALMANDER, Matthew, Sn-1792
ALMOND, Hezekiah, Mu-1816, Mu-1811
    Jacob, Gi-1812
    John, Su-1812
    Thomas, Wi-1815
ALRED, Solomon, A-1805
    Thomas, A-1805
ALROT, Herbert, Sn-1811
ALSOMBRY, James, Mt-1798
ALSOP, James, Gr-1799
    John, Gr-1799(2)
ALSUP, Drury, Gi-1812
    Henry, Gr-1821
    James, Gr-1804, Gr-1805
    John, Gi-1812(2)
    Randle, Gr-1805
    Randolph, Gr-1804
    Robert, Gi-1812, Gr-1804, Gr-1805
    Thomas, Gi-1812
    William, Gr-1805
ALTUM, James, Je-1822
ALVES, Shadrick, Sn-1811
    Walter, C-1823
ALVIS, Abraham, Sn-1811
    Ashley, Sn-1816
    Martha, Sn-1811
    Walter, C-1818
AMBROSE, David, Wa-1819
    Foster, Wa-1819
    Israel, Sn-1816
AMBROUS, Farber, Wa-1814
AMES, David, Wh-1825
AMMONS, George, Se-1799
AMOS, Thomas, Su-1796

ANCHOR, William L., Wl-1814
ANDER, Adam, Ge-1812
ANDERS, Ephraim, Wi-1815
    Mark, Wi-1801
ANDERSON, Adley, Gr-1805
    Alexander, Se-1799
    Alexander, Gen., Je-1822
    Andrew, Su-1812
    Archibald, Bo-1805, Mu-1811
    Azariah, Wi-1810
    B. John, Sn-1816
    B. William, Sn-1816
    Barnabas, Ge-1783
    Cornelius, Mt-1798
    Daniel, Wl-1804, Mt-1798
    David P., Wi-1810
    Edward, Wh-1811, Wh-1825
    Enoch, W-1812
    Francis, Wl-1804
    Gabriel, B-1812
    Graice, Mu-1816
    Henry, Mt-1798, Mu-1811
    Holmes, B-1812
    Isaac, C-1823, B-1812, W-1812,
        Wh-1811
    Jabez, Wh-1825
    Jacob, Wh-1825, J-1802, Wh-1811,
        C-1823
    James, Ge-1783, Ge-1805, Ge-1812,
        Je-1800, Je-1822(2),
        Mu-1816, Sn-1811, Sn-1816,
        Wh-1825(5), Wh-1811(2),
        Wi-1815, Wl-1804, Bo-1801,
        Wa-1819
    James Sr., Je-1822
    James (alias Little Turkey),
        Wh-1811
    James V., Wa-1814
    Joel, D-1811
    John, B-1812, D-1811(3), Ge-1812,
        Gr-1799, Gr-1804, Gr-1805(2),
        Je-1822, Mu-1811, C-1818,
        C-1823, Sn-1811, Su-1796,
        Su-1812(2), Wh-1811,
        Wh-1825(2)
    John Sr., C-1823
    John Jr., C-1823
    John, heirs, Gr-1821
    John B., Sn-1817
    Joseph, Wh-1825, Je-1822(2),
        Je-1800, Wh-1811(2)
    Joseph, Esq., R-1819
    Joseph, Jordan & James, D-1805
    Joshua, Ct-1796, Ct-1798
    Lazarus, Mu-1811
    Lewis, Wa-1814
    Mathew, Sn-1787
    Matthew, Sn-1811
    Matthias, Wh-1825
    Michael, Gr-1805
    P. David, Mu-1811
    P. William, Wl-1804
    Peter, B-1812, Wl-1804
    Phebe, Sn-1816, Sn-1811
    Philip, Fr-1812
    Pleasant, Sn-1816
    Quinton, Mu-1816
    R. G., Wh-1825
    Rachel, Ge-1812, Ge-1805
    Richard, Sn-1816, Wl-1804
    Robert, Sn-1811, Mu-1811, D-1811,
        J-1802, Gi-1812, Gi-1819

ANDERSON, Robert Sr., Wh-1825
    Robert Jr., Wh-1825
    Robert G., Wh-1811
    Samuel, Sn-1816, D-1811, Sn-1811,
        Gi-1819
    Samuel Y., Gi-1812, Gi-1819
    Sarah, Sn-1817
    Stephen, Sn-1811, Gi-1812
    Stuart, Su-1796
    Thomas, Sn-1811, Sn-1816, D-1805,
        R-1819
    Thomas Sr., Ct-1796, Ct-1798
    Thomas Jr., Ct-1796, Ct-1798
    Timothy, Mt-1798, Hu-1812
    Uriah, J-1802
    W. P., Wi-1801(2)
    William, D-1805, D-1811, Sn-1816,
        Sn-1811, Wh-1825, Wl-1804,
        Mu-1811, Je-1822, Gr-1799,
        Su-1796, Ge-1805, Ro-1805,
        Gi-1812, Wa-1814, B-1812,
        Se-1799, Bl-1815, Gr-1821
    William Sr., Je-1822
    Wm. B., Sn-1817
    Wm. C., Sn-187
    Wm. H., Sn-1816
    William P., Wl-1804, D-1811,
        Wh-1811
    William P. & Jno., Wh-1811
    Zachariah, Wh-1825
    _____, C-1818
ANDES, Adam, Wa-1814
    Frederick, Wa-1814, Wa-1819
    George, Ge-1805, Ge-1812
    William, Wa-1814, Wa-1819
ANDREAS, David, Sn-1811
ANDRESS, Ann, Wi-1810
ANDREW, James, Wi-1815, B-1812
ANDREWS, Adam, Mu-1816
    Andrew, Wi-1815
    Annanias, Wi-1815
    Archibald, Mu-1816
    Athelston, Wi-1815
    Benjamin, Cl-1803
    David, D-1805, Mu-1811, Mu-1816
    Eleazar, Wi-1815, Wi-1810
    Ephraim, Wi-1810
    George, Wi-1815
    James, Wl-1804, D-1805
    John, Wi-1815(2), Mu-1811,
        Mu-1816, D-1805, Wi-1810
    Knaly?, Wi-1810
    Mark, Wi-1810, Wi-1815
    Patton, D-1805
    Samuel, Wi-1815
    Tapley B., Wi-1810
    William, Wh-1825, Rb-1812
    _____, D-1805
ANEAL, Joham, B-1812
ANGEL, Archibald, C-1823, C-1818
    James, Wh-1825
    Jessee, Wh-1825
    John, Wh-1825
    Laurence, Wh-1825
    Martin B., Wh-1825
ANGLE, Jacob, Je-1822
    Reuben, B-1812
    Ruben, B-1812
ANGLIN, Aaron, Su-1796, Wl-1804
    Caleb, Mu-1816
    Samuel, Mu-1816
ANTHONEY, Jacob, Ro-1805

ANTHONEY, Jane, Sn-1816
    William, Sn-1816
ANTHONY, Elijah, Gi-1819, Gi-1812
    Jacob, B-1812
    Jane, Sn-1816
    John, Ge-1782, K*-1815
    Joseph, Gi-1819
    Martain, Fr-1812
    Nicholas, B-1812
    William, Su-1796, Su-1797, Wi-1815,
        Wi-1810
    Wm. B., estate, Sn-1816
ANTONY, Martin, Fr-1812
ANTRIM, Robert, Ge-1812
    Thomas, Ge-1805
AOUATE, Jas., Se-1799
APPLEBY, David, Mu-1811
    John, Wi-1810
APPLEGATE, Samuel, R-1819
APPLETON, James, Rb-1812(3)
    James J. P., Rb-1812
    John, Rb-1812(2)
    John Sr., Rb-1812
    Thomas, Rb-1812
ARBUCKLE, Robert, Je-1822
ARCHER, Arron, Wa-1819
    Benjamin, Wa-1819, Ge-1812,
        Wa-1814
    Cornelius, Gr-1805, Gr-1799
    Elisha, Gi-1812
    H. John, Mu-1811
    Israel, Fr-1812
    John, Gr-1805, Ct-1798, Ct-1796,
        Gr-1804
    Richmond, A-1805
    William, Ct-1798, Ct-1796
ARCHUR, Cornelius, Gr-1804
ARCHY, Richmond, C-1818
ARINTON, Jacob, B-1812
ARLINGTON, John, Fr-1812
ARMFIELD, Isaac, Sn-1816
    John, Sn-1816
ARMISTEAD, William, Gi-1812
ARMITAGE, Isaac, Ge-1805
ARMS, Edward, Je-1822
ARMSTRONG, Abner, Fr-1812
    Alexander, Ge-1812, Ge-1805
    Andrew, R-1819
    Ann, Ge-1805, Ge-1812
    Benjamin, Ge-1783
    Daniel, R-1819, Ge-1805
    Elihu, R-1819
    Francis, D-1788(2)
    George, B-1812
    Huey, Wh-1825
    Hugh, W-1812
    J. Elias, Mu-1816
    Ja. Elias, Mu-1811
    James, Wi-1815
    James, Wi-1816(2), Mu-1811,
        B-1812, J-1802(2), Gi-1812
    Jesse, Fr-1812
    John, Wi-1801, Wi-1810, Mu-1811,
        Fr-1812, Wl-1804, K*-1815
    Joseph, Mu-1816
    Lanseylot, Ge-1783
    M., D-1788
    Martin, Mt 1798
    Martin & James, D-1805
    Mathew, Sn-1811
    Matthew, Sn-1816
    Nathaniel, D-1805

ARMSTRONG, Richard, Ro-1805, Gi-1812
    Robert, Mu-1811, D-1811, Wi-1810,
        K-1799, Ge-1783, K*-1815
    Samuel, Wa-1819
    Thomas, D-1805
    Will, Rb-1812
    William, Wi-1815, Mu-1811, D-1811,
        Bo-1801, B-1812, Fr-1812,
        W-1812, Su-1797, Su-1796,
        Gi-1812
ARNDA, Thomas, Mu-1811
ARNET, Jacob, Gr-1821, Gr-1799
    James, Gi-1819
    John, Gi-1819, Gi-1812
    Wm., Gi-1812
ARNETT, Jacob, Gr-1805, Gr-1804
    John, Mu-1811, Wi-1810
ARNEY, Peter, J-1802
ARNO, Peter, Gr-1799
ARNOLD, Elijah, Fr-1812
    Francis, Wh-1825
    Hays, Wh-1825
    Henry, K-1799
    James, Su-1797
    John, Wl-1804
    Levi, Fr-1812
    Peter, Wh-1825
    Robert, Mu-1811, B-1812, Mu-1816
    Smith, B-1812
    Thomas, Mu-1816
    William, Gr-1799, K-1799, Gr-1805,
        Wl-1804, Gr-1804, Mu-1811,
        Mu-1816
ARNOLS, Wyatt, Hu-1812
ARNOT, Holbert, Je-1822
    John, Je-1822
ARNWIN, James, Gr-1799
    John, Gr-1799
ARON, William, D-1811, Gr-1805
ARONTON, Charles, B-1812
ARRANTS, Harmon, Su-1797, Su-1812,
        Su-1796
    Richard, Su-1812
ARRINGTON, Charles, Sn-1792
    Thomas, Wa-1819, Hu-1812
ARROWWOOD, James, Wh-1811
ARTHUR, Elias, Gr-1799
ARWIN, James, Gr-1805
    John, Gr-1799, Gr-1805
ARWINE, Albertus, Gr-1821
    Daniel, Gr-1821
    James, C-1823, Gr-1804, Gr-1805,
        Gr-1821, Su-1796
    John, Gr-1804(2), Gr-1805, Gr-1821
    John Sr., Gr-1804, Gr-1805
ARWOOD, Jesse, Wa-1814
ARYES, Amon, Fr-1812
    Moses, Fr-1812
ASBURN, Alex., Bo-1800
ASHBROOKS, Moses, B-1812
    William, B-1812
ASHBURN, M., Bl-1815
    Martin, Gr-1805, Gr-1804, Gr-1799
ASHCROFT, Ichabod, W-1812
ASHE, Thomas, Ct-1798
ASHER, Amos, C-1818
    Charles, C-1818
    Daniel, Gr-1799
    David, Gr-1805
    John, Li-1812*
ASHFORD, Dempsy, Sn-1816
    Demsy, Sn-1816

ASHURST, Charles, Gr-1804
ASHLE, Solomon, Bo-1800
ASHLEN, Wm., Wi-1801
ASHLEY, John, Sn-1811
    Noah, Gr-1804, Gr-1805, Je-1800
ASHLIN, William, Wi-1815
ASHLOCK, William, A-1805
ASHMORE, Hezekiah, Je-1800
    James, Gi-1812
    James Sr., Gi-1812
    William, Gi-1812
ASHURST, David, Gr-1804
    William, Gr-1804
ASHWINE, Samuel, Mu-1811
ASHWORTH, John, Su-1797, Su-1796,
        Su-1812
    Moses, B-1812
    William, Gr-1805
ASHY, John, SDn-1811
ASKEW, Aaron, Wi-1815
    James, Sn-1811
ASKIN, James, Sn-1811
ASLEY, Nathaniel, D-1811
ASLLOCK, William, K-1799
ASSHBROOKS, George, Ct-1796
ASSHER, John, Ct-1796, Ct-1798
ASTERBUM, James, Su-1812
ASTIN, Alexander, Wl-1804
ASZMAN, Casper C., Rb-1812
ATCHESION, Nathen, Sn-1811
ATCHESON, Adam, Sn-1816
    Peter, Sn-1811
    William, Sn-1811
    Willis, Sn-1811
ATCHON, William, Sn-1816
    Willis, Sn-1816
ATECHON, Nathan, Sn-1816
ATES, Benjamin, Gr-1804
    George, Gr-1804
    James, Gr-1821
ATHA, Elijah, Wi-1825
ATHERLY, Isaac, Wl-1804
ATKINS, Corneless, K-1799
    David, Mu-1816
    Isaac, Gi-1812
    James, Rb-1812
    John, Gr-1805
    Joseph, Fr-1812
    Morris, Gr-1821
    Robert, B-1812, K-1799
    Weston, Gr-1821
    William, Mu-1816
ATKINSON, Armstead, Wi-1815
    David, Ro-1805
    Mat., Ro-1805
    Milton, Wa-1819
    Saml., Wi-1815
    William, Gr-1821, Ro-1805
ATKISON, William, D-1805
ATLASS, John, D-1805
AUGLIN, James, Wi-1815
AUGUST, John, Gr-1799
AUKLIN, H., Cl-1803
AULSTON, Johstep, D-1788
AUPH?, Henry, B-1812
AUSEMUG, Peter, Gr-1799
    Philip, Gr-1799
AUSEMUS, Peter, Gr-1799
    Philip, B-1812
AUST, Frederick, Wl-1804
AUSTELL, William, Je-1822
AUSTIN, Archibald, Je-1822, Je-1800

AUSTIN, Benjamin, C-1823, Wa-1819
    Cook, Fr-1812
    David, Wh-1825
    Edwin, Wi-1815
    Henry, Sn-1816
    Hesckiah, Bl-1815
    James, D-1811, D-1805
    John, Cl-1803, Wi-1815, Wh-1811
    John Sr., Wh-1825
    John Jr., Wh-1825
    Joseph, Je-1822, D-1811
    Landers, Gr-1799
    Nathaniel, Ge-1812, Wh-1825, Cl-1802
    Nathaniel, Gen., Cl-1802
    Robert, Gr-1799, Gr-1821
    Samuel, Wa-1819
    Saunders, W-1812, W-1811
    Stephen, Gr-1799
    Thomas, Cl-1803
    William, SN-1816, Wh-1825, Je-1822
AUSTON, Nathaniel, Gr-1799(2)
    William, B-1812
    William Jr., Gr-1799
AUTT, John, B-1812
AUTRY, Simon, Fr-1812
AVANT, Simon, Fr-1812
AVENT, Hurbert, Sn-1811
    William, Sn-1816, Sn-1811
AVERETT, Larkin, Gi-1812
AVERITT, John, Mu-1816
AVERS, Robert, Ro-1805
AVERY, Henry, Wh-1825
    Joseph, K-1799
    Peter, K-1799
    Peter Sr., Ro-1805
    Peter Jr., Ro-1805
    Thomas, Ro-1805
AVORY, Nicholas, Bo-1805
AYDELLOTTE, Jasper, Mu-1811
    Thomas, Mu-1816
    Zadock, Mu-1816
AYDLETT, Thomas, Mu-1811
    Zadock, Mu-1811
AYERS, A. O., Mo-1825
    D. Joseph, A-1805
    Hartwell, Sn-1816
    Henry, Rb-1812
    John, C-1823
AYRES, Arthur, Mu-1816
    D. B., K*-1815
    Elkna, W-1812
    Gentry, W-1812
    Henry Jr., Rb-1812
    James, Mu-1816
    John, Je-1822
    Joseph, Mu-1816, Mu-1811
    Moses, Fr-1812
    Young, Wi-1815
    Zacheus, Ro-1805
BAB, Stephen, Fr-1812
BABB, Burnett, Rb-1812
    David, Ge-1812
    James, Gi-1812
    Jesse, Wh-1811
    Joseph, Ge-1805
    Levi, Ge-1812
    Philip, Ge-1805
    Philip, son of Thomas, Ge-1812
    Phillip Jr., Ge-1812
    Seth, Ge-1805, Ge-1812
    Stephen, Fr-1812

BABB, Thomas, Ge-1805, Ge-1812
    William, Ge-1812, Wl-1804
BABBER, Daniel, Ro-1805
BABBET, Jno., W-1812
BACH, Amos, B-1812
BACHELY, John, Wa-1814
BACHER, Charles, Gr-1799
BACHMAN, Samuel, Su-1796
BACHUS, William, Wl-1804
BACKMAN, Jonathan, Su-1797
    Samuel, Su-1797
BACKSTER, James, Co-1821
    John, Co-1821
BACKSTON, Washington, B-1812
BACON, Aaron, Su-1812
    Aaron Sr., Su-1812
    Baister, K-1799
    Charles, Wa-1819(2)
    Edmond, Hu-1812
    Isaac, Wa-1819
    James, Wa-1819(2)
    Jesse, Wa-1814, Wa-1819
    John, Wa-1819(2), Wa-1814
    Jonathan, Wa-1819(2)
    Joseph, Wa-1814, Wa-1819
    Thomas, Wa-1819(2), Wa-1814
BADGER, Joshua, Wh-1811
    Briton, Mu-1816
    John, Sn-1816, Sn-1823
    Thomas, Sn-1816
BADGETT, Jonathan, Sn-1811
BADJET, John, Sn-1811
BAFORD, Charles, Wi-1810
    Edward, Wi-1810
    Gabril, Wi-1810
    James, Wi-1810
BAGGET, Burrel, Fr-1812
BAILES, Eldridge, Hw-1801
    James, Ge-1805
    John, Wa-1819
    Solomon, Ge-1805
    Stephen, Ge-1805
BAILEY, Abraham, Mu-1816
    Charles, Ct-1798, Ct-1796
    Christopher, K-1799
    Claudius, Ge-1805
    Cotteil, Ct-1796
    David, Ro-1805
    E., Gi-1819
    Edmund J., Gi-1812
    Ezekiel, C-1823
    Henry, Wl-1804
    James, Gr-1821, Ge-1805, R-1819, Rb-1812, Mu-1811
    John, Ge-1812, Ge-1805, Rb-1812
    Johnathan, Mu-1811
    Parks, Gi-1812
    Richard, Gi-1812, Je-1800
    Robert, A-1805, Bo-1801, Bo-1805
    Thomas, B-1812
BAILIS, Samuel, Co-1821
BAILS, Daniel, Ge-1805
    Eldreg, Hw-1799
    John, Wl-1804
    Solomon, Ge-1812
BAILY, Henry, Wi-1810
    James, Mu-1816
    John, Ge-1812, B-1812
    Jonathan, Mu-1816
    Joseph, Wl-1804
    Richard, Mu-1816
BAINES, Wm., Bo-1800

BAINHART, Conrod, Ge-1812
BAINS, Nichodemius, Ro-1805
    William, Ro-1805
BAIRD, David, Wl-1804
    George, B-1812(2), Mu-1811(2)
    H. Isham, Mu-1811
    James, Mu-1811
    John, D-1811, Wl-1804
    Robert, Mu-1811
    William, Mu-1811(2), Wl-1804
    Zebulon, Wl-1804
BAITS, Moses, D-1811
BAITY, John, Bo-1805
    Samuel, Bo-1805
BAKEN, Jeremiah, Wa-1814
BAKER, Abraham, Fr-1812
    Alexander, Wh-1811
    Andrew, Mu-1816, Hw-1799
    Charles, Su-1796, Su-1797,
        Su-1812, Wa-1814, Bo-1801,
        Bo-1800
    Christopher, Ge-1805, A-1805
    Colby, D-1805
    David, C-1823, Gi-1812
    Edward, Gi-1812, C-1823, C-1818
    Elisha, Ge-1782
    Esaias, Mu-1811
    George, Gr-1821, B-1812, C-1823
    George Jr., C-1818
    Green B., Wi-1815
    Humphrey, D-1805
    Isaac, Mt-1798, Sn-1811, Sn-1816,
        R-1819
    Isaac Jr., Ge-1812
    Isaac Sr., Ge-1812, Ge-1805
    Jacob, Gi-1812(2)
    James, D-1811, Wl-1804, Je-1800,
        Wa-1814, C-1823, A-1805
    John, Wl-1804, Mt-1798, Wh-1825,
        Gr-1805, Wi-1815, Gi-1812,
        Je-1800, Hw-1799, Ge-1805,
        R-1819, Ge-1812, Je-1822,
        Wh-1811, A-1805, Gr-1804,
        B-1812, Gr-1799, Ct-1796,
        Ct-1798
    John Jr., Gi-1812
    John A., Wh-1811
    Jonathan, Wa-1814
    Jonathan Jr., Wa-1814
    Joseph, Je-1800, Gr-1799
    Joshua, Gr-1805, Gr-1804
    Josiah, A-1805
    Larkin, Wh-1825
    Martin, Sn-1816
    Meredith, Wh-1825
    Michael, Ro-1805
    Morris, Hw-1799, Su-1796
    Morriss, Su-1797
    Nicholas, D-1805
    Peter, Ge-1812, Wh-1825, Ge-1805
    Robert, Wh-1825, Rb-1812, A-1805,
        B-1812, C-1823, C-1818
    Robert Jr., C-1823
    Roth, B-1812
    Samuel, C-1818, C-1823, A-1805
    Thomas, Mu-1816, Je-1822, W-1812,
        C-1823
    William, Wh-1825(3), D-1811,
        Mt-1798, Ge-1812, Wh-1811,
        Bo-1801, C-1823, Ct-1796,
        Ct-1798
    Young, Hu-1812

BALANCE, Abraham, Wi-1815
    Nathaniel, Wi-1801
BALCH, E. Thereau, Mu-1811
    Elijah, Ge-1805, Ge-1812
    George B., B-1812
    Rev. H., Dec., Ge-1812
    Hezekiah, Ge-1805, Ge-1782
    Hezekiah W., Ge-1805
    James P., Je-1822
    John, Ge-1812(2), Je-1822,
        Je-1800, Ge-1805
    P. Amos, Mu-1811
    Samuel Y., Ge-1805
BALDEN, Caleb, Sn-1811
BALDIN, John, Rb-1812
    Zonas, D-1805
BALDRIDGE, Andrew, D-1811
    Daniel, D-1811
    Francis, D-1811
    James, Mu-1816
    John, Gi-1812
    Michael, Mu-1816
    _____, Mu-1811(2)
BALDRY, William, Rb-1812
BALDWIN, Aron, D-1811
    Ezekiel, Ge-1805
    Kinson, Gi-1812
    Moses, D-1811
    Wm. & WITT, Jessee, R-1819
BALE, James, Mu-1816
BALEMAN, Isaac, Wi-1801
BALENGER, James, James, Wa-1814
BALENTINE, David, D-1811
BALES, Asher, Je-1822
    Jacob Sr., Ge-1812
    John, Mt-1798
    John Sr., Je-1822(2)
    William, Je-1822(2)
BALEW, Thomas, Sn-1787
BALEY, John, Ge-1812
    Martin, Ge-1812
    Parks, Gi-1819
    Thomas, Ge-1812
    William, Mo-1825, Ge-1812
BALIASON, Thomas, Co-1821
BALINGER, James, Wa-1819
    Lydia, Je-1800
BALIS, Haman, Se-1799
BALKER, Benjamin, Mt-1798
BALL, Anber, Sn-1816
    Isaac, Sn-1816, Sn-1811
    James, Sn-1816(2), Sn-1811
    John, Gr-1821
    Joseph, Wa-1819, Wa-1814
    Joseph H., Wa-1814
    Robert, Ge-1812
    Thomas, Gr-1821, Wa-1814, Wa-1819
    V. James, Wl-1804
BALLARD, Etheldred, Hu-1812
    John, Ct-1796
    Joseph, Sn-1811
    Joshua & Abraham, D-1805
    Leroy, W-1812
    Micajah, C-1818
    Richard, C-1823
    Samuel, A-1805
    Washington, Sn-1816
    Wiat, Fr-1812
    William, Gr-1821, Ro-1805
    _____, Mu-1811(2)
BALLENGER, James, Wa-1814
    _____, Je-1800

BALLENTINE, David, Wi-1815
    Lemuel, Wi-1815
    Robert, W-1812, W-1805
    William, D-1811
BALLINGER, G., Gr-1799
    John, Je-1822
    Moses, Gr-1805
    William, Je-1822
BALOTE, Jeremiah, Wl-1804
BANCES, Teason, Sn-1792
BAND, John, B-1812
BANDRY, Thos., Sn-1816
BANDY, Joseph, Sn-1811, Sn-1816(2)
    Parem, Sn-1811
    Parrin, Wl-1804
    Perrin, Sn-1816
    Richard, Sn-1816, Wl-1804
    Solomon, Wl-1804, Sn-1811
    Walsha, Wl-1804
BANE, David, W-1812
    Robert, Je-1800
BANER, Henry, D-1811
BANET, Barsilev, Hw-1799
BANGUS, Bunt, Mu-1811(2)
BANKHEAD, John, Gi-1812
BANKS, Eli, R-1819
    Hannas, Gr-1805
    John, K-1799, Fr-1812,
        Gr-1805
    John Hughs, Gi-1819
    Josiah, Gr-1805
    Nathaniel, K-1799
    Simon, Fr-1812
    Thomas, Wi-1815
    William, Wi-1815, K-1799, Gr-1805
BANNER, Jesse, Wi-1810
BANNETH, John, Gr-1799
BANNON, John, Sn-1811
BANORS?, Willis, D-1805
BANSEN, Lewis, D-1805
BANTER, Robert, Wi-1801
BANTON, Nancy, Wi-1801
    Wm., Sn-1811, Sn-1811
BAR, Benjamin, Su-1797
BARANUM, Thomas, Cl-1803
BARBEE, Wm., C-1818
BARBER, Farel, Sn-1816
    James, Sn-1811
    Liff, Su-1797, Su-1796
    Limin, Su-1797
    Moses, Su-1812
    Simon, Su-1796
    Thaddeus, Sn-1811
BARBERRY, Gobilon, Mu-1816
BARBIE, Elza, Gr-1821
BARCROFT, Jonathan, Wa-1814
BARDEN, John, Bl-1815
BARE, Adam, Je-1822
    Henry, Je-1822
    John, Je-1822
BAREFIELD, James H., Hu-1812
    Stephen, Wi-1815
BARETON, Thomas, Sn-1811
BARETY, Andrew, J-1802
BAREY, Jesse, R-1808
BARFORD, John, Rb-1812
BARGDON, James, Bl-1815
BARGER, George, W-1812
    Jacob, W-1812
    Willie, Wa-1819
    Wyley, Wa-1814
BARHAM, Hutcher, D-1811

BARHARD, Jacob, Sn-1816
BARKDALES, Daniel, Wl-1804
BARKEHOUSE, John, Ct-1796
BARKELY, Robert, Wa-1814
BARKER, Alexr., Mu-1816
    Allen, Hu-1812
    Ambrose, Fr-1812(2)
    Andrew, Mu-1811
    George, Mu-1816
    Harden, Mo-1825
    Isaac, Sn-1811
    John, Mo-1825, D-1811
    John Sr., D-1811
    Jonah, Fr-1812
    Josiah, Fr-1812
    Laban, D-1811
    Lavon, D-1811
    Lemon, D-1811
    Lewis, Hu-1812
    Newton, Sn-1816
    Peter R., Wi-1810
    Soloman, Mo-1825
    William, Gr-1821
    Wilson, D-1811
BARKERWELL, Robt., Sn-1816
BARKLEY, John, estate, Wi-1815
    William, Ge-1812
BARLARY, Waller, Fr-1812
BARLOW, Henson, Je-1822
BARMAN, Daniel, Bl-1815
    Jacob, Gr-1799
BARMER, John, A-1805
BARNABAS, Micheal, Gr-1805
BARNARD, Elisha, Sn-1816
    Jacob, Sn-1816, Sn-1811
    Jacob Sr., Sn-1811
    James T., Sn-1816
    John, Gr-1821, Su-1797, Su-1796,
        J-1802
    Jonathan, Gr-1804
    William, Sn-1811
    Zaduck, Sn-1811
    Zedock, Sn-1816
BARNERD, Solomon, Wi-1810
BARNERS, Wright, Sn-1816
BARNES, Amylin, D-1811
    Benjamin, D-1811, D-1805
    Callum, Sn-1816
    Elias, D-1805
    George, Gi-1819
    Henry, D-1805, D-1811
    James, Wi-1815, Rb-1812, D-1805,
        Je-1800, Wa-1819, Wa-1814
    James Sr., D-1811
    James Jr., D-1811
    Jesse, D-1811
    Joel, D-1811
    John, Mu-1816, D-1805
    Jordon, D-1811
    Joshua, Gi-1812
    Mary, Wa-1819, Wa-1814
    Nathan, D-1805, D-1811, Wa-1819
    Nathaniel, Sn-1816
    Nemiah, W-1805, W-1812
    Richard, Wi-1801
    Soloman, Sn-1811, Sn-1816
    William, Su-1797, Bo-1801, Su-1812,
        Su-1796
    Wright, Sn-1811
BARNET, Charles, Su-1812
    Hugh, B-1812
    James, Wi-1810

BARNET, John, B-1812, Fr-1812, Gi-1812
    Joseph, Bo-1801
    Michael, Je-1800
    Richard, Gi-1812
    Robert, Wl-1804, Mt-1798
    Sarah, Su-1812
    Thomas, Wi-1810, Wi-1801
    Wiley, Sn-1816
    William, B-1812
BARNETT, Elijah, Wh-1811, Wh-1825
    James, Je-1822, Su-1812, B-1812
    John, Gr-1805(2), Rb-1812, Wh-1825
    Joseph, Bo-1800
    Lewis, Hw-1801
    Michael, Je-1822
    Reubin, Su-1797
    Robert, Wi-1801
    Solomon, Wi-1815
    William, Gi-1812, W-1812
    Wrenard, Gr-1821
BARNHART, Conrod, Ge-1812
BARNHEART, Conrad, Ge-1805
    John, D-1811
BARNHILL, Robert, Je-1822
BARNLY, John, Sn-1811
BARNS, Adam, Wl-1804
    Alexr., Mu-1816
    James, Mu-1816(2), W-1805, Se-1799, Mu-1811
    Joshua, Wl-1804
    Lewis, Wl-1804, Wh-1825
    Loftam, Wl-1804
    Lowen, Sn-1816
    Nathaniel, Sn-1816
    Seth, Mu-1816, Mu-1811
    Thomas, Wl-1804, Wh-1825
    Widow, Mu-1816
    Wilkerson, Mu-1816
    William, W-1805, W-1812
    William Sr., W-1805
BARON, John, Gr-1799, Wa-1814
    William, Wa-1814
BARR, Andrew, Su-1812
    Ely, Sn-1816
    George, Su-1812
    Hugh, Sn-1816, Wi-1815, Sn-1811
    Isaac, Mu-1816
    Isaac Jr., Mu-1811
    Jacob, Su-1812
    John, Sn-1816, Wh-1825, Sn-1811(2), D-1811
    Jno. Isaac, Mu-1811
    Patrick, Sn-1811, Wl-1804, Sn-1816
    Saml., Sn-1816, Sn-1811
    Silas, Rb-1812
    Thomas, Sn-1816
    Walker, Mu-1816
    Wm., Sn-1816
BARRAN, Joseph, Gr-1799
BARRANS, Richd., Gi-1812
BARRATT, Jonathan, B-1812
BARRD, Thomas, Mt-1798
BARREN, Alex. Jr., Gi-1812
    Alex. Sr., Gi-1812
    Nancy, Gr-1821
    Thomas, Wa-1819
    Walker, Wa-1819
    William, Wa-1819, Gi-1812
BARRER, William Sr., W-1812
BARRET, John, Sn-1816
    Thomas, Wi-1815

BARRET, William, B-1812
BARRETT, David, Sn-1816, Sn-1811
    George, Sn-1811
    James, Wi-1815
    John, Sn-1811
BARRON, Henry, Fr-1812
    James, C-1818, C-1823
    John, C-1823, C-1818, Gr-1799
    Joseph, C-1818
    Thomas, Wa-1814
    Walker, Wa-1814
BARROTT, David, Sn-1816
    George, Sn-1816
    Edward, Sn-1811
    James, W-1812
    Micajah, Wl-1804
BARROW, Micajah, D-1805
    Thomas, Su-1812
BARRY, James, Wi-1801, Sn-1811
    John, Sn-1816
    Redd. D., Sn-1816
    Redmond D., Sn-1811
    Thomas, Wi-1801(2)
    Wm., Wi-1801
BARSTON, John, C-1823
BARTER, John, Wa-1814
    Moses, Wl-1804
BARTHOLOM, Joseph, K*-1815
BARTLET, James, Cl-1803
BARTLETT, Isaac, Wl-1804
    Jesse, B-1812
    John, Mu-1811
    Joseph, Wh-1811, Bo-1801
    Nathan, Wh-1825(2)
    Thomas, Rb-1812, Mu-1811
    William, Wh-1825, Wl-1804
BARTLEY, John, Ge-1805
BARTLY, John, Ge-1812
    Robert, Wa-1819
BARTON, Alexr., W-1812
    Benjamin, B-1812
    George, D-1805
    Henry, Gr-1799
    Hugh, Su-1797
    Isaac, Je-1800, Gr-1821, Ge-1783
    Isaac Jr., Gr-1805, Gr-1804
    Jessee, Gr-1805
    John, Gi-1812, Sn-1816
    Samuel, Wl-1804
    Thomas, Su-1797, Su-1796, Gi-1812
    William, Gr-1821, Sn-1811
BARTOON, Saml., D-1788
BARWELL, John, Sn-1811
BASEFIELD, James, Hu-1812
BASEY, Lewis, D-1811
BASFIELD, Danl., Hu-1812
    Fredrick, Hu-1812
BASHAM, Archibald, C-1818, C-1823
    Arthur, Bl-1815
    John, Sn-1816, C-1818
    Johnson, C-1818
    Johnston, C-1823
    Jonathan, C-1818
    Miniard, A-1805
    Richard, C-1823, C-1818
    Wm., C-1818
BASHAW, Benjamin, D-1811, D-1805
    Peter, D-1811
BASHUN, Jonsan, Gr-1799
BASINGER, George, Ge-1812
    Michael, Ge-1812
BASK, Wm., Sn-1816

BASKERVILLE, Richd., Sn-1816, Sn-1811
BASKET, Charles, Su-1812, Wa-1819
    John, Su-1796, Wa-1814, Wa-1819
    Richard, Wa-1819
    William, Su-1812
BASKIN, John, Se-1799
    Moses, Se-1799
BASKINS, John, Ge-1783
    Walter, B-1812
BASON, Henry, Sn-1811
    John, A-1805
BASS, Benjamin, Su-1796
    Benjamine J., Wi-1815
    Ezekiel, Wl-1804
    Guilford, Sn-1823
    Jeremiah, Ct-1796
    John, Wl-1804
    Jordan, Wl-1804
    Kinchen, Wi-1815
    Lamond, D-1805
    Laurence, Mu-1811, Wi-1815
    Lawrence, Mu-1816
    Nathan, Gi-1812
    Peter, D-1811, Wi-1815, Mu-1816
    William, Fr-1812
BALLEL, _____, Hw-1801
BASSENDINE, Charles, Ct-1798
BASSETT, Thomas & John, D-1805
BASSLE, George, Wl-1804
    Morgan, Wl-1804
BASSON, Peter, Sn-1816
BASTION, James, D-1805
BATE, Humphrey, Sn-1816
BATEMAN, Benniah, Wi-1815
    Enoch, Wi-1815, Wi-1810
    Isaac, Wi-1815
    Jonathan, Wi-1801, Wi-1815
    Simeon, Wi-1815
    Simon, Wi-1815, Wi-1810
    William, Wi-1815
BATEMON, Isaac, Wi-1810
BATES, Elijah, Wh-1811
    George, B-1812
    Hampton, Je-1822
    Humphrey, Sn-1811
    James, Bo-1805, B-1812
    Jeremiah, Gi-1819
    Joseph, Je-1822
    Mathew, Je-1800
    Moses, Gi-1812
    Robert, D-1811, Wi-1815
BATEY, Thomas, Gi-1812
    William, Gi-1812
BATMON, Jonathan, Wi-1810
    Simeonon, Wi-1810
    Willum, Wi-1810
BATSON, Daniel, W-1812
BATT, Thomas, Ge-1805
BATTAL, Peter, Ro-1850
BATTES, Francis, Ro-1805
BATTLE, Irin D., Rb-1812
    Isaac, D-1811
    Jacob, Ge-1812
BATTLES, Henry, Wa-1819
    William, Wa-1819
BATTS, Benjamin, Rb-1812
    Jeremiah, Rb-1812
BAUCOMB, Britain Jr., Mu-1816
BAUERMAN, Peter, Bo-1800
BAUGEN, Brian, Mu-1816
BAUGH, Bartholomew, Mu-1816
BAUGHAN, Joel, Rb-1812

BAUGHER, Jacob, Bo-1801
BAUGHMAN, Christian, Wi-1815
    Jonathan, Su-1812
    Nathan, Su-1812
    Samuel, Su-1812
BAUGHN, James, Rb-1812
BAULCH, Wiliam, Wh-1825
BAULIS, Andy, Se-1799
BAUMGARTNER, George, A-1805
BAVINS, Elija, R-1808
BAWERS, Daniel, Bo-1800
BAWLDIN, Henry, Je-1800
BAXTER, Aron, Co-1821
    James, Ge-1805
    Jeremiah, D-1811
    Ruth, Ge-1812
BAY, William, D-1811
BAYD, Henry, Wa-1819
BAYES, Reuben Jr., Wa-1819
BAYET, Ethreldrel, B-1812
    James, B-1812
    John, B-1812
BAYLES, Abner, Wa-1819
    Abraham, Wa-1819
    Barnabas, D-1811
    Damiel, Wa-1819
    Daniel, Wa-1819, Wa-1814(2)
    Daniel L., Wa-1814, Wa-1819
    George, Wa-1819
    Hezekiah, Wa-1819
    Jacob, Wa-1819
    Jesse, Wa-1819
    John, Wa-1814(2), D-1811, Wa-1819
    John Jr., Wa-1814
    Reuben, Wa-1814(4)
    Rien, Wa-1819
    Riis, Wa-1814
    Samuel, Wa-1814, Wa-1819
    Samuel Sr., Wa-1819
    Samuel Jr., Wa-1814(2), Wa-1819
    William, Wa-1819, Wa-1814
BAYLESS, Barnabas, D-1805
    John, D-1805
BAYLEY, James, W-1812
    Robt., W-1812
BAYLY, Joseph, Mu-1811
BAYSINGER, Michael, Ge-1805
BAYTY, John S., Gi-1819
BAZEL, Isaac, Wi-1801
BAZZELL, Jonathan, Sn-1816
BEACHBAUN, Samuel, B-1812
BEACHBOARD, Benjamin, Su-1796
    Levi, Su-1812
BEACHBURN, James, B-1812
BEACHIN, James, Sn-1811
    James Jr., Sn-1811
    John, Sn-1811
    William, Sn-1811
BEACON, Joshua, Gr-1805
BEADLES, Alfred G., Wh-1825
BEADY, John, Gr-1799
BEAKE, Joshua, D-1788
BEAL, Michael, Gr-1799
    Thomas, Gi-1812
BEALES, Isaac, Wa-1814
BEALS, Daniel, Ge-1812
    David, Wa-1814
    Jacob, Ge-1812
    Joseph, Ge-1812
    Solomon, Ge-1812
    Stephen, Ge-1812
BEARD, Adam, Wl-1804, Sn-1811

BEARD, Alexander, Wl-1804
    Am., Sn-1816
    Arch., Bo-1800, Bo-1801
    Capt., K-1796
    David, Bo-1800, Wl-1804, Sn-1787,
        Sn-1792
    David Jr., Sn-1811
    David Sr., Sn-1811
    Deavis, Sn-1816
GEORGE, Bo-1805, Bo-1800, Bo-1801
    H. Isham, Mu-1816
    Henry, Bo-1801, Bo-1800
    Hugh, Ge-1783
    James, Wa-1819, Bo-1800, Bo-1801
    John, Fr-1812, B-1812, Bo-1805,
        Se-1799, Li-1812*, Su-1796,
        Su-1812, Su-1797
    Joseph, C-1823
    Lewis, C-1823, C-1818
    Patrick, Je-1800
    Robert, Wa-1819, Wa-1814
    Samuel, Sn-1811, Mu-1816
    Thomas, Su-1796
    Thomas C., Sn-1816
    William, Sn-1816, Sn-1811, Gr-1821,
        C-1823, Bl-1815, Wa-1819,
        Wi-1801
BEAMER, Thomas, D-1811
BEAMES, James, Ct-1796, Ct-1798
BEAN, Barter, Wa-1814
    Edmond, R-1819
    Edmund, Fr-1812
    Elizabeth, Gr-1804, Gr-1799
    George, Fr-1812, Ge-1812
    Hagan, Gr-1805
    Hogan, Gr-1804
    Jacob (Joab?), Fr-1812
    Jesse, Fr-1812(2)
    Jesse Jr., Fr-1812
    Jessee, Gr-1799
    Joel, Gr-1804, Fr-1812, Gr-1805
    John, Wa-1814, Gr-1804, Fr-1812,
        Gr-1799
    John H., Fr-1812, Gr-1799
    John Jr., Fr-1812(2)
    Lemuel, Fr-1812
    Margaret, Wa-1814
    Mark, Wa-1814, Wa-1819
    Obediah, Fr-1812
    Robert, Wa-1819, Fr-1812(2),
        Gr-1821
    Stephen, D-1805
    William, Fr-1812, Gr-1821
    William Jr., Fr-1812
BEANE, Ralph, Wa-1814
BEANLAND, Edward, Wi-1801
BEAR, George, Su-1796
    Jacob, Su 1812
    Mathias, Su-1812
    Matthias, Su-1796, Su-1797
    Peter, Su-1796, Su-1797
BEARDEN, John Jr., Sn-1823
BEARDING, John, Sn-1816
BEASEY, Isaac, D-1811
    James T., D-1811
BEASLEY, Archabard, Wi-1810
    Archer, Wi-1815
    Barnett, Wi-1815
    Ephraim, Wl-1804
    John, Mu-1811, D-1805, Mu-1811
    Micajah, D-1811
    Philip, Wi-1815

BEASLEY, Willie, B-1812
BEASLY, Anne, Wi-1815
    Charles, D-1811
    Ephraim W., Wi-1815
    John, Fr-1812
    William, Fr-1812
BEASON, Daniel, B-1812
    Lurance, Mu-1816
    Nancy, Sn-1811
BEATMAN, Enoch, Wi-1815
BEATTY, Cypens, Wh-1825
    James, Su-1796
BEATY, Andrew, Su-1796
    Arthur, Mu-1816
    David, D-1805, D-1811, Mt-1798,
        Wi-1801
    Hugh, Ro-1805
    James, Su-1797, Mu-1816
    John, Mu-1816, Mt-1798, Gr-1799,
        Bo-1801, Bo-1800, Wi-1810
    Samel, Bo-1801
    William, D-1811
BEAVENS, Joel, D-1805
BEAVER, Christian, Su-1796
    Jessey, Sn-1816
BEAVERLY, STublefield, Sn-1811
BEAVERS, Jesse, Rb-1812
    Joel, D-1811
    Thos., Ge-1783, Se-1799
    William, Je-1800
BEAZLEY, Jesse, Gi-1812
BECHON, James G., Wi-1801
BECK, Frederick, Fr-1812
    Henry, Fr-1812
    Jacob, Fr-1812, R-1819
    Jeremiah, Fr-1812
    John, D-1811, B-1812
    Joseph, Wi-1815
    Lewis, Fr-1812
    Nathaniel, Rb-1812
BECKER, James, Gi-1819
BECKETT, Charles, Ro-1805
BECKHAM, William, D-1805
BECKNAL, Samuel, Ge-1812
BECKNALL, Daniel, Ge-1812, Je-1822
    James, Je-1822
    Nelson, Je-1822
    Pheboe, Ge-1812
    Samuel, Je-1822
    Young, Je-1822
BEDDIST, John, Fr-1812
BEDFORD, John R., D-1811
    William, D-1811
BEDLY, Josha, Sn-1816
BEDMON, William, J-1802
BEDSAUL, GEorge, Gr-1821
BEDWELL, Caleb, Gr-1805
    Ira, Wh-1811
    James, B-1812
    Jessee, Gr-1804, Gr-1805
    Jessey, Gr-1805
    John, Gr-1804, Gr-1805
    Reuben, B-1812
BEEHON, G. James, Mt-1798
BEEKER, Nicholas, D-1788
BEEL, Thomas, Wi-1801
BEELAR, Danel, Gr-1805
    John, Gr-1799
    Peeter, Gr-1805
    Richard, Sn-1811
    Abraham, Gr-1821
    Daniel, Gr-1804, Gr-1821

BEELAR, David, Gr-1821
    George, Su-1796
    Isaac, Gr-1821
    Jacob, Su-1796
    John, Su-1796
    John Sr., Gr-1804
    John Jr., Gr-1821, Gr-1805, Gr-1804
    Joseph, Su-1796, Gr-1804, Gr-1805
    Joseph Sr., Gr-1821
    Joseph Jr., Gr-1821
    Peter, Gr-1804, Su-1796
    Woolery, Su-1796
BEELOR, Daniel, Gr-1799, Su-1796, Gr-1805,
    Su-1797
    George, Su-1797
    Jacob, Su-1812(2), Su-1797
    John, Su-1812, Gr-1799
    John Sr., Gr-1805
    John Jr., Su-1812, Gr-1850
    Joseph, Su-1796, Su-1812(3),
        Gr-1799, Gr-1805
    Joseph Sr., Su-1797
    Martha, Su-1812
    Peter, Gr-1799
    Pieter, Gr-1805
    Samuel, Su-1812
    Woolery, Su-1797
BEEN, Stephen, Gr-1799
BEESLY, James, Fr-1812(Busby?), Je-1822
    Richard, W-1805
BEESON, Amarios, Je-1800
    Lamuel, Sn-1816
    Thomas, Je-1800
BEGHAM, James, Mu-1811
BELCHER, Arthur, Wh-1825
    John, Wi-1815
    Michance, Hw-1801
    William, Wh-1811
BELDEN, Bartholomew, Wh-1825
BELEMY, Elisha, Mt-1798
BELFORE, Andrew, Wa-1819
BELL, Adam, Gi-1812, Mu-1811
    Admond, Je-1822
    Andrew, Wa-1119
    Brooksey, Wa-1819
    David, Bo-1805, B-1812, Fr-1812,
        Wi-1815, D-1811
    George, D-1811(3), D-1805
    George Sr., D-1805
    Hugh, D-1805, Mt-1798
    Hugh Buckham, D-1805
    Hugh F., Wi-1815
    James, Wi-1801, Sn-1811, Mu-1816,
        D-1811(2), D-1805, Mu-1811,
        Wl-1804, Fr-1812, Wi-1814,
        Rb-1812, Wa-1819, Ge-1812(2)
    Jeremiah, Sn-1816
    John, Mu-1816, Wh-1825, D-1805,
        D-1811(2), Mu-1811, Mu-1816(2)
        D-1805, Fr-1812, C-1823,
        Bo-1801, Bo-1800(2), Wi-1815,
        Co-1821, B-1812, Se-1799,
        Wa-1814, Wa-1819, Ge-1812,
        Rb-1812, Ge-1804, Hw-1801
    John Jr., Ge-1805
    John J. Wm., C-1818
    John T., D-1811
    Johnathan, Mu-1811
    Joseph, Wi-1815, Hw-1801
    Nathaniel, D-1811
    Polley, Sn-1816
    Richard, Ct-1796, Hw-1801

BELL, Robert, D-1811(2), D-1805(2),
        Sn-1787, Fr-1812(2), Sn-1792,
        Hw-1801, Ge-1805
    Samuel, Wi-1815, D-1805, D-1811(2),
        Wi-1810, B-1812, Wa-1819,
        Je-1822
    Shederick, D-1811
    Stephen, Hw-1801
    Stephenson, Mu-1811
    Sterling, Mu-1816, Mu-1811
    Thomas, D-1811, D-1805, Mu-1811
    William, Sn-1816(2), Mt-1798, D-1811,
        Mu-1811, Mu-1816, D-1805,
        C-1823, Ge-1782, B-1812,
        Ge-1812(3), Ge-1805
    William R., D-1811, Wi-1815
BELLAMY, Elisha, D-1811
BELLE, William, Wi-1801
BELLENGER, Jacob, W-1812
BELLIW, Peter, Fr-1812
BELLOW, John, B-1812
BELLS, Daniel, Mu-1816(2)
    Isaac, Mu-1816
    John, D-1811
    Jonathan, Mu-1816
    Thomas, Mu-1816
BELLWELL, Isaac, Wh-1285
BELOTE, Henery, Sn-1811
    Henry, Sn-1816
    Jeremiah, Sn-1816, Sn-1811
    John, Sn-1816, Sn-1811
    Richard, Sn-1811
BELS, Barton, Mt-1798
    Donaldson, Mt-1798
    William, Mt-1798
    Zachariah, Mt-1798
BELSHEN, Wm., Hw-1801
BELSHER, John, Hw-1799
BELT, Thos., B-1812
BELYERE, Abraham, Hu-1812
BENCH, John, Gr-1805
BENEFIT, Peter, Su-1812
BENET, Jessy, Bl-1815
    Searcy, Mt-1798
BENETT, Grifeth, Sn-1816
BENGE, Micajah Lewis, D-1788
    Richard, Fr-1812
BENHAM, Daniel, Bo-1801
BENJAMIN, Henry, B-1812
BENLEY, John, D-1805
BENNATT, Walker, Wh-1825
BENNET, Alexander, Wi-1815, Wi-1810
    Benja., Gi-1812
    James, Bl-1815
    Jessey, Je-1800
    John, Wi-1810
    Joseph, Gi-1812
    Julias, K-1799
    Levan, Je-1822
    Levi, Wh-1811
    Miason, Mt-1798
    Nathan, D-1811
    William, Sn-1816, Wi-1815
    William Jr., Sn-1816
BENNETT, George, D-1805, Wi-1815
    James, Je-1822
    John, Wi-1815, R-1819, B-1812
    John Sr., Ge-1805
    John Jr., Ge-1805
    John T., Wi-1815
    Rachal, Ge-1812
    Thos., Ge-1783, Gr-1799

BENNETT, Walker, Wh-1811
    William, Je-1822, A-1805
    Wm. J., Wh-1825
BENNING, James, D-1811(2)
BENNINGFIELD, James, D-1811
    Robert, D-1811
BENOIT, Earnest, D-1811
BENSESS, Peter, Wi-1810
BENSON, Bable, Ge-1805, Ge-1812
    Benjamin, Gi-1812
    Chirchester, Gr-1799
    Early, Gi-1812
    Elisha, D-1805
    Elizabeth, D-1805
    Gabriel, Mu-1811(2), R-1819
    Goberas, Mu-1816
    John, B-1812, R-1819, Wi-1815,
        Sn-1811
    Leaben, B-1812
    Martin, Rb-1812, Wi-1815
    Matthias, R-1819
    Richard, Rb-1812
    Robert, Sn-1811
    Thomas, A-1805, K-1799
    William, Rb-1812
BENTHALL, Matthew, Gi-1812
BENTLEY, John, Sn-1816
BENTLY, John, Sn-1811, Gi-1812
    Richard, Gi-1812
BENTON, Benjamin, D-1805
    David, W-1812
    Edward, Mu-1811
    James, Rb-1812
    Jessee, Wi-1815
    Jessee, heirs, Mu-1811
    Mary, Wi-1815
    Nancey, Wi-1815
    Nathiel, Wi-1815
    Samuel, Wi-1810
    Thoms. H., Wi-1815
    Titus, Rb-1812
BERD, David, Se-1799
    Zebelun, Se-1799
BERGER, Frederick, Su-1812
BERKE, James, Ge-1783
BERKLEY, Ebenzer, Wa-1814
BERNARD, George, D-1811
    John, Hu-1812
    Thomas, D-1811
BERNES, Horatia, Wi-1810
    Jeramiah, Wi-1810
BERNOSTN, William, Bl-1815
BERRAMORE, Wm., Gi-1819
BERRY, Basil, Wi-1801, Wi-1815
    Bazzill, Wi-1810
    Benjamin, Hu-1812
    Bezzal, Wi-1815
    Enoch, B-1812
    Ephraim, W-1825
    George, Bo-1800, Bo-1805
    Hugh, R-1819
    James, Wi-1810, Gi-1812, Gr-1799(2)
    James & Haslerig, R-1819
    John, D-1811, Wh-1825, Gr-1799,
        Je-1800, Gr-1799
    John G., D-1811
    Jonathan, Gi-1812
    Joseph, Wl-1804
    Lawson, D-1811
    Robert, Je-1800
    Samuel, Fr-1812
    Thomas, Wi-1810, Bo-1801, Wi-1815

BERRY, Thomas, continued--Wi-1801,
        Bo-1800
    William, W-1818
    Wm., estate, Wi-1815
    Wright, Wh-1825, Rb-1812
BERRYCROFT, Danl., B-1812
BERRYHILL, Alexander, Fr-1812
    M. William, Mu-1811, Mu-1816
    William, Fr-1812
BERRYMAN, Anderson, Wi-1815
    John, B-1812
BERTHAL, Buck, Gi-1819
BERTHWRIGHT, Williamson, D-1811
BESBERS, Jarel, Gi-1812
BESHEARS, Jeremiah, Wh-1825
BESHELL, John, Je-1822
BESIER, John, Sn-1816
BESKINS, Mary, Ro-1805
BESLEY, Wm., Bo-1801
BESON, Henry, Sn-1816
BETHEL, Larkin, Fr-1812
BETTIS, Bradley, Je-1822
    David, Je-1822
    Eli, Je-1822
    Horotio, Wi-1810
    Simeon, Hu-1812
    Thomas, Je-1822
    William, Je-1822
    William J., Je-1822
BETTS, Johnathan, Mu-1811
    Jonathan, D-1811
    Zachariah, D-1805
    Zacheriah, D-1811
BEUL, William, Mu-1811
BEVEN, Abell, W-1812, W-1805
BEVERLY, John, Hu-1812
BEVERS, Joel, Wl-1804
BEVINS, James, B-1812
    Stephen, B-1812
BEWFORD, Charles, Wi-1801
    James, Wi-1801
    Spencer, Wi-1801
BEWLEY, Anthony, Ge-1812
BEWLY, Anthony, Ge-1812
    Jacob, Ge-1812
    Johon, Ge-1812
BEYLEW, John, Hu-1812
BEZER, Peter, D-1811
BIBB, Christian, Su-1797
    William, D-1811(2)
BIBBY, William, D-1811
BIBLE, Adam, Ge-1812
    Christian, Ge-1812, Ge-1805
    Christopher, Ge-1805
    George, Ge-1812
    John, Ge-1812
    Lewis, Ge-1812
    Philip, Ge-1812, Ge-1805
BIBLES, John, Bo-1801
BICE, Wm., Bo-1801
BICKERSTAFF, Henry, A-1805
    John, Mu-1816, A-1805
    Robert, A-1805
BIDDLE, James, Wa-1814
    Samuel, Wa-1814, Wa-1819
    Thomas, Wa-1814, Wa-1819
    Thomas Jr., Wa-1819
BIDWELL, Martin, Wh-1825
BIFFEL, Jacob, Mu-1816
    Nathan, Mu-1816
BIFFELL, John, Mu-1816
BIGBY, George, Rb-1812

BIGBY, Patrick, D-1811
    Thomas, Ro-1805
BIGGAR, Joseph, Wi-1810, Wi-1801
    Robert, Wi-1810, Wi-1801
BIGGS, David, Sn-1811
    John, Ge-1783, Rb-1812(2), Ge-1805,
        Ge-1812
    Joshua, Sn-1816
    Reuben, Ge-1805
    Ruben, D-1811
    William M., Je-1822
BIGHAM, James, Mu-1816
    John, Bo-1805
    Nath., Bo-1800, Bo-1801
    Samuel, Bo-1801
    Wm., Ge-1783, Bo-1801, Fr-1812
BIGLEY, Patrick, D-1805, D-1811
BIGS, Adam, Sn-1816
    John, Sn-1816
    Peter, Gi-1819
BILES, James, Bo-1800
    Stephen, Gi-1812
BILL, David, Sn-1811
    George Sr., Mt-1798
    Robert, Fr-1812, Bo-1800
BILLANDS, Thomas, Ge-1783
BILLBERT, John, Sn-1816
BILLIANSLY, Elijah, Ge-1812
BILLING, John, Su-1796
BILLINGS, Ardent?, D-1805
    John, D-1805, Wh-1825
    Peter, Wh-1811, Wh-1825
    William, D-1805, Wh-1825
BILLINGSBY, Jacob, Wa-1819
    James, Wa-1814, Wa-1819
    Jesse, Wa-1814, Su-1812, Wa-1819
    John, Wa-1814, Wa-1819
BILLINGSLEY, James, Wi-1810
    Jepthah, Ge-1805
    John, Su-1797, J-1801, Su-1812
    John Sr., Su-1812
    Thomas, Ge-1805, J-1802
    Walter, J-1802
BILLINGSLY, Thomas, Gi-1819
BILLINGTON, Ezekiel, B-1812
BILLS, Isaac, Mu-1811
BILNOR, John, Ge-1812
BINCONE, Richard, Rb-1812
BINDING, Charles, Gr-1799
BINGESS, Thomas, Wh-1825
BINGHAM, Josiah, Mu-1816
    Reubin, Hw-1801
    William, B-1812
BINKLEY, Adam, D-1811
    Adam Sr., D-1811
    Daniel, Rb-1812
    Fredrick, D-1811
    Jacob, Rb-1812(3), Wa-1814
    Joseph, Rb-1812
    Peter, D-1811
BINON, Job, Sn-1811
BINSON, Spencer, R-1819
BINTLY, James, Sn-1816
BINUM, Reason, Wl-1804
BIRCH, Elijah, Je-1822
    James, D-1811
    Richard, Je-1822
BIRD, Abraham, Sn-1811
    Alexander, Fr-1812(2)
    Amos, Mt-1798, Ge-1783
    Andrew, Se-1799
    David, Ge-1812

BIRD, Jacob, Ge-1805
    James, Wa-1814, Ge-1805, Ct-1796
    John, Gr-1805(2), W-1812, Wi-1815,
        Gr-1799, Gr-1804
    John Sr., Ge-1812
    John Jr., Ge-1812
    Jonathan, Se-1799
    Joseph, Ge-1783
    Richard, Wi-1815
    Thomas, Rb-1812
    William, Fr-1812, Se-1799
BIRDSON, John Sr., R-1819
BIRDSONG, John, Gr-1799
    John Jr., R-1819
BIRDWELL, Benjamin, Su-1796, Su-1797,
        Wa-1814
    George, D-1805, D-1811(2)
    Hugh, D-1811
    Isaac, D-1811(2)
    John, Su-1797, Su-1796, Gi-1812
    Joseph, Su-1797, Su-1796
    Mary, Su-1796, Su-1797
    Robert, Su-1797, Su-1796
    Ruben, D-1805
BISCANE, John, Ro-1805
BISHOP, Alishi, Hw-1801
    Elijah, Hw-1801
    George, A-1805
    Henry, B-1812
    John, Su-1797(2), Su-1796
    Joseph, Bl-1815
    Joseph Jr., Hw-1801
    Joseph Sr., Hw-1801
    Matt., Ge-1783
    Peter, Su-1796, Su-1797
    Samuel, Ct-1798, Ct-1796
    Thomas, Su-1796, Su-1797
    William, A-1805, Su-1796, J-1802
BITNER, John, Ge-1805, Wa-1814
    Margaret, Wa-1819
BITSERBURGY, Peter, Ge-1805
BITTEMAN, John, Mu-1816
BIVERY, Spencer, Gi-1812
BIZELL, Isaac, Wi-1815, Wi-1810
BLACAMORE, George, Sn-1811
BLACK, Alexr., Gi-1812, Wi-1801
    Cavin, Bo-1805
    David, D-1805
    G. Thos., Mu-1816
    Gavin, Bo-1801, Bo-1800
    George, Sn-1811
    George G., Fr-1812
    Hugh, D-1805
    Jacob, Je-1822, Sn-1816
    James, Bl-1815, Wa-1814, Wi-1801,
        Wi-1810, Hu-1812
    James, Esq., Mu-1816
    John, Bo-1800, Gr-1799(2), C-1823,
        A-1805, D-1805, Je-1800,
        Gi-1812, Gi-1819, Mc-1825,
        Ro-1805, Sn-1816, Sn-1811
    John Jr., C-1818
    John Sr., C-1818
    Joseph, Ge-1812
    Joseph Jr., Bo-1805
    Mark, Wi-1815
    Mical, Sn-1816
    Michael, Sn-1811
    Peter, Hu-1812
    Robert, Gi-1819, Je-1822, Ge-1812,
        Gi-1812, Wi-1801
    Samuel P., Wi-1801

BLACK, Thomas, Wi-1810, Mu-1816, Hu-1812,
        Wi-1801(2)
    Widow, Ge-1812
    William, Wi-1815, Ro-1805, Rb-1812,
        Ge-1805, Ge-1812, Wi-1810(2),
        Wl-1804, Mt-1798, D-1805(2)
    William Sr., D-1805
BLACKAMON, George, D-1805
BLACKAMORE, William, D-1805
BLACKARD, Eli, Fr-1812
    Jerimiah, Mu-1816
BLACKBOURN, Edwd., Mu-1816
    John, Mu-1816
    William, Mu-1816
BLACKBURN, A. Lemuel, Mu-1816
    Ambrose, Mu-1816
    Andrew, Je-1822
    Arch., Wa-1819
    Benjamin, Wa-1814, K-1796, Bo-1801
    Edward, Mu-1811, Je-1822
    Gidn., Wi-1815
    Gidion, Mu-1811, Bo-1800
    Gillian, Bo-1800
    Israel, Rb-1812
    James, Je-1822
    John, Mu-1816, Mu-1811, Gr-1805,
        Gr-1821, Je-1822, Ge-1805,
        B-1812, Gr-1804, Je-1800
    John & Edward, D-1805
    John W., Ge-1812
    Joseph, Fr-1812
    Robert, Rb-1812
    Thomas, Ge-1805
    William, Je-1800, Cl-1803, Se-1799,
        Wl-1804, Wa-1819
BLACKE, John, D-1788
BLACKENS, Thos., D-1788
BLACKFARE, _____, D-1811
BLACKMAN, Bennet, D-1811
    Bennett, D-1805
    Elijah, B-1812
    Elizabeth, Sn-1816
    John, Wi-1810, Wi-1815, Wi-1801
BLACKMOORE, John, Wh-1825
BLACKMOR, J., Wi-1801
BLACKMORE, G. D., Sn-1817
    George D., Sn-1816(2)
    Rachel, Su-1812
    Robert, Su-1812
    Samuel, Su-1812
    Widow, Su-1812
BLACKSTON, Jessee, heirs, Wi-1810
BLACKWELL, James, R-1819, Mt-1798
    Jesse, Ro-1805
    John, Ge-1783, B-1812
    John B., Rb-1812
    Nathan, B-1812
    Pleasant, W-1805, W-1812
BLACKWOOD, Andrew, J-1802
    Robert, Fr-1812
    William, Gr-1799
BLAGG, John, A-1805
    Joseph, Je-1822
BLAIN, Jacob, Wh-1825
    John, Wi-1815
    Joseph, Gi-1812
    Robert, Gr-1821
BLAIR, Alexander, Gr-1821, Gr-1804,
        Gr-1805
    Andrew, W-1812, Mu-1816
    Arthur, D-1811
    James, Bo-1800, Gr-1805, D-1811

BLAIR, James Sr., Gr-1799, Gr-1804,
        Gr-1821, Gr-1805
    James Jr., Gr-1804, Gr-1821,
        Gr-1805
    John, Gr-1821, Wa-1819(2), Bo-1800,
        Bo-1801, Bo-1805, Wa-1814(2),
        Wh-1811, Gr-1805, D-1811(3),
        D-1805(2)
    John, heirs, Gr-1804
    John & Parsons Ph., Wa-1819
    Jos., Gi-1819
    Jossiah, Gr-1799
    Peter, Sn-1816, Sn-1811
    Robert, J-1802, Gr-1799, Sn-1811,
        Sn-1816, Gr-1805
    Samuel, Mo-1825, Bo-1805, J-1802,
        D-1811, Gr-1805, D-1805,
        Wi-1801
    Thomas, Bo-1805, B-1812, Wl-1804
    Tom, Wa-1819, Wa-1814
    William, Gr-1799, Gr-1804, Gr-1799,
        Bo-1801, Ge-1812, Gr-1805
BLAIRE, William, Ro-1805
BLAKE, Benjamin, Je-1822 Gr-1805
    Hugh, Ge-1812(2)
    John, D-1811
    Willoby, Hw-1799
BLAKELEY, Robert, Wa-1819
    Wm., Gi-1819
BLAKELY, Alexr., W-1812
    Daniel, Wa-1814
    Forest, Mu-1811
    James, Mu-1816, Mu-1811, D-1811,
        R-1819, Wa-1819
    James, estate, Mu-1811
    Jennet, Mu-1816
    Jessee, D-1805
    John, Wa-1814, Wa-1819
    Robert, Wa-1814
    Samuel, Mu-1811, Mu-1816
    Thomas, R-1819, Wa-1814
    Thomas Jr., Wa-1814
    William, D-1811, Mu-1816, Wa-1814,
        Mu-1811
BLAKEMAN, William, D-1811
BLAKEMON, Lee C., Sn-1823
    Thomas, Sn-1823
BLAKEMORE, Edward, Sn-1816
    George, Sn-1792, Sn-1816
    James, Sn-1816(2), Sn-1811
    John D., Sn-1816, Sn-1811
    Reubin, Sn-1811
    Thos., Sn-1816(2), Sn-1811
BLAKLEY, Daniel, Wa-1819
BLAKMORE, Geo. D., Sn-1787
BLALOCK, Charles, Wl-1804
BLANCETT, Archibald, W-1812
    Henry, W-1812
    James, W-1812
    Peter Sr., W-1812
    Peter Jr., W-1812
    William, Gr-1821
BLANCHET, Peter, W-1812
BLAND, John, D-1805
BLANKENSHIP, Geo?, D-1811
    Isam, Bo-1800
BLANKINSHIP, Isom, Bo-1801
BLANTA, John, Mu-1816
BLANTEN, Isaac, W-1812
BLANTENS, John, Mu-1811
BLANTON, Alexander, B-1812
    Isaac, Wh-1811

BLANTON, John, W-1812
    Tarlton, Co-1821
    Vincent, W-1812
    Vinson, Mc-1825
    William, W-1812
BLASCOCKE, Archibald, Wa-1814
BLASENGAME, Jno. Jr., Gi-1812
    Jno. Sr., Gi-1812
    Wade, Gi-1812
BLAXTON, Argyle, Je-1822
BLAYLOCK, Henery, Wi-1810
BLEACH, Abraham, Hw-1799
BLEAK, Francis, D-1805
    Peter, Ge-1805
BLEDSAW, Abraham, Fr-1812
    James, Ge-1812
BLEDSOE, A., Sn-1816
    Abram, Sn-1811
    Anthony, Sn-1787
    Anthony, heirs, Wl-1804
    Anthony Head, Sn-1787
    Catey, Sn-1816
    Henry, Sn-1817
    Henry B., Sn-1816
    Isaac, Sn-1817, Sn-1792, Sn-1787
        Sn-1811
    Isaac, heirs, Sn-1811
    John, C-1823
    Lewis, Fr-1812
    Raty, Sn-1811
    Wm., Sn-1816
    Wm. Lytle, Sn-1811
BLERTON, HEnry, D-1811
BLESSING, Henry, B-1812
BLEVENS, Armstreat, W-1812
    William, Su-1796
BLEVINS, Armstad, Su-1797
    Armstead, Su-1796
    Cluncy, Su-1812
    Dillon, Su-1796, Su-1797
    Ditlow, Su-1812
    Hardin, Su-1812
    James, Su-1796, Su-1797
    John, Su-1797, Su-1812
    John Sr., Su-1812
    John Jr., Su-1812
    John R., Su-1812
    Matthew, Su-1812
    Moses, Su-1812
    Phillip, Wa-1819
    Stephen, W-1812, Bl-1815
    Walter, Su-1812
    William, Su-1797(2), Su-1796,
        Su-1812(2)
BLIAR, Alexander, Gr-1799
    James Jr., Gr-1799
BLISHER, Hugh, Ro-1805
BLITHE, Samuel, Wl-1804
BLIZARD, Thomas, Bo-1805, Bo-1801
BLOISE, James, Ro-1805
BLOODTHALL, Thos., Wi-1801
BLOODWORTH, Edmond, Sn-1816
    Henry, Sn-1811
    John, Sn-1816
    Joseph, Sn-1816
    Thomas, Sn-1811, B-1812
    Thos. Sr., Sn-1816
    Thos. Jr., Sn-1816
    Webb, Sn-1811, Sn-1816
    William, Sn-1816, Sn-1811, Wl-1804
BLOUNT, G. John, Wl-1804
    Isaac, D-1811

BLOUNT, Jackey S., Wi-1815
    John G., Wi-1801, Gr-1799
    Thomas, Wi-1801, Wl-1804
    William, Wi-1815
BLOW, Samuel, Fr-1812
BLOYD, Feebley, B-1812
BLOYTH, James, B-1812
BLUE, Douglass, Gi-1812
    Moses, Gi-1812
BLUFORD, Edward, Wi-1815
    Spencer, Wi-1815
BLUNT, Wiley, Gr-1821
    Willie, Gr-1799
BLYTHE, Andrew, Sn-1816, Gi-1812(2)
    Benjamin, Wi-1815
    H. Samuel, Sn-1816
    Jacob, Gi-1812
    James Sr., Wi-1815
    John G., D-1811
    Joseph, Wi-1815, Wi-1810
    Joseph Jr., Wi-1815
    Richard, Sn-1816
    Saml., Gr-1810(3)
    William, D-1805
BOASLEY, Dillard, Wl-1804
BOATMAN, Ezekiel, Gr-1821
    George, Gr-1804, Gr-1821, Gr-1799,
        Gr-1805
    Henry, Gr-1804, Gr-1821, Gr-1799,
        Gr-1805
    William, Wh-1811, Gr-1821
BOATRIGHT, Chesley H., Gr-1821
    James, Wi-1810
BOATWRIGHT, William, Gr-1821
BOAZ, Edmund, Sn-1811
    William, Mu-1816
BODENHAMER, Peter, Mu-1816
BODIN, Levi, Ro-1805
BODLE, James, Gr-1799
BODMAN, Thomas, Gi-1812
BODY, John, S-1805
BOGARD, Abraham, Gi-1819
    Cornelius, Bo-1800
    Jacob, Gi-1812, Gi-1819, Wi-1801
BOGART, Cornelius, Ct-1798, Ct-1796
    Samuel, Ct-1796
    Samuel Jr., Ct-1798
    Samuel Sr., Ct-1798
BOGAS, Bennett, Je-1800
BOGEE, H. George, Wl-1804
BOGHARD, Cornelius, Bo-1801
BOGLE, Andrew, Bo-1801, Bo-1800
    Andrew Jr., Bo-1805
    Hugh, Bo-1805, Bo-1801
    Jepht., Bo-1800
    Joseph, Bo-1801
    Joseph Sr., Bo-1805
    Joseph Jr., Bo-1805
    Samuel, Bo-1805, Bo-1800, Bo-1801
BOHANNON, George, Wh-1825
    James, Wh-1825, Hu-1812
    John, Wh-1825, Hu-1812
    Lewis, Wh-1825
    Philamon, Su-1812
    Thomas, Wh-1825
    William, Wh-1825
BOUEN, Elijah, Ct-1798
BOICE, Hez., Gi-1812
BOILS, Barnabas, D-1811
    John, Ge-1805, D-1811
BOLDEN, Wm., Sn-1787
BOLE, James, Bo-1801

BOLEN, Isaac, D-1805
    Levy, Hw-1799
    Nicholas, D-1805
    Phillip, Wa-1819
    Thomas, Wa-1819
    William, Hw-1799
BOLES, James, Bo-1800
BOLING, David, Gr-1821
BOLT, Benjamin, B-1812
    John, B-1812
BOLTAN, Joel, Wl-1804
BOLTON, John, Wi-1815, Mu-1816
    Robert, R-1819
    Thomas, Gr-1821
    Thomas Jr., Gr-1821
BOMAN, Willm., Sn-1792
BOMAR, William J., Wi-1815
BOMER, Anselm, Wh-1825
    William, Wi-1810
BON, Abraham, Fr-1812
    Edward, Fr-1812
    Jacob, Fr-1812(2)
    John, Fr-1812(2)
    Stephen, Fr-1812
    William, B-1812
BOND, Henry, Bo-1801, Su-1796, Su-1797
    Isaac, Gi-1812
    Jesse, J-1802
    Jessee, W-1812
    John, Wi-1815(2), W-1812
    Joshua, Gi-1812
    Nathan, J-1802
    Nathen, W-1812
    Page, Wi-1815
    Stephen, Mo-1825
    William, Wi-1815
    William, Su-1812, Su-1796, W-1812, Su-1797
    William Sr., Wi-1815
    William Jr., Wi-1810, Wi-1815
    Zekeriah, Sn-1816
BONDS, Isaac, C-1823
    Zacariah, Sn-1811
    Zaceriah, Sn-1816
BONDURANT, Edward, D-1805, D-1811
BONE, Abner, Wl-1804
    Azariah, Gi-1812
    Hugh, Wl-1804
    James, Sn-1792, Wl-1804
    John, Sn-1816, Wl-1804
    Thomas, Wl-1804
BONNER, James, Fr-1812
    John & James, J-1802
BOO, Rudolph, Ge-1812, Ge-1805
BOOK, William, D-1805
BOOKOUT, Charles, A-1805
    John, A-1805
    Marmaduke, A-1805
BOOKER, Barnabas, Gr-1799
    David, Su-1812
    Frederick, Su-1812
    John, Mu-1816, Su-1812(2), Su-1797
    Martin, Su-1812(2)
    Peter, Su-1812
    Peter R., Wi-1801
    R. Peter, Mu-1816, Mu-1811
    Richard, D-1811
    William, Su-1812
BOON, Bryant, D-1811
    Daniel, W-1812, W-1805
    Henry, B-1812
    Hezekiah, Ct-1798

BOON, Hiram, W-1812
    John, Gr-1805
    Mordecai, Ct-1798
    Philip, Sn-1816
    Solomon, Ct-1798, Ct-1796
BOONE, Peter, Je-1822
BOOTH, Andrew, D-1811
    David, Wa-1814(2)
    Edwin E., K*-1815
    Henry, D-1805, B-1812
    Henry Sr., D-1811
    Henry Jr., D-1811
    John, Wa-1819, Wa-1814(2)
    Joseph, Wa-1814(2)
    Nathan, W-1812
    Stephen, B-1812
BOOTHE, David, Wa-1819
BORAN, Bazel, Je-1822
    Wm., Bo-1800
BORDEN, Daniel, Ge-1812
    Hall Sims, Bl-1815
    Joel, Bl-1815
BORDERS, Michael, Ge-1783
BORDON, Daniel, Ge-1805
BOREN, Abraham, Wa-1814
    Absolom, Gi-1812
    Chaney, Wa-1814
    Chany, Wa-1819
    Elijah, Wa-1814, Wa-1819
    Francis, Rb-1812, Sn-1811
    Hezekiah, Wa-1819
    Jerock, Wa-1819
    Jöhn, Wa-1814, Rb-1812, Sn-1811
    John Jr., Sn-1811
    Sally, Sn-1816
    Tarlton, Sn-1811
    William, Wa-1814
BORIN, Abra., Gi-1812
    James, Gi-1812
BORING, Gremsley, Wa-1819
    Joshua, Wa-1819
BORRIAN, Barny, Wa-1819
BORROW, John, Su-1812
BORUM (Bowen?), John, Fr-1812
BOSHAM, John, Bl-1815(2)
    Jonathan, Bl-1815
    William, Bl-1815
BOSLEY, Beal, D-1805
    James, D-1788
    James R., D-1811
    John, D-1811
BOSTICK, Absalom, Wi-1810
    Absolom, Wi-1815
    John, Wi-1815, Wi-1810
    Nathan, Sn-1816
BOSTON, Nancy, D-1805
BOSTWICK, Charles, Su-1812
BOSWELL, Hosea, D-1811
    James, Su-1812
    Miles, D-1811
BOSWERS, Leonard, Ct-1798
BOSWORTH, Collin, D-1811
    W., D-1811
BOTERITE, Daniel, Bo-1801
BOTKIN, High, Se-1799
    Thomas, Se-1799
BOTTLE, Henry, Wa-1814
    Joshua, Cl-1803
BOTTOM, John, Mu-1811
BOTTOMS, Wm., Gi-1812
BOTTS, John, B-1812
BOUCHER, Thomas, W-1805, W-1812

BOUGHER, Jacob, Bo-1800
    John, Su-1796
BOULES, James, Hu-1812
BOULTON, Joel, K-1796
BOUNDS, George, Fr-1812(2)
    James, A-1805, Wh-1811
    Jesse, Fr-1812(2)
    Jessee, Wh-1825
    John, A-1805, Wh-1825
    Thomas, Wh-1825, Wh-1811(2)
    William, Wh-1825
BOURCHEIR, Samuel, Su-1812
BOURDEN, Adon, Bo-1801
BOURN, Jac, Mo-1825
BOUSER, George, Wa-1819
    John, Wa-1819
BOUSHING, David, Su-1812
BOUTWELL, Stephen, Bo-1800
BOW, Bartlett, D-1811
    Henry, D-1805
BOWARK, James H., W-1812
BOWDEN, James, Mu-1811(2), Mu-1816
BOWDER, Lott, D-1805
BOWEN, Abram, Ge-1812
    Arthur, Wh-1811
    Charles, Wh-1811
    David, Ro-1805
    George A., Gr-1821
    Henry, Gr-1821, Wh-1825
    Henry Sr., Gr-1805(2), Gr-1799
    Henry Jr., Gr-1805, Gr-1804,
        Gr-1799, Gr-1821
    James, Gr-1805, Wh-1811, Gr-1804,
        Gr-1799
    John, J-1802(2), Gr-1805(2),
        Gr-1804, Gr-1799, Gr-1821
    Joseph, Su-1796, Sn-1811
    Laml. A., Sn-1811
    Mary, Sn-1811
    Thomas, Gr-1821
    William, Sn-1787, D-1788, Wl-1804,
        Bo-1801
    William B., Gr-1821
BOWENS, Nicholas, Wh-1285
    William, Sn-1792
BOWER, Joel, D-1805
    John, Su-1812
BOWERMAN, John, Bo-1800, Bo-1801
    Michael, Bo-1801
    Peter, Bo-1801
BOWERS, C. William, D-1805
    Christly, Ge-1812
    Daniel, Bo-1801
    Henry, Wa-1814
    Jesse, Wl-1804
    John, Ge-1812, Ge-1804(2)
    Lemuel, D-1811
    Leonard, Ct-1796
    Nancy, Wa-1819
    William, Ge-1805
    William, Esq., Ge-1812
    William P., D-1811
BOWERY, John, Su-1812
BOWIN, Andrew, Gr-1821
BOWLAND, David, Je-1822
    Jacob, Wi-1810
    Jas., Wi-1815
BOWLER, James, D-1805
BOWLES, Chares, D-1811
    John, D-1811
BOWLIN, William, Su-1797
BOWLING, Absolom, C-1818

BOWLING, Alexander, Gr-1804, Gr-1805,
    Sn-1816
    Benjamin, A-1805
    Edmond, Ge-1812
    Jeremiah, Ge-1812
    Joel, A-1805
    John, Su-1812
    John Jr., Su-1812
    Joseph, A-1805
    Larkin, A-1805
    Thomas, Gr-1804, Gr-1805
    William, C-1818, Gr-1804(2)
BOWLS, John M., W-1812
    William, Je-1822
BOWMAN, Benjamin, Je-1822, Wh-1825
    Daniel, Wa-1814, Wa-1819, Ge-1805
    Elias, Bo-1800, Wa-1814
    Elizabeth, Ge-1812
    George, Je-1822
    Henry, Ge-1805, Ge-1812
    Hezekiah, Wa-1814
    Hiram, Wh-1825
    Jacob, Ge-1805(2), Ge-1812, Wa-1819,
        Je-1800, Mu-1816
    Jacob Sr., Ge-1812
    Jeremiah, Gr-1821
    John, C-1818, Gr-1821, Wa-1819(2),
        Je-1822, Wa-1814(2), Sn-1811
    Joseph, Wa-1819, Wa-1814, Ge-1812
    Leroy, Sn-1816
    Peter, A-1805
    Samuel, Ge-1812
    Sparling, Ge-1812
    Sperling, Ge-1805
    Sperling Jr., Ge-1805
    Thomas, Mu-1816
    William, Gr-1799(2), Gr-1821,
        Sn-1787, Wa-1819, Gr-1804,
        Wh-1811(2), Sn-1811, Gr-1805
BOWMON, John, W-1812
BOWRY, John, Su-1797
    Margaret, Su-1796
BOWSER, John, Su-1797, Su-1796
BOWYER, Luke, Cl-1803
    Michal, Su-1796, Su-1797
BOX, Edward, Ge-1783
    Henry, Ge-1783
    Jonathan, Je-1822
    Joseph, Ge-1783
    Robert, Ge-1783
BOY, Adam, Su-1812
    Andrew, Wl-1804
    Jacob, Su-1796, Su-1812, Su-1797(2)
BOYAKIN, William, Mu-1811
BOYCE, Hezekiah, Mu-1816
    James, Su-1812
    Nancy, Sn-1816
BOYD, Aaron, Wl-1804
    Abram, Wi-1801
    Alex, Bo-1800
    Alexander, B-1812, Bo-1801
    Andrew, D-1811, Mu-1816, Mu-1811,
        D-1788, Sn-1811
    Armstead, Wi-1801(2)
    Aron, Wi-1815
    B. Leard, Mu-1811
    David, Wa-1819
    Elijah, Gi-1812
    Francis, Gr-1821
    George, Bo-1801, Bo-1800
    Harison, Wi-1801(2)
    Harrison, Wi-1810, Wi-1815

BOYD, Henry, Wa-1814
    James, Je-1800, Bo-1805, Bo-1801,
        Bo-1800, Mt-1798, Wi-1801,
        Wi-1810, W-1812, Ge-1783,
        Su-1796, Su-1797, Ge-1812
    Jeremiah, Wa-1814
    John, Bo-1800, B-1812, A-1805,
        Sn-1792, Bo-1801, Rb-1812,
        R-1819, Gi-1812, Sn-1811,
        Sn-1816, Mu-1816, D-1805,
        Wl-1804, D-1788(2), Mu-1811,
        D-1811(2)
    John R., Wi-1815
    Jordon, A-1805
    Joseph, B-1812, Mu-1811
    Leroy, Rb-1812
    Margaret, Wh-1811
    Richard, D-1805, D-1811
    Robert, Gr-1799, Bo-1801, Bo-1805,
        Bo-1800, Sn-1816, D-1811,
        Mu-1811, Wi-1815
    Robert & John, D-1805
    William, Ct-1796, A-1805, Bo-1800,
        B-1812, Bo-1801, D-1811,
        Ge-1783, Je-1800, K-1799,
        Rb-1812, Su-1812, W-1812,
        Wl-1804
    William G., Wi-1815
    William J., Wi-1815
    William L., D-1811(2)
BOYDE, William, Bo-1805
BOYDSTONE, Thomas, Gr-1799
BOYDSTUN, William, Ge-1783
BOYED, Robt., Sn-1811
    William, Ct-1798
BOYER, George, Wa-1814
    Henry, Wa-1814, Sn-1811
BOYERS, Joseph, Se-1799
    Robert M., Sn-1816
BOYET, Thos.?, Wi-1810
BOYETT, Jessee, B-1812
BOYKIN, James, Sn-1816
    Milley, Sn-1816
    Mills, Sn-1816
    Robert, Sn-1816
BOYL, Thomas, D-1811
    William, D-1811
BOYLE, Hugh, Sn-1816
    Isaac, Sn-1816
    James, Sn-1816
    John, Sn-1811, Sn-1816
    Robert, Sn-1816, Sn-1811
    William, Sn-1811
BOYLES, David, Je-1800
    Jonathan, W-1812
    Joseph, W-1812
BOYLS, Charles, Wi-1801
DOYOKIN, Wiley, Mu-1816
BOYSE, Charles M., Fr-1812
    William, Fr-1812
BOYTE, Etheldrige, Wi-1810
BOZIER, Peter, D-1811
BOZOTH, Joseph, Wh-1825
    Levi, Wh-1825
BOZORTH, Levw, Wh-1811
BRABSON, Ephraim, Wa-1814
BRACHIN, William, Sn-1811
BRACHON, John, Rb-1812
BRACK, Durham, Sn-1811
    George A., B-1812
    John, Wh-1825
BRACKEN, Ferris, Ro-1805

BRACKEN, Henry, B-1812
    Isaac, Sn-1811
    James, W-1812
    John, D-1811
    Wm., Sn-1816
BRACKENRIDGE, Wm., Gi-1819
BRACKETT, Morgan, Su-1812
BRACKIN, Elisabeth, Sn-1811
    Isaac, Ro-1805
    James Jr., Sn-1816
    John Sr., Sn-1816
    John Jr., Sn-1816
BRACY, John, Sn-1811
*BRAANT, John, Hw-1799
BRADBERRY, George, Mu-1816
    Jacob, Mu-1816
    Jacob Sr., Mu-1816
    James, D-1811
BRADBURN, Wm. Y., Rb-1812
BRADBURY, George, Mu-1811
BRADEN, Alaxander, Sn-1792
    Alexander, Rb-1812
    Andrew, A-1805
    Charles, Wl-1804
    Edward, Gr-1799, Gr-1804, Rb-1812
        Gr-1805, Gr-1821
    George, C-1818
    John, C-1818, Gr-1799, Gr-1805,
        Mu-1816, Gr-1804
    Joseph, Wi-1815
    Samuel, Wi-1810
BRADFORD, Benjamin, Je-1800, Gr-1799,
        B-1812, Ct-1796
    Benjamin J., D-1811
    Green, D-1805
    Hamilton, B-1812
    Henry, Wl-1804, Sn-1816, Je-1800
    I. Benjamin, D-1805
    James, Je-1822
    John, Wh-1825, B-1812, D-1811
    Thomas G., D-1811
    William, Wh-1825, Sn-1816
BRADHURST, Joseph, Ge-1812
BRADICK, John, Wl-1804
BRADIN, Alexander, Wl-1804
    Robert, Rb-1812
BRADLEY, Anselm, Wh-1825
    David, Sn-1816, Sn-1811
    Edward, Sn-1816
    Elisha, Gi-1812
    George, Gi-1812
    Henry, Sn-1811
    Isaac, Gr-1821
    Isham, Wh-1825, Wh-1811
    James, Gr-1821, Wi-1815, Wl-1804
    John, Bo-1800, Bo-1801, Wh-1825
        Sn-1811
    John Sr., Wl-1804
    John Jr., Wl-1804
    Jonathan, Su-1796, Su-1812, Su-1797
    Lamuel, Sn-1811
    Moses, Sn-1816
    Nathaniel, Rb-1812
    Richard, Sn-1811, Sn-1816
    Robert C., Wi-1810
    Sam., Gi-1812
    Terry, Wi-1815
    Theny, Sn-1811
    Thomas, Wl-1804, Sn-1816, Wh-1825
    William, Fr-1812, Gi-1812
BRADLY, Abram, Sn-1816
    Danial, Sn-1816

BRADLY, Edward, Sn-1811
     Henry, Sn-1816
     James, Sn-1811
     John, Sn-1816
     John D., Sn-1811
     Joshua, Sn-1816(2)
     Luke, Sn-1816
     Richard G., Sn-1816
     Richard T., Sn-1811
     Thomas, Wi-1815, Sn-1816, Sn-1811
     William, Sn-1816
BRADON, Joseph, Wi-1810
BRADSHAW, Benjamin, Je-1822
     Charles, Wh-1825
     Christopher, Ge-1812
     David, Sn-1811
     Fielding, Sn-1816
     G. Eli, Mu-1816
     George, Wh-1825(2)
     Henry, Wl-1804, Mu-1811
     Hugh, Mu-1816
     James, Je-1800
     Joel, Wh-1811
     John, Sn-1811, Wh-1811
     John C., D-1811
     Peter, Wl-1804
     Richard, Je-1822
     Samuel, Je-1800, Fr-1812
     Solomon, Mu-1811
     Thomas, Su-1796, D-1811
     Will, Mu-1816
     William, Wh-1811, Je-1800, Sn-1811,
          Wh-1825, D-1805, Mu-1811
BRADY, Charles, R-1819
     Edward, Wh-1811
     Jeremiah, R-1819
     Jolasse, Mu-1811(2)
     Joseph, Gr-1804
     Thomas, Sn-1811
BRAG, Richd., Mu-1816
BRAGG, Charles, Su-1796
     David, Su-1812, Su-1796, Su-1797
     Hugh, Gr-1804, Gr-1805
     John, Je-1822
     Joseph, Su-1812
     Moore, Wi-1801
     Nicholas, Je-1822
     Thomas, Su-1796, Su-1812, Su-1797
BRAHAM, John, Wh-1811
BRAIDEY, Thomas, Bo-1800
BRAINS, John, B-1812
BRAKE, Shearwood, Je-1822
BRAKEBILL, Henry, R-1819
BRALEY, Walter, Wl-1804
BRAN, John, Je-1800
BRANAM, James, C-1818
     John, Hw-1799
     Martin, Hw-1799
BRANCH, Benjamin, D-1811, D-1805
     Henry, Mu-1816, Mu-1811
     James, Mu-1816
     John, B-1812, Mu-1816
     Nicholas, B-1812, Wi-1815
     Robert, Wl-1804
BRANDIN, Thomas, Ge-1812
BRANDON, Abel, Sn-1811
     Christopher, Hu-1812
     James, Fr-1812(4)
     John, Gi-1819, B-1812
     Richard, Gi-1819
     Thomas, Fr-1812
BRANER, Casper, Je-1822

BRANHAM, Ephriam, C-1818, A-1805
     James, C-1818, C-1823
     James Sr., Gr-1804
     James Jr., Gr-1804
     Martin Sr., C-1818
     Sarah, C-1818
     Talmon, C-1818
     Thomas, Gr-1804, A-1805
BRANNAM, James Sr., Gr-1805
     James Jr., Gr-1805
     T. G., Cl-1803
BRANNER, George, Je-1822
     John, Ct-1798
     Michael, Je-1800, Je-1822
     Michael Sr., Je-1822
BRANNON, Thomas, Wa-1814
     William, D-1811, Wa-1814
BRANNUM, James Jr., Gr-1805
     James Sr., Gr-1805
     Thomas, Gr-1805
BRANSCOMB, Joseph, C-1818, C-1823
BRANSFORD, Nathan, Sn-1816
BRANSON, Andrew, Bl-1815
     Daniel, Je-1822
     David, Gr-1821
     John, Gr-1805, Bl-1815
     Jonathan, Gr-1805
     Lemuel, Gr-1805, Gr-1804, Gr-1821
     Nathaniel, Gr-1821
     Thomas, D-1811
BRANTLEY, Abraham, Wi-1810
     Charles, Mt-1798
     John, Wi-1815
BRANSTETTER, Peter, Ct-1798, Ct-1796
BRARROW, Mathew, Wi-1815
BRASFIELD, John, J-1796
BRASHEARES, Robert, Gi-1819
     Bazzle, Ro-1805
     Robert S., Ro-1805
BRASON, Thomas, Wa-1814
BRASSEL, Gorge, K-1799
     William, Sn-1816
BRASSFIELD, James, C-1823
BRATCHER, Benjamin, C-1823
     Charles, Je-1800, C-1823, C-1818
     Isaac, C-1823
     John, C-1818
     Johnson, C-1818
     Samuel, C-1823
     Sherman, D-1805
     William, Mt-1798, Ge-1805(2),
          C-1823(2), C-1818
BRATCHERS, John, D-1805
BRATON, George, Wi-1801
BRATREY, James Sr., Sn-1816
     James Jr., Sn-1816
     Robert, Sn-1816
BRATTEN, Hugh, Gi-1812
     James Jr., Sn-1811
     Robert, Sn-1811
     Thomas, Gi-1812
BRATTON, Hugh, Gi-1819
     Paul, Gi-1812
     Thos., Gi-1819
     William, A-1805, Sn-1816, Sn-1811
BRAWLEY, John, Gi-1812
BRAWNER, William, A-1805
BRAY, George, Wh-1825
     James, Wh-1825(2)
     John, K-1799
     Solomon, Su-1812
BRAYENT, James, D-1788

BRAZAELE, Elijah, Ro-1805
    Henry, Ro-1805
    James, Ro-1805
BRAZEL, Morgan, K-1799
    Richard, K-1799
    Valintin, K-1799
    William, Sn-1811, K-1799
BRAZELTON, Isaac, R-1819, A-1805, K-1799
    Jacob, Je-1822
    John, Je-1800, Ro-1805
    Lanty, Je-1822
    Will, Je-1800
    William, Je-1822, Gi-1812
    William Sr., Je-1800
    William Jr., Je-1822
BRAZLE, George, K-1799
    William, A-1805
BRAZLETON, Isaac, A-1805
BREADEN, Edward, Gr-1805
BREAVIT, William O., D-1811
BRECKENRIDGE, Alexr., heirs, Mu-1816
    George, Mu-1816
BRECKER, John, Wa-1814
    William, Wa-1814
BREDIN, Samuel, Su-1812
BREDWELL, Wm., C-1823
BREEDING, Byrum, R-1819
    John, W-1812
BREEDON, Mason, B-1812
BREEZE, Thomas, Bo-1800, Bo-1801
BREKEM, John, Fr-1812
BRENSFORD, Arthur, Sn-1811
BRENTHILL, Edward, Wi-1815
BRENTSFUND, James, A-1805
BRESHAMS, Robert, Ro-1805
BRESHEARS, Isaac, Wh-1825
    Jeremiah, Wh-1825
    John, Wh-1825
    Thomas, Wh-1825
BRESHERS, John, Gi-1812
BRESSON, James, W-1812
BREVERT, John, Je-1800
BREWANTON, John, Fr-1812
BREWER, Aaron, Wh-1825
    Elisha, D-1811
    Elisheal, D-1788
    Henry, Mu-1816
    Oliver, Wl-1804, Je-1800
    Philip, Ge-1805
    Russell, W-1812
    Samuel, Sn-1816, Ge-1805, Ge-1812
    William & Francis, D-1805
    Zion, Gr-1804, Gr-1805
BREWS, Robert, Sn-1816
BREYDON, Joseph, Wi-1801
BRIAN, Andrew, Ge-1812
    Daniel, Ge-1812
    Elizabeth, Ge-1812
    Jesse, Ro-1805
    John, Ge-1812
    Philip, Wi-1815
    Thomas, Je-1800
BRIANT, Adrian, Wh-1825
    Ann, D-1805
    Archelas, Wi-1815
    James, Je-1822
    John, D-1811, C-1823, Fr-1812, C-1818
    Joseph, Gr-1799, Gr-1805
    Mason, Fr-1812
    Morgin, Hw-1799
    Samuel, Wl-1804, D-1805

BRIANT, Shederick, D-1811
    Thomas, Fr-1812
    William, D-1811
    Willis, Mu-1816
BRICKER, John, Wa-1819
    Michael, heirs, Wa-1819
    William, Wa-1819
BRICKIN?, G. James, Mt-1798
BRICKS, William, Ro-1805
BRIDEN, Spencer, Gr-1805
BRIDGEMAN, Wm., C-1823
BRIDGES, Barns, Mu-1816
    Britin, Rb-1812
    Brittain, Mu-1816
    Daniel, Mu-1816
    Drury, Mu-1811(2)
    Edmund, Sn-1811
    Henry, Mu-1811(2), Mu-1816
    James, Wi-1801, Mu-1816, Mu-1811(2)
    Joseph, D-1805
    Reddick, Sn-1816
    Redick, Sn-1811
    S. Daniel, Mu-1811(2)
    Saml. B., Wi-1815
    Thomas, Cl-1803, Gr-1799
    William, Gr-1799
    _____, Wi-1810
BRIDGET, George, Gr-1805
BRIDGEWATER, Isaac, Gi-1812
BRIDGEWATERS, Isaac, D-1805
BRIDWELL, Sandford, Su-1812
BRIENT, John, W-1812
BRIGANCE, Charles, Sn-1811
    David, Sn-1811, Sn-1787, Sn-1792
    Elija, Sn-1811
    Elizabeth, Sn-1816
    James, Sn-1811, Sn-1816
    John, Sn-1811, Sn-1787
    Wm., Sn-1787
    Wm., heirs, Sn-1816
BRIGG, Anselem, Sn-1816
BRIGGS, James, Wh-1825
    John, Wh-1811, Je-1800
    Nathan B., Wh-1825
    Richard, Gi-1812
BRIGHAM, David, Mt-1798
    James, Mt-1798, Su-1797, Su-1796
    John, Su-1796
    Thomas, Mt-1798
BRIGHT, James, Su-1812, Li-1812*
    Michael, Ge-1812(2)
    Wm., Li-1812*
BRIGHTBILL, Peter, Su-1797, Su-1796
BRIGHTWELL, William C., Wh-1811
BRILES, John, Wh-1825
    Reuben, Wh-1825
    Samules, Co-1827
    William, Wh-1825
BRILEY, Abraham, Hu-1812
    Cottrel, Ct-1798
    John, D-1811
    Joshua, Hu-1812
    Samuel, Sn-1811, Sn-1816, Mu-1811
    Wiliam, Sn-1811
BRILL, Richd., Sn-1816
BRILY, William, Sn-1816
BRIM, Abraham, Bo-1800
    Edmond, Bo-1801
    Henry, C-1823, C-1818
    Joseph, C-1818, C-1823
    Lewis, Gr-1804, A-1805, C-1823, C-1818

BRIMER, Joseph, Ct-1796
BRINKLY, Thomas, Sn-1816
BRINSON, Gaus, Mt-1798
    James, Wl-1804
BRINTO, Jacob, C-1818
BRINTON, John, C-1818
BRISCOE, John, Fr-1812
BRISON, Hugh, Ge-1783
    Samuel, Wa-1814
BRISTO, John, Gr-1799
BRISTOL, John, D-1805
BRISTOW, John, Cl-1803
BRIT, Edmond, Wh-1825
    John, Wa-1819, Wa-1814
BRITAIN, Benjamin, C-1823
    Cullen, Wi-1815
    David, Wh-1825
    Nathaniel, Su-1796
    William C., Wh-1825
BRITON, James, Ge-1812, Sn-1816
    Thomas, Sn-1792
BRITTAIN, Abraham, Su-1796(2)
    Abram, Su-1797
    Benjamin, B-1812
    Joseph, B-1812
    Nathan, Su-1797
    Richard, Su-1796, Su-1797
    William, Je-1800
BRITTAN, Abraham, Wl-1804
BRITTE, Robert, D-1805
BRITTEN, Abraham, Wa-1814
    William, Ge-1805
BRITTON, Andrew, Je-1822
    Benjamin, C-1818, Je-1800
    Cornelius, Wa-1814
    James, Je-1800
    John, Su-1812
    Joseph, Je-1822
    Joseph Sr., Wa-1814, Wa-1819
    Joseph Jr., Wa-1814
    William, Ge-1812
BROADAWAY, John, B-1812
BROADMAN, John P., Wi-1815
BROADWAY, John, B-1812
BROCK, Allen, Gr-1799, A-1805
    Charles, Gr-1821
    Cornelius, W-1812
    David, Gr-1805
    Durhan, Sn-1816
    George, Gr-1799, Ge-1783, Gr-1805,
        Gr-1821, Gr-1805
    James, J-1802, Gr-1821, Fr-1812
    Jehue, Gr-1821
    Jessee, Gr-1805
    Jessey, Gr-1805
    John, Wh-1811, Gr-1804, Mu-1811
    Leonard, Gr-1821
    Lewis, Mt-1798
    Moses, Gr-1804, Gr-1805
    Obadiah, Gr-1821
    Reubin, Ro-1805
    Sarah, C-1818
    Sherrod, A-1805
    Thomas, Gr-1821
BROCKAS, William, Gr-1804
BROCKS, Allen, A-1805
    Isaac, Ro-1805
BROCKUS, John, Gr-1821
BROADAWAY, John Jr., B-1812
BRODERICK, William, Su-1797
BRODINAX, Thomas, D-1811
BRODY, Joseph, Gr-1805

BROGANS, Reynolds, Wh-1811
BROGDEN, David, W-1812
BROILES, John, Ge-1805
BROILS, Aron, C-1818
    George, Bo-1800, Bo-1801
BROKIS, William, Gr-1799
BROLING, John, Su-1812
BROMFIELD, Elisha, Wi-1815
BROMIT, Owen, Je-1800
BROMLEY, James, Bo-1801
BRONSON, Charles, B-1812
BROOK, George, Gr-1805
    Tho., Sn-1816
BROOKE, William, D-1805
BROOKES, William, B-1812
BROOKING, Isaac, Sn-1816
BROOKS, Archabald, Fr-1812
    Archibald, Wl-1804
    Arthur, Wl-1804
    Christopher, Ge-1812, Mt-1798
    Dabney, Gi-1812
    George, Mu-1816, Sn-1811, Wi-1815
    Henry, Mu-1816
    Hezekiah, Mu-1816, Mu-1811
    James, W-1812(2), Wi-1815, D-1805,
        Fr-1812
    James Jr., Wi-1814
    John, Sn-1811, D-1805, Su-1796
    Joseph, R-1808
    Mary, R-1819
    Mathew, D-1811
    Mathew, heirs, Sn-1816
    Matthew, D-1805, Wl-1804
    Micajah, Mu-1811
    Moses T., D-1811
    Philip, C-1818
    Price W., Wi-1815
    Robert, Mu-1811, Fr-1812
    Samuel, Mu-1811
    Stephen, Wl-1804, Wi-1815, Ge-1805
    Stephen, Dec., Ge-1812
    Tarlton, Je-1822
    Thomas, Mu-1816, Mu-1811
    Thomas Sr., Ge-1812
    Thomas Jr., Sn-1816, Ge-1812
    William, W-1812, D-1811, Fr-1812
    William B., Gi-1812
BROOKSHAW, Thomas, Sn-1811
BROOKSTON, Thomas, Fr-1812
BROOM, Miles, Ro-1805
BROOTH, Samuel, Mu-1816
BROTHERS, Edward, W-1812
    Philip, Sn-1811, Sn-1816
BROTHERTON, John, Ge-1812
    William, Ge-1812, Ge-1805
BROUN, Jeremiah, Wl-1804
    William, Wl-1804
BROUTSFUND, James, A-1805
BROW, Absalom, W-1812
BROWDER, Federick, Wi-1810
    Fredorick, Wi-1810
    Fredrick, Wi-1815
    John, Ro-1805, D-1805
BROWDY, Joseph, Gr-1805
BROWLES, Davies, Ro-1805
BROWN, Abraham, Wa-1819, Gi-1812, Wa-1814
    Abraham Jr., Wa-1819
    Absalom, Mu-1811, B-1812
    Alexander, Wh-1825, Ge-1805,
        Fr-1812
    Anny, Sn-1811
    Asa, Hu-1812

BROWN, Avery, A-1805
    Benjamin, Wh-1825, Wi-1810, W-1812,
        Ge-1805, Su-1797, Wa-1814,
        Wi-1815
    Benjamin M., Sn-1811
    C. John, Ct-1798
    Caldwell, Ct-1798
    Charles, Sn-1811, Wi-1815
    Christian, Wa-1819
    Claiborne, Je-1800, A-1805
    Clancen?, Mt-1798
    Conrad, Wa-1819, Wa-1814
    Daniel, Mu-1816, Mu-1811(2), Mu-1816,
        Wi-1815, J-1802
    David, Sn-1816, Wl-1804, Gr-1805,
        Wa-1819(2), W-1812, Je-1800,
        Ge-1812, Wa-1814(3), Gi-1812,
        Bo-1800, Bo-1801
    Davis, Sn-1816
    Duncan, Mu-1811, Mu-1816, Gi-1812
    Durden, Hu-1812
    Edward, Wl-1804, Gr-1805, Gr-180
    Eli, C-1818
    Elijah, Bo-1801
    Ephraim, Wi-1810, Wi-1815
    Fedrick, Sn-1816
    Francis, Fr-1812, Sn-1816
    George, Mu-1811, D-1811, Je-1800,
        Su-1812, Su-1797, Wa-1814,
        Ge-1805(2), Ge-1812(3)
    George M., Wh-1825
    Henry, D-1811(2), D-1805, Su-1812,
        Wa-1814, Gr-1821
    Hezekiah, B-1812
    Hugh, Mu-1816(2), Wa-1814, B-1812
    Isaac, Wh-1825, D-1805, Gr-1805(2),
    Wa-1814, Wh-1811, Gr-1804
    Isaith, Bo-1801
    Jackson, Wl-1804
    Jacob, Wa-1819(2), R-1819, Wa-1814(3)
    Jacob Sr., Wa-1814(3), Wa-1819
    Jacob Jr., Wa-1819, Wa-1814(2),
        Wh-1811
    James, Wl-1804, Sn-1816(2),
        Sn-1811(2), Gr-1805(5),
        Gi-1812(3), Je-1822, Wh-1811,
        Gr-1821, C-1818, Bl-1815,
        Ge-1783, Gr-1804(2), C-1823(2),
        Gr-1799(2)
    Jarama, Gr-1805
    Jathem, Ge-1812
    Jepah, Bo-1800
    Jerremiah, Gr-1805
    Jesse, Wa-1819, W-1812, Wa-1814
    Jessee, Wh-1825, Mu-1811
    *Jeremiah, Wl-1804, Bo-1805, Gr-1804
    Jethro, Mu-1811(2)
    Joel, Sn-1811, Sn-1816
    Johannon, Wh-1825
    John, Wl-1804(3), Sn-1816(2), R-1819,
        Sn-1811(3), Mu-1816, R-1808,
        Ro-1805, W-1812, Wa-1819(3),
        Gr-1821, D-1788, Wh-1825(2),
        Mu-1811(3), Mu-1816(2),
        D-1811(2), Gr-1805, Gi-1812,
        Wa-1814(4), C-1818, Su-1797,
        Ge-1805, Ge-1812, Je-1822,
        A-1805, Bo-1801, C-1823,
        Bo-1800, Gr-1799
    John Sr., Wa-1819
    John Jr., Wa-1819, Wa-1814
    John B. C., Wl-1804

BROWN, John C., Wa-1814
    John C. Sr., Wa-1819
    John C. Jr., Wa-1819
    John J. H., C-1818
    Jonathan, B-1812, Ge-1805(2)
    Joseph, Wh-1825
    Josiah, Mu-1816
    Leonard, Sn-1816, Sn-1811, Hu-1812
    Lewis, Gi-1812
    Lieper, Fr-1812
    Lindsey, Wh-1825, Wh-1811
    Mary, Mu-1816, Wa-1814, Wa-1819
    Matthew, Wl-1804, Gi-1812
    Maxwell, Ge-1805
    Michael, Wa-1819, Wa-1814
    Morgan, Mt-1798, Gi-1812
    Moses, D-1805(2)
    Nathaniel, D-1811, Fr-1812
    Noah, C-1823
    Noell, Wi-1810
    Nowell, Gi-1812
    Philip, Ge-1805
    Polly, Je-1822
    Reuben, A-1805
    Reuben D., Sn-1816
    Reubin D., Sn-1811
    Richard, Sn-1816, Sn-1811(3),
        D-1805, Wi-1810, Wi-1801,
        Wh-1825, Wl-1804
    Robbert T., Sn-1816
    Robert, D-1811, Wi-1801, Mu-1811(3),
        Sn-1816, W-1812, Gi-1812,
        B-1812, C-1818, Sn-1811
    Roby, D-1805
    Ruffin, Wi-1810, Wi-1815
    Sally (widow), Gi-1819
    Salusne, Ge-1812
    Samuel, D-1811, Wh-1825, Sn-1811,
        Mu-1816, Ro-1805, B-1812(2),
        Wa-1819, Bl-1815, C-1823,
        C-1818, Wi-1815
    Shedrick, B-1812
    Soloman, Wa-1819
    Solomon, Wa-1814, B-1812
    Stephen, Wa-1814, Gr-1821
    Thomas, D-1805(2), Mt-1798, D-1811,
        Gr-1805, Sn-1816, Wa-1819(2),
        K*-1815, C-1818, Ro-1805(2),
        W-1812(3), Su-1797, Je-1822(2)
        Ge-1812(2), Su-1812,
        Wa-1814(2), Gi-1812, Fr-1812,
        Ge-1805(2), Gr-1804, Gr-1821,
        Gr-1799
    Thomas Jr., Wa-1819, Wa-1814
    Thomas G., R-1808, Ge-1805
    Thomas J., Wa-1814
    Valn., Sn-1816
    W. John, Mu-1811(2), Wa-1819
    Wadkins, D-1811
    Washington, C-1823
    Widow, Sn-1816
    Wiley, Wi-1810, Mu-1816
    William, Wa-1814(2), Mu-1816(3),
        Mu-1811(3), Gr-1805, Hu-1812,
        W-1812, Wa-1819(4), Gi-1812,
        Je-1800, Ge-1812(5), Wh-1811,
        Ro-1805, Wi-1815, Gi-1819,
        Gr-1804, Fr-1812, Gr-1821,
        Ge-1805, Gr-1799
    William Sr., Wh-1825
    William Jr., Wh-1825
    Zacharoh, Fr-1812

BROWNFIELD, Elisha, D-1811
BROWNLEE, Jno., Se-1799
BROWNLEY?, Cornelius, D-1811
BROWNLOW, John & Alexander, D-1805
    Joseph A., Su-1812
    Samuel, Su-1812
    William L., Su-1812
BROWNING, Beedy, B-1812
    Charles, Wa-1819
    David, Gi-1819
    Edward, Sn-1811
    George, B-1812
    John, Gi-1819
    Joshua, B-1812
    Ninrod, Rb-1812
    Rodger, Ge-1805
    Roger, Ge-1812, Su-1796, Su-1797
    Samuel, Wl-1804
    Thomas, Gi-1812, Sn-1816, Sn-1811
BROWNSVILLE, Amos, Wi-1810
BROYHILL, William, Mo-1825
BROYLE, James, Wa-1814
    Michael, Wa-1814
BROYLES, Abraham, Wh-1811
    Adam, Wa-1814, Ge-1812, Wa-1819
    Aron, C-1823
    Cyners, Wa-1814
    Cyrus, Wa-1819
    Ephriam, Ge-1812(2)
    Ezekial, Wa-1819
    Ezekiel, Ge-1805
    Felix, C-1823
    George, Wh-1825
    Jacob, Ge-1783
    James, Wa-1819
    Jeremiah, Ge-1805
    John, Wh-1811
    John Jr., Ge-1812
    Julias, Wa-1814
    Julius, Wa-1819
    Mathew, Wa-1814
    Matthias, Ge-1805
    Michael, Wa-1819
    Michaele, Ge-1812
    Nathan, Wa-1819
    Nicholas, Wa-1814
    Nicholas, estate, Wa-1819
    Samuel, Wa-1814
    Simon, Wa-1814, Wa-1819
    Thomas, Wa-1814
    William, Co-1827
BROYLS, Mary, Ge-1812
BRUCE, Edward, B-1812
    James, Mu-1811, Sn-1811
    Mu-1816, Mu-1811, Je-1822
    John, Je-1822
    Robert, Sn-1811(2), Sn-1816
    Ruben, Sn-1816
    Thomas, Gi-1812
    Walker, Sn-1816, Sn-1811
    William, Sn-1816(2), Sn-1811, W-1812
BRUEN, George, Gi-1812
BRUFF, James, Wi-1815(2)
BRUIS, Arret, Gr-1805
BRUK, David, Sn-1816
BRUMBLE, Lewis, Rb-1812
BRUMET, Abram, W-1812
BRUMLEY, Barnet, Bo-1801
    Cornelius, Wi-1815
    Isaac, Ge-1805
    James, Bo-1800
    John, Gi-1812

BRUMLEY, John Sr., A-1805, C-1818
    John Jr., A-1805
    Lewis, Wh-1825
    Mary, Ge-1805
    William, A-1805, Bo-1800, C-1818
*BRUMFIELD, Joseph, B-1812
BRUMLOW, Augustine, Ge-1783
    Barns, Ge-1783
    Thos., Ge-1783
BRUMMIT, James, Wa-1819, Wa-1814
    Micajah, Wa-1814
    Micasah, Wa-1819
    Samuel, Wa-1814, Wa-1819
BRUMSNET, John, Fr-1812
BRUMSON, Joseph, D-1811
BRUMSTETTER, Daniel, Su-1812
    Peter, Su-1812
BRUNDRIDGE, Stephen, Fr-1812
BRUNER, Jacob, Ge-1812
    Jacob Jr., Ge-1812
    John, Ge-1812
BRUNSON, Joseph, Gi-1812
BRUSO, John, B-1812
BRUSTON, James, Gr-1799
BRUTON, David, A-1805
    Jacob, Gr-1799
    James, Gr-1799
    John, A-1805
    Samuel, Gr-1799
BRYAN, Ambrose, Su-1796
    Andrew, Wh-1825, Wh-1811
    Asa, Rb-1812(2)
    Edmond, Rb-1812
    Hardy, Rb-1812
    Hardy J. P., Rb-1812
    Henry, D-1811
    Henry M., Wi-1815
    James, Wh-1825
    James H., Rb-1812(2)
    James R., Wh-1811
    Jerimiah, Mu-1816
    John, Wh-1811(3), Je-1800, Wh-1825
    Lamuel, Wi-1815
    Lewis C., Rb-1812
    Michal, Su-1797
    Morgan, Wh-1811
    Robert, Sn-1792
    Samuel, D-1811
    William, Su-1797, Wh-1811(2),
        Je-1800, D-1811
    Wm. L., Wh-1825
    William M., Wh-1811
    Wm. M., Sr., Wh-1825
    Wm. M. Jr., Wh-1825
BRYANS, Edward, B-1812
BRYANT, Ambrose, Su-1797
    David O., Wi-1815
    Elisha, Gi-1819
    Enoch D., Gi-1812
    James, Gr-1821, Je-1822, Gi-1812,
        Gr-1804, Gr-1805, Li-1812*,
        D-1805, K-1796
    John, Gr-1821, Gi-1812
    Joseph, Gr-1805, Gr-1821(2),
        Gr-1804
    Joshua, Fr-1812
    Nathan, D-1805
    Richard, Fr-1812
    Samuel, D-1805
    Thos., Sn-1811
    William, Su-1796, Gr-1805, Fr-1812
        Sn-1816, Gr-1804

BRYANTS, Bryant, Ge-1783
BRYMER, John, Je-1822
      Vinscent, Je-1822
      William, Je-1822
BRYNE, James, Wl-1804
BRYNNER, Daniel, D-1811
BRYSON, Abraham, R-1819
      Hannah, R-1819
      Jacob, R-1819
BUCHANAN, Andrew, D-1805
      David, D-1811
      Davis, D-1805
      Edward, Bo-1801
      James, D-1805
      John, Wi-1810, D-1788(2), D-1805,
          D-1811, Wi-1815
      Maj. John, Wi-1815
      Peggy, D-1805
      Robert, D-1805, Li-1812*
      Samuel, D-1805
      Thomas, D-1811
      William, Gi-1812, Su-1796
BUCHANNAN, Andrew, W-1805, W-1812
      John, Wl-1804, D-1805
      Peter, Su-1797
BUCHANNON, Thos., B-1812
BUCHANON, James, D-1811
      Robert, D-1811
BUCHART, George, Su-1812
BUCHETT, Richard, Wi-1801
BUCHHINSON, Jeremiah, Ro-1805
BUCK, Abraham, Ct-1798, Ct-1796,
        Wh-1825
      Isaac, Wh-1825
      John, Gi-1812
BUCKALOW, Jonathan, Su-1812
BUKET, Mathias, Je-1822
BUCKHALTER, Henry, Ge-1812
      William, Fr-1812
BUCKHAM, Andrew, Sn-1811
BUCKHANON, James, B-1812
BUCKHANNON, Benjamin, B-1812
      Hugh, Rb-1812
      John, Wi-1801(2), Mu-1816,
          B-1812
      John Jr., B-1812
      Samuel, Wi-1801
      Thos. Jr., B-1812
BUCKHORN, Willie, B-1812
BUCKINGHAM, Thomas, Wa-1814, Wa-1819,
        Ge-1783
BUCKLER, Henry, D-1805
      John, Su-1797
BUCKLES, John, Su-1796
BUCKLEY, Joseph, Wi-1801
      Nathan, Sn-1811
      Nathl., Sn-1816
BUCKLY, James, B-1812
BUCKNEL, William, Su-1796
BUCKNER, Bur, Co-1821
      Ezra, Gr-1821
      George, Wh-1811
      Henery, Co-1821
      Presley, Gr-1799, Su-1796
      Ressy, Mu-1816
      William, Ct-1796, Su-1797
BUCOME, James, Wa-1814
BUE, Angles, Gr-1804
BUFORD, Charles, Gi-1812, Gi-1819
      James, Gi-1812, Gi-1819, Wi-1801
      Spencer, Wi-1810
BUGASS, John, Wh-1825

BUGBY, Thomas, Gr-1805
BUGG, Benjamin, Wi-1810
      Jessee, Wi-1810
      Willim, Wi-1815
BUICE, William, Wi-1801
BUIS, William, R-1808
BUISE, William, R-1819
BUKMAN, Elijah, B-1812
BUKNER, Presley, Su-1797
BULL, Elisha, Wa-1819, Wa-1814
      George, Gr-1821, Gr-1799, Wa-1814
      Jacob, Wa-1814, Wa-1819(2)
      John, Bl-1815, Je-1822, Hw-1799
      John Jr., Gr-1805, Gr-1804
      John Sr., Gr-1805, Gr-1804
      Joseph H., Wa-1814
BULLA, Isaac, B-1812
      James, B-1812
BULLARD, Christopher, Fr-1812
      Isaac, Ge-1783
      John, Cl-1803
      Joseph, Fr-1812, Ge-1783
      Martha, Je-1800
BULLEN, James, Gr-1821
      Jesse, Gi-1819
BULLER, Christopher, J-1802
BULLINGER, Peter, Ct-1796, Ct-1798
BULLOCK, Amos, Wi-1810
      David, A-1805, Wh-1825
      Elijah, Gr-1821
      John, Mu-1816, Wh-1825, C-1823
      Jonathan, Mu-1816
      Nathan, Wi-1810, Wi-1815
      Richard, C-1818, C-1823
      Samuel, Gr-1805, Gr-1804
      William, Wh-1825, Su-1812
BULLS, Barnabas, Wi-1810
      William, D-1805
BULLY, Anty, Ge-1783
BUMPASS, Gabriel Jr., Gi-1812
      Gabriel Sr., Gi-1812
      Gowan, Wl-1804
      James, Gi-1812
      William, D-1811(2), Wl-1804, D-1805
      Willm. Sr., Wl-1804
BUMPERS, Jospeh, Ge-1783
BUMSTETTER, Frederick, Su-1812
BUNCH, Anderson, Gr-1821
      Christopher, Su-1812
      David, Gr-1799, Gr-1804, Gr-1805,
          Gr-1821
      James, Gi-1819
      Jessee, Gr-1805
      John, Gr-1821, Gr-1804, Wi-1801,
          K-1799(Banks?)
      John Sr., Gr-1805
      John Jr., Gr-1821
      John Sr., heirs, Gr-1850
      Josiah C., Gr-1821
      Martin, Gr-1799, Gr-1804
      Merada, Gi-1819
      Robert, Gr-1799
      Samuel, Gr-1805, Gr-1821
      Solomon, Mu-1816
      Thomas, Gr-1821, Gr-1799
      William, Sn-1811
BUNDY, David, Sn-1811, Sn-1816
      David Jr., Sn-1823
      David Sr., Sn-1823
      James, C-1823, Gr-1805, C-1818
      John, Sn-1823, D-1805
BUNHAM, Ivey, Gr-1805

BUNN, Etheldrid, Gi-1819
    Henery, Sn-1816
    Williamson, Cl-1803
BUNTIN, Joseph, Sn-1811, Sn-1816
    Wm., Sn-1816
BURBY, William, Je-1822
BURCH, George, Je-1822
    Harris, Gr-1805
    John, Su-1797, Je-1822
    Ryal, Gr-1805
    William, Gr-1805
BURCHAM, David, Mu-1816
BURCHELL, Thomas, Gr-1821
BURCHFIELD, Joseph, Je-1822
BURCHUM, David, Mu-1811(2)
BURCK, Anderson, Mo-1825
BURD, Jacob, Ge-1812
BURDEN, Elijah, Wh-1825
    Hall Sims, Bl-1815
    John, Wh-1825
    Nathaniel, Wh-1825
    William, K-1799
    William Sr. Wh-1825
BURDETT, Jiles, B-1812
    William, B-1812
BURDIN, Eli, Wh-1811
    John, Wh-1825
    Joseph, Wh-1825
    Squire, Wh-1285, K-1799, Wh-1811
    Wm. Jr., Wh-1825
BURDINS, John, Wl-1804
BURDON, John, A-1805
BURES, Spencer, Gi-1819
BURGAN, John, Su-1797
BURGAR, Michael, Ge-1805
BURGE, Polley, Wi-1815
    Wm., C-1823
BURGER, John, Ge-1812
    Michael, Ge-1812
    Tazwell T., Wi-1815
BURGES, Ben, Gi-1812
    John, B-1812
    Nathaniel, Gi-1819
    Richard, B-1812
    Will., Gi-1812
    Wm., C-1818
BURGESS, James, Wi-1810
    Josiah, Wh-1825
    Thos., W-1812
    William, Fr-1812(2)
BURGEY, Eathern, Ge-1805
BURGIS, John, C-1818
    Wm., C-1823
BURGNER, Peter, Ge-1812
BURGNES, Peter, Wa-1819
BURK, Andrew, Wh-1811
    Arter, Ct-1796
    Benj., Sn-1811
    Elihew, Ct-1796
    John, Su-1796, Su-1797
    Miner, D-1788
    Robert, Wa-1814, Ro-1805, Wa-1819
    Samuel, Wl-1804
    William, Bo-1801, Bo-1800, Bl-1815
BURKES, Harris, Gr-1804
    Hezikiah, Mo-1825
    Ryland, Gr-1804
BURKET, William, Mu-1811
BURKETT, James, Mu-1816
    Robert, Mu-1816
    William, Mu-1816
BURKETTE, Richard, Sn-1811

BURKHEART, F., Ge-1805
    George, Ge-1805
BURKIN, Wm. A., Hu-1812
BURKLAND, Daniel, C-1823
    Walter, C-1823, C-1818
BURKLY, John, Sn-1792
BURKS, Harris, Wh-1811
    John, Gr-1805, Gr-1804
    Joseph, Wi-1810
    Richard, Gr-1805, W-1805, W-1812
        Wh-1811(2)
    Riland, Wh-1811
BURKY, Christian, Ge-1812
BURLESTON, Moses, W-1805
BURLINGTON, Henry, Wh-1825
BURLISON, Isaac, Co-1821
BURLISTON, Moses, W-1812(2)
BURLSTON, Moses, W-1805
BURN, Jacob, Gi-1819
BURNBILE, John, Wh-1825
BURNES, George, Mu-1811(2)
    James, Mu-1811(2)
    William, Gi-1812
BURNET, Alexander, Wl-1804
    John Sr., Gr-1821
    Joseph, Gr-1804, Gr-1805
    Philip, Sn-1816
    Robert, D-1788
    Samuel, Wl-1804
BURNETT, Charles, Gr-1805
    Claibourne, Gr-1850
    Cornelius, Fr-1812
    George, Wi-1815
    Henry, D-1811
    James, Gr-1821
    John, Gr-1805, Mu-1816
    John Jr., Gr-1821
    Joseph, D-1811, Gr-1821
    Labourn, Gr-1805(2)
    Leonard, D-1811, D-1805
    Richard, Gr-1821
    Robert, Ge-1805
    William, Sn-1811, Je-1822
BURNEY, Adam, Gi-1812
    Charles, Gi-1812
    Samuel, Gi-1812
    Wm., Ge-1783
BURNFIELD, James, D-1811
BURNHAM, Ivy, Wi-1810
    Jonas, D-1805
    Joshua, Wi-1810
    Richardson, B-1812
    Saml., B-1812
    Thomas, B-1812
    William, B-1812
BURNINE, Moses, Je-1822
BURNINGHAM, James, Mu-1816
BURNS, Charles, Mu-1815
    Ethelred, Gi-1812
    Henry, Gi-1812, Sn-1811
    Horatio, Wi-1815
    Isaac, Je-1800
    James, Je-1800
    Jeremiah, B-1812
    John, Gi-1812, Mu-1816, Mu-1811,
        Sn-1811
    John Sr., B-1812
    John Jr., B-1812
    Josiah, B-1812
    Miles, Mu-1816, Mu-1811
    Pattick, Ro-1805
    Robert, Ge-1812, B-1812, Ge-1805

BURNS, Saml., B-1812
    Solomon, D-1811
BURNSIDE, Thomas, D-1805
BURNSIDES, Andrew, Wh-1811
BURRESS, John, J-1802
    Thomas, W-1812
BURRIS, Anthony, Fr-1812
    John, Wa-1819, Fr-1812
    William, Mu-1811, C-1818
BURROUGH, Jarald, B-1812
    Johmael, B-1812
    Truman, B-1812
BURROUGHS, Thomas, Wi-1815
BURROW, Joel, Mu-1811(2), Mu-1816
    Philip Sr., B-1812
    Philip Jr., B-1812
    William, Mu-1811, Mu-1816, B-1812
BURROWS, Boaz, B-1812
    John, Fr-1812
BURTON, Allen, Wi-1810
    Ann, D-1805
    Charles A., Wi-1801
    Daivd, D-1811, Fr-1812
    David H., Hu-1812
    Frank N. W., Wi-1815
    Henry, Wh-1811, Wh-1825
    Hutchins, A-1805
    John, Gr-1804, Fr-1812(2), Gr-1799
    John H., Hu-1812
    Lucey, Wi-1815
    Samuel, Wi-1801
    Samuel H., Hu-1812
    Seth, C-1823
    Theoderick, Wl-1804
    Thomas, Wh-1811
    William, Gr-1805, Gr-1804
    Wils, Sn-1811
BURTON & SMITH, Mu-1811
BURWITT, Walker, Wh-1825
BUSBEY, James, Sn-1811
    Stephen, Sn-1811
    Thomas, Gr-1805
BUSBIE, Mery, Gi-1819
BUSBY, Dolley, Sn-1816
    James, Wi-1810
    John, Fr-1812, Gr-1799
    Richard, W-1812
    Robert, D-1811
    Stephen, Sn-1816
    Thomas, B-1812
    William, Sn-1816, Sn-1811
BUSH, Benjamin, Sn-1816
    Calvin, Co-1827
    George, Sn-1811, Sn-1816
    William, Wl-1804, Sn-1811
BUSHREL, Euseley, D-1788
BUSLEY, Christian, Ge-1805
BUSOM, Benjamin, Mu-1811(2)
BUSSELL, John (Thunder), Wh-1825
    John Jr., Wh-1825
    John Sr., Wh-1825
    Recick, Wh-1825
BUSSEY, Elliot, B-1812
    George, Mu-1816, B-1812
    George Sr., B-1812
    Washington, B-1812
BUSTARD, Claudius, Wa-1814
BUSTER, Christian, Ge-1812
    Claudius, Ge-1805, Ge-1812
BUSTLE, John, Wh-1811
BUSTON, Jesse, R-1819
BUTCHER, Barnabas, Gr-1805, Gr-1804

BUTCHER, Barney, Gr-1799
    Elisha, C-1818
    Gasper, D-1788
    Samuel, Je-1800
BUTHE, Epapaphroditus, Gr-1821
BUTHRIE, Alexander, Je-1822
BUTLER, Elisha, Su-1812, Su-1797, Su-1796
    Henry, Sn-1816, A-1805
    Jacob, A-1805
    James, K-1796
    John, B-1812, Mu-1811, Sn-1811,
        Mu-1816, Gi-1812
    John S., D-1811
    Robert, D-1811
    Thomas, A-1805
    Thomas R., Rb-1812
    Zachariah, Mu-1811
BUTLERS, John, Sn-1811
BUTON, Asa, D-1811
    George, D-1811
BUTRAM, John, C-1823
BUTT, Benjamin, Su-1812
    Hasel, Sn-1816
    John, Su-1812
BUTTER, Aaron, Sn-1811
    Dennis? S., D-1811
    Isaac, D-1811
    S. John, Mu-1816
BUTTS, William, D-1805
BUYERS, Isaac, Mu-1816
    James, Mu-1816
    John, Mu-1816(2)
    William, Mu-1816
BUZBY, John, A-1805, Gr-1799, Gr-1805
    Sherad, Gi-1819
    Thomas, Gr-1799(2), Je-1800, Gr-1804
BYANT, Burel, Sn-1811
BYARS, John W., Sn-1811
BYAS, William, Co-1821
BYBY, Pryor, Br-1821
BYD, James, Wi-1815
BYERS, David, Wi-1815
BYERS, Herald, W-1805, W-1812
    Isaac, Mu-1811(@)
    James, Mu-1811(2)
    Nathan, W-1812
    Robert, W-1812, W-1805
    William, Mu-1811(2), Wi-1815, D-1811
BYLER, Abraham, B-1812, Ct-1798
    Jacob, Gi-1812
    John, B-1812(2)
BYNAM, Isaac, W-1812, W-1805
    James, Wi-1805
    James Jr., D-1805
    William, B-1812
BYNAN, Andrew, J-1802
    James, J-1802
BYNER, John, Sn-1811
BYNIS, James, D-1805
BYNON, William, Fr-1812
BYNUM, John, Fr-1812
    William, Gi-1819
BYRAM, Benjamin, B-1812
    Ebenr., Ge-1783
    Humphrey, B-1812
    James, B-1812
BYRAN, Benjamin, B-1812
BYRD, David, Hw-1799
    Jesse, Ro-1805
    John, Ge-1783, Rb-1812
    Thomas, Rb-1812
    William, Hw-1799, Sn-1792

BYRDWELL, John, Ro-1805
    Joshua, Ro-1805
BYRN, Charles, D-1811
    James, Wi-1801
    James Sr., D-1811
    James Jr., D-1811
    John, Sn-1816, Sn-1811
    William, D-1811
BYRNE, James, Wi-1801
BYRONS, William, Ro-1805
BYRUM, William, Gi-1819
BYSER, Lowery, Sn-1816
BYSHEARS, Jacob, Wh-1825
CABBAGE, Adam, Su-1796
    Adam Sr., Gr-1821
    Adam Jr., Gr-1821
    Alexander, C-1823
    Jacob, Gr-1821
    John, C-1823, Gr-1804, Su-1796,
        Su-1797, Gr-1821
CABE, John, Bo-1800
CABINESS, Charles, D-1805
CABLE, Adam, B-1812
CACHRAN, George, Ge-1812
CADE, Hughes, Su-1812
CADLE, Mark, Cl-1803
CAFFRAY, Peter, D-1788
    Richard, Su-1796
    William, Sn-1811
CAGBURN, Zachariah, B-1812
CAGE, Edward, B-1812
    Elizabeth, Wa-1819
    James, Wa-1819, Sn-1816
    Jesse, Sn-1816
    John, Sn-1811
    Ruben, Sn-1811
    Rubin, Sn-1816
    V. Black, Wl-1804
    Will, Sn-1817
    William, Sn-1811(2), Sn-1816,
        Sn-1792
    Wilson, Sn-1816
CAGLE, Charles, D-1811
    George, D-1811
    Jacob, W-1812, D-1811
    John, D-1811
    Valentine, W-1812
CAGOOD, Joseph, Cl-1803
CAGTE?, Charles, W-1812
CAHALL, Edward, D-1811
CAHILL, James, B-1812
CAIN, Archibald, Wh-1811
    David, Gr-1799(2)
    Hardress, D-1811
    Hugh, Gr-1799, Gr-1821, Gr-1804
    James, W-1805
    Jesse, Gr-1799
    John, Ct-1798, Ct-1796
    Mastain, D-1811
    Peter, Ct-1798, Ct-1796
    Wm., Rb-1812
CAINE, John, Ro-1805
CAISEY, William, B-1812
CAISMON, Isaac, Gr-1799
CALAHAN, Joshua, Fr-1812
    Obediah, Mu-1816
CALDHOON, David, Wa-1819
CALDWELL, A. W. & C., R-1819
    Adam Wm., Bo-1805
    Alexander, Je-1800
    Amos, Mu-1811, Mu-1816
    Anthony, Je-1800

CALDWELL, Ballard, B-1812
    Carson, Bo-1801, Bo-1805
    David, Wl-1804, Wi-1810, Bo-1801(2),
        Bo-1805, Bo-1800(2), R-1808
    George, Bo-1800, Bo-1801
    James, Mt-1798, Bo-1805, B-1812
    Jane, Wi-1810
    John, Sn-1816, Bo-1805, Bo-1801,
        Bo-1800, Wa-1814
    John & James, Je-1822
    Joseph, D-1805
    Robert, D-1811
    Samuel, Ge-1805, D-1805
    Thomas, Wi-1801, Ge-1812, Ge-1805,
        Bo-1801, Bo-1800
    William, K-1796, Wl-1804, Je-1800,
        Je-1822, Mu-1811
CALEHAN, Valentine, Mu-1816
CALES, James, Je-1800
CALFEY, Arihl, Co-1821
CALHONE, Samuel, Wl-1804
    Thomas, Wl-1804
CALHOON, Charles, Wi-1810(2)
    George, Wi-1810(2)
    George Sr., B-1812
    George W., B-1812
    John, W-1811
    William, B-1812
    Wilson, Wi-1810
CALHOUN, David, Wa-1814
CALLAHAN, Charles, Je-1800
    John, Gi-1812
    William, Gi-1812, Je-1800
CALLAWAY, David, Sn-1816
    Richard, Fr-1812
CALLEN, Charles, Je-1822
    Henry, Je-1822
    Thomas, Wi-1810
CALLER, Robert, K-1799
CALLIHAN, Valentine, Ge-1805
CALLINGS, Durham, B-1812
CALLISON, James, Gr-1804(2)
CALLOWAY, David, Sn-1823
    T. F. M., Mo-1825
    William, Gi-1812
CALLVIN, John, Gr-1804
CALTON, Thomas, Wi-1815
CALVERET, John, Wl-1804
CALTON, Thomas, Wi-1815
CALVERET, John, Wl-1804
    William, Wl-1804
CALVERHOUSE, William, Gr-1821
CALVERT, John, B-1812
    Joseph, B-1812
    Leonard, Wa-1814
    Robert, Mu-1816, Mu-1811
    William, Wa-1814
CALVERTH, David, Gi-1812
CALVIN, Francis, Sn-1816
    John, Gr-1805
    Peter, Sn-1811
    Samuel, Gr-1799
CALVINE, John, Gr-1805
CAULDWELL, William, Mu-1816
CAMBEL, Duncan, Je-1800
    John, K-1799
CAMBELL, Archd. M., Rb-1812
    James, D-1788
CAMBILL, Alexander, Gr-1805
CAMBRELL, Robert, Wh-1825
CAMEL, Samuel, Co-1821
CAMER, Thomas, Bo-1800

CAMERON, Absalem, Gr-1821
    Andrew, D-1811
    Elijah, Wh-1825
    Ewen, Wi-1810
    Ewinn, Wi-1801
    Henry, Co-1827
    James, Bo-1805, Ge-1783
    John, Wh-1825
    Joseph, Co-1821
    Samuel, Bo-1805
CAMILL, Giles, Rb-1812
CAMION, William, Wh-1825
CAMMEL, Sammuel, Wi-1815
CAMNASS, John, Ge-1783
CAMON, Samuel, Mu-1816
CAMP, Benjamin, Fr-1812
    Collin, Sn-1816
    James, D-1811
    John, D-1805, D-1811
    John H., D-1811
    Thomas, D-1811
    Vardy, Wh-1825
CAMPBEL, John, Bo-1801
CAMPBELL, A., Gr-1799
    Abel, C-1823
    Alexander, Gi-1819, Wi-1815,
        B-1812, Gr-1804, Ge-1783,
        Wa-1819, Wa-1814, D-1811,
        Gr-1805, D-1805, Wi-1810
    Andrew, Wi-1815
    Archibald, Wa-1819, Wl-1804,
        Ge-1812
    Arthur, Gr-1799
    Capt., K-1796
    Carrick, Ge-1812
    Charles, Wl-1804, Je-1822
    Daniel, Wh-1825, Ro-1805
    David, Ge-1783, Co-1821, Wi-1801,
        Wi-1810
    Donald, Gr-1799
    Francis, D-1811
    G. W., Mu-1811
    Gallaway, Gr-1805
    George, B-1812, Gi-1812, D-1811,
        D-1805
    George W., Co-1821, Je-1800, Wi-1815
    Hamm'n. C., Gi-1812
    Hiram, Mu-1816
    Hugh, Gi-1819, Wa-1819, Gi-1812,
        Mu-1816, Mu-1811
    Isaac, Ct-1798, W-1812, Ct-1796
    James, Je-1800(2), Gr-1821, Ge-1805,
        Gr-1799, Bo-1801, C-1818(2),
        Wa-1819(2), C-1823, Gr-1804,
        Sn-1792, Wl-1804, Bo-1805,
        Wa-1814, Mu-1811, Gr-1805(2),
        Gi-1812, W-1812, R-1808,
        K*-1815, Mt-1798, D-1811,
        Mu-1816(2), D-1805(2), W-1805
    James, Capt., Mt-1798
    Jeremiah, Ct-1798, Ct-1796
    John, Cl-1803, Ge-1805, Co-1821,
        Gi-1819, Wl-1804, Bo-1805,
        Fr-1812, C-1823, Je-1822,
        Su-1812, Je-1800, Gr-1821,
        R-1819, Wh-1811, Gi-1812,
        Mu-1811, Mu-1816(2), Wh-1825,
        D-1811, D-1805
    John K., Wi-1815, Wi-1810
    Joseph, Co-1821, C-1818, Bo-1805,
        C-1823, Fr-1812, Gi-1812,
        Sn-1816

CAMPBELL, Joseph Sr., Cl-1803
    Joseph Jr., Cl-1803
    Joshua, Sn-1787
    Mathew, Gr-1821, Gr-1804
    Matthew, Gr-1805
    Michael, Ge-1812, Wl-1804, D-1811
    Nathan, Wi-1810
    Nathaniel, C-1823
    Nero, Je-1822
    Owen, Rb-1812
    Philip, D-1811
    Robert, Ge-1805, Sn-1792, Wl-1804,
        Co-1821, Bo-1805, Ge-1783,
        Gi-1812, Mu-1816, Mu-1811,
        Wh-1825, Bo-1801
    Solomon, Ct-1798(2)
    Terrance, K*-1815
    Theopholus, J-1802
    Thomas, C-1818, A-1805, Bo-1805,
        Je-1822
    Thomas J., R-1819
    W. George, Mu-1816
    William, Ct-1798, Wl-1804(2),
        Co-1821, W-1812, Je-1800,
        Ro-1805, K*-1815, Wi-1815,
        D-1811, Gr-1805, Sn-1816,
        Mu-1811, Wi-1801, Wl-1804
    Zachariah, C-1823, Ct-1798(2),
        C-1818
    Zachariah Sr., Ct-1796
    Zachariah Jr., Ct-1796
CAMPBLE, Hugh, Sn-1811
    John, Gi-1812, Bo-1800
    Robert, Bo-1800
    Thomas, Sn-1811
CAMPPBELL, Geo. W., Gi-1819
CAMRON, Daniel, Mu-1816
    Ezra, Gr-1799
    John, Gr-1799
    Samuel, Bo-1801, Bo-1800
CANADY, Charles, Je-1800
    John Jr., Je-1800
    John Sr., Je-1800
    Porter, Je-1800
CANAWAY, Jesse, Bo-1805
    Joseph, Bo-1805
    Thomas, Bo-1805
CANBY, Blandent, Mu-1816
CANCANY, Henry, B-1812
CANDELL, James, Gr-1799
CANDLER, Anderson, Sn-1816
CANEDY, John, W-1812
    Walker, Bo-1800
CANEON, Joseph, Wi-1810
CANGROW, Isaac, Wl-1804
CANLEY, Wm., Sn-1811
CANN?, James, W-1812
CANNADA, John, Wi-1801
CANNEY, John, D-1811
CANNOGHAM, Paul M., B-1812
CANNON, Abner, Je-1800, Mu-1816, Mu-1811
    Andrew, B-1812
    Archibald, Wl-1804
    Burrell, Mu-1811
    Burwell, Mu-1816
    Caleb, Je-1800
    Clement, B-1812, Wi-1810, Mu-1811
    Howard, Mu-1816
    James, Wl-1804, C-1823, Je-1800
    John, Gr-1805, D-1805, Mu-1816,
        Gr-1804, Mo-1825, Je-1800,
        Je-1822, Gr-1799

CANNON, Joseph, Wl-1804
    Joshua, Wi-1801, Wi-1815
    Menes, B-1812
    Minas, Wi-1810
    Minos, Wi-1801, Wi-1815
    Moses, Wi-1810
    Newton, Wi-1810
    Patrick, Ge-1812
    Robert, Wi-1815
    Samuel, Wl-1804, Mu-1811
    Theophilus, Wl-1804
    Thomas, Je-1800, W-1812
    William, Gi-1812, B-1812, D-1811
CANNONS, Francis, Ro-1805
CANTERBERRY, John, Gr-1799, A-1805
    Zachariah, A-1805, Gr-1799
CANTHERS, Johnathan, Wa-1819
    Nathaniel, Sn-1811
CANTRELL, Aaron, Wh-1825
    Abram, W-1812
    Aron, W-1812
    Benj., W-1812
    James, W-1812, Wh-1825
    John, W-1812
    Moses, Wh-1825
    Richard, Je-1822, W-1812
    Rich., Esq., W-1812
    Sampson, W-1812
    Stephen, Sn-1816, Sn-1811, Gr-1805,
        D-1811, Je-1822
    Stephen, Insign, D-1788
    Watson, W-1812
    William, Wh-1825
CANTRIL, Stephen, Sn-1792
CANTRILL, Richard, W-1805
CANWELL, Wm., Cl-1803
CAPBELL(sic), William, B-1812
CAPELER, Henry, Rb-1812
CAPERTON, George, Fr-1812
    James, Wi-1815
    John, Fr-1812
    William, Fr-1812
CAPISH, Adam, Gr-1799
    John, Gr-1799
CAPLE, James, Mu-1816
    Samuel, Wl-1804
    William, B-1812
CAPLEN, Jas., Bl-1815
CAPLEY, John, B-1812
CAPLIN, John, B-1812
CAPLINGER, Jacob, Wl-1804
    John, Wl-1804
    Leonard, Wl-1804
CAPPS, David, Gr-1821
    Gedion, Su-1812
    Hiram, Gr-1821
    Jacob, Gr-1821, Gr-1804
    Joel, Gr-1821
    John, Gr-1821
    Thomas, Su-1812
    William, Gr-1805, Gr-1821
    William Jr., Gr-1804
    William Sr., Gr-1804
    Willis, Gr-1805, Gr-1804, Gr-1821
CAPS, Allsey, B-1812
    Jacob, Gr-1799
    Joel, Sn-1816
    William, Sn-1816, Gr-1799
CAPSHAW, James, Wh-1825
CAR, Caleb, B-1812
CARBOUGH, John, Ge-1812
CARBY, William, Wi-1815

CARCATHERS, Jonathan, Wa-1814
    Samuel, Wa-1814
CARCLOCK, John, Gr-1799
    Joseph, Gr-1799
CARD, William, Wl-1804
CARDEN, Robert Jr., Mo-1825
    William T., Gr-1821
CARDER, Dorcas, Ge-1812
    John, Ge-1812
CARDHEY, Ben, Bl-1815
CARDIFF, Frail, B-1812
CARDINE, John, K-1796
CARDWALL, Thomas, Sn-1811
    Wilson, Sn-1811
CARDWELL, Antony, Gr-1821
    Daniel, Gr-1821
    George, Wh-1825
    James, Gr-1821
    John, Cl-1803
    Nelson, Sn-1823
    Pegren, Cl-1803
    Robert, Gr-1821
    Thomas, Sn-1823, Wh-1825
CARETHERS, Samuel, Wa-1819
CAREVILE, John, Gr-1804
CAREY, Alex, Ro-1805
    James, Sn-1816
    John, Mu-1816
    Joseph, Wa-1814
CARGHRAN, Job, Co-1821
CARGILL, C. Dannias, Mu-1816
CARGO,? John, Henry & Martin, D-1805
CARITHERS, James, Wa-1819
    Samuel, Su-1812
CARLAND, James, Wl-1804
CARLEY, Henery, Sn-1816
CARLILE, James, Fr-1812
CARLISLE, William, Mu-1811
CARLOCK, Frederick, Hw-1801
    Henry, A-1805
    James, C-1823
    Joseph, C-1823, Mu-1811
    Moses, Hw-1801
    Sarah, C-1818
CARLTON, Benag., Wi-1815
    Robert, Gi-1812
CARMACK, Aquella, D-1811
    John, Su-1812
CARMAN, Samuel, D-1805
CARMARK, John, Bl-1815
CARMICAEL, Duncan, Gr-1804
    James, Gr-1804
CARMICAL, Duncan, Gr-1821
    James, Gr-1821
CARMICHAEL, Daniel, Je-1822
    James, Je-1822, Gr-1799
    Samuel, Je-1822
CARMICHEL, Duncan, Gr-1805
    James, Gr-1805, Je-1800
CARMICK, Anguish?, D-1805
CARMICLE, Archibald, Wa-1814
    Isbell, Wa-1814
    William, Wa-1819, Wa-1814
CARMIKLE, John, Co-1821
CARMON, Caleb, Je-1822
    John, Je-1822
    Skipper, B-1812
    Thomas, Je-1822
CARNAHAN, Hugh, Mu-1816
    James, Mu-1816
    John, Fr-1812
    William, R-1819

CARNEHAN, Hugh, Mu-1811
    James, Mu-1811
CARNER, Hugh, Ge-1812
    Tush, Gi-1812
CARNES, Michael, Gr-1799
    Michael Jr., Gr-1799
    Nathaniel, Wi-1815
    Nicholas, Gr-1804
    Thos., Hu-1812
CARNEY, Elisha, D-1811
    John, Je-1822, Mu-1816
    Joseph, Je-1822
    Josua, Sn-1816
    _____, B-1812
CARNNEL, Robert, Gi-1819
CARNS, Alexander, Mt-1798
    George, Wi-1815
CARNY, Kemust, D-1811
CAROTHERS, Hugh, Sn-1811
    John, Wi-1815
    Robert, Wi-1810, Sn-1811
    Robert Jr., Wi-1815
    Thomas, Sn-1811
    William, B-1812
CARPENTER, Chester, W-1812, K-1799
    George, Bo-1800
    John, B-1812
    Pharis, Co-1821
CARPER, Adam, D-1811
    Joseph, Je-1822
CARR, Anderson, Sn-1811
    David, Bo-1801
    Eawensley Gilbert, Su-1812
    Gilbert, Su-1797, Su-1796
    Henry, Gr-1821
    James, Mu-1811(2), Sn-1816,
        Sn-1811, Bo-1801, Bo-1800,
        B-1812, Su-1797
    Capt. John, S.-1811
    John, Mu-1816(2), Sn-1816, Mu-1811,
        Wi-1815, Sn-1823, Wa-1814,
        R-1819, Rb-1812
    John D., Sn-1816
    Jonathan, Wh-1825
    Joseph, Su-1812
    King, Sn-1792, Sn-1811
    King Jr., Sn-1816
    King Sr., Sn-1816
    Patrick, Su-1812(2)
    Richard, Wa-1819, Sn-1811, Sn-1787,
        Sn-1816, Wa-1814
    Robert, Mu-1811, B-1812
    Robt. Sr., Ge-1783
    Samuel, Bo-1801, Sn-1811, R-1819,
        Sn-1811, Fr-1812, A-1805,
        Wi-1815, Wa-1819, Wa-1814,
        Su-1797, Su-1796, Su-1812
    William Jr., Sn-1816
    William Sr., Sn-1816
CARREL, Andrew, W-1812
    James, Sn-1811
    Peter, Ge-1812
CARRELL, John, W-1812
    Joseph, Ro-1805
    Samuel, D-1811
    William, Fr-1812
CARRET, Benjamin, Ge-1812
CARRICK, Addison, Wh-1825
    Moses, Wh-1825
    Samuel D., Gr-1804
    Seth, Wh-1825
    Vance, Wh-1825

CARRIER, John, Su-1812(2)
    Thomas, Su-1812
    William, Su-1812
CARRIGER, Godfrey Jr., Ct-1796, Ct-1798
    Godfrey Sr., Ct-1796, Ct-1798
    Henry, Ct-1798
    Michael, Ct-1798
    Nicholas, Ct-1796, Ct-1798
CARRIT, John Jr., Wl-1804
    John Sr., Wl-1804
CARRITHERS, Samuel, Su-1796, Su-1797(2)
CARROL, Jesse, D-1811
    Lewis, Su-1812
    Samuel, D-1805
    William, Su-1812, D-1811
CARROLE, William, Su-1812
CARROLL, Bazzell, Gr-1821
    Henry, Wa-1819
    Hickman, Wa-1819
    Luke, Wa-1814
    William, Wa-1814, Su-1796, Su-1797
CARRON, Samuel, Wh-1825
CARRONS, David, B-1812
CARRUS, Ansylum, Wi-1825
CARRUT, John, Se-1799
CARRUTH, Alexander, Wl-1804
    Walter, Wl-1804
CARRUTHERS, James, Wi-1815
CARRWAY, Charles, K-1799
CARRY, James, Sn-1811
CARSON, Adam, Ro-1805
    Alexander, Su-1812
    Andrew, B-1812, Wa-1819, Wa-1814
    D., heirs, Sn-1811
    David, Je-1800, Bo-1801, Bo-1800,
        Ro-1805, Fr-1812
    Henry, Wl-1840
    James, Ge-1805, Je-1800, Ge-1812,
        Je-1822
    James Jr., Wi-1815
    James Sr., Wi-1815
    John, Je-1800, Ge-1783, Wa-1814,
        Su-1812, Je-1822
    John Jr., Je-1800
    John Sr., Je-1800, Je-1822
    Margarett, Wa-1819
    Mary, Je-1800
    Moses, Wa-1814
    Moses Jr., Wa-1819
    Moses Sr., Wa-1819, Wa-1814
    Moses W., Wa-1814
    Nancy, Wa-1819
    Polly, Wa-1814, Wa-1819
    Rachael, Sn-1816
    Robert, Je-1800, Ge-1805, Wa-1819,
        Ge-1783, Wi-1815, Ge-1812(2),
        Wa-1814
    Robert Jr., Ge-1812
    S. Charles, D-1805
    Samuel, Je-1822, Su-1797, Wa-1814,
        Su-1796, Je-1800(2), Wa-1819
    William Sr., Wa-1814
CART, Richard, Bo-1801, Bo-1800
CARTER, A. Reuben, Mu-1811
    Abraham, Ge-1812, Ge-1783
    Augustine, Gi-1812
    Basel, Ge-1812
    Benjamin, Ge-1812, Wi-1815, Mu-1816,
        Mu-1811, Sn-1816, Wi-1810
    Caleb, Ge-1812, Ge-1805
    Charles, Sn-1787, Sn-1792
    Daniel, Wi-1815, Ge-1805, Ge-1812

CARTER, Danill, Legatee, Ge-1812
    Danniel, Wi-1810
    David, Ge-1805(2), Ge-1812
    Edward, Hu-1812
    Elijah, C-1818, C-1823, Ge-1812
    Elisha, Ge-1812
    Elizabeth, Mu-1816
    Enoch, Je-1822
    Enock, Ge-1812
    Ezekiel, Ge-1805, Je-1822, Ge-1812
    Francis, Wi-1815, Wi-1810, D-1805
    Francis J., Co-1821
    Harris, Sn-1816
    Hiram, Ge-1812
    Hugh, Ge-1805, Ge-1812
    Isaac, W-1805, Ge-1805, W-1812
    Jacob, Ge-1812
    James, Wl-1804(2), D-1805, D-1811, B-1812, Wa-1819
    James Jr., Wa-1819
    James Sr., D-1811
    Jesse, B-1812, Ge-1805
    Jessee, W-1805, W-1812
    Job, J-1802
    John, Mu-1816, Hu-1812, Ct-1796, Ct-1798, Ge-1812
    John Sr., D-1811, Ge-1805, Ge-1812
    John Jr., Ge-1805
    Joseph, Sn-1816, Ge-1805
    Joseph Sr., Ge-1812
    Landon, Ct-1798, Ct-1796
    Landon, heirs, R-1819
    Levi, Ge-1805
    Lewis, D-1811
    Meshick, Ge-1812
    Michl., Ge-1783
    Micjah, Bo-1801
    Nathan, Ge-1805, Ge-1812
    Nathaniel, Je-1800
    Peter, Wh-1811
    Reubin A., Mu-1816
    Ritchard, Wi-1815
    Robert, Wi-1801
    Samuel, Mu-1811, Bo-1805
    Susanah, Ge-1812
    Thomas, Mu-1816
    Vincent, Je-1800
    William, Ro-1805, Je-1822, Wh-1825
    William L., D-1811
CARTERS, Thomas, D-1805
CARTHEL, Josiah, Mu-1811
CARTHELL, Josiah, Mu-1816
CARTHER, Hugh Jr., Ge-1812
CARTMEL?, Thomas, B-1812
CARTMELL, John, B-1812
CARTON, John, D-1811
CARTRIGHT, David, D-1811
    Isaac, Fr-1812
    Jacob, D-1811
    John, D-1811
    Joseph, Fr-1812
    Joshua, W-1812
    Robert, D-1811(2)
    Thomas, D-1811
    Vincent, D-1811
    William, Sn-1811
CARTRITE, Thomas, Bo-1801, Bo-1800
CARTWRIGHT, Daniel, D-1805
    David, D-1811
    Isaac, Wl-1804
    Jacob, D-1805

CARTWRIGHT, James, Sn-1816, Sn-1811
    Jonth., Sn-1792
    Joseph, Fr-1812
    Matthew, Wl-1804
    Robert, D-1805(2), J-1802
    Thomas, D-1805, Sn-1816, Sn-1811, J-1802
    Vinson, D-1805
CARUM, Champ, Gr-1821
    Francis, Gr-1821
    William, Gr-1821
CARUTHERS, Hugh, Sn-1816
    James, Bo-1800
    James, heirs, Sn-1816
    Robert Jr., heirs, Sn-1816
CARVAR, Nathaniel, Wh-1811
CARVEN, Thomas, Ct-1796, Ct-1798
CARVER, Edward, Wh-1825
    Michael, Wa-1814
CARWILE, John, Gr-1805
CARWILES, John, Gr-1799, Gr-1805
CARY, John, C-1823
    Milford, Wh-1825
    Thomas, D-1811
CASADY, Charles, D-1811(2)
CASSADA, James, Wa-1819
CASBUR, John, Mu-1811
    Thomas, Mu-1811
CASE, John, J-1802
    Seperate, J-1802
CASEBOLT, John, Ct-1798
CASELMON, Benjamin, D-1788
CASEY, Bey, Wa-1819
    James, Gr-1799, Gr-1804
    Joel, Mu-1816, Mu-1811
    John, Gr-1799
    Joseph, Wa-1819
    Samuel, Gr-1799, Gr-1821
    William, Mc-1825
CASH, Elisha, Wi-1801
    Howard, Wh-1811, Wh-1825
    Jacob, Sn-1811
    Joel, D-1805
    John, D-1805(2), Mu-1811, Wh-1825
    Simpson, Wh-1811, Wh-1825
    Thoms., Wi-1815
    William, D-1805
CASHADY, Patrick, Su-1797
CASHAWN, John, Su-1797
CASHUADY, James, Gr-1821
CASIN, Daniel, D-1805
    John, Rb-1812
CASKILL, John Jr., D-1805
CASKY, Thomas, Wi-1815
CASPER, Joseph, Su-1812
CASSADA, Robert, Wa-1819
CASSADY, Reuben, Wh-1811
CASSE, Abraham, K-1796
CASSELL, John, Wi-1810
CASSELLMAN, Abraham, D-1805
    Andrew, D-1805
    Benjamin, D-1805
    John Sr., D-1805
    John & David, D-1805
    Sylvanus, D-1805
CASSELMAN, Abraham, D-1811(2)
    Andrew, D-1811
    Benjamin, D-1811
    Benjamin Sr., D-1811
    Henry, D-1811
    John Sr., D-1811
    John Jr., D-1811

CASSELMAN, Joseph, D-1811(2)
    Sylvanus, D-1811
CASTALOR, Martin, Bo-1801
CASTEEL, Daniel, Su-1812
    Edward, Bo-1800, Bo-1801, Ge-1812
    Jeremiah, Ge-1812
    John, Bo-1801, Ge-1805
    Joseph, Bo-1801
    Peter, Ge-1812
    Peter, Jr., Ge-1805
    Zachari, Ge-1812
CASTILE, John, Ge-1783
    John Sr., Ge-1783
CASTLE, Peter, C-1823, Ge-1805
CASTLEBERRY, Joseph, Rb-1812
    Benjamin, Wl-1804(3)
    Sylvanus, Wi-1801
CATCHING, Saymor, Ge-1805
CATE, Charles, Je-1800
    Charles Sr., Je-1800
    Isaac, Mo-1825
    John, Je-1800, Sn-1811, Je-1822
    John Jr., Je-1822, Je-1800
    John E., Je-1822
    Richard, Je-1822
    Thomas, Je-1822
    William, Je-1800
    William Jr., Je-1822
    William Sr., Je-1822
CATBIRTH, Daniel, Gi-1819
CATES, Abner, Sn-1811
    Charles, Je-1822
    Elijah, Je-1822
    Ephraim, Sn-1816, Sn-1811
    Isaiah, Wi-1815
    John, R-1819, B-1812
    Joseph, Sn-1816
    Moses, Gr-1821
    Rowland, D-1805
    Samuel, Gr-1821
    Thomas, Mu-1811
    Wm., B-1812
CATHEART, John, Gr-1804
CATHER, Archibald, Wi-1815
CATHEY, Alexr., Esq., Mu-1816
    Alexr., Sr., Mu-1816, Mu-1811
    Alexander Jr., Mu-1811
    D. Thomas, Mu-1816, Mu-1811
    George, Wi-1815
    Griffith, Mu-1816, Mu-1811
    James, Co-1821, Sn-1811, Mu-1811, Mu-1816
    John, Mu-1811
    John Jr., Mu-1816
    John Sr., Mu-1816
    Will, decd., Sn-1811
    William, Mu-1811, Mu-1816
CATHRON, Wm., heirs, Sn-1811
CATHY, George, B-1812
    Hugh, B-1812
    John, Wi-1810, B-1812(2)
CATIMORE, Lyons, Hu-1812
CATLIN, John, Ro-1805
CATNEY, Thomas, Co-1821
CATOR, Levern, Wi-1815
    Moses E., Wi-1815
CATRIN, Adam, Ge-1812
    Francis, Sn-1811
    Valentine, Ge-1812
CATRON, Christian, Sn-1816
    Christopher, Wh-1811
    Francis, Sn-1787

CATRON, Jacob, Wh-1811
CATROW, Chrisley, Sn-1811
    Henry, Su-1812
    John, Su-1812
    Peter, Su-1812
    Phelty, Su-1812
CATS, Isaac, Wh-1811
    Robt., Sn-1811
CATTHEY, Matthew, Sn-1816
CAUBLE, Pettr., Ge-1812
CAUDLE, Joshua, Mu-1816
    Zachariah, Gr-1799
CAUGHRAN, Saml., Mu-1816
CAULFIELD, John, Su-1797, D-1811
CAULTHARP, John, Gr-1804
CAUSLY, Thomas, Rb-1812
CAUTERBERRY, John, A-1805
    Zachariah, A-1805
CAUTHERS, John, Su-1812(2)
CAVENDER, Alexander, Je-1800
    Henry, Gr-1821
    James, Wi-1815
    Stephen, D-1811
    Tho., Gi-1812
    William, Ge-1812
CAVENESS, William, Sn-1816
CAVENIST, William, Sn-1811, Sn-1816
CAVENOR, Edward, Gi-1812
    Gent, Gi-1812
    Needham, Gi-1812
CAVES, John, A-1805
CAVET, James, Sn-1816
    Richd., Sn-1792
CAVETT, John, Sn-1811
    Michael, Sn-1811, Sn-1792
    Richard, Sn-1811
CAVETTE, Michael, Sn-1792
CAVIT, John, Su-1797
CAVITT, Andrew, Sn-1816
    John, Su-1796
    Joseph, Sn-1816
CAVNAR, Joseph, Ge-1812
CAVNER, Hugh, Ge-1805
CAWFIELD, John, Su-1812
CAWOOD, John, Su-1797
    John Jr., Su-1796
    Joshua, Su-1812
    Moses, Bo-1801
    Stephen, Gr-1799
    Thomas, Su-1812
CAYCE, Shederick, D-1811
CAYES, John, Sn-1811
CAYLE, Ruben, W-1812
CEARCY, John, Wl-1804
    Rewben, Wl-1804
CEARLE, George, Gr-1799
CECIL, George, Su-1706
CENTER, Freman, Sn-1816
    Milton, Ro-1805
    Richard, Sn-1816
    Tandy, Gr-1805
CERTAIN, Asa, Wh-1825
    Charles, Wh-1825
    Eli, Je-1822
    Jacob, Wh-1825
    Jarel, Wh-1825
    Job, Wh-1825
CHAFFIN, Abner, J-1802
    Jospeh, J-1802
    Robert, Bo-1800, Bo-1801
CHAIMBERS, Moses, Wi-1815
CHAIRS, Nathaniel, Mu-1816

CHALLON, George W., D-1811
CHAM, Goldsberry, D-1811
CHAMBAS, Anthony, Wl-1804
CHAMBERLAIN, D., Co-1821
    Elizabeth, Gr-1805
    Hann, Bo-1800
    Hanna, Bo-1801
    James, Wa-1814
    Jeremiah, Gr-1804, Gr-1799, Je-1800, Gr-1821
    Margaret, Gr-1805
    Mary, Gr-1805
    Ninian, Je-1800
    Thomas, Gr-1821
CHAMBERLAINS, Heirs of, Gr-1821
CHAMBERLAND, James, Wa-1819
CHAMBERLIN, Elizabeth, Gr-1805
    Jeremiah, Gr-1805
    John, Ge-1783
    Margeret, Gr-1805
    Mary, Gr-1805
    Stout, Ge-1783
CHAMBERS, Alexander, Wl-1804
    Edwd. O., Gi-1812
    Elijah, Bl-1815
    Elisha, Bl-1815, C-1818
    Hardy, Hu-1812
    Henry T., Sn-1792
    James, Hu-1812
    John, Bl-1815, Wi-1801, K-1796
    Joshua, C-1818
    Mary, Wi-1810
    Moses, Wi-1801
    P. Elijah, Mu-1811
    Ruben, Hu-1812
    Samuel, Wi-1801
    Thomas, D-1805, C-1823
    William, Bl-1815, Gi-1812
CHAMMAS, William, Co-1821
CHAMNESS, Berry, Gr-1821
CHAMP, Richard, D-1811
    William, D-1811
CHAMPION, John, Fr-1812(2)
    William, Fr-1812
CHAMPLESS, Waters, C-1823
CHAMPLIN, Benjamin H., Ge-1812
    Thomas, Gr-1821
CHANCE, Ezekiel, Su-1796
    Philip, Ge-1805
    William, Sn-1816
CHANCY, William, Gr-1821
CHANDLER, Daniel, Gr-1821
    David, Gr-1805
    Isaac, Wa-1814
    James, Rb-1812
    Richard, Bo-1801
    Shadrach, Mu-1816
    Shadrack, Rb-1812
    Simion, Co-1821
    Thederick, K-1796
    William, K-1799, A-1805, Je-1822
CHANDLEY, William, Ge-1805
CHANEL, Elisha, Mt-1798
CHANERY, William, Wa-1814
CHANEY, Francis, Wh-1825
    Isham, W-1812
    Jacob, A-1805(2)
    John, Wh-1825
    Robert, Wh-1825
    William, Wa-1819
CHANY, Jacob, K-1799
CHAPEL, Abner, B-1812

CHAPHU(Chasshu?), Jas., Se-1799
CHAPIN, Jessee, B-1812
    Nathan, B-1812
CHAPMAN, Benjamin, Wa-1819, Wa-1814, Sn-1816
    George, Rb-1812
    I. H., Co-1821
    James, Sn-1811
    John, Sn-1811, Sn-1816, D-1811, A-1805
    John Sr., Wa-1814
    John Jr., Wa-1814
    John D., Wi-1815
    Joseph, Je-1822
    Martha, Sn-1816
    Nancy, Je-1822
    Nelson, Wi-1815, Wi-1810
    Philip, Sn-1816
    Robert, Wa-1814
    Samuel, Wa-1819, Wa-1814, Wl-1804, D-1805
    Wm., Sn-1816, Gi-1812, C-1823, Ge-1805
CHAPPELL, Samuel, Sn-1823
CHAPPLE, James, Wl-1804
    William, Wl-1804
    Woodin, Wl-1804
CHARLETON, John, Wa-1814
CHARLES, Isaac, Bo-1801
    James, Fr-1812
    Joel D., Wh-1825
    John, Ro-1805, D-1811
    Oliver, W-1812
    Richard, Fr-1812, Bo-1800
    Solomon, Wh-1825(2)
    Stephen K., Wh-1825
    William, D-1811
CHARLESTON, Painter Jr., Wa-1814
    Painter Sr., Wa-1814
CHARLTON, Pointon Jr., Wa-1819
    Pointon Sr., Wa-1819
    Thomas, Wa-1819
CHARTER, Agness (widow), Gi-1819
CHARTON, Washington, D-1811
CHASE, Jeremiah, Su-1812
    Obed., Je-1822
    Sarah, Su-1812, Su-1796, Su-1797
    Walter, Su-1812
CHASER, Michael, D-1805
CHASTON, James, Sn-1811
    Jeremiah, Sn-1811
CHAVER, Washington, D-1805
CHEATHAM, Anderson, Rb-1812
    Archer, Rb-1812
    Christopher, Rb-1812
    John B., Rb-1812
    Peter, Mu-1816, Mu-1811
    Thos. A., Rb-1812
    William, Mu-1816
CHEATWOOD, Plesant, K-1799
CHEEK, Danson, C-1818
    Davison, Gr-1805
    Dawson, Gr-1804, Gr-1799
    Eli, Mu-1816
    Elijah, Sn-1816
    Jesse, Je-1800
    Jessee, Gr-1805, Gr-1804
    William, Je-1800
    Willis, Gr-1821
    Willson, Je-1800
CHENETH, Archibald, Wa-1814
    Nicholas, Wa-1814
CHERRY, Benjamin, Bl-1815

CHERRY, Calip, D-1805
    Daniel, Sn-1811, Wi-1810
    Eli, D-1811
    Elijah, Bl-1815
    Ezekiel, Sn-1816
    Jeremiah, Mu-1811
    Jerimiah, Mu-1811
    John, C-1823
    Joshua, Sn-1811(2)
    Lemuel, J-1802
    Queals, Bl-1815
    Wiley, heirs, Wi-1815
    Wilie, Wl-1804
    Willey, heirs, Wi-1810
    William, D-1811
CHERRYL?, William, Sn-1816
CHESHER, Daniel, Gr-1805
    Thomas, Gr-1821
CHESNEY, John, Gr-1821
CHESNUT, John, Mo-1825
    Nelson, Mo-1825
CHESSEN, William, W-1812
CHESSER?, William, Mu-1811
CHESSHER, Daniel, Gr-1850
CHESTER, John, Wa-1819, Wa-1814, Su-1812,
        Su-1797, Su-1796
    John Jr., Wa-1819
    Robert, Su-1812
    Samuel G., Wa-1819
    Tenneson, Mu-1811
    Wm., Sn-1817
    William P., Wa-1814, Wa-1819,
        Wa-1814
CHETLY, Benjamin, Mu-1811, Mu-1816
CHEWNING, John, Rb-1812
    Thomas, Rb-1812
CHIANS, John, Gi-1819
CHIDERS, Henry, Wi-1801
CHILCOAT, James, Fr-1812
    John, Fr-1812
CHILDERS, Mitchell, Mu-1816
    Richard, Mo-1825
    William, Fr-1812(2)
CHILDRESS, David, Su-1796, Su-1797,
        Hu-1812
    Henry, Wi-1801
    Hiram, Wh-1825
    John, Mu-1811
    John Jr., D-1805
    John Sr., D-1805
    Joseph, B-1812
    Larkin, Hu-1812
    Nathaniel G., D-1811
    Ro. S., Gi-1812
    Stephen, Wi-1810, Wi-1815
    Thomas, D-1805, D-1811
    William, Su-1796, Su-1797, Su-1812,
        Wh-1825
    William B., Su-1812
CHILDS, John, D-1811
CHILESH?, Peter, B-1812
CHILTON, James, Je-1822
    James Jr., J-1802
    John, J-1802
    Palatiah, R-1819
    William, Gr-1799
CHILUT, Thomas, D-1805
CHILY, William, Wh-1825
CHINETH, Nicholes, Wa-1819
CHINN, Ths., Cl-1803
CHISHOLM, John, Mu-1816
CHISLOM, William, Mt-1798

CHISLON, Isham, Ro-1805
CHISM, Demsey, Hu-1812
    John, Mu-1816, Mu-1811, Wl-1804
CHISN, Berry, Mu-1816
    Bolin, Mu-1816
CHISUM, Elijah, Cl-1803, Wh-1811
    Elijah Jr., Wh-1811
    Elijah Sr., Wh-1811(2)
    Elisha, Gr-1799
    Elisha Jr., Gr-1799
    James, Cl-1803, Wh-1811(2)
    John, Wh-1825, Wh-1811(2)
    John (Hickrynut), Wh-1825
    William, Wh-1825
CHISUS, James, Gr-1799
CHITEMAN, James, Bl-1815
CHITWOOD, Daniel, C-1823
    David, C-1823
    Edmond, Wi-1815
    James, C-1823
    James Jr., C-1823
    John, C-1823
    Lazarus, K-1799, C-1823
    Pleasant, A-1805, C-1823
    Shadrach, C-1823
    Shadrach Sr., C-1823
    William, C-1818, C-1823(3)
CHIVERS, Andrew, Ge-1812
CHOAT, Abel, Rb-1812
    Austin, A-1805
    Austin Jr., Kl-799
    Benj., W-1812
    Christerfer, K-1799
    Edward, Rb-1812
    Gabriel, Rb-1812
    John, K-1799, Rb-1812, W-1812
    Joseph, Mu-1811
    Moses, K-1799
    Squire, Mu-1811
    Stephen, W-1812
CHOATE, Aron, Mt-1798
    Greene, Mt-1798
    John, Mt-1798
    Joseph, Mu-1816, Mt-1798
    Squire, Mu-1816, Mt-1798
    Thomas, Mu-1816
CHORT, Thomas, K-1799
CHOTE, Benjamin, Su-1797, Su-1796
    Justin, K-1799
CHREYEN, Aaron, Se-1799
CHRISENBY, William, K-1799
CHRISMAN, Aaron, Su-1797
    David, Su-1796
    Isaac, A-1805
    John, Su-1796(2)
CHRISTAIN, Thomas, Sn-1792
CHRISTER, James, Wh-1825
CHRISTIAN, Allen, Gr-1804, Gr-1799
    Christopher, D-1811
    George, Su-1796
    Isam, Ge-1783
    Jessee, Gr-1804, Gr-1805
    John, W-1812(2), Su-1796,
        W-1805(2)
    Margaret, Su-1796, Su-1797
    Nathaniel, Mu-1816
    Robert, Su-1796, Su-1812, Su-1797
    Thomas, Co-1821, Ge-1783
    William, Gr-1804, Bl-1815, Su-1796,
        Gr-1805, Su-1797
CHRISTIANBURY, Joshua, Ro-1805
CHRISTION, Edmond, Sn-1811

CHRISTMAN, Aaron, Wi-1810
    Abreham, Wi-1810
    David, Wi-1810
    William, Wi-1810
CHRISTY, Hugh, Su-1812
    James, Wh-1825
    John, Wh-1825
    Joseph, Wh-1825(2)
    William, Rb-1812
CHROUSEM, Ma., Se-1799
    Wm., Se-1799
CHUMBLEY, Joseph, D-1811
CHUMBLY, Joseph, D-1811
CHUMLEY, Daniel, R-1819
    John, Wl-1804
CHUNN, Samuel, Je-1822
CHURCH, Arthur, Mu-1816
    Phillip, Gi-1819, Mu-1816
    Robert, Wa-1819, Wa-1814
    Thos., Mu-1816
CHURCHILL, Richard, B-1812
CHURCHMAN, Edward, Gr-1799(3), Gr-1805(2),
    Gr-1804(2), Gr-1821
    James, Je-1822
    John, Je-1800, Je-1822, Gr-1799
    Reuben, Je-1822
    Stephen, Je-1822
    Thomas, Gr-1799, Gr-1805, Gr-1804,
    Gr-1821
    William, Je-1800
CHURCHWELL, Richard, Mu-1811
    William, Mu-1811
    William Jr., Mu-1811
CHUSEN, Richard, Se-1799
CID, Pleasant, Co-1827
CIMBERLAND, Jacob, Sn-1792
    Michael, Sn-1792
CINCLEAR, Hugh, Mu-1811
CIRYB, Malica, Wi-1815
CITOCILLER, William, Su-1796
CLABORN, John, C-1818
    Thomas, D-1811
CLACK, John, Se-1799, Gi-1812
    Spencer, Gi-1812, Gi-1819
CLAIBORNE, Thomas, D-1811
    William C., Su-1796
CLAMPET, Ezekiel, Wl-1804
    Nathan, Wl-1804
CLAMPITT, Jonathan, Sn-1811, Sn-1816
    Nathan, Sn-1811
CLANTON, Drury, D-1811
    Geo., Gi-1819
    Jno. W., Gi-1819
    Richard, D-1811
CLAP, Adam, Sn-1792(2)
CLAPENA, Lewis, Gr-1805
CLAPP, Lodawick, A-1805
CLARA, John, Wh-1811
    William, Wh-1811
CLARDY, Michael, A-1805(2)
    Richard, B-1812
CLARK, Aarley, Ro-1805
    Alexander, Wi-1815, Wi-1810
    Andrew, Gi-1812
    Avory, Rb-1812
    Benjamin, Wl-1804
    Boling, Wi-1815
    Durgess, Wh-1825
    Daniel, Wh-1825(2)
    David, Wl-1804
    Denas, Wh-1825
    Edward, Ro-1805, Gr-1799, Gr-1804,

CLARK, Edward, Cont'd., Gr-1805
    Eli, Gr-1821
    Ethan, Mu-1816
    George, Wl-1804, Wa-1814
    Henderson, Wa-1819, Wa-1814
    Henry, Gr-1799(2)
    Isaac, Sn-1816
    Isham, Gr-1799
    James, W-1812, B-1812, J-1802,
    Bo-1800
    James B., Rb-1812
    Jane, Gr-1821
    Jessee, Wh-1825
    John, Rb-1812(2), Gi-1812, Wa-1814,
    Wa-1819, Gr-1821, Fr-1812,
    Wi-1810
    John E., D-1811
    Joseph, Su-1812, Wa-1819, Cl-1803,
    Wi-1815, Wh-1825, Sn-1811,
    Sn-1816
    Josiah, Ct-1798
    Landren, D-1788
    Lever, D-1811
    Levi, Gr-1821
    Lewis, D-1811
    Malihia, Wa-1814
    Mary, Sn-1811
    Nancy, Wa-1819, Wa-1814(2)
    Parsons, Wh-1825
    Samuel, Gr-1804, Gr-1805, Gr-1799,
    Je-1800, Wh-1825, Gr-1805
    Stuart, W-1812
    Thomas, W-1812, R-1808, Bl-1815,
    Fr-1812, Wh-1825(2), D-1805,
    Gr-1799, Wl-1804(2), Wi-1801
    Thomas N., R-1819
    Walter, Ge-1812, Ge-1805
    William, Gr-1821, Sn-1811(2),
    Sn-1816(2), W-1812, Wa-1819,
    Wa-1814, Wh-1825(2), Wi-1810
CLARKE, Abraham, Wh-1811
    Isom, Cl-1803
    James, Su-1796, Su-1797
    Joseph(Josiah?), Wh-1811
    Joseph, Wh-1811
    Lewis, Su-1812
    Mary, Sn-1816
    Samuel, Ro-1805
    Silas, Cl-1803
    Thomas, W-1812, Wh-1811
    William, Wi-1810
CLARKSON, David, Gr-1804
CLARKSTON, James, Je-1822
CLARKY, John, Wh-1825
CLARY, Elisha, Sn-1816
CLATON, Wm., Wi-1801
CLAUNCH, Barnet, Gr-1799
    John, Gr-1799
CLAUSE, William, Wa-1819
CLAWSON, Jacob, Wa-1819
    Jas., C-1818
    Josiah, Ge-1805, Ge-1812
    Samuel, Wa-1819
CLAY, Eleazer, Gr-1804
    Eleezer, Gr-1805
    John, Wi-1810, D-1811, Wi-1815
    Larkin, D-1811
    William, Gr-1799, Gr-1821, Gr-1804,
    Gr-1805
    Woody, Wi-1815
CLAYBROOK, Levy, D-1811
CLAYBROOKS, Levy, D-1811

CLAYBURN, William, D-1805
CLAYMAN, George, Su-1812
 John, Su-1812
CLAYPOOL, Stephen, Gr-1799
CLAYTON, Daniel, Sn-1811, Gr-1804,
  Gr-1805
 Frederick, D-1811
 Henry, Mu-1811
 John, Mu-1816
 Richard, Sn-1816, Mu-1816
 Samuel, Gr-1805
CLAXON, Constantine, A-1805
CLAXSON, Conto, K-1799
CLAXSTON, Anson, Sn-1811
CLAXTON, Amous, Sn-1811
 Anthony, D-1811
 David, Gr-1805
 John, B-1812
 Joshua, Sn-1816(2), Sn-1811
 Mathew, D-1811
CLEARY, Elisha, Sn-1792
CLEAVELAND, Abner, Mu-1811
CLEAVER, Frederick, Ge-1812
CLEAVES, John, D-1811(2)
 William, D-1811
CLECK, John, Gr-1799
CLEEK, John, Wi-1801
CLEFT, John, B-1812
CLEMANS, John, Bo-1801
CLEMENS, Ham, B-1812
 John, B-1812
CLEMENT, Cartter, D-1805
CLEMENTS, Richard, Wh-1811
CLEMINS, John, Wl-1804(2)
CLEMM, James L., Wi-1815
CLEMMONS, Adam C., Bl-1815
 Frederick, Ro-1805
 Jacob, Ro-1805, Bl-1815
 John, Bl-1815
 Thomas, B-1812
CLENARO, Lawrence, Rb-1812
CLENDENAN, John, Je-1822
CLENDENEN, James, W-1812
CLENDENNING, James, Sn-1811
CLENGERY, George, Wa-1814
CLENNOY, Johnathon, Ro-1805
 Samuel, Sn-1816, Sn-1811
CLER, David, Ro-1805
CLERK, Davis, Bo-1800
 George, Je-1800
CLEVELAND, Eli, Mo-1825
 Larkin, Gi-1812
 Martin, Gr-1821
 Oliver C., Gi-1812
CLEVENGER, George, Je-1822
 John, Co-1821
CLIBORN, John, C-1823
CLICK, George, Wa-1819
 George L., Wa-1819
 Henry, Wa-1819, Wa-1814
 Malachi, Ge-1805
 Martin, Ge-1805, Ge-1812(2)
 Mary, Su-1812
 Melker, Ge-1812
 Michael, Su-1812
 Peter, Wa-1819, Wa-1814(2)
 James, Je-1800
CLIFTON, Anthony, D-1805
 Harden, Gr-1805
 Hardin, Gr-1805
 Hardy, Gr-1799, Gr-1805
 William, Gr-1799, Gr-1804, Gr-1805

CLIMAN, Joseph, D-1805
CLIMER, Thomas, W-1812
CLINDINING, James, Sn-1792
CLINE, Andrew, Su-1797
 Con, Sn-1816
 Jacob Jr., Je-1822
 Jacob C., Sr., Je-1822
 John, Sn-1816(2), Sn-1811, R-1819
 Martin, Sn-1816, Sn-1811
 Peter, Gr-1799
 Samuel, Je-1822
CLINGER, William P., Wa-1814
CLINNY, Jon., K-1799
CLINTON, David, D-1811
 James, B-1812
 Thomas, Mt-1798
CLIPPER, Frederick, Fr-1812
 Jacob, Wa-1819
 James, Wh-1811, Fr-1812
 John, Wa-1819
 Philip, Fr-1812
 Samuel, Wh-1811
CLIPYEAR, Lewis, Gr-1804
CLOAR, Elijah, Sn-1816
 John Jr., Sn-1816
 Wm., Sn-1816
CLODFETTER, Jacob, A-1805
CLONE, John, Sn-1811
CLOP, Jacob, Bo-1800
CLOSSON, Jacob, Wa-1814
CLOUD, Benjamin, Su-1812
 Iasum, Bo-1800
 Isaac, Su-1812
 Jason, A-1805
 Jeremiah, Su-1797, Su-1796, A-1805
 John, Wh-1825
 Phillip, Wi-1815
 Samuel, C-1823
 Thomas, Wh-1825
CLOUSE, Aaron, Wa-1814
 Adam, Wh-1825
 Elijah, Wh-1825
 William, Wa-1814
CLOW, Absalom, Sn-1811
 Eligah, Sn-1811
 John, Sn-1811
 William, Sn-1811
CLOWER, Daniel, Gr-1821
 James, Gr-1821
CLOWERS, Jacob, Ge-1783
CLOYD, David, D-1811, D-1805
 Ezekiel, Wl-1804
 James, Wa-1814, Wa-1819
 Philip, D-1811(2)
 Phillip, D-1805
 Samuel, Wa-1814(2), Wa-1819
 William, Wa-1019
 William Jr., Wa-1814
 William Sr., Wa-1814
CLUCK, Adam, Gr-1821
 Daniel, Je-1822
 Henry, Je-1800, Gr-1821
 John, Je-1800
 Mary, Je-1822
 Peter, Je-1800, Je-1822
CLUTTS, Estate, Ge-1812
CLYBOURN, B. Thomas, D-1805
 George, Sn-1811
COAD, William, A-1805
COAL, Robert, Mu-1811
COATS, Benjamin, B-1812, Gr-1821
 Charles, Gr-1799, Gr-1805, K-1796

COATS, Christopher, Su-1812
    Jessee, Gr-1799, Gr-1804
    John, Fr-1812, B-1812, Bo-1801,
        D-1811
    William, B-1812
    Wilson, B-1812
COBB, Arthur, Gr-1821
    Atheil Dredd, Ct-1798
    Dred, Ct-1796
    Jesse, Je-1822
    JOseph, Gr-1799(2), Gr-1804,
        Gr-1821, Gr-1805
    Pharoah, Ct-1796, Ct-1798
    Richard C., A-1805
    Samuel, Bo-1800
    William, Gr-1799
COBBLE, John, Ge-1812
COBLE, Adam, Wi-1810
    Daniel, A-1805
COBLER, Christopher, D-1811
    Francis, D-1811
    Harris, D-1811(2)
    Harvey, D-1811
    Hensley Sr., D-1811
    Hensley Jr., D-1811
    John, D-1811
    Nicholas, D-1811
COCHAIN, James, Bo-1801
    John, Bo-1801
COCHES, John W., D-1811
COCHORN, John, Bo-1800
    Wm., Gi-1812
COCHRAM, John, Rb-1812
COCHRAN, George, Wa-1819
    Jacob, Mu-1811
    James, Bo-1800, Mu-1811
    John, Wi-1815, Wi-1810
    Samuel, Mu-1811(2)
    William, Wi-1810
COCHRANE, David, Gr-1821
COCHRON, William, Mt-1798
COCK, B. Pleasant, Mu-1811
    Peter, Mt-1798
    Pleasant B., Mu-1816
    Richard, Mt-1798
    Richd. J., Mu-1816
    Stephen, Mt-1798
COCKARAN, Nicholas, Sn-1811
COCKBOURN, George, Mu-1816
COCKBURN, George, Gi-1819
COCKE, John, Gr-1805, Gr-1804, Gr-1799
    Sterling, Gr-1821
    Thomas, Wi-1801
    William, Gr-1799
COCKE & BROWN, Gi-1821
COCKELREESE, Jacob, Sn-1816
COCKELRUS, Henry, Sn-1816
    Nicholas, Sn-1816
COCKHILL, John, Wi-1801
COCKMAN, James, Mu-1816
COCKNER, Jacob, Wa-1814, Mu-1816
    John, Mt-1798
    William, Mu-1816
COCKRELL, Edwd., Mu-1816
    John, B-1812
    Lucy, Mu-1811
COCKRILL, John, B-1812
    John Sr., D-1805
    Lewis, D-1805
COCKS, James, Wi-1810
    John, W-1812
CODDLE, Joshua, Mu-1811

CODMER, William, Gi-1819
COE, Joseph, Mu-1816
    William, Wl-1804
COFELL, James, Gr-1799
COFFE, George, Gr-1799
    Henry, Gr-1799
COFFEE, Benjamin, B-1812, Wi-1801
    Chesley, Mu-1816
    George, Gr-1821
    James, Je-1800
    John, Wl-1804, Gr-1821, B-1812
    Meredith, Gr-1821, Gr-1805
    Merida, Gr-1804
    _____, D-1805
COFFER, James, Wa-1819, B-1812
    Thomas, B-1812
COFFEY, Chesley, Mu-1811
    Hugh, Hu-1812
    John, Wi-1815
    Meredith, Gr-1799
    Nathaniel, Mu-1811
    William, B-1812
COFFILL, John, Su-1796
COFFIN, Charles, Ge-1805
    Charles Rev., Ge-1812
    John, Fr-1812
    Nathaniel, Gr-1804, Gr-1805
COFFITT, Abraham, C-1818
    Daniel, C-1818
    George, C-1818
    Isaac, C-1818
COFFMAN, Andrew, Gr-1821, Je-1822
    Andrew Jr., Gr-1821
    Daniel, Ge-1805, Ge-1812
    David, Gr-1821
    George, Gr-1804, Gr-1821, Gr-1805
    Harmon, Ge-1812
    Isaac, Gi-1812, D-1805
    Joseph, C-1818
    Level, Gi-1812
    Loveal, Ge-1805
    Nicholas, Je-1822, Ge-1812
    Rinehart, Gr-1821, Ge-1812
    Rhineheart, Gr-1804
    Riner, Gr-1805
    Robert, Je-1822
    Sameul, Je-1822
    William, Gr-1821
COFFREY, Danelson, D-1805
    John, D-1805
    Peter, D-1811
COFFY, John, Mt-1798
    Rice, B-1812
COFMAN, David, Je-1800
    Isaac, Je-1800
    James, Je-1800
    Lovel, Je-1800
COFMON, George, Gr-1805
COGBELL, Charles C., Sn-1816
COGDALE, Joseph, Gr-1799
COGGBURN, John, Ge-1812
    Patrick, Ge-1812
COGGLE, John, D-1805
COHEN, Amos, Rb-1812
    George, Gi-1819
COHERN, Wm., Sn-1816
COHN, Peter Rb-1812
COHOL, Elisha, Wa-1814
COHOON, Charles, Wi-1815
    Charles Sr., Wi-1815
    Wilson, Wi-1815
COHSON, George, Wi-1815

COIL, Cummins, Wi-1815
COILS, George, Bo-1800
COIN, Joseph, Su-1812
COKER, Jesse, Sn-1816
  Peter, Wh-1825
COLB, Asa, K-1799
COLBACK, Henry, Su-1812
  John, Su-1812
COLBERT, Colintine, Fr-1812
COLBOTH, Jacob, Ct-1796
COLDTHARP, Nanthl., D-1805
COLDWELL, David, D-1811
  John, Bo-1800
  Joseph, D-1811
  Robert, D-1811
  Samuel, Ge-1812(2)
  William, D-1811(2)
  Wm. Sr., D-1811
  William Jr., D-1811
COLE, Abraham, B-1812
  Abram, Gi-1812(2)
  Alexander, A-1805
  Andrew, Wi-1815
  Denon, B-1812
  Edward, Mu-1811
  Elisha, Su-1812, Su-1797, Su-1796
  Hugh, Sn-1816
  Isam, Wi-1810
  Isham, Wi-1815, Wh-1825(2)
  James, Wh-1811, Sn-1816(2), Mu-1811
  John, A-1805, Gi-1812(2), Wa-1814,
    Su-1812, Rb-1812, Wa-1819,
    D-1811
  Joseph, Wa-1814, Wl-1804, Mu-1811
  Joseph Jr., Su-1796
  Joseph, heirs, Wi-1815
  Josiah, Wh-1825
  Nine, B-1812
  Philip, Ge-1812(6)
  Pilsmore?, D-1811
  Reuben, K*-1815
  Richard, Wh-1825
  Samuel, Wi-1815, Wi-1810
  Shatl., Ge-1812
  Solomon, Wh-1825
  Stephen, Wh-1825
  T. William Jr., Wl-1804
  Thomas, Wi-1815, Wi-1810, D-1811
  Thos., heirs, Wi-1815
  William, Rb-1812, Sn-1816, Wi-1815,
    Wi-1810, Mu-1811(2), D-1811,
    Mu-1816(2), Wi-1801, B-1812,
    Wh-1811
COLEBOURN, Thos., Mu-1816
COLEBURN, Richard, Ge-1812
  Thomas, Mu-1811
COLEMAN, Jessey H., Co-1821
  John, Mu-1811
  Joseph, Wi-1801, D-1811(2)
  Joshua, Wi-1815
  Thomas, Mu-1811, Mu-1816
  William, Co-1821
COLEN, Joshua, Gr-1799
COLENGER, Higgins, Wa-1814
COLESON, David, W-1812
COLGER, Charles, Rb-1812
COLIER, Wilson, Gi-1812
COLINGER, Smith, Wa-1814
COLISON, Enoch, Wa-1814
COLKER, William, W-1812
COLLINS, Aaron, Gr-1804
  Andrew, Wa-1819

COLLINS, Aron, Gr-1805
  Casler, Fr-1812
  Conly, Gr-1821
  David, Gr-1804, Gr-1805
  Dorrum, Mu-1816
  D_____, Gr-1821
  Edmond, W-1812, Gr-1821
  Edward, Wi-1801, Sn-1811, Je-1800
  Elisha, Gr-1799
  Griffee, Gr-1805
  Griffin, Gr-1804
  Griffy Jr., Gr-1821
  Hadijah, Wi-1815
  Henry, R-1819
  Jacob, Wh-1825
  James, R-1819
  John, Wa-1819, Je-1800, Je-1822
  Joseph, Gr-1805, B-1812, Wa-1814,
    Gr-1804, Gr-1821
  Joshua, Gr-1805, Gr-1804, Su-1812
  Lewis, Gr-1804, Gr-1821, Gr-1805
  Stephen, Mu-1811
  Thomas, D-1811, D-1805, Fr-1812,
    Wa-1819, Gi-1812
COLLESON, James, Gr-1799
COLLET, Abraham, Ge-1805
  Andrew, C-1823
  Isaac, Ge-1812
COLLEY, Joseph, Sn-1811
  Squire, Mu-1811
COLLIER, Henry, Wh-1811
  John, Ge-1805
  Joseph, W-1812
  Robert, Sn-1811
  Thomas, Ge-1805
COLLIFOR, William, Gr-1821
COLLINGIN, William, Mt-1798
COLLINGS, David, Wh-1825
  Peter, Wl-1804
COLLINGSWORTH, John, Gr-1821
COLLINGTON, Charles, Mt-1798
COLLINSWORTH, Coventon, Je-1800
  Edmond, D-1811
  Edward, D-1805
COLLISON, James, Gr-1805
  Johnathan, Gr-1799
  Johnathan Sr., Gr-1799
COLLIT, Andrew, Ge-1812
  Jacob, Ge-1812
COLLOM, William, Wa-1819
COLLON, Jonathan, Wa-1814
COLLONGAN, Elizabeth, Wi-1815
COLLONS, Joseph Sr., Wa-1819
COLLUM, Jonathan, Wa-1819
COLLUMS, George, Gr-1799
COLQUIT, Samuel, Fr-1812
COLQUITT, John T., Fr-1812
  Samuel, Fr-1812
  William, Fr-1812
COLSTON, Elijah, Ge-1812
  Samuel, Wa-1819
  Thomas, Ge-1812(3)
  Thomas Jr., Ge-1812
COLTER, Andw., Ct-1798
  Jno., Ge-1783
COLTHARP, Clayton, D-1811
  John, Je-1822
  Norrel, D-1811
  William, D-1811
COLVERT, Leonard, Wa-1819
  William, Se-1799, Wa-1819
COLVILLE, George, Bo-1800, Bo-1801

COLVILLE, Joseph, Bo-1800, Bo-1801, W-1812,
        W-1805
    Samuel, W-1805, W-1812
    Samuel Esq., W-1812
COLVIN, John, Gr-1821
COLWELL, James, Gi-1812
    John, Sn-1811, Gi-1812
    William, Gi-1812
COLYAR, Alexander, Wa-1814(2)
    William Sr., Wa-1814(2)
    William Jr., Wa-1814
COLYER, Alexander, Wa-1819
    Barnett, Fr-1812
    Charles, Ct-1796
    John, Ge-1812
    Morgan, Ge-1812
    Stephen, K-1799
    Thomas, Ge-1812
    William, Je-1822, Wa-1819(2)
COMBE, Philip, Gr-1799
COMBLES, Samuel, J-1802
COMBS, George, Gr-1821, Gr-1799
    Jerremiah, W-1812
    Job, Je-1800
    John, Gr-1821, Je-1800
    Jonathan, Su-1797, Su-1812
    Joseph, Je-1822
    Laburn, Hu-1812
    M. George, Gr-1804
    Nelson, Gr-1821
    Nicholas, Su-1797, Su-1812,
        Su-1796(2)
    Philip, Gr-1804
    Simon, W-1812
    William, Mu-1816, Je-1822
COMENS, Samuel, Wi-1810
COMER, John, Wa-1814
COMES, Thomas, Fr-1812
COMFORT, Andrew, Wi-1810
    James, Mu-1811
COMMINGS, John, Sn-1792
COMMINS, Wm., Sn-1816
COMMONS, Joseph, Li-1812*
COMOS, Nicholas, Su-1797
COMPTON, Henry, D-1811
    John, Ct-1798
    Richard, D-1811(2)
    Richard & John, D-1805
    Vinson, Wl-1804
    William, D-1805
    William Sr., D-1811
COMTON, James, K-1799
CONAL, Thomas, B-1812
CONAN, George, Mu-1811(2)
CONAWAY, Jesse, Bo-1800
    Joseph, Bo-1800
    Phillip, Ge-1783
    Thomas, Bo-1800
CONDAY, William, Cl-1803
CONDER, Daniel, Mu-1811, Mu-1816
    John, Mu-1811
    Peter, Wi-1815, Mu-1811
CONDERY, Nathl., Sn-1792
CONDLEY, John, Gr-1805
CONDNOS, John, D-1850
CONDON, James, D-1811
CONDRA, Benjamin, Gr-1804
    Dennis, Gr-1804
    Eliphaz, Gr-1804
    Richard, Gr-1804
    William, Mt-1798
CONDRAY, Benjamin, Gr-1805

CONDRAY, Denis, Cl-1803
    Dennis, Gr-1805
    John, Cl-1803
CONDREY, Benjamin, Gr-1799
    Dennis, Gr-1799
CONDRY, Benjamin, Gr-1805
    Cephus, Fr-1812
    Dennis, Gr-1850, Gr-1821
    Furnifold, Gr-1821
    Hammond, Gr-1821
    Richard, Su-1796, Su-1797
    Stephen, Gi-1812
CONDSAN, Wm., Bo-1800
CONDUIT, Patsey, Ge-1812
CONE, John, Rb-1812
CONGER, John, Sn-1811
CONGO, James, D-1811
    John, D-1811
CONKIN, George, Su-1797, Su-1796
CONLEY, Daniel, W-1812
    George, Rb-1812
    John, R-1819, Gr-1799
CONLY, John, Gr-1804
    Nathaniel, W-1812
CONN, James, Gr-1805
    John, A-1805
    Joseph H., Sn-1816
    Josiah, Fr-1812
CONNALLY, William & Thomas, D-1805
CONNARD, James, Bo-1805
CONNARY, Joseph, Mu-1811
CONNEL, Jiles, Mt-1798
    Mcaker, Gi-1819
CONNELL, James, Rb-1812
    John, Gi-1819
    Sampson, Rb-1812
    Will, Rb-1812
    Wm., Rb-1812
CONNELLY, Andrew, D-1811
    James, D-1811
    Peter, D-1811
    Thomas, D-1811
    William, D-1811
    William Sr., D-1811
    William Jr., D-1811
CONNELY, Christopher, D-1805
CONNER, Abraham, Wh-1825
    Archibald, Wh-1285, Wh-1811
    Edward, Wh-1811
    James, D-1811(2), Je-1822, Gi-1819
    John, Gi-1819
    Joseph, Je-1800
    Julias, Ct-1796, Ct-1798
    Lewis, Gi-1819
    Martin, W-1812
    Richard, Je-1800
    Terrance, Bo-1800, Bo-1801
    William, Sn-1792, D-1788
CONNERS, Thomas, Sn-1792
CONNEY, William, D-1811
CONNOR, Abner, Gr-1799
CONNORS, Thomas, Wl-1804
CONRAD, John, Wa-1814
CONSTABLE, Jacob, Wa-1814
CONVAN, John Jr., Wa-1814
CONWAY, Charles, Wh-1825, K-1796
    George, Ge-1805
    Henry, Ge-1812(2), Ge-1783, Ge-1805
    James, Ge-1812
    Jessee, Wh-1825
    Jessey, Bo-1801
    Joseph, Bo-1801

CONWAY, Thomas, Bo-1801
    William J., Je-1822
    _____, Ge-1812
CONWELL, Jesse, B-1812
    John, B-1812
    Thos., B-1812
    William, C-1823
CONYER, James, Sn-1816
    John, D-1855, Sn-1816
    Thos., Sn-1787
CONYERS, Bartholomew, Je-1822
    William, Mu-1811
COODY, James, Gi-1819
COOK, Alexander, J-1802
    Aron, Gr-1799, Gr-1805
    Augustine, Rb-1812
    Burrel, Fr-1812
    Charles, B-1812
    Charles Jr., B-1812
    Christian, Ge-1812
    Daniel, Fr-1812
    Drusila, Gi-1819
    Edmond, estate, Wi-1801
    George, D-1788, B-1812, Bo-1801
    George Sr., Ge-1812(2)
    George Jr., Ge-1812
    George L., Wh-1825
    Henery, Wi-1810, Sn-1811
    Henry, Wi-1815, Wi-1801
    Hugh, Gi-1819
    Jacob, Ge-1805, Rb-1812, Rb-1819,
        Sn-1816
    Joel, D-1811
    John, Gr-1821, Fr-1812, B-1812,
        Gi-1812, Ge-1812, Mu-1816
    John Esqr., Mu-1816
    John Sr., Ge-1812(2)
    John Jr., B-1812
    Joseph, K-1799, Su-1812
        Mu-1816, D-1805, D-1811, Mu-1811
    Lettie, Ro-1805
    Marcurious, Gr-1799
    Michael, Gr-1805(2), Gr-1804,
        Bo-1801
    Michel, Bo-1800
    Nicholas, Wh-1825
    Reuben, Su-1812
    Richard, Mu-1811, Wl-1804
    Robert, B-1812, Wh-1825
    Rubin, D-1811
    Simon, Gr-1805
    Stephen, B-1812
    Thomas, Mo-1825, Mu-1816
    Wandell, Wa-1814
    William, Fr-1812, Gr-1799(2),
        Gr-1804, Gr-1821, Gr-1805(2),
        Gi-1812
    Willie, D-1811
    _____, Ge-1812
COOKE, George, Bo-1800
    Henry, Wi-1815
    Jacob, Su-1812, R-1808
    Jacob Jr., Su-1812
    Jessee, Sn-1811
    John, D-1788
    Joseph, Su-1797, Su-1796
    Mareurcurus, Cl-1803
    William E., Gr-1821
    William W., D-1811
COOKS, George, Ro-1805
    Peter, Wh-1811
COOKSEY, Enoch, W-1812, W-1805

COOLEY, William, Ge-1805
COOMER, John, B-1812
COON, Adam, Wi-1815
    Catherine, Wa-1814
    Thomas, Wi-1815
COONCE, Robt., Se-1799
    Samuel, Se-1799
    Shadrick, Se-1799
COONS, Joseph, Je-1822
    Michael, Gr-1804, Je-1822
    Michael Sr., Je-1800
    Michael Jr., Je-1800
    Michal, Gr-1805
COOP, Arasha, Wl-1804
    Horatio, B-1812
    James, B-1812
    Michael, Wa-1814
    Richard, B-1812, Sn-1816
COOPE, Baracias, Bo-1801
    James, W-1812
COOPER, Abraham, Ct-1796, Ct-1798,
        B-1812
    Alexander, Wh-1825
    Andrew, Su-1797, Su-1796
    Benjamin, Se-1799(2), D-1811
    Caleb, Su-1796
    Charles, B-1812, D-1811
    Christian, Ge-1812
    Christofer, B-1812
    Christopher, Ge-1805, Wl-1804
    Cornelius, Gr-1799
    David, Wh-1825, Wi-1810
    Edmond, D-1805
    Edmund, Mu-1811
    Emond, D-1811
    Edward, Ct-1798, Ct-1796, B-1812
    George, Sn-1816, Sn-1811, Bo-1801
    Hardy, Wi-1815
    Harrison, Mu-1811
    Harson, Se-1799
    Henry, D-1805, D-1811(2), A-1805
    Huston, D-1811
    Isaac, Gr-1799, Sn-1823, Sn-1811,
        Sn-1816
    Isham, R-1819
    Jacob, Je-1800
    James, C-1823, D-1811
    James Esq., W-1812
    Jese, Se-1799
    Jesey, Se-1799
    Job, Ct-1798, B-1812
    Jobe, Ct-1796
    Joel, Ct-1798, Ct-1796
    John, A-1805, Ct-1796, B-1812,
        Mu-1816, Bo-1800, Ct-1798,
        Bo-1801, Gr-1799, Su-1797,
        Su-1796, Sn-1811, Mu-1811,
        D-1805(2), Sn-1816, K-1796,
        D-1811
    Joseph, C-1823, W-1812
    Laner, D-1811
    Levina, Gi-1819
    M. Robert, Mu-1816
    Martin, Se-1799
    Nathan, Ct-1798, Ge-1805, Ct-1796
    Patience, Ct-1796
    Peter, C-1818, C-1823
    Richard, Rb-1812
    Robert, Wl-1804
    Samuel, Gi-1812(2), W-1812, Gr-1805
    Thomas, Gr-1804, Bo-1800, Wa-1814,
        Su-1797, Su-1796, Sn-1811,
        Wh-1825

COOPER, William, Gr-1799(2), Gr-1821,
          A-1805, Gr-1804, B-1812(4),
          Se-1799, Gi-1812, Ge-1812
     William Sr., Mu-1811
COOS, Jacob, Wa-1819
     Michael, Wa-1819
COOSE, William, Gr-1821
COOTER, Abraham, Je-1822
COOTES, Fredorica, Wh-1825
COPAS, Thomas, Su-1812
     William, Su-1812
     William Jr., Su-1812
COPBURGER, Walter, Su-1812
COPE, Andrew, Wh-1825
     Baracies, Bo-1800
     Charles, Rb-1812
     Ritchard, Sn-1811
COPEA, Perry, Mu-1816
COPELAND, Anthony, Mu-1811, Mu-1816,
          Ge-1805
     Daid, Ge-1812(2)
     David, Mu-1816, Mu-1811, Ge-1783,
          Ge-1805(3), Ge-1812
     Hezekiah, Ge-1812
     James, Mu-1811, Wh-1825, Mu-1816
          Ge-1805
     John, Ge-1805, Su-1796, Su-1797
     John Sr., Ge-1812
     John Jr., Ge-1812
     Joseph, J-1802
     Rickets, Je-1800
     Soloman, Je-1800
     Stephen, J-1802, Je-1800
     Thomas, Gr-1805, Wh-1825, Gr-1804
     William, Su-1796, Su-1797
     Zacheus, Je-1800
COPELANE, Thomas, Ro-1805
COPFER?, William, W-1812
COPLAND, David, Bo-1800, Bo-1801
     Nicholas, J-1802
     Rebecca, Je-1822
     Richard, Gr-1805
     Sam., Gi-1812
     Soloman, Je-1822
     Thomas, Gr-1805
     William, heirs, Gr-1821
     Zacheus, Je-1822
COPELANE, Thomas, Ro-1805
COPFER?, William, W-1812
COPLAND, David, Bo-1800, Bo-1801
     Nicholas, J-1802
     Rebecca, Je-1822
     Richard, Gr-1805
     Sam., Gi-1812
     Soloman, Je-1822
     Thomas, Gr-1805
     William, heirs, Gr-1821
     Zacheus, Je-1822
COPP, Jacob, Wa-1814
COPPER, William, W-1805
COPPINER, Higgins, Su-1796
COPPING, Thomas, Wl-1804
COPPINGER, Higgs, Su-1812
     Huggins, Su-1797
     Huggins Sr., Su-1797
COPPOCK, Aron, Ge-1812
     Isaha, Je-1800
     James, Je-1800
     John, Je-1822
     Thomas, Je-1800
     Thomas, heirs, Je-1822
COPPS, Shadrack, W-1812

CORBAN, Johnson, Wh-1825
CORBETT, Elizabeth, Je-1800
CORBIT, Jno., Ge-1783
CORBITT, John, D-1811
     William, D-1805
CORDAN, James, Wh-1825
CORDEL, John, Rb-1812
CORDER, John, Sn-1811
     Richard, C-1823
CORDLE, Thos., Sn-1816
CORITHERS, John, Mu-1816
     Robert, Mu-1816(2)
CORLELUS, William, B-1812
CORMACK, Edward, Gr-1850
CORMICK, Patrick, A-1805
CORMLEE, James, Sn-1816
CORN, Saml., Bo-1800
CORNEALES, Jeptha, K-1799
CORNELIUS, Edmond, D-1811
     James, Wl-1804, D-1811
     John, Gr-1799
CORNELOUS, James, Sn-1816
CORNELUS, James, Sn-1811
CORNEY, Gustin, Gi-1812
CORNULIA, John, D-1811
CORRAN, James, Wa-1819
     John, Wa-1819
CORRITHERS, James, Gr-1799
CORSELIUS, John, Wa-1819
CORTHRAN, John, Sn-1816
CORTMEL, John, B-1812
CORUM, Robert, Sn-1816
COSBEY, James, Ge-1783
COSC, George, Wa-1814
     Mabury, Wa-1814
     William, Wa-1814
COSEL, John, Gr-1805
COSSASS, John, Wa-1819
COSSON, Isaac, Wa-1814
     John, Wa-1814
     Margaret, Wa-1814
COSTATER, Martin, Bo-1800
COTHEN, John, Wl-1804
COTNER, John, Gr-1821
     Martin, Gr-1821
     Peter, Gr-1804, Gr-1805
COTRAN, Francis, Sn-1792
COTS, Benjamin, Gr-1805
COTTEN, Allen, D-1805
     Wm., Hu-1812
COTTENHAM, Wm., Hu-1812
COTTER, James, Ge-1805, Ge-1812(2)
     John, Ge-1812(2), Ge-1805
     Stephen, Je-1800, Ge-1805, Ge-1812
COTTEREL, Lemuel, Su-1796
COTTERELL, Samuel, Su-1797
COTTON, Allen, D-1811
     Arthur, Sn-1811
     Cullen, Wa-1819
     Daniel, B-1812
     Jacob, Gr-1799
     John, Sn-1816, Sn-1811
     Lazarus, Sn-1792
     Moore, Sn-1816, Sn-1811
     Peter, Gr-1821
     Priscilla, Sn-1816
     Prissila, Sn-1811
     Pullen, Sn-1816
     Robert, R-1808, Sn-1816
     Thomas, Sn-1792
COTTRELL, John, K-1799
     Pryor, D-1811

COTTRELL, Rubin, Gr-1805
    Thomas, D-1811
COU, John, Wa-1819
COUCH, John, Ge-1812
    Joseph, Wh-1825
    Thomas, B-1812
    Timothy, Wh-1825
COUGHRON, William, Sn-1816
    William, heirs, Je-1822
COULSON, Elijah, Ge-1805
    Isaac, Wh-1825, Wh-1811
    John, Ge-1805
COULSTON, John, Ge-1812
COULTER, Charles, Bo-1801
COULEE, Daniel, Ge-1805
COULTER, Eli, Gr-1805
    George, Li-1812*
    James, R-1819, Ro-1805
    John, Gr-1805, Gr-1804, Gr-1799
    Richard, Bo-1805
    Richard Jr., Bo-1801
    Robert, Rb-1812
    Thomas, Gr-1805, R-1819, Bl-1815
COUNCE, Adam, A-1805
    John Sr., A-1805
    John Jr., A-1805
COUNCEL, Rodrick, D-1811
COUNGTON, John, Wl-1804
COUNSE, John Sr., Gr-1804
    John Jr., Gr-1804
    Nicholas, Gr-1804
COUNSELMAN, John, D-1811
COUNT, Josefus, Sn-1811
COUNTS, Aaron, Gr-1821
    George, Fr-1812
    Jacob, J-1802
    John, Gr-1805, Gr-1799
    John Sr., Gr-1805
    Nicholas, Gr-1821, Gr-1799
    Nicholas Jr., Gr-1821
COURFMAN, Jacob, Wi-1815
COURTHUS, Thomas, B-1812
BOURTIS, Benjamin, Wi-1815
    Joshua, Wi-1815
COURTNEY, George, Ge-1812
    James, Je-1822
    Marshall, Je-1822
COURTS, Charles, Mu-1811
    William, B-1812
COUTLER, Charles, Bo-1800
    Francis, Bo-1800
    Richard, Bo-1800
COUTS, David, Gr-1821
    John, Rb-1812
COUZINS, Abel, Wi-1815
COVE, William, K*-1815
COVENTON, James, Gi-1812
COVEY, Joshua, Je-1822
    William Sr., Mu-1816
    William Jr., Mu-1816, Mu-1811
COVIN?, James, Rb-1812
COVINGTON, William A., Sn-1811
COVINTON, Henry, Rb-1812
COVINTRY, George, Rb-1812
COVY, William Sr., Mu-1811
COWAN, Alexander, A-1805, Gr-1799
    Andrew, Bo-1800
    Arch., Bo-1801
    David, Wh-1811
    Elizabeth, Wa-1819
    George, Je-1822
    James, R-1808, Je-1800(2), Bo-1801,

COWAN, James, Cont'd., Fr-1812
    Jane, Je-1800
    Joel W., Je-1822
    John, Ge-1800, Je-1822, R-1808,
        W-1812
    John Sr., Bo-1801
    Joseph, Wi-1815, Wi-1810, R-1808
    Mathew, Je-1822
    Peter, Su-1812
    Richard, C-1818
    Robert, Wh-1825, Su-1796, Gr-1799,
        W-1812, Su-1812, Bo-1801,
        Bo-1800
    Samuel, C-1818, Bo-1800, Bo-1805,
        Gr-1799, C-1823
    Stewart, Fr-1812
    William, Fr-1812
COWANT, Johnathan, Su-1812
COWARD, John, Su-1812
COWDEN, Elijah, B-1812
    Henry, D-1811
    Josiah, Sn-1816
    Robert, B-1812
    Thomas, Wi-1810
    William, B-1812, Sn-1811, Mu-1811,
        Mu-1816, Sn-1816
    William Jr., Sn-1811
COWEN, Arch., Bo-1800
    David, D-1805
    James, Fr-1812, Ge-1812
    James P., Fr-1812
    John, Hu-1812, Bo-1800
    Joseph, Hu-1812, Mu-1816
    Robert, Fr-1812, Su-1797
    Samuel, Mu-1811
COWGILL, Abner, D-1811
    Henry, D-1811
    John, D-1811
COWIN, Robert, W-1805
COWLER, William, Wi-1801
COWLIN, Joseph, Fr-1812
COWON(Couson?), John, Fr-1812
COWSERT, Andrew, Wi-1815
COX, Abraham, Ct-1798, Ct-1796
    Abram, Su-1812
    Amon, Fr-1812
    Amos, Gr-1805
    Amos Jr., Gr-1804
    Benjamin, Wa-1819, Gr-1821
    Bosley, Su-1812
    Branton, C-1818
    Caleb, Wa-1819
    Daniel, Gi-1812
    David, B-1812
    Dudley, Je-1800
    Edmond, Gr-1804
    Edmund, Gr-1805
    Edward, Su-1797, Su-1796, D-1805
    Edward Sr., Su-1812
    Elijah, Su-1812
    Elisha, C-1818
    Ephraim, Ge-1783
    Eziel, Ge-1812
    Gale, Ge-1812
    Greenberry, Su-1797, Su-1796
    Harmon, Gr-1804, Gr-1799, Gr-1805
    Henry, Je-1800, Wh-1811
    Isaac, Wa-1819
    Isham, Esq., Ro-1805
    Jacob, Gr-1821
    Jacob, heirs, Gr-1821
    James, B-1812, C-1823, Su-1812

COX, Jeremiah, Gr-1804, Su-1797, Gr-1799
    Su-1796, Gr-1805
  Jeremiah Jr., Su-1812
  Jesse, Su-1812(2), Su-1796, Su-1797,
    D-1811(2)
  Jiles, Ge-1812
  Joab, A-1805
  John, Ct-1796, C-1818, Gr-1804,
    Wa-1819, K*-1815, Je-1800,
    W-1812, Wl-1804, Wi-1815
  John Sr., Su-1812
  John Jr., Su-1812
  Joseph, Su-1812, Wh-1825
  Joshua, Su-1812, Su-1796
  Josiah, Gr-1799(2)
  Lemuel, Ge-1812
  Matthew, Ge-1805
  Meredith, Su-1812
  Nathaniel, Ro-1805
  Reed, Je-1822
  Richard, Ct-1798, Gr-1799(2),
    Ct-1796
  Robert, Wh-1825
  Ruben, D-1811
  Samuel, Gi-1819, Gr-1804, Gr-1799,
    Gr-1821, Wi-1810, Gr-1805,
    Wi-1815
  Sam., Jr., Gi-1812
  Saml. Sr., Gi-1819, Gi-1812
  Samuel M., D-1811
  Solomon, Wh-1811(2), Je-1800
  Taker, Gi-1819
  Thomas, Gr-1799, B-1812, Su-1812(2),
    Wi-1810, D-1805, Wi-1815,
    D-1811
  Thomas, heirs, Gr-1805
  William, Je-1800, Ge-1805, Gi-1812,
    Wa-1819(2), Su-1812, Je-1822,
    Je-1800(2), Wa-1814, Gr-1805,
    Su-1812, Ge-1812, Wh-1825,
    D-1805
  William Sr., Je-1822
  William Jr., Je-1822
  William R., Gi-1819
  Zachariah, Rb-1812
COXEY, Thos., Sn-1816
COYLER, Charles, Ct-1798
  Stephen, Ct-1798
COZBY, James W., R-1819
  John, R-1819
  Robert, R-1819
COZIAH, Buston, Wa-1819
  William, Wa-1819
CRABAUGH, Charles, A-1805
CRABB, Frances, Fr-1812
  Francis, Gr-1799, Fr-1812
  John, Gr-1804, Gr-1799, Gr-1805
  Joseph, Gr-1799, Wh-1811
  Joseph, deceased, Gr-1799
  Ralph, Fr-1812
  Stephen, Gr-1804
  Thomas, Fr-1812
CRABS, James, Rb-1812
CRABTREE, Barnet, Ge-1805
  Barnett, Ge-1812
  James, Ge-1783, Rb-1812, W-1812,
    J-1802, Wl-1804
  John, Wl-1804
  Joseph, Se-1799, Wl-1804
  William, Se-1799, Wh-1811, Wl-1804
CRADAC, William, Ge-1812
CRADDOCK, William, D-1811(2)
CRADOCK, William, D-1805
CRAFFORD, Hugh, Sn-1811
  Thos., Ge-1783
  William, Fr-1812
CRAFORD, Cannoway, Bl-1815
  Hughe, Sn-1787
CRAFT, Jesse, Su-1796
  John, Mt-1798
  Michael, Su-1796
  Michael Sr. (in Long Island),
    Su-1796
  Michal, Su-1797
  Michal Sr., Su-1797
  Michal Jr., Su-1797
  Samuel, Su-1797
  Thomas, Su-1796, Su-1797, Su-1812
CRAFTON, B. John, Mu-1816
  John, Ro-1805, Wi-1810, Wi-1815
  Robert, Mu-1811, Mu-1816
CRAG, David, Wi-1810
CRAGG, David, Sn-1811
  John, Mu-1816
  Richard, Wi-1815
CRAIG, Alexander, D-1811, Bo-1800, A-1819,
    Bo-1801, D-1805
  Andrew, Wi-1815
  Crozier, B-1812
  David, Bo-1800, Bo-1801, Ge-1783,
    Wi-1815, Mu-1816, Mu-1811
  James, Bo-1800, Je-1822, Wi-1810,
    D-1805, Wi-1801, Wi-1815,
    Mu-1811
  James Sr., Ge-1783, Bo-1801, Mu-1816
  James Jr., Bo-1801, Ge-1783, Mu-1816
  John, C-1823, Bo-1801, B-1812(2),
    Ge-1783, Bo-1800, C-1818,
    Gi-1812
  Johnston, Mu-1811, Mu-1816
  P. John, Mu-1811
  P. William, Mu-1811
  Reubin, C-1818
  Robert, Je-1822
  Robert P., Je-1822
  Sammel, R-1819
  Samuel, Wi-1815, Ge-1805, Wi-1810,
    Mu-1811, Mu-1816
  Samuel, estate, Ge-1812
  Susanna, Bo-1800
  William, Mu-1811(2), Bo-1801,
    Mu-1816(2)
CRAIG & WASHINGTON, Mu-1816
CRAIGE, James, Hu-1812
  John, Hu-1812
  Robt., Hu-1812
CRAIGH, Thomas, Mt-1798
CRAIGHEAD, Alexander, Wh-1825
  B. Thomas, D-1805
  Benjamin, Gr-1821, K*-1815
  John, K*-1815
  Robert, K*-1815
  Thomas, D-1811
CRAIL, James, Ro-1805
CRAIN, Abras, B-1812
  Ezekiel, Sn-1816
  Joel, B-1812
  Joseph, Rb-1812
  Lemuel, Rb-1812
  Lewis, Sn-1792, Sn-1816
  Spencer, Rb-1812
  Thomas, D-1811
  William, Gr-1805, Sn-1811, Sn-1816
CRAINE, Abijah, Wh-1825

CRAINE, Bathel, Wh-1825
    Charles, Gr-1821
    Charles Jr., Gr-1821
    Stephen, Wh-1825
CRAMER, Henry, D-1811
CRAMT., Ezechiel, Gr-1799
CRANBERRY, Thomas, C-1818
CRANE, Abijah, Wh-1811
    Dozier, Wh-1811
    Lewis, Sn-1787, Rb-1812
    Samuel, Gr-1804
    Stephen, Wh-1811
    William, Wh-1811
    W_____, Sn-1811
CRANMORE, James, R-1819
    Josiah, R-1819
CRANSHAW, Cornelius, Wi-1810
    Oliver, Wi-1815
CRANTZ, Thomas, D-1811
CRASEY(Grady?), David, Sn-1787
CRASOCK, Samuel, B-1812
    William, B-1812
CRATHERS, Robert, Mu-1811
CRATON, James, Se-1799, Fr-1812, Wl-1804
    John, Fr-1812
CRAVAN, John, Sn-1792
CRAVEN, Joseph, C-1823, A-1805
    Joshua, C-1823
    Richard, C-1823
CRAVENS, Jack, C-1818
    James, Ge-1783
    John, Sn-1787
    Joshua, C-1818
    Robert, Ge-1783, Gi-1812
CRAVINS, James, Ge-1812
CRAW, Robert, Ct-1798
CRAWFORD, Alexander, Mu-1811(2), Mu-1816
    Alexr. C., Mu-1816
    C. Alexander, Mu-1811, Mu-1816
    Capt., K-1796
    David, Fr-1812
    Edward, J-1802
    George, Mu-1816
    Henry, Gr-1821
    Hugh, Su-1797, Su-1796, Sn-1792,
        Sn-1816, Su-1812
    Isabel, Ge-1812
    James, B-1812, Bo-1801, Wa-1819,
        Wa-1814(2), Mu-1816, Mu-1811
    John, Ge-1805, Wa-1814, J-1802
        Su-1812, Wa-1819, Ge-1812,
        Su-1797, Wi-1810, Wi-1801,
        Mu-1811(2)
    John, heirs, Mu-1816
    John W., Wa-1819
    Joseph, J-1802
    Margaret, Ge-1812
    Samuel, Ge-1805, Wa-1819, Ge-1812,
        Su-1812, Mu-1811
    T. James, Mu-1816
    William, Ge-1805, B-1812, Wa-1814,
        Su-1812(2), Sn-1816,
        Mu-1811(2), D-1805, Mu-1816
    William A., Wa-1819
CRAWLEY, Eliza, Ge-1812
    Henry, Gr-1805
    James, Wh-1825
    John, Wl-1804, Hu-1812
    Thomas Sr., Wh-1825
    Thomas Jr., Wh-1825
    William, Ct-1798
CRAWOOD, Agatha, Su-1812

CRAWSBY, Samuel, Mu-1811
CRAWSON, Samuel, Ct-1798
CREAGAN, Patrick, Su-1796
CREAMER, Daniel, Ge-1783
CREASIN, Isaac, Cl-1803
CREECH, Moses, Ro-1805
CREEDGINTON, George, Su-1797
CREEDINGTON, George, Su-1812(2)
CREEK, George, Wi-1815
    John, Wi-1815
CREEL, John, Mu-1816
    William, D-1811
CREELE, Patrick, Su-1797
CREELEY, Patrick, Su-1796, Su-1797
CREELY, John, Mu-1811
CREEMER, Daniel, Ge-1812(2)
CREGAN, Patrick, Su-1797
CREGMILES, Joseph, Ge-1812
CREMER, Daniel, Ge-1805
CRENSHAW, David, Sn-1816
    Elizabeth, Wi-1815
    Freeman, D-1811
    Joel, Sn-1816
    John, Sn-1816
    Joseph, Wi-1810
    Nancey, Wi-1815
    Nathaniel, Sn-1823, Sn-1811
    Thomas, Gi-1812
CRESHER, Anthey, D-1788
CRESILIAS, John, Wa-1814
    John Jr., Wa-1814
CRESSE, Wm., Gi-1812
CRESSOR, Thomas, Wa-1819
CRESWELL, Henry, Je-1800
    Sampson, W-1812
CRETE, William, B-1812
CREUSE, William, Gr-1821
CREWILL, Samuel, Ro-1805
CREWLY, William, Sn-1816
CREWS, Frenney?, Sn-1816
    Pleasant, Gi-1812
    William, Sn-1823, Sn-1816
    Wrinny, Sn-1811
CRIAMER, William, Gi-1819
CRIBB, Cary, Wi-1810
    William, Wi-1810
CRIBBENS, Thomas, Sn-1792
CRIBS, Jacob, Wi-1815
CRICHLOW, Henry, Wi-1810
CRICK, John, Wi-1810
CRIDER, Jacob, Je-1822
CRIDDINGTON, Elizabeth, Su-1812
    Rodger, Su-1812
CRIDDLE, Edward, Wi-1815
    John, D-1811(2)
CRIDDLETON, Brel, Ro-1805
CRIDLEY, Thomas, Fr-1812
CRIG, Alexander, B-1812
CRIM, William, Wh-1811
CRISEL, John, Rb-1812
CRISMAN, Aaron, Wi-1815
    David, Wi-1815
    Gilbert, C-1818
    Isaac, A-1805
CRISMON, Abram, Wi-1815
CRISP, Mansil, Gi-1812
    Tilman, Mu-1816
    William, B-1812, Mu-1816
CRISSWELL, Samuel, Gi-1812
CRISWELL, Henry, Mu-1811
CRISTEPHER, Daniel, Wi-1815
CRITCHFIELD, Benum, Gr-1799

CRITCHFIELD, Richard, Gr-1799
    William, Gr-1799
CRITKLIAS, John, Wa-1814
CRITTENTON, Wm., Gi-1812
CROCKET, David, Wi-1815, Sn-1816
    George, Sn-1811, Sn-1816
    James, Wi-1815(2)
    John, Mt-1798
    Robt., Sn-1816
    Samuel, Mt-1798, Wi-1801
    William, Sn-1816
CROCKETT, Aaron, Su-1812
    Andrew, Su-1812, Su-1796, Wi-1815
    Elizabeth, Su-1812
    John, K-1812, Fr-1812, Gr-1804
    John H., Wi-1810, Wi-1801, Wi-1815
    Joseph, Wi-1801, Wi-1815, Su-1797, Su-1796
    Samuel, Wi-1815(3), Su-1797, Su-1796
    Silas, Su-1812
CROCKILL, William, Rb-1812
CROFFORD, Thomas, K-1799
CROFORD, John, Ro-1805
CROFT, Washington, Gi-1812
CROMWELL, Doyian, D-1805
CROOK, Bigance?, D-1811
    John, B-1812, Wh-1825, Wh-1811(2)
    John Sr., Wh-1825
    Yearby, Sn-1811
    Zerrell, Je-1822
CROOKSHANK, George, Wa-1819
    William, Wa-1819
CROOKSHANKS, George, Wa-1814
    Robert, Wa-1814
    William, Wa-1814
CROPPER, William, D-1811
CROSBY, George, Gr-1821, Ge-1812, Ge-1805
    William, Ge-1812, Ge-1805
CROSON, James, D-1805
CROSS, Abraham, Su-1812
    Abram, Su-1796, Su-1797
    Absalom, C-1823
    Acquilla, Su-1796
    Alquilla, Su-1797
    Aquilla, Su-1812
    Arch, B-1812
    Arter, Sn-1816
    Arther, Sn-1811
    Bejemun, Gi-1819
    Britain, Ge-1805
    Caswell, C-1823
    David, B-1812
    Elijah, Su-1812, Su-1796, Su-1797
    Elijah Sr., Su-1812
    Elizabeth, C-1818
    Gibson, B-1812
    Henry, Gi-1812, Ge-1805, Ge-1812
    Isaac L., Hu-1812
    Jacob, B-1812
    James, Wl-1804
    Joel, Su-1797, Su-1796
    John, Gr-1805, Su-1812
    Joseph, Su-1812
    Larkin, C-1823
    Maclin, Fr-1812
    Martin, D-1805
    Micajah, A-1805, C-1823
    Oliver, Mu-1811
    Pleasant, C-1823
    Richard, Mt-1798
    Samuel, Wl-1804, D-1811
    Shadrach, Ge-1805

CROSS, Shadrack, Gi-1812
    William, Su-1796, D-1805, B-1812, Su-1812, Su-1797
    William Sr., Su-1812
    Zachariah, Sn-1787
    Zachary, Su-1812
CROSSARY, Nicholas, D-1805
CROSSFORD, James, D-1805
CROSSLAND, Wm., W-1812
CROSSLIN, Thomas, B-1812
CROSSLOW, James, D-1811
CROSSON, Samuel, Ct-1796
CROSSWAY, Nicholas, D-1811
CROSSWELL, Drury, D-1805
CROSSWHITE, George, Ct-1796, Ct-1798
CROSTON, Henry, Mt-1798
CROTS, Felty, Sn-1811
CROUCH, Elijah, Wa-1819
    George, Wa-1819(2), Su-1812
    James, Wa-1819
    Jesse, Wa-1819, Wa-1814
    John, Wa-1819, Wa-1814
    Joseph, Wa-1819(3), Wa-1814(3)
    Joseph (of John), Wa-1819
    Michael, Wa-1819
    Peter, Ro-1805
    Susannah, Wi-1815
    William, Wa-1819(2)
CROUESTER, Adam, Gi-1812
CROUGHTON, Charles, J-1802
CROUSE, Marshall, Wa-1814
    Matthias, Gr-1821
CROW, Isaac, Wi-1801, Mu-1811, Wi-1810
    Joanna, Wi-1815
    John, Je-1822, Gr-1804
    Levi, B-1812
CROWBURGER, Jacob, Su-1812
    Michael, Su-1812
CROWDER, James, Wh-1825
    John, Wi-1815
    Molly, Sn-1811
    Richard, Wh-1825(2)
    Thomas, D-1811
    William, Su-1796
CROWLEY, Berry, A-1805
    Henry, Gr-1804
    Jacques, C-1818
    James, A-1805
    John, Gr-1799
    Michael, B-1812
    William, Gr-1799
CROWNOVER, Dorey, Wh-1811
    Joseph, Wh-1811, Wh-1825
    William, Wh-1825
CROWS, Henry, Gr-1805
    Matthias, Gr-1805
CROWSON, Abram, Gi-1812
    Isaac, Gi-1812
    Jacob, Gi-1812
    John, Gi-1812
    Moses, Gi-1812
    William, Ge-1783, Gi-1812
CROZIER, Arthur, A-1805
    John, K*-1815
CRUDDLE, John, D-1811
CRUDUPE, John, Wl-1804
CRUIM, John, Wh-1811
CRUISE, Adam, Bo-1805
    Samuel, Sn-1811
CRUM, Henry, Su-1796, Su-1797
    John, Ge-1812
    John, estate, Ge-1812

CRUM, William, Sn-1816
CRUMB, Jacob, Ge-1812
    William, Sn-1811
CRUMBLEY, William, Ge-1812, Ge-1805
CRUMBLY, Samuel, Ge-1812
    William Jr., Ge-1812
CRUMLEY, Daniel, Su-1796, Su-1797, Su-1812
    George, Su-1812, Su-1796(2), Su-1797
    Jacob, Su-1812
    Jesse, Su-1797
CRUMP, Edmund, Ge-1783
    Fendal, Wi-1815(2)
    George, B-1812
    Isaac, Ge-1805
CRUMPTON, Thomas, A-1805
CRUNK, John W., Wi-1815
    Richard, Rb-1812
CRUPPER, William, D-1811
CRUSBY, Samuel, Mu-1816
CRUSENBERRY, James, C-1823
    Joseph, C-1818
CRUSOE, Jack, Wa-1814
    John, Wa-1819
CRUSP, Adam, Sn-1811
CRUTCHER, Edmund, Wl-1804
    James, D-1811
    Larkin, Wi-1815
    Thomas, Wi-1801, D-1811, D-1805,
        Wh-1811(2)
CRUTCHFIELD, Charles, D-1811
    William, Wl-1804
CRUTCHLOE, James, D-1811
CRUTCHLOW, Henry, D-1850
CRY, John, B-1812
CRYDER, George, Sn-1816
CRYER, George, D-1805
    J., Sn-1816
    James, Sn-1816
CRYERS, James, Sn-1811
    Robert, Ro-1805
CUBLEY, William, Gi-1812
CUCKEY, Zacariah, Je-1800
CUDDY, James, Su-1797
CUDE, John, Je-1800, Gr-1805, Gr-1804
CUEW, William, A-1805
CUFF, Andrew, Wi-1810
CUFFMAN, Jaratt, Sn-1816
CUISSER, Martin Sr., Wh-1825
CULBAUGH, Jacob, Ct-1798
CULBERHOUSE, William, Gr-1805
CULBERT, George, Wi-1815
CULBERTH, Daniel, Mu-1816
CULBERTSON, Benjamin, Wi-1815
    James, Rb-1812
    Wm., Rb-1812
CULBURTH, Benjamin, Mu-1811
    Daniel, Mu-1811
CULHEN, James, Bo-1800
CULLEY, Joseph, Sn-1816
    Thomas, Sn-1811
CULP, Davis, W-1812
    Henry, B-1812
CULTON, James, Bo-1801
    Philip, Ge-1812
    Robert, Bo-1800, Bo-1801
CUMMING, Thomas, Wi-1810
CUMMINGS, David, Wh-1811, Wi-1815
    John, Wh-1811
    Joseph, Wh-1811
    Joseph Sr., Wh-1825
    Joseph Jr., Wh-1825
    Moses, A-1805

CUMMINGS, Thomas, A-1805
CUMMINS, Benjamin, W-1812
    David, D-1805, D-1811(2)
    Hugh, Wa-1814, Su-1797
    James, Wi-1815
    John, B-1812, Wa-1814
    Malci, W-1812
    Margaret, Sn-1816
    Moses, W-1812
    Saml., Wi-1815
    Thomas, B-1812
    William, W-1812
CUMNEY, John, Wh-1825
CUMPTON, John, Ct-1796
    Philip, Mt-1798
CUMP(TON?), Thos., D-1788
CUNAGEN, John, W-1812
CUNAY, Samuel, Wi-1801
CUNEGEN, John, W-1805
CUNINGHAM, Aaron, Mu-1816
    Allexander, Sn-1811
    David, Bo-1800
    Thomas, Gr-1804
CUNNINGHAM, Aaron, Mu-1811, Ct-1796
    Alexander, Sn-1816
    David, A-1805, C-1818, Bo-1801
    Enoch, D-1811(2)
    Humphrey, B-1812
    James, D-1788, J-1802, Gi-1812,
        Gr-1799, Je-1800, A-1805,
        Fr-1812, C-1818, Wa-1819
    John, W-1805, Wh-1825, Ro-1805,
        W-1812, Li-1812*, Bo-1801,
        Bo-1800, Ge-1783, B-1812,
        Ct-1798, Gr-1799
    John B., Wi-1815
    Jonathan, A-1805, C-1818
    Joshua, Gr-1799
    Josiah, D-1811
    Martha, Wa-1819
    Mary, Ct-1798, Ct-1796
    Mat., Gi-1812
    Matthew, Wi-1801
    Miles, Bo-1801, Bo-1800
    Thos., Hu-1812, Gr-1799
    William, Ct-1798, Ct-1796
    _____, W-1812
CUNNINGS, John, Bo-1805
CUNTER, Stephen W., Gr-1805
CUP, David, Bo-1801
    Jacob, Bo-1805, Bo-1801
    James, Bl-1815
    Mikel, Bl-1815
CUPPER, Andrew, Wh-1811
CURCELIOUS, Isaac, Ge-1812
CURINGTON, Lewis, Ge-1805
CURKHAM, William, Gr-1799
CURL, John T., Gr-1821
CURNUTT, James Sr., Je-1822
    James, Je-1822
    William, Gr-1821
CURNY, Adam, Gi-1819
CURREN, Robt., Wi-1801(2)
CURREY, Isaac, Je-1800
CURRIN, B. P., Wi-1815
    Jonathan, Wi-1815
CURRIS, Wm., Wi-1815
CURRITH, Boyd, Bl-1815
CURRY, B. Robert, D-1805
    George, Je-1822
    George Jr., Je-1822
    Isaac, Je-1822, D-1811, D-1805

CURRY, Isaiah, D-1811
    John, Wl-1804, Mu-1816
    Jonas, D-1805
    Robert B., Wi-1815, D-1811
    Thomas, Sn-1811
CURTAIN, John, Su-1797
    Lewis, Ge-1812
    Richard, Ge-1812
    Richard Sr., Ge-1812
CURTEN, John, Su-1796
CURTICE, Nathaniel, Ge-1783
CURTIN, John, Su-1812
CURTIS, Benjamin, Wi-1810, Wi-1801
    Bolen, Ct-1796
    Edmond, W-1812
    Elijah, A-1805, C-1818, C-1823
    Henry, B-1812
    James, W-1812
    James & William, D-1805
    John, W-1812
    Joshua, Hu-1812, D-1811, Wi-1810
    Nathaniel, D-1811
    Samuel, A-1805
    Silas, Fr-1812
    Thos., Hu-1812
    Thos Sr., Hu-1812
    Wm., Hu-1812
CURTON, Richard, Ge-1805
    Thomas, Ge-1812, Ge-1805
CURYR, James, Wl-1804
CUSACK, John B., Bo-1801
CUTBERTH, Benjamin Sr., Ct-1798, Ct-1796
    Benjamin Jr., Ct-1796
    Daniel, Ct-1798, Ct-1796
    Emanuel, B-1812
CUTCHIN, Joshua, Wi-1815
CUTLER, Jesse, D-1811
CUTTS, William, Su-1812
CYER, Sameul, Wh-1825
CYLER, Joseph, Ge-1783
CYPEART, Francis, J-1802
CYPERT, Baker, W-1812
    Francis, W-1812
    John, W-1812
    Thomas, Wl-1804
CYRUS, Nimrod, Gr-1805
DABENS, William, Wi-1810
DABNEY, Charles A., Wi-1815
    John, Wi-1815, D-1805, Wi-1810, Gi-1812
    William, Gi-1812
DABREY, John, Wl-1804
DAGLEY, Benjamin, C-1823
    Elias, C-1823(2)
    Elvis, C-1818
    Jonathan, C-1823
    John, Mu-1816(2)
    Joseph, C-1823, C-1818
DAGLY, John, Mu-1811
DAIL, Abel, Gr-1821
    Abner, Gr-1821
    James, Gr-1821
    Jonathan, Gr-1821
DAIMWIID, Henry, Gr-1821
DAIRNWOOD, Mu-1816
DALE, Abel, Gr-1805, Gr-1799, Gr-1804
    Alexander, Gr-1799, J-1802
    John, Wh-1811
DALLACE, Joshua, Je-1800
DALTENS, David, Mt-1798
DALTON, Carter, Gr-1821
    David, Gr-1821

DALTON, Ennis, Gr-1804
    Enos, Gr-1821, Gr-1805
    J., Wi-1815
    John, Sn-1811
    Meredith, Gr-1821
    Nancy, Gr-1821
    Nathan, Je-1822
    Reuben, Gr-1804
    Rubin, Gr-1805
    Talbot, Wh-1811
DALY, John, Wi-1815
DAMENT, Charles, Sn-1792
DAMERON, Joseph, Je-1800
DAMEWOOD, Robert, Rb-1812
DAMODE, George, Rb-1812
DAMOSH, Samuel T., B-1812
DAMRORY, James M., Bl-1815
DANAWAY, Elijah, Bo-1805
DANCE, Archibell, Hw-1799
DANEAR, Stephen, Ro-1805
DANELSON, Robert, Bo-1800
DANFORTH, Josiah, Bo-1800, Bo-1801
DANIEL, Banton, D-1811
    Basdel, D-1811
    David, Gi-1812
    Edward, Gr-1804, Gr-1805
    Edward Sr., Gr-1821
    Edward Jr., Gr-1821
    Frances, Gr-1804
    Francis, Gr-1805, Gr-1821, Gr-1799
    Garrett, Gr-1821
    James, Gr-1821, Gr-1799, Wh-1811
    Jerimiah, D-1811
    Jesse, Sn-1816
    John, Gr-1821(2), Gr-1799, W-1812, R-1819
    John Sr., Gr-1805, Gr-1804
    John Jr., Gr-1805, Gr-1804
    Joseph, Gr-1821
    Joseph Jr., Gr-1821
    Marmaduke, Wa-1819
    Peter, R-1819
    Richard, Wa-1814, Wa-1819, Su-1797
    Robert, Ge-1805
    Thomas, Sn-1816
    Washington, C-1823
    Wats, B-1812
    William, Mu-1816, Wh-1825, Mu-1811(2), Gr-1821, C-1818, Wh-1811
    Woodson, Ct-1796
DANKAN, John, B-1812
DANLEY, Hezekiah, Ge-1812
CANNELLY, Wiliam, W-1812
DANNIEL, Edward, Gr-1805
    Richard, Su-1796
DANSET, Edmond, D-1818
    Robert, C-1818
DANWELL, Christopher, Cl-1803
DARBEY, Philip, Gi-1812
    Richard, Gi-1812
DARDEN, William, Su-1797
    _____, B-1812
DARE, John, Je-1822
DAREBERY, Jacob, W-1812
DARIDGE?, Peter, D-1811
DARINS, Wm., Gi-1812
DARK, Micajah, Mu-1816
DARKE, Benjamin, D-1805
DARMON, Joseph, B-1812
DARNEL, David, Rb-1812
DARNOLD, John, Mu-1816

DARTING, Abraham, Su-1812
    John, Su-1812
DARWIN, William, Fr-1812
DASH, John, D-1805
    Jonathan, D-1788
DATEN, Benjamin, Wh-1825
    John, Wh-1825
DATUN, Frelty, Hw-1799
DAUBINS, John, Sn-1792
DAUESE, William, Bl-1815
DAUGHERTY, James, C-1823
    William, Wl-1804
DAUGHLY, Henry, D-1811
DAUHBIN, Samuel, Wi-1801
DAUSCH, Edmond, C-1823
DAUTHIT, James, Bl-1815
    John, Bl-1815
DAUTY, Henry, D-1811
DAVAS, Seth, Wi-1815
DAVE, Denton, Wa-1819
    John, Wa-1819
DAVENPORT, Mathew, Gi-1819
    Robert, Gi-1812
DAVEY, Richard, D-1811
DAVICE, Daniel, Hu-1812
DAVID, A. King, C-1823
    Amos, Gi-1819
    Azariah, R-1819, R-1808
    Azoriah, Ro-1805
    Benjamin, Ct-1798
    Blaik, D-1811
    David, Ro-1805
    George, Sn-1811
    J. King, C-1818
    J. Simpson, C-1818
    James, D-1811
    Jenkin, R-1808
    John, Wh-1812
    John H., D-1811
    Mart, C-1823
    Owen, R-1819, R-1808
    Richard, Su-1796
    Sampson, A-1805
    Simpson, C-1823, C-1818
    Thomas, Ro-1805
    William, D-1811, D-1805
DAVIDSON, Abraham, Hu-1812
    Andrew, Bo-1801
    Daniel, Sn-1811
    David, Gr-1821, Gr-1804
    E. Ephraim, Mu-1811
    Egnew, Ct-1798
    Eph., Mu-1816
    George, Wi-1801, Mu-1816, Mu-1811(2)
    Gilbreath, Mu-1816
    Goldry, Gr-1805
    Hudson, Hu-1812
    Jacob, Je-1822
    James, Ct-1798, A-1805, Bo-1801,
        Je-1800
    John, Ct-1798, Gr-1804, Gi-1819,
        D-1805
    Joseph, Mt-1798
    Lewis, B-1812
    O. John, Mu-1816
    Robert, Mu-1816, Mu-1811
    Samule, Gr-1799, Bo-1805
    Thos., B-1812
    Watlet, Ro-1805
    William, A-1805, Ct-1798, Gr-1804,
        B-1812, Bo-1801, Mu-1816,
        Ro-1805, Gr-1805, D-1805,

DAVIDSON, William, cont'd., D-1811
DAVIDSONS, Moses, K-1799
DAVIES, George B., Su-1797
    John, Su-1796(2), Su-1812
    Joseph, Hw-1799
    Miles, Su-1812
    Robert Jr., Sn-1811
    Robert Sr., Sn-1811
    William, Sn-1811
DAVIS, Aaron, Gr-1799
    Absalom, Wh-1825
    Absalom & Miles, D-1805
    Absolom, D-1811
    Acquilla, Gr-1804
    Ammon L., Wh-1825
    Amos, Wi-1810
    Andrew, D-1805, D-1811, Gr-1821
    Anthony, Cl-1803
    Archibald, Mu-1816, Wl-1804
    Augustin, Wh-1825
    Ben, Gi-1812
    Benjamin, D-1805, Sn-1816, Je-1822,
        Je-1800, Gr-1821, C-1823
    Benson, Se-1799
    Benton, C-1283
    Blackamore, D-1805
    Blackemore, D-1811
    Bozzle, Ro-1805
    Britton, Ro-1805
    Burgan, C-1818
    Chas., D-1805, Wa-1819
    Charles Sr., Wa-1814
    Charles Jr., Wa-1814
    Colly, D-1805
    Cornelius, Wh-1825
    Danl., Sr., Gi-1812
    Daniel & Elijah, D-1805
    David, Je-1800, Gr-1804, B-1812,
        Gr-1805, Ge-1805, Gr-1799
    Edward, Ro-1805, Gi-1812
    Eli, Je-1822
    Elias, Gr-1805, Gr-1804
    Elija, Bo-1800
    Elijah, D-1805, Bo-1801
    Elisha, Mt-1798, Wi-1815
    Elnathan, Gr-1799
    Enoch, D-1805, Gi-1812
    Ephraim, Wh-1825
    F. Isham, Wl-1804
    Frederick, Wi-1815, Wi-1801
    Furklow, C-1818
    George, Mu-1811(2), Ge-1812,
        Bo-1800, C-1818, C-1823
    Harkins, Ge-1805
    Heirs, Je-1822
    Henry, Mu-1811(2), Mu-1816(2)
        Wi-1801, Wl-1804, Ro-1805,
        B-1812, Fr-1812
    Henry Sr., Fr-1812
    Isaac, D-1811(2), Gr-1805, Ge-1812,
        Ge-1805, Gr-1821, Gr-1799,
        B-1812
    Isaac Jr., Ge-1812
    J. Fielding, Se-1799
    Jacob, R-1819
    James, D-1811(2), Wh-1825, Wi-1815,
        Wl-1804, Wh-1825, D-1811,
        Gr-1805, Mu-1816, Wi-1815,
        Wa-1814, Gr-1821(2), Ge-1805,
        Gr-1804, Wa-1819, C-1818(2),
        Bo-1800(2), C-1823, K-1799,
        Bo-1801(2), Je-1800, Gr-1799

DAVIS, James H., Ge-1812
    James P., W-1812
    Janes, Ge-1812
    Jessee, Wh-1825, Ge-1812, W-1812,
        B-1812
    John, Mt-1798, Wl-1804(4), D-1811(2)
        Mu-1811, Mu-1816, Wi-1815,
        Wi-1801, D-1805, Wi-1810(2),
        Sn-1811, Sn-1816, Mt-1798,
        Gi-1812, Ro-1805, Rb-1812.
        W-1812(4), Ge-1805(2),
        Wa-1819(2), Je-1800, Gr-1799,
        Gr-1804, A-1805, Ge-1783,
        Se-1799, Gr-1821, Je-1822,
        Su-1797, Su-1812, Gi-1812,
        Wa-1814, K-1799(3), Bl-1815,
        Fr-1812, B-1812(2)
    John Jr., Gr-1821
    Johnathan, Sn-1816
    Jonathan, Wi-1801, Ge-1805, Ge-1812
    Jonathan C., Wh-1825
    Joseph, Mu-1816, Ge-1812, Ge-1783,
        Ct-1798
    Joshua, Wh-1825
    L. John, Wl-1804
    Lewis, Ro-1805
    Magness, Gi-1812
    Majr., Esqr., Mu-1816
    Martin, Wi-1815
    Mathew, Wh-1825
    Micajah, Mu-1811
    Micasah, Wa-1819
    Michael, Gr-1805, K*-1815
    Michle, Gr-1805
    Morgan, Wi-1801
    Morgin, Wi-1810
    Moses, Wh-1811, Gr-1799, Cl-1803
    Nathan, D-1805, Ge-1812, Gi-1812,
        Ct-1796, Fr-1812, Gi-1819,
        Ct-1798
    Nathaniel, Ge-1812, Ge-1805,
        Wa-1814, A-1805, Wa-1819
    Newet, Wl-1804
    Nicholas, Je-1822, Ge-1783, Je-1800
    Nicholas Jr., Je-1822
    Pelham, C-1818
    Polly, Wa-1814
    Pruilla, Gr-1805
    Richard, Su-1797
    Robert, Wh-1825, Wi-1815, Wi-1810,
        Sn-1811, Wh-1825, Sn-1816(2),
        Wi-1801, Je-1800, Bo-1805,
        Gr-1821, Se-1799(2)
    Robert Jr., Sn-1816
    Samuel, Mu-1816, D-1805, Wh-1825,
        Mu-1811, Je-1822, Ge-1805,
        Gr-1821, R-1808, Bo-1800,
        Bo-1801, Gi-1819
    Samul, Sn-1816
    Sarah, Wi-1810
    Seth, D-1805, D-1811
    Sherod, B-1812
    Sterling, Wi-1815, D-1811
    Thomas, Mu-1816, Wl-1804, Ge-1805,
        Ge-1812, Wa-1814, Wa-1819,
        Bo-1805, B-1812, Bo-1801,
        Gr-1821, Co-1827, Ge-1783,
        Bo-1800, Se-1799, C-1823
    Thomas Jr., Ge-1812
    Thomas Sr., Ge-1805
    Turner, D-1811
    Vance, Wh-1825

DAVIS, William, C-1823, Ct-1796, Ct-1798,
        D-1811, Fr-1812, Ge-1805(2),
        Ge-1812, Gi-1812, Gr-1805(2)
        Gr-1799, Gr-1821, Je-1800,
        Ro-1805, Se-1799, Sn-1816,
        Mt-1798, Mu-1811(3),
        Mu-1816(2), W-1812, Wi-1801(2)
    Wm. R., G-1812
    William, Robert, Isaac & Thomas,
        D-1805
    Willis, Gi-1812
    Wilson, C-1823, C-1818
    Wyley, Fr-1812
    Young, D-1811
    Zach., B-1812
DAVISE, Jeusha, Se-1799
DAVISON, Agness, Su-1796
    Agnew, Su-1797
    Jesse, C-1823
    John, Su-1796, Mt-1798, Su-1812,
        Su-1797
    John Sr., Su-1797
    Samuel, Su-1797, Su-1796
    Thomas, Fr-1812
    William, Su-1796, Fr-1812, Su-1797
DAVISS, Augustus, Wh-1811
DAVISSON, William, W-1812(2)
DAVLIN, Patrick, Wi-1815, Wi-1810
DAVY, John, D-1811
    Joseph, Wi-1810, D-1811
    Joseph & John, D-1805
DAWLY, Thomas, Fr-1812
DAWNHAM, James, Fr-1812
DAWSET, Moses, Sn-1816
DAWSON, Abraham, Je-1822
    Ezekiel, Wi-1810
    Hudson, Gi-1812
    Jonathan, B-1812
    Joseph, Wi-1810
    William, Sn-1823, Wi-1810
    Willis, D-1811
DAY, Aron, D-1811
    Danl., B-1812
    David, Hw-1799
    Henry, Sn-1816
    Hugh, B-1812, R-1819
    Jesse, R-1819, Je-1800
    John, A-1805, Je-1822(2), R-1819,
        Je-1800
    Joseph, A-1805
    Levi, Je-1800
    Nathaniel, Je-1800
    Thomas, Je-1822
    _____, Rb-1812
DAYED, Chatham, Wi-1810
DAYLY, Carter, Gr-1821
DAYS, John C., B-1812
    William, Gr-1805
DEADERICK, David, Wa-1814, D-1811
    David Sr., Wa-1819
    David Jr., Wa-1819
    George M., D-1811, Wi-1801
    M. George, D-1805
    Thomas, D-1805, D-1811
    William H., Je-1822
DEADRICK, Gill, Mu-1811
DEAKE, Brittain, Wl-1804
DEAKIN, John, Wa-1819
DEAKINS, Daniel, Wa-1819
    Henry, Wa-1819
    James, Wa-1819, Wa-1814
    Richard, Wa-1819

DEAL, Henry, Sn-1811, B-1812
    Jeremiah, B-1812
    Jeremiah Jr., B-1812
    Larkin, B-1812
    William, J-1802
DEAMON, George, Su-1812
DEAN, Benjamin, Je-1800
    Charles, B-1812
    Colby, D-1805
    Francis, Je-1800
    Greenberry, B-1812, Wi-1810
    Jacob, Fr-1812(2)
    John, Fr-1812, Je-1800
    Joseph, Wi-1815
    Joshua, Fr-1812, W-1812
    Micheal, W-1812
    Richard, Co-1827, Co-1821
    Robert, K-1799, D-1805
    Thomas Jr., Ge-1812
    William, Je-1800
DEANS, Jesse, Ro-1805
    Penelope, Mu-1816
    William, Mu-1811
DEARING, Anselm I., Mc-1825
DEARMAN, George, Su-1796
DeARMAND, David, Bo-1800, Bo-1801
    Richd., Bo-1800, Bo-1801
    Samuel, Bo-1801, Bo-1800
DEARSTONE, Christian, Ge-1805
DEASEN, Solomon, Wh-1825
DEASIN, John, Mu-1816
DEASON, Abraham, B-1812
    Absalom, B-1812
    Enoch, B-1812
    John, Mt-1798
    Noah, Wh-1825
    William, B-1812
DEATHERAGE, John, D-1811
    Thomas, D-1811
    John & Thomas, D-1805
DEATHRIGE, Abner, Ge-1812
DEATHERIGE, Bird, Ge-1812(2)
DEAVEDSON, James, K-1799
DEAVER, William, Wi-1801
DEBERRY, Benjamin, Wi-1815
DEBORDE, William, Gr-1804
DEBUSK, Elias, Fr-1812
DECENS?, Thomas, B-1812
DECK, Jacob, Su-1812
    John, D-1805
DEDDRICK, Cassery, Mt-1798
DEDERICK, M. George, Wl-1804
DEDRICK, G. H. Michael, Mt-1798
DEEN, Daniel, Wl-1804
    Densey, Wi-1801
    Herod, Wi-1815
DEENE, Joseph, Wi-1810
DEENY, James, B-1812
DEES, James, Fr-1821
DEESON, William, Mu-1816
DEFRIESE, Hiram A., R-1819
DEGRAFFENREAD, Mary, Wi-1810
    Matcalf, Wi-1810
DEGRAFFENREED, Matcalf, Wi-1801
DEGRAFFENRIED, Mary, Wi-1815
    Heirs, Wi-1815
DELANEY, Benjamin, Ge-1812
    Jacob, Ge-1812
    James, Wa-1814, Wa-1819
    John, Ge-1805, Ge-1812(2)
    William, Su-1812, Wa-1819, Wa-1814
DELANY, Francis, Ge-1783

DELANY, Jas., Ge-1783
    Jno., Ge-1783
    William, Fr-1812, Su-1796
DeLAP, Robert, C-1818
DELASS, Robert, A-1805
    William, Sn-1816
DELEZRES, Jesse, Ro-1805
DELK, Gabriel, C-1823
    John, C-1823
DELOACH, Boykin, Fr-1812
    John, Su-1812(2), Fr-1812
    Ruffin, Sn-1792
    William, Rb-1812
DELL, Leonard, Ge-1805, Ge-1812
DELYARD, John B., D-1811
DEMENT, Charles, W-1812, Sn-1811
    David, Sn-1811
    John, Ge-1812
    Thos. M., Gi-1812
DEMET, Charles, J-1802
DEMOND, John, D-1811
DEMOSS, James, D-1811(2)
    James Jr., D-1811
    John, D-1805
    Lewis, D-1811(2)
    Lewis & Abraham, D-1805
    Thomas, Wi-1815, D-1811
    Wm., Wi-1815, Wi-1810
DEMPSEY, George, Sn-1816
    James, A-1805
    John B., B-1812(2)
DEMPSY, James, A-1805
DEMSEY, Allen, Wh-1825
    George, Sn-1811
    John, Wh-1825
DEMUMBRUN, Felix, D-1811
    Timothy, D-1811
    Timothy Jr., D-1811
DENHAM, Hardin, K-1796
    Joseph, A-1805, K-1799
DENING, John, Sn-1816
DENINGTON, Wilkins, Sn-1816
DENIS, L., Ge-1812
DENISON, John, Gr-1804
DENKINS, John, Sn-1811
DENNES, Henry, D-1811
    Samuel, D-1811
DENNEY, William, Wh-1825
DENNING, John, Sn-1811
    John W., Wh-1825
    Matthew, Bo-1801
    Sims, Wh-1825
DENNIS, Daniel, D-1811
    Edward, Gr-1821
    James, D-1811
    Joel, Co-1821
    John, D-1811
    John Sr., Gr-1821
    John Jr., Gr-1821
    Joseph, Gr-1805, Gr-1821, Gr-1804, W-1812, Gr-1799
    Joseph Jr., Gr-1821
    Jospeh, minor, Gr-1821
    Leir, Gr-1821
    Thomas, Gr-1804, Gr-1805, Gr-1799, Gr-1821
    William,G r-1821
    Zebedee, Ge-1805
DENNISON, John, Gr-1805, Je-1800
DENNISTON, John, Je-1822
DENNY, Charley, Co-1821
    James, Co-1821

DENNY, John, B-1812
    Pharroah, Co-1821
    Robert, Wh-1825
    Wallis, Sn-1816
    Wm., Sn-1792, Wh-1811
DENSON, John, Fr-1812(2)
    Joseph, Fr-1812(2)
    Robert, B-1812
    William, Gr-1799
DENT, John, Gr-1799, Gr-1804, Gr-1821
    Josiah, Ro-1805
DENTON, Abraham, Wh-1811(2), J-1802
    Benjamin, Wh-1811
    Edwin, Gi-1812
    Elijah, J-1802, Wh-1825, Wh-1811
    Isaac, Je-1822, J-1802
    Jacob, Je-1800, Je-1822(2)
    Jacob Jr., Je-1800
    Jacob Sr., Je-1800
    James, Su-1797, Wa-1819, Su-1796
    Jeremiah, Wh-1825, J-1802, Wh-1811(2)
    Jeremiah Sr., Wh-1825
    John, W-1812, Wl-1804, J-1802, Je-1800
    Joseph, Su-1797, Su-1796, Je-1800
    Josiah, Je-1822
    Martha, Wa-1819
    Ozias, Wh-1825
    Samuel, Wh-1825, J-1802(2), Wh-1811, Wa-1814(2)
    Samuel Jr., Wh-1811
    Thomas, Ge-1805, Bo-1805
    William, Je-1822
DENVER, Morgan, Wh-1825
DENWAY, Elijah, Fr-1812
DENWODY, Samuel, Ge-1805
DENWOODY, Samuel, Ge-1812
DEPEE, Micajah, Gr-1805
DEPEW, James, Wa-1819
    John, Wa-1819
DEPRES, James, Sn-1816
DEPRIDE?, George, Wh-1825
DEPRIEST, Horatio, Mu-1816
    John, Wi-1810, Wi-1815
    Samuel, D-1805
    William, B-1812
DEPT, Thomas, Sn-1815
DEREBERY, Daniel, Wi-1801
    Jacob, Wi-1801
DERHAM, Levi, Mc-1825
DERIFIELD, John, Wh-1825
DERING, Reuben, Bo-1800
DERREBERRY, Micheal, W-1812
DERREBY, Andr., W-1812
DERRICK, George, A-1805
    Jacob, A-1805
    Simon, A-1805
    Tobias, A-1805
DERRICK, William, Wa-1814, A-1805
    William E., Wa-1819
DERRUM, William, Sn-1816
DERRYBERRY, Jacob, Mu-1816
    Michael, W-1812
DERRYLUNEY, Michel, Gr-1799
DESART, Robert, Wi-1810
DESHA, Joseph, Sn-1792
    Robert, Sn-1797, Sn-1792
    Robt. Jr., Sn-1816
DESHAM, Aaron, Gr-1821
DESHAN, Aron, Gr-1805
DESMUKES, John, D-1811
    Paul, D-1811

DEULANEY, John Jr., Ge-1812
DEVARD, William, Gr-1804
DEVAUL, Abraham, Gr-1799
DEVAULT, Adam, Su-1812
    Frederick, Wa-1819, Wa-1814
    Gabriel, Su-1812
    Jacob, Gr-1804, Wa-1819
    John, D-1805, Gr-1821
    Michal, Su-1797
    Michael, Su-1812, Su-1796
    Valentine, Wa-1819, Wa-1814
DEVAZER, John Gi-1812
    John C., Gi-1812
DEVEES, Charles, Gr-1799
    James, Gr-1799
DEVEN, Jain, Ge-1819
DEVENPORT, Wm., Bo-1800
DEVER, Charles, Gr-1799
    Matthew, A-1805
    William, Wi-1801, Mu-1811
    Wilm, Gi-1819
DEVERY, Amos, Wi-1810
DEVINCE, John, W-1812
DEVOR, William, Mu-1816
DEVOUGH, Isaac, Su-1797
DEW, John, D-1805
    Robert, A-1805
    William, D-1811
DEWALT, Baily, B-1812
DEWARINE, John, Gi-1819
DEWEESE, William, Wh-1825
DEWEISE, Henry, Wh-1811
    James, Wh-1811
    Morgan, Wh-1811
    William, Wh-1811
DEWITT, Frederick, Ge-1812
DEWOODY, William, Ge-1805, Ge-1812
DEWSON, David, Hw-1801
DIAL, James, Wi-1815
    Jeremiah, Wl-1814
DIAN, Thomas, D-1805
DIBRELL, Anthony, Wh-1825
    Charles Sr., Wh-1825
DIBRILL, Joseph B., Wh-1825
DIBYELL, John, Bo-1800
DICASON, William, Sn-1816
DICK, Henry, Je-1800, Je-1822
    Jacob, Je-1822
DICKASON, James, Sn-1816
    Jas Jr., Sn-1816
    John, Sn-1816
    Oliver, Sn-1816
    William, D-1805
DICKENS, John, R-1819
    William P., Wi-1815
DICKERSON, Elisha, D-1811
    Francis, Je-1800
    James, Sn-1816
    John, Sn-1816
    Thomas, Sn-1816, D-1811
    Willis, Sn-1816
DICKES, William, Ge-1812
DICKESON, Nathaniel, Rb-1812
    William, Rb-1812
DICKEY, Benonai, Mu-1811
    Ephraim, Fr-1812
    Ephraim Jr., Fr-1812
    George, Fr-1812, Mu-1811, Mu-1816
    James, R-1819, Je-1822
    John, Mu-1816, Fr-1812
    M. Geo., Mu-1816
    Peter, D-1811
    Samuel, R-1819

DICKIE, John, Mu-1816
DICKIN, Thomas, Je-1800
DICKINGS, Samuel, Wl-1804
DICKINS, James, Gr-1804
    Townley, Ro-1805
DICKINSON, David, Wi-1810, Wi-1815
    Jack, D-1805
    Jacob, D-1811
    Jacob Sr., D-1811
    John, D-1811
DICKISON, John, Sn-1811
    Nathaniel, Sn-1811
    William, Sn-1811
DICKMAN, Elliott, Wi-1810
DICKSON, Benjamin, Sn-1811
    Edmond, Fr-1812
    Ephraim D., B-1812
    Hugh, Hu-1812
    James, Wi-1801, Mu-1816, D-1805,
        Mt-1798(2), B-1812
    John, Mu-1816, D-1805, Mt-1798,
        Bo-1801, Bo-1800, B-1812,
        Ge-1812
    Joseph, Mt-1798(2)
    Joseph, Dec'd., Sn-1791
    Matthew, B-1812
    Michael, Hu-1812
    Nathaniel, Mt-1798(2)
    Robert, Li-1812*
    Samuel, Bo-1800, Mu-1816, Bo-1801
    Thomas, Mu-1811, Bo-1801
    Wiliam, Mu-1816
    William, Mu-1811, Mt-1798(3),
        D-1811, Ge-1805, Ge-1812
DIE, Martin, B-1812
DIEL, James, J-1802
    John, J-1802
DILAND, Joel, Wi-1810
DILARD, Lisha, Se-1799
DILDINE, James, Wh-1825
    Jonathan, Wh-1825
DILEDINE, Jonathan, Wh-1811
DILL, Asa, Wl-1804
    Joab, D-1805
    Job, Mu-1816
    John Sr., Wl-1804
    John Jr., Wl-1804
    Roland, Wh-1825
    Thomas, Wl-1804
    William, Wl-1804
    _____, A-1805(2)
DILLAHUNTY, John, D-1811
    John Sr., D-1805
    Silas, D-1811, D-1805
    Thomas, D-1805
    William, D-1811
DILLARD, Ezacirick, Se-1799
    James, Ge-1783
    Joel, Wi-1815
    John, Se-1799
    John B., D-1811
    Martha, Wa-1819
    Owen, Wl-1804, Sn-1816
    Peter, Ge-1783
    William, Sn-1792
    Zach., Wl-1804
    Zachh., Sn-1792
DILLEN, Garrett, Ge-1805
    James, Co-1827
    John, Co-1827
DILLIARD, Joel, Wi-1801
DILLIN, John, Wi-1815

DILLINDER, Joseph, Wi-1810
DILLINGHAM, Merlem, K-1799
DILLINHAM, Peter, K-1799
DILLON, Carter, J-1802, Wh-1811
    Ganat, Ge-1812
    Isaac Sr., Sn-1816
    James, Wh-1825, Ge-1805, Ge-1812
    John, Wi-1815
    Peter, Ge-1812, Ge-1805
    Thomas, D-1805, J-1802
    William, Ge-1812, Ge-1805
DILZILL, John, Bo-1801
DIMENT, Thos. M., Sn-1816
DINNEL, Thomas, Je-1822
DINNING, David, Sn-1811, Sn-1816
    Jos., Sn-1816
    William, Sn-1811, Sn-1816
DINSMOORE, Samuel, Ge-1805
DINSMORE, James, R-1808
DINWIDDIE, James, Ge-1812, Ge-1805(2)
DIRGAN, John, Wh-1811
DIRKHAM, John, D-1805
DIRRUM, Henry, Sn-1811
DISLY, John, Bl-1815
DISMUKES, Daniel, D-1811
DISMUKS, David, D-1805
DISON, Josiah, B-1812
    Patrick, D-1805
DITTEMORE, Michael, Ge-1812
DITTIMORE, Michael, Ge-1805
DITTO, William, B-1812
DITTY, Abraham, Wh-1825
    John Sr., Wh-1825
    John Jr., Wh-1825
DIVEN, Alexr., Sn-1792
DIXEN, Reuben, Gr-1821
DIXON, Douglas, Mo-1825
    James, D-1811
    Jeremiah, Gr-1805
    John, Su-1797
    Joseph, Gi-1812(2), Sn-1787
    Leonard, W-1812
    Mathew, Wi-1815
    Reuben, Gr-1805
    Reubin, Gr-1804
    Thomas, Ge-1783
    William, D-1805, Sn-1811, Su-1812
DOAK, David, C-1823
    John Rev., Wa-1819
    John, C-1818, Se-1799
    Robert, C-1823, C-1818
    Thomas, C-1818, C-1823
DOAKE, John Rev., Wa-1814
    Samuel B., Wa-1814
COAKS, John, Wl-1804
    Robert, Wl-1804
DOAN, John, Go-1812, Wa-1810
    Thomas Sr., Ge-1812
DOBBIN, David, Mu-1816
DOBBINS, Alex., Sn-1816
    Alexr., Mu-1816, Sn-1811
    Andrew, Ge-1805
    Carson, Sn-1816, Sn-1811
    David, Mu-1816, Mu-1811
    Hugh, Wi-1815, Wi-1810
    James, Mu-1816(2), Mu-1811(2)
    John, Gi-1812, Sn-1811, Mu-1816
    Reuben, Je-1800
    Robart, Sn-1811
    Robert, Sn-1816
    William, Wi-1815
DOBBS, David, B-1812

DOBBS, Henry, B-1812
    James, B-1812
    Joseph, B-1812(2)
    William, B-1812
DOBINS, Andrew, Ge-1812
DOBKINS, Soloman, Cl-1803
DOBS, John, Fr-1812(Doles?)
    William, Sn-1816
DOBSON, Benja., Wl-1804
    Daniel, Ge-1812
    Henry, Wi-1810
    John, Ge-1805
    Joseph, Ge-1805
    Joseph Sr., Ge-1812
    Robert, Ge-1812, Ge-1805
    Samuel, Ge-1812
DOCOUIER, Thomas, Ro-1805
DODD, James, Je-1822
    Joab, A-1805
    John, Ge-1812(2), Ge-1805, Mt-1798
    Mark, B-1812
    Robert, D-1811
    Solomon, Fr-1812
    William, Ge-1805, Ge-1812(2),
        Je-1822
DODDY, Anson, B-1812
DODE, James, Mo-1825
DODSON, Allen, D-1811
    Charles, Sn-1816
    Daniel, Wh-1825
    Eli, Wh-1825
    Elijah, W-1812, W-1805, D-1811,
        Gi-1819
    Elisha, W-1812, Wi-18180, Wi-1801,
        W-1805
    George, Mu-1816
    Gibbons, Wh-1811
    Hightower, Wi-1815
    Hiram, Wh-1825
    Isaac, Wh-1825
    James, Gr-1799
    Jesse, W-1812, Wh-1811, Cl-1803
    Jessee, W-1812(2), Wh-1825, W-1805(2)
    Jessee Sr., Gr-1799
    Jessee Jr., Gr-1799
    John, Gr-1805
    John Sr., Wh-1811, Gr-1804, Wh-1825,
        Gr-1801
    John Jr., Wh-1811, Gr-1804, Wh-1825,
        Gr-1805
    Lazarous, Wi-1801
    Lazarus, Wi-1815, Wi-1810
    Nimrod, W-1812, Gr-1799
    Presley, Wi-1815
    Raleigh, Gi-1812
    Rawleigh, Wi-1815
    Rolley, Wi-1810
    Samuel, Gr-1799, Wh-1825, Gr-1805
    Samuel H., Wi-1810
    Solomon, Gr-1804, Gr-1805
    Thomas, J-1802, Wh-1811, Gr-1805
        Gr-1804(2)
    Thomas Sr., Gr-1799
    Timothy, D-1811
    William, Wh-1825(2), Mu-1816, Wi-1810
DOGATT, Miller, Gi-1812
DOGGETT, Jesse, Je-1822
    Miller, Je-1800
    Thomas, Je-1822(2)
DOGWOOD, Charltan, Ro-1805
DOHERTY, Andrew, A-1805
    Cornelius, J-1802

DOHERTY, Dennis, Rb-1812
    Francis, Gi-1812
    George, Ge-1783, Je-1800
    George Jr., Je-1822
    George Sr., Je-1822
    James, J-1802(2), Je-1800
    John, Gi-1812, J-1802, Bo-1801
    Joseph, B-1812, Je-1800, Ge-1783
    Joseph Jr., Je-1800
    Josiah, Je-1822
    Mary, Wi-1815
    Robert, J-1802, B-1812
    William, Je-1822, Ro-1805, B-1812,
        Je-1800, Ge-1783
    William Sr., Gr-1799
    _____, A-1805
DOLARHIDE, Cornelius, Fr-1812
DOLIN, Thomas, D-1805
    Timothy, Su-1812
DOLLARHIDE, Cornelius, Fr-1812
    Quillon, Sn-1792
DOLLINS, Tyree, Mu-1816
DOLLS, James, Wh-1825
DOLLSON, William, Mu-1816
DOLSON, Fortunatus, Mu-1816
    Jordon, Mu-1816
DOLTON, Bradley, A-1805
    John, Sn-1816
    Timothy, Su-1796
    Tolbert, Wh-1825
    William, Wh-1825, Sn-1811
DONAHO, Elija, Sn-1811
DONAL, Peter, Ro-1805
DONALD, Matthew, R-1819
    McNicols, Wl-1804
DONALDLY?, Moses, Wi-1815
DONALDSON, Andrew, J-1812, Je-1822,
        Je-1800
    Buckley, Wi-1815
    Moses, Rb-1812
    Robert, Bo-1801
    William, Ge-1812, Je-1800
DONALL, Thomas, Wl-1804
DONALSON, James, Gi-1812
    John, Je-1822
    L_____, Wi-1810
    William, Wi-1801
DONATHAN, Elijah, Gr-1804, Gr-1799
DONATHEN, James, Fr-1812
DONE, John, Wa-1814
DONELSON, Alexander, D-1805, D-1811(2)
    Andrew, Wl-1804(2)
    Ebenezar, Wl-1804(2)
    Ebenser, Se-1799
    Francis, Wi-1810
    Humphry, Se-1799
    James, D-1788
    John, D-1805, Mu-1816, Wi-1801(3),
        Wl-1804, Wi-1815
    John Sr., D-1811
    John Jr., D-1811
    Lemuel, D-1811
    Leven, D-1811, Wi-1815
    Lewis, D-1805
    Robert, Wi-1815
    Saml.?, K-1796
    Severn, D-1811(2)
    Sisern, D-1805
    Stockley, Gr-1799
    William, Wi-1810, Se-1799,
        Wl-1804(2), Wi-1801, D-1805,
        Wi-1815, D-1811

DONELY, Hezegiah, Wa-1814
DONESS, James, D-1805
DONICA, Thomas, Ge-1805
DONNAL, Dr. Thomas, Sn-1792
DONNALD, Thomas, Wi-1815, Sn-1811
    William, Sn-1792
DONNALDSON, Francis, Wi-1810
DONNALLY, William, W-1805
DONNALSON, Andrew, B-1812
DONNEL, George, Mt-1798, Wl-1804
    James, Wl-1804
    John, Wl-1804, Wi-1801
    Robert, Wl-1804
    Samuel, Wl-1804
    Samuel Jr., Wl-1804
    Thomas, Sn-1816, Sn-1817, Wl-1804
    William, Wl-1804(3), Se-1799
    William Jr., Se-1799
DONNELLY, James, D-1805, D-1811
    John, D-1805, D-1811
DONNELSON, Mary (widow), Gi-1819
    Robert, Mu-1811
DONNELY, Alexander, Se-1799
    Samuel, Se-1799
    William, Se-1799
DONNOLDSON, Barnet, Wi-1810
DONOHO, Archebald, Sn-1811
    Archibald, Sn-1816
    Charles, Sn-1811, Sn-1816
    Francis, Sn-1811
    Isaac, Sn-1816
    James, Sn-1811, Sn-1816(2)
    John, Sn-1816, Sn-1787
    Thomas, Wl-1804
    Wallis, Sn-1816
    William, Sn-1816, Wl-1804
DONAHOE, Charles, Bo-1801
DONAHOO, Benjn., Sn-1811
    Henry, Cl-1803
    Isaac, Sn-1811
DONOLD, John A., K-1799
DONOVEN, A. W., K*-1815
DONSON, William, Wi-1815
DOOGAN, Saml., B-1812
DOOLEY, James, Mu-1811(2), Mu-1816
    James Jr., Mu-1811
    Michael, Mu-1811, Wi-1815
    Thomas, Wl-1804
    William, Wi-1801, Mu-1811, Mu-1816
DOOLING, Wm., Gi-1812
DORAH, John, Gr-1805, Gr-1799
DORAN, William, Wl-1804
DORCH, Isaac, Mt-1798
DOREL, Levy, Sn-1816
DORHIRTY, Edmond, Wh-1825
DORMART, JEsse, B-1812
DORMERT, Benjamin, B-1812
DOROUGH, John, Gr-1804
DORRAS, Thomas, D-1811
DORREBURY, Daniel, Wi-1810
DORRELL, James, Wh-1811
DORRES, Levi, D-1811
DORRICE, William Sr., Sn-1811
DORRICKSON, Josiah, D-1811(2)
DORRIES, William Jr., Sn-1811
DORRIS, Elijah, Sn-1816
    Henry, Rb-1812(2)
    Isaac Jr., Rb-1812
    John, Sn-1816, Rb-1812(2)
    Robert, D-1811
    Samuel, Sn-1816(2), Sn-1811(2)
    Samuel Sr., Rb-1812

DORRIS, Shaven, D-1811
    William, Sn-1811, Sn-1816(3)
DORRISS, Wm., Rb-1812
DORSEL, Willis, Sn-1811
DORSET, Thomas, Sn-1811
DORSEY, Mathew, Mt-1798
DORTCH, Isaac, Rb-1812
DORTON, Alexandria, Wi-1810
    Andrew, Wi-1810
    James, Mu-1816, Wi-1810
    John, Wi-1801, Mu-1816
DORTY, Tyler, B-1812
DORWELL, William, Mu-1816
DOSE, John, Bl-1815
DOSON, John Eld., Sr., Wh-1815
DOSS, Azariah, Rb-1812
    Ayers, Mu-1811
    Greenberry, Fr-1812
    James, Rb-1812
DOSSETT, Robert, C-1823
    William H., Gi-1819
DOSSLEY, John, Gi-1819
DOTHERO, Michel, Bo-1801
DOTHRIDGE, George R., Wh-1825
DOTSON, Bradley, A-1805
    Caty, Sn-1816
    Chas., Ge-1783
    David, Sn-1816, Mu-1816
    Elisha, Wi-1801(2)
    Foster, Mu-1811
    Hightower, Mu-1816
    James, Fr-1812
    Joel, Gr-1821
    Jno., Ge-1783, Gr-1821, D-1811
    Jonas, Wh-1825
    Lazarus, Wi-1801
    Mary, Ge-1812
    Moses, Ge-1812
    Oliver, A-1805
    Reubin, Wi-1801
    Samuel, Gr-1821
    Samuel H., Gi-1819
    Thomas, Wi-1815
    William, Gr-1821, Wi-1815, Sn-1811
    Willis, Wi-1801
DOTY, Enoch, Ge-1805
    Ezeriah, Ge-1812
    Isaac, Ge-1805, B-1812
    Isriah, Ge-1805
    James, Mu-1816
DOUGAN, James, Fr-1812(3)
    John, Fr-1812(3)
    Robert, Fr-1812, Sn-1792
    Sharp, Fr-1812
    Thomas, Fr-1812(2)
DOUGLAS, Alexander, Je-1822
    John, Je-1822, Wa-1814
    Joseph, Gr-1805
    Thomas, Wa-1814
DOUGLASS, Alexander, D-1811
    Alfred, Sn-1816
    Benj.?, Sn-1816
    Danl., Gi-1812, Mu-1816
    Edward, Sn-1792(2), Sn-1811
    Ezekeal, Sn-1792
    Ezekiel, D-1805
    Ezekile, D-1811
    Henry, D-1811, D-1805
    Hugh, D-1811, Mu-1816
    James, Sn-1811, Sn-1816, Sn-1792
    John, D-1805(2), Sn-1816, Mu-1816,
        Sn-1811, Wi-1815, Wi-1812

DOUGLASS, Mathew, W-1812
    Matthew, C-1818, C-1823
    Nathl., Gi-1812
    Rhodeham, B-1812
    Rubin, Sn-1816
    Ruebin, Sn-1792
    Thomas, D-1811, Fr-1812, B-1812, C-1823
    William, D-1811, Sn-1811, Sn-1792, C-1823, C-1818, W-1812
    William H., Sn-1816
DOUGLESS, Edward, Sn-1787
    Howard, Sn-1811
    James, Sn-1816
    William & Thomas, D-1805
DOUNEN, William, B-1812
DOUTHIT, Absalem, Bl-1815
DOW, Andrew, D-1788
    Luther, D-1805
DOWD, John, Wi-1810
DOWDY, Alfred, B-1812
    Danl., B-1812
    Howel, B-1812(2)
    John, B-1812
    Joseph, Wi-1815
    Micajah, B-1812
    Thos., Wi-1810, B-1812
    Wm., Wi-1815
DOWEL, David, Sn-1816
    John, Sn-1816
    Page, K-1799(Vowel?)
    William, Sn-1816
DOWELL, Archibald, D-1811(2)
DOWLIN, John, D-1811
DOWLY, Mathew, Fr-1812
DOWNEN, James, Wi-1801
DOWNEY, Jonathan, Benj., Robt. & John, D-1805
    Robert G., Wh-1825
DOWNING, James, Fr-1812
    John, Sn-1811
    William, Sn-1811
    William H., Wi-1815
DOWNS, Ambros, Mt-1798
    Benjamin, Su-1797(2), Su-1796
    James P., D-1811
    Joshua, Mt-1798
    Major, Sn-1816, Sn-1811
    William, Mt-1798, Sn-1811, Sn-1816, Su-1796(2), Su-1797
DOWTHERD, Evan, Gr-1799
    Jeremiah, Sn-1816, Sn-1792
DOXEY, Jeremiah, Sn-1811
    John S., Sn-1816
DOYL, Joshua, Wi-1815
    John, Wh-1825
    Redem, Wh-1825
    Simson, Wh-1825
    Sunot?, Wh-1825
DRAIN, Benjamin, Wa-1814, Wa-1819
    John, Ge-1812
DRAKE, Abraham, Ct-1796, Ct-1798
    Benjamin, D-1811, Ct-1798, D-1811, Ct-1796
    Edwd., Mu-1816
    Elijah, W-1812
    Ephraim, Wa-1814, Fr-1812, Wa-1819
    Harbert, Mu-1816
    Henry, Gr-1821
    Isaac, D-1811(2), Ct-1798, W-1812, D-1805, Wi-1801
    Jacob, Su-1812, W-1812

DRAKE, James, Fr-1812, Gr-1804, Gr-1805
    Jesse, D-1811
    John, Wi-1801, W-1812, D-1805, Mt-1798, D-1811
    John Sr., D-1811
    John Jr., D-1811
    Jonathan, D-1811(2)
    Joshua, D-1811
    Peter, Su-1812
    Thomas, B-1812
    Widow, Su-1812
    William, D-1811(2)
    Zachariah, Wi-1810, B-1812
    Zacheriah, Wi-1815
DRAPER, John, A-1805
    Joshua, Sn-1816, Sn-1823, Sn-1811
    Thomas, Gr-1821
    William, Sn-1816
DRAUGHAN, Miles, Rb-1812
DRAUGHTON, John, Rb-1812
DREAPER, William, Sn-1811
DRESSER, Henry, Gr-1805
DREW, Benjamin, Wl-1804
    Edward, Wl-1804
    John, Bo-1801
DRICHES, Stephen, Wh-1825
DRINKARD, Daney, Ro-1805
    William, Wi-1815
DRINNER, David, Wh-1825
DRISKELL, Mahal, Je-1800
DRISKILL, Jesse, Rb-1812
    Obediah, B-1812
    Samuel, Wh-1825
DRUDGE, Enoch, D-1811
DRUE, Benjamin, Ge-1805
DRUMGOLD, James, Mt-1798
DRUMGOLE, James, D-1788
DRUMMON, David, Wh-1811
    Milton, Su-1812
DRURY, John, D-1811
    Smith, Wh-1811
    William, Su-1812
DRYDEN, David, Ge-1812, Su-1812, Su-1797, Su-1796
    Joel, Ge-1805, Ge-1812
    John, B-1812
    Jonathan, B-1812
    Nathanl., B-1812
D. BARRY, Redman, Wl-1804
DUBERRY, Wm., Mu-1816, Wi-1810
DUCAN, Peter, Hu-1812
    Roten, Ro-1805
DUCKERY, Matthew, B-1812
DUCKWORTH, John, A-1805, Mu-1811, Mu-1816
    Johnson, A-1805
DUDLEY, Francis B., Wi-1815
    Jn., K*-1815
    Joseph, Mu-1816
    Theodereck B., Wi-1815
DUDLY, Gains, Mu-1811
    Watson, Ge-1812
DUE, Jedi. C., Wh-1825
    John, Wh-1825
DUFF, Jonah, Bl-1815
    Thomas, Wh-1825, Wh-1811
    Wm., Sn-1811
DUFFEL, John, Wi-1810
    Wm., Wi-1815
    _____, D-1805
DUFFIELD, George, Ge-1812
    John, D-1811
DUFFILL, John, D-1788

DUGAN, Robert, Wi-1801
    William Rev., Wa-1819
DUGER, Alexander, Ge-1812
    Claburn, Ge-1812
    Daniel, Ge-1812
    Thomas, Sn-1811
DUGGARD, Julias, Ct-1798, Ct-1796
    William, Ct-1798, Ct-1796
DUGGER, Alexander, Mu-1816, Ge-1805
    Claiborne, Ge-1805
    David, Mu-1815, Ge-1805
    Edwd., Sn-1811
    Flood, Sn-1816
    Fred, Sn-1816
    James, Mu-1811, Sn-1811, Ge-1805,
        Gi-1812
    John, Sn-1811, Sn-1816
    Joseph, Mu-1811, Mu-1816, Ge-1805
    Lannord, Sn-1811
    Leonard, Sn-1816
    Luck, Sn-1811
    Luke, Sn-1816
    Shadrack, Mu-1816
DUGGIN, Edward, D-1805
    Robert, Wl-1804
DUGH, William, B-1812
DUGLAS, Thomas, Gi-1819
DUGLASS, Elmore, Sn-1787
    Ezekiel, Sn-1787
    George, Ct-1798
    James, Gi-1819
    John, Wa-1819
    John Jr., Wa-1819
    Joseph, Gr-1805
    Robert, Bo-1805
    Thomas, Ct-1798
DUKE, H., Ge-1812
    James, Sn-1811
    John, Gr-1805, Sn-1816, Gr-1804,
        Fr-1812
    Pleasant, Gr-1805, Gr-1799, Gr-1804
DUKERY, Matthew, B-1812
DUKES, George, Mu-1811
DUKEY, Alexr., Gi-1812
    John, Gi-1812
    Robert, Gi-1812
DUKSON, John, Mu-1811
DULANEY, David, Ge-1812
    Elkanah R., Su-1812
    W. L., Su-1812
DULANY, Elkena K., Su-1812
    William, Su-1797
DULEY, Abraham, Ge-1783
DULIN, Daniel, C-1818
DULL, Nicholas, D-1811
DULY, William, Sn-1811
DUMAS, Henry Jr., Wh-1825
    Henry Sr., Wh-1825
DUMBILLE, Robert, Gr-1805
DUMENT, Reubin, Mu-1816
DUMVELL, Robert, Gr-1799
DUMVILL, Richard, Gr-1804
    Robert, Gr-1804
DUMVILLE, Richard, Gr-1805
DUN, James, J-1802
    John, Wi-1801
    William, Wi-1801
DUNAGAN, Samuel, Wh-1825
DUNAGIN, Wm., Wi-1810
DUNBAR, Thomas, Mt-1798, D-1788
DUNBARR, Alex., Ro-1805
DUNCAN, Andrew, Wa-1814, Wa-1819

DUNCAN, Brice, Wa-1814
    Charles, Fr-1812, Wa-1814
    Charles, estate, Wa-1819
    Craven, Je-1800, Ge-1783
    Elias, A-1805
    Elijah, Hu-1812
    Francis, Wa-1819
    James, Hu-1812, Wa-1819, Wa-1814
    Jane, Je-1822
    Jere, Je-1800
    Jesse, Wa-1814, Wa-1819
    Joel, Wh-1811
    John, Wh-1811, Wh-1825, D-1811(2)
        Wa-1819, Ge-1783, Bo-1801,
        Bo-1800, Rb-1812, Je-1800
    Joseph Sr., Wa-1819, Wa-1814
    Joseph Jr., Wa-1814, Wa-1819
        (est. of Jane Allison & heirs
          of Robert Allison)
    Joshua, C-1823
    Josiah, B-1812
    Levi, W-1812
    Marshal, Wh-1825
    Martin, Rb-1812
    Martin J. P., Rb-1812
    Rice, Wa-1819
    Robert, Wa-1819
    Rolly, A-1805
    Russel, Wh-1825
    Samuel, Wa-1819
    Solomon, Wh-1825
    Tandy, Sn-1811
    Thomas, Wh-1825, Ct-1798
    Thomas L., Fr-1812(2)
    Washington P., Wh-1825
    Will, Mu-1816
    William, Wh-1825, Gr-1799, Wa-1819,
        Gr-1804, Fr-1812, W-1812(2),
        Rb-1812
    Zachariah, D-1805
DUNCOME, Benjamin, Gr-1821
DUNEHUE, Patrick, Hw-1799
DUNGAN, Jacob, B-1812(2)
    Jeremiah, Ct-1798
    Jonathan, B-1812
    Mary, Wa-1814, Wa-1819
    Wm., Wi-1815, Wa-1814, B-1812
DUNGWORTH, Charles, Wa-1814
    Thomas, Wa-1814
DUNGY, Berrel, Wh-1825
    Richard, Wh-1825
DUNHAM, Charles, Wa-1819
    Daniel, D-1811
    Henry, Ge-1783
    Isom, D-1805
    John, D-1811, Wi-1815, D-1788
    Jonathan, W-1805, W-1812
    Joseph, Ge-1783, B-1812
    Larance, Ct-1798
    Lawrance, Ct-1796
    Matheny, Gr-1805
    Peter, Gr-1799
    Samule, Ge-1812, Gr-1799
    Wm., Sn-1816
    _____, Ge-1812
DUNKUM, Philip, Gr-1821
DUNLAP, Adam, Bo-1800, Bo-1801, Bo-1805,
        Fr-1812
    George, Bo-1801
    James, Bo-1805, Bo-1801, Bo-1800
    John, Bo-1805, Bo-1801, Bo-1800
    Joseph, Ge-1812

DUNLAP, Robert, Ro-1805
    Samuel, Ct-1796, Ct-1798, Wi-1815,
        Gr-1804
DUNMION, John, D-1788
DUNN, Allen, D-1805
    Andrew, W-1812
    Azariah, Rb-1812
    Benjamin, D-1805, D-1811
    Daniel, Ge-1805
    Daniel Jr., Ge-1812
    Daniel Sr., Ge-1812
    David, Wi-1810
    Francis, C-1823
    John, Wh-1825
    John C., B-1812
    Joseph, Fr-1812, Ge-1783
    Levi, Rb-1812
    Lewis, D-1811
    Michael, D-1811
    Michael C., D-1811
    Michael & Mickey, D-1805
    Robert, Fr-1812
    Thomas, Gr-1799, Gr-1804, Gr-1805,
        Su-1796
    William, D-1811, Wh-1825, Ge-1783
DUNNAM (Durrum?), Wm., K-1799
DUNNIGAN, William, Wi-1810
DUNNING, James, Sn-1816
    Robert, Mt-1798
    William, Gr-1821
DUNNINGHAM, Edwd., Wh-1825
DUNNUM, James, Mu-1816
    Joseph, K-1799(Durrum?)
    Robert, Mu-1816
DUNSMORE, James, A-1805
    Samuel, Su-1797, Su-1796
DUNTON, Daniel, Su-1812
    James, Su-1812
DUNWAY, Joseph, Fr-1812
    Samuel, Fr-1812
    William, Fr-1812
DUNWOODY, James, Fr-1812
DUNWORTH, Charles, Wl-1804
DUNY, Richard & Nesly, D-1805
DUPREE, James, D-1805, D-1811
DURAL, Joseph, D-1811
DURAN, George, Sn-1811
    James, D-1811
    Morning, D-1811
    Thomas, Sn-1811
DURDON, Holland, Rb-1812
DUREN, Daniel, D-1811
DURHAM, Charles, Wa-1814
    Elijah, C-1823
    James, Sn-1811
    John, W-1812, B-1812, Sn-1811
    William, Gr-1799, Bo-1800, Bo-1801,
        Bo-1805, Sn-1811(2)
    Wm. Sr., Sn-1816
DURKIN, George, C-1823
    Henry, C-1823
    Isaac, C-1823
    Jessee, W-1805
    John, W-1805
    Peter, C-1823
    Reubin, C-1823
DURLEY, William, Sn-1816
DURNY, James, Mu-1816
DUROSSETT, Elijah, Wh-1811
DURRAN, William, Bl-1815
DURRATT, Joseph, D-1805
DUSON, Joseph, Gi-1819

DUTTON, Timothy, Su-1797
DUTY, Eliza, Sn-1816
    George, Sn-1816
    John, Sn-1811
    Richard, Sn-1811
    Solom, Sn-1823
    Solomon, Sn-1811
    Thomas, Wi-1815
    William, Sn-1811, Sn-1816, Sn-1812
    William Rev., Wa-1814
DWIGGENS, Daniel, B-1812
DWIGGINS, John, A-1805
DWIRE, Daniel, Ro-1805
DYAL, James, Wi-1810
    Joseph, Wi-1810
DYAR, Abner, Gr-1804
    Abram, Ge-1812
    Josiah, Gr-1804
    Manoah, Gr-1804
    Peter, K-1796
DYCHE, Christian, Ge-1812
    Christian Jr., Ge-1812
    Henry Sr., Ge-1812
    Manuel, Gr-1812
    Michael, Ge-1812
DYER, Abner, Gr-1805
    Baldy, D-1805, Wh-1811
    Charlton, Gr-1805, Gr-1821
    David, Su-1797, Su-1796
    Edward, Wa-1819
    Elisha, Gr-1805
    Elizabeth, Gr-1821
    George, Mu-1816, Mu-1811, Gr-1821
    Isaac, Gr-1821(2)
    Jacob, Ge-1812
    James, Gr-1799, Gr-1804, Gr-1821
    James, minor, Gr-1821
    James Sr., Gr-1821
    James Jr., Gr-1821, Gr-1805
    Joel, Gr-1805, D-1805, Gr-1821
    John, Wi-1815(2), Wi-1825, Ct-1798,
        Ct-1796
    Joseph, Gr-1805, Gr-1804, Gr-1821
        Gr-1821(2)
    Josiah, Gr-1805
    Manoah, Gr-1805
    R. Thomas, D-1805
    Robert, heirs, Gr-1821
    Samuel, Wh-1811
    Spilsby, R-1819
    Thomas, Gr-1805, Gr-1821
    William, Gr-1805, Wh-1825, Gr-1821,
        Gr-1804, Je-1800, Wh-1811
    William (Redhead), Gr-1821
    William Sr., Gr-1821, Gr-1805
    William Jr., Gr-1821(2)
    Williams, Gr-1805
DYERS, Joshua, D-1811
DYFFELL, John, D-1805
DYKE, Christian, Ge-1805
    Henry, Ge-1812
    Henry Sr., Ge-1805
    Henry Jr., Ge-1805
    Jacob, Ge-1812
    Marten, W-1812
DYRE, Thomas, Gr-1804
DYSARD, Robert, Wi-1815
DYSART, James, Mu-1816
DYSER, James, Wi-1801
    Robert, Wi-1801
DYSERT, John, Wi-1801
DYZARK, Robert, B-1812

DYZARK, William, B-1812
DYZEAK?, Francis, B-1812
　　　John, B-1812
EADEN, William, D-1811
EAGIN, Barnabas, Wl-1804
　　　James, Wl-1804
EAGINS, Edward, Ge-1783
EAGLETON, David, Ge-1783
EAKELS, Joel, Sn-1792
EAKER, Philip, Ge-1805
EAKIN, David, D-1811
　　　Moses, D-1811, D-1805
EALAM, Edward, Wi-1810
EALIM, Jonathan, B-1812
EALL, David, Rb-1812
EALY, Jacob, Je-1822
EALY's heris, Je-1822
EANES, Davis, W-1812
EANS, Daniel, Fr-1812
EAREY, Houston, D-1805
EARHART, Henry, Bo-1800
　　　Micnolas, Bo-1800
EARHEART, David, D-1811
　　　　Elijah, D-1811
　　　　Jacob, D-1811(2)
　　　　Moses, D-1811
　　　　Philip, D-1811
EARL, James, Rb-1812
EARLES, Harris, Wh-1825
　　　Martin, Wh-1825
　　　Nathan, Wh-1825
　　　Pleasant, Wh-1825
EARLEY, GEorge, Wh-1825
　　　James, Sn-1811
EARLS, Frederick, Je-1800
EARLY, Benjamin, Fr-1812
　　　Levy, Gr-1810
　　　Samuel, Wa-1819
　　　Thomas, Wa-1819
EARNEST, Felix, Ge-1812, Ge-1805
　　　Geo., Gi-1812
　　　George & Andy, Su-1812
　　　Henry, Ge-1805
　　　Jacob, Ge-1812(2), Ge-1805
　　　Lawrence, Ge-1805, Ge-1812
　　　Peter, Ge-1805, Gi-1812, Ge-1812
EARTHMAN, Isaac, D-1811
　　　Jesse, D-1805
　　　Lewis, D-1811, D-1805
EARWOOD, Will., Gi-1812
EASELY, Peleg, Sn-1816
EASFREY, _____, D-1788
EASLES, William, Wh-1825
EASLEY, Benjamin, Su-1812
　　　Daniel, Gr-1821, Su-1812
　　　John, Su-1812
　　　Joseph, Sn-1811, Su-1796
　　　Miller, Gr-1805
　　　Miller W., Gr-1821
　　　Peter, Su-1796, Su-1797, Su-1812
　　　Robert, Su-1812, Su-1796, Su-1797
　　　Stephen, Su-1796, Su-1812, Su-1797
　　　Stephen Sr., Su-1812
　　　Warham, Gr-1821
EASLY, John, Fr-1812
　　　War, Fr-1812
EASOLS, Joel, Sn-1811
EASON, John G., Wa-1819, Wa-1814
　　　Reddick, Wl-1804
EAST, Edward A., D-1811
　　　John, Mu-1811
　　　John W., B-1812

EAST, Joseph, Mu-1816
　　　Tarlton, D-1811
　　　Thomas, D-1811
EASTER, John, D-1788
EASTERLIN, Thomas, Su-1797, Su-1796
EASTERLY, John, Gr-1821, Ge-1812
　　　Philip, Ge-1805
EASTES, Laban, D-1811
EASTHAM, George W., Wh-1825
　　　William, Mu-1816
EASTIS, Andrew, Fr-1812
　　　John, Fr-1812
EASTISS, Reuday, Gi-1812
　　　Will., Gi-1812
EASTLAND, N. W., Wh-1825
　　　Thomas, Wh-1285
EASTON, James, heirs, R-1819
　　　William, D-1811, D-1805
EATHERLY, Harison, D-1805
　　　John, D-1805
　　　Jonas, D-1805
EATHIN, William, D-1805
EATON, Andrew, Gr-1804
　　　Clement, Je-1822
　　　D. Robert, Gr-1804
　　　James, Gr-1805
　　　John, Wi-1810
　　　John H., Wi-1815
　　　Joseph, Je-1822, Gr-1804, Ge-1783,
　　　　Gr-1799, Gr-1805
　　　Dr. Robert, Gr-1805
　　　Robert D., Gr-1821
　　　William, Gr-1821(2)
　　　Wm. B., Wi-1815
EAULT, James, Wi-1815
EAVES, Jonathan, Fr-1812
　　　Solomon, Wh-1811
EAVIS, Andrew Jr., Bo-1800
EBLEN, James, Ro-1805
　　　John, Ro-1805
　　　William, Ro-1805
ECHALE, John, Wi-1810
ECKEL, Flemon, Je-1822
　　　Peaer, Je-1822
ECHOLS, Elkanah, Wl-1804
　　　John, Wl-1804, Wi-1815
　　　Moses, Wl-1804
ECSTER, James, Hw-1799
EDDE, James, B-1812
　　　John, W-1812
EDDLEMAN, Leonard, Ge-1812
　　　Michael, Ge-1812
EDDY, Lloyd, Gr-1804
EDEN, Alexander, Bl-1815
　　　Archibald, Bl-1815
　　　Austin, Ct-1798
　　　James, Ct 1706, Bl 1815
　　　James Jr., Ct-1798
　　　James Sr., Ct-1798
　　　William, Bl-1815
EDGAR, Alexander, Je-1800, Je-1822
　　　Anderson, Je-1822
　　　Andrew B., Je-1822
　　　George, Je-1800
　　　John H., Je-1822
　　　Samuel, D-1811
　　　William, Mu-1811
EDGE, Henry, W-1805, W-1812
　　　Moses, Rb-1812
EDGEMAN, Braxton, Su-1812
　　　George, Su-1797
　　　Samuel, Su-1812, Su-1797

EDGEMAN, William, Su-1812
EDGEN, Daniel, Su-1796
EDGER, James, Mu-1816
EDGES, William, Mu-1816
EDGINGS, William, Fr-1812
EDGMAN, Samuel, Su-1796
    William, Su-1796
EDGOR, John, Wi-1810
EDINGTON, David, Gr-1805
    James, Gr-1805
    John, Bo-1801
    Thomas, Gr-1805
EDISTON, William, Ge-1812
EDLEMAN, David, Mu-1816
    John, Mu-1816
EDLINGTON, James, K*-1815
EDMINSTON, Will Esq., Mu-1816
    Will Jr., Mu-1816
EDMISTON, David, Wi-1815, Ge-1812
    David, heirs, Wi-1810
    John, Wi-1815
    Saml., Wi-1810, Wi-1815
    U. James, Mu-1811
    William, Ge-1812(2)
EDMON, Meshack, Gi-1812
EDMOND, John, Je-1800
    Robert, Mu-1811
EDMONDS, Anthony, A-1805
    George, Je-1822
    John, Bo-1800, W-1812
EDMONDSON, Andrew, D-1805, D-1811
    James, Bo-1801, Mu-1816
    John, Bo-1800, Bo-1801, Wi-1815,
        Wi-1801(2)
    John Sr., D-1811, D-1805
    Moses, Wi-1810
    Robert, D-1811(2)
    Samule, Ge-1805
    Solomon, Ge-1805
    Thomas, Wi-1801
    Will, Mu-1816
    William, Wi-1810
    Wm., Wi-1815
EDMONS, James, Bo-1800
EDMONSON, David, Wi-1801
    John Jr., Wi-1810
    John Sr., Wi-1810
EDMONSTON, Archibald, Mt-1798
    John, Mt-1798
    John & James, Mt-1798
    Robert, Mt-1798
EDMUND, Robt., Mu-1816
EDMUNDS, Jno., Ge-1783
EDMUNDSON, John, Mu-1811
    William, Mu-1811
EDNEY, Alson, Wi-1815, Wi-1816
    Given, D-1811
    Newton, Wi-1815
EDWARD, Adam, Wa-1814
    Arthur, Wa-1814
    Hudson, Sn-1811
    John, W-1812, Wa-1814
    Joshua, Je-1800
    Peter, Wi-1801
    Stephen, Mu-1811
    Thomas, Wa-1814
EDWARDS, Abel, Wa-1819, Su-1797, Su-1796
    Adonijah, Mu-1811
    Alec, Wa-1819
    Andrew, B-1812
    Andrew S., B-1812
    Arthur, Wa-1819

EDWARDS, Charles, Rb-1812, Sn-1816,
        Bo-1800, Mu-1811, Sn-1811
    David, Gi-1812
    Edmund, Rb-1812
    Edward, Rb-1812
    Eli, Wa-1814(2)
    F. Mack, Mu-1811
    Fredrick, Sn-1792
    Graveat, Rb-1812
    Gray, Gi-1812
    Henry, Gr-1799, Je-1800
    Jacob, Wi-1801
    James, Wl-1804, W-1812, Rb-1812
    John, Hu-1812, Sn-1816, Bo-1801,
        Wl-1804, C-1818, Su-1797,
        Rb-1812, Su-1796, Gr-1799,
        Je-1800, Wa-1819
    Joseph, D-1805
    Joshua, Su-1812
    Laben, Je-1800
    Mark, Bo-1800, Bo-1801, Wl-1804
    Mary, Gr-1821
    Nathan, Sn-1811, Sn-1816
    Oliver, Rb-1812
    Owen, Su-1812
    Peter, Wi-1801
    Richardson, Mu-1811
    Robt., Wl-1804
    Sampson, D-1811
    Solomon, Ct-1796
    Thomas, Sn-1811, Mt-1798, Mu-1811(2),
        Sn-1792, Wa-1819
    Walter, C-1818, R-1819, R-1808
    William, Wl-1804, Sn-1816(2),
        Sn-1811(4), Gi-1819, Sn-1792,
        Rb-1812(3)
    Wilson, Mo-1825
EDWARDSON, Robert, D-1805
    Thomas, D-1805
EDWELL, John, Rb-1812
EDWIN, William, Wa-1814
EGAN, John & William, D-1805
EGANS, Seward, Bo-1800
EGGNEW, Thomas, Sn-1787
EGNEW, George, Mu-1811
    Jesse, Mu-1816
    Thomas, Sn-1792
    Thomas, heirs, Sn-1811
EGNIES, John, Rb-1812
EGRIM, John, Su-1796
EHTES, Robert, Gr-1799
EILLINGS, Abraham, Sn-1792
EIMMET, Jacob, Mo-1825
EISLEY, Christian, C-1823
    John, C-1823, C-1818
ELAIR?, Samuel, D-1811
ELAM, Edward, Wi-1815
    William, B-1812
ELARD, William, B-1812
ELBRIDGE, Nathan, Ro-1805
ELDER, Andrew, Gr-1821
    John, K-1796, Mc-1825
    William, K-1796, Je-1822
ELDERS, James, Wl-1804
ELDRIDGE, Jesse, Ro-1805
    Machariah, J-1802
    Obed., Ge-1812
    Samuel, J-1802
    Suicon, Ro-1805
    Thomas, Ro-1805, Ge-1783
    William, Su-1796
ELERSON, John, Mu-1811

ELERSON, Richard, Mu-1811
    Thomas, Mu-1811
    Theophilus, Mu-1811
ELIGES, Joseph, Wl-1804
ELIM, Jyen?, B-1812
    William, B-1812
ELIOT, Barthalomew, Mo-1825
    P. John, Mu-1811
    Thomas, Fr-1812
    William, Ro-1805
ELIOTT, John, Mu-1811
    Simon, heirs, Mu-1811
ELIS, Elijah, Wa-1814
ELKIN, Gabriel, W-1812
ELKINS, Abraham, Ct-1796
    David, Gr-1821
    James, Gr-1804, Gr-1805
    Joseph, Gr-1821
    Larkin, Su-1812
    Nathan, W-1812
    William, Je-1822, Gr-1821
    _____, Gr-1805
ELLACE, Robert, Sn-1816, Sn-1811
ELLASON, James, Wi-1801
ELLEDGE, Joseph, Esq., W-1812
ELLEGE, Joseph, W-1812
    Whitefield, W-1812
ELLEGGMAN, Thomas, D-1805
ELLEM, Stephen, heirs, Wi-1815
ELLENTON, Stephan, Sn-1816
ELLER, John, Co-1821
ELLERGE, Edmun, Se-1799
ELLET, Andrew, Wi-1810
    James, C-1823
ELLICE, Lewis, Je-1800
ELLIFF, John, Gi-1812
ELLIDGE, Joseph, Je-1822
ELLIGE, John, W-1812
ELLINGTON, James, Co-1827
ELLIOT, Abraham, Gr-1804
    Archibald, Wh-1825
    Benjamin, Gr-1799
    Jacob, Gr-1804
    John, Wa-1819
    Patrick, Wa-1819
    William, Gr-1804
ELLIOTT, Abraham, Gr-1805
    Amos, A-1805
    Andrew, Gi-1812
    Barnett, D-1805
    Barney, Wi-1810
    Benjamin, Gr-1804, Rb-1812, Gr-1805
    Elizabeth, Sn-1811
    Enock, Mu-1816
    Faulkner, Mt-1798
    George, Wa-1819, Sn-1816
    Hugh, Sn-1811, Mu-1816
    Isaac, Sn-1816
    Jacob, Gr-1805, Gr-1799
    James, Sn-1816(2), Wi-1815, Wi-1810,
        Sn-1811, Mt-1798, C-1823,
        Rb-1812
    James Sr., Wi-1815
    John, Wi-1810, Wi-1815, Mu-1816,
        Wa-1814, Gi-1812
    Lewis, Mt-1798
    Matthew, Gr-1805
    P. John, Mu-1816
    Patrick, Wa-1814
    Piggy, Sn-1811
    Robert, Wi-1810, Wi-1815, Je-1822,
        C-1818, C-1823

ELLIOTT, Samuel, Wl-1804
    Simon, B-1812
    Stephen, W-1812
    Thomas, Ct-1798
    William, B-1812, Je-1800, W-1805,
        W-1812
ELLIS, Abraham, D-1811
    Edmond, W-1812, W-1805
    Elijah, Wa-1819
    Ellis, dec., Ge-1812
    Enos, Ge-1812
    Ezekiel, Wa-1814, Wa-1819
    George, Hu-1812
    Humphrey, Su-1812
    Isaac, Sn-1811, Sn-1816
    Jacob, Wa-1814, Wa-1819, Sn-1811
    James, C-1823, Wi-1815, Gi-1819
        Wa-1819, Je-18000, Wa-1814,
        Wi-1810
    Jehu, Je-1800
    Jeremiah, D-1805
    John, Je-1800, B-1812, C-1823
        B-1812, Wa-1814, Ge-1805,
        Wa-1819
    Jonathan, W-1812, W-1805
    Joseph K., Wi-1810
    Nehamiah, Je-1800
    Richard, Ge-1812
    Robart, Sn-1811
    Robert, Sn-1816, Gr-1804
    Samuel, Ge-1805, Ge-1812, Sn-1816
        Shobal, Ge-1805
    Simons, Rb-1812
    Stennel, Sn-1816
    Snalen, Sn-1811
    Thomas, Ge-1805
    Thomas, dec., Ge-1812
    William, Je-1800, Gr-1821, Ct-1798,
        Ge-1812, Ge-1805, Gi-1812,
        D-1811(2), Wi-1810
    William Sr., Rb-1812
    William Jr., Rb-1812
ELLISON, Andrew, Gi-1812
    Henry, Sn-1811
    John, Wa-1814
    Jonathan, Hu-1812
    Joseph T., Wi-1815
    Robert, B-1812
    William, Je-1822
ELLISTON, Joseph T., D-1811
    T. Joseph, D-1805
ELLOR, Jacob, Su-1797, Su-1796
ELLUM, Robert, Wi-1815
ELMORE, Charles, Wl-1804
    Christopher, D-1811(2)
    David, Je-1822, Je-1800
    Elijah, Wh-1825
    George, D-1811, Wh-1825
    Henry, Rb-1812
    Joel, Je-1800
    Julius, Rb-1812
    Mordecai, Je-1822
    Thomas, Je-1822, Wh-1825
    William, Je-1822, Su-1796
ELNEY, Newton, D-1811
ELROD, James, Wh-1811(2)
ELSEY, Isaac, Wa-1819
    John, Wa-1819, Wa-1814, Gr-1804
    Thomas, Wa-1814, Wa-1819
    William, Fr-1812
ELSON, Samuel, Mu-1811
ELSWICK, Andrew, C-1823

ELSWICK, Frederick, C-1823
  Jonathan, C-1818, C-1823
  Stephen, C-1818, C-1823
ELY, George, Ge-1805, Ge-1812
  Nicholas, Ge-1812
ELZA, John, Su-1796
EMBERSON, George, Fr-1812
  John, Su-1796, Fr-1812
  Walter, Su-1796
EMBOY, Reubin, Fr-1812
EMBRY, Britain, Fr-1812
  James, Fr-1812
  Jesse, Fr-1812
EMBUSON, James, Fr-1812
EMERSON, H. James, Mu-1816
  James, D-1811
  John, Mu-1816
  William, Mu-1816
EMERTON, Thomas, D-1811
EMERY, Isaac, C-1823
EMETTON, William, D-1811
EMMERSON, John, Mu-1811
  Tho., K*-1815
  William, Mu-1811
EMMERT, George, Su-1797, Su-1796,
   Ct-1796, Ct-1798
  Jacob, Su-1797, Su-1796
EMPSON, William, Rb-1812
EMRY, Bohr, Fr-1812
ENCHOR, William L., Wa-1814
ENDMON, John, Gi-1812
ENGLAND, Aaron, Wh-1811, Wh-1825
  Corban, K-1799
  Elijah, Wh-1811, Wh-1825
  HOger, Wh-1825
  Jacob, Rb-1812
  James, Rb-1812
  Jesse, Wh-1811
  Jessee, Wh-1825
  John, Wh-1825, Su-1797, W-1812,
   Su-1796, Wh-1811, K-1799(2),
   A-1805, Bo-1800
  Joseph, Wh-1825, Wi-1805, Ro-1805,
   W-1812, K-1799
  Joseph G., W-1805, W-1812
  Matthias, Wh-1825
ENGLE, George, Ct-1798, Ct-1796
  Peter, Ct-1798
  William, Ct-1798, Wa-1814
ENGLEMAN, Joseph, D-1811
ENGLES, William, estate, Wa-1819
ENGLISH, Alexander, Ge-1812
  Andrew, Ge-1812, Ge-1805
  Andrew Jr., Ge-1812
  Edward, Mu-1816
  Henry, Ct-1798, Ct-1796
  James, Su-1812, Wl-1804, C-1818
  James Sr., W-1812
  James Jr., W-1812
  John, W-1812, Wa-1814, Wa-1819
  Joseph, Ge-1783
  Joshua, A-1805, C-1818
  Richard, A-1805
  Robert, Ct-1796, Ct-1798
  Samuel, Wh-1811
  Thomas, Mu-1816, Wa-1814
  William, Su-1812, Ge-1783
  Wilson, Gr-1804, Gr-1805
ENNIS, John R., Rb-1812
ENOCH, Gabriel, Isaac, Enoch & John,
   D-1805
  Nevill, K-1796

ENOCHS, Robert, Wl-1804
ENOCK, Robert H., B-1812
  Sarah, Ge-1812
  William, Ge-1812
ENSLEY, Enoch, D-1811
EOFF, Joseph, B-1812
  William, B-1812
EOFFE, Isaac, B-1812
EPERSON, Benja., Gi-1812
  Joseph, Sn-1811
EPPERSON, Anderson, D-1811
  Anthony Sr., Wa-1814
  Anthony Jr., Wa-1814
  Benjamin, Wa-1814
  Joseph, Ge-1783
  Samuel, Wa-1814
  Thomas, Wa-1814
EPPISON, Anderson, Wi-1815
EPPLER, John, Gi-1812
  Jonathan, Gi-1812
EPPS, John, B-1812
ERP, Josiah, R-1819
ERTHAM, William, Mu-1811
ERVIN, Andrew, Mu-1816
  David, Mu-1811
  Joseph & Charles Dickinson,
   D-1805
  William, Wi-1801
ERVING, Wm., Wi-1810
ERWIN, Alexander, Mu-1816
  Benjamin, R-1819
  David, Su-1796, D-1811, Su-1812
  George, Wa-1814, Wa-1819
  James, Mu-1811, D-1811, Wh-1825
  James Sr., Mu-1816
  James Jr., Mu-1816
  Jesephire, B-1812
  John, Su-1812, D-1811, D-1805,
   Wi-1815, Su-1812, Sn-1816
  Joseph, D-1811
  Nat., Sn-1816
  Robert, K-1796
  S. James, Mu-1816
  Vincent, Wi-1815
  William, Su-1812, Wa-1819(2),
   Wa-1814, Wh-1811, Wl-1804
   Sn-1816, Mu-1811, Wh-1825
   Mu-1816, Wi-1801
  William B., D-1811
ERWINE, Francis, C-1818
ESBRIDGE, Samuel, Ro-1805
ESCUE, Robt., Li-1812*
ESDALE, David, D-1811
ESEX, Thomas, Sn-1816
ESLINGER, Andrew, Je-1822, Ge-1812
ESPIN, James, heirs, Sn-1816
ESPY, Robert, Sn-1787, Sn-1792
ESSARY, Thos., W-1812
ESSERAY, James, W-1812
ESSERY, Thomas, Bo-1801
ESSURY, Thomas, Bo-1800
ESTEP, James, Hw-1801
ESTERLY, Conrod, Ge-1812
  Gasper, Ge-1812
  George, Ge-1812
  John, Ge-1812
  Moses, Ge-1812
  Philip, Ge-1812
ESTES, Absolom, Wl-1804(2)
  Armstead, Wi-1815
  Barnet, Gr-1799
  C. John, Gr-1804

ESTES, Chesley, Mu-1816
    Ezekiel, Gr-1799
    Floyd, Gr-1821
    John, Gr-1799, Gr-1804, D-1788,
        Gr-1805, Mu-1811
    John Sr., Gr-1821
    John B., Wa-1819
    John Big, Gr-1821
    L. B., Mu-1811
    Micajah, Gr-1805, Gr-1799
    Moses, D-1788
    Peter, Wi-1815
    Saml., Wi-1815
    Thomas, Gr-1804, Gr-1799
    Washington, Gr-1821
ESTES & ARMSTRONG, Mu-1811
ESTILL, Isaac, Fr-1812
    James, Fr-1812(2)
    Wallace, Fr-1812
ESTIS, Benjn. H., Sn-1811
    Peter, Wi-1810
    Robert, Wi-1810
ESTRIDGE, Richard, Ct-1798, Ct-1796
    Tho., Gi-1812
ESTRIGE, Richad., Se-1799
ESTUS, John, Wl-1804
ETCHLEY, Joseph, Su-1797
ETHELDRED, Williams, Gr-1804
ETHELDRIDGE, David S., D-1811
ETHREDG, Peter, W-1812
ETHREGE, Aaron, Sn-1811
    Mathew, Sn-1811
    Thomas, Sn-1811(2)
ETHRIDGE, John, Sn-1816
    Mathias, Wl-1804
    Terrell, Sn-1816
    Thomas, Wl-1804, Sn-1816
ETON, James, Wa-1814
ETTER, John, Ge-1812
ETTLEMAN, Leonard, Ge-1805
EUBANK, James, Rb-1812
    Martin, Rb-1812
EUBANKS, Elijah, Rb-1812
    James, Sn-1816
    John, Gi-1812, Sn-1811
    Lewis, Gi-1812
    Marton, Sn-1811
    William, Sn-1816, Sn-1811
EURE, John, Su-1812
EVAN, John B., Wi-1801
EVANES, Mary, Wi-1810
EVANS, Absalem, Gr-1821
    Andrew, Gr-1821, Gr-1799
    Archer, Ct-1796
    Benj., Wi-1815, Wi-1810
    Daniel, Gi-1812, Mu-1811
    David, Gr 1799, Gr 1804, Gr-1805,
        Gr-1821, Je-1822
    Davis, Gr-1799
    Edward, Bo-1801
    Ethelred, Wi-1810
    Evan, Ge-1783, Ge-1812
    Evin, Ro-1805
    Ezekiel, Je-1822
    Ezer, Mu-1816
    George, Gr-1804, Je-1822
    George Jr., Gr-1821
    George Esq., Je-1800
    Henry, Gr-1805
    Jacob, Je-1800, Je-1822
    James, Fr-1812, W-1812, Je-1800,
        Mu-1816

EVANS, Jane, Gr-1821
    Jeremiah, D-1805
    Jesse, B-1812, Mu-1816
    Jesse (Hatter), Cl-1803
    Jessee, Wi-1815, Mu-1811
    Joel, Gr-1799, W-1812
    John, Hw-1801, Wi-1815(2), Fr-1812,
        Gr-1821, Ge-1812(2), Wi-1810,
        D-1805
    John B., by J. H., Je-1800
    Jonathan, Ge-1812
    Joseph, Fr-1812, Mu-1816
    Lewis, D-1805
    Mary, Wi-1815
    Nathaniel, Wh-1825
    Robert, Ge-1812, D-1811, D-1805
    Samuel, Ct-1798, Ct-1796, Je-1822,
        Su-1812
    Thomas, Fr-1812
    Walter, C-1818, Je-1822
    Whitsell, Je-1822
    William, Cl-1803, Gr-1804, Gr-1799,
        Fr-1812, Je-1822(2), Ge-1812,
        Su-1797, D-1805(2), D-1811,
        Gr-1805
    William B., D-1811
    Williams, Su-1796
EVEINGS, Daniel, D-1788
EVENS, Bird, D-1811
    Daniel, Wi-1801
    Even Sr., Ge-1805
    George, Mt-1798
    Harelin, Ro-1805
    Harmon, Cl-1803
    Henry, Ge-1805
    Jesse, heirs, Wi-1801
    Jno., Cl-1803
    Jonathan, Ge-1783, Ge-1805
    William, Hw-1810, Ro-1805, Sn-1816
    Capt. Wm., D-1811
EVERET, David, Sn-1816
    Philip, Ge-1805
EVERETT, Carey, D-1805
    Ellez., Sn-1811
    James, D-1811
    Jesse, D-1811
    John, D-1811
    Joseph, Su-1797
    Robert, Bo-1800
    Simon, D-1811(2)
    Thomas, D-1811
    Thomas & John, D-1805
EVERETTE, Jonathan, D-1805
EVERIT, Philip, Ge-1812
EVERITT, Benjamin, Su-1812
    Joseph, Su-1812
EVERLY, Daniel, Sn-1811
EVERY, George, Wl-1804
    John, Ro-1805
EVIN, Alexander, Wl-1804
    James, Hw-1799
    John, Gi-1819
    Samuel A., R-1819
EVINS, Andrew Bogle, Bo-1805
    David, Wi-1815
    David C., D-1811
    Evin, R-1819
    Jesse, Cl-1803
    Jonathan, R-1819
    Matthew, Ro-1805
    Thomas, Hw-1801
    William, Cl-1803, J-1802, Hw-1799

EVRSS, Bailey, C-1818
EWEING, Elijah, Sn-1792
EWEL, John, B-1812
EWEN, James, Sn-1792
EWIN, Henry, D-1811
    Henry C., D-1811
    Nathan, Wi-1815
    William, Wi-1801
EWINS, Alexander, Mu-1811
EWING, Alexander, Wi-1801, D-1805
    Andrew, Wi-1810, Wi-1815, D-1811(2)
    Andrew Jr., D-1805
    Andrew & Nathan, D-1805
    Edley, D-1811
    Elijah, J-1802
    Esley, D-1805
    George, B-1812, Bo-1800, Bo-1801,
        Bo-1805
    James, D-1811, Bo-1801, B-1812,
        Bo-1800
    John, Bo-1800(3), Bo-1801, Bo-1805
    John L., Wi-1815, D-1811
    Joseph, Mu-1816
    Nathan, Wi-1801, Mt-1798, D-1811
    Nathaniel, Bo-1800
    Patrick & Francis, D-1805
    Robert, B-1812
    William, Mu-1816, D-1805, Wi-1815,
        Bo-1801, Bo-1800, B-1812
EWINGS, Andrew, Gi-1819
EXUM, Arther, Sn-1811
    James, D-1811
    Joseph, Sn-1811, Sn-1816
    Will, Sn-1811
EZEKIEL, Lyon, Ge-1812
EZEL, Balam, Wi-1810
    Bancel, Wi-1810
EZELL, Balam, Wi-1815
    Jeremiah, D-1811
    Parham, Mu-1816
    Pasham, Mu-1811
    Timothy, Gi-1812
    William, Gi-1812, Gi-1819
    William H., W-1812
EZLL, Frederick, Wi-1815
FAGAN, John, Su-1796
FAIN, Charles, B-1812
    David, B-1812
    Ebenzer, Wa-1814, Wa-1819
    Jesse, Bo-1805
    John, Wa-1814, Je-1822
    Nicholas, Su-1812, Gi-1812
    Samuel, heirs, Wa-1814
    Thomas, Wa-1819
    Thomas & John, Wa-1814
    William, Wa-1814
FAINT, John, Ge-1783
FAIRLESS, James, Sn-1811, Je-1822
    Polly, Sn-1816
    William, Je-1822
FAIRLING, Robert, D-1805
FAIRMAN, John, Wl-1804
FAITH, Alexander, Mt-1798
FALKNER, James, Bo-1800
    Joseph, Bo-1800
    Lewis, W-1812
FALLS, James, Gc-1805
FALLWELL, Elisha, B-1812
FALWELL, John, D-1811
FANCHER, Jacob, Wh-1811
FANE, Geo., Gi-1812
FANN, George, Ge-1812

FANN, John, Ge-1812
    Philip, Ge-1812
    Soloman, Ge-1812
FANNAN, Joseph, Gi-1812
FANSHER, James, Je-1800
FANSWORTH, John, Ro-1805
FANVEEL?, John, Wl-1804
FANWITH?, Asa, B-1812
FARE, Ephraim, Wl-1804
    John, Wl-1804
FARIS, Absolom, Fr-1812
    Boler, Gi-1819
    Charles, Fr-1812
    George, Fr-1812
    Gideon, Wa-1819
    Gidion, Wa-1814
    Heyekiah, Fr-1812
    Isaac, Mu-1816
    James, Wi-1801, Fr-1812(2)
    James Sr., Mu-1816
    James Jr., Mu-1816
    John, Fr-1812, Mu-1816
    John Jr., Mu-1816
    Nimrod, Gi-1812
    Richard, Fr-1812(2)
    Samuel, Mu-1811, Mu-1816
    Smith, Fr-1812
    Stephen, Fr-1812
    William, Mu-1816, Fr-1812
FARLESS, Robert, Rb-1812
FARLEY, Isham, Wh-1825
    Jeremiah, Wh-1825
    John, W-1812, Wh-1825, Sn-1811
    Pleasant, Wh-1825
    Stephen, Wh-1825
    William, Wh-1825
FARLIN, Evan, A-1805
FARLOR, Clay, B-1812
    Jessee, B-1812
    William, D-1805
FARMBOROUGH, East, D-1805
FARMBROUGH, Stuart, D-1811
FARMER, Andrew, A-1805, K-1799
    Conrod, Hu-1812
    David, Fr-1812, K-1799, K-1796
    Felty, Hu-1812
    Frederick, Ro-1805
    George, D-1805
    Hamen, Fr-1812
    Henery, K-1799
    Henry, A-1805(2), K-1799
    John, Hu-1812, Ct-1796, A-1805,
        K-1799
    Joseph, B-1812
    Leonard, Rb-1812
    Miller, Ro-1805
    Nathan, Gi-1812
    Samuel, Rb-1812
    Stephen, Wl-1804, Gi-1812
    Thomas, Wl-1804, Ct-1798, Ct-1796,
        Gi-1812, Rb-1812
    William, Wl-1804, Bl-1815, K-1799,
        Fr-1812, A-1805, Gi-1812
    Zachariah, Fr-1812
FARNER, John, Ge-1812, Wi-1801
    Lemuel T., D-1811
    Nathan, Wi-1801
FARNERS, John, Mu-1811
FARNSWORTH, Benjamin, Ge-1812, Ge-1805
    David, Ge-1805, Ge-1812
    George, Ge-1805
    Henry, Ge-1783

FARNSWORTH, Henry Sr., Ge-1812, Ge-1805
    Henry Jr., Ge-1812
    John, Ge-1805, Ge-1812(4)
    Nancy, est. of G. Farnsworth,
        dec., Ge-1812
    Robert, Ge-1805
FARR, James, Sn-1811, Sn-1792
    Walter, A-1805, Sn-1816
    William, A-1805
    William, dec'd., Wl-1804
FARRAR, Clement, Wi-1810
    Joseph, Wi-1810
FARRELL, Martin, Fr-1812
FARREN, John, Sn-1811
FARRESS, Champ, W-1812
    James, W-1812
    Nathen, W-1812
FARRINGTON, Joshua, Wi-1815
FARRION, George, B-1812
FARRIOR, George, Wl-1804(2)
FARRIS, Calip, D-1805
    Lewis, Wh-1825
    Stephen, C-1823
    William, D-1811
FARRISS, Caleb, Mu-1811
    Craig, Mu-1811
    Isaac, Mu-1811
    James Sr., Mu-1811
    James Jr., Mu-1811
    John Sr., Mu-1811
    John Jr., Mu-1811
    William, Mu-1811
FAULKNER, William, Wi-1815
FAUST, George, Su-1812
    Lewis, Su-1812
FAWBUSH, Hugh, Wa-1814
FAZEL, Martin, Wa-1819
FEANU, JOhn, Wa-1814
FEARS, William, W-1812
FEASTON, Abraham, Wa-1819
FEAT, Edward, B-1812
    Timothy, B-1812
FEATHERSTON, Charles, Sn-1816
FEERS, Jacob, Gr-1799
    James, Gr-1805
FEES, William, Je-1800
FEEZLE, Henry, Ge-1812
FEGAN, John, Su-1797
FEINT, Phillip, Ge-1783
FELIPPIN, Jesee
FELKER, William, Je-1822
FELKES, Thomas, D-1811
FELKIMER, Jacob, Rb-1812
FELLERS, Abraham G., Ge-1812(2)
    Jacob, Ge-1812
FELLONS, Jacob G., Wa-1819
FELLOW, Jacob, Ge-1805
FELLOWS, Abraham, Ge-1805
FELTNER, James, Je-1822
FELTNOR, John, Su-1796
FELTON, Haral, Mu-1811
    John, Wh-1825, Su-1797
FELTS, Cader, Wh-1811
    Cary, D-1811
    George, D-1811
    Roland, D-1811
    Thomas, D-1811
    William, D-1811, Wa-1814, Je-1822
FENALIN, Frederick, Wa-1819
FENBERY, James, Wh-1811
FENLEY, James, Gr-1799
FENNAR, Robert & Richard, Mt-1798

FENNEL, John, B-1812
FENNEY, James, Gi-1819
FERAL, Thomas, Sn-1811
FERALE, James, Sn-1811
FEREL, Len, Sn-1811
FERGASON, Edward, Sn-1816
FERGUSON, Alexander, R-1819, D-1811
    Benjamin, Gr-1799
    Eli, R-1819
    Elias, R-1819, Bo-1805
    Henry, Wa-1819, Rb-1812, Wa-1814
    Hiram, Wh-1825
    James, Wh-1825(2), Gr-1799, Gr-1821
        Mt-1798
    John, A-1805, Wa-1814, R-1819,
        R-1812(2), Gr-1821
    John T., Wa-1814
    Jonathan, Rb-1812
    Larkin, Wa-1819
    Mathis, Wh-1825
    Moses, Su-1797
    Nelson, Sn-1816
    Olly, D-1811
    Robert, K-1796, R-1819
    Thomas, Wa-1819, Wa-1814
    William, D-1811, B-1812
FERRAR, William, Wi-1810
FERREL, Charles Jr., B-1812
    Charles Sr., B-1812
    John Sr., B-1812
    John Jr., B-1812
    Mathew, Sn-1811
    William, B-1812
FERRELL, Benson, Sn-1816
    Burtis, Sn-1816
    James, Je-1822
FERRILL, David, Mu-1816
    James, Je-1800
    John, Mu-1816
    Levi, Mu-1816
    Thomas, K-1796
FERRINGTON, Jehu, Wl-1804
FETHERSTON, Charls., Sn-1811
FEUSTON, John, Ge-1805
FEW, Edmond, Gr-1805
FEWQUA, Joshua, D-1811
    Peter, D-1811
FGERL, John, Mc-1825
    Moss, Mc-1825
FIELD, David, Su-1797
    Golder, W-1812
    Joel, Gr-1821
    Robert, Gr-1821
    Stephen, Su-1796, Su-1797
FIELDEN, John, D-1805
    Nimrod, Wi-1815
FIELDER, Avery, Wl-1815
FIELDING, James, Je-1822
    William, Je-1822
FIELDON, John L., Wi-1810
    Meredith, Wi-1810
FIELDS, Daniel, Ge-1812, Gr-1805
    David, Gr-1850, Se-1799, Gr-1804,
        Wl-1804
    Joab, Wh-1811
    John, Mu-1816, Mu-1811, D-1811
    Capt. John, Mu-1816
    Joseph, Gr-1804, Gr-1805
    Nelson, Wi-1815
    Richard, Wh-1811
FIELS, Thomas, Ge-1783
FIFER, Caleb, Wl-1804

FIGUERS, Mathew, Mt-1798
FIGURES, Matthew, Wl-1804
FIKE, Elisha, Rb-1812
    Elkin, Rb-1812
    John, Rb-1812
    Leroy, Rb-1812
    John, Rb-1812
    Simon, Rb-1812
FILAND, James, D-1811
    William, D-1811
FILEMON, Ralph, D-1788
FILES, James, Mu-1816, Mu-1811
    Manly, W-1805
FILLEN, Jacob, Ge-1812
FILLPOT, Joseph, Je-1800
FILPOT, Timothy, Je-1800
FIN, Jessee, W-1812
FINCH, Calvin, Wa-1819, Wa-1814
    Edward, Wl-1804, Fr-1812
    Thomas, Wa-1814, Wa-1819
    William, B-1812, Wa-1819
FINCHER, John, Ge-1812
FINDLEY, Alexander, B-1812
    Daniel, Wa-1814
    James, Wa-1819
    John, B-1812
    William, Gi-1812
FINE, A., Co-1821
    Abraham, Co-1821, Wa-1814, Wa-1819
    Elijah, Wa-1814, Wa-1819
    John, Wa-1819, Ge-1783, Wa-1814
    Jonathan, R-1808, R-1819
    Peter, Ge-1783
    William, Gi-1819
FING, George, Su-1796
FINICHE, Frederick, Wa-1814
FINK, George, Su-1797
    Michael, Su-1812
FINLEY, Archibald, W-1812
    Daniel, W-1812
    George, B-1812
    Hugh, Sn-1811, Sn-1816
    James, Gr-1799, A-1805
        John, Ro-1805, Bo-1805(2),
        Bo-1800(2), Bo-1801, W-1812
    Joseph, Bo-1801, Bo-1800
    Michael, Rb-1812
    Robert, Bo-1800, Bo-1805, Bo-1801
    Samuel, Gr-1799, Cl-1803
    William, Ge-1805
FINN, Harison, B-1812
    Jesse, Bo-1801
    Peter, Sn-1816
FINNEY, Andrew, D-1811
    James, D-1811
    Joseph, Ge-1805
    Pleasant, Fr-1812
    Riley, Gi-1812
    Samuel, D-1805
    William, D-1811
FINNING?, Lemuel, D-1811
FIRTHING, Solomon, Rb-1812
FISER, Jacob, Rb-1812
    Peter Sr., Rb-1812
    _____, Rb-1812
FISHER, Anthoney, Ct-1798, Ct-1796
    Archibald, Sn-1792
    Benjamin, Sn-1816
    Caleb, W-1812
    Francis, W-1812
    Frederick, D-1811, Mu-1811
    Frederick Sr., Mu-1816

FISHER, Gasper, D-1805
    George, Mu-1816
    Jacob, B-1812
    John, B-1812(2), Bo-1801, Sn-1816
    Michael, B-1812(2)
    Peter, Sn-1816, Sn-1792, Sn-1811
    Samuel, Bo-1800, Ro-1805
    Thomas, Mu-1816, B-1812
    William, Wh-1811, Ct-1796, B-1812,
        Wh-1825, Wi-1801, Sn-1811,
        Wi-1810, Sn-1816
FISHTER, William, Ct-1798
FISK, Elias, Co-1821
    Madison, Wh-1825
    Moses, Wl-1804, Wh-1811
FISOR, _____, Rb-1812
FITCH, William, B-1812
FITTLE, Adam, W-1812
FITTS, Joseph, Wi-1815
    Lanford, Sn-1823
    Reuben, Rb-1812
FITZGARALD, John, Wi-1815
    William, Wi-1815
FITZGARELD, John, Wi-1810
FITZGARROLD, Pattrick, Ct-1798
FITZGERALD, Ambrose, Mu-1816
    Christopher, Mu-1816
    Edmund, Mu-1816
    Emond, Mu-1811
    Garrett, Wh-1811
    Garrot, J-1802
    James, Mu-1816, Mu-1811
    John, Mu-1816
    Martin, Mu-1816
    Patrick, Bo-1801
    William, Wh-1811, Mu-1816
FITZGERALDS, Christopher, Mu-1811
    John, Mu-1811
FITZGERILL, Aiken, Wa-1819
    James, Wa-1819
FITZGERREL, Jabey, Fr-1812
FITZHUGH, Ezekiel, D-1811, D-1805
    John, D-1811
FITZPARTRICK, John, Hw-1801
    Thomas, Hw-1801
FITZPATRICK, Andw., Wi-1810, Wi-1815
    John, Wi-1810
    Morgan, Gi-1812, Mu-1811
    Samuel, Wi-1815, Wi-1810
FITZSIMMONS, Thos., by G. D., Je-1800
FLACK, James, Mu-1816, Mu-1811
FLANAGAN, Samuel, Mu-1816
FLANARY, Jacob, K-1799
    William, Ct-1796
FLANNINGHAM, John, Ro-1805
FLATFORD, Nathaniel, Je-1822
FLATT, Benja., Gi-1812, Wh-1811
    David, Gi-1812
    John Jr., Ro-1805
    John Sr., Ro-1805
    Poeny, Ro-1805
FLAWD, John, Wi-1815
FLEENER, Adam, Sn-1792
FLEENEY, Adam, Sn-1792
FLEMIN, Julias, Mu-1816
FLEMING, D. John, Mu-1816
    David, B-1812
    F. Thomas, Mu 1816, Mu 1811
    Hannah, Wi-1801
    James, Sn-1816
    John, B-1812, Gi-1819
    John W., C-1823

FLEMING, Juless, B-1812
    Ralph, Wi-1801
    Robert, Sn-1811, Sn-1816
    Samuel, Wl-1804, B-1812(2)
    Thirmond G., Sn-1811
    William, Sn-1816, Sn-1811
FLEMINGS, James, estate, Mu-1811
    Ralph, heirs, Wi-1801
FLEMMING, Alexander, Rb-1812
    John, W-1812
FLEMON, Plunket, Wi-1815
FLEMSMON, W. John, C-1818
FLENIGAN, John, K-1796
FLENNEKIN, Capt., K-1796
FLETCHER, Elijah, W-1812
    John, Rb-1812(2)
    Lewis, Wh-1825
    Richard, Mt-1798
    Simon, Mt-1798
    Thos., D-1788
    Thomas H., D-1811
    William, Wa-1819, Rb-1812
FLETNOR, Jacob, Su-1796
FLEWALLEN, William, Rb-1812
FLIN, George, Su-1797, Su-1796
FLINGAWAY, John, Sn-1811
FLINN, Geo., Gi-1812
    James, B-1812
    William, Wh-1825
FLINT, Abijah, Gi-1812
    Martin, Gi-1812
    Meriday, Gi-1812
    Richard, D-1805, Gi-1812
FLIPPEN, John, Je-1822
FLIPPIN, Wm., Gi-1812
FLIPPS, Garrett, Rb-1812
FLOID, William, Gr-1805
FLOOD, Seth, Rb-1812
    Thomas, Wl-1804(2)
FLORONS, John, Gr-1821
FLOURNOY, Silas, D-1811
FLOWERS, Benjamin, Wl-1804
    Henry, Wl-1804
    Holdy, Wl-1804
    John, Wl-1804
    Thos., Hu-1812
FLOYD, Alexander, Fr-1812
    David, R-1819, Fr-1812
    David Sr., B-1812
    Davies, B-1812
    Elisha, Fr-1812
    Isaac, Wa-1819, Wa-1814
    William, Wi-1810, Fr-1812, R-1819
FLUNOR, Jacob, Su-1797
FLY, Elisha, Wi-1810
    Jeremiah, Mu-1816
    Jesse, D-1811(2)
    John, D-1811, Mu-1816, Mu-1811, Wi-1810
    John D., D-1811
    M. John, D-1805
FLYNN, John, Wh-1825
    Mark, Wh-1825
    William, Wh-1825
FOALY, Henry, Ge-1783
FOARD, Horatio, Wa-1814
    Horatio Jr., Wa-1814
    James of Loyd Jr., Wa-1814
    John of Loyd Sr., Wa-1814
    Joseph, C-1818
    Loyd Sr., Wa-1814
    Mary, Wa-1814

FOARD, Mordica, Wa-1814
    Thomas, Wa-1814
    Thomas Sr., Wa-1814
    Thomas Jr., Wa-1814
FOGALMON, Michal, Mu-1811
    Samuel, Mu-1811
FOGLEMAN, Michael, Mu-1816
    Samuel, Mu-1816
FOGORTH, William, Mu-1816
FOLAND, Jacob Sr., Hu-1812
    Jacob Jr., Hu-1812
FOLK, William, Su-1812
FOLKE, Wm., D-1788
FOLKNER, James, Bo-1801
    Joseph, Bo-1801
FOLLET, George, Wa-1814, Wa-1819
    Jeremiah, Wa-1814
FOLLIES, William, Mu-1816
FOLLIS, Abram, Gi-1812
FOLSOM, Nathaniel, Ct-1796, Ct-1798
FONKHOWSER, Christr., Sn-1792
FOOD, Also, Hu-1812
FOOSHEE, John, Ge-1805
FOOT, Richard, Rb-1812
FOOTER, Enoc, Ge-1812
FORANA, Woodson, Ro-1805
FORBES, Alexander, R-1819, John, Gi-1812
    James, Gi-1812(2)
FORBIS, Thomas, Je-1800
    William, Fr-1812
FORBUSH, Samuel, Hu-1812
    Thos., Hu-1812
FORD, Alex., Bo-1800, Bo-1801
    Alexander, Sn-1811, Su-1797, Su-1796, Sn-1816
    Benjamin, J-1802
    David, Fr-1812
    Dye, Su-1796, Su-1797
    Edward, R-1819
    Esther, Je-1822
    Ezekial, Wa-1819
    Frederick L. C., Su-1812
    Grant, Wa-1819
    Henry, W-1812
    Horatia Jr., Wa-1819
    James, Wa-1819, Gi-1812
    James Sr., Mt-1798
    John, Wa-1819(2), Wa-1814, Su-1797, Je-1800(2), Su-1796
    John Jr., Wa-1819
    John D., Su-1812
    John W., Wh-1825
    Joseph, Ct-1796, Ct-1798
    Josn., Ge-1812
    Loyd, Wa-1819
    Loyd Jr., Wa-1819
    Mary, Wa-1819
    Mathew, Co-1827
    Micasah, Wa-1819
    Modicai, Wa-1819
    Mordicai, Wa-1819
    Mose, Mt-1798
    Ralph, Gr-1805, Gr-1804, Ge-1812
    Silas, Su-1812
    William, A-1805, Ge-1812(2), Ge-1805
FORDS, Henry, Wl-1804
FORE, A. P., Dr., Je-1822
    Augustin P., Ge-1805
FOREHAND, Allen, D-1811
    John, D-1811
FOREHET, John, Gr-1799
FOREST, John, Su-1797

FORESTER, Enoch, Bl-1815
    Robert, Bo-1800
FORGASON, Edward, Sn-1811
    Samule, Sn-1811
FORGERSON, Isaac, Wi-1815
    Joel, Wi-1815
FORGEY, Andrew, Gi-1812
    John, Gi-1812
FORGUSON, Edward, Sn-1823
    Henery, Bo-1801
    Hugh, Bo-1801, Bo-1800
    James, Gr-1804, Gr-1805
    Jeremiah, Mu-1811
    John, Bo-1801, B-1812
    Pleasant, Gr-1805
    Robert, Bo-1800, Bo-1801
FORGY, Andrew, Mu-1816
    John, Mu-1816
FORMAULT, John Sr., Gr-1799
FORRES, Thos., Hu-1812
FORREST, Nathan, B-1812
    Richard, W-1805, A-1805, Fr-1812,
        K-1799
    Shedrack, B-1812
    Shedrack Jr., B-1812
    William, Hu-1812
FORRESTER, Isaac, Sn-1811
    Wm., Sn-1816
FORRICE, James, Je-1800
FORSON, Benjamin, J-1802
FORSYTH, Andrew, Je-1822
    John, Mu-1816
    William, Fr-1812
FORT, Elias Sr., Rb-1812, Mt-1798
    Elias Jr., Rb-1812
    Elias B. C., Rb-1812
    James, Rb-1812
    Josiah, Rb-1812, D-1805
    Josiah J. P., Rb-1812
    Sugg, Rb-1812
    Whitmel, Rb-1812
    William A., Rb-1812
FORTENBERRY, John, Fr-1812
FORTNER, Archiley, W-1812
    Blake, Hu-1812
    Jonathan, Hu-1812
    Josiah, W-1812
FOSHER, Frederick Jr., Mu-1816
FOSSETT, Richard, Mu-1811
FOSTER, Alexander, Wl-1804
    Anthony, D-1805, D-1811
    Anthony Jr., D-1811
    Archilles, Fr-1812
    Benjamin, Su-1797, Su-1796
    David, Sn-1811
    Enoch, A-1805
    George, Fr-1812, B-1812, D-1805,
        Mu-1816, Mu-1811
    Isaac, Fr-1812
    James, W-1812, Wl-1804, Bl-1815
    Jeremiah, W-1812
    Jesse, Gi-1812(2)
    John, Se-1799, Wl-1804, Gi-1812,
        Sn-1816
    Joseph, Fr-1812, Gi-1812
    Lederick, D-1805
    Levy, Ge-1812
    Martin, Gr-1799, Ge-1805
    Peter R., Wa-1819
    Richard, Mu-1816, Mu-1811
    Robert, Wl-1804; Ge-1805, Ge-1812,
        D-1805

FOSTER, Robert Esq., Mu-1816
    Robert C., D-1811, Wi-1815
    Samuel, W-1812
    Thomas, Fr-1812(Forbis?)
    Thomas, Wa-1819, W-1812(2), Mu-1816,
        W-1805
    W. George, Mu-1811
    William, Wh-1811, W-1812, Wh-1825,
        Sn-1816, Sn-1811, D-1811
FOUST, John, Su-1796
    Peter, Su-1796
    Philip, Su-1796
FOUSTER, Robert, Bo-1801
FOUT, Jacob, Je-1800
FOUTE, Jacob Sr., Je-1822
FOWIN, Samuel, Wa-1814
FOWLER, Daniel, D-1811(2)
    Jack, D-1805
    James, B-1812
    John, R-1819, J-1802, D-1811
    Mason, D-1811
    Moses, D-1811
    Obediah, B-1812
    Richard, Wi-1810
    Selvester, J-1802
    William, B-1812, Rb-1812, Su-1812,
        D-1811
FOWLKS, Gabriel, Gi-1812
    John G., Gi-1812
FOX, Andrew, Ge-1805
    Andy, Ge-1812
    Enoch, J-1802
    Fetus, B-1812
    Huge, Wi-1815
    Jacob, Wa-1814
    James, D-1811(2)
    Jesse, Ge-1812
    John, Mu-1816
    Joseph, Mu-1816, Mu-1811
    Joshua, Wh-1825, Wh-1811
    Lewis, Rb-1812
    Peter, Co-1821
    William, Mu-1816, Wh-1825
FRAIKER, Adam, Ge-1805
    Christian, Ge-1805
    Frederick, Ge-1805
    Michael, Ge-1805
    Robert, Ge-1805
FRAIL, Elizabeth, Sn-1816
    Jos., Sn-1816
FRAIM, David, Ge-1783
    William, Su-1797(2)
FRAINCE, William, Su-1812
FRAKER, Michael Sr., Ge-1812
FRAME, Archibald, Wa-1814
    Daniel, Gi-1812
    Hugh, Ro-1805
    William, Su-1796
FRANCE, Archibald, Wa-1819
    Daniel, Wa-1819
    John, Wa-1819(2)
FRANCES, David, Je-1822
    Joseph, Je-1822
FRANCIS, Joseph, R-1808
    Linden, B-1812
    Miller, R-1819, R-1808
    Moses B., Wi-1815
    William, D-1811(2), Ge-1783
    Woodson, R-1819
FRANCISCO, John, Mt-1798
FRANK, John, Je-1822
    Martin, Fr-1812

FRANKER, Adam, Ge-1812
    John, Ge-1812
FRANKAM, Jary, Wi-1815
FRANKLIN, Aron, D-1811
    Alexr., Mu-1816
    Edward, A-1805
    Henry, Je-1822
    Henry Jr., Je-1822
    Isaac, Sn-1816
    James, Sn-1816, Sn-1811, D-1788,
        Sn-1792
    John, Sn-1811, Wh-1825
    John A., W-1812
    John M., Je-1822
    Joseph, Wa-1814
    Lewis, Je-1822
    Olver, Mu-1811
    Owen, Je-1822
    Richard, Sn-1823
FRANKS, Britton, Gi-1812
    Frederick, W-1812
    Henry, Wh-1811
    James, Wh-1811
    Jessee, Wh-1825
    John, Bo-1801, Bo-1800, Wh-1811
    Joseph, Ro-1805, Wh-1811
    Lemuel, Wh-1811
    Richard, Ct-1796
    Robert, Mu-1816
FRANSHARE, Richard, Se-1799
FRANTUM, Aaron, Wi-1801
FRASER, James, Sn-1787
    William, Sn-1787
FRASHER, Munford, Wh-1825
FRASHIER, Alexander, Wh-1811, Ge-1805
    Charles, Fr-1812
FRASLEN, Alexander Sr., Wh-1825
    Alexander Jr., Wh-1825
    Thomas, Wh-1825
    William, Wh-1825
FRASOR, HEnry, Wa-1814
FRAYNES, Edward, Ro-1805
FRAZER, D., D-1788
    Daniel, D-1805
    George, D-1788
    Hugh, Je-1800
    Jas., Gi-1812
    John, D-1788, B-1812, Gi-1812(2)
    Moses, Je-1800
    Walker, Gi-1812
    William, Je-1800, Gi-1812
FRAZIER, Abner, Ge-1805
    Beriah, R-1819
    Caleb, R-1819
    Daniel, D-1811
    David, Ge-1812, Ge-1805
    Ezekiel, Ge-1805
    George, Ge-1812
    James, Su-1812(2), Su-1796, D-1811,
        Mu-1816
    John, B-1812, D-1811(2)
    Martin, Wa-1814
    Moses, D-1811
    Robert, Fr-1812
    Samuel, R-1819, Ge-1812, Ge-1805,
        D-1811
    Thomas, Ge-1805
    Thomas Sr., Ge-1812
    William, Je-1822
FRAZOR, Abner, Je-1800
    James, Sn-1816, Sn-1792
    William, Sn-1816, Sn-1791

FREASHER, Re____?, Se-1799
    Wm., Se-1799(2)
FREDERICK, Moises, Gr-1805(2)
    Phillip, Je-1822
FREDRICK, Calap, Sn-1816
FREE, Philip, Gr-1804, Gr-1821, Gr-1805
FREELAND, D. James, Mu-1816
    George, D-1788
FREELS, Anderson, A-1805(2)
    Edward, A-1805
    Thomas, A-1805
FREEMAN, Asa, Wi-1815
    Griges, Gi-1812
    Howel, Hu-1812
    John, K-1796, Wi-1815
    Polly, Wi-1815, Wi-1810
    Richard, Rb-1812
    Sanders J., Wi-1815
    William, Ge-1812
    William C., Wh-1825
FREEMON, Reuben, R-1819
FREERSON, G. Moses Esq., Mu-1816
FREESE, George, Ge-1812
    Jacob Sr., Ge-1812
    Jacob Jr., Ge-1812
    Michael, Ge-1805, Ge-1812
FREET, John, Ge-1812(2)
FREGOTT, _____ Sr., Gi-1812
FREILS, Isaac, A-1805
FRENCH, Henry, Ge-1805
    Hugh, W-1812
    John, Bo-1805
    Moses, Je-1822
    Robert, Mu-1811
    Samuel, Mt-1798
    Samuel Sr., Hu-1812
    Thomas, Mt-1798
    William, R-1819, Wl-1804, Je-1822
    William L., Wa-1819
FRESHER, Gong, Se-1799
FREW, Arch., Bo-1800
    Archd., Bo-1801
FREZOR, James, Sn-1811
    William, Sn-1811
FRIE, John, Ge-1812
FRIER, John, Bo-1801
FRIERSON, David, Mu-1811, Mu-1816
    E. Samuel, Mu-1816
    Elias, Mu-1811, Mu-1816
    Elias, Maj., Mu-1816
    G. Moses, Mu-1811
    George, Mu-1811, Mu-1816
    J. Thomas, Mu-1811, Mu-1816
    J. Will, Mu-1816
    J. William, Mu-1811
    Jef. Thomas, Mu-1811
    Jeff Thos., Mu-1816
    John, Mu-1816
    Joshua, Mu-1811, Mu-1816
    M. James, Mu-1816
    Robert, Esq., Mu-1816
    Robert, estate, Mu-1811
    Samuel, Mu-1811
    Samuel, Esq., Mu-1816
    William, Mu-1811, Mu-1816
FRIESE, Jacob, Ge-1805
FRILEY, Caleb, A-1805
    John, K-1796
    Reuben, A-1805
FRINCH, Henry, Ge-1812
FRIOR, John, Ge-1783
FRISBY, Isaac, Ge-1805

FRISBY, James, Wh-1825(2)
    Josiah, Ge-1805
FRIZZEL, Abraham, B-1812
    James, B-1812
    William, B-1812
FRONLEN, Isham, W-1812
FROOKS, John, B-1812
FROST, Edward, A-1805, K-1799
    Elijah, A-1805, K-1799, Wh-1825
    John, Su-1797, Su-1796, A-1805, K-1796
    John Sr., A-1805
    Jonas, Gr-1821
    Joseph, K-1799
    Joshua, A-1805
    Josiah, K-1799
    Micajah, Wh-1825, K-1796, A-1805
    Nicholas, C-1823
    Robert, Hw-1799
    Samuel, A-1805, K-1799
    Stephen, Gr-1821
    Thomas, K-1799
FRUETLY, Weller, B-1812
FRUSHOUR, George, Ge-1812
    John, Ge-1805
    John Sr., Ge-1812
    John Jr., Ge-1812(2)
FRY, Absalom, B-1812
    Christian, Gi-1812
    Gabrial, Gr-1805
    Henry, Rb-1812
    Jacob, Rb-1812
    John, A-1805, Wa-1814, Rb-1812, Gi-1812
    Joseph, Rb-1812
    Peter, Rb-1812
    Philip, A-1805
FRYE, Benjamin, Gr-1821
    Gabriel, Gr-1799
    Robert, Gr-1821
FRYER, Jery, Bl-1815
    John, Se-1799
    Martin, D-1811, D-1805
FUALK, Onan, Sn-1811
FUANS, William, Ro-1805
FUGET, Moses, B-1812
FUGGS, Jacob, S-1811
FUGOT, Andrew, Gi-1812
    John, Gi-1812
FULCHER, Francis, Ro-1805
FULGHUM, Arthur, Wi-1815
FULGUM, Author, Wi-1810
FULK, George, Wa-1819
    Henry, Wa-1819
FULKERSON, Abraham, Wa-1814
    Alexander, Wa-1819, Wa-1814
    James, Wh-1811, Wa-1819
    John, Su-1796, Su-1797, Wa-1814(2), Wa-1819(2)
    Michael, Wh-1825
    William, C-1818
FULKERSON & BRADLEY, R-1819
FULKS, David, Wa-1819, Wa-1814(2)
    John, Mu-1811
    Sherod, Gi-1819
FULLE, Carrey, D-1805
FULLER, Alshua, Wl-1804
    Darling, B-1812(2)
    Isaac, B-1812
    Henry, Sn-1811
    Jacob, B-1812
    John, Sn-1811

FULLER, Margret, Sn-1816
    Stephen, Fr-1812
FULLERTON, James, D-1805
    Nehamiah & David, D-1805
    William, Gi-1812
FULMER, George, Su-1812
    John, Wa-1819
FULOY, Stephen Jr., Fr-1812
FULSE, George, Ge-1812
FULTON, Arthur, R-1819
    James, B-1812
    John, Ro-1805
    Nathaniel, Rb-1812
    Paul, Mu-1811, Mu-1816
    _____, Wh-1811
FULTS, Ephraim, W-1812
    Henry, Mu-1811
FULTZ, Daniel, W-1812
    John, W-1812
FUNDERBURK, George, D-1811
    Henry, Mu-1816, D-1811
FUNDERBUSH, Lany, Je-1822
FUNK, Henry, Mt-1798
    John, Su-1796, Su-1797(2)
FUNKHEIME, Jacob, Su-1797
FUNKHOUSE, Christ., Sn-1792
FUNKHOUSER, John, Su-1796
FU!UA, Thomas, D-1811
FURGESON, Isaac, Wi-1810
    James, Gr-1805
    William, Wi-1810
FURGUS, J., Wi-1801
FURGUSON, Daniel, Mu-1816
    Nathaniel, Mu-1816
    Pleasant, Gr-1804
    _____, Wa-1819
FURMAN(Turman?), James, Ge-1783
    John, B-1812
FURR, George, Mu-1811
FURRUS, John, Mt-1798
FURSELL, William, Fr-1812
FURSER, John, Bo-1800
FUSSELL, John, Wi-1815
FUSTON, John Jr., Ge-1805
FYLLER, Clayton, Sn-1811
GABBARD, Jacob, Ct-1798
GABLE, Barnebas, Ge-1812
    Barney, Gi-1812
GABRIEL, Israel, D-1811
GADDAS, Nemiah, Wh-1825
GADDY, Elijah, Wl-1804(2)
GADIS, Samuel, Mt-1798
GADON, Alex. D., Sn-1816
GAFF, Andrew, Wi-1801
GAFTIN, Jno., W-1812
GAGE, James, B-1812
    James Jr., B-1812
    Jeremiah, Gi-1812
    Jonathan, B-1812
GAILEY, James, Bo-1800, Bo-1801
GAIN, Joshua, Wa-1814
GAINEROW, Geo., Gi-1819
GAINES, Ambrose, Su-1797, Su-1812
    Benjamin, Rb-1812
    Francis, Su-1797
    Francis H., Su-1796
    James, Su-1797(2)
    James, Esq., Su-1796
    James L., Su-1812
    James T., Su-1796
    John, Sn-1816, Bo-1800
    Lewis, Mu-1811

GAINES, Robert, Gr-1805, Gr-1821, Gr-1799,
    Gr-1804
    Thomas, Rb-1812
GAINS, John, Wa-1819
    Moses, Sn-1811
    Moses Jr., Sn-1816
    Robert, Gr-1805
    Samuel, Sn-1811
    William, Sn-1811
GAINSTAFF, Michael, Ct-1798
GALASPEY, James, Ge-1783
GALASPY, Daniel, Wi-1801
GALBRAITH, Andrew, Sn-1816
GALBREATH, Andrew, Sn-1811
    James, R-1808, Ge-1812
    James, heirs, R-1819
    Margoret, Ge-1812
    Robert, A-1805
    Samuel, A-1805
    Thomas, A-1805
GALBREITH, Thomas, Je-1800
GALBRETH, James, Ge-1812(5)
GALD, Samuel, Bo-1800
GALE, William N., Su-1812
GALES, John, Wa-1814
GALIGLA, Garner, B-1812
GALL, George, Mu-1811
GALLAHER, David, K-1799
    John, A-1805
    Joseph, A-1805
GALLAN, James, Su-1797
GALLAND, Joseph, Gr-1821
GALLASPIE, Rev. John, Wi-1815
    Zacharia, Bo-1800
GALLASPY, George, Mt-1798
GALLAWAY, James, Mu-1811
GALLE, Thomas Jr., Ro-1805
GALLEHER, James, Ro-1805
GALLEHIM, David, Ro-1805
GALLEUN, Josiah, Gr-1805
GALLEWAY, Lamuel, Sn-1811
GALLIMORE, Abram, Su-1797, Su-1796
GALLING, H. John, Mu-1816
GALLION, John Jr., Gr-1805
    Joshua, Gr-1805
    Thomas, Gr-1805
GALLOWAY, James, Ro-1805
    Jesse, Ro-1805
    John, Su-1812
    Marshall, Su-1812
    Ro., Gi-1812
    Samuel, D-1805
GALLYIN, James, Gr-1821
GALLYON, William, Gr-1821
GALOWAY, John, Wa-1819
    Thomas, Wa-1819
GALUWAY, James, Wi-1810
GALWAY, Robert, B-1812
GALWORTH, John, Wa-1814
GALYEAN, Jacob, Gr-1804
    John, Gr-1804(2)
    Josiah, Gr-1804
    Thomas, Gr-1804
GAMBELL, Benjamin, Wi-1810
    Thomas, Gr-1799
GAMBIL, James, Sn-1792
GAMBILL, James, Rb-1812
    Melton, Wi-1815
GAMBLE, Aaron, B-1812
    Andrew, Ge-1805, Bo-1800(2),
        Bo-1801(2), W-1812, Wh-1825,
        Mu-1811, W-1805

GAMBLE, Charles, R-1819, R-1808
    Edmond, D-1811
    Henery, Sn-1792
    James B., B-1812
    James H., D-1811
    John, Ge-1805, Bo-1801, Bo-1800,
        Wh-1825
    Josiah, Bo-1801, Bo-1800
    Moses, Su-1797, Ge-1805, Su-1796,
        Bo-1805, Bo-1800
    Polly, Mu-1816
    Robert, R-1808, Wh-1811, R-1819,
        Ge-1805, Wh-1825
    Samuel, Wa-1814, Su-1797(2), Su-1812,
        Mu-1816
    Samuel, Su-1796 (in Hawkins Co.)
    Samuel, heirs, Wa-1819
    Thomas, Bo-1800, Wh-1825
    William, A-1805
GAMBLER, Andrew, Wh-1811
GAMBLING, James, Sn-1816
GAMBREL, Millan, D-1810
    Polly, Mu-1811
GAMBRIL, Martin, Gr-1805
GAMBROL, Martin, Gr-1804
GAMBRULL, Henry, Sn-1787
GAMELL, James H., Wi-1815
GAMER, Wm., Wi-1801
GAMIL, David, Ge-1783
GAMMELL, James, B-1812
    Joseph, B-1812
GAMMON, George, Su-1812
    James, K-1796
    Richard, Su-1796, Su-1812, Su-1797,
        Su-1812(2)
    William, Wh-1825
GAMREL, Martain, Gr-1805
GAN, Issac, Co-1827
GANAWAY, Gregory, Mu-1816
    James, Mu-1816
GANBLE, Edmondson, D-1805
GANES, Ambrose, Su-1796
    James, Ro-1805
    John, Bo-1800
GANEWAY, Burrel, B-1812
GANN, Adam, Wa-1819, Wa-1814
    Daniel, Wh-1825, Wa-1814, Wa-1819
    George, Wa-1819
    Isaac, Wa-1814, Wa-1819
    Jacob, Wa-1819
    John, Wa-1814, Wa-1819
    Nathan, Wa-1819, Wa-1814
    Reuben, Wa-1819
    Samuel, Wh-1825
    William, Wh-1811, Wa-1814
GANT, James, G-1812, Mu-1811
    John, Bo 1800
    Lewis, B-1812
    Wm., Bo-1800
GAMTT. R. & Edward, heirs, R-1819
GARAGUS, William, Mu-1811
GARDEN, John, Wi-1805
    Parish, Je-1800
GARDENHIRE, George, Ro-1805
GARDENSHIRE, Jacob, Ro-1805
GARDINER, James, Bo-1805
GARDNER, Britton, Mu-1811
    Conrod, Ge-1812
    Francis, Wa-1814
    George, Rb-1812
    Harriet, Sn-1816
    Henry, Rb-1812, Mt-1798

GARDNER, James, K-1799, Rb-1812
    Jesse, Rb-1812
    John, Sn-1811, Sn-1816, Mo-1825,
        B-1812, Bo-1801, A-1805,
        Rb-1812
    Joseph, A-1805
    Mary Ann, Sn-1811
    Nathan Sr., Mu-1811
    Nathan Jr., Mu-1811
    Obediah, Je-1800
    Robt., Sn-1811
    Shadric, Mu-1811
    Thomas, A-1805, B-1812
    Wm., Wi-1815
    Wm., heirs, Wi-1810
GARESON, John, Bo-1800
GARGLE, Caleb, R-1808
GARITT, Gray, Co-1821
GARLAND, Ambrous, Ct-1796
    Daniel, Wa-1819
    Elisha, D-1805, D-1811
    Elisha Jr., D-1811
    Gutradge, Ct-1798
    Guttradge, Ct-1796
    Harper, Ct-1796(2), Ct-1798, Sn-1811
    Humphrey, Wa-1814
    Jesse, D-1811
    John, Ct-1796, Ct-1798
    Joseph, C-1823, Ct-1796, Ct-1798
    Joshua, Wa-1819, Wa-1814
    Samuel, Ct-1796(2), K-1799
    Samuel Sr., Ct-1798
GARMAIN, William, D-1805
GARMAN, Robert, D-1805
GARMON, John, B-1812
GARNAGAN, Chesley, Gr-1799
    Thomas, Gr-1799
GARNAR, William, Bo-1805
GARNER, B., Wi-1801
    Brice M., Li-1812*
    Brill M., Wa-1814
    Brindle, Wi-1810
    Britain, Wi-1801
    Eli, W-1812
    Griffin G., Wa-1814
    Harper, W-1812
    Jacob, Fr-1812
    James, K-1799
    John, Wi-1815, A-1805, Gi-1819
    Lewis, Mu-1816
    Nathan, Mu-1816
    Nathan Sr., Wi-1801
    Nathan Jr., Wi-1801
    Obediah, Gr-1799
    Parish, B-1812
    Thomas, B-1812, W-1812
    Thomas Jr., W-1812
    Willis, W-1812
GARNOR, James, Bo-1801, Bo-1800(2)
    John F., Bo-1801
GARNS, Adam, Wa-1819
GARRAGUS, John, Mu-1811
GARRATT, Isaac, B-1812
GARREL, Thomas, Ge-1812
GARREN, Peter, B-1812
GARRET, Able, Wi-1810
    Hazen, B-1812
    Leonard, K-1796
    Lewis, Wi-1810
    Odel, Gi-1812
    William, D-1811
GARRETSON, John, Ct-1796

GARRETT, Allen, Co-1821
    Daniel, Wh-1825
    Eli, D-1805
    Francis, Sn-1811, Sn-1816
    George, D-1811
    Henry, Ge-1805
    Jacob, Wi-1810
    James, Je-1822, Sn-1816, Hu-1812,
        Sn-1811
    John, Sn-1816, D-1811, Sn-1811
    Jonathan, Fr-1812
    Martin, D-1805, D-1811
    Morris, D-1811
    Moses, B-1812
    Pleasant, Je-1822
    Polley, Wi-1810
    Richard, D-1811
    Thomas, D-1811(2), Wi-1801
    Thomas & Morris, D-1805
    William, Gi-1819, Ro-1805
GARRIGEN, Matthias, Mu-1816
GARRIGUS, John, Mu-1816
    William, Mu-1816
GARRISON, Elijah, D-1811
    Ephram, Sn-1811
    Isaac, Wl-1804
    Job, Gr-1821
    John, Bo-1801, Gr-1821
    John Sr., Sn-1816, Sn-1811
    John Jr., Sn-1811, Sn-1816
    Parish, B-1812
    Paul, J-1802
    Richard, Sn-1816
GARROT, Absalom, Gr-1799
    Isaac, Gr-1799
GARSON, John, D-1805
GARSUS, George, Fr-1812
GARVE?, Elisha, Thomas & Charles, D-1805
    Samuel & William, D-1805
GARVIN, John, Ge-1812, Ge-1805
GARVIS, Luke, Gr-1799
GARY, William, Wh-1811
GASHERE, Les, Wa-1814
GASKILL, Even, Hu-1812
GASLIN, John, Wh-1825
GASS, Andrew, Je-1822
    David, Je-1822
    George, Ge-1805, Ge-1812
    James, Ge-1812, Je-1822, Ge-1805(2)
    John, Hw-1799, Je-1822
    John, Esq., Ge-1812
    Joseph, Je-1822
    Samuel, Je-1822
    William, Ge-1812
GASSAWAY, William, Gr-1805
GASTON, Alexander, A-1805
    Joseph, Ge-1812, Ge-1805
GATES, Alan, G-1812
    Allen, B-1812
    Benjamin, B-1812
    Philip, Fr-1812
    Valentine, Fr-1812
GATLAND, Dempsey, Wl-1804
    Dempsy, Wl-1804
    Isaac, Wl-1804
GATLIN, Edward, D-1805
    Jessee, Wi-1810
    Jessee & Thomas, D-1805
    Lazarus & Nathan, D-1805
    William, Wi-1810, Wi-1815
GATTEN, Edmd., Gi-1812
GATTS, John, Wa-1819

GAUEBLES, Samuel, Su-1812
GAUGH, Ambrose, Gr-1805
    Daniel, W-1812
    John, Gi-1819
GAULD, Samuel, Bo-1801
GAUNT, Robert, Bo-1800
    William, Mu-1811
GAUT, John, Je-1800, Je-1822, Bo-1801
    John Jr., Je-1822
    Mathew, Je-1822
    William, Je-1822, Bo-1801
GAVEY, Archibald, D-1811
GAVIN, Hugh, Ge-1812
GAY, Lemon, Sn-1811
    Wm., Bo-1800
GAYHILL, Smallwood, D-1811
GAYLER, James, C-1823
    John, C-1823
GAZAWAY, Samuel, Wh-1825
    William, Gr-1805
GEAR, Jacob, Je-1822
GEARY, Archibald, D-1811(2)
    John, Wi-1810(2)
GEBBEAH, Joseph, B-1812
GEDDENS, Wm., Gi-1812
GEDDERS, James W., Gi-1812
GEE, David, Wi-1801, Wi-1810
    Edmund, Wi-1810
    Fredirica, Wh-1825
    James, Wi-1815, Wi-1810
    John, Wi-1815, W-1812
    Jones, Wi-1810
    Thomas, Wi-1810
    William, Wi-1810
GEFFERY, Joseph, K-1799
    Jeremiah, K-1799
GEIGER, John, Je-1800
GELASPEY, Richard G., Sn-1816
GELBEAK, James, B-1812
GENNINGS, John, Su-1797
GENT, Josiah, K-1799
    William Hall, Ge-1805
GENTRY, Allen, Mc-1825
    Ayers, Je-1800
    Bartlett, Je-1800
    Charles, Je-1822, J-1802
    Claiborn, D-1811
    Dowel, J-1802
    George, Wi-1815, Wi-1801, Wi-1810
    Hugh, Fr-1812
    John, Je-1822, Ge-1805, D-1811
    Joseph, Ct-1798, Fr-1812, Ct-1796
    Martin, Je-1800, Je-1822
    Nicholas, Wi-1801
    Niclos, Wi-1815
    Robert, Je-1800
    Samuel, Wi-1815, Wi-1810, Wi-1801
    Simon, Ge-1812
    Thomas, Rb-1812
    William, Gi-1819, Rb-1812
GEO, Reuben, C-1818
GEORGE, Daniel, Mu-1816
    David, Sn-1816
    Edward, Je-1800
    Garrett, Sn-1811
    Greer, D-1805
    Haykock, Mu-1816
    Isam, Sn-1811
    James, Su-1797, Su-1796
    James J., Su-1812
    Jessee, Wl-1804
    John, Sn-1811, Mu-1816

GEORGE, Joseph, Sn-1811, Sn-1816
    Presley, Wl-1804
    Reuben, Je-1800
    Saml., Bo-1800, Bo-1801
    Silas, Je-1800
    Solomon, Wl-1804, Fr-1812
    Thomas, Sn-1811, Sn-1816, Wl-1804,
        Rb-1812, Sn-1792
    Travis, A-1805
    William, Sn-1816, Wi-1815
GERARD, Charles, Mt-1798, Wl-1804
GERDNER, Joseph, Ge-1812
    Michael, Ge-1812(2)
GEREN, Eallorran, Ro-1805
    Simeon, R-1819
GERMAIN, Joseph, Wi-1801
GERMAN, Daniel, Wi-1810, Wi-1815
    Joseph, Wi-1815, Gi-1812, Wi-1810,
        Wi-1801
    Stephen, Mu-1811, Mu-1816
    Zacheus, Wi-1815
GERRAD, Isam, Gr-1799
GERRARD, Andrew, D-1805
GERRET, Eli, Wl-1804
GERRISON, Kitty, Sn-1816
GESEL, Archibald, Fr-1812
GESS, William, Gr-1805, W-1812
GEW, Thomas, Mu-1811
GHILLION, Henry, Bl-1815
GHOLSON, Benjamin, Wi-1815, Mu-1816
    Francis, Mu-1811
    John, Mu-1811(2)
    Nathaniel, Mu-1811, Mu-1816
    William, Mu-1811, Mu-1816
GHOLSTON, Francis, Fr-1812
GHOMLEY, Joseph, Bo-1800, Bo-1801
GHRATCHER, George, Fr-1812
GHRIST, Hauldsworth, Mu-1816
GIBBENS, William, Gr-1821
GIBBERT, Mickal, Sn-1792
GIBBONS, James, Je-1822
    Patrick, Je-1800, Je-1822
    Thomas, Cl-1803
GIBBS, Bartee, Wh-1825
    George W., Wh-1811
    James, W-1805, W-1812(2)
    Jessee, W-1805, W-1812
    John, Sn-1816, Gr-1799
    John Sr., W-1812, W-1805
    John Jr., W-1812, W-1805
    Jonathan, Rb-1812
    Miles, D-1811
    Samuel, W-1805, W-1812
    Shadrack, Rb-1812
    Thomas, Wh-1825, D-1805
    William, K*-1815
GIBS, Richard, K-1796
GIBSON, Andrew, Bo-1801, Bo-1800
    Archelaus, Gr-1805
    Archibald, Gr-1804
    Benjamin, Su-1812
    Brison, W-1812
    Garret, Je-1800
    George, Gi-1812
    George M., Gi-1812
    Hezeriah, Wi-1815
    Hugh, Gi-1819
    Isaac, Gr-1804(2), Gi-1812, Gr-1805
    Jacob, R-1808, Gr-1799
    James, Ge-1805, Gr-1799 Ge-1812,
        Wl-1804, B-1812, K-1799
    Jeremiah, B-1812

GIBSON, Jeremiah D., Wa-1814, Wa-1819
    Jesse, Wi-1801
    John, Wi-1810, Mt-1798, D-1788,
        D-1811, Ge-1805, Gi-1812,
        Wl-1804, B-1812, Bo-1805,
        Bo-1801
    John S., Wi-1815
    Jorden, Sn-1787
    Neely, B-1812
    Patrick, Wi-1815, Wi-1810
    Randolph, R-1819, Wi-1801
    Rodger, Sn-1792
    Roger, Sn-1811
    Samuel, Sn-1811, Sn-1816, Ge-1783
    Saml., Ge-1783
    Sarah, Gr-1821
    Spencer E., Wa-1814, Wa-1819
    Thomas, D-1805, Wa-1814, Wa-1819,
        Bo-1800, Bo-1801
    Valentine, Gr-1799
    William, D-1811, Ge-1805, Je-1822,
        B-1812, Bo-1800
    Wm. Sr., Hu-1812
    Wm. Jr., Hu-1812
    Capt. William, Mt-1798
    Wilson, Mt-1798
GIDDENS, Clark, Su-1797
    Francis, Wi-1815, Wi-1810
    James, Wi-1815, Wi-1810
GIDDINS, Clark, Su-1796
    Francis, Wi-1801
GIDEAN, Isham, Wa-1819
    James, B-1812
GIDEON, Francis, Wi-1801
    Isaac, Bo-1805
    Isaac Sr., B-1812
    Isaac Jr., B-1812
    John, B-1812
    Richard, Mu-1811
GIESLER, Samuel, Wa-1819
GIFFELER, Adam, Su-1796, Su-1797
GIFFERD, Joseph, Su-1797
GIFFORD, George, Fr-1812
    Jabes, Su-1797
    Jabez, Su-1796
    John, Su-1812
    William, Su-1812, Mu-1816, Mu-1811
GIGER, George, Je-1800, Je-1822
    Peter, Rb-1812
GILASPIE, Lewis, Fr-1812
    William, Sn-1792
GILASPY, George, Mu-1811
GILBER, William, Gi-1819
GILBERT, Charles, Gr-1804, Gr-1805
    Edward, B-1812, Mu-1816
    Felix, K-1799, A-1805
    James, Rb-1812
    John, Gi-1812, Wa-1814, Rb-1812,
        Gi-1819, Gr-1799, Gr-1805,
        D-1811
    Michael, J-1802
    Thomas, Gr-1804, Gr-1805, D-1811
    Webster, Rb-1812
    William, D-1811(2)
GILBERTS, Saml., Ge-1783
GILBREATH, Hugh, Bo-1801, Mu-1811, Mu-1816
    James, Je-1822
    John, Mu-1816, D-1811
    Samuel, Je-1822
    Thomas, Bo-1800, Bo-1801
    Thomas Sr., Je-1822
    Wm., Bo-1801

GILBRETH, Jno., Ge-1783
    Wm., Ge-1783
GILCHRIST, Daniel, B-1812
    Duncan, Mu-1816, Mu-1811
    John, Mu-1811, Mu-1816
    Malcom, B-1812
    Malcomb, Mu-1811, Mu-1816
GILDWELL, Mark, Wh-1811
GILE, Eli, Sn-1816
GILES, Eli, Sn-1811
    Ely, Sn-1816
    James, Co-1827
    Josiah E., Sn-1816
    William, Wi-1815
GILESON, John, Bo-1800
GILL, George, Mu-1816
    James, D-1811
    Jno., Mu-1816
    Robert, Mu-1816
    Thomas, Mu-1816, Mu-1811, Gr-1821
    William, D-1805
GILLAM, Anthony, D-1805
    Calin, D-1805
    Jacob, Gr-1805
    John, Ct-1796, Ct-1798
    Mrs., Wi-1801
GILLASPIE, Alenn, Mu-1811
    Alex, Bo-1800, Bo-1801(2)
    James, Bo-1800(2), Bo-1801(2)
    John, Mu-1811, Bo-1800
    Robert, Bo-1800, Bo-1801
    William, Bo-1800(2), Bo-1801(2),
        Sn-1811
    Zachariah, Bo-1801
GILLASPY, Daniel, Wi-1801
GILLENTINE, Nicholas, Wh-1811
GILLENWATERS, William T., R-1819
GILLES, John, Ge-1783
GILLESPIE, Alexander, Mu-1816
    Capt., K-1796
    George, Wi-1801, R-1819
    John, Mu-1816, Sn-1816, Wi-1815
    Robert, Wi-1810
GILLESPY, Thomas, Ge-1783
GILLEY, Charles, W-1812
    Daniel, W-1812
    Edward, W-1812
GILLIAM, John, R-1819, Wl-1804, Fr-1812
    John Jr., Fr-1812
    Lemuel, W-1805, W-1812
    Nathl., D-1811
    Thos., Mu-1816, Fr-1812
GILLIAN, William, Wa-1814
GILLIESPIE, John, Bo-1801
GILLIHAND, Jno., Ge-1783
GILLILAND, David, Je-1822
    Haten? John, D-1805
    James, Co-1821
    Robert, Co-1827, Co-1821
    William, Wa-1819, Co-1821
GILLIM, Thomas, D-1805
    William, Wh-1825
GILLINGTON, Nicholas, Gr-1799
GILLINTINE, John, Wh-1825
GILLIS, Alexander, Fr-1812
    George, Wa-1814, Ge-1812
GILLISPIE, Allen, Ge-1812
    D., Mu-1816
    David, Wi-1815, Wi-1801
    George, Sn-1816, Mu-1816, Wi-1815
    George F., Ge-1812
    George H., Ge-1812

GILLISPIE, George L., Wa-1814
    George T., Wa-1819
    Isaac, Wi-1815, Wi-1810
    James, Wa-1819, Mu-1816
    Jno., Wi-1810
    Robert, Wi-1815
    Thomas, Wi-1815(2), Mu-1816(2),
        Wi-1810, Wa-1814, Wa-1819
    Thomas, by son George, Ge-1812
    Thos., Jr., Wi-1810
    William, Sn-1816
GILLUM, James, D-1811
    Thomas, Mu-1811, D-1811
    William, Mu-1811
GILLY, James, Mu-1816
GILLYLAND, Jno., Gi-1812
GILMAN, Henry, D-1805
GILMER, Abner, Sn-1811, Sn-1816
GILMORE, Alma, Je-1822
    Hugh, Gr-1821
    James, Mu-1816, Mu-1811, Gr-1821
    John, Mt-1798, Gr-1805, Bo-1801,
        Gr-1799(2)
    John Sr., Gr-1804
    John Jr., Gr-1804
    Joseph, Rb-1812
    Nancy, Gr-1805
    Peter, Gr-1805, Gr-1821, Gr-1804
    Samuel, Gr-1821
    Thomas, Gr-1821
    William, Mu-1811, Mt-1798, Gr-1821
GILPATRICK, George, Wh-1825
    John, Wh-1825
GILS, Richard, Wa-1819
GILSON, Bengemon, Sn-1816
GINKINS, Aaron, Wa-1819
    John, Wa-1819
    William, K-1799
GINNINGS, Hezekiah, Gr-1799
    Royal, Gr-1799
    Thomas, Gr-1799
    William, Gr-1799
GIPSON, Archeles, Gr-1799
    Garrot, Gr-1799
    Isham, B-1812
    James, Gr-1799
    John, D-1788, B-1812
GIRTMAN, Daniel, Su-1812
GIST, Benjamin, Wh-1825, Ge-1783, Wh-1811
    George, Wh-1825
    John, Wh-1825, Ge-1783
    Russell, Wh-1825
    Thomas, Wh-1825, Ge-1783, Wh-1811,
        Wh-1825
    William, Je-1800, Wh-1811, Wh-1825
    William Jr., Wh-1825
    Wm. Sr., Wh-1825
GITGOOD, Alexander, Su-1812(2)
GITT, Jacob, Su-1812
GITTAN, Regis, Ro-1805
GITTINGS, Alexander, Wh-1825(2)
GIVANS, Daniel, Fr-1812
GIVEN, David, D-1811
    George, Hw-1799
    Isam, D-1811
    Mical, Hw-1799
GIVENS, James, J-1802
    John, Ro-1805
    Russell, Elisha, Robert & William,
        D-1805
GIVIN, Edward, Sn-1816
GIVINGS, James, Wl-1804

GIVINGS, John, Sn-1816
GIVINS, James, Fr-1812
FLACO, John, Fr-1812
GLAIZE, Laurens, Ge-1783
GLASCOCK, Archibald, Wa-1819
    John, Ge-1805
GLASCOCKE, Gregory, Wa-1814
GLASGO, Cornelias, Wi-1801(2)
GLASGOW, Asa, Wh-1825
    Cornealius, Sn-1792
    Cornelious, Sn-1816
    Cornelius, Sn-1787
    J., Ro-1805
    James, D-1811
    Jesse, D-1811
    Jessee, D-1805
    Spencer, D-1805
    Thomas, Gr-1821
    Will, Sn-1811
GLASS, Alexander, Mu-1816
    Francis Sr., Ro-1805
    Francis Jr., Ro-1805
    Hiram, Wa-1819
    James, Ro-1805
    John, Mo-1825, Bo-1800, Ro-1800,
        Ro-1805, Je-1800, Ge-1812
    John Sr., Ge-1805
    John Jr., Ge-1805
    Joseph, Cl-1803
    Robt., Mu-1816
    Samuel, Bo-1801, Bo-1800
    Saml. F., Wi-1815
    Thos., Mu-1816
    Wiley, Mo-1825
    William, Wa-1819, Bo-1800, Bo-1801,
        Mu-1816
GLASSCOCK, George, Ge-1812
    Gregory, Wa-1819
    John, Ge-1812
GLAZE, Henry, Wa-1819, Wa-1814
    Lawrence, Ge-1812(2)
GLEANER, Absalom, D-1805
    Michael, D-1805
GLEASON, Benjamin, D-1805
GLEAVES, Matthew, Mu-1811
    Michael, D-1811, Wl-1804
    Michel, D-1788
    Thomas, D-1811
GLEESON, Edward, Wh-1811, Wh-1825
    John W., Wh-1825
GLEEVES, Matthew, Mu-1816
GLENN, Abraham, Wi-1815
    Alexander, Wh-1825, Wh-1811
    Henry B., Wh-1825
    James, C-1818, C-1823, Gi-1812
    Jesse, Wh-1811
    John, Wh-1825
    Joseph Sr., Wh-1825
    Joseph Jr., Wh-1825
    Robert, C-1818, C-1823, Wh-1811,
        Gr-1799
    Robert Sr., Wh-1825
    Robert Jr., Wh-1825
    Samuel, Wh-1825
    William, Wh-1825(2), Wh-1811
    Wilson, Wh-1825
GLIDEWELL, Mark, Wh-1825
GLIMPH, George, Wi-1815
GLOSSUP, Jonathan, Gr-1821
GLOSTER, Thomas, Mt-1798
GLOVER, Absolom, D-1811
    D., Sn-1811

GLOVER, George, Fr-1812
    James, Su-1812
    Jesse, Gi-1819
    John, Wl-1804, Wi-1815, Su-1812
    Jones, Wi-1815, Wi-1801
    Joseph, B-1812
    Joshua, Gi-1812
    Lancaster, Wi-1810
    Richard, Ge-1812, Su-1812
    Samuel, Fr-1812
    Thomas, D-1805, Su-1812
    William, Wi-1810, Wi-1801, Sn-1817
GLUSLIP, William, Mo-1825
GLUTHERY, George, K-1799
GOAD, Ayers, A-1805, C-1823, C-1818
    Edward, R-1819
    Gabriel, Su-1797, Su-1796
    Hyram, C-1823
    John, Su-1797, Su-1796, A-1805
    Joshua, C-1818, C-1823
    Margaret, Su-1796, Su-1797
    Peter, Su-1796, Su-1797
    Reubin, Mu-1816
    Robert, R-1819, Wh-1825, Mu-1816
    Robert Sr., Mu-1816
    Thomas, R-1819, Mu-1816
    William, R-1819(2), Su-1796, Su-1797
GOALDSON, John, K-1799
GOALSON, Reubin, K-1799
GOAR, Ambious, J-1802
GOARD, James, Wh-1811
GOATS, George, Gi-1812
GOBORTH, Samuel, Ge-1812
GODARD, Edmond, Wh-1825
    Moses, Wh-1811
    Moses Jr., Wh-1825
    Moses Sr., Wh-1825
GODDARD, Thomas, Su-1797, Su-1796, Su-1812
    William, Su-1812(3), Su-1796
    William Sr., Su-1796
GODFREY, Rem, C-1823
GODSEY, Bartlet, Je-1822
    Berryman, Su-1812
GOEN, Daniel, Je-1800
    Ezekiel, Je-1800
    James, Gr-1799
    John, Gr-1799
    Thomas, Gr-1799
    William, Je-1800
GOFF, Ambrose, Gr-1805, Su-1797, Gr-1804
    Andrew, Wi-1815, Wi-1801, Mu-1811
    John, Mu-1811, Wi-1801(2), Wi-1810
    Thomas, Gi-1812, Wi-1801, Wi-1815
    William, D-1805, Wi-1815, Sn-1816
    H. Andrew, Mu-1811
    Hiram, Mu-1816
    John, Bo-1805
    William, Ge-1805, Ge-1783
    Zacharia, Bo-1800, Bo-1801
    Zachariah, Wa-1814, Bo-1805
GOGLE, Curtiss, W-1812
GOHEAN, James, Sn-1811
GOICES, James, Ro-1805
GOIN, Amos, Sn-1811
    Daniel, Gr-1804
    James, Gr-1804, Rb-1812
    Jeremiah, Rb-1812
    John, Gr-1804
    Levi, Gr-1799
    Ruiah, Gr-1799
    Thomas, Gr-1799
GOING, Caleb, Gr-1805

GOING, Claiborne, Gr-1805
    Daniel, Gr-1805
    David S., Gr-1821
    James, Gr-1805
    John, Gr-1805
    Labom, Gr-1805
    Shaderick, Gr-1805
GOINS, Abraham, Sn-1816
    Claborn, Gr-1805
    Daniel, Gr-1821
    Drury, Gr-1821
    Isham, C-1818, C-1823
    James, Gr-1805
    John, Gr-1805, Bo-1801
GOLDEN, Charles S., Wh-1825
    Enoch, Wh-1825
    Jacob, Gr-1821
    Thomas, D-1811
    William, Gr-1804, Je-1822
GOLDENS, Peter, Su-1812
GOLDESIN, William, Gr-1805
GOLDING, Enoch, Wh-1811
GOLDSBERRY, Henry, D-1811
GOLLAHER, John, A-1805
    Joseph, A-1805
GOLLIHER, James, Je-1822
GOLSON, Stephen, A-1805
GOLSTON, John, Wl-1804, A-1805
    Reuben, A-1805
GOOCH, David, Wi-1815, Wi-1810
    James, Rb-1812
    Nathan, Wi-1815
GOOD, David, Wa-1814
    Emanuel, Wa-1819
    Joel, B-1812
    Wm., Wi-1801, Gr-1799, Su-1812
GOODE, Charles, Wi-1815
    Saml., D-1811(2)
GOODEN, George, Hu-1812
GOODGREW, William, Mu-1816
GOODING, James, D-1805
GOODLINK, Michael, Ge-1812
GOODLOE, Robt., heirs, Wi-1815
GOODLOW, Rezon & James, D-1805
GOODMAN, Amos, Bo-1805
    Andrew, Su-1812
    Archable, Wi-1810
    Benajah, Wi-1815
    Benjamin, Ge-1783
    Benjamin Jr., Ge-1783
    Henry, Rb-1812
    James, Ge-1783
    Jessee, Mu-1811, Mu-1816
    Joab, Wi-1801
    John, D-1811(2)
    Joseph, Bo-1800
    Michael, D-1811
    Shered, Hw-1799
    Stephen, Bo-1801
    Thomas, Mu-1816, Ge-1783, Mu-1811
    William, D-1805
    _____, Mu-1811
GOODNER, Conrad, Su-1796
GOODPASTURE, Abraham, J-1802
    John, J-1802, Wh-1811
GOODRICH, Caleb, D-1811
    Edward, D-1811
    John, D-1811(2)
    William, D-1811
GOODRUM, John, Sn-1811
GOODSEN, Andrew, Wh-1825
GOODSON, John, D-1811, B-1812, Su-1812,
    Su-1812, Su-1796

GOODSON, Joseph, Je-1800
    Micajah, W-1805, W-1812
    Sparrow John, D-1805
    William, Je-1800
GOODWIN, Britton, Ro-1805
    Henry, Fr-1812
    James, D-1811
    Jesse, Fr-1812
    John, D-1811, Fr-1812
    Peter, Gi-1812
    Solomon, Gr-1821
GOOGE, James, A-1805(2)
    Josiah, A-1805
    William, A-1805
GOOLSBY, John, Wh-1811
    Kibby, Wh-1811
GOPLING, James, Gi-1812
GORDAN, Samuel, Wi-1801
GORDEN, Alexander, Rb-1812
    Benjamin, Wi-1801
    David, Wi-1801
    John, Wi-1801
    John Sr., Mu-1811
    John Jr., W-1805, Mu-1811, W-1812
    Moses, Wi-1810
    Robert, W-1805, W-1812
    Samuel, Mu-1811
    William, Mu-1811
GORDIN, Ambros, K-1799
GORDON, C. Robert, Gr-1804
    Charles, Wi-1815
    David, B-1812, D-1805
    George, Ge-1812, Ge-1805, Je-1822,
        J-1802, Je-1800
    George Jr., Ge-1812
    James, W-1812, Wi-1815, D-1805,
        Mu-1816, W-1805
    John, Gi-1812, W-1812, D-1805,
        Mu-1816(2)
    John, Esqr., Mu-1816
    Josiah, Mu-1816
    Robert, Ge-1812(2)
    Robert C., Ge-1812
    Thomas, Ro-1805
    Tho. H., Gi-1812
    William, D-1805, Mu-1816
GORE, Ambrose, Ge-1800
    William, B-1812
GOREY, Michael, Ro-1805
GORJE, Henry, Gi-1812
GORMAN, John, Ro-1805
GORREL, Thomas, Ge-1805
GORVIN, John?, Gr-1821
GOSEA, James, Wi-1815
GOSHEN, Henry, B-1812
    Jacob, Su-1812
    James, B-1812
GOSHIN, John, Bl-1815
GOSNER, William, D-1805
GOSOY, James, Wi-1810
GOSS, Benjamin, J-1802
    Isaac, Gr-1805
    Jacob, B-1812
    Samuel, Bl-1815
GOSSAGE, Daniel, Wh-1825
    Wm., C-1823
GOSSELL, Saml., W-1812
GOSSET, Elijah, Mu-1811
    John, Mu-1816, Mu-1811
    William, Mu-1811, Wi-1815
GOSSIT, William, Mu-1816
GOSWAY, Robert, Mu-1811

GOTCHER, Henry, Fr-1812(2)
    Joshua, Fr-1812
GOTHERD, Geroge, R-1819
GOTICHER, Joshua, Fr-1812
GOTT, John, Wa-1819, Wa-1814
    Joshua, Wa-1814
    Lot B., Su-1812
    William, Wa-1819
GOTZ, Seth, Cl-1803
GOUD, Ayers, A-1805
    John, A-1805
GOUDGES, Thomas, Wh-1811
GOUDY, John C., Sn-1817
    Robert, Sn-1817
GOUGE, James, R-1808
    James Sr., R-1808
    Jessee, Gr-1805
    John, Wh-1825, R-1808
    Joseph, Wh-1825
    Josiah, R-1808
    Martin, R-1808
    William, Wh-1825, Gr-1821
GOUGH, John W., Wh-1825
GOURLEY, Hannah, Ct-1798
    Hugh, Sn-1811
    John, Sn-1811
    Thomas, Ct-1796
GOURLY, Hugh, Sn-1811
GOWDY, C. John, Sn-1816
    Edmond, B-1812
    John, Sn-1811
    Robert, Sn-1811, Sn-1816
GOWEN, Amos, Sn-1816
    John, D-1811
    Robert, Mu-1816
    William, D-1811
GOWER, Alexander, D-1811
    Elisha, D-1811
    Matthew, Bo-1800
    Robert, D-1811
    Russel, D-1788, D-1811
    William, D-1811
GOWERS, Nathan, Ro-1805
GOWIN, James, Wi-1810
GOWSON, Johnathan, Mu-1811
GRABBY, Jacob, Gr-1821
GRACE, Jacob, Rb-1812
    James, Wh-1825
    Leven, J-1802
    Richard, Je-1800
GRACEE, John, Mu-1811
GRACEY, John, D-1811
    Newel, Wi-1815
GRACY, Hugh, Wh-1825
    Newell, D-1811
    William Sr., Wh-1825
GRADDY, Wm., Co 1821
GRADESHIRE, William, Ro-1805
GRADY, John, C-1818
    William, Sn-1816
GRAFFITH, Amos, Ro-1805
GRAGG, Harmon, J-1802
    Henry, Ge-1812
    John, Ge-1805, Ge-1812(2), B-1812
    Malsom, Ge-1812
    Robert, B-1812
    Thomas, Ge-1812
    William, Ge-1812
    William Jr., Ge-1812
GRAHAM, Abner, W-1812
    Alexander, Fr-1812, Sn-1811, A-1805,
        Sn-1816

GRAHAM, Andrew, Ge-1812
    Charles, Wa-1819
    David, Gr-1805, Wh-1811, Gi-1812
    George, Je-1800, Ge-1805, Je-1800
    Henry, Mu-1816
    James, Sn-1816, Wi-1810, Sn-1811,
        B-1812, Ge-1812(2)
    James Sr., Ge-1805
    John, Wi-1810, Wh-1825, Fr-1812,
        B-1812, Wi-1815, Su-1797,
        Su-1796, Ge-1805, W-1812,
        Wi-1801
    Joseph, W-1812, Je-1822
    Lewis, Sn-1816
    Loyd, Mu-1816
    Nathan, Sn-1816
    Nathaniel, Gr-1805, K-1796
    Nichols?, Mu-1811
    Richard, W-1812
    Robert, Wi-1810, Wi-1815
    Samuel, Wa-1819
    Spencer, A-1805, C-1818, C-1823
    Thomas, K-1796, Gr-1821, Ge-1805
    William, Wi-1810, Gr-1821, Wa-1819,
        Ge-1812(2), W-1812, Ge-1805,
        Je-1822
    _____, Esq., W-1812
GRAIGHEAD, David, D-1811
GRAINGER, John, Sn-1811
    Thomas, Sn-1811
GRALEY, John, Gr-1799
GRAMER, Joseph, W-1812
GRAMES, John, Je-1822
GRANARD, William, Su-1797
GRAND, James, Wh-1825
GRANFOR, James, Sn-1816
GRANGER, Bengimon, Sn-1811
    Benjamin, Sn-1816
    David, Sn-1811
    Lewis, W-1812
    Nancy, Mu-1816
    Nathan, Gi-1812
    Will, Sn-1811
    Wm., Sn-1811
GRANSHAW, J., D-1811
GRANT, Isaac, Gr-1804, Gr-1799, Je-1822,
        K*-1815
    John, Je-1822, Rb-1812
    John Sr., C-1818, C-1823
    John Jr., C-1818, C-1823
    Richard, Fr-1812
    Thomas, Mu-1816(2)
    William, Ge-1812, D-1811
GRANTHAM, James, Wh-1811, Wh-1825
GRANTHEM, Richard, Gr-1821
GRANTOM, Amos, Gi-1812
GRAVE, David, Gi-1819
GRAVES, Alexander, D-1805
    Benjamin, Ct-1798
    Fedrick, Sn-1816, Gi-1812
    G. John, Wl-1804
    George, Ro-1805
    Henry, D-1811, Gr-1821
    Jacob, Sn-1816, Fr-1812, Gi-1812
    James, Ct-1796
    John, D-1805, Sn-1816, Gr-1805,
        D-1811, Ct-1798, Gi-1812(3),
        W-1812
    John Jr., Gi-1819
    Nathanl., Mu-1816
    Ralph, Gi-1812
    Stephen, Bo-1805, Bo-1801, Bo-1800

GRAVES, Starling, Gi-1819
    William, Fr-1812, Sn-1816
    William B., Gi-1819
GRAVS, John, Gi-1819
GRAY, Abner, Ge-1805, Ge-1812
    Alexander, D-1805, Fr-1812
    Asa, Ge-1812
    Benajah, D-1805, D-1811
    Burk, Gi-1819
    Charles, Mu-1811
    Curtis, Rb-1812
    David, Ge-1805
    Deliverance, D-1805
    Dorras, D-1805
    Edward, Ge-1805(2), Ge-1812(2)
    George, Fr-1812
    Henry, Wi-1815
    Jacob, Je-1800, Ge-1805, C-1818,
        Wi-1815, C-1823, Mu-1816,
        Wi-1810
    James, Wa-1814(2), Wa-1819, C-1818,
        Co-1821, C-1823, Wi-1815,
        D-1811, Wi-1810
    James M., Wi-1815
    John, Gr-1805(2), Gr-1821, Je-1822,
        Wa-1814, B-1812, Wi-1801
        Wi-1815, Gr-1804, Wi-1810
    Joseph, D-1811, C-1823, C-1818,
        Su-1812
    Lucky, Wi-1815
    Mary, Ge-1812
    Michael, Gr-1821
    Moses, Gr-1821
    Nathan, Wa-1814, Wa-1819
    Nathen, C-1818
    Nathienal, C-1823
    Price, Wi-1815
    Rachel, Ge-1812
    Robert, Wa-1819, Wi-1815, Wi-1810,
        Mu-1811, C-1818, Wa-1814(2),
        Ge-1812(5), Ge-1805
    Samuel, B-1812, Wl-1804
    Walter, Gr-1799
    William, Mu-1816, Mu-1811, Wl-1804,
        Fr-1812, Bo-1800, Bo-1801,
        Bo-1805, Gr-1821
    Willis,   Gr-1799
    Young, D-1805
GRAYHAM, Andrew, Wa-1814
    David, Gr-1805
    John, A-1805
    Nathaniel, Gr-1805
GRAYSON, Berry, Bl-1815
    Charles, Wa-1814
    James, Gr-1805, Wa-1814, Gr-1804
    Joseph, A-1805, Mo-1825
    Ren, Bl-1815
GREAR, Martin, D-1805
GREAVES, Jonathan, B-1812
    Joseph, B-1812
    Samuel, B-1812
    Therman, B-1812
GREEG, James, Su-1812
    John, Su-1812
GREEN, Abednego, W-1812
    Andrew, B-1812
    Ann, Wl-1804
    Archibald, B-1812
    Arnold, Wa-1814, Wa-1819
    Aron, D-1805
    Arthur, Wh-1825
    Asa, Rb-1812

GREEN, Avery, Wh-1825
    Charles, D-1811
    Daniel, B-1812
    David, Sn-1811, Rb-1812
        Edmund, Sn-1811
    Edward, Sn-1816, Sn-1822
    Eldridge, D-1811
    Elias, Wh-1825
    Elisha, Sn-1811
    Elopan, B-1812
    Evin, Rb-1812
    Francis, Co-1821, Je-1800
    Frederick, Wa-1819
    Fredrick, W-1812
    Furny, Gr-1799
    George, Mu-1811, Mu-1816
    Gideon, Rb-1812
    Greenbery, Sn-1816
    Ira, Wa-1819
    Isaac, B-1812, D-1811, Sn-1816
    Jacob, Ge-1783
    James, Wl-1804, Wa-1819, K-1799,
        Gr-1799, Rb-1812(3)
    James B., B-1812
    Jesse, Sn-1792
    John, Wl-1804(2), Sn-1816, Gr-1799,
        Wh-1825(2), Co-1821, Fr-1812,
        Wh-1811
    Jonathan, Wl-1804, D-1805
    Joseph, D-1811, Wh-1825, Gr-1804,
        Gr-1799, Je-1800
    Joseph(heirs, by Aliphas Condray),
        Gr-1805
    Joshua, Wa-1819, Wa-1814
    Lewis, D-1805
    Littleton, D-1811
    Michael, Sn-1811
    Needham, Sn-1816
    Philimon, Gi-1812
    Phillamore, Ge-1805
    Saml., W-1812
    Shedrick Sr., W-1812
    Sherwd., Wi-1815(2)
    Solomon, K-1799
    Thomas, Mu-1816, Wh-1825, D-1811,
        B-1812
    Wesley, Wh-1825
    William, Ct-1798, Wh-1825(2),
        Co-1821, B-1812
    William, heirs, Mu-1816, Gr-1821
    Willis, B-1812
    Zach., Sn-1811
    Zachariah, Sn-1792, Sn-1787
    Zackariah, Sn-1816
GREENAWAY, James, Bo-1800, Bo-1801
GREENE, Betsy, Wa-1814
    Gnl. Heirs, Mu-1811
    Ira, Wa-1814
    John, Je-1822, Je-1800
    John Sr., Je-1822
    John Jr., Je-1822
    Susannah, Wa-1814
    Thomas, Ge-1805
    William, Ge-1805
GREENFIELD, T. Gerrard, Mu-1816
GREENING, William, Rb-1812
GREENLEE, John, Gr-1821, Hw-1799
    William, Fr-1812
GREENLEY, James, Fr-1812
    John, Je-1800
GREENWAY, George, Su-1812
    Joseph, Su-1812
    William, Wa-1819, Wa-1814

GREENWAY, William Sr., Wa-1819
GREENWOOD, Caleb, Gr-1799
    H. Bailey, A-1805
    Joseph, Wl-1804
    William, Wl-1804
    William H., Fr-1812
GREER, Alexander, Ct-1796, Ct-1798
    Andrew, Ct-1796, Ct-1798, Su-1797
    Andrew Jr., Su-1796
    Anny, Sn-1811
    Arthur, Bo-1800, Bo-1801
    Benjamin, D-1811, D-1805
    Berry, D-1811
    Daniel, Gi-1819
    George, D-1811
    Greenberry, D-1805
    Henry, Hu-1812
    Isaac, D-1811
    James, Sn-1811, Sn-1816
    John, Gr-1805, Ct-1798, Wa-1819,
        Je-1800, Wa-1814
    Joseph, D-1805
    Little P., Ro-1805
    Martin, D-1811
    Nathan, Gr-1805
    Samuel, Wa-1814
    Samuel Sr., Wa-1819
    Samuel Jr., Wa-1819
    Stephen, Gr-1805, Gr-1821
    Thomas, Wa-1819, Je-1800
    Vance, Li-1812*
    Vincent, Wi-1810
    Walter, J-1802
    William, D-1811
GREESS, William, Gr-1804
GREFF, Nathan, Su-1797
GREGG, Isaac, Je-1800
    James, Su-1796, Su-1797
    Nathan, Su-1796
    Samuel, Mu-1816
GREGGORY, Major, Rb-1812
GREGGS, Ear, estate, Su-1812
GREGOREY, John, Sn-1811
GREGORY, Abel Jr., Sn-1823
    Bannister, Sn-1816
    George, Je-1822
    Henry, D-1805
    Isaac, Sn-1811, Je-1822
    John, Sn-1811
    Joseph, Je-1822
    Richard, Je-1822
GREGRY, Jacob, Sn-1816
GRESHAM, Collins, Mo-1825
GRESSON, John, Wa-1814
    Thomas, Wa-1814
GRESSUM, Chas., W-1812
GREY, John, Gr-1804
    Samuel, Mu-1811
    Thomas, Wi-1815
GRIDEN, Samuel, Wi-1801
GRIDER, Wm., Li-1812*
GRIER, John, Je-1800
GRIFF, Jacob, Sn-1811
GRIFFEE, John, Wi-1815
GRIFFEN, Brooken, Gr-1804
    Owin, Mu-1811
    Spencer, Gr-1804
    William, Mu-1811
GRIFFET, John, Gr-1804
GRIFFETH, Amos, A-1805
    Isaac, A-1805
    John, W-1805, B-1812, W-1812
    Joseph, W-1805

GRIFFETH, Richard, C-1823
    William, D-1805, A-1805
GRIFFETS, Levi, Gr-1821
GRIFFETT, James, Gr-1799
GRIFFEY, Richard, C-1818
GRIFFIES, Anderson, Gi-1812
GRIFFIN, Benj. E., Co-1821
    Humphry, Sn-1811
    James, D-1811
    Lott, Wi-1815
    Noah, Co-1821
    Rosen, Mu-1816
    Stansberry, Wa-1819
    Thomas, Je-1822
    Wiley, Mu-1816
    William, D-1811, Ct-1796, Ct-1798,
        Je-1800
    Wilson, Mu-1816, Mu-1811
GRIFFINS, Thomas, Gr-1821
GRIFFIS, John, Mc-1825
GRIFFIT, John, Gr-1805
GRIFFITH, Amos, Bl-1815, A-1805
    Caroline, C-1823
    David, Bl-1815, Ro-1805
    Don, Wh-1825
    George, Wh-1825, Bl-1815, Gr-1799
    Griffee, Gr-1805
    John, Mu-1816, Mu-1811, J-1802
    Jones, J-1802
    Joseph, W-1812
    Matthew S., Bl-1815
    Samuel, Mu-1816, Mu-1811
    Thomas, Bl-1815, C-1818
    Timony, Bl-1815
    Viney, Bo-1800
    William, Wh-1825, C-1818, Bo-1801,
        A-1805, Gr-1799
    William & George, Wh-1811
GRIFFORD, George, Gr-1805
GRIFFY, Thomas, A-1805
GRIFITH, George, Gr-1799
    John, Gr-1799
GRIGGS, Join, Wi-1815
    John, Wh-1811, Mu-1811
    Michael, Gr-1805
GRIGORY, Thomas, Wi-1815
GRIGS, Samuel, Wi-1801
GRIGSBY, Aaron, Gi-1812
    Amos, Gi-1812
    Thomas, Su-1797
GRIGSLY, John, W-1812
GRILLS, Elliot, A-1805
GRIM, Isaac, Sn-1811
GRIMES, Alexander, Mu-1816
    David, Gr-1804
    Francis, Sn-1816
    George, Sn-1811, C-1823
    Henry, Mu-1811
    James, Rb-1812, D-1805, Mu-1816,
        Mu-1811
    John, Gi-1812, Gr-1799, D-1805,
        Wi-1801, Mu-1811, Wi-1810,
        Mu-1816
    Joshua, B-1812
    Nathaniel, Gr-1804
    Philip, D-1811
    Richard, Wi 1815
    Samuel, C-1823
    Stephen, Hw-1799
    William, Hw-1801, Rb-1812, Mu-1811,
        Mu-1816(3)
    William Sr., D-1811

GRIMES, Wm. Jr., D-1811
GRIMM, Geo., C-1818
    Samuel, C-1818
GRIMMER, Jacob, Wi-1815
GRIMMET, Samuel, Mo-1825
GRIMNUT, John Jr., Mo-1825
GRIMSLEY, John, Wa-1814, Wa-1819
    Loften, Wa-1819
    Lofton, Wa-1814
    William, Wa-1819, Wa-1814
GRIMSLY, Fielding, Sn-1811, Sn-1816
GRINDER, John, D-1811
    Robert, Wi-1801, Mu-1811
GRINDSTAFF, Henry, Ct-1796, Ct-1798
    Isaac, Ct-1798
GRINNING, John, D-1805
GRIPPEY, Martin, C-1823
GRISHAM, Benjamin, Ro-1805
    Ezekiel, Je-1800
    George, Wa-1819(2), Je-1822
    James, Gr-1799
    John, Je-1822
    Joseph, Je-1822
    Moses, Gi-1812
    Price, Wa-1819
    Richard, Je-1800
    Thomas, Je-1800, Wa-1819(2)
GRISSAM, Hardy, Rb-1812
GRISSOM, Robert, Je-1800
    Thomas, Gi-1812
    William, Sn-1816
GRISSON, John, Gi-1812
GRIST, Robert, Wa-1819
GRISTER, Watson, Sn-1816
GRIZZARD, Jeremiah, D-1805, D-1811
GROGG, Samuel, Ro-1805
GROOMS, Isaac, Mu-1811
    James, B-1812
GROSE, John, Gr-1799
GROSS, Edmond, C-1823
    Edward, C-1818
    Frederick, B-1812
    George, Su-1797, Su-1796, Su-1812
    Henry, D-1811
    Isaac, C-1823
    John, Su-1797, Su-1796, Cl-1803,
        Gr-1804
GROVE, Reuben, Gr-1804
GROVER, William E., D-1811
GROVERSON, John, Su-1797
GROVES, Allen, Sn-1816, Sn-1811
    David, Rb-1812
    Eady, Sn-1816
    John, Gr-1805, Gr-1799
    Reuben, Gr-1821
    Reubin, Gr-1805
    Thomas, Sn-1811, Sn-1816
    Thomas Sr., Sn-1811
GRUBB, Abram, Su-1812
    Jacob, Su-1812, Gr-1821, Su-1796
    John, Su-1797(2), Su-1796(2)
    Josn., Su-1796
GRUBBS, Jacob, Su-1797
    Jacob Jr., Su-1797
GRUBS, Edward, Ge-1812
    William, Ge-1812, Sn-1811
CRUGG, Jacob, Su-1797
GRUM, John, Wa-1819
GRUNDY, Felix, D-1811(2)
GRYDER, William M., Wi-1815
GRYMES, John, Gi-1812
GUARDIAN, Britian, Mu-1816

GUARDNER, Josiah, Gr-1805
    Thomas, Gr-1805
GUARREN, James, B-1812
GUDERCEN, C. F. M., Wh-1825
GUESS, Chrisr., D-1788
    David, Sn-1811
    Samuel, Je-1800
GUEST, Isaac, W-1812
    John, Hw-1801
    Joseph, Hw-1799, W-1812
    Joshua, Mu-1816
    Moses, W-1812, Hw-1799, Hw-1810
    William, Hw-1799, W-1812
GUFFEE, Ephrim, Gr-1799
GUFFY, Henry, Hw-1801
    John, Hw-1801
GUIN, Cornelious, Se-1799
    Daniel, Ge-1812
    Edward, Sn-1811
    Evan, Ge-1805
    Hugh, Ge-1805
    James, Ge-1812, Ge-1805
    Jesse, Fr-1812
    John, Ge-1805, Ge-1812, Se-1799
    Moses, Fr-1812
    Randolph, Ge-1805
    Robert, Ge-1805
    Robert Esq., Ge-1812
    William, Ge-1805, Wa-1819
GUING, Christopher, Rb-1812
GUINN, Benjamin, Mu-1816
    James, Wa-1814
    John, Je-1822
    Joseph, Je-1822
    Ransom, Wl-1804
    Thomas, Wa-1819
    William, Gr-1799
GUIRE, Benjamin, Mu-1811
GUITH, Wm., Bl-1815
GULLEFORD, James, D-1811
GULLEN, Wm., D-1788
    _____, K-1799
GULLET, George, Mu-1811
    Richard, Ge-1783
    Samuel, Mu-1816
GULLETT, Samuel, Mu-1811
GULLEY, Lazarus, Ge-1805
    Lewis, Ge-1805(2)
GULLIAM, James, C-1823
GULLICK, James, D-1805
    Reece, Ro-1805
GULLIFORD, James, D-1805
GULLY, Enoch, D-1811
GUNN, James, Rb-1812
    Richard, C-1823
GUNNING, David, Su-1812
    Robert, Su-1812
GUNSON, Daniel, Rb-1812
GUNTER, Augusten, W-1812
    Charles, Wi-1810, Wi-1815
    Claibourne, W-1812
    Francis, Wi-1810, Wi-1801, Wi-1815
    Hawkins, Gi-1812
    James, W-1812
    John, W-1812(2)
    Martin, Wi-1810
    Sterling, Wi-1815
GUPPETH, Wm., C-1818
GURLEY, Benjamin, Wi-1815
    Davis, Mu-1816
    Jeremiah, Mu-1811
    Jeremiah Sr., Mu-1811
GURLY, Jerimiah, Mu-1816
GURTNER, David, Ge-1805
    Michael, Ge-1805
GURY, John, Wi-1815
GUSPETH, Joseph, Gi-1812
GUTCHREY, Robert Sr., Wi-1815
    Robert Jr., Wi-1815
GUTHERY, Moses, K-1799
GUTHREY, William, Wi-1815
GUTHRIE, F. William, Mu-1816
    Henry, D-1805
    James, Sn-1811, Ge-1812, Ge-1805
    Robert, Wi-1810, Sn-1811, Gi-1812
    _____, K-1796
GUTHRY, Alexander, Je-1800
    James, Sn-1816
    John, Ge-1805
    Robert, Sn-1816
GUTRY, Francis, Mu-1811
GUTTSHALL, Frederick, Ge-1812
GUY, Samuel, Wh-1825
GWATHMEY, John G., D-1811
GWIN, Alexander, Sn-1811
    Edward, Mt-1798
    Edward Jr., Sn-1816
    James, Sn-1811
    James Esq., Sn-1816
    John, Mu-1811, Sn-1816, D-1811
    William, Sn-1816(3), Sn-1811,
        Hu-1812
GWINN, Champ, Ct-1798
    James, Ct-1798
    James, Sr., Ct-1798
GWINS, Ephraim, Wi-1815
GWYN, John, J-1802
    William, Gr-1804
GYIN, John, Sn-1811
    William, Ge-1812
GYN, James, Ct-1798
GYNE, Henry, Wa-1814
    Jacob, Wa-1814
GYNNE, James, Ct-1798
GYRE, Henry, Wa-1819
    Jacob, Wa-1819
HAAS, Albert, W-1812
    Philip, W-1812
HACK, Andw., Bo-1801, Bo-1800
HACKER, John, Su-1796
    Julius, Su-1796
    Julius Sr., Su-1796
HACKNEY, Hugh, Bo-1800, Bo-1801
    Jack M., Gi-1812
    James, D-1805
    John, Bo-1800
    William, D-1805
HACKWORTH, Austin, K-1799
    Gabriel, K-1799, A-1805
    Henry, Mc-1825, R-1819
    John, A-1805
    Nichodemus, R-1808
    Peter, K-1799
HADDEN, Hugh, D-1811
    John, Gi-1812
    Saml., Gi-1812
    Thos., Gi-1812
    William, Gi-1812
HADLEY, Ambros, Wi-1815
    Joseph, Wl-1804
    Joshua, Sn-1816, Wi-1810
    William, Wi-1815
HADLY, Joshua, Wi-1801, Wi-1815
HAEL, George, D-1811

HAFACRE, Peter, Gr-1799
HAFAKER, Michael, Gr-1799
HAGAN, Arthur, Su-1797, Su-1796
    George, D-1811
    Jonathan, D-1811
HAGARD, William, Mt-1798
HAGE, George, Mu-1811
HAGEN, Henry, Gi-1812
    John, B-1812
HAGGARD, Edmund, Mu-1816, Mu-1811
    Edward, Wi-1810
    Henry, Je-1800, Se-1799, Je-1822
    James, B-1812
    John, D-1788(2)
    Nathan, Wh-1825
    Samuel, Wi-1810
HAGGERTY, George, D-1811
HAGGS, Samuel, Bo-1800
HAGIN, Richard, Sn-1787
HAGINS, Barnard, D-1811
HAGLER, Abraham, A-1805
    Thomas, A-1805
HAGWOOD, Tapley, Gr-1804
HAIG, Amos, Sn-1816
HAIL, Aledinga, Wa-1819
    Alexander, Su-1812, Su-1797, Su-1796
    Amon, Wa-1819(2)
    Bird, Wa-1819
    Chase, Wa-1819
    George, Su-1812, Wa-1819
    Hezekiah, Wa-1819
    Isom, Bo-1801
    James, Sn-1811, Wa-1819, Gr-1804
    John, Mu-1811, Wi-1810, D-1811,
        Ct-1796, Bo-1800
    Joseph, Wa-1819
    Joshua, J-1802, Wa-1819
    Luke, Bo-1800
    Mad, B-1812
    Mashee, Ge-1812
    Mark, Gr-1821
    Meshack, D-1811(2)
    Micasah R., Wa-1819
    Nicholas, D-1811
    Richard, Su-1797
    Robert, K-1799
    Shadrack, Wa-1819
    Sherrod, D-1811
    Stephen, Wi-1810
    Thomas, D-1811
    Tolbot, Gi-1819
    William, J-1802, D-1811, Wi-1810,
        Bo-1801, Ge-1783, Gi-1819,
        Bo-1800
    Wilson, Sn-1816
HAILE, Jonathan, Je-1800
    William, Je-1800
HAILEY, Aaron, Wh-1825
    Barnebas, Gr-1799
    David, Gr-1799(2)
    James, Wh-1825
    John, Gr-1805
    John Sr., Wh-1825
    John Jr., Wh-1825
    Richard, Wi-1815
HAILS, Cage, Sn-1816
    William, Sn-1816
HAILY, David Sr., Gr-1805
    David Jr., Gr-1805
    Edward, Gr-1805
    John, Gr-1805
HAINES, Abraham, Ge-1805

HAINES, George, Su-1812
    John, A-1805, Gr-1804
    Richard, Gr-1804
    Robert, Sn-1811
HAINEY, Samuel, S-1811
HAINS, Abriham, Ge-1812
    Austin L., Sn-1816
    Benjamin, Sn-1816
    Henry, B-1812
    John, Gr-1805
    William, Gr-1805, Wl-1804
HAIR, Henry, Ge-1805, Wa-1814
    Isaac, Wa-1819
    Jacob, Wa-1819, Wa-1814
    John, Su-1812
    Joseph, Su-1812
HAIRE, Daniel, Ro-1805
HAIRISS, Richard, Gr-1799
HAIS, Henry, Wa-1819
HAISTINGS, Henry, B-1812
    John Jr., B-1812
    Joseph, B-1812
    Joseph Jr., B-1812
    Richard, B-1812
    Robert, B-1812
    Stephen, B-1812
HAKER, John, Gr-1805
HALBERT, William, Wi-1810
HALBON, Martin, B-1812
HALE, Abronigo, Wa-1814
    Alexander, Ge-1812
    Amon, Wa-1814(2)
    Archibald, Wa-1819, Wa-1814
    Asa, B-1812
    Bird, Wa-1814
    Cage, Sn-1811
    Christopher, Ge-1812
    Elisha, Wa-1814
    Frederick, Ge-1812
    George, Wa-1819, Wa-1814
    Guin, Wa-1814
    Henry, Wa-1819(2)
    Henry Sr., Mu-1816
    Hugh D., Ge-1812
    Jeremiah, Mu-1811
    Jesse, B-1812
    John, Wi-1801, Sn-1816, Wi-1815
    Joseph, Mu-1816, Wa-1814
    Lewis, Mu-1816
    Mark, Wa-1814, Wa-1819
    Mesbach, Wa-1819
    Nathan, A-1805, Wa-1814, Wa-1819
    Nicholas, Wa-1814
    Philip, Ge-1812, Ge-1805
    Richard, Wa-1814
    Richard Sr., Wa-1814
    Richard of John, Wa-1814
    Robert, Wa-1819
    Ruts, Wa-1814
    Samuel, Wi-1815
    Shadrock, Wa-1814
    Thomas, Wa-1814, Wa-1819
    Walter, Wa-1819, Wa-1814
    William, B-1812(2), Wi-1801,
        Wa-1814, Su-1812
    Wm., heirs, Sn-1787
    Zachariah, Wa-1819, Wa-1814
    _____ (Hall?), R-1819
HALEUM, Hiram, Rb-1812
HALEY, Abraham, Wh-1811
    Claibore, Gr-1821
    David Sr., Gr-1805, Gr-1804

HALEY, David Jr., Gr-1804, Gr-1805
    Edward Hawkins, Gr-1805
    John, Wh-1825, Gr-1804
    William, Wh-1825
HALFACKER, Jacob, Wi-1815
HALFACOR, Michael, Ge-1783
HALFACRE, Peter, Gr-1799
    Sewell, Wh-1825
HALFAKER, John, Wh-1825
HALFLEY, Conrod, Bo-1801
    Cransad, Bo-1800
HALL, Almond, Gr-1821
    Andrew, Ge-1805, Bo-1800, Bo-1801
    Archibald, D-1811
    Benjamin, Mu-1811, Wi-1810
    Carter, Sn-1816
    Charles M., D-1811
    Clement, D-1811
    Corbin, Rb-1812
    David, Sn-1811, Mu-1811, K-1799, A-1805
    Dickinson, Rb-1812
    E. R., Gr-1810
    Elihu S., D-1811
    Elisha, B-1812(2)
    Forges, Sn-1811
    Francis, Hu-1812
    George, Sn-1816, D-1805
    Henry, Mu-1811(2)
    Henry Jr., Mu-1816
    Hillard, Ro-1805
    Isaac, Mu-1811
    Jack, B-1812
    James, Gr-1799(2), Wa-1819, Wa-1814, D-1805(2), D-1788, Sn-1816, Sn-1811, B-1812
    James Lee, Fr-1812
    Jediah, Mt-1798
    Jehu, Wi-1801
    Jeremiah, B-1812
    John, B-1812, Gr-1799, Ro-1805, Su-1797, Ge-1805, Wi-1810, Sn-1811, Wl-1804, Sn-1816, Mu-1816
    John Sr., Gr-1804, Gr-1805, Mu-1816, Mu-1811
    John Jr., Mu-1811, Gr-1804
    John B., D-1811
    John C., D-1811
    John H., Wi-1815
    Joseph, Gr-1804, B-1812, Mu-1811, Bl-1815
    Joshua, Wa-1814, Wa-1819
    Josiah, Mt-1798
    Lemuel B., Wi-1815
    Levi, B-1812, Sn-1811, Sn-1816
    Mansil, Gi-1812
    Margaret, Gr-1804, Gr-1805
    Marley, Sn-1816
    Matthew, Mu-1816
    Michael C. A., Ge-1812
    Moses, Je-1822, Sn-1816
    Mosly, Sn-1811
    Nathaniel, Rb-1812, Ge-1805, Fr-1812
    Nathon, K-1799
    Richard, Sn-1816(2)
    Robert, Ge-1805
    Samuel, Su-1812, Su-1797, Ge-1812
    Samuel P., Wh-1825
    Simon, B-1812
    Stansall, Sn-1792
    Thomas, Mu-1816, B-1812(2), Fr-1812(2)

HALL, William, Fr-1812, Gr-1804(2), Ge-1812(2), Sn-1811(3), D-1805, D-1811, Sn-1816, Mu-1816, Mc-1825, B-1812
    William Jr., Ge-1805
    Willis, Sn-1811
HALLAWAY, John Jr., Je-1800
    Senator John, Je-1800
HALLES, John, W-1812
    Wm., W-1812
HALLON, William, Su-1796
HALLOWAY, James, Wh-1811
    John, K-1799
HALLUM, George, Wl-1804
    Heny, Wl-1804
    John, Wi-1810
    John Sr., Wl-1804
    William, Wl-1804
HALOWAY, John, Bo-1800
    Joseph, Bo-1800, B-1812
HALPRIN, Joseph, B-1812
HALTERMAN, John, Wh-1811, Wh-1825
HALTON, John, Bo-1800
HALY, John, Wi-1815
    Ham, David, Wi-1815
    Isaac, Wa-1814
    James, Gi-1812
    Jessee, Wi-1815
    John, Gi-1812, B-1812
    Samuel, D-1811, D-1805
    Thomas, Gi-1812
    William, D-1811
HAMBERGUGH, Smith, Sn-1792
HAMBY, Eli, Mo-1825
HAMBLE, James H., Je-1822
    Robert, Je-1822
HAMBLETON, Francis, Wi-1815
    James, Sn-1811(2), Mu-1811
    John, Sn-1811, Sn-1787, Sn-1792
HAMBLIN, John, Gi-1812, Gr-1799
HAMBY, Isaac, B-1812
    Wm., Gi-1812
HAMECH, James, Gr-1805
HAMELTON, Jas., Sn-1792
    Jonston, Hw-1801
    Jos., Sn-1792
    Robart, Sn-1792(2)
    Thos., Sn-1792(2)
    Thos. Sr., Sn-1792
    Thos. Jr., Sn-1792
HAMER, H. John, Mu-1816
HAMERS, John, Wi-1810
HAMES, John, A-1805
HAMIL, John, Gr-1805
HAMILL, Andrew, B-1812
HAMILTON, Abram, Su-1796, Su-1797
    Alexr., Gr-1810, Gr-1805, Gr-1805, Gr-1821
    Andrew, Sn-1811, D-1805
    Asa, Fr-1812
    Benjamin, Su-1797, Su-1796
    Dant, Su-1797
    David, Mu-1816, Mu-1811
    Eleazer, D-1788
    Elijah, Wi-1815
    Francis, Ge-1783
    George, D-1811(2)
    Haines, Mu-1811
    Hanes, D-1805
    Henre, D-1805
    Henry, Sn-1816
    Horne, Mu-1816

HAMILTON, Isaiah, Hu-1812
        James, Sn-1811, D-1805, Sn-1816,
            D-1788, Gr-1805, Hu-1812,
            D-1811, Gr-1799, Sn-1787,
            Wi-1815, Gr-1804, Je-1822,
            R-1808, Su-1812
        John, Sn-1792, Fr-1812(3), B-1812,
            Su-1797, Su-1812(2), Su-1796
        John Jr., Sn-1792
        John H., Sn-1816
        John W., Sn-1811
        Joseph, B-1812, Je-1800
        Joseph Sr., Je-1822
        Joseph Jr., Je-1822
        Joshua, Su-1812, Su-1796, Su-1797
        Middleton, Rb-1812
        Peter, Gr-1805, Gr-1804, Gr-1821
        Richard, Su-1796
        Robert, Sn-1811(2), Sn-1816, Je-1822
            Rb-1812
        Samuel, Su-1797, Wa-1819
        Thomas, Wl-1804(3), Sn-1811, Sn-1816,
            Hu-1812, Mu-1811, Fr-1812,
            Su-1812, R-1819(2), Su-1796(2)
        Thos. Sr., Hu-1812
        Thos. Jr., Hu-1812
        Timothy, Su-1812
        William, Sn-1816, Gr-1805, D-1788,
            Gr-1799(2), Gr-1804, Rb-1812,
            Gr-1821
HAMLET, Berryman, Wh-1825
        Bird, Wi-1815
        Littleberry, Mu-1816
        Thomas, Sn-1823
HAMLETT, Berryman, Wh-1825, Wh-1811(2)
        George, Wh-1811
HAMM, Joshua, B-1812
        Richard, Wa-1814
HAMMACK, Danel, Gr-1805
        John, Gr-1805
        Peter, Gr-1805
        William, Gr-1805
HAMMAM, Woodson, W-1812
HAMMANS, Obediah, Cl-1803
HAMMANTREE, James, Bo-1800
        John, Bo-1801
HAMMEL, Thomas, Mu-1811
HAMMELTON, Alexander, Gr-1805
        William, Gr-1805
HAMMER, Elisha, Je-1822
        Isaac, Je-1822, Wa-1814, Wa-1819
        Jacob, Wa-1814(2)
        Jesse, Je-1822
        John, Wa-1819
        John Sr., Wa-1814
        John Jr., Wa-1814
        Johnathan, Wa-1814
        Jonathan, Wa-1819
HAMMERS, Enos, Gr-1821(2)
        Enos Jr., Gr-1821
        Joel, Gr-1804, Gr-1821
        William, Gr-1805
HAMMILTON, George, Sn-1811
HAMMOCK, Daniel, Gr-1821, Gr-1804
        David, Gr-1805
        James, Gr-1804, Gr-1805
        John, Gr-1804, Gr-1821, Gr-1805
        Peter, Gr-1805, Gr-1804
        William, Gr-1804, Gr-1821, Gr-1805(2)
HAMMOCK, Daniel, Gr-1821, Gr-1804
        David, Gr-1805
        James, Gr-1804, Gr-1805

HAMMOCK, John, Gr-1804, Gr-1821, Gr-1805
        Peter, Gr-1805, Gr-1804
        William, Gr-1804, Gr-1821,
            Gr-1805(2)
HAMMON, Richard, D-1811
        Thomas, Wa-1814
        William, Sn-1811, Wh-1825
HAMMOND, Abram, Mu-1816
        David, Wi-1810
        Moses, Je-1822
        Robert, Je-1822
        William, Je-1822
HAMMONS, Abraham, Mu-1811
        Christ, Gi-1812
        Eli, W-1812
        John, W-1812
        John Esq., W-1812
        John Sr., W-1812
        Joseph, W-1812
        Lerroy, W-1812
        Thomas, Hw-1799
        William, Fr-1812
HAMMONTREE, Jeremiah, Bo-1800
HAMMOTT, John, Su-1812
HAMMUCK, Isaac, Je-1800
        John, Mu-1811
HAMON, Wm., Bl-1815
HAMONDS, John, Sn-1811
        Wm., Sn-1811
HAMONS, David, Wi-1815
HAMONTREE, James, Bo-1801
        Jeremiah, Bo-1801
HAMPTON, Anthony, D-1805, D-1811
        Jacob, W-1812
        James, Rb-1812, Ge-1805, Wi-1810
            W-1812
        Jesse, Wa-1819, Wa-1814(2)
        John, Rb-1812, Wa-1819, Wa-1814
        Joshua, Bo-1800, Bo-1801
        Robert, Wa-1819(2)
        Ruben, W-1812
        Samuel, Su-1796, Su-1797
        Smith, Rb-1812
        Thomas, Wi-1810, Sn-1792(2),
            Wa-1819
        William, W-1812
HAMSON, Briant R. Alex, C-1818
HAMTON, Thomas, Wi-1801
HANBACK, Mitchell, B-1812
HANBY, Dennis, B-1812
HANCE, John, K-1796
HANCOCK, Daniel, C-1818
        George, C-1823, C-1818, Wi-1815
        Joel, A-1805
        John, C-1818, A-1805, D-1811
        John Sr., C-1823
        John Jr., C-1823
        Joshua, W-1812
        Lewis, Ge-1812
        Major, Ge-1812
        Martha, C-1818
        Martin, C-1823
        Nancy, Mu-1816
        Robert, Se-1799
        Thomas, C-1823
        Wm., C-1823
        William Sr., A-1805
        William Jr., A-1805(2)
        Wilson W., Ge-1812
HAND, Samuel, D-1811
HANDERSHELL, Henry, Sn-1787
HANDLEY, Samuel, Fr-1812

HANDLY, John, Fr-1812
    Langsdon, Wa-1814
HANDY, Thomas, D-1811
HANES, C. Richard, Mu-1811
    Christopher, Je-1822, Je-1800
    George, Ct-1798, Ct-1796
    James, Wa-1819
    John, Je-1800, Mu-1816
    John S., B-1812
    Joseph, Hw-1801, Mu-1816
        Overton, Sn-1816
    Peter, Sn-1816
    Richard, Hw-1801
    Thomas, Wi-1815
    William, Je-1822, Sn-1816
HANEY, David, Sn-1792
    James, Mu-1816, Sn-1816
    Jeremiah, Gr-1821
    Tho. B., Gi-1812
HANKINS, Abel, Gr-1799
    Allen, Hu-1812
    Arthur, Wl-1804
    David, Mu-1816
    Edward, Je-1822, Je-1800, Gr-1799
    Eli, Gr-1821
    James, Ro-1805, Je-1822
    John, Je-1822(2), Gr-1805(2),
        Gr-1804
    John Jr., Gr-1805
    Margaret, Wi-1810
    Rebecca, Ge-1812
    Richard, Wl-1804, Je-1822, Je-1800
    Sherrod?, Mu-1811
    Thomas, Je-1822, Je-1800(2), D-1811,
        Gr-1805
    William, Gr-1805(2), Gr-1821(2),
        Ge-1812, Gr-1804, Gr-1799,
        Hu-1812
    William Jr., Ge-1812, Gr-1821
HANKS, George, Mu-1811, Mu-1816
    John, D-1805
    Moses Sr., Mu-1816, Mu-1811
    Moses Jr., Mu-1811
    Richard, D-1805, D-1811
    Thomas, Mu-1811, Mu-1816
    William, Mu-1816
    Zechariah, Wh-1811
HANLEY, Saml., Bo-1801, Bo-1800
    Saml. for J. Cowan, Bo-1801
    Ware, Wi-1815
HANN, Jacob, Gr-1805
HANNA, Andrew, Bo-1801
    George, B-1812
    James, A-1805
    James Sr., R-1819
    James Jr., R-1819
    John, R-1819, A-1805, C-1818
    John Jr., Bo-1800, Bo-1801
    John D., Sn-1811
    Joseph, Bo-1801
    Joshua, R-1819
    Martha, Sn-1816
    Robert, R-1819
    Robert Sr., Bo-1801
    Robert Jr., Bo-1801, Bo-1800
    Wm., Bo-1800
    Wm. Sr., Bo-1801
    Wm. Jr., Bo-1801, Bo-1800
HANNAH, Andrew, Su-1797, Wa-1814, Su-1796,
        Ge-1812, Wa-1819
    Isaac, Fr-1812
    James, Gi-1812, Sn-1792, Mu-1816,

HANNAH, James, cont'd, Sn-1787
    John, Gi-1812, Wl-1804
    John Doak, Sn-1787
    Joseph, D-1805
    Robert, B-1812(2), Bo-1805
    Samuel, Ge-1812, Ge-1805, B-1812
    William, Ge-1812, Ge-1805, B-1812
HANNE, Christopher, Ge-1812
HANNER, Wm., Sn-1816
HANNION, L. Washington, Mu-1811
HANNIS, Samuel, D-1805
HANOLD, Jonathan Jr., Ge-1812
HANS, John, Wa-1819
    Thomas, Wa-1819
    Young B., D-1811
HANSHAW, Washington, Ge-1812
HANSON, William, Ro-1805
HANSROD, JOh n, C-1818
HANSROE, John, C-1823
HANTS, Samuel Old, Co-1821
HANY, Francis, Sn-1787, Bl-1815
    James, Bl-1815
    John, Bl-1815
    Richard, Bl-1815
HANYMAN, Charles, D-1805
HARBER, Mills Theod., Mu-1816
HARBERSON, John, D-1811
HARBERT, David, Gr-1799
    Event, Sn-1816
    William, Wi-1801
    _____, Su-1796
HARBIN, Jarrett, A-1805
    Nathaniel, Rb-1812
HARBISON, James, K*-1815, B-1812
HARBOUR, Elisha, W-1812, Su-1812
    Elijah, Wl-1804
    Samuel, W-1812
HARBURT, James, Wh-1825
HARCEL, Eli, Wl-1804
HARDAMAN, N. P., Wi-1810
HARDAWAY, Edward, Rb-1812
    Joseph, Rb-1812(2)
HARDCASTLE, James, Fr-1812
    Robert, Fr-1812
    Eleazar, Wi-1815
    Elezeer, Wi-1810
    John, Wi-1801, Wi-1815
    N. P., Wi-1815
    Nichs., Wi-1801
    P. N., Mu-1816
    Peter, Wi-1810, Wi-1815
    Thos., D-1788, Wi-1815
    Thos. J., Mu-1816
HARDEMON, Robert, Mu-1816
    Thomas J., Wi-1810
HARDEN, Benjn., D-1788
    Edward, D-1805
    Francis, Wa-1819
    James, Mu-1816
    Jeremiah, Wi-1815
    Jerimiah, Wi-1810
    John, Wi-1810
    Johnson, Mo-1825
    Joseph, Wi-1810, A-1805, Ro-1805
    Presley, Wi-1801
    Thos., Wi-1801
    Thomas H., B-1812
    William, Ct-1796
HARDER, Jacob, Wi-1810
    James, Wi-1815, Wi-1810
    Jeremiah Jr., Wi-1815
    William, Wi-1815, Wi-1810, Wi-1801

HARDGRAVE, Francis, D-1811(2)
    Jas., Wi-1815
HARDGROVE, James, Wi-1810
HARDIMAN, John, Wi-1810
    N. P., Mu-1811
HARDIMON, Blackstone, Mu-1816
HARDIN, Bailey, Wi-1815, Wh-1811
    Burges, B-1812
    Calloway, Mu-1816
    Henry, Mu-1811
    Isaac B., Mu-1816
    John, Wi-1815, Ge-1812
    John Sr., Sn-1787
    Joseph, Ge-1783
    Jos. Sr., Sn-1787
    Mark, B-1812, Mu-1816(2), D-1805, B-1812
    Robert, Je-1822, Ge-1812
    Swan, Mu-1816
    Thomas, Wi-1810
    Thomas J., Wi-1815
    William, D-1805(2), Ct-1798, Ge-1812
HARDING, Giles, D-1805
    John, D-1811(2)
    Thomas, D-1805
HARDISON, Chas., Mu-1816
    James, Mu-1816
    Thos., Mu-1816
HARDMON, Joshua, Mu-1816
HARDY, Coleman, Gi-1812
    Hensley, D-1811
    Henson, D-1811
    Thomas, D-1811
HARE, William, Wa-1819
HARELSON, John, Gr-1799
    William, Gr-1799
HARETT, Joshua, B-1812
HARGIS, James J., Wh-1825
    William, Wh-1825
HARGISS, Abraham, Fr-1812
    John, Fr-1812
    Thomas, Fr-1812
    William, Fr-1812
HARGRAVE, B. William, D-1805
    Benj., Je-1800
    Eli, Je-1800
    Francis, D-1805
    George, D-1805
    Thomas, Co-1827
HARGROVE, John, Sn-1811
    Joseph, Je-1800
    Stephen, Wi-1815
HARINGTON, Charles, Sn-1792
HARIS, Thomas, Cl-1803
HARISON, Gillian, Bo-1800
    Jeremiah, Co-1821
    Thomas, Fr-1812
HARISS, Benchy, D-1805
    Humphrey, Fr-1812
    Richard, Gr-1805
HARKEN, Willm., Sn-1792
HARKER, John, Gr-1805, Sn-1792(2)
    Julias, Ro-1805
    Moses D., Mu-1816
    Willm., Sn-1792
HARKINS, Daniel, Wl-1804
HARKLEROAD, Henry, Su-1812
    Henry Jr., Su-1812
    Lawrence, Su-1812
    Martain, Su-1812
    Martin, Su-1812
    Samuel, Su-1812

HARKNESS, John, B-1812
HARKNEY, William, D-1811
HARKRIDER, John, Ro-1812
HARLAN, Elijah, Mu-1811
    Joseph, Sn-1792
HARLE, Baldwin, Je-1822
    Baldwin Jr., Je-1822
HARLESS, George, A-1805
    Henry Sr., A-1805
    Henry Jr., A-1805
HARLEY, Elisha, Gr-1799
    James, Su-1812
    John, Fr-1812
    Thomas, Fr-1812
    William M., Gi-1819
HARLIN, Thomas, D-1811
HARLISS, George, A-1805
    Henry Sr., A-1805
    Henry Jr., A-1805
    Philip, A-1805
HARLLY, John, Ge-1812
HARLOW, Esquire, Wh-1811
    John, Wh-1825
    Obadiah, Wh-1825
    Squier, Gr-1805
    Thurman, Wh-1825
    William, Wh-1825(2), Gr-1805
HARLS, Linton, D-1811
HARLSON, Andrew, Gi-1812
    William, Gr-1805
HARLY, James, Ge-1812
HARMAD, William, Gr-1804
HARMAN, John, D-1811
    Sterl., Mu-1816
HARMENTAGE, Isaac, Ge-1812
HARMON, Adam, Hu-1812, Wa-1819, Wa-1814
    Agness, Ge-1812
    Chrisley, Ge-1812, Ge-1805
    Christopher, Je-1800
    Esaiah, B-1812
    George, Ge-1805
    Gideon, B-1812
    Henry, C-1823, Ct-1798, B-1812
    Isaac, Ge-1812, Ge-1805
    Jacob, Ct-1798, Ge-1812, Ge-1805, Je-1822, Je-1800
    James, Gr-1804
    John, C-1823, B-1812, C-1818, Su-1812
    John Sr., Ge-1812
    John Jr., Ge-1812
    Jonathan, B-1812
    Joseph, Wa-1814
    Lewis, A-1805, B-1812, Gr-1804, B-1812, Je-1822, Je-1800, Gr-1805
    Miller, Gr-1805
    Moses, Ge-1812
    Paul, A-1805
    Paul Jr., C-1823
    Peter, Ge-1812
    Peter Sr., Ge-1805
    Philip, R-1819, Ge-1805
    Stephen, Ge-1805, Ge-1812
    Thomas, Ge-1805
    William, Gr-1805, Gr-1799, R-1819
HARN, Jacob, D-1811
    Levi, W-1812
HARNAY, William, D-1805
HARNESS, John, Mu-1816
    Joshua, C-1818
HARNEY, Thomas, D-1811

HARNNON, William, Gi-1819
HARON, James, Wi-1801
HARP, Beverly, W-1812
    Clabourne, W-1812
    Sampson, Wh-1825
    Thomas, W-1812
    William, Wh-1811, J-1802, C-1818
HARPEL, Robert, Mu-1811
HARPER, Britain, D-1811(2)
    Henry, Sn-1816, Sn-1811
    James, Sn-1811
    John, Sn-1811, D-1805, D-1811,
        W-1812
    Joseph, Sn-1811
    Richard, Cl-1803
    Rummers, Sn-1816
    Samuel, B-1812
    Summers, Sn-1811
    Thomas, Je-1800
    Wilkins, Wi-1815
    William, Sn-1816, D-1811
HARPETH, Bigg, Wi-1801
    West, Wi-1801
    Wm., Sn-1811
HARPOLE, Adam, Wl-1804, Sn-1792
    John, Wl-1804, Sn-1792
    Martin, Wl-1804, Sn-1792
    Paul, Wl-1804
    Solomon, Wl-1804
HARRALD, Richard, Wl-1804
    Uriah, Ge-1812
HARRASON, Isach, Ge-1812
HARRASS, Robert, Sn-1816
HARREL, David, B-1812
HARRELL, Charles, Wi-1815
    James, Fr-1812, Wi-1810
    William, Gr-1821
HARRELSON, David, J-1802
    John, Mu-1811
    William, Gr-1805
HARRIL, Shedrach, Mu-1811
HARRINGTON, John, Rb-1812
    Peter, Wa-1819, Su-1812, D-1811(2)
    Richard, D-1805
    Whitmill, Rb-1812
HARRIS, Abijah, R-1819(2)
    Alfred M., Gi-1812
    Allin, Wl-1804
    Andrew, Wl-1804
    Archibald H., D-1811
    Arthur, Wl-1804
    Bartlett, Wh-1825
    Benjamin, Wh-1825, Wa-1814, Wa-1819
    Blair, Sn-1816
    Bright B., Sn-1816
    Caddy, D-1811
    Christy, C-1823
    David, Je-1822
    Edmond, Mu-1811, Mu-1816
    Edward, Wl-1804, Wi-1801
    Elmor, Sn-1816
    Elmore, Sn-1811
    Evan, B-1812, Gr-1804, Gr-1821,
        Gr-1799, Gr-1805
    George, Je-1822, Wa-1819
    George C., Wa-1819
    Gideon, Rb-1812
    Howell, Rb-1812
    Isaac, Wh-1825, Gr-1821
    James, Hu-1812, Sn-1811(2), W-1805,
        Su-1796, Wa-1819, B-1812,
        Gr-1804, Fr-1812, Gr-1805(2),
        D-1811

HARRIS, James G., Gr-1821
    James W., Sn-1816
    Jeremiah, Su-1797, Su-1796
    Jesse, Gr-1821, W-1812, W-1805
    Joham, B-1812
    John, Mu-1816, Sn-1811, Wl-1804(2),
        Ge-1812, Gr-1821, B-1812(2),
        Bo-1801, Gr-1799, C-1818,
        Mu-1811
    John C., Wa-1814, Wa-1819
    Jonathan, Wh-1825, Bo-1801
    Jos., Sn-1816
    Mathew H., Sn-1816
    Matthew, Rb-1812
    Moody, D-1811
    Moseley, B-1812
    Nathaniel, B-1812, Wi-1815, Gi-1819
    Nehemiah, Gr-1805
    Newsom, D-1811
    Nimrod, Fr-1812
    Peter, Gr-1821(2), Gr-1799, Gr-1804,
        Fr-1812, Cl-1803, Gr-1799
    Peter Sr., Gr-1805
    Peter Jr., Gr-1805
    Rewben, Wh-1825
    Richard, Gr-1804, Gr-1805
    Richd. C., Mu-1816
    Robert, Gr-1805, Gr-1821, Wh-1811,
        Gr-1799, Gi-1819, Gr-1804,
        Sn-1811
    Robert, estate, Sn-1811
    Samuel, Gr-1799, Wi-1810, A-1805,
        Bo-1800, Wl-1804(2), Fr-1812,
        Bo-1801
    Samuel H., Fr-1812
    Shadrick, B-1812
    Simpson, D-1805
    Simson, Mu-1811
    Stuart, Gr-1805
    Susannah, D-1805
    Thomas, Gr-1821, Sn-1816
    Thomas A., Wi-1810
    Thomas K., Wh-1811(2)
    Thompson, Mt-1798
    Timothy, Wh-1825
    Wallas, Sn-1811
    West, Wl-1804, Mu-1816
    William, Sn-1816, Bo-1801, Gi-1819,
        Gr-1821, D-1805, D-1811(2),
        Gr-1805
HARRISE, Saml. B., B-1812
HARRISON, Alexr., Mu-1816
    Andrew, Rb-1812
    Ann, Wi-1815
    Benjamin, Je-1800
    C., Je-1822
    Daniel, Wa-1819, Fr-1812, Hu-1812
    Edmond, D-1811, Wh-1811
    George, Ge-1805
    Henry, Sn-1811
    Isiah, Ge-1805
    James, Fr-1812, Sn-1787, Sn-1792,
        Je-1800, Sn-1816, D-1805
    Jeremiah, Ge-1812, Ge-1805
    John, Hu-1812, B-1812(2), Je-1800
    Jonathan, Bo-1800, B-1812, Wh-1811
    Josiah, Co-1821
    Lewis, D-1811
    Mast, Mu-1816
    Matthew, Mu-1816
    Peter, Je-1822
    Reuben, Co-1821

HARRISON, Richard, D-1811
    Robert, B-1812
    Sally, Je-1822
    Samual, Wa-1819
    Samuel, Hu-1812
    Stith, Wl-1804
    Thomas, B-1812, Gr-1799
    Thomas Sr., Fr-1812
    Thomas Jr., Fr-1812
    Washington L., D-1811
    William, Su-1812, Wi-1815, Fr-1812,
        Wa-1819, Ct-1798, Ge-1805,
        Je-1800, Su-1797, Ge-1812,
        Wi-1810
    William P., Wi-1810
    Zacheriah, D-1811
    _____, Sn-1811
HARRISS, Alexander, Wh-1825
    Alinn, Fr-1812
    Archibald, D-1805
    Cornelius, Wh-1825
    Ephraim, D-1805
    Igerges?, Hu-1812
    John, Fr-1812, Wi-1815
HARRISSON, Jessee, D-1805
    John, D-1805
    John, Thomas & John, D-1805
    Joseph, W-1812
    Thomas, D-1805
HARROL, William, B-1812
HARROLD, Hedac?, Sn-1816
    John, D-1805
HARRYMAN, Charles, B-1812
    John, B-1812
HARSBERGER, John, Su-1812(2)
HART, Alexander, Bo-1801
    Alice, Bo-1800
    Andrew, Mo-1825
    Ann, Mt-1798
    Calep, Co-1827
    David, Sn-1816, B-1812
    Elisha, Mu-1816
    Hardy, Gr-1799
    Henry, Sn-1811, Rb-1812, Sn-1816
    J. Brown, C-1818
    James, Sn-1811, Sn-1816
    John, Mu-1816, Su-1812, Sn-1812
    Joseph, Mu-1816, Bo-1800, C-1818,
        Mu-1811, A-1805, C-1823,
        Bo-1801
    Leonard, Su-1796
    Matthew, Sn-1816
    Moses, B-1812
    Philip, D-1811
    Richard, D-1811, Mu-1811, D-1805
    Robert W., D-1811
    Susanah, Mt-1798
    Thomas, A-1805, Ge-1783
    Thomas, heirs, Mu-1811
    Wm. D., C-1823
HARTEN, James, Sn-1811
HARTGRAVE, John, Mu-1811
HARTLEROAD, Henry, Su-1796
    Martin, Su-1796
HARTLERWAR, Henry, Su-1797
    Martin, Su-1797
HARTLEY, Charles, D-1811
HARTMAN, George, D-1811, D-1805
    Henry, Wa-1819, Wa-1814
    Jacob, Su-1812
    John, Wa-1819, Wa-1814, D-1805
    Joseph, Wa-1819(2)

HARTMAN, Joseph Sr., Wa-1814
    Levi, Wa-1819, Wa-1814
HARTON, Josiah, D-1811
HARTS, Linton, D-1811
HARTSELL, Abraham, Wa-1814
    Hannah, Wa-1819, Wa-1814
    Isaac, Wa-1819, Wa-1814
    Jacob, Wa-1814, Wa-1819
HARTUL, James, Wh-1825
HARTWICK, Ayers, heirs, Sn-1811
HARTY, Daniel, Ge-1812
    Dennis, Ge-1805
    Jacob, Wh-1811
HARVELL, John, Gr-1821
HARVER, James, R-1808
HARVEY, Alexander, Gi-1812(2)
    Andrew, Gi-1812(2)
    James, Wa-1819(2), Wa-1814
    John, Je-1800, J-1802, Gi-1812
    Littleton, D-1805
    Martin, Wi-1801
    R. Littleberry, D-1805
    Robert, Gi-1812(2)
    Thos. G., Mu-1816
    Will Jr., Gi-1812
    Wm. Sr., Gi-1812
HARVY, John, Mt-1798
HARWELL, Abraham, Gi-1812
    Herbert, Rb-1812
    James, Gi-1812
    _____, Gi-1812
HARWICK, Jacob, Wh-1825
    Nicholas, Wh-1825
HARWOOD, Eli, D-1805
    John, D-1811(2), D-1805
    Thos., Gi-1812
    William, D-1811, D-1805
HASE, James, Mu-1811
HASKEL, Peter, Sn-1811
HASKELL, Joshua, D-1811
HASKET, John, Je-1800
HASKILL, John, K-1796
HASKINS, Thomas, Gr-1799, D-1811
HASLERIG, Richard, R-1819
HASLET (Hasley?), John, Rb-1812
HASLEY, David, A-1805
    John, Ge-1812, Rb-1812
HASPETH, Saml., Wi-1801
HASSEL, Elijah, Wi-1810
    Joseph, Wi-1810
    Zebulon, Wi-1810
HASSELL, Jarret, Sn-1811
    Jessee, Sn-1811, Wi-1815
HASSILL, Asa, Sn-1816
    Jesse, Sn-1816
    Jinnett, Sn-1816
HASTIN, Daniel, Wh-1811, Wh-1825
    David, Wh-1825, Wh-1811
    Joseph, Wh-1811, Wh-1825
HASTLER, Michael, A-1805(2)
HASWELL, Benjamin H., Wh-1825(2)
HATCH, Edward, D-1805
HATCHEL, Herod, B-1812
HATCHER, James, Su-1812
    John, Su-1812
    Thomas, Su-1812
    William, Su-1812, Se-1799, Su-1796,
        Su-1797
HATCHET, John, Mu-1811
HATCHETT, Archibald, Fr-1812
    Banister, D-1811
    John, Mu-1816

HATELY, Robert, B-1812
HATEN, David L., Wh-1825
HATFIELD, Andrew, C-1818, C-1823
    Davis, C-1823
    Esewick, C-1818
    George, A-1805
    Hyram, C-1823
    James, C-1818, C-1823, D-1805
    Jerimiah, C-1823
    John, Gr-1799, A-1805
    Jonothan, C-1818
    Jonthan, C-1823
    Joseph, A-1805, C-1818
    Richard, A-1805
HATHCOCK, Auston, B-1812
    Charles, B-1812
    Elisha, B-1812
    Howel, B-1812(2)
    John, B-1812(2), Gi-1812
    Philip, B-1812
HATHWAY, Leonard, Su-1797
HATLEY, John, B-1812
    Robert, B-1812
HATMAKER, Francis, C-1823, A-1805, C-1818
    Jacob, C-1823
    Wm., C-1823
HATTER, Michael, Je-1800
    Phillip, Je-1800
HATTS, John, Ro-1805
HAUK, Paulson, Ge-1812
HAULT, Jacob, D-1811
HAUMA, James, Mu-1811
HAUN, Abraham, Ct-1796, Je-1822
    Adam, Je-1822
    Christopher, Ct-1796
    Jacob, Je-1822, Gr-1821
    Mathias, Ct-1796
    Sebaustein, Ct-1796
HAUQUICK, John, Su-1812
HAUTON, James, B-1812
HAUTZ, Christopher, Ge-1812
    Jacob, Ge-1812
HAVARD, David, Sn-1792
HAVELY, Jacob, Ge-1805
HAVEN, John, Fr-1812
HAVENS, Daniel, Hw-1799, Fr-1812
    James, Je-1800
    John, Je-1800
    Zacharis, Hw-1801
HAVRON, James, Su-1796, Su-1797
HAW, John, D-1805
HAWK, Christopher, Fr-1812
    George, W-1812
    Jacob, W-1812
    Paulser, Ge-1805
HAWKE, John, Su-1796, Su-1812
HAWKIN, William, K-1799
HAWKINS, Benjamin, Mt-1798, Wh-1811
    Edward, A-1805
    Henry, Gr-1805, Su-1796, Gr-1799,
        Gr-1821, Su-1797
    Henry Jr., Gr-1805
    James, D-1805, Ro-1805
    John, Sn-1811, Sn-1816, Gr-1799,
        Gi-1812, Ro-1805, Su-1812,
        W-1812, Su-1796
    Mathew, K-1799
    Matthew, A-1805
    Nathan, Su-1796
    Nicholas, Su-1796, Su-1797
    Rebecah, Ge-1812
    Samuel B., Gr-1799

HAWKINS, Stephen, Mu-1811, Mu-1816
    Thomas, Gr-1805, Mu-1811, Gr-1799
    William, Je-1822, Mu-1816, Gi-1812
HAWKS, Jacob, Su-1812
HAWLEY, Francis, Su-1812
    James, Su-1812
HAWN, Abraham, Ct-1798
    Christopher, Ct-1798
    George, Ct-1798
    Jacob, Ct-1798
    Mathias, Ct-1798
HAWORTH, Absalom, Ge-1805
    Absalom Sr., Ge-1805
    George, Ge-1783
    James, Ge-1805(2), Je-1800
    Richard, Je-1800
    Willi, Je-1800
    William, Je-1822
HAWSLY, Jonathan, Sn-1811
HAY, Aron, D-1805
    Balaam, Wi-1815
    Basham, D-1805
    Benjamin, Wi-1801
    James, Bo-1800
    Jeremiah, Mu-1811
    John, Wi-1810, Wi-1815, Wi-1801
    Joseph, Wl-1804
    Richard, Wi-1810, Wi-1801, Wi-1815
    William, Wl-1804, Wi-1801, Wh-1825,
        Wi-1810
HAYES, Hugh, D-1811
    James, Mu-1816
    Oliver B., D-1811
    Robert, Rb-1812
    William, Rb-1812
HAYGOOD, Tapley, Gr-1799, Gr-1805
HAYLEY, William, Rb-1812
HAYLOR, Hugh O., Jr., Gr-1821
HAYNE, George, Hu-1812
HAYNELL, James, Gi-1812
HAYNES, Andrew, Gi-1812
    Elijah, Sn-1816
    George, Wi-1815
    Henry, R-1819
    James, Gi-1812
    James S., Gi-1812
    Jessee, Sn-1816
    John, Gr-1821, Gi-1812, Sn-1792(2),
        D-1805, Wh-1811(Harper?)
    Joseph, B-1812
    Peter, Sn-1811
    Richard, A-1805
    Robbert, Sn-1816
    Stephen, Rb-1812
    Sterling, C-1818, Gr-1821
    Thomas, Je-1822, Rb-1812
    William, Gr-1821
HAYNIC, George, Sn-1823
    Jesse, Sn-1823
    William, Sn-1823
HAYNIS, Jesse, SN-1811
HAYNS, Anderson, Wi-1815
    James, Mu-1811
    Joseph Sr., B-1812
    L. Alexander, Mu-1811
    Richard, A-1805
HAYS, Agnes, Mu-1816
    Alexander, Je-1822
    Andrew, D-1805, D-1811
    Balam, D-1811
    Battrick, W-1812
    Campbell, D-1811

HAYS, Charles, Wl-1804, D-1805(2), D-1811,
        B-1812
    David, D-1805, D-1811(2), Ge-1805
    Eleanor, Mu-1811
    Elijah, Wa-1819
    Ezekiel, Wa-1819
    George, Mu-1811
    Henry, D-1811
    Hugh, D-1805
    Jacob, Fr-1812
    James, D-1805, D-1811, Sn-1792,
        Ge-1812(2), Ge-1805(2), W-1812,
        Je-1822
    John, Mu-1811, Wi-1801, Wl-1804,
        Je-1800, Ge-1783, Wa-1819
    Jonathan, Mu-1811
    Joseph, D-1805, Sn-1792, Ge-1812,
        Ge-1805
    Lewis, Ge-1812
    Nicholas, Ge-1805
    Oliver B., D-1811
    Rachel, Mt-1798
    Robert, D-1805, D-1811, Wl-1804,
        Wi-1801, D-1788, Mt-1798,
        C-1818, Ge-1805, Ge-1812
    Samuel, D-1811
    Thomas, B-1812
    Tobert, Mt-1798
    W. Joseph, D-1805
    William, D-1805, Gr-1805, D-1811(2),
        Wi-1815(2), Gr-1804, Gr-1799,
        C-1823, A-1805, W-1812,
        Ge-1812
HAYSE, James, Sn-1787
HAYSLET, William, B-1812
HAYSTET, John, Sn-1816
HAYTER, Abraham, C-1818(2)
    Abraham Sr., C-1823
    Abraham Jr., C-1823
HAYWOOD, John, Mt-1798(2), D-1811
    William, Hw-1799
HAYWORTH, Abraham, Ge-1812
    Absom, Ge-1783
    Jas., Ge-1783
    Stephen, Je-1800
    William, Gr-1821
HAYWORTHY, Absolom, Ge-1812(2)
HAZLET, John, Sn-1816
HAZLEWOOD, Blaney, Je-1822
    Thomas, Je-1822
HEAD, Henry, Sn-1816
HEADERICK, Abraham, Wa-1814
    Charles, Wa-1814
    Jacob, Wa-1814
HEADLEY, Caleb, Gi-1812
HEADRICK, Henry, Ge-1805
    Jacob, Ge-1812(2)
    John, Ge-1805
    William Sr., Ge-1805
HEARD, James, A-1805, K-1799
    Jessee, W-1812
    Stephens, A-1805
HEART, Henry, B-1812
HEATH, John, Wh-1825
    Matthias, A-1805
HEATHER, Thomas, C-1823, C-1818
HEATHERICK, Jacob, Ct-1796
HEATHERLY, Ewins, Ct-1798
    Hugh, C-1823
    John, Ct-1798, Ct-1796, C-1823
    Thomas, C-1823
    Wm., C-1823

HEATAN, Enock, Wi-1815
HEATON, Elizabeth, D-1805
    John, Ct-1798, Ct-1796
    Robert, D-1805, D-1811(2)
    Thomas, D-1811
HECKNEY, Preston, B-1812
HEDDON, Hugh, Gi-1812
HEDDRICK, Joseph, Su-1812
HEDERICK, Henry, Ge-1812
    William, Ge-1812(2)
HEDGE, Robert, Sn-1817
HEDLEY, Blake, Se-1799
    Joseph, Se-1799
HEDRICH, John, Je-1822
HEDRICK, Abram, Su-1812
    John, Ge-1812
HEFFERTON, Archd., Gi-1812
HEFFNER, David, Wh-1285(2)
HEFTNER, George, Wh-1825
HELAM, Jonathan, Ge-1812
HELL, Caron, Mu-1811
    James, Mu-1811
HELLEY, John, Wi-1801
HELLUMS, James, A-1805
    Jonathan, A-1805
HELSLEY, Christian, Ge-1812
HELM, Fielding, Wi-1815
    Henry, Wa-1819, Wa-1814
    Henry & William B., Je-1822
    John, Wa-1814
    John, heirs, Wa-1819
    Meredith, Mu-1816
    Henry, Wa-1819
    Jacob, W-1812, W-1805
    James, Mu-1816
    John, Ro-1805, W-1812, J-1802,
        W-1805, Mu-1816
    Lonay?, Mu-1816
    Thos., Wi-1812
    William, Ro-1805
HELONS, Joseph, Sn-1816
HELTON, Abraham, B-1812
    Abraham Jr., B-1812
    Ann, Je-1822
    Edward, Wh-1825
    James, Mu-1811, Mu-1816
    Jesse, A-1805
    Mosses, Ct-1798
    Peter, Ct-1796(2), A-1805
    Petet, Ct-1796
    William, Je-1800
HEM, John, Bl-1815
HEMPHILL, Joseph, Gr-1799
    William, Wi-1815, Wi-1810
HENALSON, Abner, Mu-1816
HENDERSON, Alex., Bo-1800
    Andrew, Je-1800, Je-1822
    Benjamin, Wi-1810
    Bennet, Sn-1816
    Charles, Sn-1811
    Daniel, Ge-1805
    Danill, Sn-1811
    David, Je-1800
    Edward, Bl-1815
    Francis, D-1805
    George, Je-1822, Hw-1801
    James, Fr-1812, C-1818, Ge-1783,
        Se-1799, Ge-1812, Je-1822,
        J-1802
    John, Bl-1815, Je-1800, Ct-1796,
        Bo-1800, Bo-1801, Ge-1805,
        Ge-1812, Gi-1812, Gr-1821,
        D-1811, Sn-1816

HENDERSON, John (son of A.), Je-1822
    John Jr., Ct-1796
    Joseph, Bo-1801, Bo-1800, Ge-1812,
        Ge-1805
    Lawson, Sn-1816, Mu-1811
    Logan, Mu-1811(2)
    Loston, Mu-1811
    Nathan, Gi-1812
    Nathaniel, Wi-1810(2), Mu-1816,
        Mu-1811
    Noden, JE-1822
    Patsy, Sn-1816
    Peter, Ct-1796
    Pleasant, W-1812, W-1805
    Richard, Gr-1799, Mu-1816, Mu-1811
    Richard & Co., Gr-1799
    Robert, Je-1800, Wl-1804, Se-1799,
        Ge-1805, Ge-1812, W-1812,
        Wi-1810, Mu-1811
    Robert N., Je-1822
    S. William, Mu-1811
    Sammuel, Wi-1815
    Samuel, Fr-1812, Ge-1812, Ge-1805
    Shadrick, Bl-1815
    Thomas, Gr-1804, Gr-1799, Cl-1803,
        Co-1827, Sn-1816, Mu-1811,
        Gr-1805
    William, Gr-1799, Gr-1804, Ge-1783,
        Bo-1800, Bl-1815, Se-1799,
        Bo-1801, Je-1822, W-1812,
        Gi-1812(2), Wi-1801, Sn-1811,
        Mu-1816, Mu-1811, D-1805
    William, heirs, Je-1822
    William S., Mu-1816
    Wm. T., B-1812
    Wilson, Mu-1816
HENDLEY, George, Wa-1814, Wa-1819
    Isaac, Wa-1814(2), Wa-1819
    James, Wa-1819
    Joshua, Wa-1814, Wa-1819
    Elijah, A-1805
HENDRICH, Thomas, Sn-1787
HENDRICK, David, Fr-1812
    Jacob, Wa-1819
    James, Cl-1803
    Jeremiah, Sn-1811
    Jessee, Mu-1811
    Samuel, Wa-1819
HENDRICKS, Abner, Mu-1816
    Drucilla, Wl-1804
    Elijah, Hu-1812
    Jeremiah, Wl-1804
    John, Ct-1798, Ct-1796
    Jos., Sn-1792
    Joseph D., Wl-1804
    Solomon, Ct-1796, Ct-1798
    Tolbert, Sn-1816
    Wm., Gi-1819
HENDRIN, Abner, Mu-1811
HENDRIX, Albert, Sn-1811
    Thomas, Wi-1815
HENEGAR, Henry, Ge-1812
HENERY, Joseph, Wh-1825
    Samuel, Bo-1801(2)
    Thomas, Wh-1285
HENESLY, Benjamin, Wh-1825
HENGER, John, J-1802
HENLEY, Abner, J-1802
    Caleb, Mu-1816
    George, Hu-1812, Rb-1812
    John, Sn-1811
    William, Rb-1812(3), Sn-1811

HENLY, Caleb, Mu-1811, Mu-1816
    John, Fr-1812
    Moore, Fr-1812
    Samuel, Rb-1812
    William, Fr-1812
HENDRIX, Squire, A-1805
HENERY, Charles, Bo-1801
    James, Bo-1805
    Samuel, Bo-1805
    William, Bo-1805, Bo-1801
HENNEGER, Javon, Ge-1805
HENNESSEE, James, W-1812, W-1805
HENNEY, John, Sn-1816
HENNING, Alsua, Wl-1804(2)
    Pace, Wl-1804(2)
HENRDY, Thompson, Wa-1814
HENREY, Newton, Sn-1811
HENRY, Abraham, Ct-1796, Ct-1798
    Andrew, Wi-1801
    Benjamin, Je-1822
    Charles, Bo-1800
    David, Mt-1798, Sn-1811, Rb-1812,
        Sn-1816, Je-1822
    Eli, Wa-1819
    Ewen, Je-1822
    Ezekiel, Ro-1805, R-1808
    George, Wh-1825
    Hately, B-1812
    Hugh, Wl-1804, Je-1822
    Hugh Jr., Je-1822
    Isaac, Fr-1812, B-1812
    Isaiah, Mu-1816
    James, Fr-1812, Ge-1812, Gi-1812
    James Sr., Gi-1812
    James L., Gi-1819
    John, Wi-1810, Wh-1825, Wh-1811,
        Je-1822, R-1819
    John J., Wi-1815
    Josiah, Mu-1811
    Lofty, Je-1822
    Moses, Sn-1816
    Newton, Sn-1816
    Quist?, Wh-1825
    Robert, Gr-1850, Ge-1812
    Samuel, Fr-1812, Bo-1800
    Silas, Je-1822
    Spencer, Wa-1819
    Squire John, R-1808
    Thomas, Wl-1804
    Thomas B., Gi-1819
    William, D-1811(2), Sn-1811,
        Sn-1816, Je-1800, Bo-1800,
        Gi-1819, Ge-1812, Ro-1805,
        Je-1822, Gi-1812, Co-1821
HENSE, John, Sn-1811
HENSFORD, Andrew, Fr-1812
    Henry Sr., Fr-1812
    Henry Jr., Fr-1812
    John, Fr-1812
HENSHAW, John, Gr-1805
    William, Fr-1812
HENSLEY, Charles, Wh-1285
    Isam, Su-1797
    Obediah, Fr-1812
    Samuel, J-1802
    William, D-1805
HENSLY, John, Wa-1819
HENSON, Allen, Ro-1805
    David, Wh-1825
    Elisha, D-1811
    Green, Ro-1805
    Jesse, Sn-1816

HENSON, John, J-1802, Sn-1816
    Josiah, Sn-1816, Sn-1811
    Pall, Gr-1799
    Solomon, Sn-1816, Sn-1811
    Thomas, Sn-1816
    William, Sn-1811, Sn-1816(2)
HERALD, Elijah, Mo-1825
    John, Wa-1819, Mu-1816
HERBERT, Nathaniel, D-1811
    Richard, Wi-1815
HERD, James, Wh-1825
    Joseph, Wh-1825
HERENDEN, George, Je-1822
HERING, Heli, Sn-1811
HERMAN, Richard & Thomas, D-1805
HERMEN?, William, Mu-1811
HERMER, William, W-1812
HERNDEN, Samuel, Gr-1799
HERNDON, Benjamin Sr., Mu-1811, Mu-1816
    Benjamin Jr., Mu-1816, Mu-1811
    Cornelius, Sn-1811, Sn-1816
    John, Hu-1812
    Joseph, Mu-1816, Mu-1811
    Mary, Sn-1823
    Reuben, Fr-1812
    Stephen, Mu-1816
    William, Sn-1816
HERNERY, REuben, Co-1821
HERNEY, Augustin, D-1811
HEROD, John, Se-1799
HERRALD, Raba, Sn-1816
    William Sr., Gr-1804
    William Jr., Gr-1804
HERRAMON?, Stephen, W-1812
HERREL, Mashe, Ge-1812
HERRELSON, Major, Gi-1812
HERREN, A_____, D-1811
    Andrew, Wi-1810
    Beverly, D-1811
    Isaac, A-1805
    James, Wi-1815
    John, Hu-1812
    Lamuel, D-1811
HERRIN, Abner, Mu-1816
    Andrew, Wi-1815
    Delaney, C-1823
    James, Wi-1810
    John, Wi-1810
    Solomon, Mu-1816
HERRING, Peyton, Gi-1812, Wi-1810, Mu-1811
    Solomon, Mu-1811
    Stephen, Rb-1812
HERRINGTON, John, Gi-1812
HERROD, John, Wl-1804, Fr-1812
    Levi, Wl-1804
HERRON, David, Wh-1825, Wh-1811
    Eli, Sn-1816
    Ferguson, Wh-1825
    James, Wh-1811(2)
    Richard, Wh-1825
    William, Wh-1825(2), D-1811, C-1818
    William W., Gi-1819
HERSE, John, Bo-1801
HERSFERD, Chaels, Sn-1811
HESKET, George, Mu-1816
HESLEY, James, D-1811
HESLIP, Thomas, Fr-1812
    Wallace, Fr-1812
HESS, William, Wi-1801, Wi-1810
HESSE, John, Bo-1805
HESSELL, Asa, Sn-1811
HESTER, Henry, Gi-1819

HESTER, Robert, Wh-1825
    Stephen, Mu-1816
HESTON, Samuel, Mu-1816
HETER, Thomas, Wi-1815
HETHAWAY, Leonard, Su-1796
HETTON, William, Mu-1816
HEUY, Jesse, Rb-1812
    Joseph, Rb-1812
    William, Rb-1812
HEW, David, Mu-1816
HEWET, Patrick, Wh-1825
HEWITT, Benjamin, B-1812
    William, Su-1796
HEWS, James, Wi-1815
    Richard, Wi-1815
HEZIAH, Richard, Gr-1799
HIACH, T. M., K*-1815
HIBBARD, Lemuel, Gr-1799
HIBBERD, Jedediah, Je-1800
    Jediah, Gr-1804
HIBBS, Malon, A-1805
HICE, James, Ge-1812
HICK, Jacob, Hu-1812
    William G., Cl-1803
HICKASON, David, Sn-1811
    Richard, Sn-1811
    Samuel, Sn-1811
HICKERSON, Charles, D-1811
    John, Sn-1787
HICKEY, David, Ge-1783
    John, Wh-1825, Ro-1805
    Joseph, Mo-1825, Wh-1811
    Joshua, Wh-1825, Gr-1821, Gr-1804,
        Gr-1805
HICKLAND, John, Bo-1800
HICKLIN, John, D-1805
HICKMAN, Abner, D-1811
    Adam, Su-1812
    Benjamin, Wh-1825, Je-1800
    Bowen, D-1788
    Caleb, Je-1822
    Edward, Mt-1798
    Edwin, J-1802
    Elias, Je-1822
    Elisha, Je-1822
    Francis, Je-1800, Je-1822
    Henry, Je-1822
    Jacob, Su-1812
    James, Gr-1799, Je-1800
    John, A-1805
    Joseph, Sn-1811
    Joshua, Je-1822
    Mary, Sn-1816
    Peter Sr., Su-1812
    Snody, Wl-1804
    Stephen, Wh-1825
    Thomas, D-1811, D-1805
    William, Wi-1810, D-1805, Je-1822
    Wm. Sr., Wi-1810
HICKNEY, Michael, Ro-1805
HICKON, Charles, Wh-1825
HICKS, A. N., Gi-1819
    Abel, Sn-1816
    Alex, Se-1799
    Arthur, Gi-1812
    B. Smith, Su-1812
    Benjamin, B-1812
    Derry, Mu-1811
    Elijah, Mu-1816, K-1799
    Harrison, Gi-1819
    Henry, Sn-1792, Su-1796, Su-1812,
        Su-1797

HICKS, Isaac, Su-1797, Bl-1815(2)
    Isaac Sr., Su-1797
    Isaac Jr., Su-1797
    Jacob, Su-1797, Su-1796, Su-1812
    James, Wl-1804, Wi-1801, Wi-1810,
        Wi-1815
    James G., D-1811
    Job, Hu-1812
    Joel, Su-1812
    John, Wi-1801, Wi-1810(2), Sn-1811,
        B-1812, Sn-1787, Wi-1815(2),
        Gi-1819, Su-1812
    Joseph, Co-1821, Wa-1819
    Joshua, Mu-1811
    Nathaniel, Su-1812
    Richard, Su-1796, Wl-1804,
        Su-1797(3)
    Seat, Rb-1812
    Shadrach, Su-1796
    Shadrick, Su-1797
    Smith B., Su-1812
    Stephen, Su-1812(2), Su-1797,
        Su-1796
    Thomas, Mu-1811, Wi-1815
    William, B-1812, Su-1812, R-1819
    Willis, A-1805
    Zebedee, Wl-1804
HICKSON, Daniel, Gr-1821
    John, Gr-1821, Ge-1812
    Susanah, Ge-1812
HICKUM, Jacob, Su-1812
HIDE, Henry, Wl-1804
    William, C-1818
HIDEN, David, R-1819(2)
HIDER, Adam, Ct-1796
    Elizebeth, Ct-1796
    John, Ct-1796
    Michael, Ct-1796
HIGDON, James, Wl-1804
HIGGASON, David, Sn-1816
HIGGENBOTHAM, William, B-1812(2)
HIGGENBOTTON, Curtis, Rb-1812
HIGGINBOTHAM, Aron, W-1805, W-1812
HIGGINBOTTOM, Gabl., Gi-1812
    Wm., B-1812
HIGGINS, Barry, D-1811
    Bernard, Sn-1816
    Burrel, R-1808
    James, Wi-1810
    Joel, R-1808
    John, J-1802
    Martha, Wi-1810
    Phelomon, J-1802
    Samuel, Sn-1816
    Samuel D., Sn-1816
    Thomas, Wa-1819
    Wm. B., Li-1812
HIGGS, James, Mu-1816
HIGHBARGER, David, Ge-1812
HIGHS, Robert, B-1812
HIGHSMITH, Daniel, Rb-1812
    John, Mu-1811
HIGHTOWER, Abijah, A-1805
    Austin, Ge-1783
    Epaphroditus, Gr-1821
    Hardy, Gi-1812
    James, A-1805
    Joshua, Gr-1821
    Richard, Wi-1801, Ge-1783, Wl-1815
HIGS, John, B-1812
HIIPSHUR, Henry, Gr-1805
HILL, Abel, Gr-1821

HILL, Abraham, Wh-1811, Je-1822, Je-1800
    Alexander, Wl-1804, W-1812
    Alexander, Esq., W-1812
    Allen, Fr-1812, Wi-1815
    Allin, Wl-1804
    Benjn. F., B-1812
    Bennet, Mt-1798
    Caleb, Gi-1819
    Daniel, Fr-1812, Je-1800, Je-1822
    Daniel Jr., Je-1822
    Dann, Wi-1815
    Elijah, C-1823, Wh-1811, Je-1822,
        Wh-1825
    George, B-1812
    Green, Wi-1801, Wi-1815
    Henry, Fr-1812
    Hill, Je-1800
    Isaac, W-1812
    J. D., Wi-1801
    James, Gr-1799, Wi-1815, Wl-1804,
        B-1812, A-1805, Ge-1783,
        Cl-1803, Gi-1812, Wh-1811(2),
        Je-1822, Wi-1801, Mu-1811,
        Mu-1816
    James Sr., Gr-1821
    James Jr., Gr-1821
    Jeremiah, Fr-1812
    Jessee, B-1812, W-1812
    Jimmy, Wi-1815
    Joab, Gr-1799, Cl-1803
    John, Gr-1799, Cl-1803, Wi-1815,
        A-1805, Ct-1796, W-1812(2),
        R-1819, Je-1822, Gr-1821,
        Wh-1811, Ge-1800, Wi-1810,
        Wi-1801(2), Wi-1815, Mt-1798
    John D., Wi-1815, Wi-1810
    Jonas, Fr-1812
    Jonathan, K-1799
    Joseph, Je-1822, Je-1800
    Joseph Sr., Gr-1821
    Joseph Jr., Gr-1821
    M. Charles, D-1805
    Mathew, C-1823
    Matthew, C-1818
    Moses, Gi-1819
    Noddy, Hi-1822
    Peter, Bo-1800
    Phanoah, W-1812
    Pleasant, Ge-1812
    Richard, Wh-1811, W-1805
    Robert, B-1812, Wi-1815(2), J-1802,
        Je-1822, Je-1800, Mu-1811,
        K-1796
    Samuel, Ge-1805
    Samuel Sr., Je-1800
    Samuel Jr., Je-1800
    Spencer, Wi-1810, B-1812
    Stephen, Mu-1811
    Stephen D., Wh-1825
    Thomas, A-1805, Fr-1812, Gi-1812
        Wh-1811, Wi-1815, D-1811(2),
        Wh-1825(2), Mu-1816
    Thomas Jr., A-1805
    Walter, Wi-1815, Wi-1810
    William, Gr-1799, B-1812(2), Wh-1811
        Su-1812, Je-1800, Je-1822,
        D-1811(2), Wi-1815, D-1805,
        Wh-1825
    William C., Wi-1810
    William G., Sn-1816
    Wm. H., Wi-1815
    Winfield, Wh-1825

HILL, Heirs, Je-1822
HILLARD, Joel, Bl-1815
    Kemp, D-1805
HILLCUM?, Jepthah, W-1812
HILLES, Isaac, W-1812
HILLHOUSE, George, Gi-1812
    Robert D., Gi-1812
    Samuel, Fr-1812
HILLIARD, Isaac, Wi-1815
HILLS, Richard, B-1812
HILTON, Alexander, Gr-1821
    Arnold, Su-1796
    Charles, Su-1812, Su-1796
    James, Gr-1821, Su-1812, Su-1797
    John, Gr-1821, Su-1796, Su-1812
    Joshua, Gr-1805
    Richard, Gr-1805
    Stephen, Gr-1821
HIMALL, Robert, Ge-1783
HIMAN(Henson?), Edw. H., Fr-1812
HINCHA, William, Je-1800
HIND, Stephen, D-1811
HINDS, David, Mu-1811
    James, Gr-1821
    John, Wl-1804
HINES, Robert, Fr-1812
    Zachariah, Gr-1821
HINKEDD, John, Gr-1799
HINKLE, Anthony, Rb-1812
    George, Je-1800
    George Jr., Wa-1819
    Henry, A-1805
    Nathan, A-1805
    Peter, Rb-1812
HINSDON, Pumphrit, Fr-1812
HINSHAW, Ena, Je-1822
    George, Gr-1821
    John, Gr-1799, Gr-1804
    Margaret, Je-1822
    Uriah, Je-1822
HINSHEERS, Mathias, Gr-1799
HINSON, Houston, Bl-1815
    John, Ct-1798, Bl-1815
HINTER, Orthneal, Gr-1805
HINTON, Jeremiah, D-1805, D-1811
HIPSHEAR, Henry, Gr-1804
HIPSHEER, Henry, Gr-1799
HIPSHIRE, Henry, Gr-1821
    William, Gr-1821
HIRELY, Widow, Su-1812
HIRSE, John, Bo-1800
HISE, Jacob Sr., Ge-1812
    Jacob Jr., Ge-1812
HISSON, Andrew, Gi-1812
HIST, Meshack, D-1805
HISTON, James, A-1805
HITCHCOCK, Elijah, Wh-1811
    Ezekiel, Wh-1811, Wh-1825
    George, W-1812, W-1805
    James C., Wh-1825
    John, Wh-1811
    Moses, Hu-1812
    William, Wh-1811
    William Sr., Wh-1825
    William Jr., Wh-1825
HITE, Jacob, Wa-1819, Wa-1814
    John, Wa-1819, Wa-1814, D-1811
HITS, Richard, Fr-1812
HITSSON, John, Bl-1815
HITTERICK, John, Su-1796, Su-1797
    William, Su-1797, Su-1796
HIX, Abraham, Wa-1819, Wa-1814

HIX, Archibald, W-1812
    Harrison, Gi-1812
    Henry, W-1812
    John, Wi-1801, Gi-1812, Wa-1819
        Wi-1801
    Jonathan, Ge-1783
    Mashack, W-1812
    Robert, Mu-1816
    William, W-1812
HIXSON, Andrew, Ge-1812, Ge-1805
    Ephraim Sr., Bl-1815
    Ephriam Jr., Bl-1815
    John, Bl-1815
    Joseph, Bl-1815, Ge-1805
    Timothy, Ge-1805
    William, Bl-1815, Bo-1815, Ge-1805
HIZER, John, J-1802
HOBACK, Frederick, Su-1812
    Philip, Su-1812
HOBBS, Collin S., D-1811
    Edward D., D-1811
    Enos, A-1805
    Henry, Wh-1811
    James, A-1805, K-1799, Wl-1804,
        Bl-1812
    Job, K-1799
    Joel, Wi-1815, Wi-1810
    John, Wi-1815
    Poc?, K-1799
    Solomon, Gi-1812
    Stephen, D-1811
    Thomas, Gr-1805
    William, D-1811, Wi-1815
HOBDEY, Wm., Sn-1816
HOBMS?, Dannel, Bl-1815
HOBS, John, Wi-1810
HOBSON, Davison, Gi-1819
    Henry, Mu-1811
    John, D-1811
    Lawson, Gi-1812
    William, D-1811
    Younger, Gi-1819
HODD, Robert, R-1819
HODGE, Ambrose, Gr-1805, Gr-1804
    Ceban, Sn-1811
    Edmond, Wa-1819
    Francis, D-1811, D-1805, Su-1797,
        Su-1812, Su-1796
    George, D-1811
    Howel, Wa-1814
    James, Mu-1816, Gr-1805, D-1811,
        D-1805, Sn-1792, Gr-1804,
        Gr-1821
    Jesse, Gr-1821
    John, Gr-1805, Mu-1816, Sn-1811,
        Gr-1804, Wa-1819, Gr-1821
    John Jr., Gr-1805
    John D., Sn-1811
    Joseph, Sn-1811
    Lamuel, Sn-1816
    Luther, Gr-1805
    Mesheck, Gr-1804
    Moses, Gr-1804, Gr-1805
    Philip, Gr-1821
    Robert, Sn-1816
    Rolin, Wa-1814
    Thomas, C 1823, Wi-1815
    Welcome, Gr-1805, Gr-1804
    William, B-1812, Sn-1811
    _____, D-1788
HODGES, Abner, Wh-1825
    Allen, Su-1812

HODGES, Ambrose, Gr-1799, Gr-1804
    Asa, Sn-1811
    Calloway, Je-1822
    Charles, B-1812, Je-1800
    Charles Sr., Je-1822
    Charles Jr., Je-1822
    David, Sn-1811
    Drury, Ge-1783
    Edmond, Gr-1821, Je-1822, Je-1800
    Edmond Sr., B-1812
    Edmond Jr., B-1812
    Edward, Wa-1819
    Eli, Gr-1821
    Henry J., Je-1822
    James, Gr-1805(2), Gr-1804, Wl-1804,
        Gr-1799
    Jesse, Wl-1804, Gi-1812, Wl-1804
    John, Gr-1805, Fr-1812, Gr-1804,
        Je-1822, Gr-1821
    Joseph, Sn-1816
    Josiah, Wl-1804
    Moses, Gr-1799, Je-1822
    Robin, Wa-1819
    Welcome, Ge-1783
    William, Gr-1805, Su-1797, Su-1796,
        Wl-1804, Su-1812
HOFFMAN, Balcher, D-1805
    Michael, D-1805
HOG, Absalom, Wh-1811
    Thomas, Mt-1798
HOGAIN, William C., Je-1822
HOGAN, Daniel, D-1805
    David, Mt-1798, Mu-1811
    Edward, W-1805, D-1788, Sn-1792,
        Sn-1787, W-1812
    James, Bo-1800
    John, Mu-1816
    John Sr., Mt-1798
    John Jr., Mt-1798
    Richd., Sn-1792
    Thomas, Mt-1798
HOGARD, James, Wa-1819
HOGE, Abner, Wh-1825
    James, Fr-1812
    Jno., Wi-1801
    Joseph, A-1805
    Miles, Fr-1812
HOGEN, Daniel, D-1788
HOGES, Ashford, Sn-1811
HOGG, Archilis, Gr-1804
    John, D-1811
    John B., B-1812
    Obediah, Gr-1799
    Reubin, Gr-1799
    Saml., Bo-1801
HOGGARD, James, Su-1812
HOGGATT, Anthony, Ge-1805
    John, D-1811, D-1805
HOGGET, Soloman, Je-1800
HOGGETT, Anthony, Ge-1812
HOGH, Andrew, W-1812
HOGIN, Edward, Sn-1787
HOGSHEAD, William, A-1805
HOGUE, James, Mo-1825
    Jonathan, Mt-1798
HOKETT, Michael, B-1812
HOLADAY, Benjamin, K-1799
    Peter, Wi-1810
    William, K-1799
HOLAWAY, Henry Sr., Wi-1815
    John, Bo-1801
    William, Je-1800

HOLBERT, Enos, W-1812, W-1805
    James, Wi-1810
    Joel, Wi-1810
    John, Wi-1810
HOLBROOK, George, B-1812
    Henry, B-1812
HOLCOMB, James, Mu-1816
    Lewis, Mu-1816
    Will., Mu-1816
HOLD, David Sr., Gr-1799
    Nickolas, D-1805
HOLDAWAY, Timothy, Je-1800
HOLDEN, John, B-1812
    John Jr., Wh-1825
    Joseph, Wh-1825
HOLDER, Bledsaw, Fr-1812
    John, Fr-1812(2), Wh-1811
    John Sr., Wh-1825
    Mastin, Fr-1812
    Moses, Fr-1812
    Ridech, Mu-1816
    Solomon, D-1811(2), Fr-1812
    Spencer, Wh-1825
    Yassy, Fr-1812
HOLDMAN, John, Bl-1815
HOLDWAY, Henry, Je-1822
    John, Je-1822
    Joseph, Je-1822
    Preston?, Sn-1811
    Timothy, Je-1822
    William, Je-1822
HOLDY, Thomas, D-1805
HOLEBROOK, Ezekiel, B-1812
    Henry, B-1812
HOLEMAN, Charles, Wl-1804
    Daniel, Rb-1812, Mo-1825
    James, Rb-1812
    Joshua, Rb-1812
    Nathan, Wl-1804
    Thos., Rb-1812
    William, Mt-1798
    Yancy, Wi-1815
HOLEMON, Absolom, J-1802
    Thos., Sn-1816
HOLES, James, Mt-1798(2)
HOLIDAY, Henry, Wi-1810
    Thomas, Sn-1811
HOLINGER, John, Wa-1814
HOLINSWORTH, Jacob, W-1812
HOLKRUM, Merida, Hu-1812
HOLLAND, Daniel, Wh-1811
    Fedrick, Sn-1811
    Gustavus, Wi-1815
    H. Thomas, Mu-1811
    Harphry, B-1812
    Harrison, Wh-1825, Wh-1811
    Hemp, Wi-1810
    Isaac, R-1819
    James, Rb-1812(2), Sn-1811, Mu-1811
        D-1805, Mu-1816, Wh-1825
    John, Su-1797, R-1819, W-1812
        Rb-1812, Ro-1805
    Kempt, Wi-1815
    Nathan, Wh-1811
    Samuel, R-1819
    Thos., B-1812(2), Hu-1812
    Wilie, Rb-1812
    William, Ro-1805, Su-1797, Rb-1812,
        Wh-1825
HOLLANSWORTH, John, Mu-1811
HOLLAWAY, John, K-1799
HOLLEN, Gustavis, Wi-1810

HOLLEY, John, Gr-1804, Gr-1805
    Jonathan, Sn-1816
HOLLIDAY, David, Wi-1810
HOLLIMAN, John, Wi-1815
HOLLINGSWORTH, Daniel, C-1818, C-1823
    E. V., C-1818
    James, C-1818, C-1823
    John G., Mu-1816
    Joseph, D-1811
    Josiah, Gr-1821
HOLLINSWORTH, Daniel, Wh-1825
HOLLIS, Isaac, Mu-181
    James, Mu-1811, Mu-1816, Sn-1811
    Jesse, Sn-1811, Sn-1816
    Morgan, Sn-1816
    Samuel, Rb-1812
    Stephen, Mu-1816
HOLLOWAY, Bramillion, R-1819
    James, Fr-1812
    Jeremiah, C-1818, C-1823
    John, Su-1797, Su-1796, Wi-1815, C-1823
    Richard, Sn-1816
    Robt., Sn-1816
    William, Ge-1805, C-1823
HOLLUM, William, Wh-1825
HOLLUMS, James, K-1796
    William Jr., K-1796
HOLLUP, Wm. T., D-1811
HOLLY, Elizabeth, Ge-1783
    James, Fr-1812
HOLMES, Abijah, D-1811
    Albert, Sn-1811
    Ann, Mu-1816
    Archd., Mu-1816
    Edward, Wh-1825
    Isaac, B-1812
    James, W-1812, B-1812
    John, B-1812, D-1811
    Moses, Mu-1816
    Phineas, B-1812
    Robert, Mu-1816, Sn-1816
    Robert Jr., Sn-1816
    William, D-1805
HOLMAN, James T., Wh-1825
    Malichea, Sn-1811
    Peter, by G. S., Je-1800
    William, Bl-1815
HOLMARKS, William, A-1805
HOLMEN, William, Mu-1811
HOLMS, James, Wa-1819
    Moses, Mu-1811
    Solomon, Mu-1811
HOLOMAN, Alx., Sn-1816
    Benjamin, Rb-1812
HOLOWAY, Samuel, Sn-1811
HOLSTEAN, Westley, D-1811
HOLSON, Henry, Gr-1805, Gr-1821
    John, Mo-1825
    William, Mo-1825
HOLT, Abner, Wi-1810
    Ambrose, Mu-1816
    Barrott, Ge-1805
    Christopher, D-1805
    David, Gr-1850(2), Gr-1804(2), Gr-1799, Gr-1821, Ge-1812
    Edmond, Gr-1805, Gr-1804, B-1812
    Edward, Gr-1799
    George, D-1805
    Hardin P., Wi-1815
    Henry, Gr-1821, C-1818, Wh-1811
    Irby, Bl-1815

HOLT, Jacob, Wa-1814, Wa-1819
    James, B-1812(2), Gr-1804, Gr-1821, Gr-1805(2), D-1805, Sn-1816
    John, Wa-1819, Wh-1811, Wi-1815(3), D-1805, Mu-1816
    John Sr., Gr-1805(2)
    Joseph, Gr-1805, D-1811, B-1812, Be-1805, Ge-1812(3)
    Michael, Gr-1804, Gr-1805
    Nicholas, B-1812
    Norman, Wa-1819
    Robert, D-1811
    Shedrick, B-1812
    Simon, Su-1796, Su-1797
    Will, Sn-1811
    William, D-1811, Mu-1811, Mu-1816, B-1812
HOLTEN, Daniel, Bo-1801
HOLTON, John, Bo-1801
    William, Mu-1811
HOLTSINGER, John, Wa-1819
HOLWAY, Whitfield, Sn-1816
HOMER(Horner?), David, K-1799
HOMER, John, Gi-1819
HOMES, James, Wi-1815
    Luke, Wi-1815
    Robert, Sn-1811
    Thomas, D-1811
HONEYCUTT, John, Mu-1811
    Robert, Gr-1804, Gr-1805
    William, Mu-1811
HONLEY, John S., Wa-1819
HONN?, Jeremiah, W-1812
HOOD, Abraham, Ge-1805
    Alexr., Gi-1812
    Austin, W-1812
    Charles, Hu-1812, Bo-1805
    David, D-1805
    Demsey?, W-1812
    Edward, Wi-1815
    Huthson, C-1818
    Isaac, W-1812
    James, W-1812, Gr-1804, Gr-1805
    John, Co-1821, Mu-1811, Ge-1812
    John B., Ge-1812
    Nathaniel, Ge-1805
    Robert, R-1819, Ge-1783
    Samuel M., Ge-1812
    William, W-1812, Ge-1805, Gr-1805, Gr-1804(2), Hu-1812, Wh-1825
HOOFMAN, William, Sn-1816
HOOKER, John, Fr-1812, Wa-1819
    Nathan, B-1812
    Richard, B-1812
    Robert, Ct-1798
    Thomas, Wi-1801
    William, Ct-1798, Ct-1796, W-1812, Wi-1810
HOOKS, James, Gi-1819
    Robert, Bo-1800, Bo-1801
HOOP, Absolom Jr., D-1811
HOOPER, Absolom, D-1811
    Arron, D-1805
    Baily, Hu-1812
    Church, D-1805
    Edward, Wh-1825
    Innis, Bl-1815
    James, Wi-1804
    Jesse, D-1811
    Jessee, D-1805
    John, B-1812
    Joseph, D-1811, D-1805

HOOPER, Nimrod, D-1811
    Obadiah, B-1812
    Richard, B-1812
    Thomas, D-1805, D-1811
    William, Mt-1798
HOOSER, John, Ct-1796
    Randolph, Ct-1798
HOOVER, Andrew, Sn-1816, Sn-1811
    Henry, Sn-1816
    J. C., C-1823
    Martin, B-1812
    Michael, Su-1812
    Valentine, W-1812
HOPE, Adam, D-1805, D-1811, Sn-1811
    Eli, Wi-1810, Gi-1819
    James, Mu-1811, Wi-1810, Wi-1801,
        Ro-1805
    James, heirs, Wi-1815
    John, D-1811
    Samuel, D-1811
    Thomas, D-1811, A-1805
    William, Wi-1815
HOPKINS, Benjm., W-1812
    Davd., Sn-1811
    James, Wi-1815
    Jason, Wi-1815
    Joseph, D-1805, Mu-1816, Mu-1811
    Lahugh, Gi-1819
    Thomas, Sn-1816, Gr-1821, Su-1812,
        Wh-1811
    William, Wh-1825, B-1812
HOPPER, Archabald, Gr-1805
    Archebel, Gr-1805
    Archeble, Gr-1799
    Archibald, Gr-1804
    Charles, Gr-1805, Gr-1804, C-1823,
        Je-1800
    Frederick Sr., D-1811
    Harris, Ge-1812
    James, D-1811
    Joseph, D-1811
    Seamore, Gr-1821
    Thomas, Gr-1805, D-1811, Gr-1804,
        Gr-1805
    William, Ge-1805
HOPSON, William, Ro-1805
HOPTON, Aron, Ge-1812
HOPWOOD, William, B-1812
    Willis, B-1812
HORACE, William, D-1811
HORD, William, Gr-1799, Cl-1803
HORDAN, John, Wa-1814
HORIDGE, Henry, A-1805
    William, A-1805
HORN, Etheldred, D-1811
    Jabez, D-1811
    Jacob, Ge-1812
    John, Su-1812
    Joshua, Gi-1819
    Mathew, D-1811
    Philip, Su-1797
    Tom, Gi-1819
    William, Gi-1812
HORNBACK, John Sr., Je-1800
HORNBARGER, Philip, Mt-1798
HORNBERGER, Jacob Sr., Wa-1814
    Jacob Jr., Wa-1814
HORNDAY, Solomon, B-1812
HORNE, Richard, Wh-1811
    Sherod, Wh-1811
    Thomas, Wh-1811
HORNER, Cavalier, Je-1822

HORNER, George, Je-1800
    Isaac, Je-1822
    James, Gr-1799
    John, Gr-1804, Gr-1799
    Thomas, Gr-1805, Je-1822, Gr-1804
    William, Gr-1805, Je-1800, Gr-1804
    William Sr., Je-1822
    William Jr., Je-1822
HORNES, Thomas, Ro-1805
HORNESLEY, Burrell, Ro-1805
HORNEY, Alexander, Je-1822
    Thomas, D-1805
HORNLEE, Jacob, D-1805
HORSEAM, Joab, Hw-1799
HORSEAN, Joseph, Hw-1799
HORSLEY, Charles, Sn-1823
    James, Sn-1823
    Robert, Sn-1823
    William, Sn-1823
HORTEN, Daniel, Wa-1814, Wa-1819
    Isaac, Wa-1814, Wa-1819, C-1823
HORTON, James, A-1805, C-1823
    John, Ge-1812, Ge-1805
    Joseph, A-1805
    Nathaniel, C-1823
    William, K-1799, C-1823
HOSBRING, William, Gr-1799
HOSKERG, Ninly, Cl-1803
HOSKINGS, Thomas, Cl-1803
HOSKINS, Elias, Gr-1799
    George, A-1805
    James, Je-1822
    Jesse, Je-1800, A-1805
    Jessee, B-1812
    John, A-1805
    Niley, Cl-1803
    William, Je-1822, A-1805, Je-1800
    William Ck., Je-1822
HOSONBERGER, Jacob, Wa-1819
HOSS, Abraham, Wa-1814, Wa-1819
    Adam & Mather, D-1805
    George, Wa-1814(2)
    Henry, Wa-1814, Wa-1819
    Isaac, Wa-1814, Wa-1819
    Jacob, Wa-1814
    John, Wa-1814, Wa-1819(2)
    Margaret, Wa-1819
    Sarah, Wa-1819, Wa-1814
HOST, Dudley, B-1812
HOSTLER, Michael, A-1805(2)
HOTCHHISS, Jared, Ro-1805
HOTNER, Isaac, B-1812
HOTSIPILLER, Jacob, Wa-1819
HOTSPILLER, Jacob, Wa-1814
HOTTON, Charles Jr., D-1811
HOUBER, Christian, B-1812
    Jacob, B-1812
HOUKS, Matthias, Wl-1804
HOUSE, Cagan, Sn-1811
    Elizabeth, Sn-1811
    George, Sn-1811
    Isaac, Wi-1801, Wi-1815
    Isham, Wi-1815
    Jacob Sr., Wl-1804
    Jacob Jr., Wl-1804
    James, Wi-1815, Wh-1811
    John, Sn-1816, Wi-1815, Sn-1811,
        Wl-1804
    Joseph, B-1812
    M_____, Sn-1816
    Thos., Sn-1816
    William, Wi-1815, Je-1800

HOUSELEY, Robert, Su-1797, Su-1796
HOUSELY, John, Je-1822
HOUSER, George, Su-1812
    John, Su-1797, Wa-1819, Su-1796,
        Ct-1796
    John P., Mu-1816
    Josiah, Mc-1825
    Michael, Su-1812
    Nicholas, Su-1796, Su-1797
HOUSLEY, Joseph, C-1823
    Robert, Su-1812
HOUSON, R., K*-1815
HOUSTIN, James, Mu-1811
HOUSTON, Archabel, Wi-1801
    Archibald, Gi-1819
    Aron, Wi-1815
    David, Wi-1801, Wi-1815
    Edwd., Mu-1816
    James, Wi-1801, Mu-1811, Mu-1816(2),
        Ge-1805, Bo-1801, Gi-1819,
        Bo-1800(2), Ge-1783, Bo-1801
    John, Wi-1801, Mt-1798, Wa-1814,
        Ro-1805, Bo-1800, B-1812,
        Bo-1801, Wa-1819
    Richard, Mu-1816
    Robert, K-1796, C-1818, C-1823
    Samuel, Bo-1800, Bo-1801
    Walter, Wh-1811
    William, Wi-1801, Ge-1805, Ro-1805,
        Wa-1819, Bo-1800, Bo-1801
HOUTS, Christopher, Ge-1805
HOVAL, Jacob, Ge-1805
HOVAS, Peter, Li-1812*
HOW, Benjamin, Mu-1816
HOWARD, Abraham, Gr-1804, R-1819(2),
        Gr-1805
    Abram, W-1812
    Adol Sr., Ro-1805
    Adol Jr., Ro-1805
    Alexr., Je-1800
    Baldwin, Su-1812
    Bolen, Gr-1799
    Cannon, Mu-1811
    Chichester, Sn-1811
    Elisha, Wh-1825
    Ezekiah, Ge-1812
    Ezekiel, Ge-1805
    F_____, Sn-1811
    George D., Wh-1825
    Green B., Sn-1816
    Henry, Je-1800
    Isaac, Wh-1825
    Jacob, Wa-1819
    James, Fr-1812, Je-1800, Mu-1811,
        Sn-1811, Sn-1816, Mu-1816
    John, Ct-1796, Ct-1798, Gr-1804(3),
        Wa-1819, Ro-1805, R-1808
    John Sr., Je-1800
    John Jr., Je-1800
    Joshua, D-1788
    Nathan, Rb-1812, A-1805
    Nees, Wh-1825
    Perminas, estate, Mu-1811
    Peter, Wh-1825
    Portman, Wh-1825
    Richard, Gr-1799, Gr-1804, Ge-1783,
        Gr-1805(2)
    Robert, Gr-1799, Wh-1811, Su-1812,
        Wh-1825(2)
    Samuel, A-1805, Mo-1825, Je-1822
    Samuel P., Rb-1812
    Sarah, Sn-1811

HOWARD, Shadk., Gi-1812
    Thomas, A-1805
    William, Gr-1799, C-1818, Gr-1804,
        W-1812, Wh-1811, Wh-1825(2),
        Gr-1805, D-1811
HOWATH, Absalom, Ge-1805
HOWDERSHELL, Henry, Ge-1812
HOWDESHALL, Henry, Sn-1792
HOWE, Charles, Wa-1819
    _____, Bl-1815
HOWEL, Benjamin, Gr-1805, Gr-1799
    Caleb, Gr-1805, Gr-1804
    Calib, Gr-1805
    Calip, Gr-1799
    Henry, Gr-1805, Gr-1799
    James, D-1811, Gr-1805
    John, Mu-1811, Gr-1805, Wl-1804,
        Wh-1825, Gr-1799, Gr-1821
    Malikiah, Gr-1805
    Melchiah, Gr-1799
    Meleciah, Gr-1805
    Philip, Ge-1805, Ge-1812
    Phillip, Wl-1804
    Thomas, Sn-1811
    William, Gr-1805, Gi-1819
HOWELL, Benjamin, Gr-1805
    Christopher, Ro-1805
    Elijah, W-1805, W-1812
    George, Mu-1811
    Henry, Gr-1805, Gr-1804
    James, Gr-1804, Gi-1812
    John, Gr-1804, Gr-1821, Gi-1812,
        Mu-1811
    Joseph, Wi-1810, Wi-1815
    Joseph B., B-1812
    Malachi, Gr-1821, Gr-1804
    Thomas, Sn-1811
    William, Gr-1799, Gr-1804, Je-1822,
        Gr-1805
HOWERTON, Edward, R-1819
    Grief, R-1819
    Jackson, R-1819, R-1808
    Jerimiah, R-1819
    John, R-1819, Je-1822
    Micajah, R-1819
HOWETH, William, Gr-1799
HOWEY, Richard, Je-1822
HOWITT, Robert, D-1805
HOWLE, Blackstone, Wh-1825
    Lewis, Wh-1825
HOWLETT, William, D-1811(2)
HOWLLETT, George, D-1811
HOWSTON, David, Wi-1810
    Liddy, Wi-1810
HUBARD, Edward, Wl-1804
    James, W-1812
    Joseph, Wl-1804
    L., Ge-1783
    Thomas, D-1805
    Zebulun B., Sn-1792
HUBBART, Bengamin, Sn-1811, Sn-1816
    John, Sn-1811, Sn-1816
    William, Sn-1811, Sn-1816
HUBBERD, Robert, Bo-1805
HUBBERT, Matthew, R-1819
    Michand, D-1811
HUBBS, Thomas, D-1805
HUBERT, Nathaniel, B-1812
HUBS, Caleb, Ge-1783
HUCHESON, Samuel, Bo-1801
HUCHISON, William, Sn-1816
HUCKABY, James, C-1823

HUCKABY, John, C-1818(2)
    Thomas, C-1818
    William, C-1818, C-1823
HUCKER, Normand, B-1812
HUCKERSON, John, Sn-1792
HUDDLESON, John, K-1796
HUDDLESTON, David, Gr-1805
    David Sr., Gr-1804, Gr-1805
    David Jr., Gr-1804
    Daniel Sr., Gr-1805
    James, J-1802, Mu-1811
    John, Rb-1812, Gr-1805
    Jonathan, Rb-1812
    Joseph, Mu-1816, Mu-1811
    Josiah D., Rb-1812
    Robert, Gr-1821
    Samuel, J-1802
    Thomas, Gr-1805, Gr-1804, R-1819
    Wm. Sr., Rb-1812
    Wm. Jr., Rb-1812
HUDEBURGH, Thomas, Ct-1798
HUDEBURK, Thomas, Ct-1796
HUDELTON, John, Gr-1799
HUDGENS, Edward, D-1811
    James, D-1811
    William, D-1811
HUDGINGS, Ambrose, Gr-1799
    James, Wh-1825
    Robert, Gr-1805
HUDGINS, Robert, Gr-1799, Gr-1804
HUDLESTON, Robert, Gr-1805
HUDLON, John, Rb-1812
HUDSON, Abel, Wh-1811
    B. Adam, Mu-1811
    Benjn., Hu-1812, Gr-1804, Gr-1799,
        Gr-1805, Sn-1811
    Burrel, Wh-1811, A-1805
    Chamberlin, Hu-1812, Sn-1811
    Dawsey, Hu-1812
    Drury, Sn-1811
    E. G., Hu-1812
    Edward, Mu-1811, Mu-1816
    Ezekiel, Gr-1799
    George, Wh-1811, Wh-1825
    Isaac, D-1811, Wh-1825
    James, Gr-1799
    Jessee, B-1812(2)
    John, Gr-1799, Wi-1815, Rb-1812,
        Sn-1816(2), Sn-1811
    John Jr., Rb-1812
    Jos.?, D-1805
    Obediah, Gr-1799
    Pink, Wh-1811
    Richard, Bo-1801, Bo-1800
    Thomas, D-1805, Fr-1812
    Thomas Sr., Rb-1812
    Thomas Jr., D-1811
    William, D-1811, Wh-1825, Wi-1810
    William T., Je-1822
    Zadich, Gi-1819
HUDSPEATH, Thos., Mu-1816
HUDSPETH, Charles, J-1802
    Connel, Mu-1811
    Council, Mu-1816
    John, Ge-1812
    Robert, Fr-1812
    Thomas, Mu-1811
    William, Fr-1812
HUELLE, Samuel, Je-1800
HUES, John, Ro-1805
HUESTON, Saml., orphans of, Wi-1815
HUEY, James, Mu-1811

HUEY, John, Rb-1812, Mu-1816
HUFF, John, Ge-1812
    Joseph, Ge-1812
    Leonard, Ge-1805
    Voluntine, Gi-1812
    William, Co-1827, Wh-1825
HUFFAKER, Michel, A-1805
HUFFMAN, Andrew, Ge-1805
    Balren, Rb-1812
    Christopher, Wh-1825
    Daniel, Ct-1798, Ct-1796
    David, Wa-1819
    Jesse, Ge-1805
    John, B-1812, Je-1800
    Matthias, Su-1812
    Michael, Rb-1812
    Peter, Su-1796, Su-1797
    Wm., Rb-1812
HUFFSTADLER, David, Ge-1805
HUFFY, Henry Jr., Hw-1801
HUFHINE, Philip, Wa-1814
    Phillip, Wa-1819
HUFMAN, Adam, Wa-1814
    David, Wa-1814
    Henry, Wa-1814, Wa-1819
    Jacob, Wa-1814
    Jesse, Wa-1819
HUGGINS, Bernard, Mu-1816
    Charles, Mu-1816
    John, D-1805
    Rubin, Wi-1810
HUGGONS, Charles, Mu-1811
    James, Mu-1811
HUGH, George, B-1812
    Joel, B-1812
    John, D-1811
    John Scott, Sn-1811
    William, Fr-1812
HUGHBANKS, William, D-1811
HUGHES, Aaron, Je-1800
    Abner, Su-1797, Su-1796
    Alewen, Su-1812
    Christopher, Wh-1825
    David, Su-1796(2), Su-1812, Sn-1792,
        Su-1797
    Elijah, Rb-1812
    Elira, Su-1797
    Ezekiel, R-1819
    Francis, C-1818
    George, Su-1812, W-1812
    Henry, Su-1797
    James, Wi-1810(2), Wi-1815, Su-1797,
        Su-1812, Ge-1805
    Jessey, D-1788
    John, Mt-1798, Sn-1792, Je-1800,
        Ge-1805, Gi-1812
    Moses, Bo-1800
    Nicholas, Wi-1810
    Oin, Wi-1815
    Richard, Wi-1810
    Rowlend, Sn-1792
    Thomas, Su-1797(2), Su-1812(2),
        Su-1796(2)
    William, Su-1796
HUGHEY, G. JOhn, Mu-1811
    James, Wi-1801
    Lewis, J-1802
HUGHLET, John W., Gi-1812
HUGHS, David, Sn-1792
    Francis, Ge-1812, Ge-1783
    Goodman, B-1812
    Hardy, Gr-1799

HUGHS, Jessee, B-1812, Sn-1787
    John, W-1812, B-1812, Sn-1792,
        Gr-1799, Sn-1792, Bo-1805,
        Mu-1811, Mt-1798
    Joshua, W-1812, W-1805
    Josiah, B-1812
    Moses, Bo-1801, Ge-1812, Mo-1825
    Nicholas, W-1812(2)
    Rice, B-1812, Wl-1804
    Robert, Bo-1800, Gr-1799, Bo-1801
    Samuel, Wl-1804, B-1812
    William, Wl-1804, D-1811
HUGHS, William, D-1811
    William S., B-1812
HUGHSON, James, R-1819
HUGHSTON, Hugh, B-1812
HUGNIGHT, Joseph, Rb-1812
HUGHSTON, William, Ge-1812(5)
HUKEN, Harreit, C-1823
HUL, Richard, W-1812
HULKERSON, Reuben, A-1805
HULL, Able, W-1812
    Alfred, Je-1822
    Frederick, Su-1812
    Isaac, Je-1822
    John, Ge-1805
    John Sr., Ge-1812
    John Jr., Ge-1812
    Jos., Sn-1792, Bl-1815
    William, Su-1796
HULME, George, Wi-1810, Wi-1815
    John, Wi-1810
    Robert, Wi-1810
    Thomas, Wi-1815
    William, Wi-1815
HULS, William, Su-1797
HULSE, James P., Su-1812
    William Sr., Su-1812
HULVY, Conrod, Ge-1812
HUMBARD, Eden, Ge-1805
    John, Wl-1804
HUMBER, Jesibel, Gr-1821
    Samuel, Gr-1821
HUMBERD, Jacob, Gr-1821
    Reason, Gr-1821
    Samuel, Gr-1821
    William, Gr-1799, Gr-1821, Gr-1805
HUMBERT, Edon, Ge-1812
    Jonathan, Ge-1812
    Thomas, Ge-1805
    William, Gr-1805
HUMBIRD, William, Gr-1804
HUMBLE, Daniel, Su-1812
    George, Su-1812
    Henry, Gr-1821, Su-1812
    Josiah, W-1805
    Peter, Su-1812
HUME, Charles, Gr-1821
    William, D-1811
HUMES, Thomas, Je-1800
HUMLEY, William, A-1805
HUMMONS, Thomas, Wa-1819
HUMPHRES, W. Perry, Wl-1804
HUMPHREY, Charles, Sn-1811
    David, Sn-1811
    George, Wa-1814
HUMPHREYS, David, Wa-1814
    Elisha, Ct-1798
    George, Wa-1819
    Horatio, Hu-1812
    Jesse, Ct-1796
    John, Gr-1804, Wa-1819, Gr-1821

HUMPHREYS, Lesley, Wa-1814, Wa-1819
    Moses, Wa-1819, Wa-1814(2)
    Thomas, Wh-1811
    William, Wa-1814
HUMPHRIES, James, D-1811
    Moses, Su-1797
HUMPHRIS, John, Wh-1825
HUMPHRY, Charles, Sn-1816
    David, Sn-1816
    Elijah, Sn-1811, Sn-1816
    George, Rb-1812
    Hester, R-1819
    John, Gr-1799
    Nathan, Gr-1821
    Solomon, Sn-1816
HUMPSTON, Reuben, Je-1822
HUN, Stephen, Fr-1812
HUNGERFORD, Jon., Mu-1816
HUNICUT, Joseph, Je-1800
HUNICUTT, Leonard, Wh-1811
    Robart, Gi-1812
HUNLEY, William, Sn-1823
    Willis, Sn-1811
HUNNELL, Peter, Mu-1811
HUNNYCUTT, John, C-1818
HUNSLEY, Christian, Ge-1805
HUNT, Abraham, Ge-1783, Fr-1812
    David, Cl-1803, Fr-1812(2)
    Elizabeth, Wa-1819
    G., Wi-1815
    George, Fr-1812, Cl-1803
    Hardy, Sn-1816
    Henry, Fr-1812, Rb-1812
    James, Sn-1811, Fr-1812, Gi-1812
    Jesse Sr., Wa-1814
    Jesse Jr., Wa-1814
    Jessee, Sn-1811
    John, Sn-1816, K-1796, Cl-1803(3),
        Gr-1799, Fr-1812, Su-1812,
        Rb-1812, Su-1797, Wa-1814,
        Su-1796
    Jordan, Rb-1812
    Joseph, Wa-1819
    Joshua, Wa-1814, Wa-1819
    Leon, Sn-1811
    Levi, Sn-1811
    Lewis, Fr-1812
    Memuccan, Wi-1801
    Nathaniel, Fr-1812
    Nathaniel Sr., Fr-1812
    Peter, Wa-1819
    Philip, D-1811
    Samuel, Wa-1819, Wa-1814
    Shadrack, Rb-1812
    Sheaderick, D-1811
    Simon, Wa-1814
    Sion, Sn-1816, D-1805
    Smith, Wa-1819, Wa-1814
    Thomas, Sn-1816(2), Sn-1811, Wa-1814,
        Wa-1819
    Urah, Wa-1814(2)
    Uriah Sr., Wa-1819
    Wesley, Wa-1814(2), Wa-1819
    William, Rb-1812, Fr-1812
    Wilson, Gr-1810
HUNTER, A. James, Wl-1804
    Aaron, Mu-1811
    Abraham, Gr-1799
    Adam, Sn-1816, Sn-1811
    Alexander, Wl-1804
    Andrew, Gr-1805
    Benjamin Sr., Wh-1825

HUNTER, Cades, Sn-1811
    Cador, Sn-1816
    David, D-1811, Wa-1819, C-1818
    Demsy, Sn-1816
    Elijah, Wi-1815
    Elijah, Mu-1811, Wi-1810, Mu-1816
    Elijah Sr., Wi-1815
    Elish, Wi-1810
    Francis, Gr-1821, Gr-1804, Gr-1805
    Francis Jr., Gr-1821
    George, Je-1800
    Henry, Mu-1811, Gr-1799, C-1823,
        Wi-1815, Gr-1799
    Jacob, Wa-1814, Wa-1819
    James, Wh-1825, Je-1800, Je-1822
    Jeremiah D., Wa-1819
    Jessee, Wh-1825
    John, Mu-1811, Wh-1825(2), Gr-1804,
        Gr-1821, Wa-1819, Ge-1812,
        Gr-1805(2), Wa-1814(2)
    John Sr., Wa-1814
    John Jr., Mu-1816
    John Brook, Wa-1819
    John T., Wh-1825
    Joseph, Wa-1819, Wh-1825, Ge-1812
    Luis, Sn-1816
    Manuel, D-1811
    Mary, Mu-1816
    Matthew, Gr-1804, Gr-1805
    Neadom, Sn-1811
    Nicholas, Sn-1816
    Samuel, Ge-1812, Je-1800
    Squire, Wh-1825
    Stephen & William Hugins, D-1805
    Theophilus, Sn-1811, B-1812
    Thomas, Mt-1798, Ge-1812, Ge-1805
    William, Wh-1825, Sn-1816, Mu-1811,
        Gr-1821
    William Sr., Wh-1825
    William Jr., Wh-1825
HUNTOR, Elijah, Wi-1810
HUPPEN, John, D-1811
HUREK, Benjamin, B-1812
HURET, Robert, Wh-1825
HURLEY, Daniel, Ge-1812
    John, Gr-1799
    Winney, Ge-1812
    Zachariah, Ge-1812
HURLY, Joseph, Ge-1812
    Thomas, Fr-1812(2)
HURNY, Thomas, Ge-1805
HURST, Abraham, Ge-1805
    Absolem, Cl-1803
    Elegg, Cl-1803
    Elijah, Ge-1805
    James, Cl-1803
    John, Cl-1803(2), Gr-1799, B-1812
    William, B-1812
HURT, Anderson, Mu-1816
    Bird S., Mu-1816
    Floyd, D-1811
    John, Ro-1805
    Robert, Ro-1805
    S. Bird, Mu-1811
    Saml., Gi-1812
    Sion, Wi-1815
    Zach. Sr., Gi-1812
    Zach. Jr., Gi-1812
HUSBAND, John Jr., Mu-1816
HUSE, John, Ge-1812, Ge-1812, Wi-1810
HUSETAN, James, Ge-1812
HUSEY, Elija, Bo-1800

HUSON, Richd., Gi-1819
    William, Bl-1815
HUSONEY, Conrad, Ro-1805
HUSSE, Elijah, Bo-1801
HUSSEY, Christopher, Bo-1800, Bo-1801
HUST, Elijah, D-1811
    William, D-1811
    William B., Wi-1815
HUSTER, David, D-1805
HUSTON, David, Gi-1819, Wi-1801
    George, Su-1812
    John, Wi-1801
    Joseph, Wi-1805
    Pleasant, Rb-1812
    Preston, Wa-1819
    Robert, Wi-1801, Ge-1783
    Saml., Ge-1783
    Thomas, Mo-1825
    Walter, Wh-1825
    William, Rb-1812
    William Sr., Rb-1812
HUSTORS, James, Wi-1815
HUTCHENS, Jenks, K-1799
HUTCHERSON, Charles, Gr-1799, Gr-1805
    Colman, Gr-1805
    James, Gi-1812
    Jessee, Gr-1805
    John, Gi-1812
    Paul, Gr-1799
    William, Gr-1805
HUTCHESON, Ambrose, Rb-1812
    Charles, Gr-1804, Bl-1815
    Sandford, Rb-1812
    Thomas, Bl-1815
    William, Hw-1799, Gi-1812
HUTCHINGS, Aaron, Wh-1825
    Benjamin, Wh-1825
    Christopher, B-1812
    Christopher & John, D-1805
    G., Sn-1811
    John, B-1812, Wh-1811, Wh-1825
    Lemuel, B-1812, Wl-1804
    Moses, Wh-1825
    Richard, Rb-1812
    Smith, Ge-1783
    Thomas, Wl-1804, Wh-1825
    Webster, Wh-1825
    William, Rb-1812
    _____, Rb-1812
HUTCHINS, Smith, K-1799, J-1802
    Thomas, Mt-1798
HUTCHINSON, Danl., Mu-1816
    John, Mu-1816, Fr-1812, Rb-1812
    Paul, Gr-1805
    William, D-1805
HUTCHISON, Daniel, Mu-1811
    David, Je-1822
    George, Ge-1805
    Harris H., Ge-1805
    James, Mt-1798
    John, Sn-1792, Rb-1812
    Samuel, D-1805
    Thomas, Mt-1798, Ge-1812
HUTNER, Dudley, Wh-1825
HUTSON, Abel, Wh-1825
    Adam, Sn-1816
    Benjamin, Wh-1825
    Burrel, Gr-1805
    David, Ge-1805
    Freeman, Wi-1810
    Isaiah, Wh-1825
    Issom, Gi-1819

HUTSON, James, A-1805, Wh-1825
    John, Wh-1825
    Matthias, Wh-1825
    Obediah, Wl-1804
    Robert, Ge-1812, Ge-1805
    Thomas, Ge-1805, D-1811
    Thomas Sr., D-1811
    William, Fr-1812, Ge-1805, Bo-1890
HUTTEN, Jno., W-1812
HUTTON, Charles, D-1805
    Charles Sr., D-1811(2)
    Charles Jr., D-1811
    Charles B., D-1811
    John, Fr-1812
    Joseph, W-1812
    Josiah, Bo-1800, Bo-1801
    Peter B., Maj., W-1812
    Samuel, D-1811(2)
    William, Fr-1812
HUTTONS, Patrick, Mu-1811
HYAS, Nathaniel, D-1805
    Zacheriah, D-1811
HYATT, Simon, Wh-1825
    Simson, Wh-1825
HYDE, Edmond, D-1811
    Hartwell, Wi-1815
    Henry, D-1805
    John, Rb-1812
    Richd. W., Wi-1815
HYDER, Adam, Ct-1798
    Elizabeth, Ct-1798
    Jacob, Ct-1798, Wh-1811, Wh-1825
    John, Ct-1798
    Michael, Ct-1798
HYLES, Peter, Fr-1812
HYMMS, George, Su-1797, Su-1796
HYMPHREYS, Jesse, Ct-1798
HYNDS, John, B-1812
HYNES, Andrew, D-1811
    Robert, Sn-1816
    William, Mu-1816
ICE, Frederick, Hw-1799
IMBER, John, Mu-1816
IMES, John, Gr-1821
IMPSON, John, Wl-1804
ING, Alford, Sn-1816
    Joseph, Sn-1816
INGAM, John, B-1812
INGLAND, John, Bo-1800
    Thomas, Bo-1801
INGLE, Adam, Wa-1814, Wa-1819
    Adam Jr., Wa-1819
    John, Wa-1819
    Mary, Wa-1819
    Peter, Ct-1796
    William, Wa-1819
INGLEMAN, Joseph, D-1805
INGLES, Estate, Wa-1814
INGLISH, James, C-1823
    John, A-1805, Gr-1799
    Joseph, Gr-1799, A-1805
    Joshua, C-1823
    Joshua Jr., C-1823
    William, Gr-1799
    William, deceased, Gr-1799
INGRAM, Aaron, Mo-1825
    James, Su-1812
    John, Ge-1805, Su-1797
    Marmaduke, Sn-1816
    Samuel, Wi-1810
    Wm., Hu-1812
INGRUM, Samuel, B-1812

INHENS, Aron, Wa-1814
    John, Wa-1814
INMAN, Abednego, Je-1800, Je-1822
    Benjamin, Je-1822
    Berry, Co-1827
    Ezekiel, D-1811
    Ezikel, Sn-1816
    Green, Co-1827
    Henry, Wi-1810, Co-1827, Wi-1815
    Jeremiah, Je-1822(2)
    Joseph, Gr-1799
    Lazarus, D-1805
    Lazerus, D-1811
    Samuel, D-1811
    Shadrach, Je-1822
    Shadrack, Je-1822
    Shadrick, Ge-1783
    Shedrick, Je-1800
    Wiliam H., Je-1800
    William, Gr-1799
INNMAN, Wm., Wi-1815
IRBY, Charles, Sn-1816
    Tapley, Mu-1811
IREDALE, William, D-1811
IREDELL, John Sr., D-1811
IRELAND, David, Wl-1804
    John, Fr-1812
    Thomas, Wa-1819
IRESON, James, D-1788
    Joseph, Sn-1816
IRION, John P., Wi-1815(2)
IRONS, Edward, J-1802
IRVIN, Benj., Bo-1800
    Daniel, Gr-1805
    Eph., Mu-1816
    James, Bo-1801
    Patrick, Wa-1819
    Robert, Bo-1801
IRVINE, George Esq., Je-1822
IRVING, Saml., Co-1827
IRWIN, Alexander, Wh-1825, Wh-1811
    Christipher, Wi-1815
    David, Su-1797, Wh-1811
    George, C-1823, Je-1800
    Henderson, Wh-1825
    James, Wh-1825, Wh-1811
    John, Wl-1804, Sn-1811, C-1823
    Nathaniel, Sn-1811
    Robert, Bo-1800
    Samuel, Je-1800, K*-1815
    Thomas, Wh-1825
    William, Wh-1811, Wh-1825, D-1805
ISAAC, Elijah, Gr-1799
ISAACKS, Caleb, C-1818
ISACKS, Jacob C., Fr-1812
ISANBARGER, Nicholas, Wa-1819
ISBEL, Hickman, Su-1796
ISBELL, Abraham, Wh-1825
    James, W-1812
    Jason, W-1812
ISBELS, Levi, Se-1799
    Muler, Se-1799
    William, Se-1799
ISBEN, James R., Wa-1814
ISELEY, Conrad, Su-1797
    Conrod, Su-1796(2)
    Jacob, Su-1797, Su-1796
ISELY, Christian, A-1805
ISENBERG, Nicholas, Wa-1814
ISEY, William, Wa-1814
ISH, Alexander, R-1819
    Elizabeth, Bo-1800, Bo-1801

ISH, Jacob, W-1812
    John, W-1812
ISHAM, Charles, Wh-1825, Wh-1811(3)
    Elijah, Wh-1825(2)
    James, Wh-1811(2)
    John, Wh-1825
    Washington, Wh-1825
ISHIRE, Samuel, Ro-1805
ISHMAEL, Benjamin, Ge-1805
    Thomas, Ge-1805
ISHOY, Thomas, Ro-1805
ISLES, William, Wa-1819(2)
ISOLAND, Thomas, Wa-1814
ISOM, Arther F., Mu-1816
    Elizabeth, Mu-1816
    George, Mu-1816
    James, Mu-1811
    John, Gi-1812, Mu-1811
    Jonathan, Mu-1811
    William Sr., Mu-1811
    William Jr., Mu-1811
IVER, Solomon, D-1805
IVEY, Backster, Gr-1799
    Baxter, Gr-1805
    Elisha, A-1805
    Frederick, D-1811
    Henry, Gr-1805, Gr-1799, B-1812
    James, Ct-1796
    John, D-1805, D-1811(2)
    Joseph, B-1812
    Mathey, Gr-1805
    Matthew, Gr-1805
    Philip, Je-1822
    Phillip, Gr-1805
    R. Thomas, Mu-1811
    Vandimon, Gr-1799
    Verdiman, A-1805
    William, D-1805
IVY, Baxter, Gr-1804
    Benjamin, Gr-1821
    Daniel, C-1823
    Frederick, Wi-1815
    Henry, Gr-1821, Gr-1804
    John, Gr-1821
    Mathew, Gr-1804
    Philip, Gr-1804
    Thomas, Gr-1821
IZELL, Archibald, Mu-1811
    George, Gr-1821
    Jesse, Gr-1821
IZOR, Darby, Rb-1812
JACK, Alexandria, Gr-1821
    F. John, Gr-1805, Gr-1804
    James, Ge-1812(2)
    Jeremiah, Ge-1812
    John, R-1819, Ge-1812
    John F., Gr-1821
    Thomas, R-1819, Gr-1799
JACKS, Jeason, Bl-1815
    Jeremiah, Gi-1812
    Richard, Je-1822
    William, Bl-1815
JACKSON, Alexander, Sn-1823
    Andrew, Wh-1825, Wl-1804, D-1811,
        Sn-1816, Bo-1801, Bo-1800
    Benjamin, Wa-1814
    Branch, Mu-1816
    Burrel, Wh-1811
    Daniel, Ge-1805
    David, Wl-1804, B-1812, Wh-1825
    George, Wa-1819(2), Wa-1814(3)
    Gillian, Fr-1812

JACKSON, Graham, Wh-1825, B-1812
    Hennery B., Wi-1815
    Henry, Wh-1825, D-1811, Wi-1810
    Jacob, A-1805, Wa-1819, Wa-1814
    Jame, W-1812
    James, D-1811, Mu-1816, Wh-1825,
        Gr-1805, Sn-1811, Sn-1816,
        Wi-1815, B-1812, Gr-1804,
        Wl-1804, W-1812
    Jeremiah, B-1812
    Joel, B-1812
    John, D-1811(2), Mu-1811, D-1805,
        Wh-1825, Mu-1816, Bo-1800(2),
        Wi-1815, Bo-1801, Je-1822
    Jonathan, Wa-1814
    Josiah, Je-1800
    Joshua, Su-1797(2), Su-1796
    Larken, Sn-1811
    Linders, D-1805
    Mark L., Wi-1815
    Martin, Fr-1812
    Mathew, D-1811
    Nathan, Je-1800, Gr-1799, W-1812
    Nelson, Mu-1816
    Peter, Su-1796, Wa-1819, Su-1797
    Reuben, Gr-1804
    Reubin, Gr-1799
    Richard, Fr-1812
    Robert, B-1812, Wl-1804, Rb-1812
    Samuel, Wi-1801, Fr-1812, Wa-1819(2)
        Gr-1804, Je-1800, Wa-1814
    Simeon, R-1819
    Stephen, Sn-1816
    Thomas, D-1811, W-1812, Wi-1815
    Vincent, Ge-1812, Ge-1805
    Washington, D-1805
    William, Mu-1811, D-1811(2), Wl-1804
        Sn-1811, Sn-1816, Ct-1796,
        Gr-1799, Wa-1819(2), Wa-1814(2)
    Zacariah, Wi-1801
    Zacheriah, Wi-1810, Wi-1801
JACKSON & Co., Wl-1804
JACOB, Perry, K-1799
    Samuel, Je-1822
JACOBS, Edward, Wl-1804(2)
    Jeremiah, Wl-1804(2)
    John, B-1812
    Joseph, Wl-1804(2)
    Rebecca, Je-1822
    Samuel, Wl-1804(2)
    Thomas, Je-1822
    William, B-1812
JACSON, James, Sn-1816
JADWIN, Solomon, Wl-1804
JAGGERS, John, Mu-1816
    Love, Mu-1816
    Simon, Mu-1816
    William, Mu-1816
JAMES, Abraham, Gr-1805, Gr-1804, Fr-1812
    Amos, D-1805
    Anguish, D-1805
    Bennet, Bo-1801, Su-1796, Su-1797
    Charles, Ro-1805
    Daniel, D-1788, Mt-1798
    David, Mu-1811
    Edward, Je-1822
    Elisha, Su-1812
    Enock, Hu-1812
    Hugh, B-1812
    Isaac, Fr-1812
    Isaac Jr., Fr-1812
    Jackson, Gr-1821

JAMES, Jessee, Gr-1805, Gr-1799, Gr-1804
    John, Bo-1801, Wh-1811, Gr-1821,
        Je-1822
    Joseph, Ct-1798, Fr-1812
    Joshua, D-1805(2)
    Nicholas, Gr-1821
    Rawlings, Ct-1796
    Rolling, Gr-1821
    Samuel, Bo-1801, D-1805, W-1812
    Stephen, Fr-1812
    Thomas, D-1805, D-1788, Gr-1799,
        Gr-1804, Gr-1805
    Walter, W-1805, Su-1797(2), Su-1812(2)
        Su-1796
    William, Wh-1825, D-1811, Gr-1821,
        D-1805, Gr-1799(3), Gr-1804(2),
        A-1805, Gi-1812, Gr-1805,
        Je-1822
    William Sr., Gr-1804
JAMESON, Benjamin, Ge-1805
    George, Ge-1805
    James, D-1805
    John, Wi-1815, K-1799
    Robert, Ge-1805
    Thos., D-1788
JAMISON, Benjamin, Ge-1783, Ge-1812
    George, Ge-1783
    James, D-1811
    John, Mu-1816, Mu-1811
    Thomas, Sn-1787, Sn-1792
    W. C., Mt-1798
JAMSON, John, Gr-1821
JANE, Daniel, D-1805
JANKENS, Wilton F., Gi-1819
JANN?, Richard, Gi-1812
JANNEN, John, Wi-1810
JANUARY, Isaac, W-1812, W-1805
    John, Gr-1821
    William, Gr-1805, Gr-1804
JARLIN, Benjamin, D-1805
JARMAN, Ezekiel, D-1805
    John, Je-1800
    William, Wh-1825
JARMEN, Robert, Wl-1804
    Shadrach, Wl-1804
JARMON, Robt., Hu-1812
JARNAGAN, Drury, Gr-1799
    John, Gr-1799
    John Sr., Gr-1799
    Noe, Gr-1799
JARNAGIN, Asa, Gr-1821
    Chesley, Gr-1804
    Clesley, Gr-1805, Gr-1821
    Drury, Gr-1804(2), Gr-1805
    Jeremiah, Gr-1805, Gr-1804, Gr-1821
    John, Gr-1821, Gr-1804, Gr-1805
    Mary, Gr-1804
    Mary, by Noah Jarnagin, Gr-1805
    Noah, Gr-1804
    Thomas, Gr-1821
    Thomas, heirs, Gr-1805
    William, Gr-1821
JARNIGAN, Benjamin, heirs, Je-1822
    Chesley, Je-1822
    Noah, Gr-1821
    Silas, D-1805
    Thomas, Je-1800
JARRELL, Asa F., Mc-1825
JARROT, Thomas, Gr-1799
JARVIS, Abner, W-1812
    Cornelious, Wh-1825
    Elijah C., Wh-1825

JARVIS, John, Wh-1825
    Joseph, Wh-1825
    Levi, Wh-1825
    Rezen, Wh-1825
    William, B-1812
JASO (Juro?), Andre, Fr-1812
JASPER, Nicholas, Fr-1812
JAY, David, Fr-1812
    John, Fr-1812
JAYNE, Nathaniel, Gr-1821, Je-1822
JAYSON, F., Bl-1815
JEAMS, Isral, Ro-1805
JEANS, Carter, Co-1821
    Hardy, B-1812
    John, Co-1821
    Philip, Fr-1812
    William, Co-1821
JEFFERIES, James, C-1818
    William, C-1818
    Thomas, Gr-1799
    William, Ge-1812
JEFFERSON, F. Peter, Sn-1811
    Peter F., Sn-1816
JEFFERY, Jeremiah, A-1805, Fr-1812
    Joseph, A-1805
JEFFRIES, David, Cl-1803
    James, W-1812
    James Sr., W-1812
    John, C-1823
    Thomas, Cl-1803
    William, Bo-1805, C-1823
JENASON, William, heirs, Sn-1811
JENINGS, Daniel, Co-1821
    Ryal, Gr-1805
JENKINS, George, Wa-1814
    Hugan, Ct-1798
    Hugh, Ct-1796
    James H., Wh-1825
    Jenky, Wh-1825
    Jesse, Fr-1812, Co-1827
    John, B-1812, Co-1827, Mu-1811
    John Sr., Wh-1825
    John A., Wh-1825
    Mathew, Je-1822
    Nimrod, Wi-1810
    Philip, Wi-1810, Mu-1816, Co-1821
    Roand, Ct-1798
    Roland, Ct-1796
    Thomas, Gi-1812(2), B-1812, Co-1827
    Thomas H., Mu-1816
    William, R-1808, Fr-1812
JENNINGS, Daniel, A-1805
    David, Mu-1816, Mu-1811
    Doctor, Mu-1811, Mu-1816
    Edward, J-1802
    Edwin, Cl-1803
    Isam, Cl-1803
    James, Gi-1819
    Jess, Co-1821
    Jesse, Sr., Gr-1805(2)
    Jessee, Gr-1804
    John, Su-1796, Su-1812
    Martin, Fr-1812(2)
    Obediah, W-1805, W-1812
    Rial, Gr-1804
    Richard, Mu-1816
    Royal, Gr-1821
    Samuel, Mu-1816
    Thomas, Co-1821
    William, Fr-1812(2), Co-1821,
        Gr-1821, Je-1800, Ge-1812
JENNINS, Obediah, Cl-1803

JENNINS, William, Cl-1803
JENNY, Able, Mt-1798
JENTRY, Samuel, Mu-1811
JERMAN, Robt., Se-1799
    Shadr., Se-1799
JERNIGAN, David, Rb-1812
JERRAL, Aron, Mc-1825
JERVAS, John, Sn-1792
JERVIS (Juins?), Allen, Fr-1812
    Martin, Fr-1812
JERVIS, James, Ge-1783
JETERS, Joseph, Bl-1815
JETSON, Richard, Wh-1825
JETT, John, Wh-1811, Wh-1825
JILES, Danele, Co-1821
    Holleway, Co-1821
    Jessey, Co-1821
    John, Co-1821
    Meadoe, K-1799
    William, Wa-1814(2), Co-1821
JILLING, Isaac, Ge-1812
JIMMESON, Thomas, Rb-1812
JININGS, George, Gr-1805
JINKINS, Henry, Gr-1799
    James, Gr-1799
    Josiah, Bl-1815
    Phillip, Mu-1811
    Thos., Gr-1799
    Timothy, Gr-1799
    William, Gr-1799, R-1819,
        K-1799(Ginkins?)
JINNINGS, Clem, Wl-1804
    Edmund, Wl-1804
    John, Mt-1798
    Richard, Wl-1804
    William, Gr-1799
JINNINS, George, Cl-1803
    John, Cl-1803
    William, Cl-1803
    Zekiah, Cl-1803
JIST, John, Wh-1811
JOAB, Jacob, Su-1797, Su-1796
    Nathan, Su-1796
    Samuel, Su-1797, Su-1796
JOAH, Nathan, Su-1797
JOB, Abraham, Mu-1816, Wa-1814
    Aron, Wi-1810
    Caleb, K-1796
    Daniel, J-1802
    Elisha, W-1812
    Enoch, Wa-1814, Wa-1819
    Isaac, K-1799
    James, Mu-1816
    Jesse, Mu-1816
    John, Wi-1810
    Moses, Wa-1819
    Nathan, Wa-1814, Wa-1819
    Ruben, W-1812
    Wm., Ge-1783
JOBE, Abraham, Wa-1819
    Enoch, Wa-1819
    Jacob, Su-1812
    Jacob, deceased, Su-1812
    James, Mu-1811
    Jessee, Mu-1811
    John, Wa-1819
    Laban, Wa-1819
    Lockarich, Su-1812
    Nathan, Su-1812
    Samuel, Su-1812
JOHN, Jesse, D-1811
    John, D-1805

JOHN, Joisla, Ro-1805
    Persons, Sn-1811
    Stan William, C-1818
JOHNINGS, John P., Gr-1821
JOHNS, Isaac, Sn-1811
    John, D-1811
JOHNSON, Alexr., Wi-1815
    Amos, Mu-1811
    Andrew, Wi-1810
    Ann M., Sn-1811
    Aquila, K-1799
    Aquilla, A-1805
    Archibald, Sn-1816, Sn-1811, Wl-1804
    Benjamin, Sn-1816, Gr-1804, Fr-1812,
        K-1799, Se-1799
    Brans?, Sn-1816
    Britton, Wh-1825
    Cader, Mu-1816
    Catharine, Wi-1810
    Charles, Wi-1815
    Craven, A-1805
    Daniel, Rb-1812
    Dankin, Wl-1804
    David, Wi-1815
    Edward, Hu-1812
    Elijah, Mu-1816, Mu-1811
    Enoch M., Mu-1816
    Enus, Je-1800(2)
    George, Sn-1811, Mu-1811, Sn-1816,
        Fr-1812
    Gidion, Mu-1811
    Guyan, W-1812
    Hanes, Mu-1811
    Hardy, W-1812
    Harrison, Fr-1812
    Henry Sr., Rb-1812
    Hezekiah, Hu-1812
    Isaac, D-1788, Hu-1812, Ge-1805
    Isham Sr., Mu-1816
    Isham Jr., Mu-1816
    Isom, Mu-1811
    J. B., Sn-1816
    Jacob, Ge-1783
    James, Mu-1816(2), Wh-1825, Sn-1811,
        Mu-1811(2), Ge-1812, Rb-1812,
        Je-1822, A-1805, C-1823,
        Sn-1816
    Jesse, Gr-1805, Fr-1812, Hu-1812
    Jessee, Gr-1805
    Jessey, D-1805
    John, Wh-8125, Mu-1816(3),
        Mu-1811(3), Wi-1815, Hu-1812,
        R-1808, Ge-1812, Rb-1812(3),
        W-1812, Wi-1815, Sn-1792,
        Bl-1815, Gr-1799
    John B., Sn-1811
    John M., Mu-1816
    Joseph, Mu-1811, Mu-1816, Je-1822,
        R-1819, W-1812
    Kinza, K-1799
    Kuiza, A-1805
    Lemuel, Fr-1812
    Lewis, Sn-1811, Gr-1821
    Liness, Sn-1816
    Luke, Wi-1810
    Matthew, Mu-1816, Mu-1811(2)
    Moses, Wi-1801
    Nathaniel, Mu-1811, D-1788
    Nicholes, Ro-1805
    Richard, Mu-1811, Sn-1811, Wh-1825,
        Sn-1816
    Richard C., Sn-1816

JOHNSON, Robert, Mt-1798, Wh-1825, Mu-1811
    Samuel, Wh-1825, Mu-1816, Mu-1816,
        A-1805, Fr-1812, Je-1800
    Selas, Fr-1812
    Simon, Mu-1816, Mu-1811
    Solomon, Wl-1804
    Stephen, Wi-1815, Gr-1810, D-1811,
        Ge-1812
    Swanson, Wi-1815
    Theophilus, R-1819
    Thomas, Mt-1798, Gr-1805, Rb-1812,
        Gr-1821, Je-1822, R-1819,
        C-1823, Mt-1798
    Thomas Jr., Rb-1812, Gr-1821
    Thomas D., Je-1822
    William, Mu-1816(2), Mu-1811(3),
        Sn-1816(2), Mu-1816, Rb-1812(2)
        Je-1822, R-1819(3), Je-1800(2)
        A-1805(2), Mo-1825, K-1799,
        Wh-1825
    William, heirs, Je-1822
    William C., Sn-1811
    Willis, Mu-1811
    Zepheniah, Mu-1811
JOHNSTON, Abner, D-1805
    Abraham, D-1805
    Alex, Gi-1812
    Alexander, D-1805, W-1812
    Amos, Esq., Mu-1816
    Andrew, Wi-1801
    Archibald, Sn-1811
    Armstead, D-1811
    Asa, Gr-1810
    Bean, Gr-1805
    Benjamin, Su-1812, Ge-1812
    Chapman, B-1812
    Charles, D-1811, Hu-1812
    Daniel, Gr-1799, Rb-1812
    David, Wi-1810, W-1812(2)
    Elijah, D-1805
    Elisha, B-1812
    Exum, Sn-1811
    Frances, Bo-1800
    Francis, W-1812, Ge-1805
    George, D-1811
    George, Esq., Mu-1816
    Harrison, Ge-1805
    Hugh, K-1799, Ro-1805
    Hugh Sr., Ro-1805
    Hugh Jr., Ro-1805
    Isaac, D-1805, D-1811
    Jacob, Wh-1811, W-1812, Su-1812,
        Ge-1805
    Jacob Jr., W-1812
    James, Sn-1811, D-1805(3), Sn-1816,
        C-1823, B-1812(2), Bo-1805,
        Gi-1812, Su-1797, Wa-1814(2),
        Ge-1812(2), Ro-1805, Ge-1805,
        Gr-1821, Su-1812, W-1812,
        Wa-1814
    James Sr., Ge-1812
    James Jr., Ge-1812
    James S., Wa-1819
    Jeffrey, D-1811(2), Wi-1810
    Jesse, Sn-1816, Sn-1811, Ge-1805
    John, D-1811, D-1805(3), Sn-1811,
        Bo-1800, Ct-1796, Ge-1783,
        Wi-1815, Je-1800, W-1812,
        Ro-1805
    John Sr., D-1811, Wi-1810, D-1805
    John Jr., D-1811, Bo-1801
    John D., D-1811

JOHNSTON, Jonathan, D-1811
    Joseph, Su-1812, Ge-1805, Ge-1812
    Joshua, Su-1812
    Lewis, Mu-1811, Mu-1816
    Littleton, D-1811
    Martin, W-1812
    Mathew, Wi-1810
    Meredith, D-1811
    Molest, D-1805
    Moses, Ge-1805
    Oliver, D-1811, D-1805
    Peter, D-1811
    Philip, Su-1797, Su-1796, Su-1812(2)
    Pleasant, C-1823
    Robert, D-1811, W-1812, Ge-1805,
        Wi-1810, Wa-1814
    Robert M., Mu-1816
    Samuel, Wl-1804, Mo-1825
    Saml., heirs, Gr-1821
    Sargent, Fr-1812
    Stephen, Gr-1805, B-1812, Gr-1799,
        Gr-1821
    Swanson, Wi-1810, Wi-1801
    Temple, W-1812
    Thomas, W-1805, Gr-1805, D-1805,
        D-1811, Gr-1821, Gr-1804,
        B-1812, Su-1797, Su-1796,
        W-1812, Su-1812, Ge-1805(2)
    Walter, Su-1797, Su-1812
    Walter, Esq., Su-1796
    Will, Jr., Gi-1812
    William, D-1805, Wi-1810, A-1805,
        Ge-1783, Wa-1819, Wa-1812(3)
        Ro-1805, Je-1800, Ge-1812,
        Ge-1805, Gr-1821
    Wm., Sr., Gi-1812
    Zachariah, D-1805
JOHNSTONE, Isaac, Gr-1821
    Joseph, Gr-1821
    William, Gr-1821
JOILS, John, K-1799
    William, K-1799
JOINER, Charton, D-1811
    Cullin, Sn-1811
    Drury, Gi-1812
    Isham, Sn-1811
    Jessee, Sn-1816
    Jessey, Sn-1811
    Jethro, Mu-1816
    John, Su-1812, Sn-1811
    Levi, D-1811
    Littleton, Sn-1816, Sn-1811
    Solomon, Fr-1812
    Thomas, Sn-1811, Sn-1816
    Whitehead, Sn-1816
    Wm., D-1788
    Willin, Bl-1815
JOINING, Harpeth, Wi-1801
JOLLEFF, William, Su-1797
JOLLIFF, Dudley, Su-1796
    William, Su-1796
JOLLY, Aury, Wa-1819
    Dudley, Wa-1814
    Henry, Wa-1814
    William, Ge-1812(2)
JONAKIN, Isaac, Gr-1805
    John, Gr-1805
JONAS, Jacob, Gr-1821
JONES, A., Ge-1805
    Aaron, Ge-1812
    Abiram, Wh-1811
    Abner, Mu-1816, C-1823

JONES, Alex, Gi-1812
    Alston, Gi-1812
    Andrew, B-1812
    Ann, Bo-1801
    Anthony, Rb-1812(2)
    Aqualla, Gr-1799
    Aquilla, D-1811, Gr-1804
    Azariah M., Rb-1812
    Benjamin, Mu-1811, Wi-1810, Su-1812,
        Fr-1812
    Berry, Wh-1825
    Biram, Wh-1825
    Britain, Fr-1812(2)
    Bryan, Wh-1825
    Calib, Ge-1812
    Charles, Su-1812
    Crafford, Ge-1805
    Daniel, D-1811, Sn-1811
    Daniel & Jarvis, D-1805
    Darling, Wa-1814
    David, Mu-1816, D-1805, Gr-1799,
        Je-1800
    Ebenezar, Bo-1801
    Ebenezer, Wh-1811, Bo-1800
    Edmon, Wi-1810
    Edward, Sn-1811, Sn-1816, Ge-1812,
        Sn-1792
    Elijah, Mu-1811
    Elisha, Sn-1811
    Elizabeth, Sn-1816
    Ely, Rb-1812
    Evan, Ge-1783
    Evan Sr., Ge-1805
    Evan Jr., Ge-1805
    Ezekiel, Su-1812
    Foster, Sn-1816
    Frances, Bo-1800
    Francis, Fr-1812
    G. W., Wh-1825
    Gabriel, Fr-1812
    George, Gr-1805, W-1812, Ge-1805,
        Be-1812
    Hardy, Wh-1811
    Harwood, Gr-1799
    Henry, Su-1812, Su-1797, Su-1796,
        Ge-1783
    Hercules, A-1805
    Hezekiah, Mu-1816, Gi-1819
    Hugh, Gr-1821
    Isaac, D-1805, D-1811, Ge-1812(2),
        Ge-1805, Je-1822, Su-1812,
        Gr-1799
    James, Sn-1816(2), Mu-1811, Sn-1811,
        Mu-1816, D-1805(2), Rb-1812,
        Ro-1805, Ge-1812, Ge-1805(2),
        Ct-1798, Ct-1796
    James Sr., Su-1812
    James Jr., Rb-1812
    James G., Wi-1815
    Jarvis Jr., D-1811
    Jeremiah, Bl-1815
    Jesse, Rb-1812
    Jessee, Wi-1815
    John, Wh-1825(3), Sn-1816, D-1811,
        Mu-1816(2), Sn-1811, Wl-1804(3),
        Mu-1811, Gr-1805, W-1812(2),
        Gi-1812(2), Ro-1805, Gr-1821,
        Ge-1812(3), Ge-1805, Su-1797,
        Fr-1812(3), Gr-1804, Bl-1815,
        Wi-1815, A-1805, B-1812(2),
        Cl-1803, Ge-1783, Wi-1815
    John Sr., Ge-1805

JONES, John Jr., Su-1812
    John M., Mu-1816
    John N., Wh-1825
    John W., Gi-1819
    Johnston, Bo-1801
    Jones Jr., Je-1800
    Joseph, Wh-1825, Mu-1816, Mu-1811,
        Gi-1812, W-1812, Ge-1812
    Joshua T., W-1812
    Josiah, Wl-1804
    Judson, Wi-1815
    Kinchen, Rb-1812
    Laban, Gr-1805
    Lackary, Su-1812
    Lemuel, D-1811
    Len, Mu-1816
    Leod. Sr., Gi-1812
    Leod. Jr., Gi-1812
    Lewis, Mu-1816, Mu-1811, Ct-1798,
        Bo-1801, Bo-1800, Ct-1796
    M. John, Mu-1811
    Mark, C-1818, C-1823
    Mary, Ge-1812, Wi-1815
    Michael, Su-1812
    Miles, Je-1822
    Morton, B-1812
    Moses, D-1811, Wl-1804
    Nathaniel, Wa-1814, Wa-1819(2),
        W-1812
    Owen, Hu-1812
    Pateman, Bo-1800
    Peter, Wl-1804, Gr-1805(2)
    Philip, Fr-1812
    Phineas, Ge-1805, Ge-1812
    Pistimas, Bo-1801
    Pleasant, Mu-1811
    Richard, Sn-1811, Sn-1816, Rb-1812,
        Sn-1792, Bl-1815
    Richard Jr., Rb-1812
    Richard H., D-1811
    Rilon, Wh-1825
    Robert, Wi-1801, Mu-1816, Sn-1792,
        Fr-1812(3)
    Samuel, Mu-1811, Ge-1812, Wa-1819,
        Su-1812(2), Mu-1816, Bo-1801,
        Bo-1800
    Shadrack, D-1805
    Solomon, Su-1812, Su-1796, Su-1797,
        C-1823
    Squire, Sn-1816
    Stephen, Mu-1811, Gr-1821
    Sugar, A-1805, C-1818
    Thomas, Mu-1816(2), Sn-1811,
        Wh-1825, Sn-1816, Wi-1801,
        Ro-1805, Ge-1812, Su-1812(3),
        Ge-1805, Je-1800(2), Wa-1819,
        Su-1796, Rb-1812, Sn-1787,
        Bo-1801, Bo-1800, Ct-1798,
        Ct-1796, Gr-1799
    Thomas E., Wi-1815
    Timothy, D-1805, D-1811
    Waddy, Rb-1812
    Wells, Ct-1796
    William, Sn-1816, Mu-1811, Gr-1805,
        K-1796, Mu-1816, Sn-1811(2),
        Wl-1804, D-1805, D-1811,
        Su-1812, W-1812, Wa-1814,
        Wi-1815, C-1823, Gr-1799(2),
        Gr-1821, C-1818(2)
    William Sr., Su-1812
    William Esq., Ge-1812
    William D., Wa-1819

JONES, Willum, Wi-1810
    Wood, B-1812
    Wyley, Su-1812
    Wyllie, Gi-1812
    Zachariah, Wh-1825
    Zechariah, Wh-1811
JONLINS, George, Wa-1819
JONS, Ezikiel, Gi-1819
JONSON, Cornelious, Wi-1815
    David, Ge-1812
    Donogel N., Mu-1816
    James, Ge-1783
    Margaret, Ge-1812
    William, Ge-1812
JONSSON, Amos Sr., Hw-1801
    Amos Jr., Hw-1801
    James, Hw-1801
JONSTON, Amos, Cl-1803
    David, Ge-1783
    James, Ge-1783
    William, Ge-1783
JOPLING, James, Wi-1810
JORDAIN, Ezekiah, Cl-1803
JORDAN, Archer, Wi-1810
    Benjamin, Mu-1811, Mu-1816
    Burton, Wi-1810
    Clemmon, Wh-1825
    Ezekiah, Gr-1799
    George, Wi-1810
    James, Hu-1812
    Jesse, Rb-1812
    Johnson, Wi-1815
    Solomon, Wh-1811
    Stephen, Wi-1815
    Thomas, Mu-1816, Wi-1815
    William, Wi-1815
    William Sr., Wi-1815
    Woodford, Gr-1821
JORDEN, Briton, Wi-1801
    Elias, Fr-1812
    John, Fr-1812(2)
    Levi, Fr-1812
    Reubin, Fr-1812(2)
    Wm., Wi-1801
JORDON, Archer, Wi-1815
    Benjamin, D-1811
    James, Hu-1812
    Lewis, Wa-1819, Wa-1814
    Merideth, D-1811
    Richard, Rb-1812
    Rover, D-1811
    Thomas, Mu-1811
    William, Wi-1810
    Williamson, D-1811
JORINZEN, John, Gr-1799
JOSE, Anderson, B-1812
JOSEA?, James, Mu-1816
JOSEPH, Alexander, B-1812
JOSEY, John, Mu-1816
    Mary, Mu-1816
JOSIAH, Warmack, Wh-1825
JOSLIN, Bird, D-1811
    Daniel Sr., D-1811
    Daniel Jr., D-1811
    James, D-1811
    Samuel, D-1811
JOSN, Kelly, R-1819
JOURDAN, William, Mt-1798
JOURNEY, Elizabeth, Li-1812*
JOWELL, Joseph, Sn-1816
JOY, James, Mu-1811
    Thomas, Mu-1816

JOYCE, Thomas, D-1811
JULIAN, Benjamin, Wh-1825
    Isaac, Mo-1825
    Kelley, Wh-1825
    William, A-1805
JULIAS, Tobias, K-1799
JULIN, Geo., K-1799
    George E., B-1812
    Jn., K-1799
JURASSET, Elijah, Wh-1825
JURDEN, John, Gi-1819
JURKEY, Jessee, W-1812
JURKY, John, W-1812
JURL, Lewis, Gr-1821
JURNIGAN, Braden, Rb-1812
    Felix, B-1812
    Jesse, Rb-1812
    Lewis, B-1812
JUSTER, William, Ro-1805
JUSTICE, Buckner, Rb-1812
    Isaac, Ge-1812
    Jacob, Ct-1796, Ct-1798
    Johnithan, Ge-1812
    James, Wh-1825
    Moses, Bo-1800, K-1796
    Thomas, Ge-1812
    William, Mt-1798
JUSTIN, Julius, Rb-1812
JUSTIS, Isaac, Ge-1805
    Thomas, Ge-1805
JUSTUS, Alfred, Rb-1812
KAGH, George, D-1805
KAGLER, Andw., Wi-1810
    John, Wi-1810
KAIGLER, Andw., Wi-1815
    Wm., Wi-1815
KAIGN, John, Wl-8104
KAIN, Hugh, Gr-1805
    James, Su-1797
    John, K*-1815
KAINE, James, Su-1812
KALER, Frederick, Su-1797, Su-1796
KALLEWON, James, Ge-1805
KAMP, Andrew, Ro-1805
KANADY, William, Gi-1812
KANARD, William, Wh-1825
KANEDY, Walter, Bo-1801
KARNEY, Elijah & Vinson, D-1805
    John & Henry, D-1805
KARR, James, Wi-1810
    John, Wi-1810
    Samuel, D-1805
    William, Wi-1810
KATEY, _____m, Gi-1819
KAUBLE, Adam, Ge-1805
    Michael, Ge-1805
KAVANAUGH, Andrew, Wl-1804
    Charles, Wl-1804
    William, Fr-1812
KAY, Allen, D-1805
    James, W-1812
KEAF, Thomas, Sn-1816
KEAN, Jonah, Wa-1814
KEANE, James, Su-1812
KEAREY, Ricd., Wh-1825
KEASE, John, Wa-1814
KEASELIG, John S., Gi-1819
KEASLER, Jacob, Ge-1812
KEATH, William, B-1812
KEATON, Elijah, Je-1822
    James, Je-1822
KEBLE, William, Bo-1805

KEE, Hugh, K-1799
    Zachariah, A-1805
KEEBLE, Wm., Bo-1801
KEEBLER, Jacob Sr., Wa-1819
    Jacob Jr., Wa-1819
    James, Wa-1819, Wa-1814
    John, Wa-1814, Wa-1819
KEEF, Thomas, Wl-1804
KEEFE, John, W-1805
    Thomas, Sn-1811
KEEL, James, Ge-1805
    John, Ge-1805
    John Jr., Ge-1805
    William, Ge-1805
KEELBER, Jacob, Wa-1814
KEELE, James, Ge-1783
    Richd., Ge-1783
KEELEY, William, Sn-1816
KEELING, George, D-1811
    Leonard, D-1811
KEEN, Ashford, Sn-1811
    Eli, Su-1812
    James, Su-1812
    Joseph, Su-1812
    Leonard, Su-1812
    Mathhias, Su-1812
    Robert, Su-1812
KEENAN, Martin, B-1812
KEENE, Jonah, Wa-1819
KEENEN, John, B-1812
KEENER, Housen, Gi-1812
    Joseph, Wa-1819
    Peter, Wa-1819
    Ulrich, Wa-1819
    William, Wa-1819
KEENEY, Joseph, Ge-1783
KEENON, John, Gi-1812
KEEP, Rubin, W-1805
KEES, Isaac, Wa-1819
    John, Wa-1819
KEESEE, George, Sn-1811
    George Faris, Sn-1811
KEESEY, Thomas, Bl-1815
KEESS?, John, W-1812
    Rubin, W-1812
KEESSE, Thomas, Fr-1812
KEETCH, James, Su-1812
KEETH, David, Bl-1815
    Ely, Bl-1815
    James, Bl-1815
    Nichodmus, Bl-1815
    Stephen, Bl-1815
KEETON, George, Mu-1811
    John, Fr-1812
KEEZEE, George Sr., Sn-1816
    George Jr., Sn 1816
KEFAVER, Nicholas, Wa-1819
KEFF, Jn., Cl-1803
    Reuben, Cl-1803
    Thomas Sr., Cl-1803
    Thomas Jr., Cl-1803
KEGWOOD, Thomas, Su-1812
KEHERLY, Wm., C-1823
KEIR, James, Mu-1811
    M. Andrew, Mu-1811
KEITH, Andrew, Gi-1812
    George, Fr-1812
    James, Je-1800, K-1799, Bl-1815
    Joseph, Wh-1811
    Nicholas, Je-1800
    Nickemus, K-1799
    Richard, Gr-1804

KEITH, William, Gr-1805, K-1799, Gr-1805,
    Wh-1825
KEITHERLY, John, Wh-1811
    John Sr., Wh-1811
KEITHLEY, Jessee, Wh-1825
KELEY, Mathew, Ge-1812
KELLAR, Daniel, Ge-1805
KELLDEA, Henry, Ge-1805
KELLER, Benjamin, Ge-1812
    Daniel, Ge-1812
    David, Ge-1812, Ge-1805, K*-1815
    Henry, Ge-1812, Ge-1805
    Hezekiah, Wa-1819
    Jacob, Ge-1812
    John, Ge-1805
    William, Wa-1819
KELLET, James, Gi-1812
KELLEY, Alex, Bo-1800
    Alfred, B-1812
    George, W-1805
    John, Ge-1783, Bo-1800, Ge-1783,
        Se-1799
    Joshua, J-1802
    Thos., B-1812
    William, J-1802
KELLIN, Robert, B-1812
KELLUM, Custus, D-1811
    Jesse, D-1811
KELLY, Alexander, Mu-1811, Mu-1816,
        Bo-1801
    Anthony, Ge-1805
    Anthony, Dec., Ge-1812 (Legatee,
        William Kelly)
    Benjamin, Su-1812, W-1805
    Charles, Je-1822
    Dennis, Wl-1804
    Durham, Fr-1812
    George, Wa-1819, W-1812
    Hugh, Hu-1812, D-1805
    Isaac, Je-1800
    Jacob, Je-1800
    James, D-1805, Fr-1812(2),
        Ge-1805(2), R-1819(2)
    Jessheca, Se-1799
    John, Bo-1801, Fr-1812, B-1812,
        Wl-1804, Su-1797
    John Sr., Ge-1812
    John Jr., Ge-1805, Ge-1812
    Jonathan, W-1805, W-1812
    Joshua, Wl-1804, Wa-1819, B-1812,
        Wa-1814
    Kinchen, Wa-1814
    Kincher, Wa-1819
    Mathew, W-1812, W-1805
    Mordica, D-1811
    Nathan, W-1812, W-1805
    Polly, Mu-1816
    Reuben, B-1812
    Simms, Fr-1812
    S____, Fr-1812
    Thomas, R-1808, R-1819
    William, Mu-1811, K-1796, B-1812,
        Ge-1805, R-1819, Je-1822
        Ge-1812(see Rodgers, Jane)
    William, Capt., Ge-1812
KELM, Jesse, Hu-1812
KELSEY, Alexander, Ge-1805
    John, Wa-1819
    John Sr., Ge-1805
    Robert, Mu-1816
    Thomas, Mu-1816
KELSLAW, Widow, Su-1812

KELSO, Alexander, Je-1800
    Hugh, Je-1800
KELSOE, Hugh, Bo-1801
KELTNER, Henry Jr., Gi-1812
KELTNOR, George, Gi-1812
    Henry Sr., Gi-1812
KEMP, Barnett, Wh-1285
    Fielding, Ro-1805
KEMRY, George Sr., Gr-1804
KENADY, Henry, Je-1800
    Rebecah, Je-1800
KENDAL, Thomas, B-1812
KENDALL, William, Wa-1814
KENDRICK, Jessee, Mu-1811
    John, Mu-1811, Mu-1816
    Thomas, Mu-1816, Mu-1811
    William, Mu-1811, Mu-1816
KENDRICKS, Jesse, Mu-1816
    Obadiah, Mu-1816
KENEDAY, William, Fr-1812
KENEDY, Andrew, Bo-1800
    Jessee, Wi-1815
    John, Bo-1801, Bo-1800
    Joseph, B-1812
    Thomas, Fr-1812(2)
    Walker, Bo-1800
    William, Mu-1816
    Wm. E., Li-1812*
KENER, Joseph, Wa-1814
    Peter, Wa-1814
    Ulrick, Wa-1814
KENERLY, Thomas Jr., Fr-1812
KENEY, Daniel, Wi-1801
    John, Ge-1783, Fr-1812
KENMORE, Wm., Gi-1819
KENNADA, Charles, Wh-1825
KENNADY, John, D-1788, Mu-1811
    William, Mu-1811
KENNALLY, Edward, Wh-1825
KENNEDAY, William, Sn-1792
KENNEDEY, Samuel, Ro-1805
KENNEDY, Abraham, D-1805
    Ada M., Je-1822
    Andrew, Mu-1816, Bo-1801
    Benjamin, Je-1822
    Daniel, R-1808
    Eli, Mu-1816
    Enoch, D-1811
    Francis, Mu-1811, Mu-1816
    G. Washington, R-1819
    George, Bo-1805
    Grace, Wa-1814
    Hugh, Wa-1819
    Isaac, D-1805, Mu-1816, D-1811
    Jacob, R-1808
    James, Mu-1816, Gr-1805, Mu-1811
    John, D-1805, D-1811, Mu-1811,
        Sn-1816, Bo-1801, Wa-1819,
        Ge-1805, Wa-1814, Ge-1812(3)
    Margaret, Ge-1812
    Robert, D-1805, D-1811(2)
    Robert Sr., D-1805
    Robert Jr., D-1805
    Samuel, Ge-1812, Wa-1819
    Thomas, Ge-1812, Ge-1805, Mu-1816
    William, D-1805, Wa-1819, Gi-1812(2)
        Wa-1814, R-1819
KENNERLY, George, J-1802
    Thomas, J-1802
KENNEY, James, Ge-1805, Gr-1812, Gr-1799
    William, Wi-1815
KENNON, Thomas M., R-1819

KENNON, William, Sn-1811
KENNY, Daniel, B-1812
    James, D-1811
    John, Je-1800
KENON, John, Gi-1819
KENOR, David, Wh-1825
KENT, John, D-1811
    William, D-1811(2)
KEPLENGER, Jacob, Wa-1814(2)
    John, Wa-1814
    Samuel, Wa-1814(2)
KEPLINGER, Jacob, Wa-1819
    John, Wa-1819, Wa-1814
    Samuel, Wa-1819
KEPPLE, Jacob, Ge-1812
KERBOUGH, John, Ge-1805
KERBY, Christopher, Ge-1805
    Daniel, Ge-1805
    Jesse, Ge-1812
    John, A-1805
    William, Wh-1825(2)
KERKENDALL, Mathew, Sn-1792
KERKPATRICK, David, Je-1800
    Hugh, Je-1800
    Jacob, Je-1800
    James, Je-1800
KERLAND, Joseph, Wa-1819
KERLEY, Wm. M., Gi-1812
KERLIN, Joseph, Wa-1814
    William, Wa-1819, Wa-1814
KERLING, Leonard, D-1805
KERNEY, James, C-1823
KERR, Andrew, Je-1800
    Catherine, Je-1822
    David, Je-1822, Je-1800
    Hugh, D-1811
    James, Su-1812(2), Ge-1783,
        K-1796, Mu-1816
    Jane, Je-1822
    John, Ge-1812, Wh-1825
    Joseph, Wh-1825(2)
    King, Sn-1792
    Mathew, K-1796
    Molent, D-1788
    Richard, Ge-1805
    Robt. Jr., Ge-1783
    Samuel, Mu-1816
    Thomas, Fr-1812
    William, Wh-1811, Ge-1783, B-1812(2)
        Wh-1825(2), Sn-1816
    William, heirs, Wh-1811
KERRY, John, Wi-1810
KERTON, George, Mu-1816
KESTERSON, John, Ge-1805, Ge-1812
    Peter, Ge-1812
    William, Ge-1812
    William Sr., Ge-1812
KETLER, Joseph, Gi-1819
KETNER, John, Je-1822
KETO, Philip, Su-1812
KETTLES, Frederick, B-1812
KETTON, ichard, Gr-1810
KEY, Bingham, Sn-1816, Sn-1811
    David, Ge-1805, Ge-1812
    Job, Su-1812
    John, Ge-1805
    Jos., Su-1796
    Macklin, Sn-1816
    Ruffin, Sn-1816
    Thos., Wi-1815
    Washington, Su-1812
    William, Sn-1816, Sn-1811, W-1812

KEY, William W., D-1811
KEYKENDALL, John, Fr-1812
    Mathew, Fr-1812
    Peter, Fr-1812
    Simon, Fr-1812
    William, Fr-1812
KEYS, Isaac, Wa-1819
    Joab, Su-1797
    Phillip, Wa-1819
    William, Su-1797
KEYSER, Philip, B-1812
    Valentine, B-1812
KEYWOOD, Benjamin, Gr-1799
    John, Su-1797, Su-1796
    Stephen, Gr-1799
KEZER, George, Wh-1825
KIBERLEY, William, C-1818
KIBLE, John, Mt-1798
KIDD, Benjamin, Wi-1815
    James, B-1812
KIDDY, Jacob, B-1812
KIDLY, Elijah, Wa-1819
KIDWELL, Charles, Gr-1805, Gr-1804
    David, Gr-1821
    John, Gr-1821, Hw-1799, Je-1822
    Joshua, Ge-1812
    Josiah, Gr-1805, Gr-1804, Gr-1799
KIETH, Bird, A-1805
    James, Fr-1812
    John, Fr-1812
    Noble, Gr-1805
    William, A-1805
    Zacheriah, Gr-1805
KIFER, Jacob, Ge-1812
    John, Ge-1812(2), Ge-1805
KIKER, Conrad, Wa-1819, Wa-1814(2)
    John, Wa-1814
    Joseph, Wa-1814(2)
KILBOURN, Benjamin, Bo-1805
    Daniel, Wi-1815
KILBRATH, Thomas, Ge-1783
KILBRETH, Alexander, Ge-1783
KILBRUK, James, Sn-1816
KILBURN, Gooden, Bl-1815
KILBURNE, Amos, Gi-1812
KILE, Thomas, Gi-1812
    William, Gi-1812, Gi-1819
KILEBRUN, Buckner, Mt-1798
KILES, Eli, Sn-1811
KILGORE, Charles, Ge-1783, Ge-1812
    James, Ge-1812
    John M., Ge-1812
    Johnston, Sn-1792
    Thomas, Fr-1812, Sn-1792, Rb-1812
    Thomas Sr., Rb-1812
    William, Ge-1812
KILLAMAN, Matthew, Sn-1811
KILLDEA, John, Ge-1805
KILLGORE, Charles, Ge-1805
    William, Ge-1805
KILLINGWORTH, Jere., Gi-1812
KILLINSGWORTH, Freeman, B-1812
KILLOUGH, Joseph, R-1819
KILNEY, John, Wa-1814
KILPATRICK, Ebenezer, Mu-1816, Mu-1811(2)
    Eleazor, Mu-1816
    Elihu, Mu-1816
    Joseph, Mu-1816, Mu-1811
    Joshua, Mu-1816
    Robert, Sn-1816, Sn-1792
KIMBALL, Buckner, W-1812
KIMBELL, James, Rb-1812

KIMBRO, George, B-1812
    James, Gi-1812
    George, B-1812
    James, Gi-1812
    Jesse, Je-1800
    Nathl., Gi-1812
    Solomon, Gi-1812
KIMBROUGH, Duke, Je-1822
    Isaac, Je-1822
    Jesse, Je-1822
    John, Fr-1812, Je-1822
    John, heirs, Je-1822
    L. Goldman, Mu-1811
    M. D., Sn-1811
    Ogilvie, Wi-1810
    William, Je-1822
KIMES, Conrad, Ge-1805
KIMLINE, James, Wi-1810
KIMMENS, Robert, Wa-1814
KIMMIT, Thomas, C-1818
KIMMON, Joseph, B-1812
KIMMONS, Joseph, Ge-1805, Ct-1798, Ct-1796
    Robert, Wa-1814
KIMRA, Conrad, Gr-1805
    George, Gr-1799
    George Jr., Gr-1805
    George Sr., Gr-1805
KIMBRY, Conrad, Gr-1804
    George Jr., Gr-1804
KINARD, Philip, B-1812
KINCADE, Joseph, Mu-1811
    Thomas, C-1823
    William, C-1818
    Wm. Sr., C-1823
    Wm. Jr., C-1823
KINCAID, James, Gr-1799, D-1811
    Joseph, Mu-1816
    Thomas, Gr-1799
    William, Fr-1812
KINCHALOW, George, Wa-1819
    James, Wa-1819
    William, Wa-1819
KINCHELOR, George, Wa-1814
    John, Wa-1814
KINCHLIE, John, Su-1796
KINCHLOW, Enoch, Wa-1819
    John, Wa-1819
KINDER, Jacob, Gr-1821
    Joseph, Gr-1821
KINDLE, George, Ge-1812
    John, Ge-1812
    William, Ge-1812
KINDRICK, Drury, R-1819
    James, R-1819
    John, Sn-1792, Mu-1811
KINEDY, Andrew, Mu-1811
KINEY, William, Mu-1811
KINF?, John, Sn-1816
KING, Abraham, Sn-1811
    Adam, Bo-1805
    Alan, B-1812
    Amos, D-1805, Su-1812, Mc-1825
    Anthony, Mc-1825
    Anval, Fr-1812
    Baker, W-1812, W-1805
    Benjamin, Su-1812, Wi-1815, Wi-1801, Mu-1811, B-1812
    Billy F., estate, Wa-1819
    Charls., Sn-1811
    David, Su-1812
    Davis, Sn-1811

KING, Elias, Wi-1815
    Ellis, Ge-1812
    Edwd?, Sn-1811
    Edward, B-1812
    George, Ge-1812, G-1812
    H., Wh-1811
    Harmon, Ge-1783
    Henery, Bo-1805
    Henry, Wa-1814, Wa-1819
    Hillsman, Gr-1804
    Hugh, Mu-1811, Mu-1816
    Jacob, B-1812
    James, Su-1797, Su-1796, Su-1812,
        Wi-1810, Fr-1812, Wl-1804
    James, Esq., Su-1796, Su-1797
    James, Rev., Wa-1819
    James & Donelson, Stockley, Gr-1799
    Jeremiah, B-1812
    Jesse, Fr-1812(2)
    John, Fr-1812(5), Je-1822, Su-1796,
        Su-1812(2), Je-1800, Rb-1812,
        Su-1797, Mt-1798, Sn-1811,
        Mu-1816, Bo-1801, Gr-1821,
        Bo-1805
    John Jr., Rb-1812
    John A., Gi-1812
    Johnson, Fr-1812(3)
    Johnston, Bo-1801, Bo-1800, Bo-1805
    Jonathan, Wi-1810, Wa-1819
    Martha, Su-1812
    Mary, Je-1800
    Meredith, Fr-1812
    Moses, Sn-1811
    Nathaniel, B-1812
    Nelson, Wi-1810
    Ransom, Wl-1804
    Richard, Sn-1811, Sn-1792
    Robert, Bo-1801, Gr-1805, Ro-1805,
        Ge-1783, Ge-1799, Gr-1821,
        Gr-1804(2), Sn-1792
    Robert, alias James Calkahoon,
        Gr-1799
    Robert & Thomas, Gr-1799
    Samuel, Mu-1816, Bo-1801, B-1812,
        Ge-1805, Bo-1800, Sn-1811,
        Wl-1804, Mu-1811
    Suzanah, Je-1822
    T. Murray, C-1818
    Thomas, Fr-1812, Su-1796(2),
        R-1819, Su-1812, Wa-1814,
        Su-1797(2), Gr-1799, Wa-1819,
        C-1818, Mc-1825
    Thomas Sr., Su-1812
    Thomas Jr., Mc-1825
    Thomas M., C-1823
    Walter, Wa-1819, Wa-1814, Su-1796,
        Su-1812
    William, Ct-1796, Gr-1804(2),
        Gr-1799, Su-1812(2), Gr-1805,
        Su-1796, Mt-1798(2), Wi-1815,
        Sn-1811(2), Ct-1798, Wa-1819,
        Su-1797, Sn-1816, B-1812,
        Gr-1799, Fr-1812, C-1823,
        C-1818, Su-1812
    William, estate, Wi-1815
    William S., Su-1812
    Heirs, W-1805, Su-1812
KING & KICKSON, Ge-1812
KINGSLEY, Alpha, D-1811
KINGSTON, Paul, D-1805, D-1811
    Richard, D-1811(3)
KINGTON, John, Su-1812

KINKAID, Thomas, A-1805
KINLEY, John, Fr-1812
KINNARD, John, Wl-1825, Wa-1819
    Michael, Wi-1801, Wi-1815
    Thomas, Wa-1819
    Walter, Li-1812*
KINNEY, James Sr., Hw-1801
    James Jr., Hw-1801
    Willam, Wi-1810
KINNON, Bengamon, Sn-1816
KINNY, Jessy, Hw-1801
KINSELY, James, Su-1812
    John, Su-1812
    Michael, Su-1812
KINSER, Jacob Sr., Ge-1812(2)
KINSOR, Jacob Jr., Ge-1812
    John, Ge-1812
    Peter, Ge-1812
KINSUR, Alexr., Wh-1825
    Jacob, Wh-1825
KINTMAN, Zacheriah, Ge-1812
KIOFHAVEN, Nicholas, Wa-1814
KIOTSINGER, Martin, Ge-1812
KIRBEY, Joseph, Bo-1801
    Richard, Bo-1801, Bo-1800
KIRBY, Archibald, Wh-1825
    Bennet, Mu-1816
    Henry, W-1812
    Henry Sr., W-1812
    Henry Jr., W-1812
    James, Mu-1816
    John, A-1805
    Richard, Wh-1825
    Wallace, Wi-1810
    William, Wh-1825
KIRK, Alexander, C-1823
    Armstead, Gr-1821
    Ezekial, Gr-1821
    George, Wa-1819, Wa-1814
    Henry, Mu-1811, Mu-1816
    Jessee L., Wi-1815
    John, Ge-1812, Mu-1816, Mu-1811
    John Sr., Ge-1805
    Lewis, Gi-1812
    Natey, Mu-1811
    Natus, Mu-1816
    Parham S., Wi-1815
    William, Gr-1804, Wh-1825, Mu-1811,
        Gr-1821
KIRKHAM, James, D-1805
    William, Gr-1805, Gr-1810, Gr-1804
KIRKINDALL, Simon, Sn-1787
KIRKINDOL, Abram, Gi-1812
    Jno., Gi-1812
KIRKLAND, Archibald, A-1805
    Daniel, Bl-1815
    Elisha, Bl-1815
    George, A-1805
    Jesse, Gi-1812
    Levi, Hu-1812
    Moses, B-1812, Gr-1799
KIRKMAN, Thomas Jr., D-1811
KIRKPATERICK, David, Ge-1812
KIRKPATRICK, Alexander, Wl-1804
    Ann, Sn-1811
    Charles, Bo-1800, Bo-1801, Bo-1805
    David, Wl-1804
    Fanney, Sn-1811
    Fanny, Sn-1816
    Felix, Mu-1811
    Frances, Bo-1805
    Henry, D-1811

KIRKPATRICK, Hugh, Sn-1811, Sn-1816
    Jacob, Je-1822
    James, Sn-1811, Hu-1812, Sn-1816, Gr-1799, A-1805, B-1801
    John, Wl-1804(2), Wi-1801, D-1805, Gr-1799, A-1805, Je-1822
    Peter, Mu-1816
    Thomas, Bo-1800, Bo-1801
    Wallis, Sn-1811
    Wilkins, Je-1822
    William, D-1805, Sn-1811(2)
KIRKSEY, T., Gi-1819
KIRKWOOD, David, Ge-1783
KISER, Joseph, Ge-1805
KISLING, George, D-1805
KISSELL, Nicholas, Su-1812
KISSESSIT, Jas., Gr-1799
    Thomas, Gr-1799
KISSINER, Jacob, Gr-1821
KITCHEN, Jesse, Gr-1805
    Jessee, Gr-1804, Gr-1799, Gr-1805, A-1805
    John, Gr-1804, A-1805, Gr-1805
    Semore, Ge-1812
    William, Gr-1805, Ro-1805
KITCHENN, William, Mu-1816
KITCHENSON, John, Wh-1825
KITCHERSIAS?, James, Wh-1825
KITCHINSON, James, Wh-1825
KITE, Isaac, Ct-1798, Ct-1796
    Jacob, Ge-1812
    James, A-1805
    Philip, Su-1796
    Richard, Ct-1798, Ct-1796
KITSMILLER, Martin, Wa-1819
KITT, Philip, Su-1797
KITTS, John, Gr-1821
KIVEIL, Elijah, Gr-1821
KIZOR, Francis, Wh-1811
    Michael, Wh-1811
    Peter, Wh-1811
KIZZOR, Phillip, Sn-1811
KLINE, Isaac, Gr-1821
    Jacob, Gr-1821
KLOYD, Drurey, Wi-1815
KNABB, Jacob, Je-1800
KNARD, George, Wi-1815
KNAUL, Martin, Wi-1810
KNEWBY?, Thompson, W-1812
KNIGHT, George, C-1823
    John, Su-1796
    John Sr., R-1819
    Josiah, Wi-1815, Wi-1810
    Thos., Sn-1811, Hu-1812
    William, D-1811, Sn-1816
KNISELEY, John, Su-1796
    Jonas, Su-1797
KNOTT, David, B-1812
    Jno., B-1812(2)
    William, B-1812
KNOWLES, James, Wh-1811, Wh-1825
    John, Wh-1811(2)
    John Sr., Wh-1825
    John Jr., Wh-1825
    William, Wh-1825
KNOX, David, R-1819
    James, R-1819, Gi-1812
    John, Gr-1805, Gi-1812
    Joseph, Bo-1801, Gi-1812
    Peggy, Mu-1811
    Saml., B-1812
    William, R-1819, B-1812

KNUCKLIS, Peter, Wh-1825
KOBBLE, Walter, D-1811
KOGER, Nicholas, C-1823
KOHER, George, Gi-1812
    William, Gi-1812
KOKING, John, Wa-1814
KONSOR, Jacob Jr., Ge-1812
KOONCE, Catherine Wa-1819
    George, Wi-1815, D-1811
    James, D-1811
    Jesse, Wl-1804
    Jessee, Se-1799
    Lamuel, Wl-1804
    Peter, Wa-1819
    Philip, Se-1799
    Phillip, Wl-1804
KOONER, Henry, Mu-1811
KOONROD, Nicholas, Wl-1804
KOONS, Henry, Mu-1816
KORTS, John, Wa-1819
KORTZ, _____, Wa-1814
KOUYHENDAL, Petter, Sn-1787
KOYLE, Benjm., W-1812
KRANTZ, David, D-1811
    John, D-1811
KRIS, Philip, Wa-1814
KRISLEY, John, Su-1797
KRISSELL, John, W-1805, Su-1812
KUDY, John, Gr-1805
    Lewis, Gr-1805
KUMMINS, Joseph, Wh-1811
KUNCE (see Counce), A-1805
KUNEY, G. Henry, Mu-1811
KUNS, Adam, Bo-1800
    Henry, Bo-1800
KUNSE, Adam, Bo-1801
    Henery, Bo-1801
    John, Bo-1801
KUNSLEY, Samuel, B-1812
KURFF, Joseph, D-1811
KUTCH, Daniel, Mu-1816, Mu-1811
KUYKANDAL, Mathew, Sn-1787
KUYKENDALL, Igents, D-1788
    John, Sn-1792(2), D-1788
    Jos., Sn-1792(2)
    Mathew, Sn-1792
    Simon, Sn-1792, D-1788
KUYKINDAL, Adam, Ge-1783
    Jno., Ge-1783
    Jos., Ge-1783
KUYKINDALL, Benjamin, Sn-1787
KYGAR, John, J-1802
KYKENDALL, Jean, Sn-1792
KYKER, Conrad, Wa-1814, Wa-1819
    John, Wa-1814, Wa-1819
    Joseph, Wa-1819
    Peter, Wa-1819
KYLE, George, Gr-1805
    Jacob, Ge-1805
    John, Ge-1805, Ge-1812
KYSER, Phillip, Sn-1816
    Phillip Jr., Sn-1816
LAAKS, William, Gr-1804
LABAN, James, Gr-1804
LABOW, Henry, Gr-1821
    John, Gr-1821
LACEWELL, John, Gi-1812
LACEY, Josiah, Wh-1825
    William, Je-1800
LACK, John, Gi-1819
LACKEY, Adam, Gi-1812
    Andrew, Bo-1800, Bo-1801

LACKEY, Archd., Ro-1805, Bo-1800, Bo-1801
    James, Sn-1811, Sn-1816
    John, Bo-1800, Je-1822
    John S., Mu-1816
    Thomas, Ct-1798, Wa-1819
    W., Bo-1801
    W. Jr., for Mayhew, Bo-1800
    W. James Agt., Bo-1800
LACKLAND, John, Ge-1805
    Joseph, Ge-1805
    Joseph Sr., Ge-1812
    Joseph Jr., Ge-1812
LACKY, Jas., for Maj. Lackey, Bo-1801
    James W., for Mayben, Bo-1801
    Robert, Fr-1812
    Thomas, Wa-1814
LACY, Amos, J-1802, Wh-1811
    Elijah, B-1812
    Isaac, W-1812
    James, Gr-1821, Ct-1798, Ct-1796
    John, Ct-1798, Ct-1796
    Philimon, Ct-1796
    Phillimon, Ct-1798
    Thomas, Wa-1819
    William, Mu-1816, Gr-1821, Gr-1805
LADD, Amos, B-1812
    Constantin, Mu-1816
    Jehoshephat, Mu-1816
LADEN, George, B-1812
LADY, Henry, D-1811
    Jacob, Su-1812
LAFEAVER, John, Wh-1825
    Zacheus, Wh-1825
LAFERTY, Samuel, Wh-1825
    William, Wh-8125
LAFFERTY, Andrew, Mu-1811
LAFORCE, Robert, Gr-1804
LAGOW, Richard, Ge-1812
LAIN, Benjamon, Gr-1821
    Dutton, Ge-1812
    Elias, Hu-1812
    Isaac, Sn-1811
    James, Sn-1811
    John, Ge-1812
    Samuel, Ge-1805, Ge-1812
    Thomas, Ge-1812
    William, Mu-1811
LAINE, John Porter, Wi-1815
LAIRD, Alexander, D-1811
    James, Ge-1805
    John, Gi-1812
LAKE, George, D-1811
    Jacob Rev., Su-1797
    John, D-1811
    William, Je-1800
LALE, Henry, D-1811
LALLINER, Leslie, Sn-1811
LALLUM?, Jonathan, Sn-1811
LAMASTERS, Isaac, D-1805
LAMB, A., Bl-1815
    Alexander, Bl-1815
    David Sr., Wi-1815
    David Jr., Wi-1815
    Gross, C-1818
    Hannah, C-1818
    Hugh, Bl-1815, J-1802
    Isaac, Gi-1812(2)
    Jesse, Gi-1812
    John, C-1823, A-1805, Gi-1812
    Joseph, Wi-1815, C-1823, C-1818
    Richard, Ro-1805
    Thomas, Wi-1810, Ge-1805

LAMB, Thomas Sr., Wi-1815
LAMBERT, Aaron, Wl-1804
    Avery, Wl-1804
    David, Wl-1804
    William, Wl-1804
LAMBETH, Demsey, Wh-1825
    James, Fr-1812
    William, Sn-1816(2), Sn-1811
LAMMON, Joseph, Wa-1814, C-1818
LAMON, David, Wa-1814(2)
    Emanuel, Wa-1814
    Jacob, Wa-1814
    John, Wa-1814(2)
    Nancy, Wa-1814
LAMOR, James, Je-1800
LAMPKIN, Ezekiel, Ro-1805
LAMPKUS, John G., Wi-1810
LAMSEY, H., K*-1815
LAMY, Andrew M., K-1799
    Robert M., K-1799
LANCASTER, Aron, Mu-1811
    John, Mt-1798
    Michal, Mu-1811
LANCE, Henry, Wh-1811
    Martin, Wh-1811
    Moses, Wh-1825
    Samuel, Wh-1825, Wh-1811
    Valentine, Wh-1811
LAND, Abraham, D-1805
    Eli Nek, Co-1821
    James, D-1805
    John, D-1805
    Joseph, D-1805
    Newman, Je-1800
    William, Co-1827
LANDCASTER, Aaron, Mu-1816, B-1812
    Joseph, Mu-1816
LANDER, William, D-1805
LANDERS, Abraham, Sn-1792
    Edward, Sn-1816, Sn-1811
    Henry, Ro-1805
    Isaac, B-1812
    Jacob, Sn-1792
    James, Sn-1811
    Jos., Sn-1816
    Wm., Sn-1816, B-1812
LANDMAN, Josiah, D-1811
    Sheppard, D-1811
LANDRATH, George, D-1811
LANDREW, Thomas, A-1805
LANDRUM, James, Ge-1812
    Mary, Wi-1810, Wi-1815
    Meriman, Wi-1815
    Merrimon, Wi-1810
    William, Ge-1812
    Young, Ge-1805
LANDRY, Hubbard, Sn-1811
LANE, A. B., Wh-1825
    Abraham, Wa-1814
    Anthony, Wh-1825
    Aquilla, Je-1800
    Aquilla, heirs, Je-1822
    Bennett, Sn-1823
    Charles, Ge-1805
    David, B-1812
    Dutton, Ge-1805, Ge-1783
    Dutton Jr., Ge-1805, Ge-1812
    Ephraim, Ge-1805
    Garrett, Je-1822
    George, W-1812
    Henry, Wh-1825
    Isaac, Gr-1799, Sn-1816, Cl-1803, Je-1822

LANE, Jacob A., Wh-1825, Wh-1811(2)
　　　James, Sn-1816, Gr-1805, D-1805,
　　　　　Su-1796, Gr-1821
　　　Jeremiah, Ge-1812
　　　Jesse, D-1811
　　　Joel, B-1812
　　　John, B-1812, D-1805, Sn-1811,
　　　　　Ge-1805, A-1805, Su-1812,
　　　　　Gr-1821
　　　Lidenu, Wa-1814
　　　Martin, Gi-1812
　　　Nathan, Mu-1811
　　　Noah, Je-1822
　　　Richard, Je-1800
　　　Rowlin, Fr-1812
　　　Samuel, Wa-1814(2), Je-1822
　　　Thos., Gi-1812
　　　Tidence, Je-1822
　　　Tidence Sr., Je-1800(2)
　　　Tidence Jr., Je-1800
　　　Turner, Wh-1825, Wh-1811
　　　William, Wl-1804, Sn-1816, Gr-1805,
　　　　　Gr-1799, Gr-1804, Gr-1821
LANES, James, Gr-1799
LANEY, Jeremiah, Ge-1805
LANFORD, Robert, Mu-1811
LANG, Edward, K-1799
　　　Elijah, Gr-1805
　　　Robert, Bo-1800, K-1799
　　　Tobias, K-1799
LANGDON, Joe, Je-1822
　　　Jonathan, Je-1822
　　　Joseph, Je-1800
LANGFORD, Merran, Ro-1805
　　　Thomas, Mt-1798, W-1812
LANGHAM, Abel, Gr-1799
　　　John, D-1805
　　　Robert, Fr-1812
　　　Solomon, Fr-1812
LANGHAM & LATHIM, Gr-1799
LANGLEY, Joseph, C-1823, C-1818
LANGLY, Joseph, Fr-1812
LANGSTON, Jacob, Wi-1815
LANKASTER, William, B-1812
LANKFORD, Hickman, Mu-1816
　　　John, Mu-1816
LANIAR, Buchanan, D-1811
LANIER, Washington, J-1802
LANKIN, Marget, Wi-1815
LANN, Richard, Gi-1819
LAPS, Benjamin, D-1811
LARAMORE, Charles, D-1805
LARANCE, John, Sn-1811
LARD, James, Wi-1810
LARDE, James, Ge-1812
LAREMORE, Hugh, Gr-1799
LARENCE, Thomas, Sn 1816
LAREW, Samuel, Ct-1796, Ct-1798
LARGE, Isham, Je-1822
　　　John, Co-1821, Gr-1821
　　　Joseph, Ct-1798, Ct-1796, Je-1822
　　　Robert, Su-1796, Je-1822
　　　Thomas, Je-1822
　　　William, Je-1822
LARGENT, John, Wh-1825
LARIMONE, Hance, B-1812
LARIMORE, George K., Je-1822
　　　Hugh, Gr-1805, Je-1822
　　　John, Gr-1821
　　　Reuben, Je-1822
LARKEN, Edward, B-1812
LARKINS, David, Fr-1812

LARKINS, John, Fr-1812
LARRAMORE, Hugh, Gr-1804
LARRAMORRE?, Daniel, D-1805
LARRIMORE, James, B-1812
LARSON, Andrew, D-1805
LARUE, Isaac, Mu-1811
LASACTE, Burrel, Bl-1815
LASATER, Abner, Fr-1812
　　　Hezekiah Sr., Fr-1812
　　　William, Fr-1812
LASETER, Frederick, D-1805
LASHHART, Thomas, D-1805
LASHLEY, Jesse, Wa-1814, Wa-1819
　　　John, Hu-1812
LASITER, Enos, Sn-1816
　　　Fedrick, Sn-1816
　　　Fredrick, D-1811
　　　Wilie, Sn-1816
LASK, Julius H., Ro-1805
LASLEY, John, Sn-1816
LASSETER, Burrell, Bo-1800
LASSITER, Burrel, Bo-1801
　　　Thos., Hu-1812
LASTER, Alexander, D-1811
LASTLEY, Peter, D-1811
　　　William, D-1811(2)
LATHAM, Benjamin, Je-1822
　　　James, Gr-1821
　　　John, Gr-1821, Sn-1816, Hw-1801
　　　John Jr., Gr-1821
　　　Lewes, K-1799
　　　Samuel, Je-1800
　　　William, D-1811(2)
LATHAN, John, Je-1800
LATIMER, Betheul, Sn-1811
　　　Charles, Sn-1816, Sn-1792
　　　Daniel, Sn-1811
　　　Griswold, Sn-1816
　　　Nathl., Sn-1792
　　　Robert, Sn-1792
LATIMORE, Danal, Sn-1816
　　　George, Sn-1816
　　　James, Hu-1812
　　　Joseph, Sn-1792
　　　Witt, Sn-1811
LATTA, John, Mu-1816
　　　Thomas, Mu-1816
LATTIMER, Lucinda, Sn-1816
　　　Robt., Sn-1811
LATURE, Christopher, Su-1812
　　　Hamber, Su-1812
LAUDERDALE, David, Sn-1823, Sn-1816
　　　Sn-1811
　　　James, Sn-1811
　　　James, heirs, R-1819
　　　James Sr., Sn-1811
　　　James Jr., Sn-1811
　　　John, Sn-1816, Sn-1816, Ge-1812
　　　John Jr., Ge-1812
　　　Josiah, Sn-1816
　　　Samuel, Sn-1811
　　　William, Sn-1816, Sn-1811(2)
LAUDERMILK, George, Je-1800
LAUGHINER, Christopher, Ge-1805
LAUGHLIN, Alexander, Su-1812
　　　Anna, Su-1812
　　　James, D-1811
　　　Robert, Sn-1811
LAUGHNER, Christopher, Ge-1812
LAURANCE, Edmond, Wi-1815
LAURENCE, Adam, Sn-1792
　　　Ezekiel, Je-1822

LAURENCE, James, Je-1822
    James, heirs, Je-1822
    John, Wl-1804(2), Je-1822(2)
    Martin, Bo-1801
    Richard, Je-1822
LAUSON, John, Gr-1805
LAVEN, Golston, Sn-1811
LAVENDER, William, Sn-1811
LAW, Archibald, Wa-1819
    David, B-1812, Fr-1812
    Edward, Sn-1816
    Henrey, Sn-1816
    Isaac, Sn-1816
    Jacob, Ct-1798
    James, Wl-1804
    James Harris, Ge-1812
    John, Sn-1816
    Will M., Mu-1816
    William, Fr-1812
LAWER, Andrew, A-1805
LAWES, Thomas Sr., Gr-1805
LAWHORN, William, Sn-1816
LAWHURS, George, Hu-1812
LAWING, William, W-1812
LAWLER, Jehu, A-1805
    John, A-1805
LAWLOR, James, A-1805
    Levi, A-1805
LAWRANCE, John, Sn-1792
LARENCE, Adam, Sn-1792
    David, B-1812
    Edward, Wi-1810
    Elias, Rb-1812
    James, Je-1800
    Joseph, B-1812
    Lemuel, Sn-1816
    Lorn, D-1811
    Martin, Bl-1815, Bo-1800
    Samuel, Wl-1804
LAWS, John, Su-1812
LAWSON, David, C-1818(2), C-1823, Gr-1805
    David Jr., Gr-1805
    Drewry, Hw-1801
    Edward, C-1818(2), C-1823
    Elijah, C-1818
    Hampton, Hw-1801
    Jacob, C-1823, C-1818
    James, D-1811
    John, Gr-1805
    Joshua, C-1818
    Nathan, Hw-1801
    Nathaniel, Gr-1805
    Pleasant, Wh-1825
    Randal, C-1818
    Randolph, Hw-1801
    Robert, K-1799, C-1818, C-1823
    Thomas, Hw-1801, Mu-1816
    Ulysses, C-1818
    William, C-1818
LAWTY?, William, D-1805
LAX, Edward, Wh-1811
    William, Gr-1805
LAXSON, Thomas, Wh-1811
LAY, Berry, Gr-1805
    Bird, C-1823
    Elias, C-1823
    Jesse, Je-1822, C-1823(2), C-1818(2) Ct-1796
    Joel, A-1805
    John, Gr-1821, C-1818(2), C-1823(2) A-1805

LAY, John Sr., A-1805, C-1823
    John Jr., A-1805, C-1818, C-1823
    John D., C-1823
    Peter, C-1823, C-1818
    Thomas, Gr-1805
    William, Je-1822, C-1823
LAYET, William, Wi-1815
LAYMAN, Christopher, Je-1822
    Daniel, Je-1800
    Jacob, Je-1822
    Joseph, Je-1800
LAYMON, Jacob, Je-1800
    Thomas Sr., R-1819
    Thomas Jr., R-1819
LAYNE, Aquilla, A-1805
    George, Ro-1805
    Thomas, Wi-1815
    William, Wi-1815
LAYSAND, John Adam, Wi-1815
LAYTON, Francis, D-1811
    Micael, Wi-1815
    Michael, Wi-1810
LAZWELL, David, A-1805
LEA, Abner, Gr-1799
    Chafley, J-1802
    David, A-1805, Ro-1805
    Francis, Ro-1805
    Hernden, Je-1822
    James, R-1819, Je-1800
    John, Gr-1805, J-1802, Gr-1804
    Joseph, A-1805
    Luke, Gr-1805, A-1805
    Major, Gr-1805, Je-1800, Gr-1799(2) Gr-1821, Gr-1804
    Rhody, Je-1822
    Robert, Je-1822
    Rowland, A-1805
    Samuel, Ro-1805
    Stephen, Gi-1819
    Thomas, Je-1822
    William, Fr-1812
    Zachariah, A-1805
LEABO, Henry, Gr-1799
    Jacob, Gr-1799
    John, Gr-1799
LEACH, David, Mu-1811
    George, Su-1812
    James, A-1805, Wa-1814, Wa-1819
    John, A-1805, K-1799
    Jonah, Fr-1812
    Neffle, Fr-1812
    Nevel, Fr-1812
    William, Wa-1814, Wa-1819
LEAH, Isaac, Sn-1816
    James, D-1811
LEAHY, Eli, B-1812
LEAK, Samuel P., Wh-1825
    Thomas, Wh-1825
LEAKEY, Jerrh., W-1812
    John, W-1812
    William, W-1812
LEAMAN, David, Je-1800
LEARD, Benjamin, Mu-1811
LEAREY, Edr. General, Mt-1798
LEAS, Tolsmon, Su-1797
LEATH, Isaac, Sn-1811
    James, Sn-1811, Sn-1816
    Joseph, Je-1800
LEATHEM, Jonathan, K-1799
    Lewes, K-1799
LEATHERDALE, James, R-1808
LEATHERDELL, John, Hu-1812

LEATHERWOOD, Thomas, Co-1821(2)
LEAVERIS, Joseph, R-1819
LEBO, Henry, Cl-1803
      Jacob, Cl-1803
      John, Gr-1805, Gr-1804, Cl-1803
LEDBETTER, G. W., Wh-1825
      Isaac, Wi-1815
      Joseph, Wi-1815
      Walter, Wh-1811
LEDFORD, Wm., Rb-1812
LEDGERWOOD, John, Ge-1805
      Nathaniel, Ge-1812, Wa-1814
LEDS, George, A-1805
LEE, Abner, Ge-1783
      Bareston, D-1805
      Benjamin, Wi-1801
      Braxton, D-1811
      Burwell, Wl-1804
      C. E., Gr-1799
      Cader, Fr-1812, Wl-1804
      Edward, Sn-1811
      George, Gr-1805, Ge-1783
      Henry, D-1811
      James, Wl-1804, D-1811, Wh-1825,
            Gr-q799, Mc-1825
      John, Wl-1804, D-1805, B-1812,
            Fr-1812, Ge-1783, Co-1827,
            Bl-1815, Gr-1799(2), Gi-1812
      John Sr., D-1811
      John Jr., D-1811
      Jos., Sn-1816
      Kiny, Wh-1825
      Lewis H., D-1811
      Mathew, Wi-1815
      Peter, B-1812(2)
      Robert, B-1812
      Samuel, Mu-1811, Mu-1816
      Stephen, W-1812
      Thomas, Gr-1799
      William, Gr-1799, B-1812, Wi-1801,
            Gi-1812
LEE (Bee?), Zachariah, K-1799
LEECH, George, R-1808
LEEKEY, Mary, Ge-1812
LEEKY, Christian, Ge-1812
      Christian Jr., Ge-1812
LEEMIN, David, Wi-1815
LEEPER, Hugh, Mu-1811
      Hugh B., B-1812
      James, B-1812
      John, Mu-1811
      Math, Ge-1783
      Mathew, Je-1822
LEERD, Samuel, Fr-1812
LEETH, Ebenezer, Je-1822, Je-1800 (Esq.)
      George, Je-1800, Je-1822
      James, Je-1822
LEETHE, Ephram, K-1799
LEEVIS, Jacob, Sn-1811
LEFFEW, Elisha, Gr-1821(2)
      Joseph, Gr-1821
LEFTWICK, Jefferson, Wh-1825
      Waman, Wh-1825
LEGAT, Salley, Sn-1816
LEGATE, Charles, Wi-1815
      William, Wi-1801
LEGATT, Charles, Wi-1810
LEGERWOOD, John, C-1823
      Joseph, C-1823
LEGG, Ambrose, Bo-1800
      Johnothan, Bo-1805
      Jonathan, Bo-1801, Bo-1800

LEGG, Matthew, Bo-1801
      Samuel, Bo-1805, Je-1822
LEGGET, Daniel, Sn-1811
      William, Mu-1816
LEGGITT, William, Hu-1812
LEHAN, Henry, Sn-1811
LEIGH, Benjamin, Wi-1815
LEIL, John, A-1805
LEIN, John, D-1788
LEITCH, Humphreys, Gi-1812
LELBURN, Andrew, Wa-1814
LEMANS, Peter, Gi-1812
LEMAR, Buchanon, D-1811
      James, Je-1822
      John, W-1812
      William, A-1805, Sn-1787
LEMARR, Benjamin, B-1812
LEMASTER, John, Rb-1812
      Thomas, Sn-1792
LEMAY, Daniel, Wh-1825
LEMEANZ, William, B-1812
LEMMON, Abraham, Wa-1814
      Chrisley, Wa-1814
LEMMONS, Jacob, R-1808
      Levi, R-1819
LEMON, Chrisley, Wa-1819
      David, Wa-1819
      Emanuel, Wa-1819
      Jacob, Wa-1819
      John, Wa-1819
      Samuel, Ge-1812
      Willm., Sn-1792
LEMONS, John, Gi-1812
      Peter Sr., Gi-1812
LEMSIL?, Wm., Rb-1812
LENARD, Jacob, A-1805
LENNING, Isaac, Je-1822
      John, Je-1822(2)
LENOR, Young, Gr-1799
LENRE (Lewis?), John, Se-1799
LENTON, Alson, D-1811
      George, D-1811
      John, D-1811
LENTZ, Martin, Ge-1805
LEONARD, John, D-1805
      Joshua, Wh-1811
      William, D-1805
LEPER, Andrew, Ge-1783
LERUE, Abraham, Je-1800
LES, Gashere, Wa-1814
LESBY, Mathew, Sn-1811
LESCOLEET, John, Ge-1812
LESCOLLECT, John, Ge-1805
LESCOMB, John, Mu-1816
LESLEY, Henry, Gr-1805
LESLIE, John, Wa-1819
LESTER, Fountain, Gi-1819
      German, Gi-1010(?)
      Henry, Wi-1815
      Jacob Jr., K-1799
      James, Wi-1815, K-1799
      John, Gi-1812
      John Sr., Gi-1812
      John Jr., Gi-1812
      Mary, Ge-1812
      William, K-1799
LESTRY, John, K-1799
LETHERMAN, Nicholas, Wa-1819
LETLER, John, Ro-1805
LETNER, John, Je-1822
      Lewis, Je-1822
LETRAL, John, Gr-1804

LETT, James, Fr-1812
LETTERALL, Wm., Rb-1812
LEUTAR?, John, A-1805
LEUTY, William S., R-1819
LEVAN, Benj., W-1812
    John, D-1805
LEVI, Jefferson, Wh-1825
    Thomas, D-1811
LEVY, William, D-1811
LEWALLEN, Claiborne, Mu-1816
    Richard, A-1805
LEWALLIN, Richard, Gr-1799
LEWBOW, Henry, Cl-1803
    John, Cl-1803
LEWFIELD, Joseph, Rb-1812
LEWIS, Abner, Gr-1799
    Alexander, D-1805
    Amos Sr., Je-1800
    Amos Jr., Je-1800
    Andrs., Ro-1805
    Andrew, Je-1800
    Aron, Je-1822
    Benjamin, Wh-1825(2), K-1796,
        Gr-1821, Wh-1811, Su-1812
    Benj. H., Mu-1816
    Charles, Sn-1816, Sn-1811
    Daniel, Co-1827
    David, Su-1797, Su-1796
    Docr., Gi-1812
    Eli, Je-1822
    Elijah, Wh-1811
    Eliza F., Mu-1816
    Errel, Wi-1810
    Evan, Je-1800, Je-1822
    F. William, D-1805
    Fielding, Gr-1799
    Gabriel, Je-1822
    George, Je-1800, Co-1827, Su-1796,
        Je-1822
    George M., R-1819
    Henry, Je-1822
    Hercules, Su-1812
    Hiram, Sn-1823
    Isaac, R-1819
    Jacob, Wl-1804, Je-1800
    James, Fr-1812, Ro-1805
    Joel, D-1805, D-1811, Wi-1801,
        Mt-1798, Rb-1812
    John, Wi-1801, D-1805, Wh-1825,
        R-1819(2), Rb-1812
    Jonathan, Sn-1816
    Joseph, Wl-1804
    Joshua, Hu-1812
    Levi, Gi-1812
    M. James, D-1805
    McJames, D-1811
    Micajah G., Wi-1801
    Nathan, Su-1797
    Nathan, Su-1796 (in Washington)
    Parish, Gi-1812
    Rachel, Je-1822
    Richard, Mu-1816, A-1805, Je-1822
    Sam, W-1812
    Samuel, Wa-1819, Gi-1812
    Seth, Wl-1804, Mt-1798
    Stark, Sn-1816, Sn-1811
    Stephens, A-1805
    Thomas, Gr-1821, Hu-1812, D-1788,
        Wh-1825(2)
    Washington, Rb-1812
    William, Wh-1825, Je-1800, Su-1812,
        Su-1796

LEWIS, William Sr., Wh-1825, Wh-1811
    R-1819
    William Jr., Wh-1825, R-1819,
        Wh-1811
    Wm. B., D-1811
    Wm. Ferral, Mt-1798
    William T., D-1811, Mu-1816, Wi-1801,
        Wh-1811
    William T., heirs, R-1819
LEWISION, Nathan, Su-1797
LEWISON, William, Hw-1801
LEZELL, Abner, A-1805
LEZENBY, Robert, D-1811
LICANE, John, Bo-1800, Bo-1801
LICKLITER, Frederick, Je-1822
LIDDY, John, Bo-1801
LIDE, John Wilds, Gr-1821
LIDGEWOOD, John, C-1818
LIEGLER, Jacob, Sn-1787
LIGETE, William, Wi-1801
LIGGET, Jno., Ge-1783
LIGHT, George, Ro-1805
    John, Ge-1812
    Michael, Hu-1812
    WRight, Hu-1812
LIGHTEN, Christain, Wa-1819
LIGHTFOOT, Thomas, D-1811, D-1805, Wi-1810
LIGHTNER, Christian, Wa-1814
LIGHTTOWER, Thomas, Co-1827
LIKE, Joseph, Ge-1812
LIKENS, William, Ge-1805
LILE, George, D-1811
    Malicha, D-1811
LILER, Daniel, Robert, Hugh & William,
    D-1805
    Malichy, George & Henry, D-1805
LILLARD, Abraham, Co-1821, Co-1827
    James, Co-1827
    John, Co-1827, Co-1821
    Owen, Sn-1811
LILLERSEN, Andrew, Wa-1819
    Andrew Sr., Wa-1819
LILLEY, Benjamin, D-1805
LIME, Lamuel L., Sn-1816
LIMONS, John, Wi-1815
    Samuel, Wi-1815
LIMPS?, John, D-1811
LINARD, Jacob, A-1805
LINCE, Martin, Ge-1812(2)
LINCH, George, J-1802
    Hugh, D-1811, D-1805
    James, D-1811, D-1805
    Jeremiah, Gr-1799
    John, Gr-1799
LINCHORN, Elijah, D-1805
LINCIN, Niclos, Wi-1815
LINCOLN, Isaac, Ct-1798, Ct-1796
    Jessee, Wh-1825
LINDER, Jacob, A-1805
    John, W-1812
    Josiah, K-1799
LINDLEY, James, Mu-1816
LINDSAY, Abraham, Mu-1816
    Charles, Je-1822
    Edward, Mu-1811
    Isaac, Wl-1804, Sn-1787
    Isaac B., Mu-1816
    John, Mu-1811, Mu-1816
    Moses, K*-1815
    P. Jacob, Mu-1811
    Robert, Mu-1811
    Wm., K*-1815

LINDSEY, Isaac, Sn-1792
    James, Mt-1798, Gi-1812
    James J., Wh-1825
    John, Wi-1806, Sn-1811, Wl-1804, R-1808
    JOhn L., Gi-1819
    Robert, K*-1815
    Wiat, Sn-1811
LINE, Nathaniel, Je-1822
    William, Je-1822, Je-1800
LINEAR, Benjamin, D-1811
LINEBERGER, Nicholas, Wa-1819, Wa-1814
    Nicholis, Wa-1814
LINEBOUGH, Daniel, Ge-1812, Ge-1805
    Jacob, Ge-1805(2)
    Jacob Jr., Ge-1812
    John, Ge-1812, Ge-1805
LING, John, Wa-1819
LINGINFELTER, Jacob, Ge-1805
LINIT, John, D-1811
LINLEY, James, Fr-1812
    William, Fr-1812
LINS, James, Cl-1803
LINSEY, David, Ge-1783, Cl-1803
    Isaac, Sn-1816, Sn-1811
    James, Gi-1812
    Jesse, Ge-1805
    Moses, Wi-1815
    Saml., Gi-1812
    Zack, Sn-1811
LINSLAY, George W., Je-1822
LINSY, Nancy, Sn-1816
LINVAL, Thomas, Wa-1814
LINVILL, Richard, Gi-1812
LINVILLE, Abraham, C-1818
    Andrew, A-1805
    Richard, A-1805, C-1818
LIONS, Anderson, Gi-1819
LIOUH, John, Ct-1796
LIPES, John, Mu-1816
LIPIN, Allen, B-1812
LIPSCOMB, Anderson, Gr-1821
    John, Rb-1812, Mu-1816
    Thomas, Rb-1812
LIPSCOMBE, Spotswood, Gr-1821
LISBE, Aron, Gr-1805
LISBY, Aaron, Gr-1804
LISENLY, William, Wa-1819
LISINLY, Charles, Wa-1819
LISK, John, Wh-1825
    William, Wh-1825
LISTER, Abraham, Ro-1805
LITE, Henry, Su-1796, Su-1797
    Vatchel, Su-1797
    Vitchel, Su-1796
    William, Su-1796, Su-1797
LITEFOOT, Thomas, Wi-1815
LITERL, Richard, Gr-1804
LITLER, John, Ge-1805
LITRAL, John, Gr-1804
LITSINGER, George, Sn-1816
LITTEL, George, Su-1812
    John, Wi-1810
LITTER, George, Su-1797
    Thomas, Wh-1825
LITTLE, Abraham, Wi-1810
    Absolam, Bo-1805
    Benjamin, B-1812
    George, B-1812, Su-1812, Su-1796
    Harmon, Hu-1812
    Hosea H., Wh-1825
    Isaac, Wa-1819, D-1811

LITTLE, John, B-1812, Su-1812, Wi-1801, Wi-1815, D-1805
    John, estate, Wa-1819
    John M., Wh-1811, Wh-1825
    Jonas, estate, Wa-1819
    Lewis, Mt-1798
    Martin, Fr-1812, J-1802
    Matthias, Su-1812, Su-1797, Su-1796
    Stephen, Rb-1812
    Thomas, Bo-1800, Bo-1801, Bo-1805
    Valentine, Su-1812
    William, Mt-1798, Rb-1812
    William P., Mu-1816
    _____, A-1805
LITTLEFIELD, Edward B., Mu-1816
LITTLEPAGE, Thomas, Ro-1805
LITTON, James, C-1823, C-1818
    Rachel, C-1823, C-1818
LITTRELL, Kug, Wi-1801
    Lott, W-1812
LIVELY, Benjamin, Ro-1805
    Emond P., Je-1822
    Jacob, Je-1800
    John, A-1805, Bo-1800, K-1799
LIVENLY, Wiliam, Wa-1814
LIVERMORE, William, Gi-1819
LIVESEY, Jesse, Mu-1816
LIVINGSTON, Jacob, Gr-1821
LIVSEY, Carter, Wi-1810
    Jessee, Wi-1810
LLOYD, Joseph, Gr-1821
    Thomas, Gr-1821
LLYDA, Henry, Wh-1811
LOCH, Walter, Gi-1812
LOCK, Charles, D-1805
    James, Mu-1816, J-1802
    Joseph, D-1811(2)
    Matthew, heirs, Wi-1810
    Richard Sr., J-1802
    Richard Jr., J-1802
    Walter, Wi-1801
LOCKARD, Robert, Ct-1798
    William, Ct-1798
LOCKE, Jacob, B-1812
    John, R-1819, R-1808
    Jonas, B-1812
    Matthew, W-1812
    Robert, R-1819
    William, R-1819, B-1812
LOCKET, John, Wl-1804
LOCKEY, W. James, Bo-1800
LOCKHARD, Thomas, Mu-1811
LOCKHART, Banjm., Esq., W-1812
    Benjm., W-1812
    Hugh, D-1811
    John, Wh-1825, D-1811
    Robert, Ct-1796
    Thomas, Sn-1816, Mu-1816
    William, Ct-1796
LOCKHEART, Andrew, W-1812
    James, W-1812
    John, Je-1822
LOCKRICH, James, Jr., Mu-1816
    Robert, Mu-1816
LOCKRIDGE, James, Mu-1816
LOCKWOOD, John, Gr-1799
LOCUES, Andrew, Ro-1805
LODERWICK, John, Wa-1819
LODSPEACH, Christian, Ge-1812
    John, Ge-1812
    William, Ge-1812
LOE, Fielding, C-1823, C-1818

LOFLEN, Joseph, Mu-1816
LOFTEN, ___an, Se-1799
LOFTIN, Thomas, D-1805
LOFTON, Thomas, D-1811
LOGAN, Alexander, Bo-1801
    Charles, Bo-1800
    David, Wi-1801, Ge-1812, Ge-1805
    George, Ct-1798, Ct-1796, Sn-1811
    Henery, Bo-1801
    Isaac, Hu-1812
    Issac, Bo-1805
    James, Bo-1801, Bo-1800
    Manafee, D-1805
    Marrach, Mu-1816
    Robert, Mu-1816
    Samuel, R-1819
    William, Wi-1815, Fr-1812, B-1812,
        Bo-1801, Bo-1800
LOGANS, Wm., D-1788
LOGGINS, Samuel, Mu-1816
LOGGITT, Absolem, Hu-1812
LOGGS, Widow, heirs, Wl-1804
LOGSON, Eppy, Rb-1812
    Peter, Rb-1812
LOGUE, Caviner, D-1811
    David, D-1811
    Ezekiah, D-1811
    Menasse, D-1811
LOFTON, William & Thomas, D-1805
LOHORN, John, B-1812
LOID, William, B-1812
LOLLAR, James, Wh-1811
LOLLER, John, Wh-1825
LOMAS, Benjamin, D-1805
LONAS, Adam, Ge-1812
LONDON, Amos, Mu-1816
    James, Su-1812
LONEGE, James, Mu-1811
LONEY, Abrm., Mu-1816
LONKING, Moses, Wa-1814
LONG, Aaron, Gi-1812
    Alexander, Fr-1812
    Christian, Wa-1819
    David, Mu-1816, Wi-1801(2)
    Edward, Wl-1804, Gr-1804
    Gabriel, Gi-1812
    George, Wh-1811, Wh-1825
    Henery, Bo-1801
    Henry, Ge-1805, Gr-1804, Wa-1819,
        Je-1822
    Isaac, Gr-1821, Gr-1805, Mu-1811
    Isaac Sr., Gr-1804, Gr-1805
    Isaac Jr., Gr-1804, Gr-1805
    J. J., Mu-1816
    J. John, Mu-1811
    Jacob, Ge-1812(5)
    James, Rb-1812, Ro-1805, Wa-1814,
        Bl-1815, B-1812
    John, Fr-1812, Ge-1805(2), B-1812,
        W-1812, Gr-1804, Gr-1821(3)
    Joseph, Gr-1804, Je-1822, Gr-1805,
        Mu-1816, Mu-1811
    Michael, Wi-1815
    Moses, Je-1800
    Nicholas, Ge-1805, Ro-1805, Je-1822,
        Mt-1798
    Nicholas, Esqr., Mu-1816
    Nicholas, estate, Mu-1811
    P. Matthew, Mu-1811
    Patruke, Gi-1812
    Pirtman, Gr-1821
    Reuben, Gr-1821, Bl-1815

LONG, Richard, B-1812
    Robert, Gr-1804, Rb-1812, Gr-1799,
        Gr-1821, Gr-1805, Mu-1811
    Samuel, Wi-1801
    Silas, Bl-1815
    Tobias, A-1805
    William, B-1812(2), Ge-1805, Fr-1812,
        Gi-1812, Rb-1812, R-1819,
        R-1808, Mt-1798, D-1788
    William C., Mu-1816
    _____, Bo-1800
LONGACRE, Benjamin, Ge-1800
    John, Ge-1800
    Iverson, Su-1812
    Richard, Je-1822
LONGFORD, Gassten, Ct-1798
LONGMARS, Elijah, C-1823
LONGMIRE, John, C-1823
    Joseph, Wa-1814
    Sarah, Wa-1814
LONGMIRES, Wm., Wl-1804
LONGMORE, Joseph, Wa-1819
LOOIS, John, Co-1821
LOOK, Richard T., Wi-1810
LOOKERS, Charles, Sn-1816
LOONEY, Abraham, Mu-1811
    Abram, Su-1812
    David, Su-1797
    Isaac, Sn-1816, Sn-1811
    Jessee Jr., Ro-1805
    John, W-1812
    Joseph, Su-1812, Ro-1805
    Martin, Sn-1811
    Mesha, Sn-1816
    Moses, Su-1797
    Peter, Sn-1816, Sn-1811, Wi-1810,
        Sn-1792, Sn-1787(2)
    Robert, W-1812, Sn-1792
    Samuel, Su-1812
    Stephen, W-1812
LOONY, David, Bl-1815
    Moses, Ro-1805
LOOTER, Benjn., Hu-1812
    Wm., Hu-1812
LOOY, Matthew, B-1812
LORANCE, John, SN-1792, Mu-1816
LORD, Alexander, D-1805
    Benjamin, Bl-1815
    Curtiss, W-1812
LORING, Thomas, Su-1812
LOSSISSER, Conrad, Wa-1819
LOT, Casper, Wa-1819
    John, Wa-1819
LOTNER, Francis, K*-1815
LOTSPEICH, Christopher, Ge-1805
    John, Ge-1805
LOTT, John, Wh-1811
LOTTS, Henry, Su-1812
LOTTY, Therman, Mu-1811
LOUDERWICK, Henry, Wa-1819
LOUGH, Jacobs, Je-1800
LOUIS, Benjamin, Sn-1823
    James, Bl-1815
LOURY, Adam, Je-1800
    James, Je-1800
    John, Fr-1812
    Robert, Je-1800
LOUTLAW, Alexander, Mt-1798
LOVE, Charles, Ge-1812
    David, Mu-1811(2), Mu-1816
    James, Sn-1811, Mu-1811, D-1811,
        Ge-1812, Wi-1801

LOVE, John, Ct-1798, Ge-1805, B-1812,
      Ge-1812, R-1819, Je-1822
    John Sr., Mu-1811
    John Jr., Mu-1811
    John D., Mu-1816
    John G., Wi-1815, Wi-1810
    Joseph, D-1788, D-1811, Wi-1810,
      R-1819, Wi-1815
    Josiah, Gi-1812
    Robert, Mu-1811, Mu-1816, Wa-1814,
      R-1808, R-1819
    Roberte, Wi-1810
    Samuel, D-1811
    Samuel W., Mu-1816
    Thomas, Ge-1805
    W. Samuel, Mu-1811
    William, R-1819, Je-1800
LOVEALL, Zachariah, Ge-1805
LOVEING, Walter, Sn-1816
LOVEL, Colson, Sn-1816
    James & John, D-1805
    Sias, Sn-1811
    Zekiriah, Sn-1816
LOVELACE, Daniel, Mo-1825
    Wm., Gr-1799
LOVELADY, Jesse, J-1802
    Jessee, Wh-1825
    Levy, B-1812
    Simeon, B-1812
    Thomas, Wh-1811, Se-1799, Wh-1825
    Wm., Se-1799
LOVELATY, Jno., Ge-1783
    Jos., Ge-1783
    Marshal, Ge-1783
LOVELES, David, Bo-1800, Bo-1801
LOVELL, George, Gr-1805
    James, D-1811
    Jeremiah, Gr-1821, Gr-1805
    John, Gr-1805
    Robert, D-1811
    Thomas, D-1811
LOVELS, Daniel, Rb-1812
LOVELY, Rose, C-1823
LOVENS, Hough L., B-1812
LOVET, Lankester, Wi-1810
LOVETT, John, Wi-1815
LOVEY, John, Sn-1811
LOVIN, Walter, Sn-1811
LOVING, Henry, Sn-1792
LOVY, Henry, D-1811
LOW, Abner, Gr-1805
    David, Fr-1812(Love?)
    Ezekiel, W-1812
    George, Su-1796
    Isaac, W-1812, D-1805
      John, K-1799
    Marvil, Rb-1812
    Robert, Wa-1189
    Thomas & Sam C., Wa-1819
    William, D-1805, W-1812
LOWD, Abel, Ge-1805
LOWDEN, Basley, Wh-1825
    Jessee, Wh-1825
    John, Wh-1825
    Willis, Wh-1825
LOWDER, John, Mu-1811
LOWE, Abner, Gr-1805, Gr-1804, Gr-1821
    Andrew E., Bl-1815
    George, Su-1812
    Isaac, A-1805
LOWELL, Andrew, Wh-1825
    John M., D-1811

LOWER, Andrew, A-1805
    Peter, Gr-1799
LOWERTY?, Jacob, Mu-1811
LOWERY, Alexander, J-1802
    Alexander Jr., Wh-1825
    James, Wh-1825
    John, Bo-1800, C-1818, D-1805
    Nelson, D-1811
    Peter, Gr-1805
    Robert B., C-1823
    Robert E., Wh-1811
    Sarah, Wi-1810
    Thomas, J-1802
    Wm., Gi-1819
LOWES, John, C-1823
LOWREY, Alexander, Wh-1811, Wh-1825
    Charles, Ge-1805, Wh-1825(2)
    James, Wh-1825
    John, Bo-1800
    Mark, Wh-1825(2)
    Nelson, D-1811
    Wm., Bo-1800
LOWRY, Adam, Wa-1819
    Alexander Sr., Wh-1825
    Charles, Ge-1812
    Greenberry, B-1812
    Henry, W-1812, W-1805
    John, Su-1796, Su-1797, Su-1812
    John, mercht., Bo-1801
    John, atty., Bo-1801
    Joseph, Wa-1819
    Peter, Gr-1805
    Robert E., Wh-1825
    Samuel Sr., Je-1800
    Samuel Jr., Je-1800
    Squire, Mu-1816, Mu-1811
    Thos. Sr., W-1812, W-1805
    Thomas Jr., W-1812, W-1805
    Wm., for Jas., Bo-1801
LOY, Joel, A-1805
    John Jr., A-1805
    John Sr., A-1805
LOYD, Able, Ge-1812
    Daniel, Mu-1811
    Frethias, Ge-1805
    Garret, Sn-1811
    Howell, B-1812
    James, Ge-1812, W-1812, Fr-1812,
      Ct-1796, Ct-1798, Ge-1805(2)
    John, Ge-1805, Ct-1796
    Joseph, B-1812
    Levy, Ct-1796
    Lewis, D-1811
    Nathan, B-1812
    Nicholas, B-1812
    Owen, Gr-1799, Fr-1812
    Robertson, Ge-1805, Ge-1812
    Stephen, Wi-1815
    Thomas, Ge-1805, Ge-1812
    William, Wa-1814, Mu-1811
    Wilson, B-1812
LUALLEN, Richard, A-1805
LUCAS, Andrew, D-1811
    David, Wi-1801
    George, Rb-1812
    John, D-1811, Bo-1800
    Oston, Hu-1812
    Parker, Rb-1812
    Thomas, R-1819
LUCIAS, Thomas, Bo-1800
LUCK, B., Mu-1816
    Samuel Jr., Mu-1811

LUCK, Thomas, Wl-1804
    William, Wl-1804
LUCKEY, Andrew, Ge-1805
    David, Mu-1811
    James, Ge-1805
LUCKY, David, Mu-1816
    James, Ge-1812
LUCRE, Joseph, Gi-1812
LUCTON, King, Sn-1816
LUDGRETT, John, D-1805
LUEDER, Jacob, A-1805
LUGEL, Wiliam, Su-1812
LUIS, Mandy, Se-1799
LUMLEY, Joseph, Wi-1810
LUMMINS, Samuel, Ro-1805
LUNDY, Daniel, Wh-1811
LUNSFORD, Jesse, Wa-1819
LUNTZ, William, D-1811
LUNY, John, Hw-1799
LUP, Joseph, Rb-1812
LUPIN, John, B-1812
LUSH, Samuel, Ct-1798
LUSK, James, D-1811, Mu-1811(2), Mu-1816
    John, Ct-1798, W-1812
    John Sr., W-1812
    John Jr., W-1812
    Jos., Ge-1783, Bl-1815
    Josiah, Fr-1812
    Robert, Mu-1811, Mu-1816, Ct-1796, Ct-1798
    Samuel, Mu-1816, Ct-1796, Gr-1799
    Samuel Sr., Mu-1816
    Samuel Jr., Mu-1811
    Thomas, W-1812
    William, Li-1812*, W-1812, J-1802
    William Sr., Fr-1812
    William Jr., Fr-1812
LUSTER, Edward, Ge-1805
    Jacob, K-1799(Lester?)
    James, Ro-1805
    John, Ro-1805, Ge-1812
    William, Ge-1812
    Zachariah, Ge-1812
LUSTOR, Alexander & George, D-1805
LUTER, Holland, Rb-1812
    Laurence, Rb-1812
    Matthew, Rb-1812
    Matthew Jr., Rb-1812
LUTGART, John, D-1811
LUTGERT, John, D-1811
LUTHEN, George, B-1812
LUTTERELL, John, Gr-1805
LUTTREL, Richard, Gr-1805
LUTTRELL, Edward, Ro-1805
    James C., K*-1815
    Mason, R-1808
    Moses, Ro-1805
LYAL, Joseph, Wi-1815
LYCEA, Gideon, Wh-1825
LYLE, Abner, Je-1822
    David, Je-1800
    Robert, Mu-1816
    Samuel, Je-1800
LYLES, Thomas, Je-1822
LYMITH, Moses, Wh-1825
LYN, Jacob, W-1812
LYNAS, George, B-1812
LYNCH, James, Mu-1811, Mu-1816
    Jeremiah, Gr-1799
    John, A-1805
    John Sr., Gr-1799
    John Jr., Gr-1799
LYNCH, William, Gr-1799
LYNIFFIN?, Jese, Se-1799
LYNN, A., D-1788
    James, Rb-1812
LYNTZ, William, Mu-1816
LYNVILLE, Moses, Wh-1811
LYON, Andrew, Mu-1816
    Ahser, Wa-1814
    Ezekiel, Wa-1814
    Ezekiel Sr., Wa-1819
    Ezekiel Jr., Wa-1814, Wa-1819
    Henry, Wi-1815
    James, Je-1800
    Nathaniel, C-1818
    Peter, Gi-1812
    Peter Sr., Gi-1812
    Richard, Gi-1812
    William, Gi-1812, Wa-1814, K*-1815, Wa-1819
LYONS, Patrick, D-1805
    Richard, Sn-1816
LYTLE, Archibald, Wi-1801, Wi-1815
    Archable, Wi-1810
    William, D-1805, D-1811(2), Wi-1801
    William Sr., Wl-1804
LYTTLE, John, Mu-1816
LYTTLETON, John, Fr-1812
MABANE, Elexd., Wi-1801
MABANS, Alexr., Wi-1810
    James, heirs, Wi-1810
MABERRY, James, Gi-1812
    John, Sn-1811
MABERY, James, Sn-1811
MABIN, James, Wi-1801, Mt-1798
MABRY, Benjn., Sn-1816
    Hamlin, Wi-1810
    James, Sn-1816
    Levi, Sn-1816
    Oren, Sn-1811
    Seth, Sn-1811
MACADOO, John, A-1805
MACE, Ann, Ge-1812(2)
    John, Ge-1812
MACEY, Eli, Wi-1801
    Robert, A-1805
MACFARLANE, S. John, Gr-1804
MACGINAS, William, Wh-1825
MACINTOSH, Darrel, D-1811
MACK, Constantine, Mu-1816, Mu-1811
    James, Mu-1816
    James H., Mu-1816
    John, Mu-1811
    Mathias, Sn-1811
    Robert, Mu-1811
    William, Mu-1816
MACKABEE, Abnego, Mu-1816
MACKAY, Catharine, Su-1812
    John, Su-1812, Su-1796, Su-1797
    Richard, Wh-1811
    Samuel, Su-1812
MACKEN, Barnabas, Wa-1819
    Edward, Wa-1819
MACKERY, William, D-1788
MACKEY, Daniel, Wl-1804
    John, Mt-1798, Bo-1800
    Robert, Wl-1804
MACKIN, Edward, Wa-1814
MACKINY, Francis, Sn-1811
MACKLIN, James C., Wi-1801
    William, Mt-1798
MACKNEY, Jesse, D-1811
    John, Bo-1800

MACKY, Ambros, Wl-1804
    Henry, Wl-1804(2)
    John, Ge-1805
    Samuel, Wl-1804
MACLIN, John, Ct-1798, Ge-1805
MACUM, John, Wh-1811
MACY, Barechai, Je-1822
MADCALF, William, Wh-1285
MADCAP, William, Ge-1805
MADDEN, Elisha, D-1811
    William, B-1812
MADDING, Clisha, Wl-1815
MADDOX, Ellen, D-1811
    William, Wi-1815
MADDRY, Buckner, Gi-1812
    James, Gi-1812
MADEN, Andrew, Wa-1819
    Hw-1801
MADLEN, Lewis, B-1812
MADLIN, Lewis, B-1812
MADLOCK, William, B-1812, Wl-1804
MADLY, James, Gr-1805
MADOX, Wilson, Rb-1812
MADSEN, Washington D., B-1812
MAENTAIN, James, Wa-1819
MAGAHAY, Samuel, Co-1821
MAGEE, John, Wl-1804
    Lewis, Gi-1812
    Samuel, J-1802
MAGERS, John, Gr-1799
    William, Ge-1812
MAGET, William, Je-1822
MAGGORD, Henry, Su-1812
MAGHEE, George, R-1819
MAGILL, Hugh, Ge-1812
    Samuel, estate, Ge-1812
    William, R-1808, Ge-1812
MAGNESS, David, D-1811
    Johnathan, D-1811
MAGPIE, Samuel, Gr-1805
MAGRAM, Michael, C-1823
MAGRAW, Elisha, Hu-1812
MAGRESS, Robert, Wl-1804
MAGUIER, Allegany, Wi-1815
MAGUIRE, Patrick, Mu-1816
MAHAM, Archibald, Rb-1812
    James, Rb-1812
MAHAN, Alexander, K-1796, Ro-1805
    David, Ro-1805
    Isaac, R-1819
    James, K-1799, Ge-1783
    John, K-1799, R-1819
    Lant, K-1799
MAHO, Joseph, Mu-1816
MAHONEY, James, Wa-1819
    William, Wa-1819
MAIDEN, Isaac, Hw-1799
MAIFIELD, William, Wh-1825
MAILEN, Robert, D-1811
MAILICOAT, James, Gr-1805
MAIN, Isaac, Wi-1810
    James, D-1788
MAINES, David, Wa-1819
MAINS, David, Wa-1814
MAIRS, Alexander, Wi-1801
    Hugh, Wi-1801
    Isaac, Wi-1801
    John, Wi-1815
    Joseph, Wi-1801(2)
    Samuel, Wi-1801(2), Wi-1810
MAJOR, James, Se-1799
MAJORS, Abner, Je-1800

MAJORS, Absolom, Je-1800, R-1819
    Benjamin, Fr-1812
    James, R-1819
    John, B-1812(2)
    Noble, B-1812
    Peter, Je-1800, R-1819
    Robert, B-1812
    Thomas, Ct-1798, Je-1800, Su-1812
    Wm., Gi-1812
MAK, H. James, Mu-1811
    William, Mu-1811
MALACOAT, James, Gr-1804
MALCOM, Alexander, Bo-1801
    John, Bo-1800
    William, Bo-1800, Bo-1805
MALCOMB, Joseph, Mu-1816
MALDWIN, Ambros, Sn-1792
MALEN, Stephen, B-1812
MALERAY, Philip, Wh-1825
MALICK, David, Ge-1805
MALICOAT, Dedman, Gr-1821
    John, Gr-1821
    William, Gr-1821
MALISTER, James, Wa-1814
MALLAND, John, B-1812
    Thornton, B-1812
MALLARD, Joseph, Sn-1811
MALLEN, Andrew, Wa-1814
MALLICOAT, Phillip, C-1823
MALLOCK, Casell, Hu-1812
MALLORY, Philip, W-1815
MALLOY, Thomas, estate, Wi-1815
MALOANE, Richard, Gr-1821
MALONE, B. Thomas, Mu-1811
    George, Su-1812, Gi-1812, Su-1797
    Hallery, Sn-1816
    Humphry, Ge-1812
    John, Ge-1812, Su-1812, Ge-1805
    Joseph, Su-1812
    Michael, Su-1812, Su-1797
    Michael Jr., Su-1812
    Michal, Su-1796
    Miles, Gi-1812
    Richard, C-1823(2), Gr-1804, C-1818
    Sarah, Wi-1815
    Thomas, D-1811
    Thos. B., Mu-1816
    William, Ge-1812, Su-1812, Ge-1805
MALONEY, Hugh, Ge-1812, Ge-1805
    John, Ge-1812, Ge-1805
    John Jr., Ge-1812
    Joseph, Ge-1812
    Robert, Ge-1812, Ge-1805
MALOY, James, Ge-1805
MALSBERGER, John, Ge-1812
MALTSBERGER, Elenor, Ge-1812
MALUGAN, William, Wi-1010
MALUGEN, John, D-1788
MANARD, Gibson, Je-1822
MANASCOE, Jno., Gi-1812
MANDLY, Caleb, Wi-1815, Wi-1810
    Calebb, Wi-1801
MANEFEE, John, Gi-1812
    Jonas Sr., D-1811
    Jonas Jr., D-1811
    Thomas, D-1811
MANERD, James, Je-1800
MANES, George, R-1819
    Isam, Ge-1812
MANESS, James, D-1811
    John, D-1805
    Lewis, D-1811

MANEY, _____, Gr-1799
MANFIELD, William, Wa-1819(2)
MANFREE, James, Sn-1811
MANGUM, Edwin, Mu-1816
　　Littleberry, Mu-1816
MANIER, John Wm., Wi-1801
　　Nicholas, Ro-1805
MANIFEE, John, R-1808
　　Willis, Wh-1825
MANIFFEE, Jonas, D-1805
MANIFOLD, James, Se-1799
MANIGN, John, Wi-1810
MANIYARD, James, Wh-1825
　　William Sr., Wh-1825
　　William Jr., Wh-1825
MANKIN, William, A-1805
MANLENDEST, James, Se-1799
MANLEY, Ancel, A-1805
　　Caleb, Wi-1801
　　David, Gr-1821
　　Reuben, B-1812
MANLIFF, Benjamin, Mu-1811
MANLY, Archibald, Mu-1816
　　Benjamin, Je-1822
　　Cornelius, D-1811
　　William, Gr-1805, Je-1822
MANN, Robert, D-1811, Wl-1804
　　Thomas, Gr-1821, Gr-1804
　　William, Wl-1804, Fr-1812
MANNEFEE, Capt., K-1796
MANNERD, Andrew, Wh-1825
MANNESS, Thomas, D-1811
MANNET, James, Wl-1804
MANNEY, Wi-1815
MANNING, Caleb, D-1811
　　Ephraim, D-1811
　　James, heirs, Wh-1811
　　Samuel, D-1811
　　William, Wi-1815, D-1811
MANNOCK, Larsus, Gi-1819
MANNON, Burrell, Wh-1825
　　Meredith, Gr-1805
MANOR, Thomas, Gr-1805
　　William, Wh-1811
MANS, William, Wa-1811
MANSFIELD, John, Je-1822
　　Thomas, Je-1822
MANSKER, Gasper, Sn-1792
　　George, Wi-1810
　　Kasper, Sn-1787
　　Lewis, Wi-1810
MANSON, William, Je-1822
MANSSER, Jasper, Sn-1811
MANTON, Charles, D-1811
MANTOOTH, Henry, Ge-1805
　　John, Co-1821
MANUEL, Cudbert, Bo-1801
　　Cudbreath, Bo-1805
　　Fleet, Bo-1805
　　Valentine, Bo-1805, Bo-1801
MANWELL, Thos. Jr., B-1812
MAPLES, James, Je-1800
　　John, Gi-1812, Gr-1805
　　Josiah, Gr-1805
　　William, Gi-1812, Je-1800, Gr-1805
　　William Sr., Gr-1805, Gr-1804
　　William Jr., Gr-1804, Gr-1805
MARBERRY, Isaac, B-1812
　　John, B-1812
MARBOW, William, Gi-1819
MARCAL, James, W-1812
MARCEL, Levrence, Gr-1799

MARCH, Henry, Su-1812
　　Henry Sr., Wa-1819
　　Silas, D-1805
MARCHANT, Williams M., Gr-1805
MARCHBANKS, Harold, Wh-1825
　　Jonathan, B-1812
MARCHEAD, John, Mu-1811
MARCK, Gravener Jr., Ge-1812
MARCLE, Laurence, Gr-1799
　　Peter, Gr-1799
MARCUM, Elisha, Sn-1816
MARDICK, Wm., Bo-1801
MARE, Moses, Wi-1814
MARES, William, W-1812
MARFIELD, Matthias, Mu-1816
MARGOT, Henry, Su-1797
　　Samuel, Su-1797
MARGRAVE, John, Gr-1805, Gr-1804
MARGRAVES, John, Je-1800
MARHEL, Abraham, Ge-1812
MARIAN, Christian & John, D-1805
　　William, Su-1812
MARIER, Jesse, Gi-1819
MARIN, John, Su-1812
MARION, Peter, Mu-1816
MARIS, Edmond, K-1796
MARKHAM, Bartlett, A-1805
　　Beverly, Gr-1799
　　Nathaniel, Wh-1825
　　William, A-1805
MARKRUM, Josiah, Hw-1799
MARKS, William, D-1811
MARLAN, Archible, Sn-1811
MARLAND, Thos., Sn-1811
MARLIN, Daniel, A-1805
　　James, Wi-1815
　　Willm., Sn-1811
MARLOW, Charles, Gi-1819
　　Edward, Wl-1804
　　George, Wl-1804
　　Thomas, Gr-1799
　　William, Wh-1825
MARR, Gideon, Wa-1819
　　Milton, Wa-1819
　　Widon, Wa-1819
MARRCOLT, Richard, Ro-1805
MARRINER, William, C-1818
MARRIOTT, John, Ro-1805
MARRON, Leonard, Gi-1819
MARROW, Hugh, W-1812
　　John, Rb-1812, W-1812
　　Robert, W-1812
MARRS, Alexander, Wl-1804
　　Benjamin, R-1819
　　Hugh, Wl-1804, Wi-1801
MARSALL, Wm., Wi-1815
MARSH, Dennis, Wh-1825
　　Gravener, Ge-1805
　　Graviner Sr., Ge-1812
　　Henry, Wa-1814
　　Henry Jr., Wa-1819
　　John, Wh-1825
　　Jonas, Wa-1819
MARSHAL, Bartlet, Gr-1804
　　Bartlett, Gr-1805
　　David, Wl-1804
　　Dickson, Mt-1798
　　Eli, Sn-1811
　　Ezekel, Sn-1816
　　Francis, Sn-1816
　　Gillen, D-1788
　　Hardy, Sn-1816

MARSHAL, Jame, Wl-1804
    John, D-1788, Mt-1798
    Joseph, Wa-1819
    Mathew, Fr-1812
    Solomon, Wl-1804
    William, D-1788, Wi-1801
MARSHALL, Abraham, Ge-1805
    Bartly, Fr-1812
    Benjjamin, Je-1822
    Elihu, D-1811
    James, D-1805, D-1811
    Jarret, B-1812
    John, B-1812
    Loren, D-1805
    Wm., Wi-1810
MARSHEL, Bartlett, Gr-1799
    Elizibeth, Wi-1810
    Francis, Sn-1811
    Joseph, Sn-1811
    _____, Wi-1815
MARTAIN, John, Wi-1815
    Luke, Ge-1812
    Paul, Wi-1815
MARTE?, Joseph, Gi-1812
MARTEN, Tavenor?, W-1812
MARTENDALE, Wm., W-1812
MARTIAN, Obediah, Sn-1811
MARTIN, A., D-1788
    Abraham, Mt-1798
    Abrehem, Sn-1816
    Albert, Gr-1804
    Alexander, W-1812, Wh-1285, Wi-1801
        W-1805
    Andrew, Sn-1816, Ge-1783, Sn-1816
    Anny, Ge-1805
    Archibald, Wl-1804, Sn-1816
    Azarias, Wa-1814
    Barkley, B-1812
    Barton, Sn-1792(2)
    Benjamin, W-1812, B-1812
    Boston, Sn-1816, Sn-1811
    Brice, Wl-1804
    Caffrey, Wh-1811, Wh-1825
    Caffrey Jr., Wh-1825
    Campbell, Mu-1811, Mu-1816
    Canick, C-1818
    Daniel, Cl-1803, C-1823, Fr-1812,
        Gr-1799, A-1805, D-1811
    David, W-1812, Mu-1811, W-1805
    Edward, Wa-1819
    Esom, Wh-1825
    Gabriel, Rb-1812
    George, Ge-1783, Sn-1792, Gr-1799,
        Wi-1810, Sn-1816, Mu-1816(2)
        D-1811(2), D-1805, Sn-1811,
        Gr-1805
    George Sr., C-1818
    George M., D-1811
    Green, Wh-1825
    Henry, Wa-1819
    Hugh, Wa-1819, Je-1822, Su-1812,
        Je-1800
    Inglish, C-1818
    Isaac, Su-1812
    Jacob, W-1812, Sn-1811, W-1805
    James, Rb-1812, W-1812, Gi-1812,
        Wa-1814, A-1805, Bo-1800,
        Fr-1812, Bo-1801, Sn-1811,
        D-1811(3), Sn-1816, Wh-1825,
        D-1805, W-1805
    James, estate, Wa-1814
    Jesse, Wh-1811, Rb-1812

MARTIN, Joel, Gr-1821, Gr-1805, Gr-1804
    John, Wh-1811, Wh-1812(3), R-1808,
        Gi-1812, Hw-1801, Fr-1812,
        C-1818, B-1812, Gr-1799,
        Gr-1805, D-1811(2), D-1805,
        Wh-1825, Sn-1811, W-1805
    John Sr., Hw-1801
    John Jr., Hw-1801
    John D., Mu-1816
    John & Sarah, D-1805
    Jonathan W., Wi-1815
    Joseph, Gi-1812, R-1819, Wa-1814,
        Bl-1815, D-1788, Sn-1811,
        Wl-1804
    Joshua, Wh-1825, Gr-1805
    Lewis, Sn-1816, Gi-1819
    Luis, Sn-1811
    Luke, Bo-1801
    Matt, B-1812
    Michael, Wa-1814
    Nancy, Sn-1816
    Nathan, C-1818
    Nathaniel, C-1823
    Obediah, Cl-1803
    Oliver, Hu-1812
    Olliver, Sn-1816
    Orramusit, Je-1822
    Patrick, Rb-1812, R-1819
    Payton, Sn-1823
    Richard, Gi-1812, Ge-1783, Fr-1812
    Richard Sr., B-1812
    Richard Jr., B-1812
    Robert, Je-1822, Su-1812, Gr-1821,
        W-1805, D-1811
    Robert N., Wh-1825
    Samuel, Gi-1812, D-1788
    Silas, D-1811
    Stephen, Wh-1825, C-1818
    Thomas, Rb-1812(2), Gr-1799, Wh-1825,
        Hw-1799
    Thomas Sr., Wh-1825
    Thomas Jr., Wh-1285
    Warner, Bo-1800, Bo-1801, Bo-1805
    William, Rb-1812, W-1812, Gi-1812(2)
        B-1812(3), Fr-1812, C-1823,
        Gr-1821, Wi-1815, Wl-1804,
        Sn-1816(3), Sn-1811(3),
        Wh-1825, Mu-1816, Gr-1805,
        Mu-1811
    William Jr., Gi-1812
    Zacheriah, Mu-1816
    Zechariah, Mu-1811
    _____, Ge-1812
MARTINDAL, John, Gi-1812
MARTINDALE, Daniel, J-1802
MARTINGALE, Danl., Gi-1812
MARTINON, William, B-1812
MARTON, Isiah, D-1811
    John, Sn-1811, D-1811, Hw-1799
    Willis, D-1811
MARVICK, WM., Bo-1800
MARX, Thomas, Gi-1812
MARYAN, John F., Wi-1810
MASCANDER, David, Bl-1815
MASE, HEnry, Gr-1804
    John, Gr-1804
    Legin, Gr-1804
    Sharad, Gr-1804
MASENGALE, Michael, Gr-1805
MASH, John, Su-1797
MASKELL, William, Je-1822, Ge-1812
MASNER, James, Ge-1812

MASNER, John, Mc-1825
    Teter, Ge-1812
MASON, Abram, Wi-1815
    Abreham, Wi-1810
    Asa, Rb-1812
    Caleb, Wh-1825
    Calib, Wh-1825
    Charles, Wi-1815
    Dan, Wi-1815
    DAniel, Wi-1801
    Foster, Rb-1812
    Isaac, Rb-1812
    Isaac Sr., Wi-1810, Wi-1815
    Isaac Jr., Wi-1810, Wi-1815
    Jacob, Wi-1810
    James, Rb-1812
    Jesse, Rb-1812
    John, Mo-1825, B-1812, Wh-1825(2)
    Joseph, Wi-1815
    Joshua, B-1812
    Michael, Ct-1796
    Nathaniel, Ro-1805
    Reuben, Je-1800
    Reubin, Gr-1799, Gr-1804
    Robert, Wh-1285
    Samuel, Rb-1812
    Solomon, C-1823, C-1818
    Thomas, Wi-1815
    William, Wh-1825, Rb-1812
MASONER, George, Ge-1812
MASSA, John, Wh-1811
MASSANGALE, Mikel, Gr-1799
    John, C-1818
    Kinchen, Wi-1810
MASSENGILL, James, Wa-1819, Wa-1814
    John, Wa-1814
    William, Wa-1819, Wa-1814
MASSEY, Adam, Wh-1825
    Daniel R., Je-1822
    Fredrick, Sn-1816
    James, Wh-1825, Hu-1812
    John, Hu-1812, Wh-1825, Gr-1805
    Jonathan, Gr-1799, Gr-1805, Gr-1804,
        Gi-1812
    Sollimon, Ro-1805
    Wm. Sr., Hu-1812
    _____, Wh-1825
MASSINGALE, Solomon, A-1805
MASSINGALL, Henry, Su-1796
    John, Wa-1819
    William, Wa-1819
MASSINGILL, Henry, Su-1812
    James, Gr-1821
    Mary J., Gr-1821
    Michael, Gr-1804, Gr-1821
    Narcissa F., Gr-1821
    Robert, Gr-1821
MASSON, Joseph, Ct-1798
    Michael, Ct-1798
MASSY, John, Mu-1816
MAST, Obadiah, Mu-1816
    Simpson, Mu-1816
MASTEN, Thos., Sn-1792
MASTERS, George, Fr-1812
MASTERSON, Aaron, K-1799
    Hugh, J-1802
    John, K-1799, A-1805
    Lazr., Gi-1812
    Thos., Wi-1801(3), D-1811, K-1799,
        Ro-1805
MASTIN, James, Fr-1812
MASTON, Thomas, Sn-1787

MASTUMAS?, John, B-1812
MATERSON, William, W-1812
MATHEIS, James, Bo-1800
MATHENY, Duncan, Gr-1805
MATHERLY, Levi, Wa-1814
MATHERS, John, Wi-1810
MATHERSHEAD, Francis, D-1811
MATHERSON, Cornelius, Wi-1810
MATHES, Alexander, Wa-1819, Wa-1814
    Allen, D-1811
    Ebenzer, Wa-1814
    George, Wa-1819, Wa-1814
    James, D-1811
    John, Wa-1819, Wa-1814
MATHESS, John, Sn-1816
MATHEW, Allen, D-1805
    Elias, D-1805
    Joel, Ge-1783
MATHEWS, Cornelious, Wi-1810
    Cornelius, Wi-1801, Wa-1819
    Davis, Mu-1811
    Ebenezer, Wa-1819
    James, Ge-1812
    Jeremiah, Je-1800
    Joseph, Ge-1812
    Richard, D-1811
    William, Ge-1812(2)
MATIONS, Thos., C-1818
MATHIS, John, Wi-1810, Fr-1812
    Thomas, C-1818, Fr-1812
MATLOCK, James, Ro-1805
    Jason, Su-1796, Ro-1805
    John, Ro-1805
    Luke?, Hu-1812, Su-1796, Su-1797
    Moore, Ro-1805
    Smith, Hu-1812
    William, D-1805, D-1811, Sn-1816,
        Sn-1811, J-1802, Ro-1805
MATTHES, James, Bo-1801
    Jonathan, Bo-1801
MATTHEW, Cornelius, Wi-1815
    John, Gi-1819
    Johnson, Wi-1815
    Kinchen, Ro-1805
MATTHEWS, Abner, Mu-1816
    Archblad, Ro-1805
    Archiley, W-1812
    David, Mu-1816
    Isham, Wi-1810, Wi-1815
    James, J-1802
    John, Wi-1815(2), Mu-1816, Mu-1811,
        Rb-1812
    Joseph, Mu-1811, Mu-1816
    Kinchen, W-1812
    Obadiah, Ge-1783
    Richard, D-1805
    Robert, Mu-1811, Mu-1816
    Sampson Sr., Rb-1812
    Sampson Jr., Rb-1812
    Sampson, J. P., Rb-1812
    Samuel, J-1802, Ge-1782
    Thomas, J-1802, W-1812, B-1812
    Walter, J-1802
    William, Wh-1825
MATTHIAS, James, Ge-1805
    Richard, Wh-1825
    William, Ge-1805
MATTLOCK, Rial, Ro-1805
MATTOCK, Chas., Gr-1810
    George, Wa-1819
    Isham, Wa-1814
    Isom, Wa-1819

MATTOCK, William, D-1811
    Zachariah, Wa-1819, Wa-1814
MATTONLY, Walter, C-1818
MATTOX, Daniel, A-1805
    Nathan, A-1805
MAUK, Andrew, Su-1797
    Henry, Su-1797
    Samuel, Wa-1819
MAULDEN, James, D-1788
MAULDER, Henry, Gr-1805
    John, Gr-1805
    Voluntine, Gr-1805
MAULSBY, William, Je-1800
MAUPIN, Amos, C-1823
MAUR, Wm., D-1788
MAURICE, Charles, Wh-1825
MAURY, Abram, Wi-1801(3), Wi-1815(2),
    Wi-1810
    James, D-1811
    Philip, Wi-1801
    Phillip, Wi-1810
    Tho. T., Wi-1815
    William, D-1811
MAUSER, Daniel, W-1812
    George, W-1812
MAXEY, Bennet, D-1811
    James, D-1811
    John, Wl-1804, D-1811
    Walter, Wl-1804
    William, D-1811
MAXFIELD, Isaac, Je-1822
    John, W-1812
    Nimrod, Gr-1804
    Seth, Gr-1799
    Thomas, Ct-1798
MAXSERY, Edward, Sn-1792
    Wm., Sn-1792
MAXSEY, Jessee, Sn-1787
MAXWELL, A. William, Mu-1811
    Danl., B-1812
    James, D-1811, Mt-1798, D-1805,
        Bo-1801
    James, heirs, Sn-1816
    Jefrey, D-1805
    Jesse, D-1811
    Jessy, Mt-1798
    John, Bo-1801, B-1812, Je-1800,
        Su-1796, Gi-1812
    Mary, Bo-1801
    Robert, Bo-1801, Bo-1800
    Samuel, Wa-1819, Wa-1814
    Seth, J-1802
    Solomon, B-1812
    Solomon P., Mu-1816
    Thomas, Bo-1801, Ct-1796, B-1812,
        Bo-1800
    Wm., Sn-1792, Sn-1816, Sn-1811
    Will. A., Mu 1816
MAXWILL, Jonaethan, Ge-1812
    William, Ge-1812
MAXY, John, Sn-1811, Sn-1816
    William, Sn-1816, Sn-1811
MAY, Adam, Wa-1814(2), Wa-1819
    Benjamin, Wi-1815
    Cassimer, Wa-1814(2), Wa-1819
    Cradock, Sn-1811
    Daniel, Mu-1811, Mu-1816
    David, A-1805, Fr-1812
    Elijah, Sn-1816
    F., D-1805
    Francis, D-1811
    Henry, Mu-1816

MAY, Hugh, Wi-1810
    James, Mu-1816
    John, Wa-1814(2), Mu-1811, D-1805,
        Fr-1812(2), A-1805, Ct-1798,
        Wa-1819, Gr-1799
    Leroy, Fr-1812
    Obadiah, Wh-1825
    P. Charles, Mu-1811
    Peter, Wa-1819, Mu-1811
    Samuel, Wa-1819
    Samuel Sr., Su-1812
    Samuel Jr., Su-1812
    Thomas, A-1805, Ge-1812
    William, Wi-1801, Wi-1815, Wi-1810,
        Mu-1816, Je-1822, Wh-1825,
        Wh-1811
MAYBAN, James, Sn-1816
MAYBERRY, Abram, Mu-1816
    Charles, Ge-1805
    Francis, Gr-1799(2), Gr-1805(2),
        J-1802
    Frederick, Fr-1812(2)
    Isaac, A-1805
    Jobe, Wi-1815
    John, A-1805
    Owen, Sn-1816
    Zrepts, Mo-1825
MAYBERY, Chas., C-1823
MAYBOURN, David H., Wh-1811
MAYBRY, Robert S., Rb-1812
MAYERS, Jacob, Ge-1812
MAYES, Dudley, Gr-1821
    Edward, Gr-1821
    Goodwin, Gr-1821
    John, Gr-1821
    Logan, Gr-1821
    Samuel, dec'd., Mu-1811
    Sherod, Gr-1821
    Thomas, Gr-1821
    William, Gr-1821
MAYFIELD, A. B., Wi-1801
    Abraham, B-1812
    B. A., Mu-1811
    Brison M., Gi-1812
    Elisha, Fr-1812
    Elisha B., Gi-1819
    Elizabeth, Wi-1810, Wi-1801
    George, Wi-1815, Wi-1810
    Henry M., Gi-1819
    Isaac, D-1805, D-1788, D-1811,
        Gi-1819
    Isaac Sr., Gi-1812
    Isaac Jr., Gi-1812
    James, Mu-1811, Wi-1810, Wi-1815,
        W-1812
    John, Sn-1811
    John E., Gi-1819
    Micajah, K-1796
    Samuel, Mu-1811
    Randol, K-1796
    Southerd, D-1788
    Southerland, Capt., D-1788
    Stephen, J-1802
    William, Mu-1811, B-1812, W-1812,
        Gi-1812
    Wm. C., Gi-1819
MAYHEW, by W. Lackey, Jr., Bo-1800
MAYHILL, Elizabeth, Wi-1815
MAYHOE, Thomas, A-1805
MAYNOR, Drury, Wh-1811
MAYO, Jacob, Sn-1811
    Valantine, Bo-1801, Bo-1800

MAYPLES, Josiah, Gr-1805
    William Sr., Gr-1805
    William Jr., Gr-1805
MAYS, Abraham, Mu-1811
    David Sr., Mu-1816
    David Jr., Mu-1816
    Elijah, Mu-1816
    Francis, Wi-1801
    Goodrum, Mu-1816
    Goodwin, Mu-1811
    Henry, Gr-1805, Gr-1821, Gr-1799
    Isaac, Mu-1816, Mu-1811
    James, Wl-1804, Wh-1825
    James G., Wh-1825
    Jessee, heirs, Mu-1816
    John, Wh-1811, Wi-1801, Wh-1825,
        Wi-1815
    Liggin, Gr-1805
    M., estate, D-1805
    Mathew, Wi-1801
    Robert, Wh-1825
    Samuel, D-1811, Mu-1816, D-1805
    Sherod, Gr-1850, Gr-1799
    Thomas, Wh-1811, Gr-1799, Wh-1825
    Tomas, Wh-1825
    William, Je-1800, Gr-1799
MAYSEY, Charles, C-1818
MAYSON, Solomon, A-1805
MAZE, James, Je-1822
    John, Je-1822
    Lydia, Je-1822
    Wm., Sn-1816
MAZY, Solomon, Bl-1815
McABLY, Ricerd, Gi-1819
McADAM, Hugh, Sn-1823
McADAMS, Amos, B-1812
    Hugh, Wa-1814
    James, B-1812, Wa-1819
    John, Mu-1816
    Robert, Wa-1814, Wa-1819
    William, Sn-1811, Sn-1792
    Wm. R., D-1811
McADDEN, Henry, Sn-1811
McADO, Ro., Gi-1812
McADOO, Andrew, Je-1800
McADOW, James, Wl-1804
    Jno., Ge-1783
    Jno. Sr., Ge-1783
    Samuel, Wl-1804
McAFEE, Chiles, Mu-1816
McAGUE, Saml., Hu-1812
    Wm., Hu-1812
McALISTER, Barnibas, B-1812
    Charles, Wi-1815
    Daniel, Fr-1812
    James, Je-1800, Wa-1819
    John, Wa-1814, Bo-1800, Wa-1819
    Mathew, Fr-1812
    Nichol, Wi-1810
    Samuel, Ro-1805, J-1802
    William, Fr-1812
McALLISTER, David Sr., Fr-1812
McALPIN, Alexander, Ge-1805
McALPINE, Robert, Gr-1821
McALSAY, John, Bo-1800
MCALWEE, James, Ro-1805
McALWHE, John, Ro-1805
McAMIS, Isaac, Ge-1805
    James, Ge-1805(2)
    John, Ge-1805
    Thomas, Ge-1805
    William, Ge-1805

McAN, John, Sn-1816(2)
    Robt., heirs, Sn-1816
McANALLEY, Chas., C-1818
McANALLY, Charles, Gr-1804
    David, Gr-1804
    Isaac, Gr-1804
    Jesse, Fr-1812
    John, Gr-1804
McANDREW, Joseph, Je-1822
McANINCH, Jas., Gi-1812
    John, Gi-1812
McANNACK, John, Gi-1819
McANNALLY, Charles, Gr-1821, Gi-1812
    John, Gi-1812
McANS, Robert, R-1808
McANTIRE, David, Su-1796
McARNOLD, James, Bo-1800
McARTHUR, Joseph, R-1819
    William, R-1819
McARVER, William, Gr-1821
McATEE, Abednigo, Gr-1804
    John, Gr-1799
McAULEY, John, Bo-1800, Mu-1811
McAULLY, John, Wh-1811
McAUSLIN, Andrew, Mu-1816
McBATH, William, Bo-1801
McBAY, Hugh, Ge-1812
McBEAN, Daniel, D-1811(2)
McBEATH, Wm., Bo-1800
McBEE, George H., Gr-1821
    Isaac, Gr-1799
    Israel, Ge-1805, Gr-1821
    James, Fr-1812
    Jesse, Fr-1812
    John, Fr-1812, Gr-1821
    Lemuel, Wh-1825
    Samuel, Gr-1799, Fr-1812
    Silas, Gr-1821
    William, Fr-1812
    William Sr., Fr-1812
McBOYDS, John, Mu-1816
McBRDE(sic), John, B-1812
McBRICE, Andrew, Wh-1825
McBRIDE, Andrew, Wh-1811
    Daniel, Gr-1805, Fr-1812
    Francis, Mu-1811
    Hugh, B-1812, Sn-1811
    Isaac, Mu-1811, Wh-1811
    James, B-1812, Wl-1804, Gi-1819,
        C-1818, D-1811, Sn-1816
    John, K-1799, Wh-1811(2), Wi-1810
    Joseph, Wh-1811, D-1811
    Martin, Ge-1805
    Moses, Fr-1812
    Nathaniel, Fr-1812
    Patienn, C-1818
    Saml., Wi-1815
    Thomas, J-1802, Wh-1811, Gi-1812
    William, B-1812, Ge-1805, A-1805,
        Fr-1812, Ge-1812, Wh-1811,
        Su-1796, Su-1797, Wh-1825
    William J., Wh-1825
McBROOM, Henry, Ge-1805
    Stephen, Gr-1804, Gr-1805
    Thomas, Gr-1804(2), Gr-1799, Gr-1805
    William, Ge-1805, Fr-1812, Ge-1783,
        Je-1822, Je-1800
    _____, Gr-1805
McBRUM, Thomas, Gr-1805
McBRYDE, Francis, Mu-1816
    Saml., Mu-1816
McBUCKNER, Patric, Gr-1821

McBURG, Wm., Bo-1800
McCABE, Charles, Mu-1811
    Hugh, Gi-1812
    John, Gi-1812
    William, Gi-1819
McCADEN, Henry, Sn-1823
McCAFFEE, Moses, Mu-1811
McCAFFERTY, Edward, Wl-1804, Mu-1811
    J. W. Edward, Mu-1811
    Jmaes, Mu-1816
McCAFFEY, John, D-1811
McCAFFREY, Hugh, B-1812
    John, D-1811
McCAIN, Eli, Mu-1811
    James, Wi-1815
    John, D-1805, D-1811, Sn-1816
    Peter, Ge-1805
    Robert, Mu-1811
McCALBERTES, James, Gi-1819
McCALEB, William, R-1808
McCALISTER, Eneas, Mt-1798
    John, Bo-1801
McCALL, Alexander, Mu-1816, Mu-1811, R-1819
    James, B-1812
    John, Wa-1814
    John Jr., Wa-1814
    Joseph, R-1819
    Robert, Ge-1812, Wa-1819
    Thomas, Mu-1816
    William, Sn-1811, Wa-1814, Wa-1819
    William Sr., Wa-1819
McCALLAHAN, Jas., Gi-1812
McCALLAM, Alexander, Bo-1800
McCALLISTER, David, Wi-1815
    James, D-1811, Wi-1801
    Joseph, K-1796, Wi-1815
McCALLOE, David, Gi-1812
    James, Gi-1812
McCALLUM, Cloud?, Wi-1810
    Daniel, Gi-1812
    Jacob, Wi-1810
McCALPIN, Elizabeth, Wi-1810
    Widow, Je-1822
    William, Wi-1815
McCAMEY, Robert, Fr-1812
McCAMIS, Alexander, Ge-1812
    James, Ge-1812(2)
    William, Ge-1812
    _____, Ge-1812(3)
McCAMISH, Thomas, Ge-1812
McCAMMON, Hugh, Hu-1812
    Robert, Bo-1800
    Samuel, Bo-1801, Bo-1800
    Thomas, Bo-1801, Bo-1800
McCAMPBELL, James, W-1805, W-1812, K*-1815
    Jno., K*-1815
    Solomon, Bo-1800
McCAMRY, Robert, Gi-1812
McCAMY, Alex'r., Li-1812*
McCANDLASS, James, W-1812, W-1805
McCANDLESS, John, R-1819
    Richard A., R-1819
    William, D-1811
McCANLES, John, Bo-1801
    Robert, Bo-1801
McCANLESS, John, Bo-1800
McCANLISS, David, Gi-1812
    James, Gi-1812
    John, Gi-1812
    Sam., Gi-1812
McCANN, George, Wi-1810

McCANN, James, Wh-1825, Wh-1811
    John, Sn-1811
    Robert, D-1805
    Robert, heirs, Sn-1811
    William, Mu-1816, Wh-1811(2)
McCANNON, Cornelius, Bl-1815
McCANSE, James, R-1819
McCARDELL, Philip, Wa-1814, Wa-1819
McCARE, Seth, Gr-1821
McCAREY, James, Hu-1812
McCARLIN, Andrew, D-1805
    John Sr., D-1811
McCARMAC, David, Ge-1812
McCARMACK, Andrew, D-1811, Sn-1811
    Lawrence, D-1811
    Matthew, Sn-1792
    William, D-1811
McCARREL, James, Mt-1798, Wi-1810
McCARRELL, George, Fr-1812
    Talton, Gr-1821
McCARRIHAN, Charles, D-1811
McCARRY, J. Overton, C-1818
McCARTER, Mathew, D-1805
    Robert, Mu-1811
McCARTHY, Abel, Je-1822
    John, Gr-1799
McCARTNEY, Andre, Wl-1804
    John, Sn-1816, Sn-1792, Bo-1801
    Lewis, Wl-1804
    Thomas, Wl-1804
McCARTNY, Chas., Ge-1783
    Jas., Ge-1783
    Jno., Ge-1783
McCARTY, Andrew, Mu-1811, Mu-1816
    Benjamin, Gr-1799
    James, Mu-1811, Gr-1799
    James Sr., Gr-1799
    John, Ro-1805, Gr-1821
    Timothy, R-1819
    William, R-1819, Sn-1816
McCARVER, Archibald, Wh-1825, Gr-1804, Gr-1799
    Campbell, Gr-1805, Gr-1804
    John, Wh-1825
    Joseph, Gr-1804
    Joshua, Wh-1825, Gr-1805, Fr-1812
    Nathaniel, Wh-1825
McCARVERY, Joshua, Wh-1811
McCARY, Henry, Wa-1819
    John Jr., B-1812
    Robert, Sn-1811
McCASLAND, Andrew, Wl-1804
    John, Mo-1825
    Stephen, Mo-1825
McCASLIN, John Jr., D-1811
    William, D-1811
McCASTELIN, James, Wi-1815
McCUAL, Joseph, Gi-1812
McCAULEY, Alex, Bo-1805
McCAULY, John, Bo-1801
McCAY, Daniel, Ge-1812
    David, Gr-1821
    Hugh, Wl-1804
    John, Ct-1798
    Lewis, Sn-1816
    William, Gr-1821, D-1805
McCEARLY, Abram, Mu-1816
    Joseph, Gi-1812
    Thomas, Gi-1812
McCEASLEY, James, Rb-1812
    John, Rb-1812
McCEE, Silas, Sn-1792

McCHAUSEY, Thomas, Su-1812
McCHRISTIAN, Benjamin, Mu-1816
    John, Mu-1816
McCIPACK, John, Gi-1812
    Thomas, Gi-1812
McCLAIN, Andrew, J-1802
    Davis, Wi-1810
    Hackett, Hu-1812
    James, J-1802, Wh-1811, Su-1797
    Jesse, Wi-1810
    John, Wl-1804
    Thomas, C-1823, C-1818, Su-1812,
        Su-1796, Su-1797
    Will, Wl-1804
McCLAIR, Thomas, Gr-1799
McCLAMAHAN, William, Je-1800
McCLANAHAM, Samuel, Mu-1811
McCLANAHAN, Alexander, Je-1800
    David, Bo-1801, Bo-1805
    James, Bo-1801(2), Bo-1805
    Joseps, Je-1822
    Matthew, Bo-1801
    Robert, Je-1822
    William, Je-1822
McCLANE, Benjamin, Wh-1825
    Daniel, Wh-1825
    James, Wh-1811
    John, Mt-1798
McCLANNAHAN, David, Je-1800
    Robert, Je-1800
McCLARAN, Alex., Wi-1815
    Franklin, Wi-1815
    Garland, Wi-1815
    John, Wi-1815
McCLARDY, David, B-1812
    James, B-1812
    John, B-1812
McCLAREN, Daniel, B-1812
    Daniel Jr., G-1812
    Hugh, B-1812
    Reuben, B-1812
McCLARKEN, Thomas, Wi-1815
McCLARY, John, C-1823, C-1818
    Robert, Sn-1816
    Samuel, Wi-1801
    Wm., C-1818
McCLAUSON, Robert, Gi-1819
McCLEARY, Andw., Gi-1812
    James A., B-1812
    John, B-1812
    Joseph, Wa-1819
McCLELAND, John, Mu-1816
    Josiah, Sn-1811
McCLELLAN, Abram, Su-1797
    Isaac B., Wa-1819
    John, Su-1796
    Robt., Wi-1815
McCLELLAND, George, D-1811
McCLELLEAN, Abram, Su-1812
    Abram Jr., Su-1812
McCLELLIN, Daniel, Ge-1805
    Samuel, Fr-1812
McCLENAHEN, John, K-1799
McCLENDEN, Weller, Bl-1815
McCLENDON, Den---, D-1811
    John, W-1812
    William, Fr-1812
McCLENEN, John, Sn-1816
McCLERGE, James, Bo-1805
    <u>   </u>, Bo-1805
McCLESTER, William, Je-1800
McCLINTOCK, Robt., Hu-1812

McCLISTER, Andrew, Je-1822
    James Sr., Je-1822
    James Jr., Je-1822
    John, Je-1822
    William, Je-1822
McCLOUD, Alx., Hu-1812
    William, Wa-1814, Wa-1819, Fr-1812
McCLUCE, David, W-1812
McCLUNG, Charles, Mt-1798, C-1823(2),
        Bo-1801, C-1818, Je-1800,
        R-1819
    Hugh, Wi-1801, Ge-1783
    Jno., Ge-1783
McCLUNY, Hugh, Wi-1815
McCLUR, James, Mu-1811
    Nathl., Ge-1783
    S. Alexander, Mu-1811
McCLURE, Alexander, Mu-1816
    Charles, Bo-1801, Bo-1800
    Cyrus, Je-1822
    Erwin, Wa-1819
    Hugh, Mt-1798
    John, Ge-1812
    Robert, Wa-1814
    Thomas, Mu-1811
    William, Wi-1810, B-1812, Ge-1812
    William Jr., B-1812
McCLURY, Hugh, Wi-1801
McCLUSKY, George, Fr-1812
    Joseph, Fr-1812, Wl-1804
    Samuel, Fr-1812, Wl-1804(2)
McCLYEAR, Hugh, Rb-1812
McCOCKLE, Robert, Ro-1805
McCOFLIN, John, D-1811
McCOLESTER, Jessee, W-1812
    Jno., W-1812
McCOLL, Thomas, Mu-1811
McCOLLAM, John, Bo-1800
McCOLLBY, Robert, Ro-1805
McCOLLESTER, James, D-1805
    William, Mu-1811
McCOLLEY, Andrew, Bl-1815
    Samuel, Ro-1805
McCOLLICK, James, Ro-1805
McCOLLISTER, Samuel, Ct-1798
McCOLLUCK, James, Fr-1812
McCOLLUM, Daniel, Mu-1816
    Isaac, Mu-1811
    James, Ge-1812
    John, Ge-1812(2), Ge-1805, Mu-1811
    Levy, D-1811
    Thomas, Ge-1812, Ge-1805(2)
    Threshers?, heirs, Mu-1816
    Thrusher, Mu-1811
    William, D-1811
McCOMBS, Alexander, D-1811
    James, Wi-1815
McCOMES, John, Bo-1801
McCOMMUS, Stephen, A-1805
McCONALD, James, Bo-1801
McCONALL, John P., Wi-1801
McCONEL, Daniel, Sn-1811
    Gumry, Sn-1811
    John, Sn-1811
McCONICE, Garnor, Wi-1810
    Keziah, Wi-1810
McCONN, Samison, Gi-1812
McCONNAL, John, Ge-1805
McCONNALL, James A., Wh-1825
    Milan A., Wh-1825
McCONNEL, Daniel, Sn-1816
    Emanuel, Mu-1816

McCONNEL, Emory, Sn-1816
    Jacob, Ge-1783
    John, Sn-1816, Mu-1816
    Robert, Mt-1798
    Samuel, Mu-1816, Mu-1811
McCONNELL, John Jr. & Sr., D-1805
    John P., K-1812*
    William, Gi-1819
    William P., Je-1822
McCONER, Mathew, D-1811
McCONNICE, Garner, Wi-1801
    Jared, Wi-1815
McCOOL, Gabriel, Ge-1783
McCORD, David, Fr-1812, Bo-1801, Mu-1811, Wi-1810, Mu-1816
    Hugh, Sn-1816
    James, J-1802, Fr-1812
    John, Gr-1799, Wi-1810, Wi-1802
    Joseph, Wi-1815
    Robert, Mu-1816, Mu-1811(2)
    Saml., Wi-1810
    William, Wi-1815, Mu-1816, Wi-1810, Sn-1816
McCORKLE, John, Su-1812, Wa-1819
    Saml., Su-1797, Su-1796, Su-1812
McCORMACH, Wm., Bo-1800
McCORMACK, Andrew, Sn-1816
    George, D-1805, D-1811(2)
    John, D-1811
    John L., D-1811
    Masterson C., Gi-1819
    Samuel, Fr-1812
    Stephen, K-1799
    Widow, Ct-1798
    _____, Ct-1796
McCORMIC, Jared, D-1805
McCORMICK, Geo., Gi-1812
    John, Fr-1812
    John B., Wh-1825
    William, Su-1797, Ge-1805, Su-1796
    __. L., Mc-1825
McCORNY, William, Ro-1805
McCORRY, Hugh, D-1805
McCORTLE, Joseph, Mt-1798
McCORY, John, B-1812
McCOSKEY, Ezekel, Wi-1810
McCOSKY, Jno., Ge-1782
McCOUN, James, Wl-1804
    Sampson, Wl-1804
McCOUNTS, Jacob, Ro-1805
McCOWEN, John, Ro-1805
McCOWN, Archibald, Fr-1812
McCOY, Absalom, Wh-1825
    Alex, Gi-1812
    Benjamin, J-1802
    Cornelius, C-1823
    Daniel, Ge-1805
    David, Hw-1799, Gr-1805
    Gilbert, Ge-1812
    James, Gr-1804, R-1819
    Jessee, Mu-1811
    John, Wa-1819, Gr-1804, Ct-1796, Wa-1814, R-1819
    Joseph, Ge-1812
    Michel, Bo-1800
    Neal, Gr-1805, Gr-1804
    Nell, Hw-1799
    Samuel, A-1805, Mu-1811
    Spencer, C-1823
    Spruss, C-1818
    William, Wa-1819(2), Wa-1814, D-1811
    _____, Ge-1812

McCRABB, Alexander, Su-1797
McCRACKEN, Henry, Wa-1819, Wa-1814
    James, A-1805, Wa-1814, Gr-1799
    John, Wa-1819(2), Gi-1819
    John Jr., Wa-1814
    Samuel, Wa-1814(2), Wa-1819
    Thomas, Wi-1815
McCRACKIN, John, Wi-1810(2), Wa-1814
McCRACKING, Elisabeth, Sn-1816
McCRADY, Andrew, Wi-1815, Wi-1810
McCRAKEN, John, Wi-1810
    Robert, Wa-1819
McCRAKIN, Ephraim, Mu-1811
    James, Wi-1810
    Samuel, Wi-1810
    Thomas, Wi-1810
McCRAREY, Benjamin, Je-1822
McCRARY, Alexander, Wi-1815
    Hugh, B-1812, D-1811
    John, Mu-1811(2)
    Nathanl., D-1805
    Robert, B-1812
McCRAVERS, James, Gi-1812
McCRAW, David, Mt-1798
McCRAWEY, John, Wi-1810
McCRAY, Elijah, Wa-1819
    Elisha, Wa-1814
    George, Wa-1819
    Philip, Wa-1819
    Thomas, Wa-1819, Wa-1814
    William, R-1819, Wa-1819
McCREDY, Alexander, Wi-1815
McCREELY, Alexr., Wi-1810
    David, Sn-1816
    William, Wi-1810
McCREY, George, A-1805
McCRORY, John, D-1811, D-1805
    Thos., Wi-1810, Wi-1815(2)
McCUISTAIN, Jahes Jr., Je-1800
McCUISTEAN, Benjamin, B-1812
    James, B-1812
    John, B-1812
    Saml., B-1812
McCUISTIAN, Andrew, Je-1800
McCUISTON, John, D-1805
McCULLAH, John, Wh-1825
    Joseph, Je-1800
McCULLAN, Robert, Wi-1810
McCULLE, John, Je-1800
McCULLER, John & Robert McCANN, D-1805
McCULLEY, Jas., Gr-1799
    John, Bo-1801, C-1823, C-1818(2), Bo-1800
    Jonathan, C-1823
    Peter, C-1818, C-1823
    Robert, Su-1812, Bo-1801, Bo-1800
    Sollomon, Bo-1800
    Solomon, Bo-1801
    William, Wl-1804, C-1818
McCULLOCH, Alen, Bo-1800
    Alexander, Fr-1812
    David, Fr-1812
    John, Bo-1801, Bo-1800
    Samuel, Bo-1800, Bo-1801
    Thomas, Bo-1801
McCULLOCK, Benjamin, Mt-1798, Mu-1811
    James, Bo-1801, Bo-1800, Fr-1812
    Robt., Gi-1812
    Samuel, Bo-1800
    Thomas, Bo-1800
McCULLOH, Robert, Mu-1816
McCULLOUGH, Joseph, Ge-1805

McCULLOUGH, Samuel, Ge-1805
    Thomas, Ge-1805, Je-1822
    William, Ge-1805(2)
McCULLUM, Hugh, Mt-1798
McCULOUGH, James, Ge-1812
McCUN, James, Bo-1800
McCURDY, Archd., Ge-1783
    David, B-1812
    James, B-1812
    James Jr., B-1812
    Robert, Bo-1800
    William, B-1812
McCULLUM, Hugh, Mt-1798
McCULOUGH, James, Ge-1812
McCUN, James, Bo-1800
McCURDY, Archd., Ge-1783
    David, B-1812
    James, B-1812
    James Jr., B-1812
    Robert, Bo-1800
    William, B-1812
McCURKIN, Thomas, Bo-1801
McCURRY, Henry, C-1818
    James, Ge-1805, Ge-1812
    John, Ge-1812
McCURTON, Thomas, Mt-1798
McCURTY, John, Ge-1805
McCUSON, John, Gi-1819
McCUSTIAN, Joseph, Je-1800
    Sanator James, Je-1800
McCUSTION, Benj., Mu-1811
    James, Mu-1811
    John, Mu-1811
McCUTCHEN, James, D-1805(2)
    John, D-1811
    N., D-1788
    Saml., Wi-1815
McCUTCHENSON, Samuel, Wi-1810
McCUTCHER, James, D-1811
McCUTCHIN, James, Wi-1801
McCUTCHING, Patrick, D-1788
McCUTHERN, Samuel, Wh-1811
McCUTTON, Duncan, D-1811
McDANEIL, Roger, D-1805
McDANEL, James, Ge-1812
McDANELL, William, Sn-1816
McDANIEL, Abraham, W-1812(2)
    Alexander, Je-1822(2), B-1812
    Alexander W., D-1811
    Catherine, Mu-1816
    Charles, Fr-1812, Wh-1825
    Clement, D-1811
    Coalman, Fr-1812
    Daniel, D-1805, D-1811
    David, W-1812, Wh-1811, Wh-1825, D-1805
    Edward, W-1812
    Fielden, Fr-1812
    Francis, D-1805, Wi-1810
    Isaac, Gr-1804
    James, Rb-1812, W-1812, R-1819, B-1812, Wh-1825
    Joel, Wh-1285(2)
    John, Gr-1821, Wh-1811, Wl-1804(2), Wh-1825
    John Jr., Wi-1810
    Johnston, D-1805
    Joseph, W-1812, Mt-1798
    Leonard, Mu-1811
    Looney, W-1812
    Lowrey, D-1811
    Magay, Wl-1804

McDANIEL, Middleton, Wh-1825
    Moses, W-1812, W-1805
    Norman, Wh-1825
    Randel, Wh-1825
    REnchy, D-1811
    Robert, Mu-1816, Wh-1811
    Roger, D-1811
    Samuel, Mu-1816, Mu-1811
    Thomas, Wh-1811
    Walter, W-1812, Wl-1804, W-1805
    William, W-1812, Ge-1812, Fr-1812, W-1805, D-1811
McDANILE, Walter, Wl-1804
McDANNEL, Nelson, Mt-1798
McDERMENT, Thomas, Sn-1816
McDERMOTT, William P. H., Je-1822
    William T. H., Je-1822
McDONAL, George, Wa-1814
    Michael, Gr-1799
McDONALD, Alexander, Gr-1799
    Alvin, C-1818
    Aron, C-1823
    Alexr., Gi-1812
    Alexander Sr., Je-1800
    Alexander Jr., Je-1800
    Daniel, B-1812
    David, Bo-1800, Je-1800
    Henry, B-1812
    Isaac, Gr-1799
    Jacob, C-1823
    James, Wi-1810, Wa-1819, Je-1822, J-1802, Je-1800, Gi-1812
    Jane, Gr-1799
    John, J-1802, Je-1822, Je-1800
    Joseph, Gi-1812
    RAndolph, Cl-1803
    Redmon, Gr-1799
    Walter, Je-1800
    William, Sn-1792, Gi-1812, Je-1822, Ge-1805, Gi-1812
McDONELL, Collin, Wi-1815
McDONNALD, Archibald, Sn-1811
    RAndolph, Hw-1799
McDONOLD, William, Sn-1792
McDOWEL, Alexander, D-1811
    John, Bo-1800
McDOWELL, Ephraim, Ge-1783
    James, Rb-1812
    James, decd., Sn-1816
    Joseph, Mu-1816, Wi-1810, Wi-1815, Rb-1812
    Shad., Gi-1812
McDUDSON, Henry, Sn-1816
McEFEE, John, Wa-1819
McEFER, John, Wa-1814
McELDERRY, John, Su-1797, Su-1796
McELHANEY, Alexander, Gr-1821
    Elenor, widow, Gr-1821
    Henry, Wh-1825
    John, Wh-1825, Gr-1804, Wh-1811
    Joseph, Rb-1812
    Moses, Gr-1804
    Robert, Gr-1804
McELHANY, Jacob, W-1812
McELHATTEN, John, Gr-1805
McELHENEY, John, Gr-1805
McELHENY, Robert, Gr-1805
McELKENY, John, Gr-1799
    Moses, Gr-1799
    Robert, Gr-1799
McELLENEY, Thos., Sn-1811
McELROY, Andrew, Wh-1825

McELROY, Isaac, Fr-1812(McCroy?)
    James, Sn-1816
    John, D-1811
    Joseph, W-1812
    Margaret, Ge-1812, Ge-1805
    Michael, Fr-1812(McCroy?)
    Samuel, Mu-1811
    William, B-1812
McELVIE, Thomas, Mu-1816
McELWAIN, Henry, D-1811
McELWEE, John, R-1808
McELWRATH, John, Sn-1816
McELYEA, James, Wl-1804
McENALLY, Richard, Gi-1819
McENELBY, David, Gr-1805
McENELLY, Charles, Gr-1799
    Jessee, Gr-1805
McENTIRE, Archibald, R-1819
    John F., Bl-1815
McENTORE, James, Ro-1805
McENTOSH, Anguish, B-1812
McERWIN, Alexander, Wa-1814
McETEE?, Abednigo, Gr-1805
McEURATH, Joseph, Sn-1816
McEWEAN, WM., Wi-1810
McEWEN, D., Wi-1801
    James, Wi-1810
    Wm., Wi-1810
McEWIN, Alexander Wh-1825
    David, Wi-1815
    James, Wi-1815
    John, Wh-1825
    Robert, Wh-1825
    Wm., Wi-1815
McEWING, Fleming, Wh-1825
    James, D-1811
    John, D-1811
McEWINS, John, Hu-1812
McFADDEN, Candon, D-1811
    Elias, B-1812(2)
    Guy, D-1811
    Robert, Wi-1810
McFADDIAN, Joseph, Bo-1801
McFADDIN, David, R-1819
    Guy & Candry, D-1805
    John, C-1823
McFADEN, David?, Mt-1798
McFALL, Francis, Ct-1798
    John, Mu-1811, Ro-1805, Ct-1798
    Saml., Hu-1812
McFALLS, James, Co-1821
McFAREN, Andw., Ge-1783
    James, Ge-1783
McFARLAN, Duncan, Gr-1799
    Henderson, Wh-1825
    William, Su-1812
McFARLAND, ANdrew B., Je-1822
    Benjamin, Je-1800
    Benjamin Sr., Je-1822
    Duncan, Gr-1799
    James, Je-1822, Ge-1812, Je-1800
    John, Je-1822
    John Jr., Je-1822
    John, agent, Su-1797
    Robert, D-1811, Je-1800, Je-1822
    William, Je-1822
McFARLANE, John S., Gr-1805
McFARLESS, John, D-1811
McFARLIN, Andrew, Ge-1805
    James, Gr-1805, Mu-1811, Rb-1812
    John, Wl-1804, Je-1800, D-1788
McFARLING, James, A-1805

McFARLING, Robt., W-1812, B-1812
McFARREN, James, D-1805
    Samuel, Gr-1799
McFARSON, Henry, Gr-1799
McFARTHING, Alexander, Ge-1783
McFEATERS, Andrew, Gr-1804
McFEE, John, Wi-1815
    Peter, Fr-1812(McGee?)
McFEETER, Andrew, Gr-1799
McFEETRAGE, Matthew, Gr-1799
McFERRIN, James, D-1811
    John, D-1811
McFETERIDGE, William, Gr-1804
McFETERS, Andrew, Gr-1805
McFORSON, John, Mt-1798
McGAHEE, William, Ge-1805
McGAHON, Foster, Gi-1819
McGAMBLE, Littleberry, A-1805
McGAN, Eli, Wi-1815
McGANN, John, Wa-1819
    William, Wa-1819
McGARICK, David & Randal, D-1805
McGASSOCK, Rheubn., Sn-1792
McGATICK, Abner, D-1811
McGAUGH, John, D-1805, D-1811
    Matthew, Wi-1801, Wi-1815
    Robert, D-1811
    Thomas, Wi-1810, Wi-1815, D-1805
    Wm., Wi-1801
McGAUGHEY, Alexander, Wi-1810
McGAUGHY, James, Mu-1811
    W. George, Mu-1811
    Wm., Ge-1783
McGAURY, Pleasant, Mu-1811
McGAVOCK, David, D-1811
    James, Wi-1815, D-1811, Wi-1801,
        Wl-1804
    John, D-1811
    Randal, D-1811
    Rendul, Wi-1810
    _____, D-1811
McGEE, Bartley, Je-1822
    Charles, Mu-1811
    Chiles, Mu-1816
    David, Mt-1798
    Elizabeth, Sn-1816
    James, Je-1822
    John, Wi-1801, Wa-1819, Ge-1800,
        Wa-1814, Gr-1799
    Joseph, Mu-1811
    Linch, Sn-1811
    Polly, Mu-1816
    Polly Jr., Mu-1816
    Richard, Je-1800, Gi-1812
    Samuel, Gi-1812
    William, Wi-1810, Mu-1811, Mu-1816,
        Sn-1811, Wa-1819, B-1812,
        Wl-1815
    Zarah, Gi-1821
    Zera, Gr-1805
McGEEHON, Benjamin, Ge-1805
    John, Ge-1805
McGEEKEN, Brewer, Ct-1796
McGEHE, Wm., Wi-1801
McGEHEE, Jacob, Mu-1811
    William, A-1805
McGEHON, Margaret, Ge-1805
McGHEE, Abraham, Wh-1825
    Barcley, Bo-1800(2), Bo-1801
    George, Wh-1825
    James, Je-1800
    John, Wh-1825, Bo-1800

McGILL, Andrew, Hw-1801
    Charles, Ge-1805
    David, B-1812
    James, Ge-1783, B-1812
    John, Hw-1801, R-1819, Ro-1805
    Robert, Bo-1800, Bo-1801, Ge-1783,
      Ge-1805
    Rollin, Gr-1821
    Rowland, Je-1822
    Samuel, Ge-1805
    William, Gr-1821, Bl-1815, R-1819,
      Ge-1805, Wi-1815
McGILVERY, John, Wh-1811
McGIMPSAY, William, Wa-1819
McGIN, David, B-1812
McGINETY, Alexander, Wa-1819
McGINEY, James, Bo-1800, Bo-1801
McGINNES, Edward, Gr-1804
McGINNIS, Aaron, Gr-1821
    Absalem, Gr-1821
    David, Wa-1814, Wa-1819
    Edward, Gr-1805
    James, Wa-1819, Wa-1814, Gr-1805
    John, Wa-1819
    John Jr., Wa-1814
    Moses, Gr-1821
    Robert, Gr-1804, Gr-1821, Je-1822(2)
      Gr-1805
McGINSSEY, John, Mu-1816
McGIRT, John, Je-1800
McGLOGHLN, Alexander, Se-1799
McGLOTHAN, John, Sn-1816
    Joseph, Sn-1816
McGLOTHLIN, Joseph, Sn-1816
McGLOUGHLIN, Jsoeph, Sn-1811
McGOWAN, Amos, Wh-1825
    James, Wh-1825
    Joseph, Wh-1825
McGOWEN, James, Mt-1798
McGOWN, Andrew, Fr-1812
    David, Fr-1812
    John, Fr-1812
    Samuel, Fr-1812
McGRADY, John, Sn-1816
    William, Sn-1811
McGRAUGH, Robert, Wi-1810
McGRAW, Isaac, Mt-1798
    John, Wh-1825
    Mathew, Gi-1819
    Poll, Mt-1798
McGREE, George, Wa-1814
McGREGER, Ezekial, W-1812
    Ezekiel, W-1805
    William, W-1812, W-1805, Mu-1811
    Willis, W-1812, W-1805
McGREGOR, Flowers, D-1811
McGREGORY, Thoms, D-1805
McGROOM, Thomas, Gr-1821
McGRORY, Pleasant, Mu-1816
McGRUNE, Elijah M., B-1812
    John, B-1812
McGUFFY, Edmond, Fr-1812
McGUIER, Joseph, Je-1822
McGUIR, Isaac, W-1812
McGUIRE, Alegany, Wi-1815
    Charles, Wh-1825, Wh-1811
    Cornelis, Ge-1783
    Cornelius, Je-1800
    George, Sn-1811, Je-1800
    Isaac, Wh-1811, Je-1800
    James, Wi-1815
    Jessee, Wh-1825

McGUIRE, John, Rb-1812
    Patrick, Je-1800
    Silas, Gi-1812
    Thomas, Su-1796, W-1812, Su-1797
    William, D-1805, Bl-1815, A-1805
McGWYRE?, William, Mu-1816
McGYN, William, Wa-1814
MCHAFEE, John, Gr-1821
MCHALE, John, Ro-1805
McHANEY, John, Gr-1805
    Robert, Gr-1805
McHEALY, Wm., C-1818
McHEIN, James, Fr-1812
McHENRY, Robert, Ct-1798
McHINNEY, Archibald, Gr-1799
McINTIRE, Hugh, Ro-1805
    John, Mu-1816
McINTOSH, Able, Ge-1812
    Charles, Rb-1812
    John Sr., Rb-1812
    John Jr., Rb-1812
    Lashland, D-1805
    Nimrod, Rb-1812
    Peter, Su-1797, Su-1796
McINTURF, Casper, Ct-1796
    Christopher, Ct-1796, Ct-1798
    Israel, Ct-1796
    John Sr., Ct-1796, Ct-1798
    John Jr., Ct-1796, Ct-1798
McINTYRE, Ancy, Mu-1816
McIVER, Augustus, D-1811
    John, Wi-1810
McIVOR, Sqr., Wh-1811
McJOHN, Esquire, Mu-1816
McKAIL, Charles, Wi-1815
McKAIN, James, Fr-1812, Sm-1816
    James Sr., Sn-1792
    Nancy, Bo-1800, Bo-1801
McKAMEY, Andrew, A-1805
    John, A-1805
    Robert, A-1805
    William, A-1805
McKARY, Andrew, Wi-1801
    William, Wi-1801
McKAUGHAN, Archd., Su-1796
McKAY, Francis, D-1811
    Henry, Wi-1801
    William, D-1811
    William Jr., D-1811
McKEA, Thomas, Mu-1816
McKEAN, Eli, Mu-1816
    James, D-1811
    John, D-1811
    Joseph, D-1805
    Robert, Mu-1816
McKEE, Adam, Wa-1819, Wa-1814
    Jacob, Mu-1811
    James, A-1805
    John, A-1805, Bo-1800, Bo-1801
    John Jr., Bo-1801
    Matthew, Gr-1799
    Robert, Wa-1814, Wa-1819
    William, Je-1822
McKEEHAN, John, Ge-1812
    Thomas, Wh-1825
McKEEN, John, Mu-1816
McKEHAN, John, C-1818
McKEMY, James, Bo-1801
    Robert, Ge-1812
    Samuel, Ge-1805, Ge-1812
McKENDREE, Wm., Sn-1811
McKENNEY, Henrey, J-1802

McKENNEY, Jessee, Gr-1804
    Seth, Gr-1804, Gr-1821
McKENSIE, Samuel A., Mo-1825
McKENZIE, Benj., Mc-1825
    Reuben, Mc-1825
    William, Gr-1799
McKERMAN, Bernard, D-1811
McKESICH, James, B-1812
McKESICK, Daniel, B-1812(2)
    Daniel Jr., B-1812
    David, B-1812
    John, B-1812
    Joseph, B-1812
McKESSICK, John, W-1805
McKEY, John, Wi-1801
    John, James & Thomas, D-1805
    Thomas, Wi-1801(2)
    William, Wi-1815, Wi-1801
McKEYMEY, Robert, Su-1796
McKIGHEN, Saml., Ge-1783
McKIMEU, James, Bo-1800
McKIMEY, William, B-1812
McKINDRICE, James, Sn-1811
McKINDRY, James, Sn-1816
McKINESS, John, Mu-1816
McKINEY, Jesse, Gr-1805
    John, Wi-1801
    Seth, Gr-1805
McKING, William, Sn-1811
McKINLEY, Isaac, Su-1812
    James, Bo-1801
    Joseph, A-1805
    Samuel, Su-1796
    William, Su-1796, Su-1812
    William Sr., Su-1796
McKINLY, Samuel, Su-1797
    Wm., Su-1797
McKINNAY, John, Wi-1801
McKINNEY, George, Je-1822
    Henry, A-1805
    James, Gi-1812, Wh-1825
    James & John, D-1805
    John, Wh-1825
    John V., Li-1812*
    Lampkin, Je-1822
    Prestley, Je-1822
    Rolin, Gi-1812
    Samuel, D-1811
    Seth, Je-1822
    Vincent, Je-1822
    Vinscent, Je-1822
    William, Gi-1812
McKINNIE, John, Ro-1805
    Rowland, Ro-1805
    Thomas, Ro-1805
    William, Ro-1805
McKINNY, Archibald, Sn 1816
    Jesse, Bl-1815
    Jessee, Gr-1805
    John, W-1812
    Seth, Gr-1805
McKINSEY, Daniel, Bo-1800
    Wm., Wi-1810
McKINZEY, Daniel, Bo-1801
McKIPACK, Archibald, Gi-1812
McKIRKHEN, James, Gi-1819
McKISEN, Jos., D-1788
McKISSACK, A., Gi-1819
    John, Gi-1819
    Robert, Sn-1811
    Thos., Gi-1819
McKISSAK, Robart, Sn-1816

McKISSICK, John, W-1812
McKISSIE, John, Ro-1805
McKIVER, John for Hudson & Hall, Gr-1799
McKLEHANY, John, Rb-1812
McKNIGHT, B. Samuel, Mu-1811
    James, Wi-1815
    James Jr., Wi-1810
    John, Mu-1811, Wi-1801
    Robt., Wi-1815
    Samuel, Se-1799
    Saml. B., Mu-1816, Wi-1815
    William, Wi-1801, Wi-1815
    Wm., heirs, Wi-1815
    Wm. W., Wi-1815
McKOY, Daniel, Ge-1805
McKUDCHEM, Andrew, Gi-1819
McKUTCHEN, Joshieh, Wi-1810
McLAIN, James, Sn-1811
    James Sr., Sn-1787
    Jas. Jr., Sn-1787
McLANAHAN, David, Bo-1800
    Matt, Bo-1800
McLAND, Joseph, Je-1800
McLANDAN, Simon, D-1805
McLANDON, Daniel, D-1805
McLANE, Dorcas, Wi-1815
    George, D-1805
McLANNAHAN, James, Bo-1800
McLARD, Thomas, Gr-1821
McLARITON, Wit, Fr-1812
McLARN, James, Su-1796
McLAUGHLIN, James, Fr-1812
    John, Wa-1819
    Jos., Wi-1815
    Tho., Gi-1812
    Wailliam, Wa-1819
    William H., D-1811
McLAUGHN, Daniel, Se-1799
McLAURINE, Willis, Gi-1812
McLAURRY, Pleasant & Micajah, D-1805
McLAYHEN, Alexander, Se-1799
McLEAIN, Ephrm., D-1788
McLEAN, Alligam, Mu-1816
    Chas. Jr., W-1812
    Ephraim, Mu-1811, Mu-1816
    James, Mu-1811, Mu-1816
    James B., Mu-1816
    John, W-1805, W-1812
    Peggy, Mu-1816
    Robert, Mu-1811(2)
    Samuel, Mu-1811, Mu-1816(2)
    Will, Mu-1816
    William, Mu-1811, Se-1799(McMun?)
McLEAR, Laughlin, D-1811
McLEARN?, Charles, W-1812
McLEMON, Burnett, Wi-1810
    Robert, Wi-1801
McLEMORE, Baswell, Wi-1815
    Jno., Gi-1812
    John C., D-1811
    Mos., Gi-1812
    Robt., Wi-1815
    Young, Wi-1815
McLEN, Alexander, Wa-1814
McLERATH, Joseph, Sn-1787
McLEVANE, John, Wi-1815
McLILLY, Samuel, Rb-1812
McLIN, Alexander, Wa-1819
    David, Wa-1814
    Joseph, Wa-1819
    Robert, Wa-1814, Wa-1819(2)
    William, Wa-1814

McLOCKLIN, Thomas, Bo-1800
McLURE, Matthew, B-1812
McLVOY, James, Sn-1811
McMACKEN, James, Ge-1812
    John, Ge-1805
McMACKIN, Andrew, Mu-1816
    Thomas Sr., Ge-1812
McMAHAN, Daniel, Wi-1801(2), Wi-1815
    John Sr., Je-1822
    John Jr., Je-1822
    William, Wl-1804(2), B-1812
McMAHON, B. John, Mu-1811
    Daniel, Wi-1810
    James, Mu-1816
    Richd., Mu-1816
    Saml. D., Mu-1816
McMAIN, James, B-1812
McMAKIN, Andrew, Mu-1811
McMANE, Dominy, Gr-1799
McMANN, John, D-1805
McMANNS, John, Mu-1816
    Laurence, Mu-1816
McMARTY, Thomas, R-1819
McMAY, James, D-1805
McMEANS, Isaac, Be-1800
    James R., Rb-1812
    John, Mu-1811, Bo-1800, Bo-1801
    Jonathan, B-1812
    Joseph, Mu-1811
McMEENAS, Laurance, Wi-1810
McMICKEN, Andrew, Gi-1812
McMILEN, Kenan, Gi-1819
McMILLAN, Alexander, Mu-1816
McMILLEN, Alexander, K*-1815
    Andrew, B-1812
    John, W-1812, B-1812
    Joseph, Li-1812*
    Robert, Gr-1821
    Rolly, B-1812
    Thomas, Gr-1821
McMILLIN, Alexander, Wl-1804
    Robert, Wi-1810
    William, Wi-1810(2), Wi-1815
McMILLION, John, Rb-1812
McMILLON, Randoff, D-1805
    Robert W., R-1819
McMINN, James, Fr-1812(2)
McMISTION, Fr-1812
McMORE, Magnes, Gr-1799
McMORRIS, Alan, B-1812
McMUKEN, David, Gi-1812
    Wm., Gi-1812
McMULIN, Wm., Wi-1801
McMULLEN, Christian, Sn-1816
    Thomas, Je-1800
McMULLER, Thomas, Wi-1815
McMULLIN, James, Ro-1805
    John, Wi-1810, Ro-1805
    R., D-1805
    Thos., Wi-1810
    William, Wi-1810
    Wm. Jr., Wi-1810
McMURRAY, John, Wi-1801, W-1812
    Samuel, Bo-1800(2), Bo-1805
    Wm., Bo-1800
McMURREY, Joseph, Bo-1805
    Robert, Bo-1805(2)
    Thomas, Bo-1805
McMURRY, Alexander, W-1812
    David, Wl-1804, Rb-1812
    James, Bo-1801
    John, W-1812, Sn-1811, Sn-1816

McMURRY, Samuel, D-1811, Ge-1783, Bo-1801
McMURTERY, James, Ge-1812
    John, Ge-1812
    Joseph, Ge-1812
McMURTEY, James Jr., Hu-1812
McMURTREY, William, B-1812
McMURTRY, Henery, Sn-1816
    Henry, Sn-1811
    James, Ge-1805
    John Sr., Sn-1811
    John Jr., Sn-1816, Sn-1811
    John Esq., Sn-1816
    Joseph, Ge-1783
    Sd., Ge-1783
McMURY, Thomas, Ro-1805
McNAB, Wm., Bo-1801
McNABB, Baptist, Co-1827, Ct-1796, Ct-1798
    David, Ct-1798
    David Sr., Ct-1796
    David Jr., Ct-1796
    George, Co-1827
    James, Mc-1825, Co-1827
    John, Co-1827(2)
    John Sr., Co-1827
    William, Bo-1800, Ct-1798, Ct-1796
McNADE, John, Wh-1825
McNAIRY, Andrew, D-1805
    Boyd, D-1811(2)
    James, Wl-1804
    John, D-1805
    Nathniel, Wl-1804
    Nathl. A., D-1811
    Thomas, D-1805
McNALEY, John, Su-1796
McNALLY, John, Su-1812, Ro-1805
McNARY, Francis, Wi-1810
McNASH, John, D-1805
McNATT, Leven, B-1812
McNEAL, Thomas, Mu-1811
McNEALEY, Wm., C-1823
McNEARY, Andrew, Mt-1798
    John Esq., Mt-1798
McNEAS, Jacob, Wa-1819
McNEECE, James, Gi-1812
McNEEL, John, D-1811
    William, Gr-1805
McNEELEY, Hugh, D-1805
    Robert, Ro-1805
    William, Wl-1804, Se-1799
McNEELY, John, Bo-1800, Mc-1825
    Samuel, Bo-1800
    William, Sn-1787, Sn-1792
McNEES, Allen, D-1811
    Hull, D-1811
    Isaiah, Ge-1805
    Robert, Wa-1814
    Rogers, Gi-1812
    Samuel, Ge-1812
    William, Ge-1805
McNEESE, Jonas, Je-1822
McNEIL, George, Bl-1815
    James, Gi-1812, Ro-1805
    John, Ge-1783
    William, Gr-1821
McNEILL, John, D-1788
McNESS, John, D-1811
    Samuel E., D-1811
McNEW, Eliga, Ge-1812
    Elijah, Ge-1805
    Isaih, Ge-1812
    Shadrach, Ge-1805, Ge-1783
    Shederick, Ge-1812

McNEW, William, Ge-1812(2), Ge-1805, C-1818
        C-1823, Mu-1816
McNIGHT, John, Gi-1819
        Robert, Wi-1801
        Thomas, Je-1822
        William, Mu-1811
McNITE, John, Gi-1812
        Samuel, Gi-1812
McNOBLE, Andrew, Ro-1805
        Elias, Ro-1805
        John, Ro-1805
McNOOK & FINLEY, Mu-1816
McNULL, William, Mu-1811
McNULTY, John, Ct-1798
McNUT, Anthony, Wa-1814
        John, Wa-1814
McNUTT, Alex, Bo-1800
        Alexander, Bo-1801
        Anthony, Wa-1819
        Benjamin, Ge-1812, Ge-1805
        James, Ro-1805, Bo-1800, A-1805,
            Bo-1805
        John, D-1805
McPASSION?, Barthy, D-1805
McPEAK, James, Wh-1825
        Jehu, Wi-1815
        John, Wi-1815
        William, Wh-1825
McPECK, William, Wh-1825
McPEET(McFEE?), Jacob, K-1799
McPETERS, Andrew, Gi-1819, Gi-1812
        Joseph, Gi-1805, Ge-1783
McPHEETERS, John, Gr-1805
McPEETUR, Joseph, Je-1800
McPHAIL, ANgus, Wi-1815
        Daniel, Ro-1805
McPHAILS, John, Mu-1816
McPHERAN, Andy, Ge-1812
        James, Ge-1805
        James Jr., Ge-1812
        John, Ge-1805
        William, Ge-1812(2), Ge-1805(2)
McPHEREN, John, Ge-1812
McPHERSON, Bartin, Gr-1805
        Barton, Gr-1804, R-1819
        George, Fr-1812, Ro-1805
        Henry, Gr-1804, Gr-1805
        Isaac, Ro-1805
        Joseph, Ro-1805
        Richard, Gr-1805
McPHERTON, Andrew, Gr-1805, Gr-1821
        John, Gr-1821, Gr-1804
McPHETHRIDGE, William, Gr-1805, Gr-1821
McQUILLIAMS, Thomas, Ct-1796
McQUEASTON, Benjamin, Mu-1811
        James, Mu-1811
        John, Mu-1811
McQUEEN, Hannah, Ct-1798, Ct-1796
        John, Fr-1812, Ct-1796
McQUELLIN, Robert, D-1811
McQUERRY, Micajah, D-1811(2)
McQUISTEAN, Robt., B-1812
McQUISTON, David, Wh-1825
McRACHAN, Saml., Mu-1816
McRANELS, John, Bo-1801
        Joseph, Bo-1801
McRAY, Alexander, Sn-1811
        John, Rb-1812
McRAYNOLDS, James, B-1812
        Thomas, B-1812
McREA, Alexander, Mu-1816
        D. W., Mu-1816

McREA, H., Wi-1801
        Jacob, Mu-1816
McREAD, James P., D-1811
McREYNOLDS, Joseph, Sn-1811
        Walker, C-1823
McRIE, Henry, Gi-1812
McROBERTS, David, Ro-1805
        James, Mt-1798
        Samuel, J-1802, Je-1800
McROCHAN, Eph., Mu-1816
McRORY, John, Mu-1816
        Nathaniel, Rb-1812
McRURY, Hugh, B-1812
        Robert, B-1812
McSPADDEN, Archibald, Gr-1799
        Esther, Je-1800
        James, Je-1822
        Samuel, Je-1800
        Thomas, Ge-1812
McSPADEN, John, Gr-1799
        Moses, Gr-1799
        Robert, Gr-1799
McSPADIN, Thomas, D-1805
McSWENEY, Joseph, Je-1800
McTEAR, Martin, Bo-1805
        Robert, Bo-1805
        William, Bo-1805
McTEER, James Sr., Bo-1801(2), Bo-1800
        James Jr., Bo-1800
        Robert Sr., Bo-1801, Bo-1800
        Robert Jr., Bo-1800, Bo-1801
McTHANIS, Joseph, Bo-1800
McTHENY, Elijah, Ge-1812
        Powel, Ge-1812
McTRINN, Sameul, B-1812
McVAUGHAN, Hugh, Su-1797
McVAY, Claibourne W., Gi-1812
        Daniel, Su-1812
        James, Gr-1805
        James Sr., Gr-1805
        Jordan, Gi-1812
        Zedekiah, W-1812
McWHEELER, James, Wa-1814(2)
McWHISTER, James, Wa-1819
McWHORTEN, John, Bl-1815
        Ha----, Fr-1812
        James S., Fr-1812
        John, A-1805(2)
        Moses, A-1805, Wi-1801
McWHURTER, WM., D-1788
McWILLIAMS, James, Mu-1811
        John, Mu-1816, B-1812(2), Mu-1811
McWIN, James, Ge-1812
McWRIGHT, James, Mu-1816
        John, Mu-1816
MEAD, Betty, Su-1812
        Maiston, K*-1815
MEADE, David, Gi-1819
        Mahlon, Su-1796, Su-1797
MEADEN, Ely, Sn-1816
MEADERS, Jeptha, Sn-1816
MEADOR, Jack, C-1823
        Jason, C-1823
        Mastin, C-1823
MEADORS, Jack, C-1818
MEADOWS, Anderson, W-1812
        Daniel, W-1812
        John, Sn-1816, Sn-1811
        Joseph, Wi-1815
        Thomas, Sn-1811, Sn-1816
        William, W-1812
MEANLY, Beverly H., D-1811

MEANS, Griffin, B-1812
    William, B-1812, Bo-1801, Bo-1890
MEARS, Jacob, Su-1797
MEASLES, John, Wh-1825
MEASON, Samuel, Mt-1798
MEBANE, Alexander, Wi-1815
    George, Wi-1815
MEBANES, James, heirs, Wi-1815
MECHIN, Soham, Bl-1815
MEDERICK, Allen, Sn-1811
MEDLEY, Britton, Wh-1811
    James, Je-1800, Gr-1805, Gr-1804
    Jessee, Wh-1825
    John, Wh-1811, Wh-1825
    John Sr., Wh-1811, Wh-1825
    Joseph, Wh-1825
    Richard, Wh-1811
    Samuel, Wh-1811
MEDLIN, Hardy, A-1805
    Richard, A-1805
MEDLOCK, Charles, Gr-1805, Gr-1804
    John, Gr-1799, Wh-1811
    Wm., Wi-1810
MEDOW, Allen, Sn-1816
    Isaac, Sn-1816
    Jonas, Wi-1810
MEECA, John, Wh-1825
MEECE, Peter, Wh-1825
MEECHAM, William, Wi-1815
MEEK, Adam, Je-1800
    Adam Sr., Je-1822
    Adam K., J3-1822
    Alexander M., Je-1822
    Amaziah, Je-1822
    Daniel, Je-1822
    James, B-1812
    Thomas, Wh-1811, Wh-1825
    William, B-1812
MEEKS, David, Fr-1812
MEENEN, Langford, A-1805
MEGEE, William, Wi-1801
MEGEHE, Ferril, Ge-1783
MEGEHEN, Brewer, Ct-1798
MEGRADY, William, Wl-1804
MEHAFFEY, Martin, A-1805
MEHUNDRO, William B., B-1812
MEIRE, James, Je-1800
MELAND, John, Wa-1819
MELBOURN, Eliott, B-1812
MELCHER, Thomas L., W-1805
MELCOM, George, Je-1800
MELHORN, George, Su-1812
MELICOAT, James, Gr-1799
MELLER, William, W-1812
MELLIN, Partin, Gi-1812
MELOIN, William, Wh-1825
MELONA, John, Je-1800
MELONE, Lewis, Wi-1801
MELONEY, Edward, R-1819
MELONY, James, Fr-1812
MELOY, Hugh, Ge-1812
    James, Ge-1812
MELTEN, Mathew, W-1812
MELTON, Anson, W-1812
    Archelaus, Co-1827
    Cooper, W-1812
    Daniel, Sn-1811
    Elijah, Gi-1812
    Elisha, Gi-1812
    Henry, Hu-1812
    James, Hu-1812, D-1811
    Joel, Wh-1811

MELTON, John, W-1812
    Nathaniel, Gr-1805
    Thomas, W-1812
    William, Sn-1811
MELUGEON, Wm., Wi-1801
MELVILLE, Thomas A., D-1811
MELVIN, Edmond, D-1811
    James, Wa-1814
    John, Wa-1819
    Joseph, Wa-1819(2), Wa-1814
    Joseph Sr., Wa-1814
    Samuel, Wa-1814
    Thomas, D-1811
    William, D-1811
MEMURLEY, James, Hu-1812
MENDENHALL, Mordecai, Je-1822
MENDINGALL, Abraham, Gr-1799
MENDINGHALL, Josh, Je-1800
    Martin, Je-1800
    Mordica Sr., Je-1800
    Mordica Jr., Je-18-0
    Stephen, Je-1800
MENEES, James, Wl-1804
MENEFE, James, D-1805
MENEFEE, Jarrett, Gi-1812
    Thomas, A-1805
    William, Gi-1812
MENET, John, Wl-1804
MENIFEE, Hardy, Wl-1804
    John, Gi-1819
    Thomas, A-1805
MENIRE, Philip, Wi-1815
    Samuel, Wi-1815
MENIS, John W., Wi-1815
MENLEY, David, Je-1800
MENSH, Gasper, D-1788
MENURE, Benjamin, Rb-1812
    William D., Rb-1812
MENYFEE, Larkin, Gi-1819
MEPHERAN, James, Ge-1812
MERCER, Edward, Su-1797, Su-1796
    Nicholas, Su-1797, Su-1796
MERCHANT, James, Wi-1810
    William M., Gr-1805
MEREDETH, Sml., D-1811
MERES, Elias C., Gi-1819
MERIOT, John, Bo-1801, Bo-1800
MERIT, Thomas, Wi-1815
MERITT, Benjamin, Wi-1815
    Shimmey, Wi-1815
MERLOY, Abraham, Wi-1815
MERPHEY, Joseph, W-1812
MERREL, Richard, Su-1797
MERRELL, Daniel, Su-1797
    Edmund, Su-1797
    Jonathan, Su-1797
    Richard, Su-1797
    Thomas, Su-1797
MERRET, Benjamin, Gi-1812, Wi-1810
    Samuel, Wi-1801
MERRIMAN, Briant, Bl-1815
    Charles, Bl-1815
    William, W-1804, D-1805, W-1812
    William Sr., W-1805, W-1812
MERRIMON, Abednego, W-1812
MERRIOTT, John, heirs, R-1819
    Mary, R-1819
MERRIT, John, Gr-1821
MERRITERY, Atrohaean, Ro-1805
    George, R-1805
MERRITT, Edward, Gr-1821
    James, Wi-1810, Wi-1801

MERRITT, John, R-1808
    Samuel, Wi-1810
    Shemey, Wi-1810
    Thomas, Wi-1810
    William, Ro-1805
MERRY, Seth, Sn-1816
MERRYMAN, William, D-1811
MESMER, Henry, Ge-1812
MESSER, James, Wl-1804
MESSICK, William, Ge-1812
MESSOR, Joseph, Wa-1814(2), Wa-1819
    Joseph Sr., Wa-1819
METCALF, Chrisr., Sn-1811
    Ilar?, D-1811
    James, Fr-1812
    William, Fr-1812
METHERALL, James, D-1811
    John, D-1811
METHERAT, John, D-1805
METLOCK, George, Ct-1796, Ct-1798
    Gidion, Ct-1796
    William, Ct-1796, Ct-1798
METOUR?, Jerremiah, W-1812
METTON, Mary, Sn-1816
MEWTIN, Jno., D-1788
MIARS, John, Bl-1815
    Simon, Wi-1815
MIATT, Wiley, Wi-1815
MICHAEL, Barnabas, Gr-1804
MICHAL, Robert, Sn-1816
MICHEL, James, K-1799
    John, K-1799
    Mordecai, Bo-1801
MICKIE, George, Wl-1804
MICKLE, Benser, Je-1800
MICLE, Barnabas, Gr-1805
MIDCALF, Morace, Sn-1816
MIDDLETON, Drury, Mu-1816
    John, Gr-1804, Mu-1816
MIDKIFF, Isaac, Gr-1805, Wh-1811, Gr-1804
    Isaiah, Gr-1804
    Isaih, Ge-1799
    Isiah, Gr-1805
    John, Wh-1811, Gr-1799
    Thomas, Gr-1821
    William, Wh-1811
MIDLETON, John, Gr-1805
MIER, John, Mu-1816
MIERS, David, Ge-1805
    Elisha, Sn-1811
    Gasper, W-1812
    Henry, Ge-1805
    Michael, Ge-1805
    Peter, Ct-1796
    Phillip, Sn-1792
    Thomas, Sn-1811
MIKIN, George, Wh-1825
MILAM, James, B-1812
MILBURN, Ann, Ge-1812
    David, Ge-1812(3), Ge-1805
    Elanor, Ge-1812
    John, Ge-1812
    Johnathan, Dec., Adm. Ann Milburn,
        Ge-1812
    Jonathan, Ge-1805
    William, Su-1812, Ge-1805
MILEHAM, Drury, B-1812
MILES, Bird, Wi-1815
    Charles, Rb-1812
    Daniel, Wl-1804
    Hartwell, Wi-1815
    Jacob, Gr-1805

MILES, John, Je-1800, B-1812
    Joseph, Gr-1805
    Richard, Gr-1805, Mt-1798, Rb-1812
    Samuel, D-1811
    Thomas, Mu-1811, D-1811
MILHORN, George, Su-1796, Su-1797
MILICAN, John, W-1812
MILIGAN, Samuel, Ge-1812(2)
    William, Gr-1799, Gr-1805
MILIKAN, Isaac, B-1812
    George, Gr-1821
    William, Gr-1821
MILKASON, George, D-1805
MILLAN, Frederick, D-1811
MILLAR, Alex, Bo-1800
    Alexander, Bo-1801
    Andrew, Bo-1801
    David, Bo-1801, Bo-1800
    Saml., Bo-1801, Bo-1800
MILLARD, Abia, Su-1812
    Rebeccah, Su-1812
    Samuel, Su-1812
    Timothy, Su-1812
MILLBANKS, David, Ge-1812
MILLECAL?, Thomas, W-1812
MILLED, Adam, R-1819
MILLEKIN, Wi-liam, Bo-1805
MILLER, Abraham, Ge-1805, Je-1822
    Adam, Su-1812, Su-1796
    Addam, Wi-1810
    Alexander, W-1812, Ge-1783, Wl-1804,
        Wh-1825(2)
    Amos, D-1811
    Andrew, W-1812, C-1818, Ge-1783,
        Bo-1801, Bo-1800
    Andrus, Bl-1815
    B. Daniel, Mu-1811
    Catherine, Mu-1816
    Charles, Hu-1812
    Chrisley, Ct-1798, Ct-1796
    Christian, Su-1796
    Christopher, Ge-1812(2)
    Daniel, Ct-1796, Ct-1798
    David, Gr-1821, W-1812
    Easley, Gr-1804
    Elijah, W-1812
    Francis, Ro-1805, R-1819
    Fred, Sn-1811
    Frederick, Wh-1811, Gr-1799, Sn-1816
        D-1811
    Fredrick, Mu-1816
    George, Ct-1796, Gr-1821, Su-1796(2)
        Su-1812(2), Su-1797(2),
        Mo-1825, Fr-1812, B-1812,
        Gr-1799, Gr-1804, Sn-1811
    George Sr., Ct-1798
    George Jr., Ct-1798
    George W., Wh-1825
    Harman, Mu-1816
    Harmon, Gr-1799, Gr-1804, Gr-1805,
        Mu-1811
    Henry, Su-1796, Su-1797, Ro-1805,
        Ct-1798, Ct-1796, B-1812,
        Mu-1816
    Henry M., Sn-1811
    Hiram, R-1819
    Isaac, Wa-1814, Wa-1819(2), Su-1796
    Jacob, Ge-1805, Wa-1819(3), B-1812,
        Su-1812(4), Wh-1811, Su-1797,
        Su-1796, Wa-1814(3), Wh-1811,
        Ct-1798(2), Ct-1796(2),
        C-1818, A-1805

MILLER, James, Wa-1814, Ro-1805(2),
         W-1812(2), Wi-1815(2),
         Wa-1819, B-1812, Wi-1810,
         Wi-1801(2), Wh-1825
    James Sr., C-1818, Wh-1825
    James Jr., Wh-1825, C-1818
    Jessee, B-1812
    John, Ct-1796, Ct-1798(4), C-1818,
         C-1823, Gr-1804, Gr-1799(2),
         Gr-1821, Gr-1805, Ge-1812,
         Gi-1812, Ge-1805, Bo-1801,
         B-1812, Bl-1815, Se-1799
         Sn-1816, Sn-1811, Su-1797(2),
         Su-1796, Su-1812, A-1805,
         W-1812, W-1805, Wh-1811(3),
         Wh-1825(2), K*-1815, Mu-1811,
         Mu-1816, Je-1822(2), Wl-1804,
         R-1819, Wi-1815, Wi-1810,
         Wa-1814(3), Wa-1819(2)
    John Esq., Mu-1816
    John Sr., Wh-1811, Ct-1796, Wh-1825
    John Jr., Ct-1796, Wh-1825
    Johnson, D-1811
    Joseph, W-1812, Wh-1811, Wh-1825,
         Mu-1811
    Joseph Jr., Su-1812
    Joseph H., Mu-1816
    Joshia, Su-1812
    Joshua, Su-1812, W-1805
    Levi, Gr-1805, Gr-1821
    Lewis, K*-1815
    M. Pleasant, Wl-1804
    Martin, Gr-1821, Gr-17-9
    Martin Kite, Wa-1814
    Nathaniel, B-1812
    Nelson, Gr-1821
    Nimrod, C-1823
    Peter, Su-1812, Wa-1814, Wa-1819
    Peter Jr., Wa-1819
    Ralph, Mt-1798
    Richard, Su-1812, Fr-1812, Sn-1816
    Robert, Je-1822, Ge-1783
    Samuel, Wa-1814, Su-1797, Ro-1805,
         Su-1796, Wa-1819, Wh-1825
    Samuel Jr., Ro-1805
    Simon, Wa-1814, Wa-1819
    Simpson, D-1811
    Soloman, Wa-1819
    Solomon, Wa-1814
    Stephen, Gr-1821, Mu-1811, Mu-1816
    Theopholus, C-1823
    Thomas, Su-1796, Wa-1819, Wa-1814,
         Wh-1825
    Tobias, Gi-1819
    William, Ge-1812, Wa-1819, Ro-1805,
         Wa-1814(3), Ge-1805, Se-1799,
         Bl-1815, C-1818(2), C-1823,
         Mc-1825, Wi-1810, D-1788,
         D-1811, D-1805, W-1805,
         Wi-1810(2)
    William, heirs, Wa-1819
MILLHANDS, John, Ge-1812
MILLIAM, Edward, Wa-1819
    Edwards, estate, Wa-1819
    Robert, Wa-1819
MILLICAN, James, Ge-1783
MILLIGAN, David, Fr-1805
    Samuel, Ge-1805
    Solomon, Gr-1805
    Thomas, Rev'd., Su-1812
MILLIGIN, James, Wl-1804
    William, Wl-1804

MILLIKAN, Coleman, Gr-1805
    David, Gr-1805
    Elihu, Je-1822
    Solomon, Gr-1804, Je-1822
    William, Gr-1804
MILLIKEN, Alexander, Je-1822
MILLION, John, Wa-1819, Wa-1814
MILLS, Absalom, Mu-1811
    Andrew, Mu-1816
    Asa, Je-1800
    Curtius, Wh-1811
    David, Hu-1812
    David A., Mu-1816
    Eli, Je-1822
    Elijah, Je-1822
    George, Sn-1811
    Isum, Hw-1799
    Jacob, Gr-1804, Gr-1805, Je-1822
         Je-1800
    James, Sn-1811
    Jesse, Je-1822
    John, Je-1800, Gr-1821, Je-1822
         Sn-1816(2), Sn-1811, Mu-1816
         Mt-1798, Wh-1825
    John Sr., Je-1800
    Joseph, Gr-1805
    Richard, Je-1800, Gr-1805, Gr-1804
    Samuel, Je-1800, Je-1822
    Sanders, Mu-1816
    Thomas, Mu-1811, Mu-1816
    William, Je-1800(2), Ro-1805,
         Je-1822, Wh-1811, Wh-1825,
         Mu-1816
    William Jr., Je-1822
    Zachariah, Je-1822
MILLSON, Edward, Wa-1814
    Jacob, Wa-1814
MILTBARGER, Wm., C-1818
MILTON, James, W-1812
MINDOCK, John, D-1805
MINEMARCH, Patrick, Ro-1805
MINERS, John, D-1811
MINGERS, Jacob, Ct-1798
    John, Ct-1798
MINIK?, Strawboura, W-1812
MINIT, John, Gr-1805
MINNIS, John, Bo-1801
MINTER, Zacaria, Sn-1811
MINUS, Benjamin, Mt-1798
    James, Sn-1811
MIRECLE, Peter, W-1812
MIRNER, Thomas, Mu-1811
MISER, George, Bo-1801, Bo-18011
    John, Bo-1800
MISINGER, Conrod, Ge-1812
MISMER, Jacob, Ge-1812
    John, Ge-1805
    Mary, Ge-1805, Ge-1812
MISSEMORE, JOhn, Ge-1812
MISTON, Sanders, A-1805
MITAR, Jacob W., Su-1796
MITCHAL, John P., heirs, Sn-1816
MITCHEEL, Robert, Se-1799
MITCHEL, Andrew, D-1811, Mu-1811
    Benjamin, D-1811
    Daniel, D-1811, Gi-1819
    David, J-1802
    David L., Wh-1825
    Elisabeth, Sn-1811
    George, Mu-1811(3)
    Hardy, D-1811, D-1805
    Jabez G., Wh-1825

MITCHEL, James, Mu-1811(2), D-1811
    John, Rb-1812, W-1812, Wh-1825,
        Sn-1816, W-1805, D-1805(2),
        Mu-1811(2)
    John R., Sn-1811
    Robert, D-1788, Sn-1811, J-1802
    Robt. B., Sn-1811
    Sollomon, Sn-1816
    Soloman, Hw-1799
    Spencer Sr., Wh-1825
    Thomas, Mu-1811
    William, D-1811, D-1788, Wh-1825,
        Mu-1811
MITCHELL, Adam, Wa-1814, Wa-1819
    Allen L., Wh-1285
    Andrew, Mu-1816(2)
    Aquilla, Gr-1821
    Archibald, Gr-1805, Sn-1816
    Benjamin, Gr-1799, Gr-1821
    C. John, Sn-1811
    Charity, Wi-1810
    Charles, Wh-1811
    David, Wh-1811, W-1812, Wa-1819(3),
        Wa-1814(2)
    Edward, Wl-1804
    Elijah, Wl-1804
    Elizabeth, Wa-1814
    Elizabeth S., Mu-1816
    Frederick, Wi-1815
    George, B-1812, Wh-1825, Wl-1804,
        Mu-1816(4)
    Greenbury, Gr-1821
    Henry, Sn-1811, Sn-1816, D-1805
    Hezekiah, Wa-1819
    Isaac, Gr-1805, Gr-1804, Gr-1799
    Jacob, Wh-1811
    James, Mu-1816, Wa-1819(2), W-1812,
        Wa-1814(2), Je-1822, Rb-1812,
        K-1799, Mu-1816, Gr-1805
    James C., R-1819, Wh-1825
    Jeremiah, Hu-1812
    Joel D., Wh-1825
    John, Rb-1812, Wa-1819(2), Wa-1814,
        Wh-1811, Je-1800, Ge-1805,
        Je-1822, C-1823, Ge-1783,
        Gr-1804, Wh-1825(2), Sn-1811(2),
        Hu-1812, Sn-1816(2), Mu-1816(3),
        Wi-1801
    John W., Mu-1816
    Marcus, Gi-1819
    Marmaduke, B-1812
    Nathaniel, Je-1822
    Nelson, Wa-1819
    Nimrod, Fr-1812
    Oliver, Rb-1812
    Perry, Je-1822
    Richard, Gr-1804, Gr-1799
    Robert, Li-1812
    Robert, heirs, Wa-1819
    Robert B., Rb-1812
    Samuel B., R-1819
    Spence, Wh-1811
    Spencer, Wh-1285
    Thomas, Wa-1814, Ge-1812, Gr-1805,
        Ge-1805, Wa-1819, Mu-1816
    William, Rb-1812, Wh-1811, Wa-1814,
        W-1812, Wa-1819(2), Gr-1805(2),
        Gr-1804, Gr-1799, W-1805,
        Gr-1805
MITCHELL & RICE, R-1819
MITCHELS, David, W-1805
MITCHNER, William, Sn-1811

MITES, John, R-1808
MITLER, Thomas, Sn-1816
MITSTEAD, John, C-1818
MIZE, Henry, D-1811
    Jesse, B-1812
MITZELS, Levy, Wi-1815
MIZEN, John, Bl-1815
MOAD, James, C-1818, C-1823
    John, C-1818
    Sedwick, C-1823
    Thomas, C-1823, C-1818
    Wadswick, C-1818
MOBLEY, Edward, D-1811
MODE, James, A-1805
MODERAL, Robt., Wi-1810
MODEREL, Robert, Wi-1810
MODEWELL, Charles, Sh-1285
    Goodman, Wh-1825
    James, Wh-1825
    John Sr., Wh-1825
    John Jr., Wh-1825
    Samuel, Wh-1825
    Solomon, Wh-1825
MODGLIN, Henry, Wi-1815
MOFFAT, Nathanl., D-1805
MOFFET, Robert, Sn-1811
    William, Gr-1799, Sn-1816
MOFFETT, John, Gr-1805
    Robert, Sn-1816
    Samuel, Gr-1805, Gr-1821
    Shadrack, Gi-1812
MOFFIT, John, Gr-1804
    Samuel, Gr-1804
MOHLER, Henry, Wa-1814
MOIARTY, Jacob, MT-1798
MOIERS, William Jr., Ge-1805
MOLDER, Henry, Gr-1805, Je-1800
    John, Je-1800
    Polly, Je-1800
    Valentine, Gr-1805
MOLE, Joseph, Ro-1805
MOLEN, William, Gi-1812
MOLER, John, Wa-1819
MOLINIDUSE, Niker, Su-1812
MOLLOY, Daniel, Gi-1812
    Thomas, Mt-1798, Wi-1801(2),
        D-1788
MOLOIN, Edward, D-1805
MOLTON, George, Su-1812
    John, Su-1812
    Nicholas, Su-1812, Su-1796
    Nicholas Sr., Su-1812
    William, Su-1812, Su-1796
MONDRALL, John, Sn-1816
MONEGATLER, P., Gi-1819
MONEY, James, Wa-1814
MONICE, William, Gr-1804
MONRO, George, Gr-1805, Gr-1804
MONROE, P. David, D-1805
    Robert, Gr-1804
MONROW, George, Gr-1805
    Robert, Gr-1804
MONROW, George, Gr-1805
    Robert, Gr-1805
MONSON, Joseph, Wa-1814
MONTAGUE, Mary, Mu-1816
MONTEETH, George, Ge-1812
    Henry, Ge-1812
MONTGOMERY, A. N., C-1823
    Alex, Bo-1800, Sn-1792, Bo-1800
    Alexander, Wi-1815, Mu-1811(3),
        Ge-1783, Sn-1787, Bo-1801(2)

MONTGOMERY, Alexr., Sr., Ge-1783
    Daniel, Sn-1816
    David, Bo-1801, Bo-1800, B-1812
    Elijah, Wi-1810
    George, Bo-1801
    Hugh, D-1805, Bo-1801, Fr-1812,
        A-1805, Bo-1800
    Hugh W., C-1823
    Humphrey, Bo-1801
    Humphries, Bo-1800
    Jacob, Mu-1816, Mu-1811
    James, Sn-1816, Mu-1811(3), Wh-1825,
        Fr-1812(3), Bo-1800(2), Bo-1801
        Gi-1812, R-1819
    James S., Bo-1801
    John, Mu-1811(2), Sn-1816, Mu-1816,
        Fr-1812, Bo-1800(2), Bo-1801,
        Gi-1812, Gi-1819
    Lamuel Thos., C-1818
    Lemuel, D-1811
    Michael, Je-1800
    Michal, Su-1797
    Robert, Bo-1805, Bo-1801, Wh-1825
    Robert Jr., Bo-1800
    Samuel, Gi-1812, D-1811, D-1805
    Thomas, Bo-1800
    William, Wi-1815, Sn-1816, Mt-1798,
        D-1805, D-1811, Wi-1801,
        Je-1800, Sn-1787(2), Sn-1792,
        Fr-1812, Bo-1800, Ge-1812
MONTGUMERY, Wm., Wi-1801
MONYFIELD, John, B-1812
MOOD, Joseph, Su-1797
MOODEY, ANdrew, Hu-1812
MOODY, Francis, Mu-1816
    George, Gr-1821, Gr-1804, Gr-1805,
        Su-1812
    James, W-1812
    John, Sn-1811(2), Gr-1821
    Jonathan, Gi-1812
    Nathaniel, Gi-1819, D-1805
    Philip, D-1811
    Thomas, Gi-1812
    William, Sn-1811
MOODY's Orphans, by Robert Easley, Su-1796
MOON, Daniel, Wa-1819, Je-1800
    James, W-1812
    John, Se-1799
    Joseph, Je-1800
    Nathn:, Se-1799
    Nathaniel, Je-1800
    Rich, Bl-1815
    Richert, Wh-1825
    Simon, W-1812
MOONEY, Charles, Wh-1285
    Geo., Ge-1783
    James, W-1805(2), W-1812
    John Sr., B-1812
    Joseph, W-1812
    Sampson, Wh-1825
    William, Wh-1811
MOONEYHAM, Jessee, Wh-1825
    Joel, Wh-1825
    Shadrach, Wh-1825
    Thomas, Wh-1825
MOONY, James, Sn-1816
    John Jr., B-1812
MOOR, Abraham, Ge-1812
    Absalom, Ct-1796
    Anthony, Ge-1812
    Daniel, Ct-1796
    David, Ge-1812

MOOR, Isaac, Gr-1799
    James, Bo-1800(2), Ge-1812(2),
        Gr-1821, Ct-1798
    Joab, Rb-1812
    Joseph, D-1811, Rb-1812
    Mackne, Gr-1821
    Rice, Gr-1821
    Saml., Ge-1783
    Thomas, Wi-1815, Bo-1800
    William, Fr-1812(2)
MOORE, Abner, Wh-1811, Gr-1799, Gr-1804
    Abraham, Rb-1812
    Absalom, Ct-1798
    Agnes, R-1808
    Alen, Bo-1800
    Alex, Ro-1805
    Alexander, Rb-1812, Su-1796, Su-1797,
        Wh-1811, Bo-1805, Bo-1801,
        Mu-1816, Wh-1825
    Amos, Rb-1812
    Andrew, Je-1822
    Anthony, Ge-1805
    Anty, Ge-1783
    Asa, Gi-1812
    Benjamin, Gr-1805
    Bennet W., Mu-1816
    Burgess, Ro-1805
    Chaney, Je-1822
    D., D-1788
    Daniel, Ct-1798
    David, Ro-1805, Ge-1805, C-1823,
        D-1811
    David & James, D-1805
    Denton, Wh-1825
    Edmund, Wl-1804
    Edward, Mu-1816, D-1811
    Elijah, Je-1822, Wl-1804
    Elisha, Je-1822
    Ephraim, Wi-1815
    Ephrain, Je-1822
    Ephram, Wi-1810
    Ewin, D-1805
    Field, Fr-1812
    Francis, Sn-1816
    Garret, Su-1797
    Garrett, Su-1796
    George, Ro-1805, Su-1812, Ct-1798,
        B-1812, Wl-1804, Gr-1805
    George L., B-1812
    Henry, Wl-1804(2), Mu-1811
    Hugh, Wi-1815
    Isaac, Je-1822
    Isreal, Sn-1816, Sn-1811
    Jacob, Su-1797, Bo-1805, Bl-1815
    James, Ge-1805, Gi-1812, Rb-1812,
        Je-1822(2), Su-1797, Ge-1812,
        W-1812, Ge-1805(2), Je-1800,
        C-1798, Bo-1805, Gr-1799,
        Sn-1811, Mt-1798, Wi-1810,
        W-1805, Wi-1815(2), B-1812,
        Ge-1783, Fr-1812, Gr-1804(2),
        Mu-1816, Hu-1812, Gr-1805(2)
    James Esq., Gr-1799
    James Jr., Ge-1805
    James B., D-1811
    Jephta, Gi-1812
    Jesse, Je-1822(2)
    Joab, D-1805
    Joel, Rb-1812
    John, Rb-1812, Ge-1805, Je-1800,
        Ge-1812, Je-1822, Wa-1819,
        Ge-1805, Ct-1798, Wl-1804(3)

MOORE, John, cont'd.--Ge-1783, B-1812,
        Sn-1811(2), Sn-1816(2),
        D-1811(3), Hu-1812, Mt-1798,
        Wi-1810, Wi-1815, Wl-1804
    John Sr., R-1819
    John Jr., R-1819
    John F., Mu-1816
    Jonathan, Mu-1816
    Joseph, Ro-1805, Su-1797, A-1805,
        Fr-1812, Wi-1815, Wi-1810,
        Sn-1816
    Lemuel, Gr-1804
    Levi, Ge-1805
    Levi Sr., B-1812
    Levi Jr., B-1812
    Levy, B-1812
    Luci, Gr-1805
    Lucinda, Je-1822
    Mackness, Gr-1804
    Markness, Gr-1805
    Martha, Gr-1804, Gr-1805
    Mary, Bo-1801, Wi-1801
    Mathew, D-1811
    Matthew G., Wh-1825
    Morris, Ro-1805
    Moses, Ge-1805, Ge-1783, D-1805
    Nathan Jr., Ro-1805
    Nathan Sr., Ro-1805
        Nathann, W-1812
    P. John, Ct-1798
    Parker John, Ct-1796
    Perry, B-1812
    Pleasant, Gi-1812
    Rice, Gr-1804, Gr-1805
    Richard, W-1812, Sn-1811, D-1811
    Risdon D., Sn-1816
    Robert, Je-1822, Wa-1814, Wa-1819,
        Gr-1804, Se-1799, B-1812,
        Gr-1799, Mu-1816, Sn-1811(3),
        Gr-1805, Sn-1816
    Samuel, Mu-1816, Sn-1811, Su-1812(2),
        Gr-1805, Su-1797(2), Gr-1799,
        Wi-1815, Su-1796(2), B-1812
    Saml. A., Jr., Wh-1825
    Samuel A., Esq., Wh-1825
    Skelton, Rb-1812
    Somerset, Gi-1812
    Summerset, Wi-1801
    Thomas, R-1819, Ro-1805, Je-1822,
        Mu-1816, Hu-1812, Wh-1825
        Bo-1801, Bo-1805
    William, Je-1800, Je-1822, Wi-1815,
        Fr-1812(2), Gr-1804, Wh-1825,
        D-1805, Sn-1811
    William Sr., Ge-1805
    Zadok, Ge-1805
MOOREHEAD, Joseph, Mu-1816
MOOT, William, Ge-1812
MOPPIN, B. Barrows, Sn-1811
MORAIN, Georg, Hw-1801
MORAN, Abner, Wl-1804
    Daniel, Ro-1805
MORCE, Fields, Se-1799
MORE, Hugh, Ge-1783
    James, Se-1799, Gi-1819, Bo-1801
    John, Gi-1819, Sn-1816, Sn-1811
    Mae, Gr-1805
    Rice, Gr-1805
    Stephen, Mc-1825
    William, Gr-1804
MOREHEAD, Joseph, Mu-1811
MORELAND, Charles, Ct-1798

MORELAND, Jonathan, Ge-1805
    Vinson, B-1812
    William, Ct-1796, Ct-1798
MORELOCK, George, Su-1797, Su-1796
    James, Su-1797, Su-1796
MORESON, Thomas, Bo-1800
MORGAIN, Chuck, Bl-1815
    James, Hw-1801
MORGAN, Abel, Su-1797, Gr-1805, Gr-1804,
        Su-1796
    Adonijah, Ge-1783
    Ben, Sn-1787
    Benjn. & David, D-1805
    Calvin, K*-1815
    Charles, Sn-1787
    Daniel, Ct-1798
    Dotson, Gr-1821
    Edmd. R., Gi-1812
    Esward, Sn-1816
    Enous, B-1812
    Eward, SN-1811
    Gabriel, Su-1812
    George, D-1811
    Hardin, Mu-1811
    Henry, Gr-1805, Gr-1799, Gr-1804(2)
        Su-1796, Gi-1812
    Henry E., Gr-1805
    Hezekiah, Je-1822
    Isaac, Sn-1787, Mt-1798
    James, Sn-1792, B-1812, Ro-1805
    Jeremiah, Sn-1792
    John, Cl-1803(2), Sn-1792, Sn-1787,
        Gr-1821, Gr-1799, Ge-1812,
        R-1819
    Joseph, C-1818, Sn-1787, Sn-1792
    Levy, D-1811
    Lewis, Ge-1783, R-1819
    Martin, B-1812
    Mary, Gr-1821
    Nathan, Wh-1811
    Nathaniel, B-1812
    Orman, Fr-1812
    Richard, Je-1800
    Silas, Je-1800
    Solomon, Su-1812
    Theophilius, Rb-1812
    Theophilius Jr., Rb-1812
    Thomas, Ge-1783, Ge-1812
    Valentine, Gr-1821, Gr-1799, Gr-1804
        Gr-1805
    William, Sn-1811, D-1811, Sn-1792,
        A-1805, Fr-1812, Rb-1812,
        Su-1796, Je-1800, Je-1822,
        Su-1812, Su-1797, Ro-1805
    William Jr., Su-1812, Je-1822
    Williamson, Wi-1810
    Willis, Ge-1812(2)
MORGEN, Armstead, Sn-1787
    William, Hw-1801
MORGIN, John, Hw-1801
    John Jr., Hw-1801
    Joseph, Cl-1803
    Mark, Hw-1801
MORISON, Thomas, Gr-1805
MORISSON, Kenough, Wi-1810
    Patrick, Sn-1792
MORLAND, Charles, Ct-1796
MORNE, John, Ro-1805
MORPLIES, Joseph, Gi-1812
MORRAS, Henery, Sn-1811
MORREL, William, Su-1812
MORRELL, Caleb, Su-1812

MORRELL, Catharine, Su-1812
    Daniel, Su-1812, Su-1796
    Edmund, Su-1796
    Edward, Su-1812
    John, Su-1796
    Jonathan, Su-1796
    Nathan, Su-1812
    Thomas, Su-1812, Su-1796
MORRICE, Morriss, Ge-1812
MORRIS, Absalem, Gr-1799
    Absalom, A-1805, C-1823, C-1818
    Adam, Gi-1819
    Benjamin, A-1805
    Charles, B-1812
    Daniel, Fr-1812, Ro-1805
    Dempsey, D-1811, D-1805(2)
    Gideon, Je-1822, Rb-1812
    Graves, Fr-1812
    Hardy, Wa-1819
    Henry, Mu-1816, Ge-1805
    Hezekiah, D-1805
    Hezkiel, Rb-1812
    Jacob, Sn-1811
    James, Mu-1816, Ro-1805
    James M., B-1812
    Jean, Je-1800
    Jere, Rb-1812
    Jesse, Rb-1812
    John, D-1805, Wa-1819, Fr-1812(2)
        Gr-1799, Je-1822, Ge-1812,
        Je-1800
    John Esq., Ge-1812
    Josiah, D-1805
    Lemuel, D-1811
    Lester, D-1811, Gi-1812
    Levin, Ct-1796, Ct-1798
    Martin, Gr-1805, Gr-1804
    Mathew, Rb-1812
    Maurice, Ge-1805
    Micajah, D-1811
    Micajah & John, D-1805
    Michael, B-1812, Wa-1819
    Millan, Wi-1810
    Moses, Fr-1812
    Richard, R-1808
    Robert, Fr-1812
    Samuel, Sn-1811, D-1811
    Shadrach, A-1805, Gi-1812, Je-1822
    Stephen, Ro-1805
    Thomas, D-1811
    William, Sn-1811(2), Wi-1815, W-1812,
        R-1819, Ro-1805
MORRISON, Andrew, B-1812
    Elias, Wl-1804
    George, Su-1812
    Hugh, Wl-1804
    James, Su-1797, Ge-1805, Su-1796,
        Ge-1812, Fr-1812, Wi-1810
    John, Ge-1812, Wi-1810
    Joseph, Wa-1819
    Kenneth, Wi-1815
    Lawrence, Su-1812
    Mary, Sn-1811
    Moses, Ro-1805
    Peter, Fr-1812
    Peter for Wells, Su-1812
    Robert, Wl-1804
    Shanaugh, Wi-1810
    Thomas, Su-1796, Su-1812, Bo-1801,
        Bo-1805
    William, J-1802, Wa-1819, B-1812,
        Bo-1805, Sn-1792, Wh-1811

MORRISS, James, Su-1796
    John, Rb-1812, Ge-1805
    Joseph, Sn-1816
    Joshua, Sn-1792
    William, Sn-1816
MORRISSON, James, Mu-1811
MORRISY, William, D-1805
MORROW, Alexander, Mu-1816, Gr-1799
    Benjamin, Sn-1811
    Ebenezer, Ge-1812
    Hugh, W-1805
    Isaac, Rb-1812
    James, Ge-1812, B-1812
    John, R-1819, Je-1822, Je-1800,
        Ge-1812, Ge-1805, B-1812,
        Fr-1812
    Leonard, Gi-1812
    Robert, Gr-1805, W-1805, Mu-1816
    Thomas, Rb-1812, Gi-1812, K-1799,
        Gi-1819
    William, Ge-1812, Ge-1783, Fr-1812,
        Je-1800, Wi-1815
MORTAN, Samuel, Wi-1810
MORTERSON, Aron, Ro-1805
MORTIAN, Abraham, Sn-1811
    Alexander, D-1805
    Asey, D-1811
    Caleb, Wa-1819
    George, Mo-1825
    Isiah, D-1811
    Jefry, Mu-1816
    John, Wa-1819, Mu-1811
    Joseph, Gi-1819
    Nicholas, Su-1797
    Samuel, Wi-1810, Wi-1815
    Thomas D., Mo-1825
    William, Fr-1812, Gi-1812, Mu-1811
MORWICK, Jacob, Su-1812
MOSELEY, John, Su-1796, Su-1797
    Joshua, R-1819
    Thomas, Rb-1812
MOSELY, Archibald, B-1812
    Peter, Wl-1804
    William, Hw-1799
MOSER, Adam, A-1805, C-1823, Wl-1804
    Jacob, A-1805
    Nicholas, A-1805
    Philip, Su-1797
MOSES, James, D-1811
    John, D-1788, Gr-1805
    Jonathan, Gr-1805
    Mark, Wa-1814
MOSGROVE, John, Gr-1799
MOSIER, Absolum, Gr-1799
    Francis, Je-1822
    John, D-1811
    Joseph, Je-1822
    Philip, Je-1822
    William, Je-1822
MOSLEBY, John, B-1812
MOSLEY, Jeptha, D-1811
    Jesse, Ge-1805, Rb-1812
    Jesse Esq., Ge-1812
    John Sr., Su-1812
    Thomas, D-1811
    William, Su-1812
MOSS, Benjamin, D-1811
    Cate, Sn-1816, Sn-1811
    Hugh, Mu-1811
    James, Fr-1812, Ro-1805, Hu-1812
    John, B-1812, Fr-1812
    Mason, Gi-1812

MOSS, Matthew, B-1812
    Merculus, A-1805
    Obediah, Ro-1805
    Ransom, Sn-1816
    Reubin, C-1818
    Samuel, Fr-1812, Je-1822
    Spencer, Rb-1812
    Thomas, Wl-1804
    Thomas B. S., Rb-1812
    Wilkins, Sn-1811
    William, Fr-1812
    William Jr., Rb-1812
MOSSLY, Joshua, W-1812
    Thomas, W-1812
MOSWELL, Nimrod, Gr-1799
MOTHERAL, John, Wi-1815, Wl-1804
    Joseph, Wl-1804, Sn-1811
    Samuel, Wl-1804
MOTHEREAL, Joseph, Sn-1816
MOTHEREL, Joseph, Sn-1811
MOTHERILL, Joseph, D-1811
MOUIR, Hardy, Su-1812
MOULDER, George, Gr-1821
    Valentine, Gr-1804
MOUNT, Humphrey, Je-1822
    John, D-1788, Je-1822
    Julius, Mo-1825
MOUNTGUMERY, William, Sn-1811
    Wm., Esq., Sn-1811
MOURIS, David, D-1788
MOWER, Nathaniel, Gr-1799
MOWNING, Caleb, B-1812
MOWREY, John, Bo-1801
MOWRY, John, A-1805
    Samuel, Je-1822
    Valentine, A-1805
MOYER, Danl., Su-1797, Su-1796
    Gasper, Su-1796
    Jacob, Su-1797, Su-1796(2)
    Jasper, Su-1797
    John, C-1823, Su-1796, Gr-1805
MOYERS, Abraham, C-1818
    Adam, Ge-1812, Ge-1805
    Christopher, Je-1800, Ge-1812
    David, Je-1822, Je-1800
    Frederick, Gr-1821
    George, Ge-1805
    Henry, Ge-1812
    Henry Sr., Ge-1812
    Jacob, Ge-1812(2), Su-1797
    James, Je-1822, Je-1800
    John, Je-1822(2), Gr-1821, Ge-1812, Gr-1804
    Joshua, Je-1800, Je-1822
    Mary, alias Showman, M., Gr-1805
    Michael, Ge-1812, Gr-1804
    William, Je-1822
MOZER, Adam, C-1818
    Solomon, B-1812
MOZIER, George, C-1818
MUFFORD, Jaco D., Rb-1812
MULHANAN, James, D-1805
MULHERIN, James, D-1811
MULHERRIN, Charles, D-1811
    James, Wl-1804
MULHOLLAND, William, Ge-1783
MULKEN, Jno., Cl-1803
MULKEY, Ann, Ct-1796
    John, Gr-1799
    Philip, Ct-1796
    Phillip, Ct-1798
MULLEN, James, Gr-1821

MULLEN, William, D-1811
MULLENS, Ezekial, W-1812
    John, Gr-1821
MULLICAN, John, W-1812
    William, W-1812
MULLIN, Alexander, D-1811
    Flower, Su-1797
    Henry, Wi-1815
    Isaac, D-1805
    Mary, Wi-1810
    Swift, Fr-1812
MULLINS, Daniel C., W-1812
    Jesse, Wa-1819, Wa-1814
    Joel, Gr-1805
    John, Gr-1805, Gr-1799, Ct-1796
    Joseph, Gr-1805
MULUROTH, John, Sn-1811
    Joseph, Sn-1811
MUMPOUER, John, Gr-1799
MUMPOUR?, Jonathan, Gr-1805
MUMPOWER, John, Gr-1804
    Jonathan, Gr-1821, Gr-1805
MUNCOS, Benjamin, Ge-1812
MUNCUS, John, Gr-1799
MUNCY, Daniel, A-1805
MUNDAY, Wm. Sr., Rb-1812
    Wm. Jr., Rb-1812
MUNKAS, John, Gr-1799
MUNN, Francis, Wi-1815
MUNROE, George, Gr-1821
    John, Gr-1821
    Mark, Gr-1821
    Robert Sr., Gr-1821
    Robert Jr., Gr-1821
MUNROW, Robert, Gr-1799
MUNY, Thomas, Gr-1805
MURCHHERSON, John, Fr-1812
MURCHSON, David, Wi-1801
MURDOCK, John, D-1811
    Sampson, Rb-1812
MURFORD, Berry, D-1788
MURFREE, Hardy, Wi-1801
    Hardy, heirs, Wi-1815
    Mathias B., Wi-1815
MURFREY, William H., Wi-1815
MURICK, Wm., Hu-1812
MURKISON, Kenneth, B-1812
    Murdock, B-1812
MURPHA, Jeremiah, Sn-1811
MURPHEY, Archebald, Wl-1804
    Elijah, Wa-1814
    H. & E., R-1819
    Hardy, Mt-1798
    Jery, Sn-1816
    John, Ge-1783
    Samuel, R-1819
    Thomas, Ge-1805
    William, D-1805, D-1811, Gr-1799(2), Ro-1805
MURPHREE, Allen, R-1819
    Isak, B-1812
    John, B-1812, R-1819
    William, B-1812
    Wyly, R-1819
MURPHREY, Nimrod, B-1812
MURPHRY, Laurence, Wi-1815
MURPHY, Archabald, Ge-1812
    Charles, Rb-1812, Mu-1816
    David, C-1818, Je-1800
    Edward, G?-1812(4)
    George, Rb-1812
    James, Mc-1825, Rb-1812

MURPHY, James Sr., Gi-1812
    James Jr., Gi-1812
    Jesse, dec'd., Wh-1811
    John, Mc-1825, Bo-1805
    Joseph, Wa-1814
    Martha, Wi-1815
    Nathaniel, Mu-1811, Mu-1816
    Robertson, Rb-1812
    Samuel, Rb-1812
    Stephen, B-1812
    Thomas, C-1818
    Uriah, Wh-1811
    William, D-1811, Sn-1816, Ge-1783,
        K-1799, Je-1800
    William M., Su-1812
MURR, John, Wa-1819
MURRAH, Christopher, Gr-1799
    Wm., Gi-1812
    Wm. H., Gi-1812
MURRAY, Cassel, Wi-1801
    Christopher, Wa-1819, C-1818, C-1823
    David, C-1823
    Francis, B-1812
    Isaac, C-1818
    Jabash, C-1818
    James, C-1823, C-1818, Gi-1812
    Jebush, C-1823
    John, Wa-1819, Wa-1814
    Jonathan, C-1823
    Jonothan, C-1818
    Joseph, Gi-1812
    Joshua, C-1818
    Morgan, C-1818, Wa-1814
    Morzan, Mu-1814
    Robert, B-1812
    Shaderick, Wa-1814
    Shadrick, Wa-1819
    Thomas, C-1823, C-1818, Gr-1804,
        Wa-1814, Ge-1805
    Thos., Sr., C-1818
    Wm., Wi-1801
MURREL, Benjamin, Je-1800
    Jeffery, Wi-1810, Wi-1815
    John, Wh-1811
    William, Co-1827
    William, Gi-1819
MURRELL, Richard Sr., Su-1812
    Richard Jr., Su-1812
    William, D-1811
MURREN, Robert, Bo-1800, Bo-1805
MURREY, Caple, Wi-1801
    Richard, Wi-1815
    Thos., Sn-1811
    William, Wh-1825
MURRIN, Robert, Bo-1801
MURROW, Benjn., Sn-1816
    Hugh, K-1799
MURRY, Allen, Mu-1816
    Ephraim, Wa-1819, Wa-1814
    John & James, D-1805
    Jonathan, Rb-1812
    Reuben, Ge-1812
    Tileigh, Wi-1815
    Thomas, Sn-1816, Sn-1823
    William, Mt-1798, Bo-1805, Wa-1814
MUSE, Daniel, Fr-1812
    Humphrey, Sn-1816
    Isaac, B-1812
    John, Gi-1819
    Philip, Gi-1812
    Thomas, Fr-1812
MUSGRAVE, Robert, Ct-1796

MUSGRAVE, Samuel, B-1812, Ct-1796
    Wilson, Gr-1799
MUSGROVE, John, Su-1797(2), Su-1796
    John Jr., Su-1796
    Moses, Su-1797
    Robert, Ct-1798
    Samuel, Ge-1812, Ct-1798
    Thomas, B-1812
    Wilson, C-1823
MUSIC, Electons, Wh-1811
MYARS, Michael, Ge-1805
MYCELF, Owen, Ge-1805
MYER, John, D-1811
MYERS, Abraham, C-1823
    Adam, Gi-1812
    Chelly, W-1805
    Christian, Wh-1825
    Daniel, Su-1812
    Frederick, Gr-1804, Su-1812
    Henry, Su-1812(2), Ge-1812
    Henry Sr., Su-1812
    Jacob, Su-1797(2), Su-1796
    John, C-1823, Ge-1812, Je-1800,
        Gr-1805
    John C., Wh-1825
    Mary, Gr-1804
    Peter, D-1811
    Phillip, W-1812
    William Sr., Ge-1812
    William Jr., Ge-1812
MYHON, James, Wh-1811
MYNATT, John, Gr-1805, Gr-1804
    Joseph, K*-1815
    Saml., Gr-1810
    Silas, Gr-1821
    Thomas, Gr-1821
    W. C., K*-1815
MYRICK, John, Mu-1816, Mu-1811
    Moreland, Mu-1811
NAB, Caleb, Wa-1814
    Henry, Wa-1814
NABOURS, Francis, Fr-1812
NAEL, Zacheriah, D-1811
NAFF, Jonathan, Ge-1812
NAGGLE, David, Ge-1812
NAGLE, Shedrick, Sn-1811
NAIL, Andrew, Wi-1801
    John, Ro-1805
    Matthew, Ge-1783, Ro-1805
NAILE, John, Ro-1805
    Nicholas, Ro-1805
    William, Gi-1812
NAILER, John, B-1812
NAILOR, Dixon, W-1812
    James Jr., W-1812
NAIRD, John, Gi-1812
NAKES, Euriah, B-1812
NALE, Geo. C., B-1812
    John, Ro-1805, Gr-1804
NALL, James, B-1812
    John, B-1812(2), Gr-1805
    Larkin, Gr-1804
    Robt., Gr-1804
    William, Wi-1815, Gr-1805, B-1812,
        Gr-1804
NANBUSKIRK?, Cornelius, D-1811
NANCE, John, Gr-1821
    Reuben, Gr-1821, B-1812
NANNEY, Patrick Ex., Je-1800
NANNY, Ames, D-1811
NAPIER, John, D-1811(2)
    Thomas, D-1805

NAPPEN, Rane, B-1812
NAPPER, M. John, Mu-1811
NARMORE, J., Bl-1815
NARRAMOR, John, Bl-1815
NASH, Demsey, Wi-1810, Wi-1815
    Francis, Wl-1804
    John, Gr-1799, C-1823
    Thomas, D-1805, Gr-1821
    William, Mu-1811, D-1811, Wl-1804,
        Su-1812
    William, Esq., Su-1796
NATHAN?, John, B-1812
NATION, Edward, Mu-1811
    Joseph, Gi-1812, Gr-1799, Ge-1783,
        Gr-1799
    Nathaniel, Gi-1812
    Thomas, Mu-1816
NATIONS, Edward, Mu-1816
NAVE, Abraham, Ct-1796, Ct-1798
    George, Bo-1801
    Isaac, Co-1821
    John, Ct-1796, Co-1821, Je-1800,
        Ct-1798, Gi-1812
    Peter, Ct-1796, Ct-1798
NAVEL, Henry, Gi-1812
NAVILL, George, K-1799
NAXEY, George, D-1811
NAY, John, D-1805
NEAL, Benjamin, Je-1800
    Ezekiel, Fr-1812, Wh-1825
    Isaac, W-1812
    James, Gi-1812, R-1819
    Joseph, W-1812
    Mathew, Sn-1811
    Patrick, Su-1812
    Peter, Gr-1799
    Teames, Wi-1810
    Thomas, W-1812, D-1811
    William, W-1812, Sn-1816, D-1811,
        Wi-1815
NEALEY, Isaac, Wi-1810
NEALLY, Benjamin, Gr-1821
NECHRORS, John, Bl-1815
NEDEVER, George, Su-1812
    Jacob, Su-1812
    Solomon, Su-1812
NEECE, John, Ge-1812
NEEDAM, William, D-1811
NEEDHAM, Enoch, Gi-1819
    Henry, Gr-1821
    Isaac, Gi-1819
    J. Bailey, Gi-1819
    John, Gr-1821
    John Jr., Gr-1821
    Lemuel, Gr-1821
    Lewis, Mu-1816
NEEHAM, Baley, Mu-1811
    Lewis, Mu-1811
NEEL, Benjamin, Je-1822, Ge-1812
    Benjamin Jr., Je-1822
    Hamilton, Ge-1812
    James, Ge-1812, Wi-1815(2)
    James S., Je-1822
    Jeremiah, Je-1822
    Jesse, Je-1822
    Joseph, B-1812
    Nicholas, Ge-1783
    Obediah, Ge-1812
    Pallace, Wl-1804(2)
    Statherd, Ge-1812
    Thomas, Je-1822
    William, Mu-1811, Wl-1804

NEEL, William Sr., Wl-1804
NEELD, Elias, Wi-1810
    Wm., Li-1812*
NEELE, Isan, Sn-1816
    William, Mu-1816
NEELEY, George, Wi-1810
    Isaac, Wi-1815
    John, Wi-1815
    Thomas, Wh-1825
    William, Ro-1805
NEELL, Brooks, Sn-1816
    Henry, Sn-1816, Sn-1811
    James, Wi-1815, Wi-1801, Wi-1810
    John Sr., Wi-1810
    Wm., Wi-1801
    Wm. Jr., Wi-1810
NEELOY, Thomas, Wi-1810
NEELY, Alex, Sn-1787
    Alexander, Sn-1816
    Alexander, heirs, Sn-1792
    Andrew, Je-1800, Mu-1811
    Charles, Mu-1816, Gi-1812, Mu-1811
    George, Wi-1801(2)
    George Sr., Wi-1815
    Hugh, Gi-1812
    James, Je-1800, Wi-1815, Mu-1816,
        D-1805, Mu-1811(2)
    John, Je-1800, Wi-1815, B-1812,
        Wi-1810, Mu-1816
    Joseph, J-1802, D-1811(2), D-1805
    Richard, B-1812
    Robert, Mu-1816(2), Sn-1811, Mu-1811
    Samuel, Mu-1816, D-1805, D-1788,
        D-1811
    Thomas, Mu-1816
    William, Wi-1815, Sn-1792, D-1811,
        D-1805(2)
    William Sr., D-1811
NEES, Adam, Ge-1812
    George, Ge-1812
    Jacob, Ge-1812
    John Sr., Ge-1812(3)
    John Jr., Ge-1812
    Michael, Ge-1812
NEESE, John, Ge-1805
    Michael, Ge-1805(2)
NEEVS, John, Mc-1825
NEIL, Benjamin, Ge-1805
    James, Ge-1805
    John, Cl-1803
    Joseph, Cl-1803
    Robert, Wl-1804
    William, Ge-1805
NEILL, Alan, B-1812
    Andrew, B-1812
    Duncan, B-1812
    James, B-1812(2)
    John, B-1812
    Nicholas, B-1812
NEILLE, Henry, Wh-1811
NEILSON, Andrew, Je-1800
    Charles B., D-1811
    George, Ge-1805
    Hugh, Ge-1805
NEILY, Clement, B-1812
    Richard, B-1812
NEISE, John, Ge-1805
NEITHERLAN, _____, Bo-1800
NELE, James, Wi-1801
NELLOMS, Samuel, Fr-1812
NELLS, Duncan, B-1812
    Jacob, Fr-1812

NELLS, John, Fr-1812
    Samuel, Fr-1812
    Thomas, Rb-1812
NELSON, Alexander, Je-1822
    Andrew, Fr-1812
    Benjamin, Wa-1819, Wa-1814
    Charles, D-1805
    Charles B., Wi-1810
    Dan, Wa-1819
    David, Ro-1805, Wa-1819, Se-1799
    Elisha, Wh-1825
    Gabriel, C-1823
    George, Sn-1811, Ge-1812
    Henry, Wa-1819(2), Wa-1814
    Hugh, Ge-1812
    Jacob, Wh-1825
    James, B-1812, Fr-1812, Wa-1814
    James N., R-1819
    Jarratt, D-1805
    Jarret, D-1811
    John, Mt-1798(2), Mu-1811, Bo-1805,
        Bo-1801, Je-1822(2), Rb-1812,
        Gi-1812, Wa-1814, W-1812
    John Sr., Wa-1819
    John Jr., Wa-1819
    Miles, Ro-1805
    Moore, D-1805
    Moses, D-1805, B-1812
    Nancy, Wa-1814
    Nathan, Wa-1819, Wa-1814
    Nathaniel, W-1812
    Pleasant, Mu-1816
    Preston, Fr-1812
    Richard, Wh-1825
    Robert, Mt-1798, Wi-1801, Wi-1810
    Samuel, Wi-1801(3)
    Southuay, Wa-1819
    Thomas, Wl-1804, Wa-1819, Wa-1814(2)
    Timothy, Wa-1814
    William, D-1811(2), Gi-1812, Wa-1819,
        A-1805, Ge-1783, Wa-1819,
        Wa-1814(3), W-1812, Wa-1819
    William Sr., Wa-1814
    William D., Mu-1816
NEMO, Uilsey G., D-1811
NENNEY, Patrick, Je-1822
NEOL, William, Gr-1799
NESBETT, Samuel, Mu-1811
NESBITT, John, D-1805
NESTOR, Frederick, C-1823, C-1818
NETHERLAND, Richard, Su-1812
NETHERLY, William, Ct-1798
NETHERTON, Henry, Wh-1825
    James, Wh-1811
NETLES, Plummer, Rb-1812
NETTLE, George, J-1802
NEUCOMB, William, D-1811
NEUGANT, Thomas, Gr-1805
NEULY, John, Gr-1805
NEVELLE, George, Mt-1798
NEVILL, Alexander, Wh-1825
    Benjamin, Fr-1812
    George, Mt-1798
    Joseph, Wh-1825, Wh-1811
    William, Wh-1811
NEVILLE, Joseph, Mt-1798
NEW, John, Gi-1812
    Pleasant, Gi-1812
    Wm., Gi-1812
NEWAL, John, Ge-1812
    Joseph, Ge-1812
    Joseph Jr., Ge-1812

NEWALL, Jesse Cole, Ro-1805
NEWAM, Eldrige, D-1805
    William Sr. & Jr., D-1805
NEWBERRY, Alexander, Ge-1805, Ge-1812
    James, Gr-1805(2)
    John, Ge-1805
    Joseph, Ge-1783
NEWBURY, James, Gr-1804
NEWBY, Henry, Sn-1811
    James, Wl-1804
NEWCON, Chancey, Wh-1825
NEWEL, George, Mt-1798
    John, Mt-1798
NEWELL, James, Gi-1812, Mu-1811
    Joseph, Ct-1798, Ct-1796
NEWGIN, Thomas, Gr-1799, Gr-1805
NEWHOUSE, Isaac, Su-1812
NEWLAND, H. M., Gi-1812
    Isaac, D-1811
    Isaac & John, D-1805
    Jesse, Gi-1812
    Joseph, Su-1812
    William, D-1811
NEWMAN, Aaron, Ge-1805, Je-1800
    Alexander, Je-1822
    Aron, Ge-1812(6), Je-1822
    Bird, Gr-1821
    Blair, Je-1822
    Cornelus Esq., Ge-1812(2)
    Daniel, Wh-1811, C-1823
    George, D-1805, Je-1822
    Isaac, Je-1822, Je-1800
    James, Je-1800(2)
    Jarrett, Je-1822
    Jesse, Gr-1821
    John, D-1811(2), A-1805, Ge-1812,
        Ge-1805, Je-1822
    John Sr., C-1818
    John Jr., C-1818, Je-1822
    Johnathan, Je-1822
    Jonathan, Je-1800
    Joshua, Mu-1811, Mu-1816, Je-1822
    Peter, Wa-1814
    Robert M., Je-1822
    Samuel, Je-1822
NEWPORT, Carana, Gr-1799
    Cavghen, Gr-1799
NEWSOM, Francis, D-1811
    James, D-1811
    Robert, Wi-1815
    Sterling, B-1812(2)
    William, B-1812, D-1811
    _____, B-1812
NEWSOME, Micajah, W-1812, W-1805
NEWTON, Benjamin, W-1812
    Benjamine, W-1815
    Charles, Su-1812
    Henry?, Sn-1811
    Henry, D-1805
    John, W-1805, Gi-1812, W-1812
    Robert, D-1811
    Saml., Gi-1812
    William, Mu-1816, W-1805, D-1811,
        Sn-1792, W-1812
    William Sr., Mu-1811
    William Jr., Mu-1811
NICALS, Lewis, Ge-1812
NICELY, Catherine, Gr-1821
    David, Gr-1821
    James, Gr-1821
    John, Gr-1804, Gr-1821
    William, Gr-1821

NICHDEMUS, Frederick, Su-1812
NICHLESON, Malachi, Wi-185
NICHLISON, Cordy, Wi-1815
NICHOL, Josiah, D-1811
NICHOLAS, Coleman, B-1812
    Daniel, Ct-1796
    David, Wh-1811
    Henry, Wh-1825
    John, Mo-1825, Wi-1801
    Richard, Su-1812
NICHOLASON, George, Mu-1811
NICHOLDS, Jacob, B-1812
    Turner, Li-1812*
    William, B-1812
NICHOLLS, John, Sn-1811
NICHOLS, Agrippa, Mu-1816
    Agripper?, Mu-1811
    Benjamin, B-1812, D-1805
    Daniel, Ct-1798
    David, Gr-1799
    David Sr., Fr-1812
    David Jr., Fr-1812
    Edward, Fr-1812
    Jessee, B-1812
    John, D-1805, Mt-1798, Wi-1801,
        D-1811(3), Wi-1810,
    Joshua, Mu-1811
    Nathan, B-1812
    Robert, Mu-1816
    William, Fr-1812
NICHOLSON, Elijah, B-1812
    Elisha, D-1811(2)
    George, Mu-1816
    Jeremiah, Je-1800
    John, Mu-1816(2), Bo-1801, Ct-1796
    John J., D-1811
    O. P., Mu-1811
    Samuel, D-1811
    Thomas, Mo-1825
    Wicks, Fr-1812
    William, Mu-1811, D-1811
    Wm. & Elisha, D-1805
NICKELSON, William, Ge-1812
NICKENSON, William, Sn-1816
NICKES, John, B-1812
NICKOLS, John, D-1805, Wi-1815
NICKS, Doke, B-1812
    Jno. Sr., B-1812
    Moses, Hu-1812
    William, B-1812
NICLES, George, Bo-1801
NICLY, John, W-1812
NIDIVER, George, Su-1796
    Jacob, Su-1796
NIDWIER, George, Su-1797
    Jacob, Su-1797
NIGHT, James, Mu-1811, Bo-1800
    Moses, D-1811
    William, D-1811, Sn-1811
NILSON, John, Fr-1812
NIMON, Michael, Bo-1805
NIN, John, B-1812
NISELEY, John, Gr-1805
NIX, John, Mu-1811, Mu-1816
    Jonathan, Mu-1816
    Solomon, Mu-1816
    Thomas, Mu-1816, Mu-1811
    William, Mu-1816
NIXON, John, W-1812, Mu-1811, Mu-1816
    Will., Gi-1812
NOAH, George, Gr-1804
    John, Gr-1804

NOAH, Joseph Sr., Gr-1804
    Joseph Jr., Gr-1804
    Peter, Fr-1812
NOBBS, Stephen, Mu-1811
NOBLE, Daniel (David?), A-1805
    Keith, Gr-1804
    William, A-1805
NOBLES, John, Co-1821
    Robert, Ro-1805
    Stephen, Mu-1816
NOBLET, William, R-1819
NOBLETT, William, R-1808
NOE, Aquella, D-1811
    Berry, C-1818
    David, Gr-1821
    George, Gr-1805
    Jacob, Gr-1821, C-1823
    John, Gr-1799, Gr-1805
    John Sr., Gr-1821
    John Jr., Gr-1821
    Joseph, Gr-1821
    Joseph, Gr-1821
    Joseph Sr., Gr-1805
    Joseph Jr., Gr-1799, Gr-1805
    Littleberry, C-1823
    Peter, Gr-1799
NOEL, James, C-1818
    Lusena, Sn-1811
    Ruben, D-1811
    William, Sn-1811
NOLAN, Berry, Wi-1815
    James, Hu-1812
NOLAND, James, Hu-1812
NOLEBAY, Richard, D-1811
NOLEN, Anslom, Wi-1815
    David, Wi-1810, D-1788, Wi-1815
    Genl. L., Wi-1815
    Goldsby, Wi-1815
    Joseph, Wh-1825
    Samuel, Wh-1825
    William, Wi-1815, Wi-1810
NOLES, Butler, D-1811
    Carbin, D-1811
NOLIN, Abraham, D-1805
NOLING, Berry, Wi-1810
    John, Wi-1810
NOLL, John, Gr-1799
    William, Gr-1799
NONDAY, Daniel, D-1805
NOONER, Andrew, Wh-1825
NORADYKE, Isariel, Je-1800
    Micaja, Je-1800
NORBET, Henry, Sn-1816
NORFLEET, James, Mt-1798
NORIS, Ezekiel, Sn-1792
    James, Wi-1810
NORKETT, John, Su-1796
NORMAN, Aaron, A-1805
    Henry, A-1805
    Isaac, A-1805
    James, Je-1822
    John, Gr-1805
    Joseph, J-1802
    Moses, Gi-1812
    Robert, B-1812
    William, Fr-1812
NORMAND, Robert, Wi-1810
NORRELL, Robbt., Sn-1816
NORRIS, Abraham, Wh-1811
    Absalom, Wh-1825
    Ezekiel, Li-1812*
    Gallant, Gr-1821

NORRIS, George, Gr-1799, Gr-1804, Gr-1821,
        Gr-1805
    James, Gr-1821
    Jarred, Gr-1805
    Jarrett, Gr-1821
    jeremiah, Gr-1804, Gr-1805
    Jerret, Gr-1804
    John, Sn-1792
    Philip, Wa-1819
    Reuben, Gr-1821
    Saml., Ge-1783, A-1805, W-1812
    Simon, Wh-1825
    Stephen, Sn-1816
    Terul, Sn-1792
    Thomas, Gr-1821, Mu-1811
    William, Gr-1804, Sn-1816, Wl-1804
    William Sr., Gr-1821, Gr-1805
    William Jr., Gr-1821, Gr-1805
    Wm. H., D-1811
NORRISS, John, Sn-1787
NORSWORTHY, William, Hu-1812
NORTH, Elisha, Wi-1815, Wi-1810
    Gabriel, Ge-1805, Ge-1812
    George, Wa-1814, Wa-1819
    Gilbert, Co-1821
    Ibram, Wi-1815
    James, Je-1822
NORTHCUT, William, Fr-1812
NORTHERN, William, Je-1822
NORTHINGTON, Andrew, Rb-1812
    Davd., Gi-1812
    Michael, Rb-1812
    Will, Rb-1812
NORTON, Edward, Fr-1812
    John, Wl-1804
    Joseph, D-1805
    Nathan, Gr-1799
    William, Gr-1799, Gr-1821, Fr-1812,
        Wl-1804, Gr-1805
NORVELL, William, Gr-1799
NORVIL, William, Sn-1811
NORVILLE, John P., Gi-1819
    Joshua, D-1811
    Phillip, Gr-1799
NORWELL, Cleaton, B-1812
NORWOOD, Samuel, Bo-1800, Bo-1801, Fr-1812
NOSEWORTHY, James, B-1812
NOTITELL, William, Fr-1812
NOTSON, Nicholas, Gr-1821
NOWELL, James, B-1812
    John, B-1812
    P. John, Mu-1811
    Riley, Hu-1812
    William, B-1812
NOWLAN, Bryan W., B-1812
    John, B-1812
    Peetor, B-1812
    Tobias, B-1812
NOWLAND, John, Ct-1796
    William, Wh-1811, Ct-1796
NOWLIN, Abraham, D-1811
    David, Mu-1816
NOYLS, Luis, Rb-1812
NOZWORTHY, James, Fr-1812
NUCKOLS, Richard, Rb-1812
NUCOMB, Joseph, D-1811
NUGEN, Thomas, Gr-1821
NULL, Jacob, Sn-1816
    John, Bo-1800
    John Sr., Bo-1801
    John Jr., Bo-1801
NULY, Benjamin, Wa-1819

NUMON, Peter, Wa-1819
NUN, Zephoniah, Mu-1811
NUNALLEE, Henry, K-1799
NUNLY, Arch., W-1812
    John, W-1812
    Moses, W-1812
    Thos., W-1812(2)
    Wm., W-1812
NUNN, Francis, D-1805
    William R., Wi-1815
    Zephaniah, Mu-1816
NUSAM, Eldridge, D-1811
NUSMAN, Joseph, D-1805
NUT, Kidar, Mu-1816
    William, Gi-1812
NUTTING, David, Ge-1812
NUTYON, Hutchins, A-1805
NYE, Shadrick, Sn-1816
NYMAN, Margaret, Bo-1801
    Michal, Bo-1801
    Michel, Bo-1800
OAKES, Alexander, Gr-1805
    Joshua, C-1823
    Josiah, A-1805
OAKLEY, James, Wi-1810
OAKLY, Henry, Mu-1816
    James Sr., Mu-1816, Mu-1811
    James Jr., Mu-1811, Mu-1816
    Jessee, Mu-1816
    Thomas, Mu-1816
    Will Jr., Mu-1816
    William, Mu-1811
    Wi-liam Jr., Mu-1816
OAKS, Hezekiah, B-1812, J-1802
    Isaac, Gr-1821, A-1805
    Joshua, Gr-1821, Gr-1805
    Richard, C-1823
OAR, Sarah, Wi-1815
    William, Sn-1792
OATES, Roger, K-1799
    William, B-1812
OATS, David, Bo-1800
OATTS, David, Bo-1801
OBANYAN, John, J-1802
O'BRYAN, James, Su-1812
O'CALLAHAN, Patrick, Li-1812*
OCLEAR, William, Ro-1805
OCLES, Dennis, Gr-1805
O'CONNER, Thomas, Bo-1801
ODALE, John, Wi-1810
ODAM, James, Sn-1816, Sn-1811
    John, Mu-1816, Mu-1811
ODANIEL, Henry, Hu-1812
    John, heirs, Gr-1821
ODEL, Enoch, Wh-1825
    Samuel, Wh-1825
ODELL, Abraham, Wa-1814, Wa-1819
    Bartlett, Wa-1814
    William, Wa-1814
ODEN, Ezekiel, Rb-1812
    John, Je-1822
    Solomon, Wi-1815
    Thomas, D-1811
ODERN, Sebern, Wh-1811
ODIER, Furnes, W-1812
ODINEAL, Waillium, Wa-1819
ODLE, Anderson, Wi-1815
    Daniel, J-1802
    Enoch, Wh-1811
    James, Wl-1804
    Jeremiah, J-1802
    John, Mu-1816, Wi-1815

ODLE, John H., Gr-1821
    Jonthan, Je-1800
    Obedum, Wi-1815
    Thomas, Su-1812
    William, Su-1797, Su-1796, Su-1812
ODOM, James, Sn-1792
O'DONAL, John, Gr-1799
O'DONALD, Michel, Gr-1799
ODONALE, William B., Wa-1814
ODUM, Seburn, Wh-1825
OFFELLS, James, Su-1812
OFFICE, James, Wh-1825, Su-1797
OFFICER, James, J-1802
    John, W-1812
    Thomas, J-1802
OFFILL, James, Su-1796
OFFMAN, James, Li-1812*
OGAN, John, Gr-1821
OGDEN, John, Hw-179, Co-1821
    William C., Hw-1799
OGELSBY, Elisha, Sn-1792
OGGDON, Francis, Bl-1815
OGILVEY, Harris, D-1805
    William, D-1805
OGILVIE, Harris, D-1811
    John, Wi-1810, Wi-1815
    Richard, Wi-1810
    William, Wi-1810, D-1811
OGLE, Hercules, Wh-1811(2), Wh-1825
    John, Wh-1811, Gr-1805
    Wyat, Wh-1825
OGLEBY, David, Bo-1801
OGLES, Dennis, Gr-1805
    Harculus Sr., Gr-1804
    Harcules, Gr-1805
    John, Gr-1805
    Thomas, Gr-1805(2), Gr-1804
OGLESBY, Daniel, Sn-1816, Mu-1811
    Elisha, Sn-1787
    James, Mu-1811
    John, Bo-1800
    Samuel, Mt-1798
    Wm., Wi-1801
OGWIN, Hardy, Hu-1812
OHANNAN, John, D-1805
OKES, Joshua, Gr-1804
OLD, Jordan R., Wi-1815
    Thomas, Wi-1810, Wi-1815
OLDEM, George, Wi-1801
    Moses, Wi-1801
OLDENGER, Daniel, Wa-1814
OLDFIELD, William, Fr-1812
OLDHAM, Conewey, Wi-1810
    Elias, Fr-1812
    George, Wi-1810, Mt-1798
    James, Se-1799
    Jessy, Mt-1798
    Lee, Mu-1816
    Moses, Wi-1810, Wi-1815
    Moses Sr., Wi-1810, Mt-1798
    Moses Jr., Mt-1798
    Nicholas E., Wh-1825
OLDHANCE, John, Je-1822
OLDRIDGE, Andrew, Bl-1815
    Nathan, Wi-1810
OLERRAL, Doctor, Mt-1798
OLFORD, Hutson, Wl-1804
OLINGER, Daniel, Ge-1812
    Jacob, Su-1812
    John, Ge-1812(2)
OLIPHAN, James, Ge-1812
    Thomas, Ge-1812

OLIPHANT, James, Ge-1805
    John, Ge-1783, Ge-1805
    Robert, Mu-1811
    Samuel, Mu-1811
    Thomas, Ge-1805
OLIVE, Robt., Wi-1815
OLIVER, Ananias, Wi-1815
    Charles, A-1805
    Charls, K-1799
    Daniel, C-1823
    Douglas, K-1799
    Edward, D-1805
    Enoch, D-1811
    Frederick, D-1805
    George, Wi-1815, Wi-1801
    John, Wa-1814(2), Wa-1819, D-1811
    Levi, Wh-1825
    Richard, Ro-1805
    Robert, D-1812, D-1805
    William, Fr-1812
OLLIPHANT, Robt., Mu-1816
    Saml., Mu-1816
OLLIVER, Durrett, Wh-1811
    John, K-1796
OLSTER, William, Sn-1811
OMSHUNDRO, William, Wl-1804
ONEAL, Benjamin, Je-1800
    Cornelis, Ge-1783
    John, B-1812
    Peter, Mt-1798
    Robert, Ge-1783
    Samuel, Wh-1825
    Timothy, D-1805
ONEEL, Jonathan Sr., Mu-1811
    Jonathan Jr., Mu-1811
ONEELE, Polly, Mu-1811
ONEIL, Robert, Bl-1815
ORANDAL, James, Mu-1816
ORE, James, Gr-1805, Gr-1799, Gr-1804
    Joseph, Gr-1805, Gr-1799, Gr-1804,
        Gr-1821
    Joshua, Mu-1811
    Robert, Wl-1804, D-1805
    William, Gr-1821, D-1788
    Wilson, Gr-1821
OREAR, Jno., W-1812
OREEGHLEY, C. James, Mu-1811
ORIELLY, James C., Mu-1816
ORLON, David, Mu-1811
ORM, Evan B., Wi-1815
ORMAN, Adam, Wi-1815
ORMES, Evan B., Wi-1810
ORR, David, Sn-1811
    Greenbary, Sn-1811
    James, Mu-1816
    John, Sn-1811, D-1811, B-1812
    Joseph, Bo-1800, Bo-1801
    Joshua, Mu-1816
    Philip, Wi-1815
    Robert, B-1812
    Robert Jr., B-1812
    Samuel, Wa-1819
    William, Wi-1810, Wi-1815, R-1819
ORSBURN, Barthomew, Sn-1811
ORTER, James, Wi-1815
ORTON, John, D-1811
    Joseph, Wi-1815
    Richard, Wi-1815, Wi-1801(2)
    Samuel, D-1811
OSBORN, Noble, Mu-1811
    Solomon Sr., Hw-1799
OSBORNE, Alexr., Mu-1816

OSBORNE, James, Wh-1811
    John, Mu-1816
    Noble, Mu-1816
    Thomas, Mu-1816
OSBURN, Alexander, Mu-1811, Bo-1801
    Bartholomew, Sn-1816
    Benjamin, Sn-1816
    Daniel, Ro-1805
    Ephraim, Hw-1799
    Luke, Se-1799
    Soloman, Je-1800
    Solomon, Hw-1799
    Thomas, Mu-1811
OSBURNE, Ben., Gi-1812
    John, Gi-1812
OSMORE, William, D-1811
OSTEN, Tho., Sn-1816
OSTIN, Nat, Cl-1803
    Wm., Cl-1803
OTIVATUS?, Joseph, Wh-1825
OUR, Rober, D-1811
OURHOTSON, Samuel, Wa-1819
OURTE, John, Mu-1811
OURTON, Jessee, Mu-1811
OUTLAW, Alexander, Je-1800
    Alexander S., Je-1822
    John, Sn-1816
OUTLAY, Alexander, Je-1800
OVEBY, Nichalls, Sn-1816
OVERALL, Nat., D-1788
OVERBEE, Nichalls, Sn-1816
OVERALL, Nat., D-1788
OVERBEE, Nicholas, Wh-1825
OVERBY, Daniel, Sn-1816
OVERHOLT, Samuel, Wa-1814
OVERSTREET, James, Mu-1816
    Lewis, C-1818
OVERTON, Benj., Sn-1816, Sn-1811
    David, D-1805
    J. Thomas, Wl-1804
    Jessee, Mu-1816
    John, D-1805, D-1811, Wl-1804
        Wi-1801
    John Jr., C-1823
    Joseph, A-1805
    Moses, Gr-1799
    Samuel, D-1811
    Thomas, D-1811, D-1805
    Thomas G., Wl-1804
OVERTURF, Philip, W-1812
OVERTURP, John, J-1802
OWEN, Arthur, D-1805
    Benjamin H., Gr-1821
    David, B-1812, Sn-1811
    Edmond Jr., D-1811
    Edmond, Robert & Judith, D-1805
    Edmund Sr., D-1811
    Elijah, D-1811
    Frederick Jr., D-1811
    Glen, Wi-1815
    Glenn, Wi-1810
    Henry, R-1819, D-1811
    Jabiz, Wi-1815
    James, Wi-1815, Wa-1814
    John, Gr-1799, Mu-1816
    John Sr., Gr-1799
    Jno. & James, Mu-1816
    Jonathan, Su 1707, Su-1700
    Joseph, Gr-1804
    Joshua, D-1811
    Moses, Wl-1804
    Nathan, Wi-1815

OWEN, Peter, Mu-1816, D-1811
    Reuben, Mu-1816
    Richard, D-1811
    Richard B., D-1811
    Robert, D-1811
    Sammul, Bl-1815
    William, Gr-1799, Mu-1816, D-1811(2)
OWENS, A., D-1788
    Aron, Sn-1811
    Arthur, D-1811
    Benjamin, Mt-1798, Gr-1799
    Benj., Nathan & Joshua, D-1805
    Christopher, Mt-1798
    Elias, Wa-1819
    Elijah, heirs, Wi-1815
    Ezekiel, Fr-1812
    Frederick, D-1811
    George H., Ro-1805
    Henry, D-1811
    Isaac, Gr-1799
    James, Gr-1804, B-1812, Gr-1805
    Jesse, A-1805
    John, Gr-1804, Fr-1812(2), Su-1812
    John Sr., Gr-1799
    John Jr., Gr-1799
    Joseph, Je-1800, Gr-1805
    Matthew, Gr-1799
    Purnell, D-1811
    Rachel, Wa-1814(2), Wa-1819
    Samuel, B-1812, Su-1812
    William, A-1805, W-1812, D-1811
    Willis, A-1805
OWIN, George, Sn-1816
OWINES, William, Gr-1799
OWINGS, William, Bl-1815
OWINS, Elijah, heirs, Wi-1810
OWNBY, James, Rb-1812
OWRY, Thomas, Su-1812, W-1805
OXBORNE, Mae, Su-1797
OXEN, John, Ge-1805
OXFORD, Abel, Gi-1812
    Isaac, Gi-1812
    John, Gi-1819, Gi-1812
    Sam., Gi-1812
OZBORN, Mae, Su-1797
OZBORNE, Jnac., Su-1796
OZBOURN, Albert, D-1811
    John, Wi-1810
    Noble, Wi-1810
    Thomas, D-1811
    Thompson, D-1811
OZBROOKS, Michal, Sn-1816
OZBURN, Edward, Fr-1812
    John, Rb-1812
    Mac, Su-1812
    Noble, Wi-1815
PAARRE, Joshua Sr., Wi-1815
PACE, Also, D-1811
    Wm., Rb-1812
    William Jr., Rb-1812
PACK, Bartimins, Rb-1812
    Benjamin Sr., D-1811
    Benjamin D., D-1811
PAFKER, Josiah, Wa-1814
PAGE, Absolom, D-1811
    Achilles, Gr-1821
    James, D-1811, Hu-1812, D-1805
    John, Hu-1812, D-1811, G-1812
        Su-1796, Su-1797, R-1819
    Nathan, Ge-1812
    Robert, D-1811, Bl-1815, Je-1822
    Thomas L., Fr-1812

PAGE, Vincent, D-1811
    Wm., Wi-1815
PAGGETT, John, Sn-1816
PAIL, Hardy, Cl-1803
PAIN, Dempsy, Rb-1812
    Isaac, B-1812
    Jesse, Wa-1819
    Jesse Jr., Wa-1819
    Josiah, Bo-1800
    Robert, Sn-1811, Wa-1819
    William, Wa-1819
PAINE, Charles, Gi-1812
    Dudley, Rb-1812
    Gideon, Rb-1812
    James, Rb-1812
    John, Gi-1812, Rb-1812
    Joseph, Gi-1812, Rb-1812
    Lewis, Gi-1812
    Orville, R-1819
    Philip, Gi-1812
    Solomon, Rb-1812
    Thomas, Rb-1812, Gi-1812
    Warren, Rb-1812(2)
    William, Gi-1812
PAINTER, Adam, Wa-1814, Ge-1805, Wa-1819(2)
    David, Wa-1819
    Henry, Fr-1812
    John, Ge-1805, Fr-1812
    Phillip, Wa-1819
    William, Wa-1819, Wa-1814
PAISLEY, James, Mu-1811
    Robt., Rb-1812
    Wm., Rb-1812
PALLET, Abram, Su-1797
    Anna, Su-1797
    Anne, Su-1812
    Robert, Su-1797, Su-1812
    William, Su-1812
PALMAR, Wm., Bo-1800
PALMER, Dempsey, Wh-1825
    John, Wh-1825
    Joshua, Je-1822
    Robert, Wi-1815
    Samuel, Bo-1801
    William, Wh-1825, Sn-1816
PALMORE, William, Bo-1805(2)
PALSEL, David, Ge-1812(4)
PANE, Jessee, D-1805
PANGLE, Frederick, Je-1822, Je-1800
    James, Je-1822
    John, A-1805, Sn-1811
PANKEY, Edward, Je-1822
    James, Je-1822, A-1805
    John, A-1805, Sn-1811
    Nancy, D-1805
    Stephen, A-1805
PANNEL, Thomas, Gr-1799
PANNELL, John, D-1811
PANNETTON, John, D-1805
PANTER, William, Ge-1812
PANTHER, Alexander, Bo-1801
PARCE, Ezra, Wa-1819
    William, Wa-1819
PARCHMAN, John, Gi-1812
    Philip, Wi-1815, Gi-1812
PARDAY, Robert, D-1805
PARETT, John, Sn-1811
PARHAM, Ephraim, Li-1812*, D-1811
    Ephram, D-1811
    George, Wi-1815
    William, Wi-1815, D-1811
PARIS, Robt., Ge-1783

PARISH, Hannah, D-1805
    Joab, Sn-1811
    Joel, Wi-1801
    John, Fr-1812
    Susan, Wi-1815
PARK, Andrew, Ge-1812, Ro-1805
    Hugh, Mu-1811, Mu-1816
    Jacob, Sn-1811
    Jeremiah, Sn-1816
    John, Wi-1815, Sn-1816
    Joseph, D-1811, D-1805, Wi-1810
    Robt., Sn-1811
    Rubin, Wi-1810
    Samuel, Mu-1816
    William, heirs, Je-1822
PARKE, Samuel, Fr-1812
PARKER, A. Isham, Wl-1804
    Aaron, Ge-1812
    Allen, Rb-1812
    Aron, Ro-1805
    Arthur, Wh-1285
    Benjamin, Ge-1812, Ge-1805
    Benjamin C., A-1805
    C. L., Mo-1825
    Calib, Ge-1812
    Daniel, Sn-1811, Sn-1816
    David, D-1811
    Elijah, B-1812, Wl-1804, R-1819
    Felix, Gr-1805
    Francis, Mu-1811
    George, Ro-1805
    Hannah, Su-1796, Su-1797
    Isaac, Sn-1816, Sn-1811
    Isaiah, W-1812
    Isham A., D-1811
    James, Mu-1816, Gr-1805, D-1805,
        Ct-1796, B-1812, Wa-1814,
        Rb-1812, Wa-1819, Gr-1821
    Jeremiah, Wi-1810
    Jesse, D-1811(2)
    John, Sn-1816, Wh-1825, Sn-1811(2),
        Hu-1812, Gr-1804, Bl-1815,
        Se-1799, Wa-1814, Rb-1812,
        Su-1812(2), Ro-1805, Wa-1819,
        R-1819
    John B., W-1812
    John C., D-1811
    John S., R-1819
    Joseph, Wh-1825, Wh-1811(2)
    Joshua, Hu-1812
    Josiah, Wa-1819
    Jud, Sn-1816
    Leonard, D-1811(2)
    Matthew, D-1805
    Nathaniel, Sn-1811(2), Sn-1816,
        Sn-1792
    Noah, Su-1811
    Peter, Wl-1804
    Phelix, Gr-1805
    Phillip, Gr-1805, Bl-1815
    Richard, Sn-1816, Sn-1811(2), A-1805
    Roaly, Bl-1815
    Robert, Sn-1811
    Samuel, Hu-1812
    Thomas, Hu-1812, D-1805, D-1811,
        Sn-1811(2)
    W. Johnson, D-1805
    William, Wl-1804, D-1811, D-1805,
        Hu-1812, Wh-1825, Ge-1805,
        Gi-1812, Su-1812, Su-1797,
        Rb-1812, Su-1796
    Winburn, B-1812

PARKER, Zachariah, Wi-1810
PARKERS, John, Wi-1810
PARKERSON, John, Sn-1811
PARKES, Bilben, Wi-1815
    Joseph, Je-1800
    Samuel, Wi-1815
    William, Je-1800
PARKEY, Jacob, Je-1800
PARKHILL, David, Bo-1801, R-1819
PARKINS, David, Ge-1805
PARKISON, Daniel, Wh-1811
PARMAN, Giles, Ge-1805
    Giles Sr., Ge-1812
PARKMAN, William, D-1811
PARKS, Alfred, Wa-1819
    Benjamin, D-1805, Wi-1815, Wi-1810
    Enos, Ge-1812
    George, Fr-1812, Mu-1811
    James, Sn-1816
    John, Wi-1815, Wi-1810, Mu-1811,
        Ge-1805, Bo-1801, Rb-1812,
        Ge-1812
    John Sr., Wi-1810
    Moses, Wi-1810
    Philip, Wa-1819, Wa-1814(2), Gr-1799
    Reubin, Wi-1801
    Robert, Sn-1816, R-1819
    Samuel, Je-1822, Fr-1812, Bo-1800
    William, Wi-1810, Wi-1801, Rb-1812,
        Ge-1812
PARMER, John, A-1805
    Stephen, Wh-1811
PARMLY, Sam., Gi-1812
PARMON, Emanuel, Ge-1812(2)
PARNAL, Henderson, Sn-1811
    Wiley, Sn-1811
PARNUL, John, Sn-1816
PARR, Ephraim, Sn-1792
    John, Mu-1811
    Will, Sn-1811
    William, Sn-1816
PARRADISE, William, D-1811
PARRESS, Jonathan, W-1812
PARRET, John, Sn-1811
PARRHAM, William, Wi-1810
PARRISH, David M., Sn-1816
    Henry, Wl-1804
    Joel, Wi-1801
    John, Sn-1816
PARROT, Elijah, C-1823, C-1818
    Jack, C-1823
    James, C-1818
    Joel, C-1818
    Lewis, C-1818
    Samuel, W-1812
PARROTT, Henry, Je-1822
    John, Je-1822
PARRY, Bartley, B-1812
    Talbot, Je-1800
PARRYT?, Richard, W-1812
PARSLEY, James, Wi-1815
    John, Wi-1815
PARSON, Able, Wh-1825
    James, Ge-1812
    Jesse, Ct-1798
    Samuel, Gi-1819
    Thomas, A-1805
PARSONS, George W., Wi-1810
    James, Wa-1819
    James W., Wi-1815
    John, W-1812
    Petet, Wa-1814

PARSONS, Robert, Ct-1796, Ct-1798
    Thomas, A-1805, J-1802, B-1812,
        Wi-1810, Wi-1815
    Thomas S., Wi-1810
PARRISH, Nicholas, Mu-1816
PARTEE, Abner, Mu-1811
    Charter, Mu-1816
PARTEN, John, Gi-1812
    William, Hw-1801
PARTIN, Leonard, Gi-1812
    Samuel, Bo-1801
PARTON, Emanuel, B-1812
    John, B-1812(2)
    Vinsen, Cl-1803
    William, Cl-1802
    Winston, Hw-1801
PARTRUH, Ephriam, Gi-1812
PARWELL, Abner, Mu-1816
PASCAL, Asa, B-1812
    Eli, B-1812
    James, B-1812
PASCHALL, Nicholas, Ro-1805
PASHER, Phillip, Gr-1804
PASMORE, B. Richd., Wl-1804
    David, Mt-1798
PASOR, John, A-1805
PASS, James, Wh-1825
    Joel, D-1805
PASSENS, Major, Wh-1825
PASSLEY, Moses, Rb-1812
PATE, Anthony, W-1812
    Bird, Je-1822
    Daniel, Je-1822
    Godfrey, Bo-1805
    Hugh, Je-1822
    Jeremiah, Ro-1805
    Jesse, D-1811
    Jessee, Wi-1815
    Job, D-1811
    John, Gi-1812, W-1812, Ro-1805
    Kintchin, Wi-1815
    Matthew, Ge-1783
    Stephen, K-1799
    Thomas, Wi-1815
    William, Rb-1812, Je-1822
PATERSON, Hugh, Sn-1811
    Jno., Ge-1783
    John Sr., Gr-1804
    John Jr., Gr-1804
    Samuel, Sn-1816
    William, Wi-1810
PATES, John, Wl-1804
PATIAN?, George, D-1811
PATON, Henry, Mu-1811
PATRICK, Hugh, Wl-1804
    James, W-1812, Wi-1815
    John, W-1812, B-1812
    Levi, W-1812
PATTEN, Benjamin, Wh-1825
    John, Ct-1796, W-1812
    Robert, Sn-1811
    William, Wi-1810
PATTENS, Thomas, Sn-1792
PATTERSON, Alex, Wl-1804
    Andrew, Wi-1801(2), D-1805, B-1812,
        Ge-1812(3), Gr-1821
    Ann, Mu-1811
    Benjamin, D-1811
    Burwell, Wl-1804
    Gawin, Ct-1798
    H. James, Mu-1811
    Isham, Wl-1804

PATTERSON, Jacob, Wl-1804
    James, Mu-1811(2), Gr-1805, Ge-1805,
        B-1812(2), Wa-1814, Gr-1821
    James Sr., Ge-1805
    Joab, Wi-1810, Je-1822
    John, Hu-1812, Mu-1811, D-1811,
        Wl-1804, Gr-1805, Wi-1815(2),
        Gr-1799, B-1812
    John Sr., Gr-1805
    John & Nathan, D-1805
    Jno. T., Mu-1816
    King, Fr-1812
    Lewis, Mo-1825
    Luke, Wi-1810
    Mark, Wi-1801
    Martin, Hu-1812
    Mathew, D-1811
    Moses, Mu-1816
    Nathaniel, Ge-1805
    Patrick, Rb-1812
    Reuben, Sn-1816
    Robert, Wl-1804, Gr-1799, B-1812(2),
        R-1808
    Robt. Sr., Hu-1812
    Robt. Jr., Hu-1812
    Saml., Wl-1804
    Sarah, Su-1797, Su-1796
    Thomas, B-1812(2), Gr-1821, D-1811
    William, Wl-1804, Wi-1815, Ge-1805,
        B-1812, Wa-1814, Ge-1812,
        St-1798
    Heirs, Je-1822
    _____, B-1812
PATTESON, Neal, Gi-1812
PATTISON, Patrick Jr., Rb-1812
PATTON, Alexander, Wi-1801, D-1805, D-1811
    Andrew, Wi-1801
    Cueston, Wi-1801
    David, Ro-1805
    Elijah, Mu-1816, Mu-1811
    Elizabeth, Wi-1815
    George, Mu-1811, D-1805
    Hannah, Wi-1815
    Isaac, D-1805, Wi-1810, Wi-1815
    Isreael, Je-1822
    Jacob, Wi-1810, Wi-1801
    James, Wi-1815(3), Wi-1810, Mt-1798,
        B-1812(5), Fr-1812, Wi-1815
    James C., Mo-1825
    James W., B-1812
    Jason, Wi-1815
    John, Wi-1815, B-1812(3), Fr-1812,
        Wa-1819, Je-1800, Ct-1798
    John Sr., B-1812
    John Jr., B-1812
    John M., Je-1822
    Joshua, B-1812
    Mathew, D-1811
    Neely, B-1812
    Robert, Sn-1816, Wi-1815, Sn-1811,
        Rb-1812, Je-1822, Je-1800
    Samuel, Gr-1805, D-1811, Sn-1811,
        Wi-1810, Gr-1805, Sn-1787,
        Wi-1815, B-1812, Je-1822,
        Je-1800
    Thomas C., Wa-1814, Wa-1819
    Tristram, Wi-1810, Wi-1815
    William, D-1811, D-1805, Gr-1805,
        Sn-1811, Mu-1816, Gr-1804,
        B-1812, Fr-1812, Wa-1814,
        Wa-1819, B-1812
PATTON & IRVINE, Mu-1811

PATTRICK, Jesse, Ct-1798
    John, Ct-1796
PAUL, Moses, R-1819
PAULEY, James, Mu-1816
    Valentine, Mu-1816, Ge-1805
PAUULS, Anthony, Wi-1815
PAULS, Elias, Sn-1816
PAULSELL, David, Ge-1805
PAUSON, John, Ro-1805
PAW, William, Mu-1816
PAWLETT, Abram, Su-1796
    Ann, Su-1796
    Robert, Su-1796
PAWLEY, Valentine, Mu-1811
    William, C-1823
PAXTEN, Isaac, D-1811
PAXTON, David, Su-1812
    Samuel, Bo-1801, Ge-1783, Bo-1800,
        Gi-1812
    Thompson, Mu-1816
PAYN, Meryman, Ge-1812
    Robert, Sn-1816
    Thomas, Ct-1798
PAYNE, Aquilla, Gr-1821
    Daniel, Su-1812, W-1812
    George, D-1805, D-1811
    Green, D-1811
    H. Thomas, A-1805
    Hardin, Gi-1812
    Henry, Wa-1814
    Isaac, Gr-1821
    Isaiah, Gr-1821
    James, W-1812
    Jesse Sr., Wa-1814
    Jesse Jr., Wa-1814
    Joel, Wl-1804
    John, Sn-1811, W-1805, Wh-1825,
        Gr-1821, W-1812(2), Ro-1805
    Joseph, D-1811
    Joshua, Fr-1812
    Josiah, D-1805
    Mathew, D-1805
    Moses, Gr-1821, B-1812
    Nathaniel, W-1812
    Robert, Wa-1814
    Ruben, D-1811, D-1805
    Squire?, D-1811
    Sylvester, B-1812
    Thomas, W-1812, Ct-1796
    Thomas H., W-1812
    William, Wa-1814
PAYSINGER, Jacob, Ge-1805
PAYTON, Ephram, Sn-1792, Sn-1787
    John, Sn-1816(2)
    John Jr., Sn-1811
    Joseph, Ct-1796, Mu-1811, Wl-1804
    Robert, Mu-1811
    W. John, Wl-1804
    Wiliam, Sn-1811
    William, Sn-1816, Ct-1798
    Y. George, D-1805
PAYZER, George, D-1811(2)
PEA, George, Fr-1812, J-1802
    Joseph, Fr-1812, J-1802
PEABLY, Thomas, C-1823
PEACE, John, B-1812
    John Sr., B-1812
    John Jr., B-1812
    Thomas A., B-1812
    William, B-1812
PEAIRS, George W., Sn-1816
    Isaac, Sn-1816

PEAK, Anney, Sn-1816
    Jacob, K-1796, A-1805
    John, Wi-1815, A-1805
    John Sr., A-1805
PEANS, James, C-1823
    Robert, C-1818
PEARCE, Charles, D-1805
    George, Ge-1812
    Isaac, Sn-1816, Sn-1792
    James, Ge-1805, Bo-1801, Bo-1800,
        Wa-1814
    John, W-1805, Bo-1801, Bo-1800,
        W-1812, Ge-1812
    Johnathan, Sn-1811
    Jonothan, Sn-1792
    Nathaniel, Wh-1825
    Richard, Wh-1825, Ge-1805
    Robert, D-1805, Bo-1801, Bo-1800
    Thomas, Wh-1285, D-1805, Ge-1812
    Thomas, Heirs, Ge-1812
    Wm., Hu-1812, Ge-1812
PEARCEFIELD, John, Gr-1804
PEARCELL, James, Mu-1816
PEARES, Robert D., C-1818
PEARIE, Lewis, C-1818, C-1823
PEARSALL, Jos. H., Mu-1816
PEARSAN, William, A-1805
PEARSON, Abel, Ct-1798, Ct-1796
    Henry, Wh-1825, A-1805
    James, Wh-1825

    Mahlon, Je-1822
    Major, Wh-1825
    Samuel, Rb-1812
    Thomas, Ct-1796
    William, A-1805, Rb-1812
PEARY, James Sr., Bo-1805
    James Jr., Bo-1805
    Samuel, Gr-1805
PEASE, William, Cl-1803
PEAWEL, Charles, Wi-1815
PEAY, Elias, D-1811
    Nathl., Wi-1815
    Thomas, Wi-1815
PEBELEY, Jeremiah, Gr-1799
PEBELLEY, Elisha, Gr-1799
PEBLEY, James, Gr-1799
PECK, Abner, D-1805
    Adam, Je-1822
    Benjamin, Je-1822
    Elizabeth, Je-1822
    Elliott, Je-1822
    Henry, Je-1822
    Jacob, Je-1822
    John, Fr-1812(Pick?)
    Moses L., Je-1822
    Nathaniel, D-1811
    Norman, Sn-1811
PECOL, Frederick, Su-1812
PECTOL, Henry, Su-1812
PEDEN, Henry, Gi-1819
PEDIGREW, Matthew, Bo-1801
PEEBLES, Wm., Wi-1815
PEEK, Adam, Je-1800
PEEL, James, Ge-1812
    John, Sn-1811
    Thomas, Ge-1805, Sn-1787, Ge-1812
PEELER, Abner, Gi-1812
    Fredk., Gi-1812
    Hiram, Gi-1812
PEELS, Zedediah, Wi-1801
PEER, Jacob, B-1812

PEERE, Barton, D-1811
PEERS, Washington, Wh-1825
PEERY, John, A-1805
    Robert, A-1805
    Samuel, Gr-1805
PEETERS, Christopher, Ge-1812
    Nathaniel, Gr-1799
    William, Gr-1799
PEETERY, Adam, Gr-1805
PEETREY, John, Gr-1805
PEEVLOR, Jacob, Su-1812
    Lewis, Su-1812
PEINTER, Adam, Ge-1783
PEIRCE, Absalom, Su-1796
PELEER, Jsoeph, Bo-1800
PELLEY, Henry, Wi-1801
PELM, Jesse, W-1812
PEMBERTON, James, D-1805
    Jesse, Wl-1804
    John, Gr-1804, Su-1797, Su-1796
    Rachel, Su-1796
    William, Su-1797, Su-1796
PEMENTO, Malichi, Mu-1816
PEMLEY, Wm., C-1818
PENAPILE, Christian, Gr-1805
PENCE, John, D-1811
PENDEGRASS, Jessee B., Sn-1811
PENDERGRASS, Joel, J-1802
    Spencer, J-1802
PENDEXTER, Lovell, Gr-1805
PENDLETON, Benjm., W-1812
    John, W-1812
    William, Wh-1811
PENHITE, James, D-1811
PENION, William, Gr-1805
PENN, Aaron, B-1812
    Catherin, Gr-1805
    Gilbert, B-1812
    Nathan, B-1812
    Richard, Je-1800
PENNEY, James, Ge-1805
PENNINGTON, Absolom, Ge-1783
    Andy, Gr-1799
    Benn, Gr-1799
    Charles, Wh-1825
    Clement S., Wi-1815
    Elijah, B-1812
    Graves, D-1811
    Greaves, D-1805
    Isaac, heirs, Wl-1804
    Jacob, Mu-1816, Gi-1812
    John, Wh-1825, Mo-1825
    Joshua, Wh-1825
    Theophelus, Gr-1799
    William, Mo-1825
PENNY, James, Wa-1814
    James Esq., Ge-1812
    Wm., Wi-1815
PENROD, Samuel, Wh-1825
PENROSE, Joseph, Mt-1798
PENTECOST, Milly, Sn-1816
PEOFERS, Abram, Su-1797
PEOPLES, James, Ct-1798
    Joel, Mu-1811
    John, Ct-1798, Su-1797, Ct-1796
    Nathan, Wa-1814, Hu-1812, Su-1796,
        Ct 1796
    William, Wi-1810, Ct-1798, Ct-1796
PEPPER, Elisha, Wl-1804, W-1805, W-1812
    Joseph, W-1812, Wl-1804, W-1805
    Wm., Rb-1812
    William B., Gi-1812

PERCEFIELD, Thomas, Wh-1825
PERCELL, Jeremiah, Mu-1811
PERCIFUL, Jeremiah Sr., C-1818
    Jeremiah Jr., C-1818
PERCUPILE, Daniel, Gr-1821
    John, Gr-1821
    Michael, Gr-1821
    Reuben, Gr-1821
PERDEW, Daniel, Sn-1816
PERDUE, Daniel A., Fr-1812
    John, A-1805
PEREMORE, Jas., Gi-1812
PERIE, Jas., Ge-1783
PERIN, Joseph, Gr-1804
PERKEPILE, Daniel, Je-1822
PERKEY, Christopher, Gr-1821
PERKINS, Abraham, D-1811
    Charles, Wi-1801
    Daniel, Wi-1810, Wi-1801, Wi-1815
    David, D-1811, Ge-1812
    Edward, Su-1796, Su-1797, C-1818
    George, Ct-1798
    Henry, Gi-1819
    Isham, W-1805, W-1812
    Jacob, Ct-1798
    James, Gr-1850
    Jesse, Fr-1812(Pickens?)
    John, Ro-1805
    John B., W-1805, W-1812
    Jno. P., Wi-1815
    Joseph, Gi-1819
    Leah, D-1805
    Levi, Wh-1811(2), Wh-1825
    Levy, Ge-1812
    Nicholas, Wi-1815(2)
    Nichs. T., Wi-1815
    Nicolas, Wi-1810
    Peter, C-1818, C-1823
    Robert, Ge-1812
    Saml., Wi-1815
    Thomas, Mu-1811
    Thomas H., Wi-1815, Sn-1811
    Washington, D-1811, Wh-1825, Wi-1815,
        D-1811(2), D-1805, Gi-1812
PERMENTER, Malachi, Mu-1811
PERREMON, John, R-1819
PERREN, Aaron, Wh-1811
    Joel, Gr-1805
    Joseph, Gr-1805
PERREY, Obediah, Sn-1816
PERRIN, Joel, Gr-1799
    John, Gr-1821
    Joseph, Gr-1799
    William, Gr-1821
PERRION, Joel, Gr-1805
    Joseph, Gr-1805
PERRON, Henry, Sn-1811
PERRUS, William, Gi-1819
PERRY, Burwell, Wl-1804
    Darling, Wi-1810
    David, Su-1797
    David Esq., Su-1796
    David Sr., Su-1812
    David Jr., Su-1812
    Dempsey, B-1812
    Drury, Wl-1804
    Edmond, C-1823
    Edwin, Sn-1811
    George, D-1805, D-1811
    James, Mu-1816
    Jeremiah, Gi-1812
    John, Fr-1812, Gi-1812, Mu-1816,

PERRY, John, Cont'd.--Sn-1816, Wi-1815,
    Sn-1811
    Joiner, D-1811
    Jonathan, Gi-1812
    Joseph, B-1812, D-1811
    Josiah, Sn-1816
    Lemuel, B-1812
    Littleton, D-1811
    Martin, B-1812(2)
    Nathanil, Se-1799
    Nathl., Wl-1804
    Norflet, Sn-1816
    Robert, Rb-1812
    Rolls, Sn-1816
    Roundtree, Rb-1812
    Rowland, Su-1812, Su-1796
    Samuel, Gr-1799
    Sion, Sn-1792
    Solloman, Co-1827
    Soloman, Co-1821
    Thomas, Ge-1805, B-1812, D-1811
    Thomas H., Wi-1810
    Thornton, Wi-1815
    William, Mu-1816(2), Mu-1811,
        Rb-1812, Wi-1810, Sn-1816
PERRYMAN, John, B-1812
PERSON, Benjamin P., D-1811
    Christian, Hw-1799
    Cristifer, Hw-1799
    Haney, Se-1799
    Sarah, R-1819
PERSONS, George, B-1812, Sn-1811, D-1788
    John, Sn-1816
PERVINE, John, Wi-1801
PERY, James, Mt-1798
    Samuel, Gr-1804
    William, Gi-1819
PETECOCK, Stephen, Fr-1812
PETER, Joseph, Rb-1812
PETER (Negro), Gr-1799
PETERS, Abraham, Ge-1805, Ge-1812(3)
    Benjamin, Su-1812
    Bruton, Gr-1821
    Christian, Ct-1798
    Conrad, Su-1797
    Conrod, Su-1796
    George, Su-1796
    Henry, A-1805
    Isaac, Su-1812
    James, Mu-1816
    John, Ct-1796, Gr-1804, Su-1812,
        Su-1797, Su-1796, Gr-1821,
        Ct-1798, Gr-1805
    Joseph, R-1819, Gr-1805
    Joshua, Gr-1804, Gr-1805
    Landon, Ge-1812
    Nathaniel, Gr-1805, Gr-1804
    Reuben, Ct-1798
    S. M. JOhn, Ct-1796, Ct-1796
    Samuel, Ct-1798, B-1812, Ct-1796
    Tobias, A-1805
    William, Gr-1804, Ro-1805, Gr-1805
PETERSON, Isaac, Mt-1798
    Isaac, Capt., Mt-1798
    Joseph, C-1823, C-1818
    William, Wi-1810
PETICOAT, Thos., Ct-1798
PETICORD, Thomas, Ct-1796
PETILLI, Lewis, Wh-1825
    William, Wh-1825
PETIT, Nehemiah, Ge-1812
PETRA, Adam, Gr-1805

PETRA, George, Gr-1805
    John, Gr-1805
PETRE, Adam, Gr-1799
    Adam Jr., Gr-1804
    George, Gr-1799, Gr-1804
    John, Gr-1799, Gr-1804
PETREE, Adam, Ct-1796, Ct-1798
    Adam Sr., Gr-1804
    Daniel, Ct-1796, C-1823, Ct-1798
    George, C-1818, C-1823
    James, Gr-1805
    John, Gr-1821, C-1818, C-1823
    Samuel, C-1818
    Thomas Sr., Wh-1825
    William, Wh-1825
PETTIJOHN, Samuel, Wh-1811
PETTIS, Horatio, Wi-1815
PETTIT, George, Je-1822
    Jones, C-1823
PETTIWAY, Henchey, D-1805
PETTY, Henry, Wi-1801, Wi-1810, Wi-1815
    James, Fr-1812
    John, A-1805
    Theophilus, B-1812
    William, Je-1800
PEVEEHOUS, Abraham, Gr-1799
PEVYHOUSE, Daniel, W-1812
    John, Ct-1798
PEW, Daniel, Gr-1805
    Samuel, Mt-1798
    Williby, Wl-1804
PEWET, James, Wi-1810
    Joel, Wi-1810
    Thomas, Wi-1810
PEWIT, James, Wi-1815
    Joel, Je-1800
PEYOR, Luke D., Wi-1810
PEYTON, Elias, Mu-1816
    Joseph, Mu-1816
    Robert, Mu-1816
PHAGAN, James, Su-1812
    John, Su-1812
PHANN, George, Ge-1805
    John, Ge-1805
    Philip, Ge-1805
PHAPPALL, Amos, Sn-1816
PAR, Ephram, Sn-1811
    Jane, Sn-1811
PHAREN, Willis, Wh-1825
PHARR, Jonathan, B-1812
    Samuel, Sn-1792
PHELIN, Richard _., D-1811
PHELPS, David, Wh-1811
    Elisha, Rb-1812
    Josiah, D-1811
    Randol, Gi-1812
PHENIX, Henry, D-1811
PHEPS, Jordan, Gi-1812
PHERSON, Robert, Ro-1805
    Thomas, Ro-1805
    William, Ro-1805
PHETTS, Isham, Rb-1812
    James, Rb-1812
    John, Rb-1812
PHIBS, Mathew, Sn-1816
PHILIP, William Sr., Wi-1815
PHILIP, Philips & Campbell, Mt-1798
PHILIPS, Abraham, Bo-1800
    Alexdr., D-1805
    Andrew, Gr-1821
    Bennet, B-1812
    Burwell, D-1805

PHILIPS, Caleb, Mt-1798
    David, B-1812
    Dyer, Ge-1812
    Ezekiah, Gr-1804
    GAbriel, Ge-1805
    Isaac, B-1812, Mt-1798, Wi-1810
    Isearel, Wi-1814
    James, Gi-1819
    John, B-1812, D-1805, D-1811
    Jonah, B-1812
    Jonathan, Su-1797, Mt-1798
    Joseph, D-1805, D-1811, D-1805,
        Wi-1810
    Lewis, Wh-1825
    Matthew, B-1812
    Merrill, D-1805
    Moses, J-1802
    Nathan, Gr-1804
    Nathan B., B-1812
    Noah, Wh-1825
    Samuel, B-1812, D-1811, D-1805
    Thomas, K-1799
    William, Gr-1804, Sn-1816, D-1811,
        D-1795
    Wm. Jr., Wi-1815
    Zaddoch, D-1805
PHILLIP, George, Su-1812
PHILLIPS, Abraham, Bo-1801
    Amos, Wl-1804
    Andrew, J-1802
    Benjamin, Wl-1804(2), D-1805,
        Su-1812, Rb-1812
    Benonley, R-1808
    Charles, Su-1797, Su-1796. Su-1812(2)
    Clemmons, Ro-1805
    David, Sn-1811
    Ebbing, Sn-1816
    Ebbins, Sn-1811
    Edmond, Je-1800
    Ezekiah, Rb-1812
    Hezekiah, Gr-1799
    James, Gi-1812
    Jesse, Ct-1798
    Joel, Gi-1812
    John, Wl-1804, Wh-1825, C-1823,
        C-1818, Co-1821, Gi-1819,
        Gi-1812
    Jonathan, D-1805, C-1823
    Joseph, Wi-1801, Wi-1815, C-1823
    Lewis, Wh-1811
    Nathan, Gr-1805
    Sam, Gi-1812
    Stephen, Wh-1825
    Thomas, C-1818, Gi-1819, Gi-1812(2)
    Wade, Ge-1812
    William, Wi-1810, Wl-1804, Sn-1811,
        C-1823, Gi-1812, W-1812
PHILPOT, Isaac, A-1805
    John, A-1805
    Warren, W-1812
PHIPPS, E. E., W-1805, Su-1812
    James, Gr-1821
    Jordan, Wi-1815
    Joseph, Gi-1812
    Joshua, D-1805
    Lewallen, Rb-1812
    Richardson, D-1805, D-1811
    Wm., Sn-1811
PHIPS, John, Fr-1812
PHITTS, Lansford, Sn-1811
PHLIPPEN, Thos., Ge-1783
PIATT, John, Je-1822

PICARD, Alexr., Mu-1816
    John, Mu-1816
PICKARD, Isaac, Mu-1811
    John, Mu-1811
PICKENS, David, Su-1812, Mu-1811
    G. John, Mu-1811
    George, D-1811
    Henry, Su-1812, Mu-1816
    Israel, Gi-1812
    Israeil, Gi-1819
    James, Gi-1812
    James Jr., Su-1812
    John, Bo-1800, Bo-1801, Mu-1816, Mu-1811
    Jonathan, Mu-1811, Mu-1816
    Joseph, Li-1812*, Gi-1819
    Nicholas, Mu-1811
    Robert K., Su-1812
    Thomas, B-1812
    Will, Gi-1812
    Will H., Mu-1816
    William, Su-1812, Mu-1811, Mu-1816
PICKERIN, Ellis, Ge-1812
    Samuel, Ge-1812
PICKERING, Benjamin, Ge-1805, Ge-1812
    Charles, Rb-1812
    Ellis, Ge-1805, Ge-1812
    Enos, Ge-1805
    Samuel, Ge-1805
    Spencer, Rb-1812
PICKERTON, Thomas, Gr-1799
PICKET(Pucket?), Ebenezer, Fr-1812
PICETT, Claburn, Gi-1819
    Douglass, D-1811
    Elijah, Mu-1816
PICKINS, Andrew, Gi-1812
    James, Su-1796
    James, Ge-1812(2), Su-1797
    John, Mu-1816
    Joseph, Ct-1798
PICKLE, Henry, B-1812
PICKRELL, John, Wh-1811
PICKRING, Enos, Ge-1812
    Rabeca, Ge-1812
PICORD, Henry, Mu-1816
    Isaac, Mu-1816
    William, Mu-1816
PIERCE, Aron, Je-1822
    Caleb, Je-1822
    Daniel, Ge-1805
    David, Je-1822, Ge-1812
    George, Ge-1805, Je-1822
    James, Wh-1811
    James Jr., Ge-1812
    John, Ge-1805
    Lewis, Ge-1812
    Robert, Je-1822
    Solomon, Je-1822
    Spencer, Mu-1811
    Thomas, Su-1812
PIERCEFIELD, John, Gr-1805
    Samuel, Gr-1799
PIERCIFULL, Thos, Ge-1783
PIERSON, Henry, Wh-1811
    John, R-1819
    Nathan, Ro-1805
    Thomas, Wh-1811
    William, Ro-1805
PIGG, James, Wi-1815, D-1811
PIKE, George, Sn-1811, Sn-1816
    John, Rb-1812
    Jonas, Rb-1812

PIKE, Thomas, Fr-1812
    Wm., Rb-1812
PILAND, Elisha, D-1811
PILANT, James, Gr-1821
PILCHER, John, Su-1796
    Joshua, D-1811
PILE, Coonrod, J-1802
PILES, Conrod, Gr-1799
    Jesse, Je-1800
    Leonard P., D-1811
    Peter, Gr-1804
PILL, John, D-1805
PILLIPS, Bl-1815
PILLOW, Abner, Mu-1811, Mu-1816
    Allen, Mu-1816
    Claiborne, Mu-1816
    Gideon, Mu-1811, Mu-1816
    Gidion, Wl-1804
    John, Wi-1815
    Mordecai, Wi-1815
    Will., Wl-1804
    Will (Col.), Mu-1816
    William, Wi-1801, Mu-1811, Mu-1816
PIMBERTON, Benjamin, Su-1812
    James, Su-1812
    Thomas, Su-1812
PINCKSTON, Turner, Wi-1815
PINE, Charles, Sn-1816
PINEGAR, Matthias, Wh-1825
    Peter, Wh-1825
PINES, Allen, Gi-1812
PINKERTON, David, Wi-1815, Wi-1810
    Jas., Se-1799, Wi-1815
    Joseph, Wi-1810, Wi-1815
    Matthew, B-1812
PINKEY, Henry, George, Crobart & William, D-1805
PINKLEY, Frederick, D-1811, D-1805
    Frederick, Jacob & Joseph, D-1805
PINKSTON, Daniel, A-1805
    Edward, Je-1822
    Hugh, Wi-1810
    James, D-1805
    John, A-1805
    Meshack, D-1811
    Peter, Wi-1801
PINSON, Duke, Rb-1812
    Larkin, Rb-1812
PIPER, John, Gi-1819
    Nutter, Hu-1812
    Saml., Sn-1811
PIPIN, James H., Gi-1819
PIPKENS, Enos, Mu-1816
PIPKIN, Lemas, D-1805
    Mark D-1805
    Philip, D-1811, D-1805
    William, D-1805
PIPKINS, Enos, Mu-1811
PIPPIN, Richard, Rb-1812
    William, Gi-1819
PIRKINS, George, Ct-1796
    Jacob, Ct-1796
PIRTH, George, D-1805
PISEN, Michael, Rb-1812
PISTOLE, John, Wh-1825
PITCHER, John, Su-1812
PITCOCK, Thomas, Wa-1819
PITMAN, Lewis, Wi-1810, Mu-1811
    Louis, Wi-1810
    William, W-1812, W-1805
PITNER, Micheal, Wl-1804
PITRARCHE, Thomas, Wa-1814

PITS, John, W-1812
PITSINBERGER, Peter, Ge-1812
PITT, Arthur, Rb-1812
    Henry, Sn-1811
    John, Sn-1811
    Joseph, Sn-1811
    Stephen, Sn-1811
    William, Sn-1816
PITTMAN, Thomas, b-1812
    William, Rb-1812
PITTNEY, William, Wi-1815
PITTS, Bartlett, Rb-1812
    Burrell, Rb-1812
    Drury, Rb-1812
    John, B-1812, Sn-1816
    Joseph, Rb-1812
PITTWAY, H., Wi-1815
PLASTER, Isaac, Sn-186
PLASTERS, Thomas, Rb-1812
PLERMMER, John, Rb-1812
PLUMBLEY, Samuel, B-1812
PLUMBLY, Thos., B-1812
PLUMER, Thomas, Gr-1799
PLUMLEE, Isaac, Wh-1811
    Rachel, Su-1797
    Solomon, Wi-1815
    Daniel, Su-1812
PLUMLY, Denton, Wh-1825
    Isaac, Wh-1825
    Joel, Wh-1825
    Jonathan, B-1812(2)
    Solomon, B-1812
    William, Wh-1825
PLUMMER, Henry, D-1811
PLUNKETT, James, Hu-1812
POAGE, Robert, Je-1800
POBART, Nicless, Gr-1799
POCH, John, Wh-1811
POCK, Thomas, Gr-1799
POE, Hardy, Cl-1803
    Jedethen, Fr-1812
    John, Fr-1812, Wl-1804
    Lindsey, A-1805
    Logan, C-1818
    Rhoden, Fr-1812, Wi-1801
    Zedethon, Wi-1801
POES, Also, D-1811
POGUE, Farner, Ge-1812
    John, Ge-1805
    John Sr., Ge-1812
    Thomas, Ge-1812
    William, B-1812
POINDEXTER, John, Gr-1821
    Lowwell, Gr-1805
POKE, James, Cl-1803
    John, Mu-1811
    Thomas, Mu-1811
POLACK, B. Wm., D-1788
POLAND, John, Ct-1798, Ct-1796
    Mosesss, W-1812
POLE, Peter, B-1812
POLEN, Jacob, Wa-1814
POLIN, Jacob, Wa-1819
POLK, Amos, Mu-1811
    Charles, estate, Mu-1811
    Daniel, Mu-1811
    Ezekiel, Mu-1811, Mu-1816
    John, B-1812, Mu-1811, Mu-1816,
        Wi-1810
    Joseph, Wi-1815, Wi-1810
    Richd., Wi-1815, Wi-1801, Wi-1810
    Samuel, Mu-1811, Mu-1816

POLK, Silas, Sn-1816
    Thomas, Mu-1811(3)
    William, Mu-1816, Mu-1811(2),
        Wi-1801(2), Wi-1815(2),
        Wi-1810
    Wm. N. C., Mu-1816
POLL, M. Pelty, D-1805
    William, Sn-1816
POLLARD, John, B-1812
    Joseph, Wi-1815
    Rheuben, Mt-1798
    Samuel, Gr-1821
    William, B-1812
POLLARRES, Joseph, B-1812
POLLET, Thomas, Wa-1819
POLLEY, Edward, Ct-1798
POLLOCK, B. William, Mt-1798
    James, Mu-1816
    John, Mt-1798, A-1805
    Joseph, A-1805
    Purley, Mt-1798
    Robert Sr., A-1805
    Robert Jr., A-1805
POLLY, John, D-1805
POND, James, D-1805
PONTSON, Absalom, C-1823
POOL, Asa, Rb-1812
    Ephriam Jr., Rb-1812
    John, Gi-1812
    Tho., Gi-1812
    William, Mu-1816, B-1812, Rb-1812
POOLE, John, Ro-1805
POOR, Aaron, K-1799
    Benjamin, J-1802
    David, Su-1812
    Jesse, Su-1812
    Joseph, J-1802
    Moses, Ge-1783
    Peter, A-1805
POPE, Elijah, Mu-1811
    Jahue, Je-1800
    John, Wi-1810, D-1805, Wi-1815,
        B-1812, Je-1800
    Lemuel, Wi-1815
    Leroy, Mu-1811
    Mary, Su-1796, Su-1797
    Simon, Ge-1812
    Thomas A., Wi-1815
    Williamson, Gr-1804
POPEJOY, Nathaniel, Gr-1821
PORCH, Thomas, D-1811
PORMEN, Samuel, B-1812
PORTER, Abner, Mu-1816
    Alexander, D-1811, Wh-1811
    Alexander B., Rb-1812
    Ambros, Sn-1811, Wi-1810
    Benjamin, W-1812, Rb-1812, Ro-1805
    Charles, D-1805
    Charles T., Je-1822, Je-1800
    David, Wi-1810, D-1805
    David W., Gi-1812
    Hanner, Wi-1801, Wi-1815
    James, D-1811, Mu-1816, K-1799,
        Gi-1812
    Jessee, Wh-1825
    John, Wi-1801, Wi-1810, Wh-1825,
        Mu 1811, Wi-1815
    John Jr., Wi-1810
    Joseph, Wi-1801, D-1811, Mu-1811
    Joseph B., Wi-1801(2)
    Joshua, Wh-1825
    Rees, Wi-1810

PORTER, Rice, D-1805
    Richard, Wl-1804
    Robert, Wi-1810, Bl-1815
    Samuel, Bo-1805, Mu-1811
    Stephen, Ge-1812
    Thomas, D-1811
    William, Wi-1810, Wl-1804, Mu-1811,
        D-1805, Mu-1816(2), Wi-1815
    William B., Rb-1812
PORTERFIELD, Francis, Li-1812*, Wh-1811
    James, D-1811
    Richard, Wh-1811
    Samuel, Su-1812
    Seth, Su-182, Su-1796, Su-1797
PORTHEROW, David, Cl-1803
PORTMAN, John, Bl-1815
PORTWOOD, Page, A-1805
POSEY, Daniel, Bo-1801, W-1812
    Joseph, Bo-1801
POSTWOOD, Page, K-1799
POTEAT, Pleasant, Wh-1825
POTEET, James, Wi-1815
    Mark, Sn-1811
    Thomas, B-1812, Wa-1814
POTEETE, Isaac, Wi-1810
    James, Wi-1810
    Thomas, Wi-1810
POTSON, John, Wh-1811
POTTER, Archibald, Wi-1810
    Begeman, K-1799
    Donalson, Wi-1815
    Donneldson, Wi-1810
    John, Ct-1798, K-1799, Gi-1812,
        Ro-1805, Je-1822
    Paul, Je-1822
    Telnson?, W-1812
POTTERFIELD, Richard, Je-1800
POTTETH, Danl., D-1805
POTTINGER, Robert, J-1802
POTTS, George, Wh-1811, Wh-1825
    James, Wi-1815, Wh-1811, W-1812,
        Wh-1825
    Jonathan, Wi-1815
    Nathan, W-1812
    Patrick, Wh-1825
    Peter, Wi-1810
POTZ, Daniel, Wi-1815
POUGE, Samuel, B-1812
POUNDERS, Richard, Gr-1805
POWEL, Dempsey, D-1805, D-1811
    Demsey, Sn-1811
    Hartwell, Wi-1815
    John, Sn-1811
    Joseph, Gr-1799
    Nathan, D-1811
    Peter, Gi-1819
    Thomas, D-1811
POWELL, Alexander, W-1812
    Ambrose, Mu-1811, Mu-1816
    Benjamin, Rb-1812
    Charles, Rb-1812
    Cyrus, Mu-1816
    Edward, Ro-1805
    Elisha, Mu-1816
    Henry, Gr-1821
    Isaac, Sn-1792
    James, R-1808, R-1819
    John, Gi-1819, Wa-1819, D-1805,
        Mu-1816
    Lawson, Mu-1816
    Lewis, Fr-1812, W-1805, Mu-1816,
        Mu-1811

POWELL, Lucis, W-1812
    Obed, Fr-1812
    Pauley, Mu-1816
    Peter, Mu-1811
    Thos., Gi-1812
    Willie, Rb-1812
POWER, Thomas, Su-1797
POWERS, Charles, C-1823
    Elijah, Hu-1812
    Jesse, C-1823
    Jessee, Gr-1799
    John, Hu-1812
    Lewis, Hu-1812
    Patrick, Ge-1805, Ge-1812
    Riggins, C-1818
    Robert, Gi-1812
    Yancy, Wi-1815
PRAT, John, Wi-1815
PRATER, Andrew, Gi-1812
    Isaac, K-1799, Ge-1812
    Thosl?, Gi-1812
    Thomas, Ge-1812
PRATHER, John, Ge-1812
    Reese, Ge-1805
    Thomas, Ge-1805
PRATT, George, B-1812
    James, Ge-1805, Wi-1815
    Jesse, Gi-1812
    John, Ge-1812
    Samuel, Wi-1815
    Thomas, A-1805
    William, Ge-1805, Gi-1819
PREAST, John, Wi-1801
    William, W-1812
PREATOR, Thomas, Ge-1783
PRENDERGAST, Jno. B., Gi-1812
PRESGROVE, Andrew, B-1812
    George, Wi-1810
PRESGROVES, George, Mu-1816
PRESLEY, John, Wl-1804
PRESLY, William, Mo-1825
PRESSGROVE, George, Gr-1799
PRESTON, George, Ro-1805
    James, R-1819, Ro-1805
    Robert, Wi-1815, Wi-1801
    Thos., Sn-1811, Sn-1816
PRETCHET, Crowell, A-1805
PRETHERO, Alexander, Ge-1805, Ge-1812
PRETHEROW, Alexr., Ge-1783
PREWET, Isaac, Wh-1811
    Lemuel, Mu-1811
    Thos., Wi-1801
PREWETT, John, Mu-1816
    Michael, B-1812
    Saml., Mu-1816
PREWIT, Hercless, C-1818
PRICE, A. S., Mo-1825
    Andrew, Wh-1825
    Christopher, Wa-1819
    Elisha, W-1812
    George, Wh-1825, D-1811
    Isaac, Gi-1812
    James, Ct-1798, Ct-1796, B-1812,
        Wa-1819
    John, Wh-1825, D-1811, Ct-1796,
        Fr-1812, Ge-1783, W-1812
    Jonathan, B-1812(2)
    Joseph, Mo-1825
    Kinchen, W-1812
    Kit, Wa-1814
    Matthew, Wi-1810
    Meredy, W-1812

PRICE, Nathan, Fr-1812
    Nathaniel, Sn-1816
    Rachel, Wa-1819, Wa-1814
    Ralph, Je-1800
    Reece, B-1812
    Reubin, W-1812
    Richard, B-1812, W-1812
    Richard Jr., W-1812
    Shadrick, Wh-1825
    Simon, B-1812
    Solomon, Ct-1798, Ct-1796
    Thomas, Wh-1825, Wi-1801, Ct-1798,
        Ct-1796, Wa-1814, Su-1797,
        Su-1796, Wa-1819
    Thomas L., Wh-1825
    William, Wh-1825, Wi-1810, Ct-1798,
        B-1812, Gi-1812, R-1808
PRICHARD, Carvel J., Fr-1812
    Henry, Mu-1816
PRICHETT, Thomas, Ro-1805
PRIDE, Burtin, Bo-1801
    Bustin, Bo-1800
    John, D-1811, Fr-1812
    William, Gi-1819
PRIEST, Fuller, Ro-1805
    John, D-1811
    Miles, Wi-1815
    Thomas, Mu-1816
PRIESTLY, James, D-1811(2)
    John T., Sn-1816
PRIGMORE, Drury, Su-1796
    Joseph, Je-1800
PRIMM, Jeremiah, Wi-1810
PRIMMER, Mary, Ct-1796
PRINCE, Ceaser, D-1811
    Eli, B-1812
    Francis, Mt-1798
    Gilbert, Gi-1812
    Robert, Mt-1798
    William, Gi-1812
PRING, James, Wa-1819
    Nicholas, Wa-1814
PRINKLE, Jacob, Mu-1816
PRIOR, Jesse, A-1805
    John, Wh-1825
    Luke Sr., Wi-1801
    Richard, Ge-1783
    Sherrell, Wh-1825
    William, Wh-1825
PRITCHARD, Bengamin, Wi-1815
    Benjamin, Wi-1810
PRITCHET, Carvell, A-1805
    Charles, Wa-1814
    Singleton, Wa-1814, Wa-1819
    Thomas, Mu-1811
PRITCHETT, Benjamin, D-1811(2)
    Ephraim, D-1811
    John, D-1805
    Thomas, D-1805
PRITHEROW, Alexander, Wa-1814
PRITHESON, Alexander, Wa-1819
PRIVET, Arvin, C-1823
    Charles, C-1823
    David, Ge-1783
    Francis, C-1823
    Harless, C-1823
PRIZEMORE, Theodimur, Su-1797
PROBART, William G., D-1811
PROCK, James, Sn-1816
    Mathias, D-1811, D-1805
PROCTOR, James, Mo-1825
    John, Rb-1812

PROCTOR, William, Fr-1812, Sn-1823
PROEN, Abner, Rb-1812
    James, Rb-1812
PROFET, David, Su-1797
    James, Su-1812
    Jeremiah, Su-1812
    John, Su-1812
PROFFETT, David Sr., Su-1812
PROFFIT, David, Ge-1812
    Robert, Ge-1812, Ro-1805
    William, Ge-1812
PROFIT, David, Su-1796
    Joseph, C-1823
    William, C-1818, C-1823
PROKE?, Jacob, Rb-1812
PROPHIT, John, Ct-1796, Ct-1798
PROPLET, Nathan, Su-1797
PROTHRO, David, Su-1797, Su-1796
    John, Su-1796
PROVENCE, Thomas Sr., Hw-17-9
    Thomas Jr., Hw-1799
PROVINCE, John, Wh-1825
PROWELL, Sampson, Wi-1815
    Sarah, Wi-1815
    Thomas, Wi-1815
PRUET, Abraham, Gr-1805
    Isaac, Mu-1811
    John, Wi-1810, Mu-1811
    William, K-1799(Brent?)
PRUETT, Gabriel, A-1805
PRUIT, Abraham, Gr-1804
    Richard, Gr-1804
PRUITT, Field, J-1802
    John, J-1802
    William Sr., Ro-1805
PRUNER, John, Su-1797
PRUYER, Hezekiah, Wi-1815
PRYER, John, Su-1797
PRYOR, James, Su-1812, Rb-1812
    John, Wh-1811, Su-1812
    Joseph, Wi-1805, W-1812
    Nicholas B., D-1811
    Pleasant, Wh-1825
    Richard, D-1811
    Thomas, Wh-1811
    William, K-1799, J-1802
        Wh-1811
    William Sr., Wh-1825
PRYORS, John, heirs, Wl-1804
PUCKET, Drury, Wh-1811
    Robert, Wh-1811
PUCKETT, Edward, Mu-1811
    John, D-1811
    _____, K-1799
PUCKIT, Guad C., Wh-1825
    John, Wh-1825
PUETY, Daus, Co-1827
PUGH, David, Ct-1796, Ct-1798
    James, Wi-1815, Wi-1810
    William, Ct-1796, Ct-1798
PULHAM, Alsa, W-1812
PULL, William, Sn-1811
PULLAM, Drury, D-1805
PULLEN, Archibald, D-1811
    Elisha, Mu-1816
    Leroy, Gr-1821
    William, Je-1822
PULLENS, Cornelius, B-1812
PULLIAM, Drury, Wi-1810, Wi-1815
PULLIN, Elisha, Mu-1811
    Jessey, Sn-1811
    Moses, Gi-1812

PULLIN, William, Gi-1812
PULLIUM, Isham, Wh-1811
PULLY, David, D-1805, D-1811
PULMAN, James, Je-1822
PULSE, Frederick, Je-1822
PUNCH, John, Su-1812, Su-1797, Su-1796,
    W-1805
PURCELL, George, Wa-1814
PURDOM, Margaret, Ge-1805
PURDON, John, A-1805
    Margaret, Ge-1812
PURDY, William, Mo-1825
PURKINS, David, Sn-1811
    Joshua, Hu-1812
PURKINSON, Wm., W-1812
PURNELL, Esaw, B-1812
    Will., Gi-1812
PURSELL, George, Ge-1812
PURSEN, James, Wh-1825
PURSEY, James J., R-1819
    David, Sn-1811
    James, Mu-1811
PURTLE, Elijah, Wh-1825
    George, Wl-1804, Wh-1825, D-1811
    Jacob, Wh-1825
    John, D-1811
    John Sr., Wh-1825
    John Jr., Wh-1825
    Matthew, Wh-1825
PURVIANCE, John, Sn-1792
PURVICE, Isaac, Gi-1812
PURVINE, John, Wl-1804
PURVIS, Cullen, Sn-1811
PUTT, William, B-1812
PYBOURN, Christopher, W-1812
    Jacob, K-1799
PYBURN, Alexander, Wl-1804
    Jacob, K-1799(2)
PYRON, Charles, Wi-1815
QAREN, James, Gr-1799
QARVIS, Riziah, W-1812
QUALES, Elias O., Hu-1812
    Robert, Wh-1825
QUALLS, Abram, Su-1812
    William, A-1805
QUALS, Cannon, W-1812
    Roger, Wl-1804
QUARLES, Cannon, Wh-1811
    William, D-1811, Wh-1811
QUEENER, David, A-1805
    Henry, A-1805
    Jacob, A-1805
    John, Su-1812
QUELAR, John, A-1805
QUIET, James, Su-1812
QUILEN, William, Wi-1810
QUILLEN, Thomas, Wa-1814
QUIN, John P., Wi-18
QUINBY, Jones, Gi-1819
QUINN, Amos, Gi-1812
    James, Gi-1812
QUINNER, Daniel, C-1823, C-1818
    Henry, C-1818, C-1823
    Jacob, C-1818
    Jacob Sr., C-1823
    Jacob Jr., C-1823
    Jacob Jim, C-1818
QUISENBERY, William, Fr-1812
QUISENBURY, John, Wl-1804
    Thomas, Wl-1804
QUISINBERRY, Nicholas, Wl-1804
QUISTENBERY, Henry, D-1811

QULLER, Charles, Ge-1812
RACKLEY, Silas, Sn-1816
    Thedarick, Sn-1816
RADER, Abraham, Wa-1819
    Ephraim, B-1812
RADFORD, David, Bl-1815
    George, Bl-1815
    Haknah, Mu-1816
    Samuel, B-1812, Mu-1816
RADGERS, Thomas, Ge-1812
RADLE, John, Gr-1799
RAE, John, Gi-1812
RAFFITY, Richard, R-1819
RAGAN, Benjamin, D-1811
    Benjn. & Thomas, D-1805
    Daniel, Mo-1825, Su-1812
    Derby, Ge-1805
    James, Bo-1805, Sn-1811, Sn-1816
    Jesse, Mo-1825
    John, Ge-1805, Bo-1805
    John Jr., Ge-1805
    Michael, D-1805
    Thomas, D-1811
    William, Bo-1805
RAGDALE, Thomas, Wi-1815
RAGEN, Joseph, Bo-1800
RAGER, Owen, Ge-1812
RAGGSDALE, Baxter, B-1812
    Daniel, B-1812
    Edward, B-1812
    John, B-1812
RAGLAN, William, K-1799
RAGLAND, Reuben, Wh-1811, A-1805, K-1799
    Rewbin, Wh-1825
    Richard, A-18
    William, D-1811, A-1805
RAGLE, Adam, Su-1812
    John, Su-1812
RAGLIN, Henry, Mt-1798
    Peter, Wl-1804
RAGON, Hugh, Sn-1792
    John, Ge-1812(2)
RAGSDALE, Abner, Wi-1810(2)
    Benga., Rb-1812
    Britain, A-1805
    Briton, Fr-1812
    Dain, Wi-1810
    Daniel, Wi-1815(2)
    David, R-1819
    Edward, Wi-1815, Je-1822, Gr-1821,
        Wi-1810, Wi-1801(2), Wi-1815
    Jessee, Wh-1825
    Joel, Rb-1812
    John, B-1812, Wi-1810(2), Wi-1815
    Peter, Mu-1811, Mu-1816
    Robert, Wi-1815, Wi-1810
    Thomas, Wi-1810
    William, Rb-1812, Mu-1816, Mu-1811
RAIGER, Anthony, B-1812
RAIL, Samuel, Gr-1804, Gr-1799
RAILE, Henry, Sn-1787
RAIMY, Allen, Mu-1816
RAIN, John Sr., D-1805
    John Jr., D-1805
RAINBOLT, Adam, Ct-1798, Ct-1796
    Elisha, Ct-1798
    John, Hw-1801
    Susannah, Ct-1796
RAINES, John, Mu-1816
RAINEY, John, Wi-1810
    William, Wh-1825, Wi-1815
RAINS, Asahel, W-1812

RAINS, George, W-1812
    Henry, W-1812, Gr-1799
    James, W-1812
    John, D-1788, Je-1800, W-1812,
        Ge-1812, Co-1821, Gr-1799
    John Sr., D-1811, A-1805
    John Jr., Mu-1811, D-1811, A-1805
    Newman, A-1805
    Phillip, W-1812
    Robert, W-1812
    William, A-1805, D-1805, W-1812,
        D-1811
RAINWATER, James, Je-1822
RAINY, David, Mu-1816(2)
RALEIGH, Vinsant, C-1823
    Winston, C-1818
RALF, John, Su-1797
    Thomas, Su-1797
RALPH, Ingram, D-1811
RALSTON, David, D-1805, D-1811
    George, D-1811
    John, D-1811, Wa-1819
    Joseph, Wi-1801(2)
RAMBO, Elias, B-1812
RAMBOUGH, Enos, Ge-1805
RAMBSY, Samuel, Gr-1799
RAMSEY, Andrew, Ro-1805, Ge-1805
    Elizabeth, Ge-1812
    Francis A., Wi-1810(2), Wi-1815
    George, R-1819, K-1799, Mc-1825
    Henry, Sn-1787
    James, Mu-1811, Mu-1816, Wh-1825,
        Ge-1812, K-1799, Ge-1805
    John, Mu-1816, R-1819, Ro-1805,
        Ge-1805, Gr-1821
    Josiah, Mt-1798
    Randolph, Wh-1825, Wh-1811
    Richard, Gi-1812, Bo-1800, Bo-1805,
        Bo-1801
    Robert, Mu-1816
    Robert Sr., Mu-1811
    Robert Jr., Mu-1816
    Robert, heirs, Mu-1816
    Samuel, Gr-1805, Su-1812, B-1812,
        Gr-1804
    Thomas, Mu-1811, D-1811, Mu-1816,
        Sn-1787
    Will G., Mu-1816
    William, Mu-1811, D-1811, D-1805,
        Mu-1816, Ge-1812, Ro-1805,
        R-1819, Ge-1805
    William Sr., D-1811
RANDAL, Anne, D-1805
    Aquella, D-1811
    Greenberry, D-1811
    James, Wh-1825
    Thomas, Mu-1816
    Samuel, Wa-1819
RANDLES, James, Se-1799
    John, Se-1799
    Richd., Se-1799
RANDOLPH, Chisum, Wh-1825
    Henry, Je-1822, Je-1800
    Hezekiah, W-1805, W-1812
    Isham, Ge-1805
    James, Je-1822
    John, W-1812
    Nathan, W-1812, W-1805
    Payton, W-1812, W-1805
    Peter, D-1811
    Peyton, Ge-1805
    Robert, W-1812, W-1805

RANDOLPH, Samuel, Bl-1815
    Sarah, Je-1800
    Thomas, Ge-1805
RANES, David, D-1805
    John, Co-1827
RANEY, Augustine, Gi-1812
    David, Mu-1811
    James, Gi-1812
RANGE, Jacob, Wa-1814, Wa-1819
    James, Ct-1796
    John, Wa-1819, Wa-1814
    Peter, Wa-1819, Wa-1814
RANGER, James, Ct-1798
RANKIN, David, Ge-1805, Ge-1812, Mu-1816,
        Mu-1811, D-1805
    James, Je-1822, Sn-1811, Mu-1811
    James Sr., Sn-1823
    James Jr., Sn-1823, Sn-1811
    John, Bo-1801
    Richard, Je-1800
    Robert, Ge-1805, Gi-1819, Ge-1812(2)
        D-1805
    Samuel, Je-1822
    Senator Thomas, Je-1800
    Thomas (son of Rankin, Thomas Jr.)
        Je-1822
    Thomas Jr., Je-1800
    William, Ge-1805, Fr-1812, Je-1822
        Ge-1812
RANKING, David, Ge-1783
    Thos., Ge-1783
RANKINS, James, Je-1800, Sn-1816, Mu-1816
    Samuel, Je-1800
RANO?, William, Mt-1798
RANSBARGER, George, Gr-1804, Gr-1805
RANY, John, B-1812
RAPE, Gustavous, D-1811
    Henry, D-1811
RAPIER, John, D-1805
    Richard, D-1811
RAPPY, Henry, Ct-1798
RASBERRY, William, Mu-1816
RASH, Howell, W-1812
    Thomas, Gr-1805
    William, Gr-1799
RASHER, Alexander, Ct-1796
RASSON, Alexander, Sn-1816
    Payton, Sn-1816
RASY, James, Fr-1812
RATCLIFF, James, Wi-1801
RATHY, James, Wl-1804
RATLEY, Jeremiah, Fr-1812
    Joshua, Fr-1812
RATLIFF, Job, J-1802
RAWLEY, James, Sn-1811
RAWLING, Benjn., Sn-1816
    Charles, Bo-1805
    Hasey, B-1812
    John, Bl-1815
RAWLINGS, A., J-1802
    Asahel, Ge-1805(2)
    Asarel, R-1819
    Benjamin, Fr-1812, Sn-1811
    D. & Rezin, R-1819
    Isahel, Bl-1815
    JOhn, Ge-1805
    Michael, Bl-1815
    Roderick, B-1812
RAWLS, Luke, Rb-1812
RAWORTH, Edward, D-1811
RAWSEY, John, Mu-1811
RAY, Alexander, Wi-1810

RAY, Benjamin, Gr-1805, Ge-1783, Gr-1821,
        Gr-1805
    Christian, D-1805
    George, W-1812
    Hugh, Ge-1812
    Jacob, Gr-1805, Gr-1804
    James, Wi-1815, Rb-1812
    Jessee, W-1805, W-1812
    John, Wl-1804, Wi-1815, D-1811,
        Wh-1825, Hw-1799
    John Sr., Gr-1805, Fr-1804
    John Jr., Gr-1804, Gr-1805
    Joseph, Gr-1799, Gr-1804, R-1808
    Jos., deceased, Ge-1783
    Joseph Sr., Gr-1805
    Lewis, W-1812
    Richard, W-1812
    Samuel, Gr-1821
    Solomon, Wl-1804
    Thomas, Wl-1804, Gr-1805, Gr-1821,
        Gr-1804, Ge-1783, B-1812
    Warren, R-1819
    William, D-1805, Ct-1798, Ct-1796
        Wl-1804
RAYBOURN, Henry, J-1802
    John, J-1802
RAYBURN, Henry, B-1812
    James, B-1812
RAYFIELD, Thos., Hu-1812
RAYL, George, Gr-1821
    Samuel, Gr-1821, Gr-1805
    Washington, Gr-1821
RAYLE, William, Gr-1805
RAYMON, George W., Wh-1811
RAYMOND, Elickim, D-1805
    Nicholas, D-1811, D-1805
RAYN, Samuel, Wi-1810
RAYNER, Henry, Sn-1816
RAYNOLD, James, Gr-1805
RAYNOLDS, Edward, W-1812
    Jenkin, W-1812
    Richard, Gr-1805
RAZIER, Christian, D-1811
RAZOR, John, Ct-1798
RAZZEL, Patton, D-1805
REA, John, Gi-1812
    Joseph, Gi-1819, Gi-1812
    Margeret (wd), Gi-1819
    Thomas, Gi-1812
    William, Gi-1812, Gi-1819
REACE, Caleb, Gr-1804
    Isaac, Sn-1811
    Sampson, Fr-1812
    Thomas Sr., Gr-1804
    Thomas Jr., Gr-1804
    _____, W-1812
REACH, William, D-1811
READ, Alexander, D-1811
    Allen, C-1818
    Carson P., Gi-1819
    Charles, Gr-1821
    Edward, W-1812, B-1805
    Felps, Gr-1821
    George G., Gr-1821
    Guilford Dudley, Wi-1801
    Isaac, C-1818, C-1823
    James, Rb-1812, Gi-1819
    Jas. L., Wi-1815
    John, C-1823, C-1818, D-1811
    Josiah, Wi-1815
    Tho., Gi-1812
    Thomas J., D-1811

READ, William, Gr-1821, B-1812(2), Sn-1811
        D-1805, Sn-1816
    Wilson, Sn-1811
READE, Jacob, D-1805
    Jones, D-1811
READER, Alexander, Gr-1821
    Henry, Ge-1812
    Jacob, Ge-1812
    John, Ge-1812
    Nancy, Wa-1819
    Wm., C-1818
READERS, James, Gr-1805
    William, Gr-1805
READIN, Alijah, Mu-1811
READING, Robert, D-1805
READLES, John, Wh-1825
READY, Thomas, C-1818
REAGE, William, D-1811
REAGON, Alen, Ge-1812
    Darby, Ge-1812
REAMES, Martha, Mu-1811
REAMS, Bolin, D-1805
    John, Je-1800
REARDEN, Thomas, Je-1800
REARDON, Dennis, Wl-1804
REAS, Charles, K-1796
REASE, Geo. & Drury, D-1805
    Joel, Mu-1811
REASON, Jacob, Ge-1812
    James, Rb-1812
REASONER, Garret, Ct-1796, Ct-1798
REASONOVER, JOhn, Gi-1812
REASONS, William, Mt-1798
REASOR, Frederick, Ge-1805
REATHERFORD, Benjamin, C-1823
    Edward, C-1823
REAVES, Abner, Fr-1812
    Avery, Fr-1812
    Bolen, Wi-1815
    Burnett, D-1811
    Charles, Wh-1825
    Edmond, D-1811
    James, D-1811, Mu-1811
    James, Jordan & Burwell, D-1805
    Joel, Mu-1811
    John, Sn-1811, Sn-1816
    John, Dec., Ge-1812
    Jordan & Danl., D-1805
    M. N., D-1805
    Moses, Ge-1812
    Reuben, Mu-1811
    Samuel, Ge-1812
    William, B-1812, D-1811(2)
    Wm. & Edward, D-1805
REAVIS, Anderson, Gr-1805
RECER, Charles, Gi-1819
RECTOR, Benjamin, Wa-1819, Wa-1814
    Cumberland, Ro-1805, R-1819
    Daniel, Wa-1819
    Eli, Gr-1821
    George, Gr-1799
    John, Gr-1805, A-1805, Gr-1821
    Mack, Gr-1805
    Maximilian, Gr-1804
    Maximilien, Je-1800
    Morgan, R-1808
    Moss?, Gr-1805
    Sanders, Ro-1805
REDDETT, David, Sn-1816
    Josiah, Sn-1816
REDDICK, David, Sn-1811
    John, Sn-1811, Sn-1816

REDDILL, Theophilus, Sn-1811
REDDIN, Augustus, D-1811
    Augustus Jr., D-1811
REDDING, Abijah, Mu-1816
    Alford, D-1811
    Amstead, Mu-1811
    Armstead, Mu-1816
    Augustus, D-1811
    Robert, D-1811, Rb-1812
REDDIS, James, Gr-1799
REDDISH, Robisson, Mu-1811
REDDITT, Marmaduke, Sn-1823
REDERICK, Calep, Sn-1811
REDFERREN, Isaac, Rb-1812
    John, Rb-1812(2)
    Townley, Rb-1812
REDFORD, William, Wi-1815, Wi-1810
REDLEY, Benley, D-1805
    Thos., Wi-1801
REDMAN, Stephen, Ct-1796, Ct-1798
REDUS, James, Gr-1804
    William, Gr-1804
REDWELL, Charles, Je-1800
REE, Robert, Mu-1816
REECE, David, Mu-1816
    James, Ge-1805
    Samuel, B-1812
    William, Ge-1805
REED, Abraham, B-1812
    Abram, Ge-1783
    Alexander, Sn-1811, D-1805
    Andrew, Wi-1815, Wa-1814
    Andrew C., K-1799
    Audre, Wa-1819
    Charles, Ge-1812
    Daniel, Mu-1816
    David, Ge-1783, W-1805, Wl-1804,
        W-1812, Ge-1812
    Edward, C-1818
    Ezekiah, B-1812
    Felps, Gr-1805, Gr-1804, Gr-1799
    George, Ge-1783, Sn-1816, Sn-1811
    Hamilton, R-1808
    Henry, Mu-1816, Sn-1816
    Hugh, Mu-1811, Wi-1810(2), Mu-1816
    Hugh Jr., Mu-1816
    Isaiah, Mu-1816
    James, Mu-1816, Sn-1816, Wi-1810,
        Gr-1805, Sn-1811, Mu-1811,
        Wa-1814
    James C., R-1819
    Jesse, Ge-1812
    John, Mt-1798, Sn-1816, Wi-1810,
        Mu-1816, A-1805, Wi-1815,
        Ge-1783, Gi-1812
    John, heirs, Wi-1810
    John S., Ge-1812
    Jonas, D-1805
    Joseph, Sn-1811, Ge-1783
    Lambert Sr., Bo-1801
    Lambert Jr., Bo-1801
    Mical, Ge-1783
    Phelps, J-1802
    Robert, Wi-1801, Wl-1804
    Ruben, W-1812
    Rubent, R-1808
    Samuel, Sn-1811, Mu-1816
    Samuel R., R-1819
    Sarah, Mu-1811
    Solomon, Gr-1799, Ge-1783
    Thomas, Ro-1805, B-1812
    Thomas Sr., Gr-1805

REED, Washanton W., W-1812
    William, Sn-1816, Wi-1810, D-1805,
        Sn-1811, Mu-1816, Sn-1823,
        Wi-1815, Sn-1792
REEDER, George, Wa-1819
    Isaac, D-1811
REEDY, Nicholas, A-1805
    Shadrack, A-1805
REES, Ephraim, Mt-1798
    George, Mu-1816
    Henry, Ge-1812
    James, Mu-1816
    James H., Mu-1816
    Jesse, R-1819
    John, Ge-1812
    Moses, Ge-1812
    Roger, R-1819
    Thomas, Je-1800, Wl-1804
    William, Ge-1812
    William Sr., Ge-1812
REESE, Bensley, Wi-1815
    Calib, Gr-1805
    George, Mu-1811
    H. James, Mu-1811
    James, Mu-1811, Je-1800, Je-1822,
        Sn-1811
    Jehu, Ge-1783
    Jordan, Wi-1810
    Joseph P. M., Je-1822
    Partrick, minor, Wi-1815
    Robert, D-1811
    Robert D., Gi-1812
    Solomon, Ge-1805
    Talley, Wi-1815
    Thomas, Gr-1821
    Thomas Jr., Gr-1805
REESOR, Jacob, Ge-1805
REESS, James, Sn-1792
REEVES, David, Mu-1816
    James, Mu-1816(2), D-1811, Je-1822
    Joel, Mu-1816
    John, Mt-1798
    Moses, Ge-1805, Bo-1800
    Osburn, Wi-1815
    Peter, Mu-1811
    Robert C., D-1811
    Timothy, D-1811
    William, Ge-1805
REGAN, Ahimas, Bo-1801, Bo-1800
    Benjamin, Bo-1801
    Charles, Bo-1800, Bo-1801
    John, Bo-1800, Bo-1801
REGAR, Jeremiah, Wa-1819
REGIN, Ahymus, Bo-1805
REGISTER, Francis, Ge-1812(2), Ge-1805
REID, Allen, C-1823
    Daniel, Gi-1812
    James, Wi-1815, Bo-1805, Mu-1816
    James Sr., Gi-1812
    Jas. Jr., Gi-1812
    Jesse, Fr-1812
    John, Ge-1805, Gi-1812, Wi-1815
    Lambert, Fr-1812
    Nathan, Fr-1812(2)
    Robert, Wa-1819, Gi-1812
    Robert S., Mo-1825
    Samuel, Bo-1800, Bo-1801
    Thomas, Gi-1812
    William, Gi-1812(2)
RENAU, George, Je-1800
RENDISH, William, Je-1800
RENEAU, Hezekiah, Je-1822

RENEAU, John, Je-1822
RENEAW, Charles, Ct-1798
    John, Ct-1798
RENFORD, James, Mt-1798
RENFRO, James, Gr-1799
    Jesse, Se-1799
    Moses, Mu-1811
    Nack R., D-1811
    Peter, Mu-1811
    Peter, heirs, Mt-1798
    Robert, D-1811
    William, Mu-1811, Mu-1816
RENFROE, Mark, Ro-1805
RENFROW, Bartlett, B-1812
    Joh, Gr-1821
    John, K-1799
RENNOLDS, Elisha, D-1805
RENO, Thomas, Je-1800
RENOE, Francis, J-1802
    George, J-1802
    William, J-1802
RENOLDS, James, Gr-1805
RENSHAW, John, Wl-1804
    Moses, Mo-1825
RENTFRO, John, Mu-1816, Ro-1805
    Joshua, K-1799
    Mark, W-1805, W-1812
    Moses, Mu-1816
    Peter, Mu-1816
    Saml., Ge-1783
    Stephen, W-1812, W-1805
RENTFROE, Joseph, Ro-1805
RESER, John, Ct-1796
RESSER, George, Wi-1815
REUBEN, Norman, Sn-1811
REUBLES, Reuben, Ge-1812
REVES, Elizabeth, Ge-1805
    John, Wi-1810
REXER, William, D-1811
REY, William, Wi-1810
REYLEY, John, Su-1796
    Joseph, Su-1796
REYNOLDS, Aaron, Mu-1816
    Anson, Mu-1811
    Benjamin, Mu-1811
    Elisha, W-1812
    Farney, W-1812
    Henry, Ct-1798
    Isaac, Gi-1812
    James, Wi-1801, Wh-1811, Mo-1825
        Ge-1805
    Joe M., Bl-1815
    John, R-1819
    Joseph, Ge-1805
    Moses, Ct-1796
    Mosses, Ct-1798
    Pryor, Wi-1810, Wi-1815
    Richard, Wi-1815, W-1812, Gr-1804
    Shaver, Hw-1801
    Susannah, Wi-1815
    Thomas, Wi-1815
RGILEY, John, Su-1797
RHEA, David, Wa-1819
    Ezekiel, heirs, Wh-1811
    Ezikiel, J-1802
    Hugh, R-1819, R-1808, Bo-1801,
        Bo-1805, Bo-1800
    James, W-1805, Su-1797, Su-1812
        Bo-1800, Bo-1801
    Jesse, R-1808,
    Jessee, Bo-1801
    John, W-1805, Su-1812, Su-1796,

RHEA, John, cont'd.--Wh-1811, Wa-1814,
        Je-1800, Su-1797, Ge-1812,
        W-1812, Bo-1800(3), Bo-1805,
        Bo-1801
    John, Esq., R-1819
    John, atty., Bo-1801
    Joseph, Su-1797, Su-1812
    Matthew, Su-1812, Su-1796, Su-1797
    Matthew Jr., Su-1812
    Moses, W-1812
    Robert, Bo-1800, Su-1812, R-1819
    Samuel, Su-1812, Ge-1805
    William, Su-1812, Su-1797, Su-1796
    William P., Wh-1825
RHEAMS, John, Je-1822
RHEED, Thomas, Je-1822
RHEY, William, B-1812
RHISDON, Harvey, C-1823
RHOADES, James, Mu-1811
    Tyre, Mu-1811
RHOADHEFFER, George, Su-1812
RHOADS, Henry, Sn-1816
    James, Sn-1811
    John, D-1805
    Samuel, Fr-1812
RHODEN, Bassell, W-1812
    George, W-1812
RHODES, Elijah, Mu-1811
    Elisha, Mu-1816
    George, Bo-1801, Bo-1800
    James Sr., Mu-1816
    James Jr., Mu-1816
    Joshua, Mu-1816
    Stanley, A-1805
    Thomas, Mu-1816
    William, Mu-1816
RHUDOLPH, Jac., Mt-1798
RHUE, Matthw., Ge-1783
RHYMES, Alexander, Fr-1812
RHYMOS, Jessee, Mt-1798
RIBOURN, Edward, K-1799
RICE, Abel, Mu-1816
    Augustus, Je-1822
    Barton, Fr-1812
    Benjamin, Fr-1812
    Benjamin Jr., Fr-1812
    Dangerfield, B-1812
    David, Ge-1805, Ge-1812(2), Je-1822
        Wl-1804, Mu-1811
    Ebenezer, Mu-1811
    Ebenezer Sr., Mu-1816
    Ebenezer Jr., Mu-1816
    Gabriel, Fr-1812
    Henry, Gr-1804, Gr-1799, Gr-1810
    Hiram, Rb-1812
    Jeptha, D-1811
    Jeremiah, Rb-1812
    John, Cl-1803, R-1819, Wl-1804(3),
        Wh-1825
    Joshua, Sn-1811, Sn-1816
    Levi, Gr-1804, Gr-1805
    M. John, Sn-1811
    Nicholas, Mu-1816
    Robert, J-1802, Mu-1816
    Roland, Mu-1811
    Stephen, Ro-1805
    T. B., Wh-1825
    Thomas, Wh-1825
    William, Sn-1816, Wh-1825(2),
        Sn-1811
RICE & MITCHELL, R-1819
RICH, Jacob, Fr-1812

RICH, Joseph, Gr-1821, Gr-1804, Gr-1805
    Thomas, Gr-1799, Fr-1812, J-1802
RICHARD, Blyth, Sn-1811
    Josheua, Su-1797
    Samuel, D-1811
    William, D-1811
RICHARDS, Daniel, Su-1812, Wh-1825
    Elizabeth, Gr-1804
    Evans, Fr-1812
    Gabrial, Ro-1805
    George, Wa-1814
    Henry, Wa-1819(2), Su-1812
    John, Gr-1805, Wh-1825, W-1805,
        W-1812, Su-1812, Gr-1804,
        B-1812, Gr-1799
    Jonathan, Gi-1812, C-1818
    Joshua, Su-1796
    Rebecca, Su-1812
    Richard, Ro-1805, Gr-1821
    Sam., Su-1812
    William, Mu-1816, Wl-1804, Ro-1805
RICHARDSON, Alexander, D-1811
    Allen, D-1811(2)
    Amos, C-1823, C-1818, Mu-1816
    Arcon, C-1823
    Barnard, Wi-1815
    Booker, D-1811
    Brine, C-1818
    Conrod, Wi-1810
    Coonrod, Wi-1815
    Daniel, C-1823, D-1811
    David, C-1823(2), C-1818, Su-1812
    Edward, D-1805
    Elijah, D-1805
    George, C-1818, Cl-1803, C-1823
    James, W-1812, J-1802, D-1805,
        Gr-1805
    James Jr., Gr-1810
    Jane, Mu-1816
    John, C-1823, C-1818, Wi-1815,
        Bo-1801, Bo-1800, Ge-1783,
        Su-1812(2), Wh-1811, Mu-1816(2)
        Mu-1811(2), D-1811
    John Sr., C-1818
    John Jr., C-1823, C-1818
    Kennedy, D-1811
    Laws, C-1818
    Mason, D-1811
    Obadiah, Bo-1801
    Obediah, Bo-1800
    Radford, Wh-1825
    Shadrack, B-1812
    Thomas, C-1823, Mu-1811
    William, J-1802, W-1812, Mu-1816(2)
    Wm., Henry & Elijah, D-1805
    Willis, Mu-1816
    Wyley, Mu-1816
RICHESON, James, Gr-1804
    John, Su-1797(2), Su-1796
    William, Ge-1783
RICHEY, Andew, Bo-1801
    Anthoney, K-1796
    David, Bo-1800
    Gideon, Ge-1783
    James, Bo-1801, Fr-1812
    Thomas, Bo-1801, Bo-1800
RICHLAND, John, Do-1801
RICHMAN, Abner, Wh-1825
    John, Wh-1825, B-1812
    Joshua, D-1805
    Peter, Wh-1825
    William, Wh-1825

RICHMOND, Daniel, Se-1799
    Ebenz., Sn-1816
    Jas., Se-1799
    John, Ge-1805, J-1802
    Jorge, Sn-1816
    Mathew, Se-1799
    William, Mu-1811
RICHMORE, William, Ro-1805
RICHY, William, D-1811
RICKE, Jacob, Mu-1811
RICKER, Frederick, Ge-1812
    George, Ge-1812
    Jacob, Ge-1812
    Peter, Ge-1805, Ge-1812
RICKETS, Micajah, Wh-1825
RICKETT, Francis, D-1805
    John, Je-1822
RICKETTS, Able, Je-1800
RICKEY, William, D-1811
RICKMAN, Mark, J-1802
    Mary, Sn-1811
    Nathan, Sn-1816
    Natl., Sn-1811
    Thomas, Sn-1816
RICORD, George, Wa-1819
    John, Mu-1811, Mu-1816
    Louis, Wa-1819
    Sion, Mu-1811, Mu-1816
RICS, Jacob, Bo-1800
    Richard, Su-1812
    Wm., Bo-1800
RIDDELL, John, W-1805, W-1812
RIDDILE, Bassell, W-1805
RIDDLE, Bassele, W-1812
    Ba le, Ro-1805
    Benjamin, Fr-1812
    Charles, Rb-1812
    Harman, Fr-1812
    Harmon, Fr-1812
    James, R-1808
    Jeremiah, R-1819
    John, Fr-1812, Gi-1819, Je-1822,
        Ro-1805
    RAndolph, Fr-1812
    Zachariah, Je-1822
    Zacharish, Je-1800
RIDDLES, Cornelius, heirs, Wl-1804
RIDEN, George, Sn-1816
RIDENOUR, John, C-1823, A-1805, C-1818
RIDENOUT, Joseph, A-1805
RIDER, John, Bo-1801, Bo-1800
RIDGE, William, Wh-1811
RIDGEWAY, Jonathan, B-1812
RIDGWAY, James, B-1812(2)
    Samuel, B-1812
RIDINGS, Joel, Hu-1812
RIDLEY, George, Wl-1804, D-1805, D-1811,
        Gr-1804, Sn-1787, Gr-1805
    James, Wi-1815
    Moses, Wi-1815
    Oran, Wl-1804
    Thomas, Wi-1810, Wi-1815, Rb-1812
    Vincent, Mu-1811, Mu-1816
    Willis, Mu-1816
RIDLY, Jeremiah, Wh-1825
RIECE, Wm., Ge-1783
RIED, David, Gi-1812
    Elisha, D-1805
    Lambert Sr., Bo-1800
    Lambert Jr., Bo-1800
RIEFF, Henry, Wl-1804
RIELLY, James, Wi-1801

RIELLY, William, Mu-1816
RIEMS, Hennery, Wi-1815
    Martha, Wi-1815
RIGDON, James, Mu-1811, Wi-1801
RIGGINS, John, Fr-1812
    Pouch, C-1823
    Ephriam, Gr-1821
    Thomas, Gr-1821
RIGGLE, George W., R-1819
    Henry, R-1819
    Jacob, R-1819
    John, R-1819
RIGGS, Clisby, Je-1800
    David, Wi-1815
    Edward, B-1812, Je-1800, Je-1822
    Ellis, Gr-1821, Je-1822
    Fall, Wi-1810
    Gilsby, Je-1822
    Isaiah, C-1823, Wa-1819
    Jacob, B-1812
    Jesse, Je-1822
    Jessee, Gr-1799
    Joel, Wi-1801
    John, Sn-1816, Sn-1823, Je-1822
    Moses, Je-1822
    Neuman, Su-1812
    Ninian, Gr-1821
    Reuben, B-1812, Gr-1804, Gr-1799
    Robert, W-1812
    Rubin, Gr-1805
    Samuel, Je-1822
    William, Gi-1812
    Wyly, Je-1822
    Zadoc, Mu-1816
RIGGONS, Henry, J-1802
RIGHT, David, D-1805
    Francis, D-1805, Mu-1811
    Garret, J-1802
    George, Ge-1812
    James, D-1805, Ct-1796, B-1812, Ge-1783
    John, Mu-1811
    Moses, Gr-1821
    Perrin, C-1823
    Robert, Ct-1796
    Rogers, Wh-1825
    Thomas, D-1805, A-1805, Ct-1796
    William, A-1805
RIGHTSELL, John, Je-1822
RIGS, Reuben, Gi-1812, Gi-1819
RIGSBY, Cannady, Wh-1825
    James, Wa-1819, Wa-1814
RIHERD, Jacob, Sn-1811
RILEY, Abram, B-1812
    Benjamin, D-1811
    Edward, B-1812
    Elisha, C-1818
    John, Je-1800
    Joseph, Gi-1812
    Martain, Fr-1812
    Robert, D-1805, A-1805
    Samuel, W-1812
    William, D-1811, B-1812
RILY, Joseph, Gi-1819
    William, Fr-1812
RIMEL, Jacob, Ge-1812
    John, Ge-1812
RIN, Charles, C-1823
    Enoch, C-1823
    George, C-1823
    James, C-1823
RINEHART, Jacob, Ge-1812

RINEHART, Michael, Je-1822, Je-1800
RINEHURST, John, Wa-1819
RING, William, Sn-1816, Sn-1812, Sn-1811
RINGER, George Jr., Ge-1812
RINGO, Cornelius, Ge-1783
RINKER, George, Ge-1805
    George Sr., Ge-1812
    George Jr., Ge-1812
    Philip, Ge-1812
RION, Harris, C-1823, C-1818
    Joseph, C-1823
RIPLEY, Thomas, Ge-1805
RIPLY, Thomas, Ge-1812(2)
RIPPETOE, John, Bl-1815
    William, A-1805, Bl-1815
RIPPEY, James, Sn-1816, Sn-1811
    Jesse, Sn-1816
RISEDON, Abraham, C-1823
RITCHARDSON, James, Ge-1783
RITCHEE, Alexander, Gr-1799
RITCHESON, Abel, Ge-1783
RITCHEY, Alexander, Je-1822
    David, Bo-1801
    Eli, Wa-1814
    James, Je-1822
    John, Je-1822
    Joseph, Je-1800
    Nancy, Je-1822
    Nathaniel D., Je-1822
    Robert, Je-1822, Je-1800
    William, Je-1800, Je-1822
RITCHIE, Alex., Gi-1812
RITSELL, Barbary, Ge-1812
RITTER, Thomas, Sn-1811
RIVERS, Joel, Wi-1801
    Joel T., Wi-1810
RIZER, Christain, D-1811
RIZLEY, Jeremiah, J-1802
RNAGE, Isaac, Wa-1819
ROACH, Absalem, Gr-1821
    Bryant, D-1805
    Drury, Gr-1821
    Elijah, C-1818
    George, Mu-1816, Mu-1811
    Green, Gr-1821
    Isaac, C-1823
    James, Wl-1804
    John, Wl-1804, C-1818, C-1823
    John Jim, C-1818
    Jordan, Je-1800
    Joshua, Gr-1804, C-1818
    Phano, B-1812
    Simon, D-1805
    Sperias, Gi-1812
    Stephen, D-1805, D-1811, B-1812
    William, D-1805, C-1823
ROADES, John, D-1805
ROADMAN, Wm. C., Co-1821
ROADS, Elisha, D-1811
ROAN, George, B-1812
    James, D-1811(2)
    John, Je-18-0
ROANE, Archibald, R-1819
    Hugh, Wl-1804
ROANY, Samuel, Sn-1816
    William, Sn-1816
ROARH, Will., Gi-1812
ROARK, Barney, Fr-1812
    Joshua, Gr-1805
    Owen, Fr-1812
    Timothy, Fr-1812
    William, Fr-1812

ROASE, Jacob, Ge-182
ROB, Jonathan F., heirs, Mu-1816
ROBARDS, William, Wi-1815
ROBB, John, Mu-1816
    Joseph, Sn-1817, Sn-1816
    Robert, Sn-1811
    Samuel, Sn-1811
    William, Wl-1804, Sn-1811(2)
ROBBINS, Aaron, J-1802
    Isaac, A-1805
    John, J-1802
    Jonathan, A-1805
    Michael, A-1805
    Samuel, C-1823
    Thomas, A-1805
    William, C-1823, A-1805
ROBBS, Joseph, Sn-1811
ROBBSON, William, Sn-1816
ROBDY, Thomas, Sn-1816
ROBENET, Moses, Bo-1801
ROBENSON, Caleshan?, Sn-1816
    Daniel, Bo-1801
    Jessee, Sn-1816
ROBERS, John, Ge-1812
ROBERSON, Cornelius, A-1805
    Daniel, Gr-1805
    Daniel Sr., Gr-1805
    David, Sn-1816
    Eligah, Sn-1816
    Jacob, Wh-1825
    James, Bl-1815, Gr-1805
    John, Sn-1811, Wh-1825
    Joseph, A-1805
    Moses, Mu-1816
    Nathan, K-1799
    Thomas L., Wi-1815
    Wm., Bl-1815, A-1805, K-1799
ROBERT, Nathan, Fr-1812
    William, Wh-1825
ROBERTS, Barton, Wh-1825
    Benjamin, Fr-1812, Wi-1810, Wi-1815
    Daniel, Fr-1812
    Edmond, Gr-1799
    Edmund, Ge-1783
    Elias, Ro-1805
    George, Sn-1817, Je-1800, Sn-1816, Sn-1811
    Graham, B-1812
    H. D. F., R-1819
    Henry, Su-1797
    Isaac, Mu-1811, D-1805
    Isaac, Estate, Mu-1816
    Isham, Je-1822
    Jacob, Wh-1811
    James, Bo-1805, Hw-1799(3), Mt-1798, D-1805, Mu-1811
    Jeremiah, D-1811
    Jesse, Rb-1812
    John, Wl-1804, C-1823, C-1818, Bo-1800, Ge-1783, B-1812(2), Sn-1792, Je-1800, Hw-1799, Ge-1812, Ro-1805, D-1811, Wi-1810
    John W., Wh-1825(2)
    Jonas, Gr-1799
    Jonathan, Ge-1783
    Joseph, heirs, Mu-1816
    Joshua, Wl-1804
    Lewis, Su-1812
    Moses, A-1805
    Nathan, A-1805
    Philip, Se-1799

ROBERTS, Phillip, Je-1800
    Richard, Wa-1814(2)
    Richard, deceased, Wa-1819
    Richardson, W-1812, W-1805
    Right, Ro-1805
    Samuel, Fr-1812
    Simon, Su-1812
    Solomon, B-1812
    Stephen, Sn-1817
    Thomas, B-1812, Wi-1815, Ro-1805
    Tom, K*-1815
    Umphery, Wh-1825
    William, Ct-1798, Ct-1796, Gr-1804, B-1812(2), Ro-1805, Wa-1814, Wa-1819, Gr-1805, Su-1796, D-1805, D-1811, Wh-1825
    Willis, B-1812
    Zacheus, Ro-1805
ROBERTSON, Allen, C-1823
    Andrew, W-1812
    Bazel, Gi-1812
    Burrell, B-1812
    Charles, Ge-1783, Wa-1814(2), Wh-1811, Wi-1801, D-1805
    Daniel, Fr-1812, Gr-1805
    Daniel Sr., Gr-1804
    Daniel Jr., Gr-1799, Gr-1804, Gr-1805
    David, Wa-1814(2), D-1805, Mu-1811
    Delina, C-1823
    Duncan, D-1811, D-1805
    Elijah, D-1811, D-1788
    Elisha, B-1812, Hu-1812
    Ezekiel, Gr-1805
    F. Jonathan, D-1805
    Felix, D-1811
    Field, C-1823
    Fielden, C-1818
    Hazekiah, Gi-1812
    Henery, Sn-1792
    Hugh, Fr-1812
    Hughes, Gr-1799
    Iky, Rb-1812
    Isaac, W-1805, W-1812, Fr-1812
    Jacob, Wa-1814, Wh-1811
    James, Gr-1799, Ge-1805, B-1812(2), Wi-1801, Mt-1798, C-1818, Wh-1811, J-1802, Ro-1805, Gi-1812, D-1805(2)
    John, Ge-1805(2), Ct-1798, Gr-1805(2) Fr-1812, Ct-1798, Gi-1819, Ct-1796(2), Gr-1804(3), B-1812, Wl-1804, Gi-1812, Wh-1811, Rb-1812, R-1808, Mu-1811(2), Mu-1816, Wi-1801, D-1805
    John W., Wh-1825
    Jonathan F., D-1811
    Joseph, C-1823, Wh-1811, Rb-1812, D-1788
    Joseph Sr., C-1818
    Joseph Jr., C-1818
    Lazarus, C-1823
    Mack, D-1788
    Mark, dec'd., Wl-1804
    McNiary, D-1811
    Michal, Mu-1811(2)
    Moore, B-1812
    Moses, Mu-1811
    Nathaniel, Fr-1812
    R. Dominick, Mt-1798
    Reubin, Wh-1825

ROBERTSON, Richeson, Gr-1804
    Riddeck, Mu-1816
    Samuel, Wa-1814, D-1805
    Sarah, D-1805
    Stephen, C-1823
    Thomas, Gr-1805(2), Wh-1825
    Thos. L., Wi-1801
    Tyra, Wh-1811
    Wilie, Rb-1812
    William, Ge-1783, Gr-1804, Gi-1812,
        J-1802, Wh-1811, W-1812
    William B., Wi-1815
    William Silvester, Wh-1811
ROBESON, Jesse, Sn-1811
ROBINS, John, Fr-1812
    Wm., Hu-1812
ROBINSON, Alexr., Mu-1816
    Allen, Wa-1819
    B. Eldridge, Mu-1811
    Catharine, Su-1797
    Catherine, Su-1796
    Charles, Wi-1815, Wi-1801
    Daid, Ge-1812
    Daniel, Gr-1821
    David, Ge-1805, Wi-1815, Fr-1812,
        Wi-1810, Mu-1816
    Enoch, Wa-1819
    Fielding, Gr-1821
    Firey, R-1808
    Fleming, R-1819
    George, Ge-1812
    Hugh, Wl-1804
    James, Ge-1805, Fr-1812, W-1812,
        Ge-1812, Wa-1819, Wh-1825,
        Mu-1816, Mu-1811
    James Sr., Ge-1812
    John, Gr-1821, Fr-1812, Wi-1815,
        R-1819, Wi-1801, Wi-1810,
        Mu-1816, D-1811
    John Jr., Ge-1812
    Joseph, K-1799, Wi-1815, Ge-1812(2),
        Ro-1805, Wi-1801
    Matthew, Mu-1816
    Michael, Mu-1816
    Micheal, Wi-1815
    Miles, R-1808
    Mills, Bl-1815
    Moses, Su-1796, Su-1797, Mu-1811
    Nathaniel, B-1812
    Oliver B., Wa-1819
    Robert, Ge-1812
    Samuel, Ge-1812, Mu-1816
    Sterling, Mu-1811
    Thomas, Ge-1805, Gr-1821, Ge-1812,
        Mu-1816, Mu-1811
    Thomas L., Wi-1810
    Valentine Jr., K-1799
    Vol., K-1799
    W., Gr-1799
    William B., Wa-1819
    William P., D-1811
    Winfrey, Gr-1821
ROBISON, John, Wh-1825, Hu-1812, Wi-1810
    Joseph, Wi-1810, Ge-1783
    Moses, Su-1812
    Wm., Ge-1783(2)
ROCKETT, Frances M., Wa-1819
ROCKHOLD, Dorson, Ct-1796
    Francis, Su-1812
    Loyd, Wh-1825
    Thomas, Su-1812, Su-1797
    William, Su-1812

ROCKLEY, Micajah, Wh-1825
ROCKWELL, Dawson, Ct-1798
RODDY, Isaac, Je-1822
    James, Je-1822, Je-1800
    Jesse, A-1805
    Jessee, Gr-1799
    Thomas, Je-1822
RODDYE, Jesse, R-1819
RODEN, Jeremiah, W-1812
    John, W-1812
    Leonard, Gi-1812
    William, W-1812
RODER, William, B-1812
RODES, John H., R-1819
    Tyre, Wi-1801
    Tyree, Mu-1816
    William, Mu-1811
RODGERS, Alexander, Gr-1805, Je-1822
    David, Mu-1816
    Elijah, Wa-1814
    Ezekiel, Wa-1814
    George, Je-1822, Je-1800
    Isaac, Je-1822
    Jacob, Je-1822
    James, Mu-1816, Gi-1812, Je-1822
    James Sr., Ge-1805
    Jane, Guardian William Kelly,
        Ge-1812
    Jesse, C-1818
    John, Mu-1816, Ge-1812(2), W-1812,
        Ge-1805
    John Sr., Gr-1805
    John Jr., Gr-1805, Ge-1805
    Joseph, Mu-1816, Wh-1811, Wa-1814(2)
        B-1812
    Lam., Gi-1812
    Levy, W-1812
    Reuben, Wa-1814(2)
    Robert, Ct-1798, Ct-1796
    Tavener, W-1812
    Ward, Co-1821
    William, Mu-1816, Wi-1801, Wa-1814
RODMAN, John, Gr-1821
ROE, John, Su-1812
ROERTSON, James, Wa-1814
ROGAN, Hugh, Sn-1787
ROGER, Jacob, Mu-1811
    Joseph, Bl-1815
ROGERS, Abraham, Wi-1801, Su-1796
    Al___, Co-1821
    Armstead, Sn-1816
    Armstead Jr., Sn-1816
    Benjamin, C-1823, Bo-1805, Bo-1800
    Cornelius, Mc-1825
    D. Joseph, A-1805
    David, Co-1821, Gr-1799, Su-1812
    Elijah, Wa-1810
    George, Wl-1804
    Green B., Mu-1816
    Henry, Wl-1804, Se-1799
    Isaac, Bo-1801
    Jacob, Mu-1816
    James, Bo-1801, Ro-1805, Gr-1799,
        R-1819, Sn-1811
    Jesse, Bl-1815, Su-1812
    John, Se-1799, A-1805, Co-1821,
        Bo-1800, Bo-1801, Gr-1799(2),
        Rb-1812, Wl-1804, D-1811,
        Mu-1811, Wh-1825, Sn-1811
    John Moss, Sn-1811
    Jonathan, heirs, Sn-1816
    Joseph, B-1812, Bo-1801, Wa-1819,

ROGERS, Joseph, cont'd.--Su-1812, Wh-1825,
        Hu-1812
    Josi..., Se-1799, B-1812
    Lemuel, Sn-1816
    Nicholas, Su-1812, Su-1796
    Paul, Gi-1812
    Reuben, Wa-1819, Bo-1800, Bo-1801
    Samuel, Ge-1805, Wi-1810, Sn-1816
    Samuel J., Mu-1816
    Stanton, Sn-1811
    Stanton, heirs, Sn-1816
    Stephen, Wl-1804
    Tabitha, Sn-1816, Sn-1811
    Thomas, Bo-1801, Bo-1800, Mu-1816
    William, B-1812, Gi-1819, Su-1812,
        Gr-1799, R-1819, Wh-1825(3),
        Wl-1804, Mu-1816, Mu-1811,
        Wa-1819
ROGINS, B. Green, Mu-1811
ROLAND, Balam, D-1811
    Daniel, Fr-1812
    David, Hu-1812
    Elisha, D-1805
    Jacob, Wi-1815
    Jesse, Hu-1812
    John, Sn-1816
    Jordon, D-1811
    Mary, Wi-1815
    William, D-1811
ROLIN, John, Sn-1811
    William, Gr-1805
ROLINSON, David, Wa-1819
ROLLENS, Daniel, R-1808
ROLLER, David, Su-1812
    George, Su-1797, Su-1812
    Jacob, Su-1796
    John, Su-1796, Su-1812, Su-1797
    Martin, Su-1796(in Knox Co.),
        Su-1812, Su-1797(2)
ROLLING, Daniel, R-1819
ROLLINS, Georg, Co-1821
    Hana, B-1812
    Robert, Co-1821
    William, Co-1821
ROLSTON, Alexander, Wi-1810, Wi-1815
    John, Wa-1814
ROMINE, Aaron, Wl-1804
ROMINES, Allen, Gr-1821
    James, Co-1821
    John, Rb-1812
RONAD?, David, B-1812
RONE, George, Mu-1816
    Henry, Mu-1816
    James, Sn-1811, Sn-1816
    James Sr., Sn-1811
    Samuel, Sn-1811
RONEY, Wm., Sn-1811
ROOK, Aaron, Gr-1805
    Benjamin, Mu-1816
    Ezekiah, Gr-1805
ROOKARD, Brown B., Gr-1821
    Thomas, Gr-1821
ROOKS, Aaron, Gr-1804
    Jacob, Mu-1816
ROOLS, Rolley, J-1802
ROONEL, Adam, Fr-1812
ROOP, Frederick, Rb-1812
ROOSE, Ruben, Sn-1811
ROPER, Andrew, Hu-1812
    George, Mu-1816, Wi-1810
    John, Je-1822
    Joseph, Gi-1812, Je-1822

RORAX, Martin, Bo-1801
    William, Je-1800
RORUX, Charles, Ge-1783
ROSBOROUGH, Joseph, Mu-1811
    Samuel, Wl-1804
ROSCO, John, Wh-1825
ROSCOE, Ebenr., Sn-1811
ROSE, Benjamin, Ge-1805, Rb-1812, Wh-1811
    John, Gr-1805, Gr-1804, Wh-1811
    John Jr., Wh-1825
    John Esq., Wh-1825
    John C., Gr-1805
    Joseph, Su-1797
    Rezia, Wh-1811
    Richard, Gr-1805, Mu-1816, Rb-1812
    Taylor, Wh-1825
    William, Wh-1825, Gr-1804
    William Jr., Wh-1825
ROSEBERRY, Robert, D-1811
    Thomas, A-1805
    William, D-1811
ROSEBOROUGH, Joseph, Wi-1801
ROSEN, David, B-1812
    James, Gi-1812
    John, Gi-1812
ROSENBURG, Matthias, Wi-1815
ROSINBUM, Matthias, Wi-1801
ROSS, Adam, Gi-1812
    Benjamin F., Wh-1825
    Daniel, D-1811, D-1805, Wl-1804
    David, Gr-1804, Gr-1805
    David, heirs, R-1819
    Davil, Su-1812
    Ebenezer, D-1805
    Edward, Ge-1812
    Elijah, B-1812
    Ezekiel, Sn-1816, Sn-1811
    Francis, Gi-1819
    Henry, Wl-1804, Gi-1812
    Hugh, Mu-1811
    Isaac, B-1812
    James, Wl-1804, B-1812(2)
    Job, W-1812
    Joel, D-1805
    John, D-1805(2), Wl-1804, Wi-1801,
        D-1811, B-1812(2), Ge-1805,
        Fr-1812, Gi-1819, Bo-1801,
        Ge-1812(2), Wa-1814
    Lenord, Mu-1811
    Patrick, Ge-1805
    Randolph, Wh-1825
    Robert, A-1805, Gi-1819, Gi-1812
    Rubin, Sn-1816
    Ruebin, Wh-1825
    Thomas, Fr-1812
    William, Mu-1811, B-1812, Ge-1805
    William Sr., Ge-1812
    William Jr., Ge-1812
    William T., B-1812
ROSSAN, John, Gi-1819
ROSSEN(Ropers?), Abner, Fr-1812
    James, Fr-1812
ROSSER, David, Rb-1812
ROSSON, Charles, Gi-1819
    John, Rb-1812
ROSSOR, Charles, Gi-1812
ROTAN, William, Wh-1825
ROTTEN, William, J-1802
ROTTOM, Richard M., Wh-1811
ROTTON, Richard M., Wh-1811
    William, Wh-1811
ROTURK, William, Gr-1805

ROUEL, Phillip, Se-1799
ROULSTONE, Mathew, Je-1800
    Moses, Je-1800
    William, Je-1800
ROUND, William, D-1805
ROUNDSIFER, David, Rb-1812
ROUNDTREE, Andrew, Wi-1801, Wi-1815
ROUSAFER, Amous, Wi-1801
ROUNSAVALL, Amos, Wi-1815
ROUTEN, Richard, Wl-1804
ROUTH, James, Mo-1825
    Philip, W-1812
ROW, C. John, Gr-1804
    John, Wa-1819
    Martin, D-1811
    William, Gi-1819
ROWAN, Francis, Ge-1783
    Henry, Gr-1799
    Nathaniel, C-1823
    Samuel, Bo-1800, Bo-1801
ROWAN, William Lackey, Gr-1799
ROWARK, Bernard, Fr-1812
    John, Mo-1825
ROWDEN, Abedaigo, R-1819
    Asa, R-1819
ROWLAND, William, Mt-1798
    William, Balam & Jord n, D-1805
ROWLER, Martin Jr., Su-1796
ROWLICK, William, Wl-1804
ROWLIN, Charles, Fr-1812
ROWLING, Bledham, Sn-1811
ROXEY, Bengamon, Sn-1816
ROY, James, Mo-1825
    John, Wi-1815
    Thomas, Mu-1816
    William, W-1812
ROYSTON, Benjamin, Su-1812
    Susannah, Su-1812
RUAN, Lewis, Wa-1814
RUBLE, Henry, Wa-1814, Wa-1819
    James Banis, Wa-1819
    John, Wa-1814(3), Wa-1819
    John W., Wa-1819
    Paulser, Ge-1805
    Peter, Wa-1814, Wa-1819
RUBY, Henry, Su-1796, Su-1797
    Thomas, Gi-1812
RUCKER, Ambrose, D-1811
    Colby, Gr-1821
    Daniel, Bo-1805
    Edmond, D-1811
    Godeon, Wl-1804
    Henry T., D-1811
    Jerimiah, Mu-1816
    Ruben, D-1811
    William, Wi-1815, Gr-1821
RUCKMAN, Isaiah, A-1805
RUCKS, Josiah, Sn-1811
RUD, James, B-1812
RUDDELL, James, Ge-1783
RUDDER, Robert, Ge-1812
RUDDLE, James, Co-1821
RUE, Lewis, Ge-1805, Je-1800
RUELDS, David, Ge-1812
RUFF, George, Gi-1812
    Henry, Sn-1817
    Jno., Gi-1812
RUHL, Wm., Bo-1801
RUL, George, Gr-1799
RULE, John, Sn-1792
    Peter, Gr-1799
RULEMAN, Joshua, Gi-1812

RULTING, Blake, Se-1799
RUMAGE, Daniel, D-1805
RUMLEY, James, Sn-1816
    William, Sn-1816
RUMMAGE, Daniel, Mu-1811
RUMP, Elijah, A-1805
RUNDLE, Isaac, Gi-1819
RUNELDS, John, Ge-1812
RUNELS, John, Ge-1812
    Joseph Jr., Ge-1812
RUNESS?, Elijah, A-1805
RUNION, Freeman, B-1812
    James, Se-1799
RUNNALDS, John, Hw-1801
RUNNALS, George W., Wh-1825
    John, Gi-1812
    William, Hw-1801
RUNNELLS, Amos, Hw-1801
    David, Ge-1783
    Henry, Ge-1783
    Job, Ge-1783
    William, Ge-1783, A-1805
RUNNELS, Amos Jr., Hw-1801
    Edward, A-1805
    Furney, A-1805
    Glover, Sh-1825
    Henry, Ge-1812, Gr-1799, Ge-1812(3)
        A-1805
    James, Gr-1799
    John, Ge-1812, A-1805
    Joseph, Ge-1812
    Joseph Sr., Ge-1812
    Mathew, Hw-1801
    Samuel, Ge-1812
    Thomas, Hw-1801
    William, Hw-1801
RUNNER, John, Ge-1812
RUNNING, Isaac, Ge-1783
RUNNION, Thomas, Mu-1816
RUNNOLDS, John, Gr-1799
    Richard, Gr-1799
    William, Gr-1799
RUNOLDS, David, Ge-1812
    William, Ge-1812(3)
RUNYAN, Aron, Ge-1812
    William, Mc-1825
RUNYON, Freeman, Je-1800
RUPER, Soloman, B-1812
RUSEL, Elizabeth, Gr-1799
    Samuel, Hw-1799
RUSH, Jesse, Ge-1812, Ge-1805
    Joseph, D-1811
    William, Mu-1816, Mu-1811
RUSHALL, John, Bl-1815
RUSHAM, John, B-1812
RUSHING, Thomas, B-1812
RUSSAM, John, Bo-1801
RUSSEL, Benjamine, Wi-1815
    David, Ge-1783
    Edward, Wi-1815
    James, D-1811, D-1788, Gr-1799(2)
        Bo-1800
    John, Bo-1801
    Philip, Mt-1798
    Pleasant, Wi-1810
    Richard, Mu-1811, Mu-1816
    Samuel, Hw-1801
    William, Mu-1816, Hw-1799
RUSSELL, Abner, Je-1822
    Absalom, Fr-1812
    Alexander, Ge-1805, Ge-1812
    Andrew, J-1802, Su-1797, R-1808

RUSSELL, Anthony, Wa-1819, Wa-1814
    Bryce, Su-1797
    Buckner, J-1802
    David, Je-1800, Gi-1812
    David Sr., Wa-1819, Wa-1814
    David Jr., Wa-1819, Wa-1814
    Edmond, Fr-1812(2)
    George, Fr-1812
    George Sr., Fr-1812
    George Jr., Fr-1812
    George W., Je-1822
    Henry, A-1805, Ge-1783, Fr-1812
    Hezekiah, Ge-1805, Ge-1812
    Hiram, Je-1822
    James, Wh-1825, D-1805, D-1811,
        Mu-1811, Je-1800, Bo-1801,
        Fr-1812, Ge-1812, R-1808
    James & Wm., D-1805
    John, Wi-1815, Fr-1812(3), Ge-1783,
        Wa-1819, R-1808, W-1812,
        Gi-1812, R-1819
    John, Esq., Ge-1812(2)
    John Sr., Gr-179, Fr-1812, Gr-1804
    John Jr., Gr-1804
    John C., Sn-1816
    Joseph, J-1802
    Mathew, Je-1822, B-1812
    Nathaniel, Fr-1812
    Nevis, Fr-1812
    Pleasant, Wi-1815
    Richard, Ct-1798
    Robert, Ge-1805, Gr-1804, Ge-1812
    Samuel, Ge-1805, Fr-1812
    Thomas, D-1811, D-1805, Ct-1796,
        Ge-1812, Wa-1814, Wa-1819,
        Je-1822, Fr-1812, Ge-1805,
        Ct-1798
    William, D-1811, A-1805, Wa-1819,
        Ct-1798, J-1802
    William Sr., Fr-1812
    William Jr., Fr-1812
RUSSET, Jo, B-1812
RUSSLE, Matthew, Bo-1800
    Robert, Wl-1804
    Vance, Bo-1801, Bo-1800
RUST, Joseph, W-1812, W-1805
RUSTER, John, Wa-1819
RUSTIN, Jesse, C-1818
RUTH, Isaac, Gr-1821
    Jacob, Gr-1821
    John, Je-1822
    Samuel, Je-1800
    Stephen, Gr-1821
RUTHERFORD, Ellet, Ge-1805, Ge-1812
    Griffith, Ge-1805, Mu-1816
    Henry, Wi-1815, Wi-1810, Mu-1811
    James, Sn-1816, Sn-1811
    John, Co-1821, Sn-1811
    Noel G., Co-1821
    Thomas, Ge-1783, D-1805
    William, D-1811, C-1823, C-1818
RUTLAND, Blake, Wl-1804
RUTLEDGE, David, Wh-1811
    Elijah, Sn-1823, Sn-1816
    George, Su-1797(2), Su-1812, Su-1796
    Henry, Wh-1825
    Joel, Gi-1812
    John, Wh-1825
    Johnston, Gi-1812
    Peter, Wi-1815
    Robert, B-1812, Wi-1815, Su-1812,
        Su-1797, Su-1796, W-1805

RUTLEDGE, Samuel, Mu-1816
    Samuel J., Gi-1819
    Will, Gi-1812
    William, Wi-1801, Mu-1816
    Wm. S., Gi-1819
RUTLEGE, James, Ge-1805, Mu-1811
    William, Mu-1811
RUTLIN, Reyford, Se-1799
RUTS, William, Je-1800
RUYL, Peter, Wl-1804
RUYLEY, Joseph, Su-1797
RYAL, John, J-1802
RYAN, Butler Thos., Sn-1811
    Charles, R-1819
    Elisha, Sn-1816
    Harris, A-1805
    John, A-1805
    Joseph, Gr-1804, Wi-1815
RYDLY, James, Wi-1801
RYE, Thomas, Su-1812
RYHERD, Jacob, Sn-1816
RYLAND, John, Wa-1819
    Sylvester, Wa-1819, Wa-1814
RYLEY, Andrew, Su-1812
RYNHART, Lewis, Su-1812
RYON, Henry, Je-1800
    Joseph, Gr-1805
    Wm., Ge-1783
RYSTON, Benjamin, Su-1797
    Joshua, Ct-1798
RYSTONE, Benjamin, Su-1796
    John, Su-1797
SABURY, Thomas, Su-1796
SADDELER, John, Sn-1792
SADLER, John, Wi-1815, Sn-1792
    Thomas, D-1811
SAGE, John, Mu-1816, Mu-1811, Wl-1804
SAIL, Elias, W-1812
    James, W-1812
SAILERS, Leonard, Wh-1825
    William, Wh-1825
SAILES, Thomas, Bl-1815
SAILING, Henry, B-1812
    Peter, B-1812
SAILOR, Godfree, Ge-1812
    John, Wa-1814, Wa-1819
SAILS, John, W-1812
    William, Rb-1812
SAINS, Warren, Ro-1805
ST. JOHN, Joseph, Ge-1812
SALLEY, John, Gr-1805
    Joseph, Gi-1812
SALLY, John, Gr-1799, Gr-1821(2)
SALMON, James, Mt-1798
    John W., Fr-1812
SALOR, William, Ge-1812
SALTER, Robert, C-1818, Wa-1819
SALTS, Andrew, Wa-1819
    Daniel, Wa-1819
    John, Wa-1814, Wa-1819, W-1812
SALVADG, Jesse, W-1812
SAM, Tidons, W-1812
SAMAR, Gahlant, Sn-1787
SAMMONS, Micajah, Wa-1814
SAMONS, Newel, Wi-1815
SAMPLE, David, Ge-1805
    James, D-1811
    John, Wi-1815(2), Wi-1810
    Mathew, Je-1800
    Moses, Je-1800
    Robert, D-1811, Wi-1815
    Robert Jr., D-1811

SAMPLE, Robert, James & John, D-1805
    Samuel, A-1805, Ge-1783
    Thomas, Wi-1815
    William, Je-1800, Ge-1783, Wi-1815,
        Wi-1810, Mu-1816
    Wm., heirs, Sn-1811
SAMPLES, David, Ge-1812
    Moses, Je-1822
    Robert, Ge-1805, Ge-1812
    Ruth, Ge-1812
    William, Wa-1819, W-1812
SAMPSON, David, C-1823
    Elijah, Je-1822
    Emanuel, Su-1812, Su-1796, Su-1797
    James, W-1812
    John, Wa-1814
    Richard, Wi-1810
SAMS, Edmund, Su-1812
    John, Su-1812
    Little B., Su-1812
    Obed, Su-1812
SAMUEL, Baker, Gr-1799
    John, Gi-1819
    Steven, Gi-1819
SAMUELS, Anthony, Gi-1812
SAND, Benjamin, Wa-1814
    Isaac, Wa-1814(2)
SANDER, Jacob, Gr-1799
    John, Ge-1812
SANDERS, Andrew, Rb-1812
    Daniel, Rb-1812
    David, R-1819, B-1812
    Edward, Wl-1804, D-1805, Mu-1816
    Elisha, Wl-1804
    Francis, D-1805, D-1811
    Franklin, D-1811
    Gabriel, Rb-1812
    George, B-1812(2)
    Harris, D-1811
    Henry, B-1812
    Hubbard, Sn-1816
    Isaac, Fr-1812
    James, Fr-1812, D-1811, Wl-1804,
        Sn-1816(2), Mu-1816, Sn-1811
    John, Su-1812, Wa-1814, D-1811
    Joshua, D-1811
    Julias, D-1788
    Luke, Wl-1804
    Nathaniel, Wl-1804
    Peter, B-1812
    Philip, Gr-1799
    Reubin, Fr-1812
    Richard, Sn-1811
    Robert, Sn-1816, Sn-1811
    Roberts, Rb-1812
    Samuel, Wi-1815
    Solomon, Fr-1812
    Thomas, Wl-1804
    Thomas G., Sn-1823, Sn-1816
    Tom G., Sn-1811
    William, Rb-1812, D-1811, Sn-1811(2)
        Wl-1804, D-1805
SANDERSON, Edward, Sn-1816
    Jeremiah, Mu-1816
    William, D-1805
SANDFORD, James T., Mu-1816
    Joseph, Mu-1816
    Samuel, J-1802
SANDIFER, Abraham, D-1811
SANDS, Benjamin, Wa-1819
    Edmund, Ct-1798
    Joseph, Ct-1798, Ct-1796, Wa-1819

SANDS, Michael, Mu-1816
    Michal, Su-1797, Su-1796
    Othaniel, Wa-1819
SANFORD, James, Wi-1815, Mu-1811, Wi-1815
SAPINGTON, John, Wi-1801
    Richard, Li-1812*
    Rober B., Wi-1801
SAPP, Benjamin, Wh-1825
    John, R-1819
    Walker, Bl-1815
SAPPINGTON, B. Roger?, D-1805
    John, Wi-1815
    Roger B., D-1811
    Thos., Wi-1801, Su-1812
SARATT, Joseph, Ge-1783
SARGANT, Johnston, Fr-1812
SARGEN, Abraham, Ge-1812
SARGENT, Aaron, Fr-1812
    James, Fr-1812
    Temple, Fr-1812
    Wm., Wi-1815, Fr-1812
SARREN, Joseph, W-1812
SARRET, Milton, B-1812
SARTAIN, Harrison, Fr-1812
    John, K-1799
SARTHERDALE, James, Ro-1805
SARTIN, David, A-1805, C-1823, C-1818
    John, A-1805, Je-1822
    White, C-1818
    Wright, C-1823
SARVER, George, Sn-1811
    Henry, Sn-1811
    Jeremiah, Sn-1811
    John, Sn-1816, Sn-1811
SASSEEN, Randolph, Je-1822
SATATHITE, David, Bo-1800
SATERFIELD, Peter, Gi-1812
SATERTHITE, David, Bo-1801
SATTERFIELD, Elizabeth, Gr-1821
    John, Gr-1821
    Martin, Gr-1821
SAULS, Henry, Wh-1825
    William, Su-1812
SAUNDER, James, D-1811
    John, D-1811
SAUNDERS, Edward, D-1811
    Eliho, Wh-1811
    George, Wh-1811, Gi-1812
    Henry, Su-1797
    Isaac, Rb-1812
    James, W-1812, Se-1799
    Jesse, Su-1797
    John, W-1805(2), Gr-1805, Gr-1804,
        Su-1797, W-1812, Gr-1821,
        Su-1796
    John Sr., W-1812
    Jos., Mu-1811
    Stonford, Gr-1821
    Turner, Wi-1815, Wi-1810
    Will, W-1812
    William, W-1805, W-1812
SAVAGE, Benjamin, Ct-1798
    Joshua, Rb-1812
    Michael, Gr-1799
    Thomas, Rb-1812
    William, Gr-1799
SAVLEY, John, Sn-1816
SAWYEARS, Robert, Wi-1801
SAWYER, Sampson, B-1812
SAWYERS, Samuel, D-1811
    William, Gi-1812
SAY, Matthew, Rb-1812

SAY, William, D-1805, B-1812
SAYERS, Foster, D-1811
    Robert, Wi-1815, Wi-1810
SAYLOR, Daniel, Fr-1812
SAYLORS, Moses, Fr-1812
SCAGGS, Solomon, W-1812
    William, Je-1822, Ge-1812
SCAGS, Charles, Gi-1812
    John, Gi-1812
    Thos., Gi-1812
SCALES, Henry, Wi-1810
    John Sr., Wh-1825
    Joseph H., Wi-1815
    Nicholas, Wi-1810, Wi-1815
SCARBRO, David, A-1805
    James, A-1805
    John, A-1805
    Samuel, A-1805
    William, A-1805
SCARBROUGH, James, Wh-1811, K-1799, Wh-1825
    Robert, K-1799
    William, K-1799, Wh-1825
SCEARFE, Jessee, W-1812
SCEEDING, Benjamin, Ge-1812
SCHELL, Andrew, Su-1796
    Arnold, Su-1796
    Frederick, Su-1796
    Joseph, Su-1796
SCHOOLBRID, David, C-1818
    James, C-1818
SCHOOLER, John, B-1812
    Nathan, B-1812
SCHULTZ, Jacob, Su-1796
    Joseph, Ct-1796
SCISCO, Simion, B-1812
SCOBY, James, Wl-1804
    Joseph, Sn-1811, Sn-1816
SCOGGIN, Jessee, Wh-1825
    John, Wh-1825(2)
    William, Sn-1811
SCOGGINS, Humphrey, Fr-1812
    Jonah, A-1805
    William, Sn-1816, Sn-1823
SCOGGON, Jesse, Wh-1811
    John, Wh-1811
SCONCE, Robert, Wi-1815
SCOOT, James, Sn-1816
SCOOTE, John, Wh-1825
SCOT, Absalom, Ct-1796
    Elias, Sn-1792
    Hannah (Wd), Gi-1819
    Jacob, Mu-1811
    James, Mu-1811
    John, Esq., Su-1796
    Joseph, Mu-1811
    Simon, Rb-1812
SCOTT, Abner, Sn-1811
    Abraham, Mu-1811
    Absalom, Ct-1798
    Adam, Ge-1783
    Alexander, Gi-1812
    Andrew D., D-1811
    Archibald, D-1811
    Charles, Gr-1804
    David, Wh-1825
    Dennis, Gr-1805
    Edward, Gr-1804, Gr-1805
    Eli, B-1812
    Elias, Wi-1810
    Francis, D-1805
    George, Wh-1825, Sn-1816
    Goodman, Gr-1821

SCOTT, Hartwell, D-1805
    Isaac, Wi-1815, D-1811(man of
        colour)
    Jacob, Wi-1801
    Jacob, Esq., Mu-1816
    James, K-1796, Wl-1804(2), Wh-1825,
        Mu-1816(2), Sn-1811, Wi-1815,
        Sn-1823, Je-1800, Bo-1800,
        Bo-1801, B-1812, Ro-1805,
        Ge-1812, Ge-1805
    Jarrot, W-1812
    Jesse, B-1812
    Jessee, Ge-1812
    John, Wi-1801, Wi-1810, Mu-1811,
        Wl-1804, B-1812(2), Gi-1812,
        Su-1797, Su-1812(2)
    John, sister of, Su-1812
    Jonathan, Wh-1825, Wh-1811
    Joseph, Mu-1816, Su-1812
    Lucy, D-1805
    Marmaduke, Mt-1798
    Micajah, Wh-1825
    Patrecek, B-1812
    Pleasant, Wi-1815
    Ricard, Gi-1819
    Richard, Wi-1801, Wl-1804
    Robert, D-1811, Mu-1811, Gi-1812
    Samuel, D-1811(2), Mu-1811, Mu-1816
        D-1805, Su-1812
    Thomas, D-1811, Wi-1815
    William, D-1811(2), Wi-1801, Wh-1825
        Wl-1804, Fr-1812(2), Wi-1815,
        Bo-1805, Su-1797, Ro-1805,
        Su-1812
    William Sr., D-1805
SCRIBNER, Lewis, Mu-1811
SCRIVENGER, James, Je-1822
SCROGGINS, Barton, Gr-1799
    Benjamin, Wa-1819
    Sterling, Je-1822
SCRUGGS, Drury, D-1811
    Finch, D-1805, Wi-1815
    Gross, D-1811
    Hartwell, Wh-1825
    James, C-1818
    John, A-1805, Wi-1815
    Julius, Ge-1805
    Langhorn, D-1811
    Mary, Wi-1815
    Mayfield, D-1811
    Richard, Ge-1812, Ge-1805
    Thomas, D-1811
    Walfield, D-1811
    William, Ge-1812
SCRUGS, Theophelus, D-1811
SDERMAN, William, Su-1812
SEABORN, John, Bl-1815
SEABOURN, Benjamin, D-1811
SEAGRAVES, Bennet, Mu-1816
    Isaac, Mu-1816
    Vincent, Mu-1816
SEAHORN, George, R-1819
SEAL, Hartwell, D-1811
    John, Co-1821
SEALES, Henry, Gi-1819
SEALS, Anthony, Je-1822
    James, Rb-1812
    Jeremiah, Gr-1804
    John Jr., Wh-1825
    Thomas, Je-1822
    William Sr., Wh-1825
    Yoberg, Wh-1825

SEALS, Zachariah, Wh-1825
SEAMORE, Cardwell, Gr-1821
    James, Gr-1821
SEANS(Leans?), John, K-1799
SEAR, Henry, Mt-1798
SEARCY, Bennet, Mt-1798, D-1805
    John, Se-1799
    Reuben, Sn-1811
    Richard, Se-1799(2)
    Robert, Wl-1804(2), Mt-1798, D-1805, D-1811
    Will., Wl-1804
    William, D-1805
SEAREMOHORN, John, J-1802
SEARLOCK, John, Gr-1799
SEARLY, Jeremiah, c-1818
SEARS, John, Bl-1815
    William, Gr-1821
SEAT, Henry, D-1811
    Joseph, D-1811
    William P., D-1811
    Willis, Wl-1804
SEATE, Joseph, D-1811
SEATER, James Sr., Ro-1805
    James Jr., Ro-1805
    Mosses, Ro-1805
SEATON, Jessee, D-1805
    Thomas, Gr-1799
    Emanule, Wi-1815
    Green, D-1811
    Littleton, D-1811
SEAVERN, George, Su-1812
SEAVERS, George, Su-1796, Su-1797
SEAWELL, Benjamin, Sn-1811, D-1811, Sn-1816
    John, heirs, Wl-1804
    John B., D-1811
    Thomas, Wl-1804, D-1811
    William, D-1811
SEBASTIAN, Saml., B-1812
SEBASTION, Robert, Sn-1811
SEBASTON, Joseph, Sn-1816
SEBOLT, David, Mc-1825
SECREST, Francis, Mu-1816
SECRO, Abraham, Wi-1815
SEDGLEY, Isom, D-1805
SEDUSCUSS, Emanuel, Ge-1783
SEEBURN, Edward, Je-1800
    John, Je-1800
SEEHORN, Gabriel, Je-1800
    John, Je-1800
    Nancy, Wa-1814
SEEMORE, Henry, R-1808
    William, R-1808
SEERS, John, Ge-1812
SEET, Gerret, Sn-1811
SEETE, Jarred, Sn-1816
SEGLER, John, Rb-1812
    Philip, Gr-1805
SEGUSH?, William, B-1812
SEHORN, Alexander, Je-1822
    Cathy, Je-1822
    John, Je-1822
    Lovisca, Je-1822
SEIK, Jacob, Rb-1812
SEISM, Thomas, Wl-1804
SELAH, George, Wh-1811
SELF, Daniel, Ro-1805
    Hezekiah, Bl-1815
    Jesse, Bl-1815, Ge-1812
    Levy, Bl-1815
    Malchizadick, Wl-1804

SELF, Spencer, Bl-1815
    Thomas, Ge-1812(2), Ge-1805
    Willis, Wi-1810
SELLARDT, Nathan, Je-1800
    Samuel, Je-1800
SELLARS, Isaac, Mu-1816
    James, Mu-1816
    John, Mu-1811(2), Mu-1816
    Robert, Mu-1816
    Samuel, Je-1822(2)
    Thomas, Mt-1798
    William, Mu-1816
SELLERS, Charles, Sn-1811
    Drury, W-1812
    Edward, Je-1822
    Gorden, W-1812
    Howell, Rb-1812
    Isaac, Mu-1811
    James, Mu-1811
    John, W-1812, Je-1800
    Larkin, Rb-1812
    Mathew, W-1812
    Nathan Sr., Je-1822
    Peters, Ge-1812
    Robert, Wi-1810, Mu-1811
    Thomas, Rb-1812
SELLS, Henry, Su-1812
    Solomon, Su-1796
SELMAN, Eli, Fr-1812
    John, B-1812
    Stafford, Fr-1812
SELMON, Abner, Fr-1812
    Eli Jr., Fr-1812
    Thomas, Fr-1812
    Thomas Jr., Fr-1812
    Wiley, Fr-1812
SELVAGE, James, Je-1822
    Jeremiah, Gr-1805, Gr-1799
    Michael, Gr-1805
SELVIDGE, Jeremiah, Gr-1804
    Michael, Gr-1804
SEMLOCK, William, Wh-1825
SENCKER, Elias, Su-1812
SENTER, Drury, Ge-1812
    Freeman, Sn-1811
    Stephen, Gr-1821
    Tandy, Gr-1804
    W. Stephen, Gr-1804
    William, Ge-1812
    Willis, Gr-1799
SERAT, James, C-1823
SERATT, Elijah, Je-1822
    Thomas, Je-1822
SERCEY, Rubin, Sn-1816
    Richard, Sn-1816
SERES, Bennet, R-1808
SERHAM, Agnes, Wa-1819
SERICEE, John, Sn-1811
SERIN, James, Wa-1819
SERTAIN, Jacob, Ge-1783
    James, Fr-1812
SERVOR, Henry, Sn-1816
SESSAM, Turner, Fr-1812
SESSTAN, Milhal, Bo-1800
SETON, Roswell, Gi-1819, Mu-1816
SETZLER, John, Su-1812(2)
    William, Su-1812(2)
SUEDDER, Nathaniel, Se-1799
SEVERTON, John, Fr-1812
    Moses, Fr-1812
SEVIER, Abraham, Ct-1798, Ct-1796
    James, Wa-1814

SEVIER, John, J-2803
    John Jr., Ct-1796
    Joseph, Ct-1798, Ct-1796
    Susanah, Ge-1812
    Valentine, Ge-1812, Ge-1805
    Valentine Sr., Ct-1798
    Valentine Jr., Ct-1798
    W. V., K*-1815
SEVIR, John Cook, Fr-1812
SEWEL, Abraham, Ct-1796, Ct-1798
    Dawson, Ct-1798
    Joseph, Ct-1798, Mu-1811
SEWELL, Joseph, Mu-1816
    Samuel, Mu-1816
SEXTON, Aron, C-1818
    Timothy, C-1818
    William, C-1818, Je-1800
SEYMORE, William, R-1819
SHACKLEFID, Thoms., D-1805
SHACKELFORD, Lewis Sr., Ge-1812
    Thomas, D-1811
    William, Je-1822
SHADDEN, Alexander, Je-1800
    James, Je-1822
    James Jr., Je-1800
    Joseph, Je-1822
    Thomas, Je-1800
    William, Je-1800, Je-1822
SHADDIN, Robert, Ro-1805
SHADDING, Joseph, Wh-1811
SHADDON, Joseph, A-1805
SHADEN, John, Gi-1819
SHADICK, Martin, Hu-1812
SHADLEY, Jacob, B-1812
SHADRICK, James, Mt-1798
    Joseph, Gr-1821
SHAFER, Frederick, Ge-1812
    John, Ge-1812(4)
    Philip, Isaac & Ann, D-1805
SHAFFER, Frederick, Ge-1805
    Josiah, Rb-1812
    Richard, D-1788
SHAIFER, K. Abraham, Sn-1811
SHAKLE, Jacob, Fr-1812
SHALL, Christian, Ro-1805
SHALLY, Luke, Ge-1783
SHALPHIN, Michael, B-1812
SHANE, John, D-1811
    Morris, D-1805
    Robert, Gi-1812, Sn-1816
SHANKLE, George, Fr-1812
    Jacob, Fr-1812
    John, Fr-1812
SHANKLIN, Jesse, Rb-1812
SHANKS, Daniel Sr., Hu-1812
    Daniel Jr., Hu-1812
    Holden, Ge-1805
    Joseph, Wa-1814
    Moses, Wa-1814
    Nicholas, Ge-1812, Je-1800
    William, Wl-1804, Wa-1814
SHANNEL, John, Wh-1825
SHANNON, David, Wi-1801, Gi-1812, Wi-1815, Mu-1816
    Georg, Wi-1801, Wi-1810, Wi-1815
    James, Ge-1812, Hu-1812, Wi-1801
    John, Wa-1814(2), Ge-1812, A-1805, Sn-1816
    Joseph, D-1805, Gr-1821
    Quinton, Gi-1819, Gi-1812
    Robert, D-1811, Wl-1804, Wi-1801
    Robt. W., Wi-1815

SHANNON, Samuel, D-1805, D-1811, Wi-1801, Wl-1804, Rb-1812
    Thos., Mu-1816, Mu-1811, Wi-1815, D-1788, Wi-1801
    Thos. & Robert, D-1805
    William, Ge-1805, Gi-1812, Mu-1811, Ge-1812
SHANNON & SAWYERS, Mu-1816
SHANON, David, D-1788
    Henry, Wl-1804
    Joseph, Ge-1812
    Saml., D-1788
    William, Ge-1812(2)
SHARLOCK, John, Sn-1816
SHARP, Aaron, A-1805, Gr-1805
    Amos, Gr-1821
    Anthony, Wi-1801, Sn-1811, Wi-1806, Sn-1792
    Aron, Gr-1805, C-1823, C-1818, Gr-1804
    Balam, Ge-1812
    Carlos, Gi-1812
    Conrad, C-1818
    Conrod, C-1823, Gr-1799
    Daniel, Bl-1815
    David, Gr-1821
    Dr., Sn-1816
    Edward, Mu-1811
    Ezekiel, Wl-1804
    George, Mu-1811, C-1818, A-1805, C-1823, Gr-1799
    Henry, Mu-1811, A-1805, C-1818, C-1823, Gr-1799, Mu-1816
    Isham, C-1823, C-1818
    Jacob, C-1823, C-1818(3), Gr-1799
    James, D-1805, Fr-1812, C-1818, C-1823
    James B., Je-1822
    James D., D-1811
    John, Gr-1805(2), K-1796, C-1823, Gr-1804(2), Bo-1800, C-1818(3) Bo-1801, A-1805, C-1823, Gr-1799, Gr-1821, Gr-1805
    Joseph, A-1805, Wl-1804, C-1823, Gr-1799
    Joshua, Mu-1816
    Leroy, Bl-1815
    Martin, C-1823
    Meredith, Gr-1821
    Moses, Gr-1821
    Nahemiah, Mu-1816
    Nehemiah, Mu-1811
    Nicholas, C-1823, Gr-1804
    Peter, C-1823
    Richard, C-1818, Fr-1812
    Richard Sr., C-1818
    Robert, Wi-1815, Sn-1792
    Russell, C-1823
    Samuel, Gr-1821
    Thomas, Gr-1805, Mt-1798, Gr-1804, Ge-1812, Gr-1805
    Turner, Ge-1812
    William, A-1805(3), Mu-1811, Mu-1816 Ct-1796, C-1818, Bl-1815, C-1823, Gr-1821
SHARPE, James, B-1812
    John, Su-1797(2), Su-1796(2)
    Josiah, B-1812
    William, B-1812, Ro-1805
SHARPES, John, Su-1812
SHATTER, George, C-1818
    Martin, C-1818

SHAVER, Daniel, Sn-1811
    David, Su-1812, Sn-1816
    Jacob, Wh-1825
    John, Sn-1823, Ge-1812, Sn-1816,
        Sn-1811
    John Sr., Sn-1811
    Joseph, Sn-1811
    Michael, Sn-1787
    Peter, Sn-1811
SHAW, Alexander, Wi-1815, Wi-1810
    Basel, Sn-1811
    Benjamin, Gr-1804, Gr-1805, Gr-1799
    Christopher, B-1812
    George W., Mu-1816
    Henry G., D-1811
    Hugh, D-1805
    Jacob, Wa-1814
    James, B-1812, Rb-1812(2), Je-1822,
        J-1802, D-1805, Mu-1816,
        Sn-1811
    Jesse, Sn-1811
    John, J-1802, Ge-1805, D-1805,
        Mu-1816, D-1811, Mt-1798
    Joseph, J-1802, D-1805, D-1788
    Josn, Gr-1799
    Levi, Mu-1816
    Louisa C., Mu-1816
    Michal, Su-1797, Su-1796
    Nathaniel, Wi-1815, Wi-1810
    Robert, Sn-1792(2), Sn-1811(2)
    Samuel, Bo-1800, Bo-1801, D-1805,
        Mu-1816, Wi-1801
    Thomas, Mu-1816, D-1805, Rb-1812
    Timothy, Wi-1815
    Torrence, D-1811
    William, Wh-1811, Rb-1812, D-1805,
        Mu-1816, Wl-1804
    William Jr., D-1805, Mu-1816
SHAYGLEY, Rachel, Mu-1816
SHEA, Morgan, Wa-1819
SHEALDS, James, Mu-1811
SHEALS, William, Fr-1812
SHEARLACK, Zaddock, D-1805
SHEASTEN, William, Wh-1825
SHECKAL, Martin, Fr-1812
SHEEN, James, Bo-1800
    Jesse, Sn-1816(2)
    William, Mu-1816
SHEETS, Jacob, Bo-1801
SHEFFER, George, Ge-1812
SHEKILL, John, Sn-1811
SHELBURN, James, Wi-1815, Wi-1810
    John B., Wi-1815
    Samuel, Wi-1810
    Sammuel, Wi-1815
SHELBY, Catharine, Su-1812(2)
    David, Sn-1792, Sn-1787, Gi-1812,
        Wl-1804, Mt-1798, Mu-1811,
        Sn-1811, Mu-1816
    Evan, Mu-1816
    Isaac, Sn-1792, Su-1796, Su-1797
    John, Mt-1798
    John Sr., Su-1797, Su-1796
    John Jr., Su-1797, Su-1796
    Joseph, Gr-1804
    Thomas, Mu-1816, Su-1812
    William, Mu-1816, Sn-1811
SHELL, Aaron, Su-1812
    Andrew, Su-1797, Su-1812
    Arnold, Su-1797, Su-1812
    Christian, K*-1815, W-1805
    Christion, W-1812

SHELL, Frederick, J-1802
    Fredrick, Su-1797
    Joseph, Su-1797, Su-1812
SHELLEY, David, Wi-1801
    Joseph, Gr-1805
SHELLY, James, Ge-1812, Ge-1805
    Jeremiah, Je-1800
    Joseph, Gr-1805
    Nathan, Je-1800, Je-1822
    Peter, Su-1796
    Thomas, A-1805
    William, D-1811
    Heirs of, Mt-1798
SHELTERS, George, A-1805
SHELTIN, Steven, Gr-1799
SHELTON, Armstead, Wa-1819
    Je-1822
    Bennett, Wi-1815
    Clever, Je-1822
    David, Gr-1799
    Eli, Je-1822
    Ezekiel, Gr-1804
    Gabriel, K-1799
    George, Mu-1816
    Gilbert, Hu-1812
    Godfrey, D-1811(2)
    Jesse, D-1811
    Joel, Gr-1804
    John, Wl-1804, Gr-1805, Mu-1816
    John M., Je-1822
    Nelson, Gr-1804, Gr-1799
    Noah Y., Je-1822
    Palatian, K-1799
    Ralph, Gr-1804, Gr-1799, Gr-1821,
        Gr-1805
    Richard, Gr-1804, Gr-1799, Gr-1805
    Stephen, Gr-1805, Gi-1819, Mu-1811
    Thomas, Gi-1812, Je-1800
    William, Gr-1804, Gr-1799, D-1811,
        Wh-1825, Gr-1805
    Wiliam Sr., Wh-1825
    William Jr., Wh-1825
    William H., D-1811
    Heirs, Wl-1804
SHELY, Catharine, Su-1796
SHENALL, Isaac, Je-1800
SHENAULT, James, B-1812
SHEPARD, Isaah, D-1805
    John, A-1805
SHEPHERD, Abraham, Wh-1811
    John, Wh-1811
    John, Fr-1812, Wi-1810, Wh-1825
    Lewis, Wi-1815
SHEPLEY, Edward, Gr-1799
SHEPPARD, James, Sn-1787
    John, D-1811, Sn-1811
SHEPPERD, Benjamin, J-1802
    Nancy, J-1802
SHERANCY, William, Wa-1819
SHERD, James, Fr-1812
SHERELL, Adam, Ro-1805
    Charles R., Bl-1815
    George, Fr-1812
SHERELOCK, John, Sn-1811
SHERER?, Christian, Mu-1816
SHERFEY, Joh, Wa-1814
    Samuel, Wa-1814
SHERILL, Ambros, Wl-1804
    Ambrose, Wi-1815
SHERIRTZ, Conrad, Su-1812
    Henry, Su-1812
    John, Su-1812

SHERLEY, Balser, Gr-1821
    Champion, Wh-1825
    John, Gi-1812, Gr-1821
SHEROD, William, Fr-1812
SHERON, James, B-1812
    Thomas, B-1812
SHEROOM?, Isaiah, W-1812
SHERRAD, Joel, Mu-1811
SHERREL, Abraham, Wh-1811
    John, Bo-1801
    Uty, Mu-1811
SHERRELE, Uriah, Bo-1805
SHERRELL, Able, Wl-1804
    Abraham, Wh-1825
    Alex., W-1812, W-1805
    Elin, Wh-1825
    Jesse, Bl-1815
    Neel, Wl-1804
    W. Saml., Wl-1804
SHERRIL, Adam, Ge-1783
    Elisha, Ge-1783
    John, Ge-1783
    Phillip, Ge-1783
    Saml. Sr., Ge-1783
    Saml. Jr., Ge-1783
SHERRILL, Abraham, Ge-1805
    Ephraim, Wl-180
    Isaac, Ge-1805
    Jacob, Wl-1804
    Jesse, Ro-1805
    John, Wh-1825
    Rewbin, Wl-1804
    Samuel, Fr-1812
    Thomas, Wa-1819
    William, R-1808
SHERROD, John, Rb-1812, Bo-1800
SHERROL, John, Bo-1800
SHESON, John, W-1812
SHETLER, George, A-1805
SHEWBEARD, Charles, Je-1822
SHEWMAKE, Johnson, Wi-1815
SHEWMAKER, Blakely, K-1799
SHIELD, David, Wa-1814
    John, D-1811
LYSANDER, Gi-1812
    William, Wa-1814
SHIELDS, David, Wa-1819
    George, Gi-1812, Ge-1805
    Henry, Ge-1805, Wa-1814(2), Ge-1812,
        Wa-1819
    James, Ge-1805, Ge-1812(2), Mu-1816
    John, Je-1822(3)
    John Sr., Je-1800
    John Jr., Je-1800
    Joseph, Wa-1814, Wa-1819
    Richard, Se-1799
    Robert, Bo-1801
    Saml., Gi-1812
    Thomas, Wa-1819
    Thomas Jr., Ge-1805
    William, Je-1800, Ge-1805, Ge-1812,
        Wa-1819, Gr-1804, Gr-1805(2)
    William P., Mu-1816
SHIEN, Abraham, B-1812
SHILLER, Isaac, D-1811
SHILLY, James, Wi-1810
SHILTON, Christian E., R-1819
SHINAULT, James, B-1812
    Walter, Bl-1815
    William, B-1812
SHINLIVER, Charles, A-1805
SHIP, William, Rb-1812

SHIPE, Peter, K-1796
SHIPLEY, Adam, Gr-1821, Wa-1819
    Benjamin, Wa-1819(3), Wa-1814,
        Su-1812
    Edward, Gr-1804
    Eli, Su-1797, Su-1796
    Elizabeth, Su-1812
    Ely, Su-1812
    James, Wa-1819, Wa-1814
    Jesse, Wa-1819
    John, Je-1822, Su-1797, Su-1812,
        Wa-1819, Su-1796
    John Jr., Su-1797
    Nathan, Wa-1814, Wa-1819
    Parker, Su-1812
    Peter, Wa-1819(2), Wa-1814
    Richard, Su-1797, R-1819
    Saml., Su-1797, Su-1796, Su-1812
    Thomas, Gr-1821, Gr-1805
    Varner, Gr-1821
SHIPLING, Thomas, Mu-1816
SHIPMAN, Abraham, Fr-1812
    DAniel, B-1812
    David, B-1812
    Jacob, W-1812
    James, B-1812
SHIPPEN, Thomas, Rb-1812
    Whilliam, Wa-1819
SHIPPMAN, Christopher, B-1812
SHIRTE, Henry, Su-1812
SHIRLEY (Shurly?), Champ, Wh-1811
    John, Wh-1811
SHIST, John, K-1799
SHIVERS, James, Rb-1812
    Jonas, D-1811
    Thomas, D-1811
SHTENBERG, Margot, Ge-1812
SHOCKLEY, Booker, Wh-1825
    Caleb, Gr-1804
    Calib, Gr-1805
    Isaac Sr., Wh-1825
    Isaac J., Wh-1825
    Isaiah, Gr-1804
    Isham, Wh-1811, Gr-1804
    Isiah, Wh-1811, Gr-1805
    John, Gr-1805, Gr-1804
    Joshua, Gr-1805
    Meredith, Gr-1805
    Richard, Gr-1804, Gr-1805, Wh-1825,
        Gr-1799
    Samuel, Wh-1825
    William, Wh-1811, Wh-1825
    Wm. Sr., Wh-1825
    William Jr., Wh-1825
    Wilson, Gr-1804, Sn-1811
SHOEMAKE, Blackley, A-1805
    David, A-1805
SHOEMAKER, Charles, R-1819
    Daniel, Su-1812, Su-1797
    John, Su-1797(3), Su-1796(2), Gi-1812
    Thomas, Su-1796
    William, Ro-1805, Su-1796
SHOFF, Hugh, Wa-1819
SHOFFNER, Martin, B-1812
    Peter, B-1812
SHOFNER, Michael, C-1818
SHOLLEY, Michael, Gr-1799
SHOMAKER, Thomas, Su-1797
SHOOK, Abraham, B-1812
    William, B-1812, D-1805
    William Sr., B-1812
SHOOKMAKER, Sol, Bl-1815

SHOOPMAN, Jacob, C-1823, C-1818
    John, C-1818, C-1823
    Michael, C-1818, C-1823
    Nicholas, C-1818
SHOOT, William, Wi-1801
SHORT, Anthy., Sn-1792
    Benjamin, Sn-1811
    Drury, Wa-1819
    Enus, B-1812
    Isaac, Wi-1815, Sn-1816
    James, Gr-1799, Gr-1804, Gr-1805
    Joab, Fr-1812
    Jonathan, Wh-1825
    Mary, Sh-1811
    Moses, Fr-1812
    William, D-1811(3), Sn-1816
SHOTE, Arthur, B-1812
    Gabriel, Gr-1799
    Valentine, Sn-1792
SHOULDERS, Soloman, Sn-1811
SHOULK, Solomon, Sn-1816
SHOULTS, Valentine, Se-1799
SHOUSE, Joseph, D-1811
SHOWN, Leonard, Ct-1796, Ct-1798
SHRADER, Coonrod, Sn-1792
SHRITE, Henry, Su-1796
SHROPSHIRE, Hicks, Wh-1825
    William, Wh-1825
    Winkfield, Fr-1812
SHUCOR, Joseph, Wa-1814
SHUFFIELD, Arthur, B-1812
    Arthur Jr., B-1812
    Ephraim, B-1812
    James, Wl-1804
    Jason B., B-1812
    William, F-1812, Wl-1804
SHULL, John, Mu-1811, Mu-1816
SHULTS, Jacob, Gr-1799(2), Cl-1803
SHUMAKER, James, Ro-1805
    Robert, K-1799
    William, K-1799
SHUMATE, James, Wi-1810
SHURLY, Thomas, Wh-1811
SHURMORE, George, Mt-1798
SHURRELL, Thomas, Wa-1814
SHURWOOD, John, Sn-1816
SHUTE, John, D-1811, Wi-1815
    Philip, D-1811
    William, Wi-1815(2)
SHY, Robert, Sn-1811, Sn-1816
SIBLEY, John Sr., B-1812
    John Jr., B-1812
SIDDONS, James, Gr-1804
SIDNER, Anthoney, Ct-1798
SIDWELL, Robert, J-1802
SIEGLAR, John, Gr-1805
    Phillip, Gr-1810
SIGLAR, John, Gr-1804
SIGLER, Henry, Su-1796
    John, Gr-1805
    Philip, Gr-1804
SILAS, James, Gr-1821
    John, Fr-1812
SILER, David, C-1823
SILES, Robert, Ro-1805
SILLARS, Mathew, Mt-1798
SILLIGMAN, Thomas, Wl-1804
SILLOMAN, Thomas N., Mu-1816
SILOR, John, A-1805
SILOUS, John, Mu-1811
SIMCELL, Daniel, Wh-1825
SIMERON, William, Je-1822

SIMES, James, Gr-1799
    Matthew, Gr-1799
SIMILY, Hugh, B-1812
SIMIPSON, Thomas, Fr-1812
SIMMERLY, Adam, Ct-1796
    John, Ct-1798, Ct-1796
SIMMON, William, D-1811
SIMMONS, Benjamin, B-1812
    Charles, Ro-1805, J-1802, Fr-1812
    Flemming, Mu-1816
    Flemmory, Mu-1811
    Jacob, B-1812
    James, Gi-1812, Gi-1819(2),
        Gr-1821
    Jehu, Gr-1821
    Jesse, Mu-1816, B-1812
    Jessee, Gr-1805
    John, Hu-1812(2), Gr-1805(2),
        D-1811, Cl-1803, Fr-1812,
        Gr-1804, Gr-1821(2), Rb-1812
    Join, Sn-1816
    Joseph, Ro-1805
    Joshua, Gr-1805
    Matthew, Gr-1805
    Nathaniel, Mu-1811, Mu-1816
    Reubin, Ro-1805
    Richd., Hu-1812, Gr-1821
    Robert, Wa-1814
    Thomas, Wi-1815, Gr-1821, Rb-1812
    Volentine, Rb-1812
    William, Wi-1815, Wh-1825, Hu-1812,
        Wi-1810, Fr-1812(3), Wa-1814
    Zachariah, Wa-1819
SIMMS, Elija, Gr-1821
    James, Bo-1801, Sn-1787
    Littlepage, R-1808
    Maston, B-1812
    Millington, Wi-1815
    Nathan, D-1805
    Wm., D-1805
SIMON, Alexander, Fr-1812
    John, Bo-1800
    Larkin, Gr-1805
SIMONS, Amon, C-1818
    Charles, Fr-1812
    Ezekiel, Sn-1811, Sn-1816
    John, Bo-1801, Gr-1821
    Thomas, Je-1822
    Wm., Bo-1801
SIMPKINS, John G., Wi-1815
    Robert, C-1818
SIMPSON, Abel, Mu-1811
    Alexander, Wi-1815
    Andrew, Hu-1812
    Archd., Wl-1804
    Asbury, Gi-1819
    Bigem, Gr-1799
    Crofford, Ct-1796
    Elijah, Sn-1816, Sn-1811
    Elisha, B-1812
    George, Gi-1812, Ro-1805
    Isaac, Gi-1819, Mu-1811
    James, Wh-1825
    James Sr., Wh-1825
    John, Sn-1816, Sn-1811, C-1823,
        A-1805, Gi-1819, Ge-1805,
        Ro-1805
    John W., Wh-1825, Wh-1811
    Joseph, Ro-1805
    Mary, Su-1797, Su-1796
    Reuben, Ge-1783
    Rhodham, Su-1812

SIMPSON, Robert, Mu-1811, Sn-1811, D-1805,
          D-1811, Sn-1816
      Sanford, Mc-1825
      Sayer, Wh-1825
      Thomas, Bo-1801, Hu-1812
      Wesley, Gi-1819
      William, Wl-1804(2), Mu-1816, D-1805,
          Mu-1811, Wh-1825, Wi-1815,
          Gi-1819, Wi-1810
      William, heirs, Wi-1801
SIMS, Allen, Fr-1812
     David, D-1805
     Eli, Wh-1825, Wh-1811
     Jack, Ro-1805
     James, Cl-1803, Bo-1800, Wi-1810,
         Wh-1811
     John, Gi-1812, Fr-1812, Mu-1816,
         Sn-1811, Sn-1816
     Judath, Mu-1816
     Julius Cesar, Fr-1812
     Martin, Fr-1812
     Peter, Sn-1792
     Randolph, Je-1822
     Robert, Gi-1812
     Thomas, Mu-1816
     Watson?, Mu-1811
     Will, Gi-1812(2)
     William, Gi-1812, Gr-1805, Gr-1804,
         Mu-1816
     William Jr., Mu-1811(2)
     Wythe, D-1811
SIMSON, George, Mu-1811
      James, Sn-1811
      Thomas, Mu-1811, Sn-1792
      Wm., Wi-1801, Gi-1812
SINCLAIR, Amos, Su-1812
        Charles, A-1805
        Hugh, Mu-1816
        John, Su-1812
        Joseph, A-1805
        Robert, A-1805
SING, William, B-1812
SINGLETARY, David, D-1811
          John, D-1811
SINGLETON, Aphi, B-1812
         Edward, Wi-1815
         John, Bo-1800, B-1812, Bo-1801
         Lewis, B-1812
         Peter, B-1812
         William, Mc-1825
SINK, Jeremiah, W-1812
SIONS, Nimrod, Gr-1799
SIRUS, Nimrod, Gr-1804
SISCO, Jaiole, Bl-1815
SISCOW, John, Ro-1805
      Sandy, Ro-1805
      William, Ro-1805
SISEMORE, Edward, Hw-1799
       James, Hw-1799
SISNALLER, John, B-1812
SISSOMS, James, Sn-1811
SISSON, Moses H., C-1823
SITLER, Jonas, D-1805
SITTLER, Isaac, D-1811
      James W., D-1811
SIVERTON, Dutton, Fr-1812
SIX, John, Hw-1799
SIYRES, John, D-1805
SIZEMAN, Stephen, Wh-1811
SIZEMORE, William, D-1811
SIZLER, Henry, Su-1797
SKAYLES, William, Ge-1812

SKEAN, James, Bo-1801
SKEEN, James, Bo-1805
      John, Je-1800, Je-1822, Cl-1803
SKIDMORE, Henrix, Gr-1799
        Thomas, C-1818, C-1823
SKILES, Ephraim, Ge-1805
      George, Bo-1801
      Wm., Bo-1801, Ge-1805
SKINALL, Isaac, Ro-1805
SKINNER, Emanual, Rb-1812
       Jesse, Rb-1812
       John, D-1811
SKIPPER, Hardy, C-1818, Ge-1783
SKIPPETH, Needham, Ct-1798, Ct-1796
SKYLES, William, Ge-1805
SLAGAL, John, Wa-1814
SLAGLE, Christopher, Wa-1819
      Henry, Wa-1814, Wa-1819
      John, Wa-1819
SLAKER, Zarubable, Mt-1798
SLATER, Charles, Wi-1815
      Henry, Wi-1815
      Sarah, Wi-1815
SLATES, Lewis, Sn-1816
SLAUGHTER, Abraham, Su-1812
         Jacob, Su-1797, Su-1812, Su-1796
         William, Wa-1819
         William Sr., Wa-1814
         William Jr., Wa-1814
SLAWTER, John, Gi-1812
SLAYTON, James, B-1812
SLEDGE, John, Wi-1815
SLEEKER, George, Wi-1810
SLEMMONS, William, Wa-1814
SLEMONS, William, Wa-1819
SLIDER, John, D-1805
SLIGER, Adam, Wa-1814, Wa-1819(2)
      James, Wa-1819(2)
      John, estate, Wa-1819
      John Sr., Wa-1814
      John Jr., Wa-1814
SLIMP, Jacob, Ct-1798
     Michael, Ct-1798
SLOAN, Alexander, Bo-1800, Bo-1801
     Arthur, Ge-1805
     James, Bo-1801, Bo-1800
     James G., Sn-1816
     James J., Sn-1811
     John, Bo-1801, Bo-1800, Sn-1811,
         Sn-1816
     Robert, Bo-1801, Bo-1800
     Thomas, Bl-1815, Sn-1811
     W., D-1811
     William, Bl-1815, Bo-1800, Bo-1801,
         Wi-1815, Wi-1801(2)
SLOCUM, Riley, Wi-1815
SLOKER, Robert, W-1812
SLONE, Eusebius, Sn-1811
     Robert, Wl-1804
     Thomas C., Gi-1819
     William, Wi-1801
SLOSS, Joseph, B-1812, Bo-1801
SLOVER, Aaron, A-1805
      Abraham, Je-1800, Je-1822
      Abraham Jr., Je-1800
      Aron, Je-1800
      Isaac, W-1812
      John, Wh-1811, Je-1822
SLUDER, John, D-1811
      Thomas, D-1811
SLUMP, Christopher, D-1811
     Jonathan, D-1805

SLYGER, Adam, Wa-1814(2)
    Christian, Wa-1814
    Henry, Wa-1814
SLYMP, Michael, Ct-1796
SMALL, Daniel, Wl-1804, Se-1799, Ge-1812,
        Ge-1805
    Henry, W-1812
    John, Ge-1812
    William, Bo-1801, Bo-1800
SMALLIN, Samuel, Ct-1796, Ct-1798
    Solomon, Su-1796
    Thomas, Su-1812, Su-1797, Su-1796
SMALLMAN, Burks, Wh-1825
    Grief, Wh-1825
    John, Wh-1825
SMALLWOOD, John, W-1812, W-1805, Gi-1812
SMALLY, John, Fr-1812
SMART, Francis, Bo-1801, Bo-1800
    John, Gi-1812
    Peter, Sn-1811
    Thomas, Rb-1812
    William, Rb-1812, Mu-1811
SMARTT, Reuben, W-1812
    Wm. C., W-1812, W-1805
SMATHERS, Philip, Ge-1805
SMEAD, Allan, Su-1797
SMEDDY, Robert, Su-1812
SMEDLEY, John, B-1812
    William, B-1812
SMELEN, Stephen, Wl-1804
SMELSER, Adam, Je-1822, Ge-1805, Ge-1812
    David, J-1802
    Jacob, Ge-1783
    John, J-1802
SMELSON, Allen, W-1812
    John, W-1812
SMIDDY, James, Wh-1825
    Jesse, C-1818, C-1823
    John, Su-1812
    Joseph, Su-1812
    Patrick, Su-1812
    Robert, D-1811, Ge-1805
    Sawrus, Ge-1812
SMILY, Thomas, Fr-1812
SMITH, Aaron, Mu-1811, Gr-1805, Gr-1804
    Abe Jr., C-1823
    Abraham, Sn-1816, Sn-1811, D-1811,
        Ge-1805
    Absolem, heirs, Je-1822
    Alexander, Wi-1801, Wl-1804, Su-1812,
        Wa-1819
    Ali Sr., C-1818, C-1823
    Ali Jr., C-1818
    Amos, W-1805, W-1812
    Anderson, B-1812, C-1818
    Andrew, Mu-1816, Wh-1811, Gr-1799,
        Bo-1801, Se-1799
    Anthony, C-1823
    Aron, Gr-1805, Gr-1799
    Austin, Gi-1812
    B. Benjamin, Mu-1811
    Barnett, Je-1822
    Bartholomeu, Gr-1799
    Bartholomew, Gr-1805
    Barton, Rb-1812
    Benjg., Sn-1792
    Benjamin, Mu-1811(2), Mu-1816(2),
        D-1805, Je-1822, C-1818,
        Wi-1815, C-1823
    Berrey, Sn-1811
    Bird, Wh-1811(2)
    Bowling, K*-1815

SMITH, Brooks, Ct-1796, Ct-1798
    Bryan, Su-1812
    Caleb, Su-1812
    Calvin, Su-1812
    Charles, Wi-1810, Mu-1816, Mu-1811,
        Gr-1805, Ge-1812(2), Wa-1814,
        Ge-1805, Gr-1804, Gr-1799
    Charles Sr., Wh-1825
    Charles Jr., Wh-1825
    Charles D., Wh-1825
    Cornelius, Ge-1805
    D., Sn-1811
    Daniel, Sn-1811, Sn-1816, Wl-1804,
        Gr-1805, Su-1797, Su-1796,
        Sn-1787, C-1818, Ge-1805,
        Gr-1804, C-1823, Sn-1792
    Daniel Jr., Su-1797
    David, Sn-1811, Gr-1805(2), Sn-1816
        Wh-1811, Gr-1821, C-1823,
        Gr-1804
    Deborah, Je-1800
    Ebenezer, Mu-1816, Mu-1811
    Edmond, D-1811
    Edward, Ct-1796, Ct-1798, Fr-1812,
    Edwin, Rb-1812
    Eli, D-1811
    Elias, Je-1822
    Elijah, B-1812
    Elizabeth, D-1805
    Ely, Gr-1799
    Ericus, C-1823
    Evans, Gr-1821
    Ezekiel, Mu-1816, D-1805, Su-1812,
        Wa-1814, Gr-1799
    Felps, Gi-1812
    Francis, Fr-1812
    Frank, Gi-1819
    Frederick, Ge-1812, C-1823, C-1818,
        Ge-1805
    George, Wl-1804, Sn-1816, Sn-1811(2)
        Gr-1805, D-1811, Ro-1805,
        Ge-1812, Su-1796, Gr-1805,
        B-1812
    Geo. Sr., Rb-1812
    George Jr., Su-1796, Rb-1812
    Gideon, Gr-1799
    Guy, D-1811
    H., Ge-1805
    H. Wm., C-1818
    Handcock, Wh-1825
    Harberd, Gr-1804
    Harbird, Gr-1805
    Harry, Wl-1804
    Henry, Wl-1804, Mu-1816, Gr-1805,
        Su-1812, Su-1797, C-1823,
        Gr-1804
    Hicks B., Su-1812
    Hugh, Mo-1825
    Hugh, Geo. & William, D-1805
    Humphrey, Gr-1821, Ct-1796
    Isaac, Wl-1804, Wi-1815, Rb-1812,
        W-1812, B-1812, Wa-1819
    J. L., Wi-1810
    Jackson, Gr-1804
    Jacob, Rb-1812(2), W-1812, Ge-1812,
        C-1818, Ge-1805, Gr-1821,
        Ct-1796, Ct-1798, C-1823
    James, Wl-1804(3), Wi-1810, Mt-1798
        Wi-1801, Mu-1816, Gi-1812,
        Su-1797, Su-1796, Ge-1812(3),
        Wa-1814, Wh-1811, Gi-1819,
        Ge-1805, B-1812, Wi-1815,

SMITH, James, cont'd.--W-1812, R-1819,
    C-1823, C-1818, Fr-1812,
    Li-1812*
  James & Henry, D-1805
  James Sr., Mu-1811
  James Jr., C-1823
  James H., W-1812(2)
  James N., Mu-1816
  James W., Mu-1816
  Jeremiah, Wa-1814, Ge-1812, Fr-1812,
    Ge-1805(2), Wa-1819
  Jeremiah D., Wa-1814, Wa-1819
  Jesse, D-1811(2)
  Joel, Wh-1825
  John, B-1812(3), Bo-1805, Bo-1810,
    Bo-1800, Ct-1798(2), C-1818,
    Ct-1796, C-1823, D-1811(2),
    D-1805, Fr-1812(5), Gi-1812(2),
    Ge-1783(2), Ge-1805, Ge-1812,
    Gr-1799, Gr-1821, Gr-1805,
    Gr-1810, Je-1800, Je-1822(2),
    K-1796, Mu-1811, Mu-1816,
    Mt-1798, Ro-1805, Su-1812(6),
    Sn-1816, Sn-1811, Wi-1801,
    Wi-1815(3), Wi-1810, Wh-1825,
    Wa-1814(2), Wa-1819, W-1805,
    W-1812(3), Wl-1804(3)
  John, dec., Ge-1812
  John Jr., Wa-1814
  John (Mason), Wa-1819
  John (orphan), Gr-1804
  John A., R-1819
  John C., Fr-1812
  John H., D-1811
  John L., Wh-1825(2)
  John M., Je-1822
  Jonah, C-1823
  Jonathan, Su-1797
  Jordon, Wh-1825
  Joseph, D-1811, Su-1812, Wh-1811,
    Wa-1819, Gr-1821, W-1812,
    Su-1797(2), Su-1796(2),
    B-1812
  Joshua, Sn-1816, Mu-1816, Rb-1812
  Josiah, Gr-1821, Gr-1799, Wl-1804
  Langdon, A-1805
  Laurence, Wi-1801
  Lemuel, Sn-1811
  Lewis, Wl-1804
  Martha, Wa-1819
  Martin, D-1805, Wi-1815
  Matthew, Mu-1811, Ct-1798
  Matthias, Mu-1816
  Meral, Sn-1811
  Merriwether, Ro-1805
  Moses, Mu-1816, Mu-1811, Gr-1821
  Mumford, R-1819
  Nathan, W-1805, W-1812
  Nathaniel, Wa-1814, Gr-1821, Wa-1819
  Needham, Rb-1812
  Nicholas, Ct-1798, Ct-1796
  Olaver, heirs, Sn-1811
  Oliver, J-1802, Mt-1798
  Page, D-1805
  Patsey, Gr-1821
  Payton, D-1811
  Philip, Ge-1805
  Pleasant, Wl-1804
  Plurr, Wi-1801
  Rachel, Gr-1821
  Ransom, C-1818(2), C-1823
  Reuben, Mu-1816, Mu-1811, Gi-1812

SMITH, Reubin, Wl-1804, C-1823
  Ricard, J-1802
  Richard, D-1811, Su-1797, Wa-1814,
    Gr-1799, Wa-1819, A-1805
  Robert, Wh-1825, Mu-1816, Rb-1812,
    Ge-1812, C-1823(2), C-1818(2)
    Ge-1805(2), A-1805, Se-1799
  Robert Jr., C-1823
  Samuel, D-1811(2), Mu-1811, Gi-1812
    Su-1812(3), Su-1796, Su-1797,
    Gr-1799, Wh-1811, Ct-1798,
    Ct-1796, Bo-1801, Bo-1805,
    Fr-1812
  Samuel Sr., Mu-1816, Su-1796
  Samuel Jr., Mu-1816
  Samuel B., Wh-1811
  Samuel H., Mu-1816
  Sean, D-1811
  Sebastian, Ge-1805
  Shelton, Sn-1816, Sn-1811
  Skelton, Sn-1823
  Soloman, Wa-1819
  Solomon, Su-1812, Su-1796
  Solomon Sr., Su-1812
  Stephen, Wi-1815(2), Wi-1810,
    Mu-1811, Gr-1805, Mu-1816,
    Gr-1821, Ge-1812, Gr-1804
  Sterling, Ge-1812, Rb-1812, C-1823,
    C-1818
  Thomas, B-1812, C-1818, Ct-1798,
    D-1811(2), D-1805, Fr-1812(2)
    Gi-1812, Gi-1819, Gr-1821,
    Ge-1812, Gr-1799, Gr-1805(2)
    Gr-1804(2), Je-1800(2),
    Mu-1816, Mu-1811, Sn-1811,
    Sn-1792(2), W-1812(2),
    Wi-1810, W-1805, Wh-1825
  Thomas B., Wh-1825
  Thos. O., heirs, Mu-1816
  Turner, Ge-1812, Wa-1819
  Uricus, Wh-1811
  Vardiman, Sn-1811
  Vincent, B-1812
  Wiley, Gr-1821
  William, B-1812, Ct-1796, C-1818,
    C-1823(2), Ct-1798(2),
    D-1805(3), D-1811, Fr-1812(2),
    Gr-1804, Ge-1805(4), Gr-1799(2)
    Gi-1812(2), Je-1822(2), R-1808
    R-1819, Se-1799, Sn-1811,
    Sn-1816, Su-1812, Su-1796(2),
    Su-1797(2), Wh-1825(3),
    Wh-1811(2), Wl-1804, Wi-1801,
    Wi-1815, W-1805, W-1812(2)
  William B., Wh-1825, Wa-1819
  William J., Wh-1811
  William S., Sn-1823
  Willis, Gr-1805
  Wimer, C-1818
  Work, Wi-1810
  Wyatt (orphan), Gr-1804
  Zachariah, B-1812
  Zaddick, Sn-1811
  Zebulen, Wa-1819
  Zebulon, Wa-1814
  Zechariah, Wi-1815
SMITHERMAN, William, Mu-1816
SMITHERS, William, Wh-1825
SMITHFIELD, Henry, C-1818
SMITHSON, Clement, Wi-1815
  Nathaniel, Wi-1815
SMITS, William, W-1812

SMOOT, Samuel, Mu-1811
SMOTHER, Edmond, Sn-1816
    Edward, Sn-1811
    Ely, Sn-1816
    Jacob, Sn-1816, Sn-1811
    James, Sn-1811
    John, Sn-1816
    Margaret, Sn-1816
    Philip, Ge-1812
    William, D-1805
    Wm. Sr., Sn-1811, Sn-1816
    William Jr., Sn-1816, Sn-1811
SMYTH, George, J-1802
    Levi, D-1788
    Taylor, Bl-1815
SNAP, Samuel, Ge-1812
SNAPP, Abraham, Wa-1819, Wa-1814
    Abraham Sr., Wa-1819
    George, Wa-1814, Wa-1819
    John, W-1805, Wa-1819, Su-1812
    Laurence Jr., W-1805
    Law. Sr., Wh-1805
    Lawrence, Wa-1819, Wa-1814, Su-1812
    Lawrence Sr., Su-1812
    Lawrence Jr., Su-1812
    Peter, Wa-1819, Wa-1814
SNEED, Billey, Sn-1811
    Burwell, D-1811
    Henley, Co-1821
    James, Wi-1815
    Reed, Sn-1816
    William, D-1811
SNEFFER, David, Gr-1799
SNELL, Charles, B-1812(2)
    Rober, B-1812
    Stephen, Wl-1804
SNELSON, James, R-1808, R-1819
SNIDER, Abraham, Ge-1812
    Barney, Su-1797
    Christian, Ct-1798
    Daniel, Wa-1819
    Frederick, Gr-1804
    George, Bo-1801, Bo-1805
    John, Mu-1811, Bo-1801, Bo-1800,
        Bo-1805
    Michal, Su-1797, Su-1796
    Peter, Ct-1798(2), Ct-1796, Bo-1800,
        Bo-1805, Bo-1801
    William, Ge-1812, Su-1797
SNODDERLY, George, C-1823
    Jacob, C-1823
    John, A-1805, C-1818
SNODDY, David, Sn-1816
    John D., Je-1822
    Samuel, Wi-1801
    Thomas, Je-1822
    Thomas Esq., Je-1800
    Wm., Sn-1792
    William, heirs, Sn-1816
SNODGRASS, David, Wh-1825, Su-1812, Je-1800
    Davis, Je-1822
    James, Wh-1825(2)
    Joseph, Je-1822
    Rhea, Su-1812
    Robert, Je-1800
    William, Gr-1804, Su-1812(2), Gr-1805
        Su-1796, Je-1800
SNODY, WM., Sn-1787, Su-1797
SNOTGRASS, William, Gr-1805
SNOW, David C., D-1811
    Ebenezer, W-1812
    Ely, Gi-1812

SNOW, Jacob, B-1812
    James, Je-1822
    John, W-1812
    William, Gi-1819, W-1812(2)
SNUFFER, John, Je-1800
SNYDER, Frederick, Gr-1805
    Jacob, Je-1822
    Michael, D-1811, Ro-1805
SOBEL, Asa, Ro-1805
SODDERS, Jacob, Hw-1801
SODERS, Abrem, Hw-1801
    Henry, Hw-1801
    Peter, Hw-1801
SOIRUS, Nimrod, Gr-1805
SOLFLY?, Jessee, W-1812
SOLLARS, Sebert, Ge-1783
SOLLOMAN, Jordan, Wi-1810
SOLLOMON, Abraham, Gr-1805
    Henry, Gr-1805
    William, Gr-1805
SOLNO, Henry, D-1811
SOLOMON, Auston, B-1812
    David, Gr-1821
    Jordon, Wi-1801
SOLOMONS, Henry, Gr-1804
    William, Gr-1804
SOMERS, John, Wl-1804
SOMERVILLE, _____, Rb-1812
SOMMERLIN, John, D-1805
SONS, George, Gr-1804
SOOP, George, Fr-1812
SOREE, Samuel, Gr-1799
SORPETH, John P., D-1811
SORRELL, David, B-1812
SORRELS, William A., Wh-1811
    Wm. M., Wh-1825
SOTHARD, Charles, Wh-1825
    McLane, Wh-1825
SOTHERLAND, Daniel, Gr-1805, Gr-1799
    George, Gr-1799
SOTHERN, Nancy, Rb-1812
SOUDER, Frederick, Ge-1805, Ge-1812
    Jacob, Ge-1805
SOUND, William, D-1805
SOUNDER, James, W-1805
SOUNDS, Michall, Ge-1812
SOURUS, Bennet, Gr-1805
SOUTH, James, B-1812
    Joseph, Gi-1812
    Philip, B-1812
SOUTHALL, James, Wi-1815
    Simon, Wi-1815
SOUTHERLAND, Daniel, Gr-1805
    Thomas, Ge-1805
SOUTHERN, Isaac, Hw-1801, Cl-1803
SOWDER, Christopher, Ge-1812
SOWDERS, Jacob, C-1823, C-1818(2)
SOWELL, Lewis, B-1812
    William, B-1812
SPAIN, David, Wi-1815, Wi-1810
    Marshall D., Mu-1816
    Solomon D., Mu-1816
    Stephen, Wi-1815
SPANN, Jeremiah, Wi-1815
SPARKER, William, Su-1812
SPARKMAN, Briant, Wh-1825
    George, Wh-1825, Gr-1805, Gr-1804
    James, Gr-1821
    Jesse, Wi-1810, Wi-1815
    Kenshen, Wi-1815
    Lewis, Gr-1821
    Thomas, D-1811

SPARKMAN, William, Wi-1801, Wi-1810,
        Wh-1825, Wi-1815, Gr-1821
SPARKS, Abel, Fr-1812
        Bailey, Hu-1812
        Benjamin, Fr-1812
        George, Fr-1812
        John, Fr-1812(2)
        Samuel, Je-1822
        Solomon, Fr-1812
        Thomas, Je-1822, Mu-1811
        William, Wh-1825
SPARLEN, John, R-1808
SPEAKS, Thomas, D-1805
SPEAR, Moses, D-1805
SPEARES, John H., Bl-1815
SPEARMAN, Joshua, Rb-1812
        _____, Rb-1812
SPEARS, Joseph, Gi-1812
        Levine, Wa-1814
SPECKART, Jacob, Wl-1804
SPECKMAN, William, B-1812
SPEERE, John, W-1812
SPEID, James, Mu-1811
SPELL, Charles, Su-1812
SPELLER, Elijah, D-1811
SPENCE, Elisha, D-1811
        John, Sn-1811, Sn-1816
        Lewis, D-1811
SPENCER, Christopher, Wh-1825
        Daniel, Gr-1805
        David, Gr-1805, Gr-1804
        Elizabeth, Wi-1810
        Franklin (minor), Mu-1816
        James, Su-1812
        John, Wi-1801, Mu-1811, Wl-1804,
                C-1823, A-1805, Gr-1804
        John Sr., Mu-1816
        John Jr., Mu-1816
        Joseph, Mo-1825
        Michael, Fr-1812
        Nathan, Fr-1812
        New, Mu-1811
        Thomas, Sn-1792, Rb-1812
        William, Wi-1810, Wi-1815
        Zilman, Mu-1816
        Zilmon, Mu-1811
SPENKER, John, Wl-1804
SPERRY, Charles, Wh-1825
        Thomas, Wh-1825
SPICER, Elijah, Wh-1825
        Hardy, W-1812
        Hyett, Wh-1825
        Isaac, Wh-1825
SPIERS, William, Gr-1821
SPILLER, Benjamin, Rb-1812
        William, Rb-1812
SPILMAN, Thomas, Bo-1800
SPINCE, David, Rb-1812
SPIRGEN, William, Wa-1819
SPIVEY, Henry, Gi-1812
SPOON, Abraham, Gr-1821
        David, Wh-1825
SPOONER, Jonathan, Sn-1816
SPRADLIN, Charles, W-1812
        David, W-1812
        Obediah, Wl-1804
SPRADLING, James, Gr-1804
        Jesse, Sn-1811, Sn-1816, Gr-1804
        Jessee, Gr-1805, Gr-1804
        John, Sn-1811
        Joseph, Sn-1811, Sn-1816
        Obadiah, Sn-1816

SPRAGGIN, William, B-1812
SPRATT, Blythe, Wi-1815
SPRIGGS, Robert, Mt-1798
SPRING, John, Gr-1804
        Nicholas, Gr-1805, Gr-1804, Ge-1805
        Valentine, Bl-1815
        Voluntine, Gr-1805
SPRINGER, Edward, J-1802
        Josiah, B-1812
SPROUCE, George, Rb-1812
SPROUL, John, J-1802
SPURGIN, Drew, Co-1827
        Elizabeth, Su-1812
        John, Su-1812, Su-1797
                Su-1796(in Sumner Co.)
        William, Wa-1814
SPYKER, Jonathan, Fr-1812
SPYOY?, Henry, Mu-1816
SQUIB, Caleb, Wa-1819
SQUIBB, Caleb, Wa-1814
        George, Wa-1189
        John, Wa-1814, Wa-1819
SQUIER, David, Wi-1815
SQUIRE, David, Wi-1801(2), K-1796,
                Wi-1810
        Ezekiel, D-1811
SQUIRES, Mary, Wi-1815
SRAFFORD, Benjamin, Wa-1819
STAAT, Saml. & Archy, D-1805
STACEL, Samuel, D-1811
STACKS, Abram, Gi-1812
        David, Mu-1816
        John, Gi-1812
        Joseph, Gi-1812
        William, Gi-1812(2)
STACY, John, Wi-1815
STAFFORD, Stephen, Gr-1799, Bo-1805,
                Bo-1801, Gr-1799
STAGG, Flamon, Wi-1815
STAGGS, Felix, Wi-1815
        John, Fr-1812, Wi-1815
STAGS, Ezekiel, Fr-1812
        William, B-1812
STAIN?, Morris, D-1788
STAINBACK, Robert, D-1811
STAKELY, Wiley, Wh-1825
STAKES, Berryman, Wi-1810
STALCUP, Eli, Sn-1816, Sn-1811
        Elisabeth, Sn-1811
        George, Sn-1816
        Isaac, Sn-1811, Sn-1816
        James, Sn-1816(2)
        Swain, Sn-1811
STALLINGS, John, Rb-1812
        Thoms, Rb-1812
STALTS, Lewis, Ge-1812
STAMBURY, William, Gr-1821
STAMPS, Edmond, Wh-1825
        George, Fr-1812
        James, Fr-1812, Wh-1811, Wh-1825
        John, Fr-1812, Wh-1825, Sn-1811,
                Sn-1816
        William, Fr-1812, Wh-1811
STANBERRY, Ezekiel, Ge-1812, Ge-1805
        Solomon, Ge-1812
        William, Ge-1812
STANBOUGH, Jacob, Je-1800
STANCILL, Jesse, Wi-1815
        Nathan, Wi-1815
STANDBY, Spencer, D-1805
STANDEFER, Israel, A-1805
        James, Bl-1815, A-1805

STANDEFER, James Jr., K-1799
    Luke Jr., K-1799
    Samuel, A-1805
    William, A-1805, K-1799
STANDFIELD, Thomas Jr., Ge-1805
STANDLY, Jeptha, B-1812
    Johnathan, Mc-1825
STANDRIDGE, Alexander, Fr-1812
    James, Fr-1812
STANETT, John, D-1811
STANFIELD, Abram, Sn-1816
    Apley, Sn-1811
    Ephraim, Wi-1815
    Capt. John, Ge-1805
    Isaac, Mu-1811
    John, Ge-1812, Su-1812, Sn-1811
    Josiah, Sn-1816
    Samuel, Wa-1814, Ge-1805
    Samuel Sr., Ge-1812
    Shakespear, Wi-1815
    Thomas, Su-1812(2), Ge-1783, Ge-1812,
        Ge-1805
    William, Ge-1812
STANFILL, Isaac, Mu-1816
    John, Mu-1816(2), Mu-1811
    Joanathan J., Mu-1816
    Sarah, Mu-1816
    Thomas, Mu-1811, Mu-1816
    William, Mu-1811, Mu-1816
STANFORD, Achells, Gr-1799
    George, Gi-1812(2)
    John, Gi-1812
    Thomas, Gi-1819, Gi-1812(2)
    William, Gi-1812
STANLEY, Demerick, Wl-1804
    Ellen, C-1818
    Henry, B-1812
    Isaac, C-1823, Gr-1805
    James, Wi-1815, Wi-1810
    John, C-1823, Gi-1812
    Joseph, C-1823, C-1818
    Martin, Wi-1801, Wi-1810
    Moses, Rb-1812
    Noble, Rb-1812
    Page, A-1805
    Reuben, A-1805
    Rhodes, A-1805
    Richard, C-1818, Rb-1812
    Roads, C-1823
    Robert, C-1818
    Ruebin, C-1818
    William, Ge-1812, Wl-1804
STANLY, Isaac, Gr-1799
    Martin, Wi-1815
    Page, C-1818
    Wright, Wi-1815
STANSBERRY, Samuel, Wa-1819
STANSBERY, Elijah, Wa-1819
STANSELL, Nathaniel, D-1811
STANSIFER, Anderson, Fr-1812
STANSON, James, B-1812
STANSSHILL, David, Fr-1812
STANTER, Abram, Su-1812
STANTON, John, Wa-1814
    Richard, Gr-1799
    Thomas, Gr-1799
STAPLES, James, Je-1822
    John, Je-1822, Wh-1825, Fr-1812
    Richard G., Je-1822
STAPLETON, William, Su-1797, Ge-1812
STAR, Joseph, Su-1812
    Michael, Su-1812

STARK, Alexander, Sn-1811, Sn-1816
    James, Rb-1812, Gi-1812
    Jeremiah, Rb-1812, Sn-1811, Sn-1816
    John, Sn-1816
    Thos., Sn-1811
    Thornton, Sn-1816
    Walter, Rb-1812
    William, Rb-1812
STARKEY, Abraham, D-1811
STARKS, Thomas, B-1812
STARKY, Jacob, W-1812
    Jarvis, W-1812
    Joel, W-1812
STARN, Christian, Wa-1819
STARNES, Adam, Ge-1805
    David, Wa-1819
    Frederick, Wa-1814(2)
    George, Ge-1812, Wa-1814
    Henry, Wa-1819
    Jacob, Wa-1814
    James, Wa-1819
    Jesse, Wa-1819, Wa-1814
    John, Wa-1819, Wa-1814
    Leonard, Ge-1805, Ge-1812
    Margaret, Wa-1819
    Thomas, Ge-1805, Ge-1812, Wa-1819
STARNS, Adam, Gr-1821, Sn-1816
    Frederick, Wa-1819
    Jacob, Wa-1819
    John, Sn-1816
STARR, Francis, C-1818
    James, Gr-1799, C-1818
    Michael, Wa-1814
STARRETT, John, B-1812
START, Thos., Sn-1816
STATE, William N., Sn-1823
STATEHAM, Love, Je-1822
STATENS, Reubin, Ro-1805
STATHART, Robert, D-1811
STATON, George, W-1805
    George D., W-1812
STATT, Zachariah, D-1805
STATTER, Ambrose, C-1818
STATTON, Robert, Sn-1792
STAYLY, Peter, Sn-1816
STEAD, Moses, W-1812
STEAL, Andrew, Wi-1801
    Robert, Sn-1816
STEALE, Andrew, Wi-1810
STEARN, David, Mu-1816
STEARR, Henry, R-1808
STEDMAN, John, Su-1812
STEEL, Alexander, Wi-1815, Wh-1825
    Andrew, Wl-1804, Mu-1816, Sn-1792
    David, Su-1812
    David Jr., Su-1812
    George, Sn-1810, Sn-1811
    Graves, Gi-1819
    Henry, Sn-1816, Sn-1811
    James, Mu-1811, Mu-1816, Ge-1805
        Su-1812
    John, Wh-1825(2), Mu-1816, Sn-1792
    Jos., Sn-1792
    M. John, Sn-1816
    Moses, Wl-1804
    Minal?, Mu-1811
    Nathaniel, Wh-1825
    Richard, Wi-1815
    Robert, Sn-1816, Sn-1787, Gi-1819
    Robert G., Mu-1816
    Thomas, Gi-1819
    William, Wl-1804

STEEL, William D., Mu-1816
STEELE, Andrew, Gi-1812
    George, A-1805, B-1812
    John, Gi-1812
    Joseph, B-1812
    Moses, Wi-1810, Wi-1815
    Robert, Gi-1812
    Samuel, Gi-1812
    Thos., Gi-1812
STEELL, Robt., Sn-1792
    Zacheriah, D-1788
STEEPLETON, Jonathan, Wi-1815
STEER, John, Su-1812
STEETER, John, Gr-1805
STEFFEY, John, Gr-1805
STELL, James, A-1805, Su-1797
    Trueman, A-1805
STELY, Petter, Sn-1811
STEMPELL, John, W-1805
STEMRELL, John, W-1812
STENITT, William H., D-1811
STENNETT, William, Wl-1804
STEPHANS, John, B-1812
STEPHEINS, William Sr., Wi-1815
STEPHEN, Gilburt, Hw-1799
    Robert, D-1805
    Thomas, Mu-1811
    William, Mu-1816
STEPHENS, Andrew, Ge-1805
    Andy, Ge-1812(3)
    Bartholomew, D-1811
    Ebenezer Sr., Fr-1812
    Ebenezer Jr., Fr-1812
    Edmund, Su-1796
    Felix, Su-1812
    George, Fr-1812
    Henry Wton., K-1799
    Isaac, Su-1812, A-1805, Bl-1815
    Jame, Wi-1815
    James, Wi-1810, Fr-1812, Je-1822
    Jams, Wi-1815
    Jeptha, D-1811
    Jeremiah, Wi-1815
    Joel, Wi-1815
    John, D-1805, Ge-1783
    Jonathan, D-1805
    Joseph, Gr-1805, Gr-1804
    Josiah, Fr-1812
    Lewis, Wi-1815, A-1805
    Loami, Wi-1810
    Moore, Mt-1798
    Samuel, Su-1812, Fr-1812
    Thomas, D-1805
    Wallace, Sn-1816
    Washington, Ro-1805
STEPHENSON, Alexander, D-1805
    Edward, Je-1800, B-1812
    James W., Mu-1816
    Jesse, Sn-1811
    John, Wa-1814, Mu-1811, Sn-1816, Ge-1783
    John C., Gi-1819
    John W., Mu-1816
    John & Mathew, Wa-1819
    Jonathan, Mt-1798
    M., Mu-1816
    Mathew, Wa-1814
    Moore, Sn-1792
    Nathaniel, Mu-1811, Mu-1816
    Nicolas, Bo-1800, Bo-1801
    Robert, Je-1800
    Thomas, Mu-1811, Mu-1816

STEPHENSON, W. Hugh, Mu-1811
    W. James, Mu-1811
    W. John, Mu-1811
    William, Wa-1819, Mu-1811, Wa-1814
    Wm. W., Mu-1816
STEPHINS, James, Mt-1798
STEPLETON, Jonathan, Wi-1810
STEPP, Fredrick, Wa-1812
    John, Mc-1825
STERFIELD, Jeremiah, Mu-1811
STERLING, Daniel, Je-1800
    James, Je-1822, Je-1800
    John, Je-1800 (senator)
    Thomas B., Gr-1821
    William, Je-1800
STERN, Abraham, W-1812
    John, W-1812
STERNES, John Jr., Ro-1805
    Peter, W-1812
STERNS, Jesse, Ro-1805
    John, Sn-1792, W-1812
    John Sr., Ro-1805
    Nicholas, Ro-1805
    William, Ge-1812
STETLER, William, Ro-1805
STEVENS, Edmund, Su-1797
    Edward, Wi-1815
    Jas., Wi-1810
    Lewis, Wi-1810
    Margaret, Wa-1814
    Richard, Hw-1801
    Thomas, Wi-1815
    William, Wa-1814
STEVENSON, Alexander, Je-1822
    Edward, Gr-1799
    James, Wi-1801
    Nicholas, Su-1796
    William, Su-1796, Wi-1801
STEVERSON, George, Wi-1815
STEVESON, William, Su-1797
STEVINS, Henry, Wi-1815
STEWARD, Alec., Ro-1805
ALEXANDER, Gr-1799
    David, Sn-1792
    Payton, Sn-1811
STEWART, Alexander, Bo-1801, Wi-1815
    Benjamin, Wh-1825
    Charles, Mt-1798
    David, Ro-1805, Sn-1811
    Dempsy, Rb-1812
    Duncan, Mt-1798
    Elisha, Wh-1811
    James, Gi-1812, Mt-1798, Sn-1816
    John, B-1812, Wh-1811, Gi-1812, Je-1822, Mt-1798, Sn-1811(3)
    Joseph, Wh-1825
    Lazr., Gi-1812
    Marcus, Wi-1815
    Peter B., Wi-1801
    Richard S., Gi-1812
    Robert, Wh-1811
    Sally (Wd), Gi-1819
    Samuel, Sn-1816, Sn-1811(2)
    Samuel Jr., Sn-1811
    Stewart, D-1805
    Thos., Gi-1812, Wi-1801
    William, Wh-1811, Sn-1811, D-1788(2), D-1805, Wh-1825(2)
    William Sr., D-1805
STEWERT, Samuel P., Mc-1825
STICKNY, George, Wi-1815
STICKS, John, Wh-1825

STIEN, Frederick, Sn-1816
STIFFEE, John, Gr-1799
STIFFER, John, Gr-1805
STIFFERY, John, Gr-1804
STIFFY, John, Gr-1821
    Reuben, Je-1822
STIGALL, Benj., Li-1812*
STILES, James, Gi-1812
STILL, James, C-1823
    Jeremiah, Wl-1804
STINE, John, Ge-1812
STINGROW, John C., Mu-1816
STINNET, Benjamin, Gr-1799(2)
    Isom, Gr-1799
STINSEN, William, Wi-1801
STINSON, Alexander, Wh-1811
    George, Gr-1799(2)
    Jacob, W-1805
    James, Ge-1805
    John, Wh-1811, Ge-1805(2)
    Martin, C-1818
    Robert, Gr-1799
STIPES, Jacob, Su-1796, Wh-1811
STITTUM, Samuel, C-1818
STIVER, William, Wh-1825
STOBACK, Andrew, D-1805
STOBAUGH, John S., Wi-1810
STOBOUGH, Adam, D-1811
    Henry, D-1811
    John, Mu-1816, D-1811(2)
    William, D-1811
STOCKARD, James, Mu-1816(2)
    Joseph, Mu-1816
    Richard, Mu-1816
STOCKARD, William, Mu-1816
STOCKDON, Thomas, Ge-1805
STOCKETT, Noble, heirs, Wi-1815
    Thos. W., Wi-1815
STOCKHARD, James, Mu-1811(2)
    Joseph, Mu-1811
    William, Mu-1811
STOCKMAN, John, Wi-1815
STOCKTON, John, Ro-1805
    Marshall, Bo-1801
    Willis, Ro-1805
STOKE, Adam, Su-1797, Su-1812, Su-1796(2)
    Adam Sr., Su-1797
    John, Ge-1812
STOKES, Frederick, Wh-1825
    Isaac, R-1819
    John, Mu-1811, Wh-1825
    Kinchen, B-1812
    Robert, W-1805
    Sylvester, Fr-1812
    William, Mu-1816
STONE, Clack, Rb-1812
    Corder, Wh-1811, J-1802
    Drury, Sn-1811
    Edward, Bo-1801
    Euribus, Sn-1816
    Hendly, Wi-1810
    Henley, Wi-1815
    Iredell, Wh-1825
    James, Wi-1815
    John, Rb-1812, Wh-1811, B-1812, Wh-1825
    Nicholas, Sn-1811
    Nicklas, Sn-1816
    Robert, Gr-1821, Gr-1805, Gr-1804, Gr-1799
    Samuel, W-1812
    Stephen, Sn-1816, Sn-1811

STONE, Thomas, Wh-1811, Mu-1816, Mu-1811
    Thomas C., Gi-1812
    Uriah, Mu-1816
    William, Gi-1812, B-1812, Gr-1799, Sn-1816, Mu-1811, Sn-1811, Wi-1815
STONECIPHER, Daniel, Ro-1805
    Michael, A-1805
STONECYPHER, Absalom, Ge-1805
    Henry, Ge-1805
    Solomon, Ge-1805
STONER, Henry, W-1812
    Isaac, W-1805
STONES, David, Mt-1798
STONESIFER, Absolom, Ge-1812(2)
    Solomon, Ge-1812
STOPHEL, Henry, Su-1812
    Jacob, Su-1812
STOREY, Wm. C., Co-1821
STORM, Coonrod, Ct-1796
    Cornelius, Ct-1796, Ct-1798
    John, Ct-1796, Ct-1798
    Peter, Ct-1796, Ct-1798
    Thomas, Wh-1811
STORY, James, St-1812, Mu-1816, Sn-1816, Sn-1811
    Vincent, Gi-1819
STOTHART, Robert, D-1811, D-1805, Wl-1804
STOTT, William, Su-1796
STOUT, Benjamin, W-1812
    Benjamin C., R-1819
    Daniel, Wa-1819, Ct-1796, Ct-1798
    Ezekiel, W-1812
    George, Ct-1798
    Hoseah, Ge-1783
    Jacob Sr., A-1805
    Jacob Jr., A-1805
    John, Wa-1814, Wa-1819
    Joseph, A-1805
    Peter, Ge-1812
    Robert, W-1812
    Samuel, A-1805
STOVALL, Barthalemew, D-1788
    Bartholomew, Sn-1816, Sn-1811, Wi-1815
    Drury, Gi-1812
    Elisha, Fr-1812
    Elyah, Fr-1812
    George, Fr-1812, Sn-1816
    Josiah, Gi-1812
    Terresha, Sn-1811
    William, Gi-1812, Sn-1816(2)
STOVEALL, William, Gi-1812, Sn-1816
STOVELL, Barthulamy, Wi-1810
STOVER, Christian, Wa-1814, Ct-1796
    Christian Sr., Ct-1798
    Daniel, Ct-1798, Ct-1796
    John, Ct-1796, Wh-1825
STOW, Abram, W-1812
    William, A-1805
STOWARS, John, Sn-1816
STRAAN, John, D-1811
STRADDER, Jacob, C-1818
STRADER, Daniel, C-1823
    Jacob, A-1805, C-1823
STRAIN, James, Wh-1825
    John, Wa-1814(2), R-1808, Mu-1811
    John Jr., Wa-1819
    John, Esq., Wa-1819
    Moses, D-1811
    Robert, Wa-1819
    Robert W., Wa-1814

STRAIN, Thomas, Sn-1792
STRAMLER, George, Wi-1801
STRAMLOR, Geo., Wi-1815
STRANGE, Edmund, Ge-1805
    James, Co-1821
STRANZE, Smith, Gr-1821
STRASNER, Mykel, R-1808
STRATFORD, Clabourn, Wh-1825
STRATLER, Henry, Sn-1811
STRATON, Calvin, Sn-1811
STRATTON, James, Sn-1811, Sn-1816
    William, Mu-1816
STREADER, Conroad, Sn-1792
STREET, Anthony, Gr-1805, Gr-1804, Wi-1812,
        Ro-1805
    Asa, Gr-1805, Gr-1799, Gr-1804
    Isaac, Sn-1811, Sn-1816
    James, Sn-1811
    Jeremiah, Fr-1812
    John, Sn-1816
    Joseph, Fr-1812
    William, Gr-1805
STREWEL, William, Ct-1796
STRICKLAND, Elihue, Hu-1812
    Lot, Fr-1812
    Seth, W-1812
    Stephen, Hu-1812
    Zach., Gi-1812
STRICKLER, Jacob, Su-1812
    Samuel, Su-1812
STRICKLIN, Gideon, Mu-1816
    Jesse, Rb-1812
    John, Rb-1812
    Mathew, Fr-1812
    Samuel, Mu-1816
    Thos., Wi-1801
    William, Mu-1816, Rb-1812
STRINGER, Edward, Je-1800
    Gray, Rb-1812
    Isaac, Rb-1812
    James, B-1812
    John, Rb-1812
STRINGFELLOW, Robert, D-1811
STRINGFIELD, James, W-1812
STRONG, John, D-1811, D-1805
    John C., B-1812
    Joseph C., K*-1815
    Shirwood, Sn-1811
STROPSHIRE, James, Fr-1812
STROSSONER, Henry, Ro-1805
STROTHER, Henry, Sn-1816
    Jacob, Sn-1816
    James, Sn-1811, Sn-1816
    John, D-1811, Rb-1812
    Richd., Sn-1811, Sn-1792
    Robt., Sn-1811
    Samuel, Rb-1812
STROUD, Christopher, Gr-1821
    Jesse, Rb-1812
    Joshua, Gr-1805
    Thomas, W-1812
    William, Gr-1799, W-1812, Cl-1803
STUARD, John, Fr-1812
    William, Fr-1812, B-1812
STUART, Alexander, Wa-1819, Wa-1814,
        Bo-1800
    Andrew, Rb-1812
    Barney, Sn-1811
    Barny, Sn-1816
    Benjamin, Ge-1805
    Charles, D-1811, D-1805
    David, Wa-1819, Co-1821, Wa-1814

STUART, Dunkin, Wl-1804
    Edward, R-1819
    Henry, Gr-1821
    James, D-1805, Wl-1804(3), Ct-1798,
        Wa-1819, Fr-1812, R-1819
    James, heirs, Wa-1819
    John, Wi-1810, Wa-1819, Rb-1812,
        W-1812, Su-1796, Su-1797
    John Jr., Wa-1814
    Margret, Wl-1804
    Mercy, R-1819
    Montgomery, Wa-1814, Wa-1819
    Mumford, Sn-1816
    Peter, Sn-1816
    Peter B., D-1811
    Robert, Ge-1805, Wl-1804, Wa-1819,
        Rb-1812, Wa-1814
    Saml., Wl-1804
    Thomas, D-1805, Wa-1819, Bo-1805
    William, D-1805(2), D-1811, Fr-1812
        Bo-1801, Bo-1800
STUBB, Zachariah, D-1805
STUBBENS, Christopher, Sn-1816
STUBBLEFIELD, Armistead, Wh-1811
    Clem, Sn-1811
    Clement, Rb-1812
    Geo., Sn-1816, Sn-1811, Cl-1803
    George Sr., Sn-1811
    Jerrimiah, Sn-1811
    Jerry, Sn-1816
    Joseph, Gr-1821, Gr-1804
    Lemuel, Sn-1811, Sn-1816
    Lock, Gr-1799
    Martin, Gr-1804, Je-1822
    Stokly, Ge-1812
    Thos., Sn-1811, Sn-1816
    Tilman, Sn-1816
    Tilmon, Sn-1811
    William, Gr-1805, Gr-1804, Cl-1803
    Woodly?, Sn-1811
    Woods, Sn-1816
STUBBS, Aron, Ro-1805
STUBELFIELD, Leeck, Ge-1812
STUBLE, Jesse, Ro-1805
STUBLEFIELD, Armstead, Sn-1811
    Joseph, Gr-1805
    Martin, Gr-1805
    Stephen, D-1805
STUCKEY, Thomas, Fr-1812
STUCKLEY, Christian, Wh-1811
    Christopher, Wh-1825
STUDART, John, Mt-1798
STUTHERLAND, Geo., K*-1815
STULL, Zacheriah, D-1811
STULTS, Lewis, Ge-1805
STUMP, Christopher, D-1805
    Frederick, D-1805, D-1811
    Fredrick, Sn-1816
    John, D-1811, D-1805
STURDEVAN, Anthony, Su-1812
STURDEVANT, Sylvanius, Wi-1815
STURDIVAN, Benjamin, D-1811
    Stephen, Su-1812
STURDIVANT, John, Fr-1812
    Lewis, D-1811
    Sylvanus, Wi-1810
STURM, Jacob, Su-1812
STURMAN, Wm., W-1805, W-1812
STUTER, Abner, Gr-1805
    Joseph Sr., Gr-1805
    Joseph Jr., Gr-1805
STUTHART, Robert, Mt-1798

STUTHART, Tait, Wi-1801
STUTTS, Henry, Rb-1812
STYLES, Wm., W-1805, W-1812
STYPE, Jacob, Wh-1825
SUDDERLIN, George, Gr-1799
SUEL, Dorson, Ct-1796
    Joseph, Ct-1796
SUGARS, Nathan, Gr-1805
SUGG, Anguish, D-1805
    Edward, B-1812
    George, Wh-1811
    Harbert, B-1812
    Josiah, D-1805, D-1811
    Thomas, B-1812
    Timothy, B-1812
    William, B-1812
SUGGS, Aquilla, heirs, Wl-1804
    Jno. H., B-1812
    Timothy, B-1812
SUGLAS, Phillip, Gr-1805
SUIRLOCK, Samuel, Gr-1799
SULAVAN, John, Bl-1815
SULCER, Larkin, Wh-1811
SULF, Malchizedsck, W-1812
SULIVAN, Henry, Bl-1815, Ge-1812
    Owen, Sn-1811
SULLAVAN, John, Bo-1801, Bo-1800
SULLENS, Josiah, K-1799
SULLEVENT, Isaac, Sn-1816
    Josiah, Sn-1811
    Owen, Sn-1816
    Saml., Sn-1811
SULLINS, Joseph, Ro-1805
    Nathan, Ro-1805
    Zechariah, Wh-1825
SULLIVAN, Alcana, W-1812
    Caleb, W-1812
    Charles, Wl-1804
    Clemna, W-1812, W-1805
    Clemy, Wl-1804
    Daniel, D-1811
    Fall, Fr-1812
    Fletcher, Sn-1816, Wl-1804
    Henry, Su-1797, Su-1796
    Jacob, W-1805, Wl-1804
    Jeremiah, D-1805
    John, Wh-1811, Wh-1825
    Mary, Su-1812
    Noah, Fr-1812
    Peter, Wl-1804
    Uriah, D-1805
    William, Wh-1825, D-1805
SULLIVANT, Jesse, Sn-1811
SULLIVENT, Edmond, Sn-1816
    John, Sn-1811
    Joseph, Sn-1816
SUMERS, Alex., Sn-1811
SUMMER, Abram, Wi-1810
    Jacob, D-1805
    Joseph, D-1805
    Samuel, B-1812
SUMMERS, Abraham, Wi-1815, Wi-1801
    Bosmon, Sn-1811
    Daniel, Wa-1814
    Isaac, Wa-1814(2), Wa-1819
    John, Sn-1816, Wi-1801
    Johnson, Wa-1814
    Jonathan, W-1812
    Joseph, Sn-1816, Wi-1810, Wi-1801
    Levi, Sn-1816
    Pleasndy, Sn-1816
    Samuel, B-1812

SUMMERS, Thos., Sn-1811
    William, B-1812, Je-1800, Wa-1819,
        Wa-1814
SUMMERVILLE, John, D-1811, D-1805
SUMMET, Daniel, Je-1822
SUMMIT, Benjamin, D-1805
SUMNER, Jacob, D-1811(2)
    Joseph, Wi-1815
    Thomas E., Wi-1815
    William, Sn-1811, Gr-1799
SUMNERS, John, Wi-1810
SUMPTER, George, Hw-1801
    Henry Sr., Hw-1801
    John, Hw-1801
SUNDERLAND, James, Gr-1821
SURBOR, Henry, Ge-1805
    Jacob, Ge-1805
SURRAT, John, Wl-1805
SURRATT, Jacob, W-1812
    James, W-1812
SURRET, Joseph, Wl-1804
SUSKINSON, David, Mt-1798
SUSWRAY, Nicholas, Su-1812
SUTER, Edmon, Mt-1798
SUTHERLAND, Daniel, Gr-1804
    David, Je-1800
    Davis, Je-1822
    James, Mt-1798
    Jon Jr., K*-1815
    Solomon, Je-1822
    Thomas, Bl-1815
    William, Ro-1805, Rb-1812
SUTHERS, Isaac, Mu-1816
SUTHON, Robert, Gr-1799
SUTLIFF, James, Je-1822
SUTTAL, Presley, Sn-1816
SUTTEL, John, Wh-1825
SUTTEN, Jasper, Mu-1816
    Pailey, Mt-1798
SUTTLE, Francis, Rb-1812
    John, Wh-1811
    Presley, Sn-1811
SUTTON, Buck, R-1819
    Cornelus, Co-1821
    Dempsey, R-1819
    Jacob, B-1812
    Jasper, D-1811
    John, B-1812, Co-1821, B-1812,
        Je-1800, Gr-1805
    Oalander?, Mu-1816
    Samuel, Ge-1805, Ge-1812
    Stephen, Wi-1815
    William, Fr-1812
    William Sr., B-1812
SUTTUL, Joseph, Gr-1805
SUYARS, James, Rb-1812
SWADER, Henry, Gi-1812
SWAFFORD, Wm., C-1818, C-1823
SWAGERTEY, Abraham, Ge-1783
SWAGERTY, Frederick, Ge-1783
    Thomas, R-1808
SWAGGART, Christain, Rb-1812
SWAIM, Uriah, Rb-1812
SWAIN, Elisha, Je-1800
    John, Je-1822
SWAINEY, Alexander, K-1796
    John L., Sn-1816
SWALER, George, Fr-1812
SWALLOWS, William, Wh-1825
SWAN, Daniel, R-1819
    James, R-1819
    John, D-1805, Wl-1804

SWAN, John B., R-1819
    Jonas, D-1805
    Moses H., R-1819
    Samuel, Je-1800
SWANEY, John, Je-1800
SWANGER, John, Ct-1796
SWANN, Burch, Rb-1812
    Catharine, Je-1822
    John C., Je-1822
    Robert, Je-1822
    Thomas, Sn-1811
    William, Wi-1815
SWANSON, Edward, Wi-1801, D-1788, Wi-1810,
        Wi-1815
    James, Wi-1815
    Pater, Gi-1812
    Peter, Gi-1819
    Richard, Wi-1815
    William, Mu-1816
SWANSY, John, Wi-1815
SWANY, John, Gr-1805
    Joseph, D-1805
SWARINGHAM, John, Gi-1812
SWARTZEL, Henry, Ge-1812
    Jacob, Ge-1812
    John, Ge-1812
    Philip, Ge-1812
SWASY, Richard, Ro-1805
SWEANEY, John, Gr-1804
    William, Gr-1804
SWEAR, Valentine, Mt-1798
SWEAT, Anthoney, Sn-1816
    Anthony, Sn-1811
    Benjamin, C-1823, C-1818
    Levi, Wh-1811
    Nathan, C-1823
    Wm., C-1823, C-1818
SWEATT, John, Sn-1811
SWEET, Nathan, C-1818
SWEETIN, John, C-1818
SWEETON, Dutton, A-1805
    John, A-1805, Gr-1799
    Robert, A-1805
    William, Gr-1799, A-1805
SWENEY, James C., Je-1800
SWENY, John, Sn-1811
SWIFT, Elisha, Wh-1825
    Flower, B-1812
    Richard, Rb-1812, D-1805
    Wm., Rb-1812
SWINDLE, Casen, Wh-1811
    Cason, Wh-1825
    Christopher, Wh-1825
    George C., Wh-1825
SWINEY, John, Wi-1815
SWINGLE, George, Je-1800, Wa-1819, Wa-1814
    John, Je-1800, Ct-1798, Wl-1804
SWINGLEY, George, Wl-1804
SWISHER, Henry, Wi-1815, Wi-1810
SWOFFORD, Aaron, Bl-1815
    Abraham, Bl-1815
SWON, Lewis, Wi-1810
SWOPES, James, C-1823
    John Sr., C-1823
    John Jr., C-1823
SWOYER, John, Wa-1814
SYBART, Abraham, Rb-1812
SYDARN & WINCOFF (H--coff?), Wh-1811
SYKES, Terrell, D-1811
SYLVESTER, Jacob, Su-1797
    Joseph, Su-1796, Su-1797
SYMONS, Leonard, Ge-1805
SYMS, Gray, Ro-1805

SYMS, James, Bo-1805
SYMSON, Benjamin, Gr-1799
SYNGLY, Samuel, Mu-1811
SYRES, Bennet, Gi-1812
SYRUS, Enoch, Gr-1821
TABB, George, Fr-1812
    William, Fr-1812
TABER, William, Wh-1825
TABOR, Solomon, Wh-1811
TACKER, Benjamin, Rb-1812
    John, Gi-1812
    Joshua, Gi-1812
TACKET, Lewis, Gr-1799
TAFF, George, Je-1800
    George Sr., Je-1822
    Peter, Je-1800
TAIT, Anderson, Wl-1804
    Caleb, Wi-1815
    David, D-1811
    John, D-1805, Wl-1804
    Martha, D-1805
    Richard, D-1805
    William, D-1805, D-1811
TALBETT, Isaac, D-1805
TALBOT, Clayton, D-1811
    John Q., Gi-1812, Wi-1810
    Richard, Wh-1811
TALBOTT, Claiton, Wi-1810
    Clayton, D-1811
    Eli, D-1811
    Joseph, Je-1822
    Ross, Je-1822
    Thomas, D-1805
TALINN, Howel, D-1811
TALLANT, Thomas, Wh-1825
TALLEY, Anderson, Mu-1811
    John, Wa-1814
    Pleasant, D-1811
    Richard, B-1812
    Ruben, Sn-1811
    Ruebin, Sn-1816
TALLY, Abraham, Mu-1816
    Jacob, Fr-1812
    John, Fr-1812(2), Su-1797, Su-1812,
        Su-1796
    Martin, Wl-1804
    Mathew, Fr-1812
    Spencer, Wl-1804
    William, Mu-1816, Wl-1804
    Willie, Fr-1812
TALOR, William, Wi-1815
TALUN, Howel, D-1805
TAMSER, Wiliam, Gi-1812
TANDSHERD, John, D-1811
TANKERLY, John, W-1805
TANKERSLEY, Charles, B-1812
    John, Mu-1811
    Richd., Wi-1815
    William, Wh-1825
TANKERSLY, John R., Wi-1810
    Joseph, Wh-1825
    Richard, B-1812
    Roland, Gi-1812
TANKESLEY, Rolin, Gi-1819
TANKESLY, John, W-1812
TANKSLY, John, Mu-1816
TANNEHILL, Wilkins, D-1811
TANNER, Edward, Mu-1816
    John, Gr-1805
    Massey, Wa-1814
TANWATER, Jacob, Fr-1812
    Lewis, Fr-1812
TARDEWELL?, George, Hu-1812

TARKENTON, Jesse, Wi-1801
    John, Wi-1801
    Joshua, Wi-1801
TARKINGTON, Benjamin, Wi-1810, Wi-1815
    Isaac, Wi-1810(2)
    Jesse, Wi-1815
    Jessee, Wi-1810(2)
    John, Wi-1815
    Joshua, Wi-1810, Wi-1815
TARKINTON, John, Wi-1810
TARL, William, D-1811
TARMATER, Jacob, Bo-1800
TARNE, Hamner, Gi-1812
TARPLEY, Alex., Gi-1812
    David, Gi-1819
    Thomas, Li-1812*
TARRANT, Henry, Ge-1812
TARRANTS, Leonard, Fr-1812
TARRY, Wm., Wi-1815
TARWATER, George, Bo-1805
    Jacob, Bo-1801, Bo-1805
    John, Bo-1805
    Lewis, Bo-1800, Bo-1801, Bo-1805
TASSEY, David, W-1812
TATE, Aaron, W-1812
    Alexander, W-1812
    David, Ge-1805
    David Sr., Gr-1821
    David Jr., Gr-1821
    Edward, Gr-1821
    Hezekiah, Li-1812*
    Isaac, Bo-1801, Bo-1805, Bo-1800
    James, W-1812
    Jesse O., Li-1812*
    John, W-1812, D-1811, Mu-1811,
        Gr-1799
    Richard, D-1811
    Robert, W-1812
    Samuel, Gr-1799
    Thomas, Ge-1783
    William, D-1811, Bo-1805
    Zacariah, Ge-1812
    Zanis, D-1811
    Zedekiah, D-1811
TATESON, David, Bl-1815
TATUM, Barnard, Mt-1798
    Dabney, Wl-1804
    Howel, Wl-1804, Mu-1811, Mt-1798
    James, D-1805, Mt-1798, D-1788
    Nathaniel, D-1811
TATUM & WIGGINS, Mt-1798
TATUMS, Absalom, heirs, Wi-1810
    Howel, Wi-1801
TAYLAR, Joseph, W-1812
TAYLOR, Abraham, D-1811
    Abram, Wi-1815
    Absalom, Wh-1811
    Albert G., Je-1822
    Allen, Mu-1816, Mu-1811
    Andrew, Ct-1796, Ct-1798
    Anson, Gi-1812
    Archelus, Fr-1812
    Archibald, Su-1797, Su-1796, Wl-1804
    Aren E., Sn-1816
    Benjamin, Sn-1816
    Benjben, Sn-1811
    Billington, Wi-1815
    Billonton, Wi-1810
    Chistopher, Wa-1819
    Christopher, Wa-1814
    Cyrus, Wh-1825
    Daniel, Gr-1804, Gr-1821(2), Gr-1805,

TAYLOR, Daniel, Cont'd.--Hu-1812, Su-1796
    Gr-1799
    Daniel Sr., Gr-1821
    Daniel W., D-1811
    David, A-1805, Bo-1801, Bo-1800
        Se-1799
    Davies, Rb-1812
    Edmond, W-1812
    Eleanor, Wi-1815
    Elijah, Su-1812
    Elisha, Wl-1804
    Elkin, Gi-1812
    Fedrick, Wi-1810
    Francis, D-1805, D-1811
    Gabriel, Gi-1812
    George, Gi-1812, Fr-1812, Gr-1804,
        Bl-1815, D-1811, D-1805,
        Gr-1805
    Gilbert D., Gi-1812
    Green, Wh-1825
    Hally, Wl-1804
    Henrey, J-1802
    Henry, Wa-1819, Ro-1805, Wa-1814
    Hughs, Gr-1804, Gr-1805
    Hughs O., Gr-1821
    Isaac, Su-1796, Su-1797, Ge-1783,
        Ct-1796, Ct-1798, Wh-1825
    Isaac Sr., Wh-1811
    Isaac Jr., Wh-1811(4)
    Jacob, Su-1812, Sn-1811
    James, Je-1800, Ct-1796, Bo-1800,
        Bo-1801(2), Wh-1825(2), Mt-1798
        Gr-1805, Wl-1804, W-1812(2),
        Gr-1799, J-1802, A-1805,
        Fr-1812
    Jeremiah Jr., Su-1796, Su-1797
    John, S-1805, A-1805(3), B-1812,
        Bo-1801, Bo-1800(2), Wh-1825,
        Wi-1804, D-1811, Gr-1805,
        Sn-1811(2), Sn-1816, Su-1796,
        Su-1812(2), Wl-1804(2)
    John H., Wa-1819
    John M., Sn-1816
    Jonathan, Rb-1812
    Joseph, Wi-1810, W-1805, Gr-1805,
        Gi-1812, Fr-1812, D-1811,
        Su-1796, Su-1797, Su-1812,
        Se-1799, Sn-1792, Sn-1811(2),
        Sn-1816(2)
    Joseph B. Smith, Su-1796
    Josephus, D-1811
    Joshua, D-1805, Wl-1804
    Josiah, Rb-1812
    Lee, Fr-1812
    Lefoy, Wa-1814
    Leroy, Wa-1819, Wa-1814
    Levi, Wa 1814
    Lewis, Gi-1812, Mu-1811
    Magnus, Bo-1800
    Martin, D-1805
    Mary M., Wi-1810
    Matthew, Ct-1796
    Mekin, Wh-1825
    Miles, Rb-1812
    Morgan, Gr-1804, Gr-1805
    Nathaniel, Ct-1796, Ct-1798, Su-1812
    Nathl., heirs, Gr-1821
    Orren, Rb-1812
    Owen, Fr-1812
    Parmenas, Je-1822, Je-1800
    Perry, Wl-1804
    Philip, Fr-1812

TAYLOR, Robert, D-1805, Ro-1805, R-1819,
    Wa-1814, Gr-1805, Gi-1812, Fr-1812,
    Gr-1804, Sn-186, Sn-1811,
    D-1811
  Samuel, Gr-1804, Mu-1811, D-1811
  Sarah, Mt-1798
  Stephen, Su-1796, Su-1797, Su-1812
  Thomas, Gi-1812, Ge-1812, J-1802,
    Bo-1801, Mu-1811, D-1805
  Thomas Sr., Wh-1811, D-1811
  Thomas Jr., Wh-1811, D-1811
  Tho. E. Jr., Wh-1811
  Tildon, Sn-1816
  William, Je-1822, W-1812, Rb-1812,
    Gi-1812, Wh-1825(2), Sn-1811,
    Wi-1801, Hu-1812
  William Sr., Sn-1816
  William Jr., Sn-1816
  Willis, Je-1822
  Zachariah, Rb-1812
  Zack, Wl-1804
  Zaick, Sn-1816
  Heirs, Gr-1821
  _____, Fr-1812
TEAG, William, Wh-1811
TEAGE, Moses, C-1823
TEAGUE, David, A-1805
  Joshua, A-1805
  Nathaniel, A-1805
  Nimrod, A-1805
  Stephen, Gr-1821
  William, A-1805
TEAHORN?, William, Mu-1816
TEAL, Edward, Gr-1805
TEALES, Joseph, D-1811
TEALL, Abm., Sn-1792
TEAR, Joseph, Mt-1798
TEASE?, Charles, Hu-1812
TEDFOR, Robt., Li-1812*
TEDFORD, Alexander, Bo-1801
  George, Bo-1801
  John, Bo-1801
  Joseph, Bo-1801
  Robert, Bo-1801
  Thos., Li-1812*, Bo-1801
TEDLOCK, James, Wa-1819
  Lewis, Wa-1814
  Tom, Wa-1819
TEDWELL, Eli, Gi-1812
  Millington, Gi-1812
TEEL, Edward, Gr-1804
  Jacob, Ge-1805
  John, Bo-1801, Bo-1800
TEGNEY, Stephen, W-1812
TELFORD, Hugh, Wl-1804
  Mirriam, Wa-1819
  Samuel, B-1812, Wl-1804
  William, B-1812, Wl-1804
TELLFORD, George, Bo-1800
  John, Bo-1800
  Robert, Bo-1800
  Thomas, Bo-1800
TELLY, John, B-1812
TEMPLE, Burel, Wi-1801
  Burrell, Wi-1815
  James, Ge-1805, Ge-1812
  John, Ge-1805, Gi-1812
  John T., Ge-1812
  Josiah, Gi-1812, Ge-1805
  Major, Ge-1805, Ge-1812, Ge-1783
  Robert, B-1812
  Thomas, Ge-1812, Ge-1805

TEMPLE, William, Ge-1805
TEMPLETON, Absalom, Ge-1805
  Absalam, Ge-1812
  Edward, Ge-1812
  George, Wh-1825
  Green P., Wh-1825
  James, Gr-1799, B-1812, Wi-1815
  John, Wh-1811, B-1812, Wh-1825
  Thomas, Wh-1825
TEMPLIN, Samuel, Wa-1819
  William, Wa-1814(2), Wa-1819
TENDALL, Noah R., Sn-1816
TENFORD, James, Bo-1800
TENILL, Achilis, Gi-1819
TENISON, Zachariah, Gi-1819
TENNEN, Alexander, Gi-1819
TENNEY, Wm., W-1812
TENNISON, Mathew, D-1811
  Samuel, D-1811
TENNY, Widow, Gi-1819
TERFORD, William, Ct-1796
TERMON, Garet, Wi-1810
TERNER, Wm., Sn-1816
TERNSTILL, Alexr., Mt-1798
  Obdh., D-1788
TERREL, WM., Sn-1816
TERRELL, Benjamin, Je-1800
  James, D-1811, Wi-1815
  Obadiah, Sn-1787
  Obediah, Sn-1792
TERRILL, George, Mu-1816
TERRY, Carlin, Sn-1811
  Clement, K-1799
  Daniel, C-1818
  Elijah, C-1818, C-1823
  Garland, Sn-1816
  Jesper, Ct-1796
  Jessee, K-1796
  John, A-1805(2), C-1818, Wh-1825,
    Gi-1812, Wh-1811
  Joseph, Wh-1825, K-1799
  Josiah, C-1818, A-1805, C-1823
  Kibble, Wl-1804, B-1812
  Moses, Ct-1796, Mu-1811
  Richard, Gr-1799
  Sam, K-1799
  Sarah, widow, Ct-1796
  Thompson, B-1812
  William, Wa-1819, Gi-1812
TESHING, William, Sn-1816
THACKER, Thomas, Wa-1819
  William, Wa-1819, Gi-1812
THACKSTONE, James, Wi-1801
THAIRMAN, Joseph, Bo-1801
THARCHILL, Levy, Ro-1805
THARP, Daniel, Je-1822
  Henry, Rb-1812
  John, Bo-1805
  Wm., Rb-1812
THARRMAN, Ralph, Wh-1811
THAXTON, John, W-1812
THERMAN, Eli, A-1805
  Philip, A-1805
THERMOND, Goldsberry F., Sn-1816
THIGPIN, Amos, Mu-1811
THING, R., K*-1815
THOMAS, Adam, Bo-1805, Bo-1801, Bo-1800
  Adonigah, C-1823, C-1818
  Aduk, Sn-1816
  Alexander, Wh-1811
  Andrew, Wi-1815
  Benjamin, Mu-1816, Mu-1811, Mt-1798

195

THOMAS, Capt. Benjamin, Mt-1798
    Cesar, Mu-1811
    Charles, Se-1799, W-1812
    Christopher, A-1805
    Daniel, Mu-1816
    David, Su-1812, Ro-1805
    Elisha, C-1823, C-1818, Sn-1811,
        Mu-1816
    G. Mary, C-1818
    George, Bo-1801, Bo-1800, Su-1797,
        Wh-1811, Wh-1825, Su-1796,
        Mu-1816
    Griffith, Je-1800
    Henry, A-1805, Bo-1800, Bo-1801,
        Wl-1804
    Isaac, Lieutent, D-1788
    Isaac Jr., Se-1799
    Isaac J., Mu-1816
    Jack, R-1819
    Jacob, Bo-1801, Sn-1792, Wl-1804,
        Bo-1800, Su-1797, Su-1796,
        Su-1812
    Jacob Jr., Su-1812
    James, Wl-1804, A-1805, Rb-1812,
        Su-1796, W-1812
    James J., Wi-1815
    Jesse N., Wh-1811
    Jesse W., D-1811
    Jessee, Wi-1801, D-1805, Wh-1825
    Job H., Mu-1816
    John, A-1805(2), Bo-1800, Bo-1801,
        Se-1799, Su-1796, Su-1812,
        Ro-1805, Je-1800, Wi-1815,
        D-1811, Mt-1798, D-1788
    John P., Sn-1816
    Joseph, C-1823, C-1818, Wh-1811,
        Wl-1804, Wh-1825, Mu-1811
    Joshua, heirs, Mu-1811
    Lodewick, A-1805
    Lodowick, A-1805
    Mack & John, D-1805
    Mark, Mu-1811
    Martin, Ro-1805
    Mary, Wi-1815
    Mary Graves, C-1818
    Mery, Wi-1810
    Meuson, B-1812
    Morrison (widow of), Gr-1804
    Nevill, Wh-1811
    Pearce, heirs, Ge-1812
    Peter, Je-1800, Je-1822
    Pharras, D-1805
    Phenious, Wi-1810
    Philemon, Mt-1798
    Philip, D-1805, D-1811(2)
    Reuben, Je-1822
    Richard, Mu-1810, Mu-1811
    Robert, D-1811
    Samuel, Wh-1825, Wl-1804, Gr-1821,
        Wh-1811
    Solomon, Wl-1804
    Stephen, Mt-1798
    William, Wi-1815, Sn-1792, Wl-1804(3)
        Se-1799, Je-1800, R-1819(2),
        W-1812, Wh-1825, D-1811,
        Sn-1811, Mu-1811, Sn-1816,
        Wi-1810
    Wm. Robt., D-1805
THOMASON, Jeremiah, Mu-1816
THOMASS, Daniel, Mu-1811
THOMASSON, George, Gr-1805
    William, W-1812

THOMLINSON, Warren, Sn-1811
THOMLSON, Ebenezer, Mu-1816
THOMPKINS, John, Mt-1798
    Joseph, Ct-1796
    Thos., Mt-1798
    Thos. B., Hu-1812
THOMPSON, Abraham, B-1812
    Adam, Wa-1814
    Alexander, Ge-1812, Gr-1804, Mu-1816
    Allen, D-1811
    Amos, W-1805
    Andrew, Wa-1814
    Archabald, W-1812
    Benjamin, Fr-1812, C-1823(2),
        Mu-1816
    Blag, C-1818
    Burrell, Fr-1812
    Catharin, Sn-1811
    David, W-1812, Wh-1811, Gi-1812
    Drury, Gi-1812
    Eaphraim, D-1811
    Ebenezer, Mu-1811
    Elisha, Mu-1811
    Frederick, D-1811, Wi-1815
    Gennens, B-1812
    George, Gr-1804, Ge-1805
    Harmon, C-1823
    Henry, Ge-1805, Ge-1812, Wl-1804,
        Mu-1816
    Hensly, Mu-1811
    Herman, C-1818
    Hudson, Sn-1816
    Hugh, Wi-1815
    Isaac, Gr-1805(2)
    Jacob, D-1811
    James, Je-1800, Je-1822, Wh-1811,
        Sn-1816, R-1819, Wi-1801,
        Wi-1810, Wi-1815(2), Gr-1799,
        Gr-1804, Gr-1805(2), Gr-1821,
        Ge-1805, Ge-1812, D-1788,
        Bo-1801, Bo-1805
    James Esq., Mu-1816
    James B., Wi-1815, Wi-1801
    Jason, D-1805, D-1811, Wl-1804
    Jeese, Wa-1819
    Jeremiah, Mu-1811
    Jesse, Se-1799
    Jessee, R-1819, D-1805
    John, Wl-1804, Gr-1805, Gr-1821,
        Gi-1812(2), Wi-1810(2),
        Wi-1815, Sn-1792, Sn-1811,
        D-1805, C-1818, R-1819,
        Je-1800, Bo-1800(2),
        Bo-1801(2), B-1812
    Joseph, Wa-1819, B-1812, Sn-1787,
        Ct-1798
    Joshua, Ct-1798, Ct-1796
    Larrance, Sn-1787
    Laurence, Mu-1811, D-1811
    Lawrence, Sn-1816
    Leonard, Wi-1815
    Lewis, C-1818, C-1823
    Moses, Wl-1804, R-1819, W-1812
    Nathaniel, Mu-1811, Mu-1816
    Neal, D-1811, D-1805
    Nicholas, Rb-1812, Sn-1823, Sn-1811
    Oliver, Gi-1812
    Owen, W-1812
    Philip, B-1812
    Reuben, B-1812
    Richard, Gr-1799, Gr-1804, Gr-1805
    Robert, Bo-1800(2), D-1811(2),

THOMPSON, Robert, Cont'd.--Mu-1811(2),
         Mu-1816, D-1805(2), Wi-1801,
         Wl-1804, D-1788
    Samuel, D-1811, Mu-1816
    Seth, Wa-1819
    Stephen, Fr-1812
    Temple, Gr-1799, Gr-1804
    Terry, Mu-1816
    Thomas, R-1819, Ge-1812(3), Ge-1805,
         Sn-1787, D-1788(2), D-1811,
         D-1805
    Thomas Sr., D-1811
    W. William, Mu-1811
    William, W-1812, Je-1800, Je-1822,
         Su-1812, Wa-1819(2), Wa-1814,
         C-1818, A-1805, D-1811(2),
         D-1805(2)
    Zachariah, J-1802
    Zacheriah, W-1812
THOMSON, Azariah, Sn-1792
    Elijah, Ge-1812
    Garsham, Ct-1796
    Jas., D-1788
    James B., Wi-1801
    John, Gr-1805, D-1788
    Robert, Wi-1801
THONPSON, David, Wa-1819
THOPSON, Thompson, B-1812
THORN, John, D-1805
    Mary, Ge-1812
THORNBERRY, Jonathan, Gi-1812
    Joseph, Je-1800
    Martin, Gr-1821
    Richard, Gr-1805
THORNBERY, Joel, Je-1800
    Richard, Je-1800
    Thomas, Je-1800
THORNBURG, Benjamin, Je-1800
    John, Wa-1819
THORNBURGH, Ai, Je-1822
    Benjamin, Je-1822(2)
    Thomas, D-1811(2)
THORNBURY, Henry Sr., Je-1800
    Henry Jr., Je-1800
THORNHILL, Armsted, Bo-1801
    Barnabas & Robert, D-1805
THORNTON, Barnett, Je-1822
    James A., Je-1822
    John, Mu-1816, Ge-1805, Mu-1811
    Reuben, Ct-1796, Ct-1798
    Richard, B-1812
    Robert, Mu-1811
    Robert G., Mu-1816
    Samuel, Mt-1798
    William, Gi-1819
THORP, John, Je-1800
THORPE, William, Ro-1805
THORTON, Clark, Fr-1812
    Owen, Mt-1798
THRASHER, John, B-1812, Fr-1812
THRATCHER, John, Fr-1812
THREEWIT, Edward, Ct-1798
THRESTHER, Isaac, Wa-1814, Wa-1819
THURMAN, Eli, Bl-1815
    Graves, Wi-1815
    James, Bl-1815
THURSTON, Christian, estate, Ge-1812
THWEEAT, Harwood, Wi-1815
    William, Wi-1815
TIDWELL, Isaac, Gi-1812
    James, Ro-1805
    John, Mu-1816

TIDWELL, Josiah, W-1812
    Mark, W-1812
    Miller, Gi-1819
    Read, Gi-1812
    Richard, Mu-1816, Mu-1811
    Simon, W-1812
    Vinson, Gi-1819
TIGNAL, Isaac, Wi-1815
TIGNOR, Isaac, Wi-1810
TIGS, John, Mt-1798
TILFERD, Thomas, Wa-1814
TILFORD, Samul, Sn-1816
TILLERY, Thomas, Wh-1825
TILLEY, Edmond, Wh-1825
    John, W-1812, W-1805
TILLMAN, Francis, Wi-1810
    Geo., Wi-1810
    Hayden, Wi-1810
    Jno., Wi-1810, B-1812
    William, Wh-1825
TILIMAN, William M., Wh-1825
TILLY, Henery, Bo-1805
TILMAN, Daniel, Wl-1804
    Francis, Wi-1815
    Haden, Wi-1815
    John, A-1805, Wi-1815
    Tobias, A-1805
TILSON, John, Wa-1814, Wa-1819
    Joseph, Wa-1819
    Peleg, Wa-1819
    Peleg Jr., Wa-1819
    Pilig, Wa-1814
    Stephen, Wa-1814
    Thomas, Wa-1819, Wa-1814
    William, Wa-1814, Wa-1819
    William Jr., Wa-1819
TILTSON, William, Ge-1812
TIMBERMAN, George, Bo-1800, Bo-1801
    Jacob, Bo-1800, Bo-1801
    Jonathan, Bo-1800, Bo-1801
    Matthew, Bo-1800, Bo-1801
    Stephen, Bo-1800
TIMMONS, Thos., Li-1812*
    William, Wi-1810, Li-1812*
TINDAL, John, D-1811
TINKER, Abraham, Wa-1814
TINKLE, George, Wl-1804
TINNEN, Hugh, Sn-1792
TINNER, Dice, Wl-1804
    Moses, Wl-1804
    Robert, Gi-1819
TINNIN, John, Sn-1816, Sn-1811
TINNING, Hugh, Mt-1798
    John, Mt-1798
    Thompson, Mt-1798
TINNINS, George, Ro-1805
TINNON, Wm., Sn-1816
TINSLEY, Cornelious Sr., Sn-1811
    Cornelious Jr., Sn-1816
    Cornelius, Sn-1816
    Moses, Sn-1811
    Richard, Sn-1823
    Spencer, Mu-1816, Mu-1811
    Sterling, Mu-1816
TIPPET, Erastus, Bo-1800
    Luke, W-1812
TIPPETT, William, W-1812
TIPPEY, Abraham, D-1811
TIPTON, Abraham, Wa-1814, Wa-1819
    Benjamin, Bo-1801
    Bing, Bo-1800
    Edon, Wh-1825

TIPTON, Edward, D-1805, D-1811
    Isaac, Ct-1796, Ct-1798
    James, Su-1812
    John, Su-1812, Ct-1796, Ct-1798
    John Sr., Ct-1798
    Jonathan, Ct-1798, Ct-1796
    Jonathan Sr., Ct-1796
    Joseph, Bo-1800, Bo-1801, Ct-1796, Ct-1798
    Joshua, Wl-1804
    Masheck, Bo-1805
    Masheeck, Se-1799
    Meshech, Bo-1801
    Mordica, Se-1799
    Robert, Se-1799
    Samuel, Ct-1798, Ct-1796
    Shadrack, A-1805
    Stephen, W-1812
    Thomas, Ct-1796, Ct-1798
TISDALE, John, Wi-1815
TITSWORTH, Frederick, Su-1812
    Thomas, Su-1812(2), Su-1797(2), Su-1796(2)
TITTLE, David, W-1812
    George, W-1812
    John, Wa-1819
    Peter, W-1812
    Samuel, Wl-1804
    Thomas, W-1812
TITTSWORTH, James, Hu-1812
TITUS, George, D-1805
    James, D-1805
    U____, D-1788
TIVES, Robert, C-1823
TIVIS, Robert, C-1818
TOBAT, George, R-1808
TOBERRY, John, A-1805
    Thomas, A-1805
TOD, Amy, Sn-1811, Sn-1816
    Asa, Sn-1816
    Lamb, Sn-1816
    Robert, Wi-1815
    Susanna, Sn-1816
TODD, Daniel, B-1812
    Isaac, C-1818, C-1823
    James & Edward, D-1805
    Jesse, C-1818
    Loe, C-1818, C-1823
    Samuel, D-1811
    Samuel A., Je-1822
    William, Ro-1805
TODHUNTER, Evin, Fr-1812
    Joseph, Ge-1805
TOLAR, Needham, Rb-1812
    Robert, Rb-1812
TOLER?, Manly, W-1812
TOLIVER, Charles, B-1812
TOLLASON, Erasmus, Bl-1815
TOLLAVER, Zachariah, Gr-1821
TOLLESSON, Erasmus, Bl-1815
TOLLET, David, Bl-1815
    Henry, Bl-1815
    John Sr., Bl-1815
TOLLETT, John Jr., Bl-1815
    Mark, Bl-1815
TOLLEVER, Jesse, W-1812
    John, W-1812
    Moses, W-1812
    William, W-1812
TOLLEY, Washington G., Gi-1812
    Zacharia Jr., Sn-1811
    Zachariah Sr., Sn-1811

TOLLISON, Calib, Wh-1825
TOLLOCK, David, Sn-1811
TOM, Joseph, Mu-1816
TOMASON, George, Gr-1805
TOMBERLAIN, Gole, Wh-1825
TOMES, James, Wi-1810
TOMKINS, Francis, Sn-1811
    John, Sn-1811
    Lydee, Sn-1816
TOMLIN, David, W-1812
    Jessee, Mu-1811
TOMLINSON, Jesse, Mu-1816
    Moses, Mu-1811, Mu-1816
TOMPKINS, Humphrey, Gi-1812
    John, Sn-1816
    Thomas, D-1805
TOMPSON, John, Mu-1811
    Mary, Ge-1812
    Roben, Wi-1810
    Robert, Wi-1815
    William, Mu-1811
TOMSON, John, Wi-1815
TONCRY, Zophar, Ge-1783
TONEY, William, Mu-1811
TONGATE, Martin, Gi-1812
    Zach., Gi-1812
TONNER, Henry, Gr-1821
    John, Gr-1821
TOOAX, Timothy, Wi-1815
TOOL, Jn., K*-1815
TOOLEY, Adam, Se-1799
    Charles, Wi-1810
TOOMB, John, Mu-1816
TOPP, John, D-1805
TOPPS, John, D-1811
TORBET, Alex, Su-1797
    Alex Jr., Su-1797
    Alexander, Su-1796
    Alexander Jr., Su-1796
    John, Su-1796, Su-1797
TORBIT, John, Su-1812
    Joseph, Su-1812
TORNEY, Patton, Sn-1792
TOSH, Martin, Je-1800
TOTEN, Benjamin, Gr-1799
TOTTEN, Benjamin, J-1802
TOTTON, John, Ge-1783
TOURNER, Lewis, Wi-1815
TOWEL, Isaac, Sn-1811, Sn-1816, Sn-1787
TOWER, Benjamin, Sn-1816, Wl-1804
TOWN, William, Gr-1799
TOWNLEY, Joseph, Gr-1821
TOWNLY, William, Gr-1821
TOWNSEN, Joshua, Fr-1812
TOWNSEND, Andrew, Wh-1811
    Charles, Wh-1825
    James, Wh-1811(2), Wh-1825
    John, Je-1822, Wh-1811
    Peter, Sn-1811, Sn-1816
    Thomas, Wh-1811
TOWNSLEY, George, Bo-1800, Bo-1801
TRACEY, Michel, Sn-1816
    William, Sn-1816
TRACKER, Edward, Gr-1799
TRACY, Even, Wl-1804
    John, D-1805
TRADEWELL, Daniel, D-1811
TRAINER, Edward, Mu-1816
TRAMBLE, David, R-1808
TRAMELL, Philip, Gr-1799
TRAMMELL, David, C-1823
    James, C-1823

TRAMMELL, Peter, C-1823
    Phillip, Sn-1792
TRANCHAM, Jeremiah, Wi-1810
TRANER, William, D-1805
TRANTHAM, Martin, Wi-1815
TRAP, James, Sn-1816
TRAPP, John, Wh-1811
    Martin, Wh-1811
    Terry, Wh-1811
    William, Wh-1825
TRASHER, Alexander, Sn-1816
TRAVES, Henry, Mu-1811
TRAVIS, John, Fr-1812, W-1812
    Matthew, Rb-1812
    Robert, Fr-1812
    William, Fr-1812, Gi-1812, W-1812
TRAYLOR, William, Sn-1811
TREADWAY, Isham, Rb-1812
    John, Wa-1814, Wa-1819
TREDWAY, Allan, Su-1796
    Isom, Gr-1799
    Robert, Su-1812
    Thomas, Su-1812, Su-1797
TREMBLE, James, J-1802
    Moses, Ge-1783
TRENT, Alexander, Hw-1799
    Simon, Fr-1812
    William, Cl-1803, Hw-1799, Wa-1814
    Williamson, Hw-1801
    _____, Fr-1812
TRENTHAM, Martin, D-1788
TREVANT, David, C-1818
    John, C-1818
    Peter, C-1818
TREWITT, Abraham, Wi-1815
TRIBBLE, Peter, B-1812
TRIBEW, John, Sn-1823
TRIBLE, Abram, Sn-1811
TRICE, John, Rb-1812
TRIG, Wm. Sr., Sn-1811
TRIGG, Abram, Sn-1811
    Abm., Sn-1816
    Alenson, Wl-1804
    Daniel, Wl-1804
    Lamon, Se-1799
    Richd. A., Sn-1811
    W., W-1812
    Will, Sn-1811
    Will. V. A., Sn-1816
    William, Sn-1816(2)
    William Sr., Wl-1804
    William Jr., Wl-1804
TRIM, James, Ge-1805, Ge-1812
    William, Sn-1811
TRIMBLE, Arch, Bo-1800, Bo-1801
    James, Mu-1811, Mu-1816
    John, Bo-1800(2), Bo-1801(2),
        Ge-1783
    Richard, R-1808
    Wm., Rb-1812
TRIMBLE & CAMPBELL, Mu-1816
    Richard, R-1808
    Wm., Rb-1812
TRIMBULL, William, D-1805
TRIP, John, B-1812
TRIPLET, John, K-1799
TRIPP, Samuel, Wi-1815
TRIPPET, Jonathan, Bo-1801
TROAX, Peter, Su-1797
TROBOUGH, Frederick, Ge-1805
    Henry, Ge-1805
    John, Rb-1812

TROBOUGH, Nicholas, Ge-1805
    Wm., Rb-1812
TROGDON, Abner, Gr-1804, Gr-1821
    Ezecheal, Gr-1799
    Ezekiel, Gr-1821, Gr-1805, Gr-1804
    Solomon, Gr-1821
TROLER, Isham, Mt-1798
TRORBOUGH, Frederick, Ge-1812
    George, Ge-1812
    Nicholas, Ge-1812
    William, Ge-1812
TROSDALL, Jos., Sn-1792
TROTMAN, Curtis, Gr-1805
    John, Gr-1805
TROTTER, Benjamin, Wi-1815
    Isham R., Wi-1810, Wi-1815
    Isham R., Esq., Wi-1815
    J. R., Wi-1815
    James, Bo-1805, Je-1800
    Thos., Li-1812*
    William, D-1811
TROUSDALE, James, Sn-1811, Mu-1816,
        Mu-1811
    William, Mu-1811, Mu-1816
TROUT, Benjamin, Wl-1804
    Joseph, Wl-1804
    Michael, Je-1822
TROWER, Thomas, Su-1812
TROXALE, David, Su-1812
TROXELL, Abraham, C-1823
TROY, John, Ge-1805
TRU, John, Co-1821
TRUET, Abraham, Wi-1810
    Elijah, Wl-1804
    Henry Sr., Wl-1804
    Henry Jr., Wl-1804
    Levi, Wl-1804
TRUETT, John, D-1805
    Nicholas, D-1805
TRUHART, James, D-1811
TRUITT, John B., Sn-1811
TRUMAN, Amos, B-1812
TRUMBO, Ambrus, Sn-1811
    Eprum, Sn-1811
    George, Sn-1811
TRUN, Elijah, Mu-1811
TRUSSELL, Benjamin, Rb-1812
TRUSTY, Abraham, Je-1822
    William, Je-1822
TRYON?, James, B-1812
TUBBS, George Sr., Fr-1812
TUCKER, Aaron, Wh-1825(2)
    Anderson, Wi-1815
    Campbell, D-1805
    Drury, Mu-1811
    Edward, B-1812
    George, Wh-1825
    Henry, Gi-1812
    James, B-1812, Je-1800, W-1812,
        Je-1822
    John, Gr-1799, Wa-1819, B-1812(2)
        Gi-1812, Je-1800, Ro-1805,
        Je-1822, Sn-1811, D-1788,
        Sn-1816
    John P., Wi-1815
    Jonathan, Wa-1819
    Joseph, Wa-1819, Wa-1814, Wi-1815
    Lewis, Wi-1815
    Nicholas, Wa-1819
    Nicolas, Wa-1814
    Radford, Ro-1805
    Robert, Ro-1805

TUCKER, Silas, Fr-1812
    Stephen T., Wh-1825
    Wm., Wi-1815(2)
    Wyly, Je-1822
TUDOR, Harris, C-1818, A-1805
TUKLE, Wm. C., Wh-1825
TULGON, Silas, Sn-1816
TULL, Nicholas, D-1811
TULLEY, Mark, Bl-1815
    Zachariah, Sn-1816
TULLIS, Samuel, Ct-1796
TUMBRILL, James, D-1811
TUNE, James, Wi-1815
    Lewis, Wi-1815
TUNING, John, Su-1812
TUNKLE, Henry, A-1805
TUNLESON, John, Mu-1811
TUNLEY, Sampson, D-1811
TUNNEL, Wm., K-1799
    Wm., Jr., K-1799
TUNNELL, John, A-1805
    Stephen, Ge-1805
    William, A-1805, Ge-1805
    William Sr., A-1805
TUNNEY, Samuel, Wh-1825
TUNSTAL, Thomas, Rb-1812
TUNSTALL, James, Rb-1812
TUPPENCE, Caty, Sn-1816
    David, Sn-1816
TUPS, Benjamin, Ro-1805
TURBERVELL, Benjamin, D-1811
TURBWELL, Benjamin, D-1811
    Willis, D-1811
TURLEY, Thomas, Gr-1821
TURNBAUGH, Andrew, Mu-1811
    James, Mu-1811
TURNBOW, Andrew, Gi-1819
TURNDALE, James, Sn-1816
TURNER, Aaron, Mu-1811
    Adam, Sn-1811
    Adam Sr., Sn-1816
    Adam Jr., Sn-1811, Sn-1816
    Alexander, Mu-1816, Mu-1811
    Benjamin, Wh-1825
    Buford, Mu-1811
    Edmund, Sn-1816
    George, Hu-1812, D-1805
    Henry, Se-1799
    J. Anthony, Mu-1811
    Jacob, Sn-1816
    James, Wh-1825, B-1812(2), Gi-1812,
        Je-1800, Sn-1816(2), Wi-1815,
        Sn-1811
    Jessee, Mu-1811, Mu-1816
    John, Mu-1811, Mt-1798, K-1799,
        Je-1800, Gr-1821, B-1812,
        Rb-1812, W-1805, W-1812,
        Sn-1811(3), Sn-1816(2)
    John Sr., Sn-1823
    John E., Wh-1825, Rb-1812
    Jonas, Wh-1825
    Jonathan, Wa-1814
    Josiah, Wh-1825
    Lemaneul, Sn-1811
    Lewis, Wh-1825
    Martin, Sn-1811
    Moses, Wh-1825
    Richard, Wh-1825
    Robert, Mu-1811, Je-1800, Gr-1799
    Spratley, B-1812, Wi-1810
    Teresha, Sn-1811
    Thomas, Wh-1811, Mu-1816, Mu-1811,

TURNER, Thomas, Cont'd.--Wi-1810
    Trusha, Sn-1816
    W. L., Sn-1823
    Walter, Je-1800
    William, Sn-1816, Mu-1811, D-1811(2)
        B-1812, Sn-1811, D-1805,
        Wh-1825
    Wm. J., Sn-1816
    Willis, Rb-1812
    Yancey, Sn-1816
    Yancy, Sn-1811
    Zachariah, B-1812
TURNEY, Henry, Wl-1804
TURNLEY, George, Je-1822, Je-1800
    James, Je-1822
    John, Je-1800
    John C., Je-1822
    William, Je-1822
TURNNER, William, Sn-1811
TURNS, Charls, Sn-1816
TURPIN, Eddmon, Sn-1811
TURRENTINE, James, B-1812
TUSSEY, Jacob, Su-1812, Su-1797, Su-1796
TUTT, Benjamin, Gi-1819
TUTTLE, David, Mu-1811
    Ichabold, Mu-1816
    James, Gr-1805(2), Gr-1799, Gr-1821
    Peter, Gr-1799
    Solomon, Gi-1812
    William, Gr-1804, Gr-1805, Gr-1821,
        Wl-1804
TWIFORD, William, Ct-1798
TWIKLE, Henry, A-1805
TYE, John, Gr-1799
TYLER, Aron, Je-1822
    Jacob, Je-1822
    John, Sn-1811
    William, Wa-1814(2), Wa-1819
TYLOR, John, Sn-1816
TYNER, Jessee, Mu-1816
TYNOR, Lewis, Su-1796
TYRE, William, Ct-1798, Ct-1796
TYREE, C. Richmond, Sn-1816
    Richard, D-1811
TYREL, John, D-1805
ULESS, Adam, B-1812
UMPHRIS, JOhn, Gr-1805
UMSTEAD, John, C-1818
UMSTED, John, Wi-1810
UNDERHILL, Abra., Wl-1804
    John, Gr-1804, Gr-1805(2)
    William, Gr-1804, Gr-1799
UNDERSHILL, Daniel, Gr-1805
UNDERWOOD, Able, Wh-1825
    Anthony, Gr-1805
    Benjamin, Mo-1825
    James, A-1805
    John, Su-1812, A-1805, Mc-1825(3)
        D-1811, Sn-1816
    Leey, Mu-1811
    Levi, Gi-1812
    Perrey, Wi-1810
    Perry, Wi-1815
    Shadrach, Wh-1825
    Thomas, Wh-1825
    William, A-1805
UPCHURCH, Joseph, Wh-1811
UPSHUR, Dawrey, B-1812
UPTON, Isaac, Bo-1801
    James, Bo-1801, R-1819, Bo-1805,
        Bo-1800
    John, Ge-1783

URSURY, Samuel, Wh-1811
    William, Wh-1811
USERY, William, Wh-1825
USHER, David, C-1823
    John, C-1823
USREY, Peter, Gi-1812(2)
    Samuel, Sh-1825
    William, Gi-1812
USRY, Thomes (Thornes?), K-1799
USSERY, Philip, Ro-1805
    Samuel, A-1805, Wi-1815
    Thomas, K-1796, Mu-1816
    William, A-1805
USSREY, Thomas, Ro-1805
USSURY, Thomas, Bo-1800
USURY, Phillip, Wh-1811
UTINGER, Jacob, Ge-1812
UTTER, Abraham, Bo-1800, Bo-1801
UTTINGER, John, Ge-1805
UZEL, Jourdin, Sn-1816
UZZEL, Isom, Sn-1816
VAESTLE, Richard, Hw-1799
VAILES, Benjamin, Gr-1805
VALE, Levy, Ge-1812
VALENTINE, Henry, Co-1821
    Isaac, Sn-1816
    William, Co-1821
VALUNTINE, Isaac, Sn-1811
VAN, Edmon, Co-1821
VANBIBBER, James, Gr-1799(2)
    John, Gr-1799(2)
    Peter, Gr-1799(2)
VANCE, David, Bo-1801, Bo-1805, Je-1822
    David G., Wa-1819, Wa-1814
    Hugh, Wa-1819
    James, Je-1800, Je-1822
    John, Je-1800(2), Su-1797, Su-1812,
        Gi-1812, Ct-1796
    John Sr., Su-1812
    John Esq., Su-1796
    Patrick, Gr-1804, Gr-1805
    Robert, Je-1822
    Samuel, Ge-1812(2), Ge-1805
    Thomas, W-1812, Ge-1783
    William, Gi-1812
    William K., Wa-1814, Wa-1819
VANCES, James, Gr-1799
VANCLEAVE, Ebenezer, B-1812
VANDAVER, John, Wh-1811
VANDEGRIFF, Gilbert, Ct-1796
VANDERGRAFT, Jacob, Gr-1805
VANDERGRIFF, Gilbert, Gr-1821, Ct-1798
    Jacob, Ct-1796, Gr-1821
    Jacob Sr., Ct-1798
    Jacob Jr., Ct-1798
    Leonard, Ct-1798
VANDERPOOL, Anthony, C-1823, C-1818
    John, C-1823, A-1805
    Samuel, C-1823
    Wynant, C-1818
VANDEVENDER, Jacob, Su-1812
VANDEVENTER, Abram, Su-1796
VANDEVER, Arnett, Wh-1825
    John, Wh-1825
VANDEVERDER, Abram, Su-1812
    Peter, Su-1812
    Thomas, Su-1812
VANDIGRIFF, Garrett, Gr-1804
    Jacob, Gr-1805, Gr-1804
VANDYKE, Freeman, Je-1822, Je-1800
    Henry, Je-1822
    Thomas, Ro-1805

VANGRIFF, Garret, Gr-1799
VANHOOK, Aron, Je-1800
VAN HOOSE, Valentine, Ct-1798
VANHOOSER, Hugh, Je-1822
    Isaac, Je-1822
    John, Je-1822
    Valentine, Je-1822
    William, Je-1822
VANHOUSEL, Robert, Ro-1805
VANHUSER, Falts, Je-1800
    John, Je-1800
VANN, David, B-1812
    Jacob, Sn-1816
    Messer, Co-1821
VANNOY, William, Ct-1798
VANOY, Elijah, B-1812
    Joel, B-1812
VANPELT, Benjamin, Ge-1812, Ge-1805
    Hugh, Ge-1805
    Jesse, Fr-1812
    Joseph, Ge-1812
VANSANDT, John, Ge-1805
VANTINE, John, Rb-1812
VANTRESS, James, Rb-1812
VANTRICE, John, Wl-1804
VANTS, Saml., Ge-1783
VANVARTER, Benjamin, Wa-1814
VAN WENTER, Abram, Su-1797
VANZANT, Jacob, Fr-1812
    Jacob Jr., Fr-1812
VARNALL, Wm., Se-1799
VARNER, Henry, Su-1812
    Jacob, Wa-1819, Wa-1814(2)
    James, R-1819
    Saml., D-1788, Ge-1805
    Solomon, R-1819
VARNUM, Isaac, A-1805
VASELL, Johnathan, Hw-1799
VAUGH, Sharer, Wa-1814
VAUGHAN, Abner, Wi-1815
    James, Mu-1811
    Powel, Mt-1798
    R. C., Sn-1823
    Thos., W-1812, Wi-1805
    William, Sn-1823
VAUGHEN, Thomas, Sn-1816
VAUGHN, Baldy, D-1811
    Benjamin, Wh-1825
    Daniel, W-1812
    David, W-1812, D-1805, D-1811
    Dixon, Wi-1815
    James, Fr-1812
    Joel, Rb-1812
    John, J-1802, A-1805, Wh-1825
    Johnston, D-1811
    Paul, D-1811
    Reuben, A-1805
    Samuel, Fr-1812
    William, Mo-1825, Fr-1812, Sn-1816
VAUGHT, Andrew, Bo-1801, Gr-1799
    David, Bo-1800
    John, Wi-1810, Wi-1815, Ct-1798,
        Ct-1796
    Joseph, Ct-1798
    William, Wa-1819
VAUGN, Edmond, A-1805
VAULX, Daniel, D-1811
    James, D-1811
VAUN, William, Gr-1805
VAWTON, John, Wi-1815
VEATCH, Elijah, Ge-1783
    Jeremiah, Ge-1783

VEATCH, Nathan, Ge-1783
VENABLE, John, Gr-1799
    Richard, B-1812
    Richard Jr., B-1812
    Samuel, B-1812
    Thomas, Wi-1810, B-1812
VENNABLE, Joseph, Wi-1810
VENNATA, Jacob, Wi-1801
VENOY, William, Ct-1796
VENSON, John, C-1818
VENTERS, Acy, Sn-1811
VENUS, John, Wl-1804
VENZANT, Thomas, Fr-1812
VERNON, Miles, Bl-1815
    Thomas Sr., Bl-1815
    Thomas Jr., Bl-1815
    William, Fr-1812
VEST, William, Ct-1796
VESTAL, Jay, Wi-1815
VETCH, Elija, Se-1799
    Lander, Mu-1811
VICE, Benjamin, Ge-1812
VICECARVER, John, Ge-1812
VICK, Cooper, D-1805
    Joseph, D-1811
VICKERS, James, Bo-1800, Bo-1801
VIED, Harmon C., Su-1812
VINCEN, George, Sn-1816
VINCENT, Anthony, Wh-1825
    Benthall, Sn-1811
    Daniel, Gi-1812
    David, B-1812
    Dewey, B-1812
    George, Su-1812, Su-1797, Su-1796,
        Ge-1812, Hu-1812
    Henry, Sn-1816
    Jackson, B-1812
    James, Sn-1811
    Jesse, Gi-1812
    John, Su-1812, Wh-1825
    Michael, D-1811
    Richard, W-1812
    Thomas, Su-1796, Su-1797, Je-1800,
        Hu-1812
    William, Wh-1825
    Willis, Sn-1816
VINEGAR, David, Wa-1819
VINETT, Micajah, Wl-1804
VINEYARD, Andrew, Gr-1821
    Daniel, Gr-1821
    John, Gr-1805, Gr-1810
    John Sr., Gr-1821, Gr-1810
VINNING, John, W-1812
    Thomas, W-1812
VINSANT, George, C-1823
    James, Sn-1811
VINSON, Abner, Wl-1804
    Abram, Su-1812
    Benthal, Sn-1816
    Enos, Sn-1816
    Henry, Sn-1811, Sn-1792
    James, Sn-1816(2), Sn-1817, Ro-1805
    James Jr., Sn-1816
    John, Mu-1811, Co-1827
    Jos., Sn-1792
    Thomas, Mu-1811
    William, Co-1827
VINTREAS, John, Ct-1796, Ct-1798
VINYARD, John, Gr-1805, Gr-1799, Gr-1804
    John Jr., Gr-1821
    Nicholas, Gr-1821
    Titus, Gr-1821

VINYARD, William, Je-1822
VOANES, Philip, Cl-1803
VOORHEES, Wm. & Peter F., Mu-1811
VOORHIES, Garret L., Mu-1816
VOWELL, Manpage, A-1805
WADDELL, Charles, Wa-1814
WADDLE, Charles, Wa-1819
    Daniel, Gr-1799
    George, Wh-1825, Su-1812
    Henry, Wh-1825
    Jacob, Su-1812
    John, Wh-1825, Wa-1819, Su-1797,
        Su-1812
    John Sr., Wh-1825
    John Jr., Wa-1819
    Jonathan, Wa-1819
    Lewis, Wh-1825
    Martin, Wh-1825, Su-1797, Ge-1812
    Peter, Su-1812
    Saml. D., B-1812
WADDY, Samuel, Ro-1805
WADE, Austen M., D-1811
    Edward, B-1812
    George, D-1811
    John, Wh-1825
    Obadiah, Wi-1810
    Obediah, Wi-1815
WADELL, John, Wa-1814
    Jonathan, Wa-1814
WADKINS, Pleasant, Mu-1816
    Samuel, Mu-1811
WADLEY, Holly, Su-1812
    Thomas, Su-1797, Su-1796
    William, Sn-1816
WADLINGTON, Thos., Mt-1798
WADSWORTH, Thomas, W-1812
WAFFORD, William, Fr-1812
WAGG, John, Ge-1812
WAGGENER, Henry, Su-1797
    Job, Su-1797
    Michal, Su-1797(2)
WAGGONER, Christopher, D-1811
    Cornelias, D-1811
    Henry, Su-1796
    Jacob, D-1811
    Jesse, Gr-1821
    John, D-1811(2), Su-1796
    Joseph, Gr-1805, B-1812
    Michael, D-1805, D-1811
    Michal, Su-1796
    Moses, Gr-1821
    Samuel, B-1812
    Thomas, Gr-1821, B-1812
    William, B-1812
WAGGONNER, David, Ct-1796, Ct-1798
    Mathias, Ct-1798, Ct-1796
WAGNER, John, Fr-1812
    Joseph, B-1812
WAGONER, George, Fr-1812
    Solomon, Fr-1812
    William, Fr-1812
WAHREN, Nathaneil, D-1811
WAIN, George, Mu-1816
WAIT, Jolly, Ro-1805
WAITE, William, Wi-1815
WAITS, Ellias, D-1811
WAKEFIELD, Charles, Mu-1811
    John, Bl-1815, Ro-1805
    Joseph, Mu-1811
    William, Mu-1811
WAKFIELD, Joseph, Bl-1815
WAKING (Wobary?), Joseph, K-1799

WAKINS, Ichabod, Hu-1812
WALDEN, James, Sersey, W-1812
WALDIN, James, Se-1799
　　John, Wa-1814
　　Rubin, Se-1799
WALDON, David, J-1802, Se-1799
WALDREN, John, Wa-1819
WALDRON, William, D-1811
WALDROP, John, Gi-1812
　　_____, Mu-1811
WALDRUP, Ezekiel, Mu-1816
　　James, Mu-1811
　　William, J-1802, C-1823
WALER, John, Ge-1812
WALIS, Clem, Wi-1810
WALKENS, Joseph, B-1812
WALKER, Abr., D-1805
　　Abraham, Wi-1810
　　Abram, Wi-1815
　　Alexander, Gr-1805, Gr-1804
　　Anderson, Ge-1812(4), Ge-1805
　　Andrew, Fr-1812
　　Archibald, D-1811
　　Ausburn, Wh-1825
　　Benjamin, Gr-1821
　　Burt, Wh-1825
　　Cliton, Wi-1815
　　Daniel, Ge-1805, R-1819
　　David, Se-1799, Wl-1804, K-1796,
　　　　D-1811
　　Edward, D-1811
　　Elenore & David, D-1805
　　Elias, Wa-1819
　　Elmore, D-1811
　　Ennis, D-1811
　　Ephraim, K-1796
　　Ephrim, Ro-1805
　　Freeman, Wi-1801
　　George, R-1819, K-1799, A-1805
　　Gidion, Fr-1812
　　Halton, R-1819
　　Henry, Gi-1812, Wi-1810(2),
　　　　Wi-1801(2), Wi-1815
　　Isaac, Ge-1805
　　Isaiah, Bo-1805, Bo-1801
　　James, Ge-1805, Je-1822(2), Ge-1812,
　　　　Rb-1812, W-1812, Fr-1812,
　　　　Bl-1815; Bo-1801, C-1823,
　　　　B-1812(2), Bo-1800, K-1796,
　　　　Mu-1816, D-1805, Sn-1816,
　　　　Wl-1804(2)
　　Jeremiah, Je-1822, W-1812
　　Jesse, Ge-1812, Fr-1821
　　John, Ge-1805, Je-1822, Ro-1805,
　　　　W-1812, Wa-1814, Wa-1819,
　　　　Wh-1811, Bo-1801(2), Bo-1805,
　　　　Gr-1799, Wi-1815, Bl-1815,
　　　　Bo-1800, Ct-1798, D-1811,
　　　　K-1796, D-1805, Wh-1825(2),
　　　　Wi-1801, Wl-1804
　　John A., D-1811
　　John B., B-1812
　　Joseph, Gr-1821, Ro-1805, Bo-1805,
　　　　Bo-1801, B-1812, D-1805,
　　　　K-1799
　　Mark, A-1805, K-1799
　　Mathew P., D-1811
　　Nathaniel, B-1812
　　Noah, Wi-1815, Wi-1810
　　Peter, Wl-1804
　　Philip, B-1812, D-1811, D-1805
　　Purnell, Ge-1805

WALKER, Reubin, Wi-1810
　　Richard, R-1819, Gr-1805, Je-1800,
　　　　Gr-1804, Wi-1815, Wi-1810
　　Robert, Wh-1811, R-1819, B-1812,
　　　　Bo-1805
　　Samuel, Rb-1812, Bo-1805, Bo-1800,
　　　　Bo-1801, C-1818, Bl-1815,
　　　　D-1788
　　Saml. A., Hu-1812
　　Thomas, Ge-1805, Ro-1805, K-1799,
　　　　Gr-1821, Wa-1819, Mu-1816(2)
　　　　Wi-1815, Wi-1810, D-1805,
　　　　Wi-1801, Mu-1811(2)
　　Thos. Sr., K-1799
　　Thomas G., Wi-1810
　　Washington, Mu-1811
　　West?, K-1799
　　William, Wa-1814, W-1812, Ro-1805,
　　　　Rb-1812, D-1811(2), Sn-1811,
　　　　D-1811
　　William Jr., D-1811, Bo-1800
WALLEN, Elisha Sr., Gr-1799
　　Elisha Jr., Gr-1799
　　Evan, C-1818, A-1805
　　Evers, C-1823
　　John, Sn-1816
　　Stephen, Su-1812
WALLER, John, Su-1812
　　Joseph, Sn-1792
　　Pleasant, Wh-1811
　　Richd., Sn-1792
　　Thomas, D-1811, Bo-1800
WALLEW, Ezekiel, Mu-1811
　　James, Mu-1811
WALLIN, James, Fr-1812
　　Stephen, Su-1796, Su-1797
WALLING, Daniel, Wh-1825
　　Elisha, Wh-1811
　　James, A-1805
　　James Sr., Wh-1825
　　James Jr., Wh-1825
　　Jesse, Wh-1825
　　John, Wh-1825, Wh-1811
　　Joseph, Wh-1825, Wh-1811
　　Thomas, Wh-1825, Wh-1811
WALLIS, Archibald, Sn-1811
　　Daniel, W-1812
　　Elias, Wh-1811
　　John, Wi-1815
　　Pleasant, Wh-1825
　　Robert B., Su-1812
　　Samuel, Mt-1798
　　Stephen, Wh-1825, Wh-1811
　　Thomas, Wi-1815
　　William, Sn-1811
WALLS, Adam, Wa-1814
　　Edmund, Wi-1815
　　Fethias, Ge-1783
　　John, Gi-1812
　　Thomas, D-1811
WALON, William, Se-1799
WALTER, Ezekeil, Mu-1811
WALTERS, Champlis, Gr-1821
　　Clary, Wa-1814
　　Clay, Wa-1819
　　George, Ct-1798, Wa-1819, R-1819,
　　　　Wa-1814
　　John, Ct-1798, C-1823, Ct-1798,
　　　　Je-1800, Gr-1821
　　Obediah, Gr-1804, Gr-1821
　　Robert, Ct-1798, Ct-1796
　　Thomas, C-1823

WALTERS, Thomas G., Wa-1814
    William, Gr-1821
WALTHAL, John, Wi-1801
    Thomas B., Wi-1815
WALTHALL, John, Gi-1812
WALTON, Augustus F., Mu-1816
    Gracy, Sn-1816
    Henry, R-1819
    Isaac, Sn-1816, J-1802, Sn-1792, Sn-1787
    Jesse, Mu-1816
    Joseph, Sn-1816
    Josiah, Sn-1816
    Langhorn F., Wi-1815
    Maberry, Sn-1816
    Mabry, Sn-1811
    Martin, Rb-1812
    Merdoc, Sn-1816
    Meredith, Rb-1812
    Merideth, Sn-1811
    Simeon, Rb-1812
    William, J-1802, Mt-1798, Sn-1787
    Wm. W., Gi-1812
WAMACK, Abner, W-1805, W-1812
    David, J-1802
    John, J-1802
WAMBLE, Joshua, Gr-1799
WAMMACK, Wm., W-1812, W-1805
WAMMICK, James, Se-1799
WAMMOCK, Jesse, Wh-1811
    John, Wh-1811
WAMPLEY, Michael, Ge-1812
WANTKEN, Rich, Cl-1803
WARD, Cuttbirth, B-1812
    David, Wa-1814
    Edward, D-1805, D-1811
    Elijah, Wh-1811, Wh-1825
    Fleming D-1811
    James, Cl-1803, Ge-1783, Gr-1799
    James J., Gi-1812
    John, D-1811, D-1805(2), Gr-1799, J-1802, Je-1822
    Jonathan, Wh-1825(2), Wh-1811
    Jorden, Gi-1819
    Joseph, D-1811
    Luke, Wl-1804
    Mary, Mu-1816
    Michael, Wl-1804
    Phillip, Wl-1804
    Thomas, B-1812
    William, Wh-1825, Mu-1811, B-1805 W-1812, Gr-1799, J-1802
    William C., D-1811
WARDEN, David, Su-1796
    James, Mu-1811, Mu-1816
    John, D-1811
WARDLOW, James, Mu-1816
WARE, George, K-1799
    George T., Rb-1812
    James, Su-1812, Su-1796
    John, K-1799
    Jonathan, B-1812
    Joseph, Bl-1815
    William, B-1812(2), Gr-1799
WAREN, Michael, Bo-1801
WARING, Michael, Su-1812
WARINGTON, Edwd., Sn-1811
WARLEY, James, Gr-1805
WARMACK, Drury, Wh-1825
    William, Wh-1825
WARMATH, Henry, B-1812
WARMICK, Alexander, B-1812

WARMICK, David Jr., B-1812
    William, B-1812
WARNELL, Natty, B-1812
WARNER, John, B-1812(2), Bl-1815
    Wm., Sn-1816, B-1812
WARNICK, Jas., Se-1799, Wl-1804
    Robert, Wl-1804
    William, Wl-1804
WARNUCK, Frederick, Ge-1812
WARON, Josiah, Mu-1811
WARRAN, Robert H., Wi-1815
WARREN, Archibald, Wh-1825
    Arthur, W-1812, Wl-1804
    Benjamin, Rb-1812
    Bluford, Wh-1811, Wh-1825
    Charles, Gi-1819
    David, Fr-1812
    Drury, Wi-1815
    Edward, Ge-1812, Ro-1805, Wi-1815 D-1805
    Henry, C-1818
    Jacob, Rb-1812
    Jesse, Rb-1812
    John, Su-1796, Rb-1812(2), Su-1797, B-1812, Mu-1811, Mu-1816
    Joseph, W-1812
    Joshua, Rb-1812, Sn-1811
    Nathan, Wi-1815
    Reubin, Fr-1812
    Robert, A-1805
    Rubin, Wi-1815
    Samuel, A-1805, Gi-1819
    Sebert, Rb-1812
    R. Benjamin, A-1805
    Thomas, Ge-1805, Gr-1804
WARRICK, William, Su-1797
WARRIN, Edward, Wi-1810
WARRING, Edmond W., Su-1797
    Edmund, Su-1796
WARRINGTON, Wiley, D-1805
WARRMER, John, C-1818
    Martha, C-1818
    Thomas, C-1818
WARSAN, Joseph, Wl-1804
WARSHAM, John, Su-1812
WARTHMAN, Jonathan, D-1805
WARTMILLER, Jacob, Su-1797
    John, Su-1796
WARWICK, Anthony, D-1811
    John, A-1805
    Wiley, A-1805
WASH, Andrew & Alexander, D-1805
WASHAM, Alesan, Bo-1800
    Alexander, Bo-1801
    Jeremiah, Bo-1801
    John, Bo-1801, Bo-1800
WASHBURN, Reuben, Li-1812*
    Sherord, Bo-1801
WASHINGTON, Gilbert G., Wi-1810
    Gray, D-1805
    Joseph, Rb-1812
    Robt. W., Wi-1815
    Thomas, D-1805
WASHMON, Joshua, Gr-1821
WASON, Elisha, K-1799
    John, Mu-1811
WASSOM, John, Su-1797, Su-1812
WASSON, Jno., K-1799
    Josiah, Gi-1819
    J____, Gi-1819
    Samuel, Mu-1816
WASSUM, Jacob, R-1819(2)

WASSUM, Jones, R-1819
WATENBARGER, Jacob, Wa-1819
WATENBERGER, Adam, Wa-1819
    Adam Jr., Wa-1819
    Peter, Wa-1819
WATERHOUSE, R. G., C-1823
    Richard G., R-1819
WATERS, Ezikiel, Bo-1805
    George, Gi-1812
    John, Wi-1815, Bo-1805, R-1808
    John A., R-1808
    Obediah, Gr-1799
    Obidiah, Gr-1805
    Samuel, R-1808
    William, D-1811
WATKIN, Robert, Wh-1825
WATKINGS, Robert, Sn-1811
WATKINS, Benjamin, A-1805, J-1802
    Charles, Sn-1816, Sn-1811
    E. B., Mo-1825
    Francis, Sn-1811
    G. Thomas, D-1805
    Henry, Rb-1812
    Isaac, D-1811
    Isaac & William, D-1805
    Isaac J., Je-1822
    Isaiah, Hu-1812
    James, Sn-1811, Sn-1816
    Neel, D-1805
    Noel, D-1811
    Owen T., Wi-1815
    Philip, D-1811, Je-1822
    Richard, Je-1822
    Robert, Sn-1816
    Thomas G., Je-1822
    William, D-1811(2), Je-1822
WATLEY, Walter, B-1812
WATSON, Andrew, Gr-1821
    Archibald, Su-1797, Su-1812
    Benjamin, B-1812
    David, D-1811, Gr-1805, Gr-1821,
        Gr-1804, Gi-1819, W-1812
    Elijah, Su-1812
    George, Rb-1812
    Hardy, Sn-1816
    James, Wi-1801, Bo-1800, Bo-1801
    John, Wl-1804, D-1811, Mu-1811,
        D-1805, Mu-1816, Wi-1815,
        Su-1797
    John Jr., Wl-1804
    Lamuel, Sn-1811
    Lewis, Fr-1812
    Lewis Jr., Fr-1812
    Mary joining Baker, Su-1812
    Montilon, Sn-1816
    Peter, W-1805, W-1812
    Robert, Gr-1805, Gr-1804
    Samuel, Sn-1811
    Samuel Rev., Wa-1819
    Thomas, D-1811, Gr-1805, D-1805,
        Gi-1812, Ge-1812, Ge-1805
    William, Wi-1815, Sn-1816, Mu-1816,
        Mu-1811, D-1811, A-1805,
        Gi-1812, W-1812
    William L., Wi-1815
WATT, George, D-1805
    Hedly, D-1805
    James, Mt-1798, Bo-1800
    John, Wi-1810
    William, D-1805
WATTERBERGER, Adam, Wa-1814
    Adam Jr., Wa-1814

WATTERBERGER, William, Wa-1814
WATTERS, James, C-1823
    Joel, C-1823
    William, D-1811
WATTS, John, Mu-1811, Mu-1816
    Ruben, Sn-1816
    William, D-1811
WATTSON, Michael, Ro-1805
    William, Ge-1805(2)
WATWOOD, George, Sn-1811
WAUGH, John, D-1811
WAUTTIN, John, Mu-1811
WAY, Nathaniel, D-1811
WAYLAND, Henry, Hu-1812
WEAKLEY, Robert, D-1805, Wi-1810,
        Mt-1798, D-1811, Wi-1801
    Samuel, D-1805, D-1811
WEAKLY, Robert, Mu-1811
WEAR, Hugh, Wa-1819
WEARE, James, Su-1797
WEATHERALL, James, D-1811
WEATHERFORD, Maney, B-1812
WEATHEROW, James, Mu-1811
WEATHERRED, Francis, Sn-1811
    James, Sn-1816
    John, SN-1816, Sn-1811
    Robert, Sn-1811, Sn-1816
WEATHERS, Edmon, Wi-1801, Wi-1815
    Jesse, Wi-1801, Gi-1819
    John, Sn-1792
WEATHERY, Jesse, Gi-1812
WEAVER, Adam, Wi-1815, Je-1800
    Benjamin, Wh-1811(3), Wh-1825
    Benjn. S., B-1812
    Craven, D-1811
    Christian, Su-1796, Su-1797,
        D-1805
    Daniel, Fr-1812
    David, B-1812, Wh-1285
    Frederick, Su-1796, Su-1812
    Fredrick, Su-1797
    George, Je-1822, Ge-1812, Su-1812,
        Je-1800
    Hasikiah, Gr-1799
    Isaac, Wh-1825
    Jacob, A-1805, W-1812, Su-1796,
        Su-1797, W-1805
    Jesse, Sn-1811
    John, Gr-1799(2), Co-1821, B-1812,
        Su-1812(2)
    Joseph, Gr-1799, B-1812, Wh-1811
    Peter, Su-1812, D-1811
    Samuel, Wh-1811, Wh-1825(2)
    Samuel Sr., Gr-1799
    Samuel Jr., Gr-1799
    William, Wh-1825, B-1812(2)
WEB, John, Mu-1811, Ge-1783
WEBB, Abel, Wi-1801
    Austin, Wh-1825
    Benjamin, Su-1796(2), Su-1797(2)
        Su-1812
    Cheley, W-1805
    Chely, W-1812
    Daniel, D-1811, Sn-1816
    David, Su-1797, Su-1812, Su-1796
    Elisha, W-1812(2), W-1805, Wh-1825
    George, Su-1812, Je-1800, Su-1797
    George, deceased, Su-1812
    Henry, K-1799
    Hiram, R-1819
    Hugh, Sn-1792
    Jales, Gi-1819

WEBB, James, W-1812, Rb-1812, Wh-1825,
            Mu-1816
    Jeremiah, W-1812, W-1805, Wh-1825
    Jesse, Su-1812, Je-1800, Je-1822
    Jessee, W-1812, W-1805(2)
    Jessee Sr., W-1812
    John, Gr-1804, Gi-1819, Wi-1815,
            Gi-1812, Rb-1812, K*-1815,
            W-1812, Su-1812, Sn-1816,
            Wi-1815, W-1805, Gr-1805
    John Sr., W-1812, W-1805
    John B., W-1812, W-1805
    Jonas, W-1812
    Jonathan, Su-1797, Su-1796, R-1819
    Joseph, Su-1812
    Joshua, W-1812, W-1805
    Julia, W-1805
    Julios, W-1812
    Julius, W-1812
    Larkin, Gi-1819, Gi-1812
    Litterany, Wh-1825
    Littleberry, Gi-1812
    Mary, K-1799
    Meredith, Mu-1811
    Merry, Wa-1814
    Moses, Su-1796, J-1802
    Nathan, Su-1812
    Richard, Ge-1783
    Solomon, Mu-1816
    Thomas, K-1799, Gi-1819, Gi-1812,
            Je-1822
    William, K-1799, Gi-1819, A-1805,
            J-1802, W-1812, Je-1822,
            Gi-1812, Mu-1811, D-1805,
            Wh-1825
    William S., Wi-1815
WEBBER, Samuel, Fr-1812
    Seth, D-1811
WEBSTER, Abbigal, Gr-17-9
    Abigail, Gr-1821
    Edward, Cl-1803, Hw-1799
    Elizabeth, Fr-1804, Gr-1805
    Henry, Gr-1821
    John, Gr-1821, Hw-1801, Hw-1799
    Jonathan, B-1812, Mu-1811, Mu-1816
    Joseph, Hw-1801
    Samuel, Hw-1799
    William, Gr-1805
WEECE, James, Je-1822
WEEKELY, Thomas, Mt-1798
    David, Mt-7198
WEEKLY, Benjamin, Mt-1798
WEEKS, Abraham, D-1805
    Abram, Mu-1811
    Charles, A-1805, Fr-1812
    Daniel, Sn-1816
    John, Su-1796, Su-1797
    Zachariah, Su-1796, Su-1797
WEEMS, George, Ge-1812, Ge-1805
    John, Ge-1805(2), Ge-1812
    John Sr., Ge-1805, Ge-1812
    John, heirs, Ge-1812
    Thomas, Sn-1816, Mu-1811
    William, Ge-1805, Mu-1816, Mu-1811
WEES, John, Ge-1812
WEESE, John, Bo-1800
    Machall, Ge-1812
WEIR, Abraham, Bo-1800, Bo-1801
    Hugh, Bo-1800
    John, Bo-1801, Bo-1800, Bo-1805
    Jonathan, Bo-1801, Bo-1800
    Joseph Sr., Bo-1800

WEIR, Joseph Jr., Bo-1800
    Samuel & Son?, Bo-1805
WELB(Webb?), John, W-1812
WELCH, Andrew, Wh-1825(2)
    George, Wh-1825
    John, Gi-1812, B-1812
    Joseph & John, D-1805
    Matthew, Wh-1285
    Matthias Jr., Wh-1825
    Nich, Gi-1812
    Nicholas, Gi-1812
    Richard, Gi-1812
    Thomas, K-1796, Gi-1812
    William, Gi-1812(2)
WELCHIR, Thomas L., W-1812
WELD, Jonathan, Bl-1815
WELIMAN, Peter, Fr-1812
WELL, Wm., Wi-1815
WELLARTIN, Jonathan, Wi-1810
WELLS, Beadon?, D-1788
    Benjamin, D-1805
    Coleman, Je-1822
    David, D-1811, Hu-1812
    Ethen, Li-1812*
    Francis, Wh-1811
    George, Ge-1812(3)
    H., Mt-1798
    Hayden, Mt-1798
    Jacbo, Ro-1805
    John, Gi-1812, Wi-1815(2), Gr-1804
    John S., Gr-1805
    Lewis, Ct-1796
    Martin Sr., Mt-1798
    Martin Jr., Mt-1798
    Mary Jr., K-1799(Webb?)
    Merry, Wa-1819
    Robert, Mt-1798
    Samuel, J-1802, Wi-1815
    Thomas, D-1805
    William, Wi-1810, Gi-1812(2), Gi-1819
WELLSFORD, Thomas, B-1812
WELMAN, James Sr., W-1812
    James Jr., W-1812
WELTY, John, Ge-1812
WEMBSLY, Isaac, B-1812
WENSTMA, Charles, b-1812
WEORKLE, Andrew, Wi-1815
WERRIN, Edmund, Wa-1814
WERRY, William, Gi-1819
WERT, Edward, Ge-1812
WESLEY, Elijah, Wh-1825
    James, Wh-1825
WESNER, Henry, Gr-1821
WESSON, Edward, Wa-1819
WEST, Andrew, Sn-1811, Sn-1816
    Berry, B-1812
    Daniel, Sn-1811
    David, Sn-1816
    Edward, Gr-1804, Wa-1819, Wa-1814(2),
            Gr-1821, Gr-1805
    Elijah, B-1812
    Fountain, Wh-1825
    George, Mt-1798, D-1811
    George & Micajah, D-1805
    Isaac, Wi-1810, Wi-1815, R-1819
    James, B-1812, Hw-1799, Ge-1812
    Jeremiah, Wl-1804, B-1812, Su-1797
    Jermiah, Se-1799
    Jesse, Gi-1819, Gi-1812
    Joel, Gi-1812
    John, B-1812, W-1812, Wi-1801,
            Wi-1815, Sn-1811, Sn-1816

WEST, Logun, Sn-1816
    Matthew, Rb-1812
    Peggy, Sn-1816
    Peter, D-1805
    Rewben, Ge-1812
    Samuel, Gr-1821, Je-1800, Wa-1819
    Thomas, Rb-1812
    Thos. S., Wi-1815
    William, Ge-1812, Ge-1805
    William H., R-1819
WESTAIN, Joseph, Wa-1819
WESTBROOKS, Thomas, D-1811(2)
WESTER, Graves, Gi-1819
WESTERMAN, John W., W-1805, W-1812
WESTERN, Joseph, Ct-1796
    William, Ct-1796
WESTMORELAND, Vincent, B-1812
WESTON, Casper, Gr-1799
    Frederick, Wl-1804
    Joseph, Ge-1805
    Simon, Ge-1805
    William, Ct-1798
WETHER, James, C-1818
WETHERLY, Joseph, Wh-1811
WETHERRED, James, Sn-1811
WETHERSPOON, Wesley, Mu-1816
WEVER, John, Wh-1825
    John Sr., Wh-1825
WHALER, William, K-1796
WHALING, John, Je-1822
    John Jr., Je-1822
WHALON, George, D-1805
WHARTER, Moses W., Mu-1816
WHARTON, George, D-1811
    Jesse, D-1811
    Jessee, D-1805
    John, D-1811
    Saml. L., D-1811
    William, D-1811
WHEAT, Azariah, Ro-1805
    John, Wi-1815
    Levy, Ro-1805
WHEATON, Calvin, D-1805
    D., Wi-1801
    Jan, estate, Wi-1815
WHEELDON, Joseph, Mu-1811
WHEELER, Benjamin, C-1818(2), C-1823(2),
        Hw-1801, Gi-1812
    Carrington, Ct-1798
    Isaac, Ge-1812
    James, Su-1796, Hw-1801
    Joseph, K-1796
    Margaret, C-1818, C-1823
    Nase, B-1812
    Nimrod B., C-1823, C-1818
    Rubin, Hw-1801
    Thomas, C-1818, C-1823
    William, Fr-1812, Bo-1801, Bo-1800,
        Wa-1819
WHEELOCK, James, Wa-1814
    John, Wa-1814(2)
WHELCHAE, Dav?, W-1812
    John, W-1812
    William, W-1812
WHELCHAR?, Daws?, W-1805
WHELCHIRP, Thomas, Wi-1805
WHELEAR, Edmund, Ro-1805
WHENNERY, Thomas, Ge-1805
WHETHEN, Robart, Bl-1815
WHIDER, James, Su-1797
WHILCHAE, Francis, W-1812
WHIPPLE, David H., Sn-1816

WHIRSEY, Simms, Sn-1811
WHIRSY, William, Sn-1811
WHISTER, Jacob, Wa-1819
WHIT, Peter, W-1812
WHITAKER, David, Wh-1825
    John, Mu-1816, Mu-1811
    William, Wh-1825(2)
WHITANBY, Daniel, Wi-1801
WHITE, Abraham, Ge-1812, Ge-1805
    Adam, Wa-1814
    Alexander, Wi-1815
    Allen, Gr-1804
    Anderson, Hu-1812
    Ann, Wa-1814
    Antler, D-1811
    Arvin, Rb-1812
    Asa, D-1811
    B. J., K*-1815
    Benjamin, Ge-1812, Gi-1819, Mu-1816,
        Wi-1815, D-1811, Wi-1810
    Bloomer, Ge-1805, Ge-1812
    Branscomb, C-1818
    Burdick, Wl-1804
    C. W., K*-1815
    Chapman, Wi-1801(3)
    Charles, Wi-1815, Je-1822, Sn-1816,
        Sn-1811
    Charles H., Sn-1823
    Daniel, Gi-1812, A-1805, Wi-1815,
        D-1811
    David, Wa-1814, Wa-1819, Bo-1801,
        Bo-1800, Gi-1819, Sn-1792
    Demsey, C-1823
    Elijah, Wi-1810, Gi-1819
    Elisha, Wi-1810, Gi-1812
    Ezekiel, Wa-1819
    Francis, D-1805
    Frederick, Ge-1812
    George, Ge-1812, Wi-1815, Bo-1805
    Henry, Ge-1805, Ge-1812(2), Gi-1812,
        Gi-1819, D-1805, D-1811
    Henry Sr., D-1811
    Henry Jr., D-1811
    Hugh, Ro-1805
    Isaac, Wa-1819, Wa-1814
    Issaiah, Wi-1815
    Jacob, Ge-1812, Ge-1805, D-1805
    James, Mu-1811(2), Wi-1801, Mu-1816(2)
        Hu-1812, Ct-1798, Bo-1800,
        B-1812(2), Ct-1796, Bo-1801,
        Wa-1819, Wa-1814, Je-1822(3),
        K*-1815, Ge-1805, Su-1812
    Jeese, Wa-1819
    Jennet, Ge-1812
    Jeremiah, Wa-1819
    Jesse, Wa-1814, Wi-1810
    Jnn., Sn-1816
    Joel, A-1805
    John, Mu-1816, Mu-1811, Hu-1812,
        Gi-1819, Ge-1805, Ge-1812,
        D-1788, B-1812(2), Ro-1805,
        Wi-1815(2), Wi-1801, Wi-1810,
        Wh-1825, Wh-1811(2), Wa-1814(2),
        Wa-1819(2), Sn-1792, Sn-1811,
        Sn-1816
    John Sr., Gi-1812, Wh-1825
    John Jr., Gi-1812, Wh-1825
    John C., Wh-1825(2)
    John Dd., Mu-1811
    John F., Mu-1816
    Jonathan, Je-1822, Sn-1811
    Joseph, Ge-1812(2), Gr-1799, Sn-1792,

WHITE, Joseph, Cont'd.--Sn-1823, Sn-1811
    Joshua, Wi-1815, D-1805
    Judan, Sn-1816
    Laid, Ge-1812
    Lewis, D-1811
    Littlebury, Sn-1811
    Lucy, D-1805, Mu-1811
    Mary, Gr-1805, Gr-1804
    Matthew, Mu-1811
    Meady, Wi-1815
    Nathan, Ge-1805
    Nelley, Gr-1805
    Noah, Mu-1816
    Philemon, Mu-1811
    Philimon, Gi-1812
    Pleasant, Wh-1825
    Richard, Wa-1814, Fr-1812, Ct-1798,
        Ct-1796, Hu-1812
    Robert, A-1805, Sn-1823, Wi-1815,
        Sn-1816(2), Sn-1811(2), Wi-1810
        D-1811
    Samuel, Je-1800, Ge-1805, Ro-1805,
        Wi-1815, Mu-1811
    Samuel & Rich, Je-1822
    Sarah, Je-1822, Wi-1810
    Scion, B-1812
    Serrel, B-1812
    Sherrod, Mu-1816
    Silas, Bl-1815
    Simpson, Gi-1819
    Solomon, D-1788
    Stephen, Wi-1815, D-1811
    Stephin, D-1811
    Thomas, W-1812, Ge-1805, Su-1812,
        Wa-1814, Je-1800, Gi-1812,
        Wi-1810, D-1805, Wa-1819,
        Sn-1811, D-1811, Wi-1815
    Thomas Jr., W-1812
    Thomas B., Wi-1815
    Thos. Henry, Wi-1801
    Thomas L., D-1811
    Thompson, Rb-1812
    Tiny, Wa-1814
    Westley, Je-1800
    William, Wl-1804, Mu-1811, Mu-1816(2)
        Gr-1805, Gi-1812, Ge-1812,
        Ge-1805, Wi-1801, Wi-1810,
        Wi-1815(2), Wh-1825(2), Wa-1814,
        Wa-1819(2), W-1805, W-1812,
        Sn-1816(4), Sn-1811, Sn-1823
    William Sr., Sn-1811
    William Jr., Ro-1805
    Wilson, Bo-1805
    Woodson P., Wh-1825
WHITEACRE, Giles, A-1805
WHITECOTTON, Aron, C-1818(2), C-1823
WHITEEN, William, Bl-1815
WHITEFIELD, Neadom, Gr-1799
WHITEHAL, Francis, W-1805
    John, W-1805
WHITEHEAD, Benjamin, Mt-1798
    Jacob, Wi-1810
    John, B-1812, Ge-1812, Ge-1805
    Jn. Buchanan, D-1811
    Lazareth, B-1812
    Robert, Ro-1805, Rb-1812(2)
    William, Mt-1798, Wi-1801, B-1812
WHITELL, Laury, Sn-1811
WHITELY, Isaac, Wh-1825
WHITEMAN, David, Je-1800
WHITENBARGER, Abraham, Bo-1801
    Henery, Bo-1801

WHITENBEARGER, Abraham, Bo-1800
WHITENBERG, John, Ge-1812
    Peter, Ge-1812
WHITENBERGER, William, Ge-1812(7)
    _____, Ge-1812
WHITENBURG, Henry, Ge-1783
    Jos., Ge-1783
WHITENBURGER, Henry, Bo-1800
WHITES, Nelson, D-1811
WHITESIDE, Abraham, Wi-1801, Mu-1816
    James, Mu-1811, Mu-1816, Wl-1804
    Jenkin, Wi-1801, Wi-1815, D-1811,
        Gr-1805
    Jenkins, Sn-1811
    John, Mu-1816
    Robert, Mu-1811, Mu-1816
    Samuel, Mu-1816, Mu-1811
    Thomas, Mu-1811, Mu-1816, Gr-1821
    William, Mu-1816
WHITESIDES, Abraham, Mu-1811
    Jenkin, Gr-1804
    John, Mu-1811
    William, Mu-1811, Gr-1805
WHITESTTON, Isaac, Gr-1799
WHITFIELD, Bryant, Mt-1798
    Harrison, D-1811
    John, D-1811
    Needham, Mt-1798
    Wilkins, D-1811
    William, heirs, R-1819
WHITFORD, Leml., Sn-1811
    Martin, D-1805
    Mathew, D-1805
    William, D-1805
WHITHEAD, Wm., Wi-1801
WHITIAR, John, Ro-1805
WHITIKER, Marsh, D-1811
WHITINBURG, Fredrick, Ge-1783
WHITLEY, James, Wh-1825
    Marcus, D-1811
    Robert, Fr-1812
WHITLOCK, Abraham, D-1805
    Alexander, Su-1796, Wa-1814,
        Wa-1819, Su-1797
    Enoch, Wa-1819
    James, Gr-1799, Gr-1821, Gr-1804,
        Wa-1819
    John, Gr-1821, Wa-1819(2)
    John Sr., Wa-1819
    Mary, Gr-1805
WHITMAN, Jacob, A-1805, C-1818, C-1823
    John, A-1805, C-1823, C-1818
WHITMER, Abner, Sn-1816
WHITMORE, Frederick, Su-1812(2)
WHITNER, Henry, Gr-1805
    Lewis, Gr-1805
WHITNEY, William O., B-1812
WHITSELL, James, D-1805
WHITSET, John, Sn-1792
WHITSETT, William, D-1805
WHITSILL, James, D-1811
WHITSON, Abraham, Ct-1798, Ct-1796
    Abrahm, Wl-1804
    Ann, Mu-1816
    Anne, Mu-1811
    Charles, Ct-1796
    George, D-1805, D-1811
    James, Mu-1816, Wa-1819, Wa-1814
    Jeames, K-1799
    Jeremiah, Ct-1798, Ct-1796
    Jesse, Ct-1796, Ct-1798(2)
    John, Ct-1796

WHITSON, Stephen, Co-1821
    Thomas, Mu-1816, Wa-1819, Ct-1798,
        B-1812, Ct-1796, Wa-1814
    William, Wa-1819, Wa-1814, Ge-1783,
        Ct-1796, Ct-1798
WHITSTONE, Mathias, Wi-1810
WHITT, William, Fr-1812
WHITTEKER, Giles, K-1796
WHITTEN, Robert, C-1818
    Thos., Se-1799
WHITTENBURG, Peter, Bl-1815
WHITTENTON, Benj., Sn-1811
WHITTER, Claborn, Sn-1811
    James, Sn-1811, Sn-1816
WHITTERBERY, Ephraim, Gr-1821
    George, Gr-1821
WHITTHELL, Adam, Je-1800
WHITTLE, Robert, Gr-1799
WHITTON, Elijah, C-1823, A-1805
    John, Sn-1816
    Robert, A-1805
    William, A-1805
WHITWITH, Lauray, Sn-1816
WHITWORTH, Edward, B-1812
    Isaac, B-1812
    Jacob, B-1812(2)
    Saml. J., B-1812
    Thomas, Wl-1804
WHORTON, William, Wi-1810
WHYTE, Robert, D-1805
WIATH, James, Mu-1811
WIATT, Samuel, Ge-1783
    William, Ge-1783
WICK, Elijah, Bl-1815
WICKS, Zachariah, Su-1812
WICOFF, Peter, Mt-1798
    William, Mt-1798
WIDBY, William, Ct-1796
WIDES, David, Wh-1825
WIDNER, Henry, Gr-1799, Gr-1821
    Jacob, Gr-1821
    John, Gr-1821
    Lewis, Gr-1799, Gr-1821
    Mathias, Gr-1821
WIDNOR, Henry, Gr-1804
    Lewis, Gr-1804
WIER, Benjamin, Fr-1812
    George, Fr-1812
    Hugh, Ge-1783, Bo-1801
    James Jr., Bo-1801
    John, Bo-1800, Bo-1801
    Joseph Sr., Bo-1801
    Joseph Jr., Bo-1801
    Samuel, Bo-1800, Bo-1801
WIERE, William, Sn-1792
WIET, Jesse, Wa-1819
WIGENTON, Jno., W-1812
WIGGANS, P. John, D-1805
WIGGENTON, Archalus, Sn-1816
    George, Sn-1816
    William, Sn-1816
WIGGIN, John, Fr-1812
    Thomas, Fr-1812
WIGGINS, Mannuel, Su-1812
WIGGINTON, Martin, Fr-1812
WIGGS, Mattw., Wi-1815
WILBOURN, Daniel, Wl-1804
    Nicholas, Wl-1804
WILBUER, Nichs., Wi-1815
WILBURN, Thomas, Wh-1811
WILCHER, Booker, Mu-1811
    H. Lowdy, Mu-1811

WILCKES, Moses, Co-1821
WILCOCKSON, David Jr., Gi-1819
    Isaac, Gi-1819, Gi-1812
WILCOKSON, David Sr., Gi-1819
WILCOX, Isaac, Bo-1801
    Samuel, Mt-1798
    Thomas, D-1811
WILDER, Joab, Hw-1799
    Sampson, Hw-1799
WILDERSON, John, Ge-1812
WILDS, John, Ct-1798
WILEBOR, John, Gr-1799
WILES, John, Ct-1796
WILEY, Alex, Bo-1801
    Alexander, Je-1800, Mu-1816
    B. John, Mu-1811
    George, Gr-1804
    James, C-1818
    John, Mu-1816(2)
    Moses, Mu-1816
    Robert, Mu-1816, Mu-1811
    William, Su-1797, Wi-1801(2),
        D-1805
WILHITE, Barnard, Gr-1799
    Caleb, Co-1827
    Calip, Co-1821
    Courite, A-1805
    Daniel, Wh-1825(2)
    Elijah, A-1805
    James, Ge-1812
    John, Wh-1825
    Julis, Gr-1805
    Julius, C-1818
    Philip, Ge-1812
    Reuben, Wh-1825, Wi-1814, Co-1821
  Robin, Co-1827
    Samuel, Ge-1812
    Simeon, A-1805
    Simon, C-1823, C-1818
    Solomon, Wh-1825(2)
    William, Co-1821
WILHOIT, Solomon, Ge-1805
WILHOYT, John, Ge-1812
    Soloman, Ge-1812
WILIFORD, William, D-1805
WILIMAN, John, Fr-1812
    Peter, Fr-1812
    William, Fr-1812
WILKE, Thomas, D-1805
WILKELSON, George, Su-1812
WILKERSON, Anguis, D-1811
    Charles, Wl-1804
    Enoch J., Mu-1816
    Francis, Wi-1815
    John, Bo-1800
    Richard, Ge-1812
    Saml., Wh-1825
    Thomas, Je-1822
    Wm. G., D-1811
    Wyett, Wl-1804
WILKESON, Junoir, Sn-1811
    Thomas, Gi-1819, Sn-1811
WILKEY, William, K-1796
WILKINS, Alexander, Wi-1815
    James, Wi-1815
    John, Wi-1815, Wi-1810, Mu-1811
    Robert, Mu-1811
    Samuel, W-1812
    William, D-1805
WILKINSON, Charles, B-1812
    David, Gi-1812
    James, Gi-1812, Sn-1816

WILKINSON, John, Fr-1812, Bo-1801
    Lewis, R-1819
    Moses, Sn-1816
    Thos., Gi-1812
    William, Sn-1816, D-1805
WILKS, Amos, Mu-1816
    Benjamin, Mu-1816, D-1811
    Daniel, Wi-1815, Wi-1810
    Jesse, Mu-1816
    John, Mu-1811(2), Mu-1816(3)
    John Sr., Mu-1816
    Minor, Mu-1816
    Minor Sr., Mu-1816
    William, Sn-1816, Mu-1816
WILLARD, George, Su-1812
    John, D-1811, Wl-1804
WILLAS, Robert, Bo-1800
WILLCOCKSON, George, Je-1800
WILLEMS, Samuel, Wi-1810
WILLER, John, Ge-1805
WILLET, Frances, Wa-1814
    Nathan, Su-1812
    Nimrod, Wa-1814
    Simeron P., Li-1812*
    Thomas, D-1811
    Zachariah, Wa-1814
    Zadock, Wa-1819
WILLETT, Enath, Ro-1805
    Frances, Gr-1804
    James, Ro-1805
    Nimrod, Wa-1819
    William, Wi-1815
WILLHIGHT, Adam, Ge-1783
    Matthias, Ge-1783
WILLHITE, Conrite, A-1805
    Judus, Gr-1804
    Simeon, A-1805
WILLIAM, Francis, Mu-1811
    Griffith, Rb-1812
    Hamett, B-1812
    James, Bo-1805
    John, Bo-1805, A-1805, Mu-1811
    John Stiller, Bo-1800
    Jos., Sn-1816, Ge-1812
    Littleton, Je-1800
    Lucreatia, Ct-1796
    Nathan, D-1811
    Reaves, B-1812
    Richd., Mu-1816
    Thomas, Mu-1811
    Veverly, Wl-1804
    William, D-1811
WILLIAMS, Aaron, Ge-1812
    Abel, Je-1822, Rb-1812, C-1818
    Abraham, Ge-1805, Wa-1819,
        Wa-1814(2)
    Aleck, C-1823
    Alexander, Mu-1816, Gr-1821,
        Ge-1812(2), Ge-1805, C-1823
    Allen, Hu-1812, Je-1800
    Amos, Gi-1812
    Archibald, Ct-1798
    Arthur, Je-1800
    Balis, Su-1797
    Basil, Su-1796
    Bengimon, Sn-1811
    Benjamin, Wl-1804, A-1805, Je-1800,
        Ge-1805(2)
    Benjamin Sr., Ge-1812
    Benjamin Jr., Ge-1812
    Benjn., heirs, Sn-1792
    Bennet, D-1811

WILLIAMS, Berry, Mu-1816
    Burges, Gi-1819
    Cais, D-1811
    Carl, Su-1812
    Charles, Rb-1812
    Christopher, D-1805, Wi-1815
    Claborn, Wi-1801
    Daniel, D-1805(2), B-1812
    David, D-1811, Wh-1825, Je-1800,
        B-1812
    Edmond, Mu-1816, D-1811
    Edward, Mu-1811, Sn-1811, Mu-1816,
        D-1788, Sn-1816, Sn-1792,
        A-1805, Sn-1787
    Elijah, Wi-1801, B-1812, Fr-1812
    Elisa, Wh-1811
    Elisha, Wi-1810, D-1811(3), D-1805,
        Wi-1815(2), B-1812
    Eneas, Ge-1812
    Ethelbert C., Rb-1812
    Etheldred, D-1811, Gr-1805, Gr-1821
    Ezekiel, Je-1822
    Francis, D-1805, Wh-1825, Ct-1796,
        Ct-1798, Gr-1821
    Garland, Rb-1812
    George, Ct-1796, Ct-1798, R-1808,
        Gi-1812, Rb-1812, Cl-1803
    Green, Rb-1812
    H., Ge-1805
    H. Samuel, Mu-1811
    Hardin, W-1812
    Hardin Sr., Cl-1803
    Hardin Jr., Cl-1803
    Hecktor, Sn-1816
    Hector, Sn-1811
    Henry, Sn-1816, Wi-1815, Sn-1811(2),
        Wh-1825, Hu-1812, Ge-1805,
        Wh-1811
    Howard, Wh-1825
    Hugh, D-1811, D-1805
    Humphrey, Wa-1814
    Humphreys, Wa-1814
    Isaac, Wh-1825, Wi-1810, Mu-1816,
        D-1805, Wi-1815, B-1812(2),
        Je-1822
    Isaac Jr., B-1812
    J. John, D-1805
    Jacob, Mu-1811, Mu-1816, Fr-1812
    James, Sn-1816(2), Sn-1811(2),
        Mu-1816, D-1811, Wi-1815(3),
        Wh-1825, Co-1821, Cl-1803,
        B-1812, Hw-1801, Ge-1812(2),
        W-1812, Wh-1811
    James Sr., Gi-1812
    James Jr., Gi-1812
    James H., Mu-1816
    James J., Wi-1815
    Jeremiah, Rb-1812
    Jesse, Rb-1812, Wh-1811
    Jessee, Wh-1825, Mu-1816, W-1805,
        W-1812(2)
    Joel, Gi-1812
    John, Mc-1825, K-1799, Hw-1801,
        Fr-1812, C-1818, C-1823(2),
        B-1812, Je-1800, Je-1822,
        J-1802(2), Wi-1810, Wi-1815,
        Wh-1811, Wa-1814, Wa-1819,
        Su-1797, Sn-1792, Sn-1816,
        Rb-1812(2), Gi-1812, Ge-1812,
        Ge-1805, Gr-1821(2), Gr-1804(2),
        Gr-1799(2), Gr-1805, D-1805(3),
        D-1811, Cl-1803, Bo-1800,

WILLIAMS, John, Cont'd.--A-1805(3),
        Mu-1811, Mu-1816(3)
    John Sr., C-1818
    John Jr., Bo-1800, Bo-1805, C-1818,
        Bo-1801
    John G., W-1812
    John Stiller, Bo-1801
    Jonth., Wl-1804
    Jonathan, D-1811, Gr-1799, Gr-1821,
        R-1819
    Joseph, Sn-1816, Wh-1825, D-1811,
        Ge-1783, B-1812, Gr-1799,
        Gr-1821, Je-1800, R-1819,
        J-1802, Bo-1800
    Jos. T., B-1812
    Joshua, Mu-1811, Mu-1816, Sn-1811
    Josiah, D-1811
    Kilen, Wh-1825
    Leaderick, D-1811
    Lewis, D-1811, Gr-1799, W-1812
    Littlebery, d-1811
    Mark, Ct-1798
    Mary, Sn-1816
    Mathews, D-1805
    Matthias, A-1805
    Moses, Gi-1812(2)
    Nataniel, B-1812(2)
    Nimrod, D-1811, D-1805
    Norris, Mu-1816
    O., Wi-1801
    Oliver, Wi-1815, Wi-1810
    Owen, B-1812
    Paul, Fr-1812
    Permenas, Mu-1816
    Peter, Su-1796
    Philip, Fr-1812
    Phillip, Hw-1801, A-1805
    Richard, Mu-1811, Bo-1801, W-1812,
        Bo-1805, Bo-1800
    Robert, Sn-1816, Mu-1816, D-1811,
        Hw-1801, Cl-1803, W-1812
    Sam, K-1799
    Sammuel, Wi-1815
    Sampson, Mt-1798
    Samson, Wi-1810
    Samuel, Wi-1801, Wi-1810(2), Gr-1805,
        D-1811, Ct-1796, Wi-1815,
        Gr-1821, Ct-1798, Rb-1812,
        Ro-1805, Wa-1814, Bo-1801
    Samuel H., Mu-1816
    Shadrach, Gr-1821
    Sherod, Hw-1801
    Silas, C-1823, C-1818
    Simon, D-1805, D-1811, Su-1797
    Solomon, D-1811
    T. Joseph, Wl-1804
    Terry, B-1812
    Theophilas, W-1805
    Theophilus, W-1812
    Thomas, Ct-1798, Sn-1811, Mu-1816,
        D-1805, Gr-1805, D-1811,
        Wh-1825, Co-1821, Gi-1812,
        Ge-1812, Ge-1805, Rb-1812,
        Su-1797, Su-1796
    Thomas A., Fr-1812
    Tom, Wa-1819
    William, Mt-1798, D-1811(2), Mu-1816(2),
        Sn-1811, Wh-1825, D-1805,
        Mu-1816, Wi-1810(2), Wi-1815(2),
        Gr-1805, Ct-1798, A-1805,
        B-1812, Gi-1812, Ge-1783,
        Gr-1799, Gr-1821, Hw-1799,

WILLIAMS, William, Cont'd.--Wh-1811
    William Sr., Gr-1799
    William Jr., Gr-1799
    William F., Gr-1821
    Wilson, D-1811
    Wright, Wi-1801(2)
WILLIAMSON, Benjamin, Wi-1815
    Greene, Mu-1811
    Hugh, Mt-1798(2), Gr-1799
    James, D-1811, Sn-1811, D-1805,
        Wi-1801
    John, Wl-1804, D-1788, Wi-1801,
        Wh-1811
    John S., D-1811
    Joseph N., D-1811
    Lewis, Bo-1805
    Richard, D-1811, D-1805
    Robert, Sn-1811, Sn-1816
    S. J., Gr-1799
    Thomas, Wi-1810, D-1805(2),
        D-1811(2), Wi-1801, Wi-1815,
        B-1812, Wh-1811, Ge-1812,
        Gi-1812, Bo-1805
WILLIARD, John, Wi-1810
WILLIE, John, C-1823
    W. Edward, C-1823
WILLIFORD, Stephen, Fr-1812
    Thomas, Fr-1812
WILLINGHAM, Elijah, B-1812
WILLIOTT, Francis, Gr-1805
WILLIS, Caleb, Wi-1810
    Davis, B-1812
    Elisha, Rb-1812
    Henry, Ge-1783, Fr-1812(2)
    Henry B., Sn-1816
    Henry R., Sn-1816
    Jacob, Sn-1811, Sn-1816
    James, Bo-1801
    Jesse, Ge-1805
    John, Sn-1816, Sn-1811
    Malachi, Sn-1816
    Maluke, Sn-1811
    Mary, Sn-1816
    Meshac, Mu-1816
    Moses, Su-1797, Gr-1804, Gr-1805,
        Sn-1811
    Nathaniel, Mu-1816, Mu-1811
    Robert, Gr-1821, Mu-1816, Gr-1805
    Thomas, Gr-1805, B-1812, Sn-1816,
        Mu-1816
    William, D-1811(2), Gr-1805, Gr-1804,
        Su-1797, W-1812
WILLISON, Abraham, Je-1800
WILLIT, Jashludevay, Ge-1812
    William, Wi-1810
WILLITT, William, Ro-1805
WILLOBY, John, C-1818
    Sarah, C-1823
WILLOUGHBY, Benjamin, Ge-1812
    John, Ge-1812
    Thomas, Ge-1812
    Wallace, Su-1812, Su-1797
    William, Su-1812
WILLS, George, Sn-1792(3)
    James, Sn-1792
    John, Su-1812, Ct-1798, Wl-1804
    Lewis, Ct-1798
    Rebun, Sn-1816
    William, Rb-1812
WILLSFORD, Willis, Mu-1816
WILLSON, Abner, Je-1800
    Adam, Je-1800

WILLSON, Cornelious, Wi-1810
    George, Gr-1799
    Isaac, Je-1800
    Jacob, Je-1800
    John, Je-1800, Gr-1799, Wi-1810
    Joseph, Se-1799
    William, Wa-1814
WILMOTH, James, Je-1822
    John, W-1812
WILMOUTH, James, B-1812
    William, Wh-1825
WILS, Ranson, Gi-1819
WILSFORD, James, Gi-1812
WILSON, Aaron Sr., B-1812
    Aaron Jr., B-1812
    Abraham, Je-1822, A-1805, C-1818, Gr-1805
    Adam, Ge-1812, Ge-1805, Hu-1812
    Adam, estate, dec., By Adam Wilson, Ge-1812
    Alexander, Ge-1805(2), Ge-1812(4), Ge-1783
    Alvin, C-1823
    Amos, Wa-1814
    Andrew, Ge-1812, D-1805, D-1811, Wl-1804
    Ann, Wi-1810
    Aquilla, Gi-1812
    Archabald, heirs, Wi-1815
    Benjamin, Su-1812, Wa-1814
    Berry R., Wh-1825
    Boyd, Gi-1812
    Charles, Wa-1819
    Cornelious, Wi-1815
    Daniel, Je-1800, D-1805, Wi-1815
    David, Ge-1812(2), Ge-1805(2), Wa-1814, Bo-1801, Sn-1787, Gr-1804, Sn-1792, Wa-1819, Sn-1811, Mt-1798(2), Mu-1816, Sn-1816
    Eben, B-1812
    Ebenezar, Wi-1804
    Eli, Je-1822, A-1805, C-1818
    Elie, C-1823
    Elizabeth, Gr-1821, C-1823
    Ephraim, Ge-1805, Ge-1783
    Ephriam Jr., Ge-1812
    Ezekiel, W-1812
    Garland, Ct-1796, Ct-1798
    George, Ge-1812, Mo-1825, B-1812
    Greenberey, K-1799
    Greenberry, Ro-1805
    Hardin, Mu-1811
    Hartwell, Wh-1825
    Harvey, C-1823
    Isaac, Wa-1814, Gi-1812, Bo-1800, Bo-1801, Gr-1804, Wa-1819, C-1818, Mu-1816
    Isaac P., Mu-1816
    Israel, Je-1822
    James, B-1812, Sn-1816(2), Wl-1804(2), Mu-1816, Mt-1798, D-1805, Hu-1812, Gr-1805, Wi-1815(2), Gr-1821, Ge-1805, Rb-1812(2), Je-1800, R-1819, Bo-1801, Sn-1787
    James Sr., B-1812, Sn-1792
    James Jr., Gr-1821, B-1812
    James, heirs, Wi-1815
    James A., B-1812
    James C., Sn-1811, Sn-1816
    James J., Ge-1812, Ge-1805

WILSON, James L., Sn-1811
    James M., Wi-1815
    Jas. S., Sn-1792
    Jason, Wi-1815
    Jesse, Wh-1811, A-1805, Fr-1812
    Joel, Mu-1811
    John, J-1802, Gi-1812, Ge-1805(2), Wi-1810, Wi-1815, Sn-1787, Sn-1792, Sn-1811, Sn-1816, Rb-1812, R-1819, Mu-1816, Mu-1811, Fr-1812(2), D-1811(2), D-1805, Ct-1796, B-1812(3)
    John, Capt., Ge-1812
    John Sr., Ge-1805, Ct-1796, Ct-1798
    John Jr., Ct-1796, Ct-1798, Wl-1804
    Jonathan, Sn-1811, Sn-1816, Wl-1804
    Joseph, Ct-1796, Ge-1783, Ct-1798, Wl-1804, Sn-1816, Sn-1811
    Jos. Sr., Sn-1792
    Joseph E., D-1811
    Jos. G., Sn-1792
    Josiah, Wi-1815(2), Wi-1810
    Lamuel, Wi-1815
    Lebow, Wl-1804
    Levi, Mo-1825, Je-1822, A-1805
    Levy, C-1818
    Macklin, Ge-1812
    Mark, B-1812, Wi-1815
    Martin, Sn-1811
    Mathew, Sn-1816
    Michael, B-1812
    Moses, B-1812, C-1823, Sn-1816
    Peter, Ge-1812
    Philip, D-1811
    Richard, Gi-1812, Fr-1812
    Robert, Wi-1801, Wi-1815, Wh-1825, Mt-1798, Hu-1812, Gi-1819, Gi-1812, Ge-1812(3), Ge-1805, Bo-1801
    Saks, Gr-1805
    Samuel, Ge-1812, Ge-1783, B-1812, Ct-1796, Ct-1798, Sn-1792, Sn-1816, Mu-1816, Wi-1801, Wh-1825, Sn-1811
    Samuel, heirs, Wi-1815
    Samuel Sr., A-1805, Sn-1816
    Samuel Jr., A-1805, Sn-1816
    Samul, Wi-1810
    Sarah, Sn-1816
    Stephen, Sn-1811, Sn-1816
    Thomas, Ge-1812, Wh-1811, Gr-1821, Ge-1805, Wi-1815(3), Co-1827, A-1805, Sn-1816, Wh-1825, D-1805, Sn-1811, Wi-1801(2), Wi-1810
    Thomas Sr., Wh-1825
    Thomas Jr., Ge-1805, Wh-1825
    William, K-1799, Wl-1804(2), Je-1800, Je-1822, Wi-1815(3), Wi-1801, Wh-1811, Wa-1819, Sn-1792, Ro-1805, Rb-1812, Mt-1798, Ge-1783, Ge-1812, Ge-1805, D-1811(2), Ct-1796, Ct-1798, C-1818, C-1823, Bl-1815
    William Esq., Wi-1810
    William Sr., Su-1812, Gr-1804, Gr-1805
    William Jr., Gr-1805, Gr-1804
    Zaccheris, Sn-1792
    Zacheheus, Sn-1811

WILSON, Zacheus, B-1812, Wl-1804
    Zacheus Sr., Sn-1816
    Zacheus Jr., Sn-1816(2)
    Zackeus, Wi-1815
WILY, Edward, Sn-1816
WIMBERLY, Noah, Fr-1812
WIMBLEDUFF, George, Sn-1816
WIMPER, Teca, Fr-1812
WIMS, Butons, Hu-1812
WIN, Hiram, D-1805, Wl-1804
WINBERRY, Levent, Sn-1811
WINBONE, Josiah, Sn-1811
WINBOURN, Wm., Gi-1819
WINCHESTER, David, Mt-1798, Mu-1811
    G., Sn-1787
    Genl. James, Wi-1810
    Hage, Sn-1816
    Hays, Sn-1811
    J. & G., Sn-1792
    James, Sn-1787, Sn-1816, Sn-1811(2), Mt-1798
    Stephen, Sn-1811
    Wm., Mt-1798
WINDENS, William, Cl-1803
WINDHAM, Aaron, Ct-1796
    Rachel, Gr-1799
    William, Gr-1804, Ct-1796, Gr-1805
    William Sr., Gr-1799
    William Jr., Gr-1799
WINDS, Enoch, Gr-1804, Gr-1799
WINDSET, Asa, Wi-1815
WINDSLO, Joseph, Wi-1810
WINDSOR, Benjamin, B-1812
WINE, Robert, Gi-1819
WINES, Enoch, Gr-1805
WINFORD, John, Fr-1812, Wl-1804
WINFREY, E. John, D-1805
    Valentine, D-1811
WINHAM, Josiah, Sn-1816
    Robert, Sn-1816
    Stephen, Sn-1811, Sn-1816
WINKEL, Mathias, Ge-1812
WINKLE, Abraham, Wa-1819
    Frederick T., Ge-1812
    John, Wa-1819, Wa-1814
WINKLES, Jeremiah, Wh-1811
WINN, John, Fr-1812
    Martin, B-1812
    Mourning, Sn-1811
    Peter, Sn-1811
    Petter, Sn-1816
    Philip P., Mu-1816
WINNLY, M., Sn-1811
WINSCOTT, Christopher, Ge-1812
WINSET, Amso, Wi-1815
    John, Wl-1804
    Martin, Rb-1812
    Milley, Wi-1815
    Silas, Wi-1815
    William, Wi-1815
WINSTEAD, Anthony, D-1805
    Samuel, D-1811, Wi-1815, Wi-1810
    William, D-1811
WINSTON, Anthony, Wl-1804
    John, B-1812
    Johnson, Mu-1816
    Nathaniel, B-1812
    Thomas, Sn-1816
    William, Wl-1804, D-1805
WINTERS, Caleb, Rb-1812
    Christopher, Ge-1805
    George, Fr-1812
WINTERS, James, Gi-1812
    John, Sn-1811
    Moses, Rb-1812(2), K-1799, Ro-1805
    Samuel, B-1812, Bo-1801, Bo-1800
WINTETH, John, B-1812
WINTON, George, R-1819
    John, W-1812(2), Ro-1805
    William, Je-1800
WIRE, William, Sn-1811, Sn-1816
WIREMAN, John, Ct-1798
    Samuel, Su-1797
WISDOM, Francis, Mu-1811
    John, Gi-1812
    Larkin, Wh-1825
    William, Gi-1812
WISE, Henry, B-1812
    John, Bo-1801
    Stephen, B-1812
    William, B-1812
WISEMAN, John, Gi-1812
    Samuel, Su-1796
    William, D-1805
WISENOR, Harvy, Wi-1810
WISER, John, B-1812
WISNOR, William, D-1811
WITCHER, John, Gr-1805
    _____, Gr-1805
WITE, James, W-1812
WITHERHORN, Samuel, Mu-1811
WITHERINGTON, Abram, Wi-1815
    Joseph, Wi-1815
WITHERLEY, Isaiah, Mu-1816
WITHERLY, Job, Mu-1816
WITHERS, Edman, Wi-1810
    John, Sn-1816
    Thomas, Sn-1811
WITHERSPOON, Alexander, Wl-1804
    David, Mu-1811, Mu-1816
    James, Wl-1804, Ge-1805
    John, Wl-1804, Wi-1810, Wi-1815
    Joseph, Wl-1804
    Samuel, Mu-1816
    W., Wi-1810
WITHIS, Benjamin, Mu-1811
WITHNOW, Richard, W-1812
WITSON, Isaac, C-1823
    James, R-1819
WITT, Ayers, Je-1800
    Burger, Wa-1814
    Caleb, Je-1822, Je-1800
    Daniel, Je-1822
    Drury, Wh-1825
    Edmond, Gr-1821
    Eli, Je-1822
    Elijah, Je-1800
    Harmon, Je-1822
    James, Je-1822, W-1805
    Jesse & Baldwin, Wm., R-1819
    Jessee, R-1819(see Baldwin, Wm.)
    Joel, Gr-1799, Gr-1805, Gr-1804
    John, Je-1822
    John Sr., Wh-1825
    John Jr., Wh-1825
    Joseph, Je-1800(2)
    Noah, Je-1822, Je-1800
    Pleasant, Je-1822
    Sampson, Wh-1825
    William, Fr-1812
WODALE, George, Wh-1825
WODS, Aaron, Fr-1812
WOFFORD, Jacob, Su-1812
WOLDEN, James, B-1812

WOLF, Charles, Su-1796
    George, Su-1797
    George W., D-1811
    Henry, Wa-1819
    Jacob, B-1812
    Lewis, Su-1797
    Philip, D-1805
    William, Wi-1815
WOLFE, George, Su-1796
WOLLARD, Silas, Mu-1816
    Willoby, Mu-1816
WOLLIVER, John, Ge-1805
WOLT, Gorge, Hw-1799
WOLVERTON, John, Mu-1816
WOMACK, Abraham, Fr-1812
    David, Wh-1811, Gr-1799
    Hyram, Fr-1812
    James, Fr-1812
    Johnston, Gr-1799
    Josiah, Fr-1812
WOMBLE, Joshua, W-1812
    Redding, Mu-1816
    Simon, Mu-1816
WOMBWELL, Reading, Mu-1811
WOOD, Abraham Sr., B-1812
    Abraham Jr., B-1812
    Agnes, Wa-1815
    Alexander, Wi-1815, Wi-1801
    Charles, Fr-1812
    Christopher, Wi-1815
    Cristopher, Sn-1816
    Curtis, Mu-1811, Mu-1816
    Daniel Jr., Wa-1819
    Drury, W-1812
    George, Wh-1825
    Henry, Wh-1811, Gr-1805
    Isom, Fr-1812
    James, Mo-1825, Co-1821, Fr-1812,
        Je-1822, W-1812
    James Okley, Wi-1815
    John, Wi-1801, Co-1821, Sn-1816,
        Hu-1812, Wi-1810, Gr-1799,
        W-1812, Gr-1821, Ro-1805
    John I., Co-1821
    John L., Mu-1816
    Johnson, Wi-1815
    Johnson Jr., Wi-1815
    Jonathan, Wi-1801, Wi-1815, Wh-1811
    Joseph, D-1811, Fr-1812, W-1812
    Josiah, Wi-1815
    L. John, Mu-1811
    Lennard, Wi-1810
    Malen, Wi-1810
    Milon, Wa-1819
    Moses, Fr-1812
    Nathan, Wh-1811
    Obadiah, K-1799
    Olliver, Wi-1810
    Robert, D-1811, Ro-1805, Co-1821
    Sampson, K-1799
    Samuel, Ro-1805
    Sarah, Wi-1810
    Seth?, Sn-1816
    Tandy, Sn-1816
    Thomas, Sn-1811(2)
    William, K-1799, Hu-1812, D-1811,
        B-1812, Fr-1812, A-1805,
        Je-1822
    William Green, Wa-1814
WOODALE, Wm., Sn-1811
WOODALL, Jehu, Gr-1805
    John, Gr-1805

WOODALL, Jonathan, Sn-1816, Fr-1812
    Kit, Sn-1811
    William, Sn-1816(2), W-1812
WOODARD, Asa, Rb-1812
    Daniel, D-1805, D-1811
    Edward, D-1811
    Hezekiah, Wl-1804
    Jesse, D-1811
    John, W-1812
    Julias, Mu-1811
    Pitt, D-1811
    Richard, Rb-1812
    Thos., Sn-1792(2), Rb-1812
    William, B-1812, Rb-1812
WOODBY, William, Ct-1798(2)
WOODCOCK, John, D-1811
WOODEL, James, Gi-1812
WOODFIN, Nicholas, B-1812
WOODFORK, William, Wl-1804
WOODLEY, John, Ro-1805
WOODLY, Jacob, W-1812
    John, W-1812
WOODRAD, Noah, Rb-1812
WOODRAM, James, B-1812
    Joel, B-1812
WOODRELL, George, Sn-1811
WOODRUFF, William, Sn-1811
WOODRUM, Obediah, Wl-1804
WOODS, Andrew, Fr-1812
    Andrew, heirs, Mu-1816
    Andrews, heirs, Mu-1816
    Archibald, Fr-1812
    Benjamin, Rb-1812(2)
    Charles, Fr-1812
    Daniel, Gi-1819
    David, Gi-1812, Fr-1812
    Elijah, Su-1812, Je-1822
    Francis H., B-1812
    George W., Ge-1805
    James, Ro-1805, Bl-1815(2),
        B-1812, Fr-1812
    John, Wh-1811, Je-1822, Su-1812,
        B-1812, Fr-1812, Wl-1804,
        Bo-1800(2), Bo-1801(2),
        Mu-1811, Mu-1816, D-1805
    John Jr., Fr-1812
    Joseph, B-1812, Bo-1800
    Joseph Jr., Bo-1801
    Joseph D., Sn-1811
    Lamuel, Wl-1804
    Matthew, A-1805
    Michael, Ge-1805, Ge-1812
    Miller, J-1802
    Nathan, Wh-1811
    Patrick, Bo-1800, Bo-1801
    Peter, Fr-1812
    Richard, Se-1799, Ge-1783
    Richard M., Ge-1812
    Robert, Gi-1812
    Ryan, Ge-1812
    Saml., Gi-1812
    Susanah, D-1805
    Thomas, W-1812, Sn-1811
    William, Gi-1812, Ro-1805, Fr-1812
    Wyly, Je-1822
WOODSON, Francis, R-1819
    Joseph, D-1811
    Peter, Rb-1812
WOODWARD, Abraham, Je-1800, Je-1822
    Aron, Je-1800
    Aron, heirs, Je-1822
    Benjamin, D-1811

WOODWARD, Jesse, D-1811
    John & Chas., R-1819
    Thomas, R-1819, Ge-1783
    William, Je-1800, R-1819
WOODWIN, Jacob, Wl-1804
WOODY, Berry, Rb-1812
    Edward, Mo-1825
    George, Gr-1805
    John, Bo-1800, Bo-1801
    Samuel, B-1812
WOOLAID, Hugh, Gr-1805
WOOLARD, Hugh, Gr-1804
    William, J-1802
WOOLCARD, Hugh, Gr-1805
WOOLDRIDGE, David, Gr-1821
    John, B-1812
    Wm., Wl-1804
WOOLDRIGE, Edmond, Hu-1812
WOOLEVER, John, Ge-1812
    Philip, Ge-1812
WOOLF, Andrew, Wa-1814, Wa-1819
    Jacob, Bo-1800, Bo-1801
    John, Wa-1819
    Joseph, Wa-1819
WOOLFINBARGER, Joseph, Gr-1821
WOOLFINGBARGER, Peter, Gr-1821
WOOLFORD, George, Su-1812
WOOLHARD, Churchy, Mu-1816
WOOLLARD, Nathaniel, Mu-1816
WOOLRIDGE, Daniel, Gr-1821
    Edward, Mu-1811
WOOLSEW, William, Ge-1805
WOOLSEY, Essau, Wa-1819
    Faltnas, Wa-1819
    Gilbert, Ge-1812(2)
    John, Ge-1805
    Oliver, Ge-1812
    Stephen, Ge-1805
WOOLSY, Israel, Ge-1812
    John, Ge-1812(3)
    Nehemiah, Ge-1812(2)
WOOLVERTON, John, Mu-1811
WOORLEY, Samuel, Rb-1812
WOOSLEY, Thomas, Gr-1804
WOOTEN, Benjamin, W-1812
    Jessee, W-1812
    John, B-1812
    Leonard, Su-1797
    Rhoden, W-1812
    Saml., Sn-1816
WOOTIN, James, Fr-1812
WOOTON, Rhodans, Wh-1825
    Samuel, Sn-1811
WORD, Dempsy, Sn-1816
    Enoch, Mu-1811
    Samuel, Mu-1811
WORDLY, Gabril, Wi-1815
WORK, Alexander, D-1811(2)
    Andrew, D-1811
    Jacob, Ro-1805
    Joseph, Bo-1805
    Robert, Su-1797
WORKINS, Henry, Sn-1816
WORKMAN, John, D-1805
WORLDRUM, John, Sn-1816
WORLEY, Finch, Wh-1811
    Fleming, Wh-1825
    George, R-1808
    Jessee, Wh-1825
    John, Ct-1796, Ct-1798, Mu-1816
WORLY, Franses, Wi-1815
WORMICK, David, B-1812

WORMINGTON, Edwd., Sn-1816
WORMSLEY, John G., Mu-1816
WORRICK, John, Gr-1821
    William, Gr-1805
WORTERS, Johnathan, Mu-1811
WORTHAM, Charles, B-1812
    John, B-1812
    Thomas, Mu-1816
    William, B-1812
WORTHEM, James, B-1812
WORTHEN, Silvester, Fr-1812
WORTHINGTON, James, A-1805(2), K-1799
    Sam, K-1799
    Samuel, A-1805, K-1799
    Thomas, A-1805, K-1799
    William, K-1799
WORTHY, Martin, Gr-1804
WOTTEN, James, Su-1797
WRAY, Alexander, D-1805
    Joseph, Mt-1798
    Richard, Wh-1825
    Samuel, D-1811
    Stephen, Sn-1823
    William, D-1811, D-1805, Mu-1811
WREN, David, D-1811
    James, Mu-1816
    Solomon, W-1812
    William, D-1811
WRENN, Gnl. Richard, Mu-1811
    George, Mu-1811
    P. Phillip, Mu-1811
    Thomas, Mu-1811
WRIGHT, Alexander, Sn-1811
    Catron, Mu-1816
    Charles Sr., D-1811
    Charles Jr., D-1811
    Christr., Gi-1812
    David, Gi-1812, Su-1796
    Edward, Je-1800
    Elijah, Sn-1811, Sn-1816, Mu-1811
    Esaw, C-1823(2), C-1818
    Ezekiel, Wa-1814
    Francis, Mu-1816
    George, B-1812, Sn-1816, D-1811
    Henry, B-1812
    Hollis, D-1811
    Isaac, Je-1800(2), Wi-1810
    Jacob, Wi-1801
    James, B-1812, Ct-1798, Ct-1796,
        Ge-1805(2), Ge-1812, Sn-1811,
        Gr-1799(2), D-1811(2),
        D-1805, Mu-1816, Sn-1816,
        D-1788
    James Sr., D-1811
    James Jr., D-1811
    Jeremiah, B-1812
    Jesse, Gr-1805, Ge-1812
    John, Gr-1821, B-1812, Mc-1825,
        Gi-1812(2), Wl-1804, Mu-1816,
        Sn-1816(2)
    John M., D-1811
    Joseph, Se-1799, Ge-1805, Wl-1804,
        Wi-1810, D-1811
    Joshua, Je-1800
    Nathan, Je-1800
    Patrick, Su-1812
    Peter, D-1812, D-1811
    Richard, Gi-1812
    Robert, Ct-1796, Je-1800
    Samuel, Je-1822
    Thomas, Ct-1796, Ct-1798, A-1805,
        B-1812, Wi-1810, D-1805

WRIGHT, William, B-1812, C-1818, A-1805,
        Fr-1812, D-1805, D-1811
WRITE, Charles, Ro-1805
    James, W-1812
    Nicholas, Mu-1811
    Peter, Fr-1812
WROTHY, Martin, Gr-1805
WYAND, Henry, D-1811
WYAT, John, Fr-1812
WYATT, John, A-1805
    Joseph, A-1805
    Reuben, Je-1822
    Samuel, Gr-1799(2), A-1805, Ct-1798
    Solomon, Ge-1812, Ge-1805
    Thomas, Ge-1805(2), Ct-1798, Ct-1796
    William, A-1805, B-1812, Ct-1796,
        Ct-1798
WYCKE, Nathaniel, D-1811
WYCLIN, George, D-1805
WYCOFF, Isaac, Mt-1798
WYLEY, Abell, Wa-1814
    William, Su-1796
WYLY, Robert, Ge-1805
    Robert, est., Ge-1812(8)
WYMAN, Henry, Ct-1796
WYNDS, Enock, Gr-1805
WYNN, James, Rb-1812
    Mourning, Sn-1816
WYNNE, Devereaux, Wl-1804
    George, Wl-1804
    Isham, Wl-1804
    K. John, Wl-1804
    Peter, Sn-1816
WYOTT, William, Ge-1812
WYRICK, Frederick, Gr-1821
    Henry Sr., Gr-1821
    Henry Jr., Gr-1821
    John, Gr-1821
    Martin, R-1819
    Michael, Gr-1821
    Peter, Gr-1821
    William, Gr-1821, Su-1812
WYSER, Jacob, Su-1812
YADEN, David, Gr-1821
    Jacob, Gr-1821
    Joseph, Gr-1804, Gr-1821
    William P., Gr-1821
YALAM, Absolem, Wi-1801
YALEMAN, _____, D-1811
YANCEY, Ambrose, Gr-1804, Gr-1805
    James, Bl-1815
    Robert, Gr-1804
    Squire, Su-1796
    William, Sn-1816
YANCY, Ambrose, Gr-1799
    John, Gi-1812, Su-1797
    Robert, Sn-1800, Gr-1799, Su-1797
    Tyre, Sn-1823
    Widow, W-1805, Su-1812
    William, Mu-1816
YANDEL, John, Sn-1816
YANDELL, Wilson, Sn-1816
YANDLE, John, Sn-1811
    Saml., Sn-1811, Sn-1816
    Will, Sn-1811
    Wm., Sn-1816
    Wilson, Sn-1811
YARBARY, Hanary, Wi-1815
YARBOROUGH, Absalom, Mu-1816, Mu-1811
    Brittain, Mu-1811
    Edward, J-1802
    James, D-1811

YARBOROUGH, Lee, Mu-1811
    Solomon, Mu-1811
    William, Wi-1810, Wi-1815
YARBROUGH, Brittan, Gi-1812
    James, D-1811
    Jeptha, Wh-1825
    John, Gi-1812
    William, D-1811
    Wm. Sr., Wh-1825
    Wm. Jr., Wh-1825
YARDLY, David, W-1805
YARICK, John, Ge-1812
YARIEN, Frederick, Bo-1801
    Michael, Bo-1801
YARNELL, Stephen, Wl-1804
YARRE, Abraham, K-1799
YATCH, Daniel, Mu-1811
YATES, Absolam, B-1812
    Benjamin, Ge-1812
    Henry F. D., D-1811
    James, Rb-1812
    James Jr., Rb-1812
    Jessee, B-1812
    John, B-1812, Gr-1821
    John Sr., Rb-1812
    John Jr., Rb-1812
    Jonathan, B-1812
    Joshua, B-1812
    Meredith, Gr-1821
    Nicholas, Ge-1812
    Samuel, B-1812
    Thomas, B-1812
    Wm. Sr., Rb-1812
    Wm. Jr., Rb-1812
YEADEN, Joseph, Gr-1805
YEAGER, Daniel, Wa-1819, Wa-1814
    Elias, Wh-1825(2)
    James, Wh-1825
    Joel, Wh-1825
    Samuel, Fr-1812
    Solomon, Wa-1814
    Solomon Sr., Wh-1825(2)
    Solomon Jr., Wh-1825
YEAKLEY, Henry, Ge-1805
YEARGIN, Bartlet, Wi-1815
YEARLY, Samuel, Wa-1814
    William, D-1805
YEARSLEY, David, Su-1812
YEATES, Benjamin, Ge-1805
    George, Wh-1811
    John, Wh-1825
    Samuel, Ct-1796
    Thomas, Wh-1825
    Washington, Wh-1825
YEATMAN, John, Wi-1815
    Thomas, D-1811
YEATO, James, Sn-1792(2)
YELL, James, B-1812(2)
    Moses, B-1812, Je-1800
YEOKUM, Isaac, Gr-1799
    John, Gr-1799
    Valentine, Gr-1799
YERIN, Matthew, Bo-1800
YERRICK, John, Ge-1805
YOAKEN, George, Mo-1825
YOAKUM, George, Gr-1799
    John, Wh-1811
YOCUM, Jacob, K-1799
    Michal, K-1799
    Solomon, K-1799
YOE, Peregrine G., Je-1822
YOKELEY, John, Su-1796

YOKELY, John, Su-1812(2)
    Peter, Su-1812
    William, Su-1812
YORK, Daniel, B-1812
    Enoch, Gr-1821
    Henry, Wa-1814
    Jabaz, Gr-1799
    James, Sn-1811, Sn-1816
    Jeremiah, Gr-1799
    Joel, Mu-1816
    Jonathan, B-1812
    Richard, Wi-1810
    Seamore, Gr-1805
    Seamore, heirs, Gr-1821
    Semore, Gr-1799, Gr-1804
    Thos., Gi-1812
    Uriah, W-1812
    William, C-1823, Je-1822
YOUNG, Abraham, Sn-1792, Rb-1812
    Abraham Jr., Rb-1812(2)
    Abram, Sn-1811
    Adam, Wl-1804
    Alexahan, Sn-1792
    Archd., Sn-1811, Gi-1812
    Berrey, W-1812
    Catherine, Wa-1819
    Coty, Wa-1814
    Daniel, D-1811(2), D-1805, Gr-1799
    David, Wl-1804, B-1812
    Edward, B-1812
    Elijah, Sn-1816
    Ezeeal, Sn-1811
    Francis, Fr-1812, Je-1822
    Franciss, Sn-1816
    Henry, W-1812, A-1805
    Isaac, Fr-1812, W-1812(2)
    James, Wa-1814(3), Mu-1816, D-1811
        Sn-1816, Wl-1804, B-1812,
        Fr-1812, Wa-1819(2),
        Rb-1812(2), Su-1796, Su-1797
    John, Mu-1811, D-1811, D-1805,
        Wh-1825(2), Ct-1798, Wa-1819,
        Bo-1801, Sn-1792(2), B-1812,
        Fr-1812, K-1799, Ge-1805,
        Ge-1812, Rb-1812, W-1812
    John, heirs, Sn-1811
    John G., Gi-1819
    John L., D-1811(2)
    Jonathan, Wa-1819, Wa-1814
    Jones, Fr-1812
    Joseph, Mu-1816, Mu-1811, Sn-1816,
        Sn-1823, Wa-1819, Wa-1814
    Martin, C-1818, C-1823
    Mary, Sn-1816
    Merlin, Mu-1811
    Moses, Sn-1811
    Nathaniel, Mu-1811, Mu-1816
    Nicholas, D-1811
    Perry, Fr-1812
    Peter, Wi-1810, Mu-1816
    Polley, Sn-1811
    Polly, Wa-1814, Wa-1819
    Robert, Wa-1814, Gr-1805, Wi-1801
    Samuel, C-1818
    Thomas, Wi-1815, Wa-1819, K-1799,
        Fr-1812
    Wilkos, Wa-1814
    Wilks, Wa-1819
    William, Wi-1810, D-1788, Sn-1811,
        Sn-1792, Gr-1821, Fr-1812(2),
        Bo-1800, B-1812, Bo-1801,
        C-1823, Wa-1819, Wa-1814

YOUNG, William Sr., Wh-1825
    William Jr., Wh-1825
    Willis, Fr-1812
    _____, Rb-1812
YOUNGBLOOD, Aaron, Gi-1812
    Andrew, Fr-1812
    Henry, Gi-1812
    Jonathan, W-1812
YOUNGER, Alexander, Mu-1811
YOURE, Alexander, Sn-1811
    Francis, Sn-1811
YOUREE, Patrick, Sn-1811
YOUREY, Partrick, Sn-1816
YOURK, Uriah, Gr-1805
YOURY, Patrick, Wl-1804
YUNG, John, Wi-1810
ZACHARY, Charles, Mu-1811
    William, Gr-1821
ZACHERY, Caleb, D-1811
    James, Gr-1805
ZACK, Joshua, D-1805
ZAES?, John, Rb-1812
    Nathan, Rb-1812
ZAMER, Adam, Sn-1811
    Henry, Sn-1811
    Philip, Sn-1811
ZARCHER, John, Sn-1816
ZETTY, Christian, Wa-1819, Wa-1814
    Samuel, Rev., Wa-1819
ZIGLER, John, D-1811
ZILLAND, M., D-1788
ZOLLICOFER, George, Mu-1816
    J. J., Mu-1816
ZOOLYCOFFER, George, Mu-1811
    J. John, Mu-1811
ZWINY, Henry, D-1788
_____, Anthony, W-1812

www.ingramcontent.com/pod-product-compliance
Lightning Source LLC
Chambersburg PA
CBHW081810300426
44116CB00014B/2301